GEORGIA CODE

TITLE 16

CRIMES AND OFFENSES

2018 EDITION

GEORGIA LEGISLATURE

TITLE 16. CRIMES AND OFFENSES

Table of Contents

CHAPTER 1. GENERAL PROVISIONS

§ 16-1-1. Short title

This title shall be known and may be cited as the "Criminal Code of Georgia."

§ 16-1-2. Purposes of title

The general purposes of this title are:
(1) To forbid and prevent conduct which unjustifiably and inexcusably causes or threatens substantial harm to individual or public interests;
(2) To give fair warning of the nature of the conduct forbidden and the sentence authorized upon conviction;
(3) To define that which constitutes each crime; and
(4) To prescribe penalties which are proportionate to the seriousness of crimes and which permit recognition of differences in rehabilitation possibilities among individual criminals.

§ 16-1-3. Definitions

As used in this title, the term:
(1) "Affirmative defense" means, with respect to any affirmative defense authorized in this title, unless the state's evidence raises the issue invoking the alleged defense, the defendant must present evidence thereon to raise the issue. The enumeration in this title of some affirmative defenses shall not be construed as excluding the existence of others.
(2) "Agency" means:
(A) When used with respect to the state government, any department, commission, committee, authority, board, or bureau thereof; and
(B) When used with respect to any political subdivision of the state government, any department, commission, committee, authority, board, or bureau thereof.
(3) "Another" means a person or persons other than the accused.
(4) "Conviction" includes a final judgment of conviction entered upon a verdict or finding of guilty of a crime or upon a plea of guilty.
(5) "Felony" means a crime punishable by death, by imprisonment for life, or by imprisonment for more than 12 months.
(6) "Forcible felony" means any felony which involves the use or threat of physical force or violence against any person.
(7) "Forcible misdemeanor" means any misdemeanor which involves the use or threat of physical force or violence against any person.
(8) "Government" means the United States, the state, any political subdivision thereof, or any agency of the foregoing.
(9) "Misdemeanor" and "misdemeanor of a high and aggravated nature" mean any crime other than a felony.
(10) "Owner" means a person who has a right to possession of property which is superior to that of a person who takes, uses, obtains, or withholds it from him and which the person taking, using, obtaining, or withholding is not privileged to infringe.
(11) "Peace officer" means any person who by virtue of his office or public employment is vested by law with a duty to maintain public order or to make arrests for offenses, whether that duty extends to all crimes or is limited to specific offenses.
(12) "Person" means an individual, a public or private corporation, an incorporated association, government, government agency, partnership, or unincorporated association.
(13) "Property" means anything of value, including but not limited to real estate, tangible and intangible personal property, contract rights, services, choses in action, and other interests in or claims to wealth, admission or transportation tickets, captured or domestic animals, food and drink, and electric or other power.
(14) "Prosecution" means all legal proceedings by which a person's liability for a crime is determined, commencing with the return of the indictment or the filing of the accusation, and including the final disposition of the case upon appeal.
(15) "Public place" means any place where the conduct involved may reasonably be expected to be viewed by people other than members of the actor's family or household.
(16) "Reasonable belief" means that the person concerned, acting as a reasonable man, believes that the described facts exist.
(17) "State" means the State of Georgia, all land and water in respect to which this state has either exclusive or concurrent jurisdiction, and the airspace above such land and water.
(18) "Without authority" means without legal right or privilege or without permission of a person legally entitled to withhold the right.
(19) "Without his consent" means that a person whose concurrence is required has not, with knowledge of the essential facts, voluntarily yielded to the proposal of the accused or of another.

§ 16-1-4. When conduct constitutes a crime; power of court to punish contempt or enforce orders, civil judgments, and decrees

No conduct constitutes a crime unless it is described as a crime in this title or in another statute of this state. However, this Code section does not affect the power of a court to punish for contempt or to employ any sanction authorized by law for the enforcement of an order, civil judgment, or decree.

§ 16-1-5. Presumption of innocence; standard of proof for conviction

Every person is presumed innocent until proved guilty. No person shall be convicted of a crime unless each element of such crime is proved beyond a reasonable doubt.

§ 16-1-6. Conviction for lesser included offenses

An accused may be convicted of a crime included in a crime charged in the indictment or accusation. A crime is so included when:
(1) It is established by proof of the same or less than all the facts or a less culpable mental state than is required to establish the commission of the crime charged; or
(2) It differs from the crime charged only in the respect that a less serious injury or risk of injury to the same person, property, or public interest or a lesser kind of culpability suffices to establish its commission.

§ 16-1-7. Multiple prosecutions for same conduct

(a) When the same conduct of an accused may establish the commission of more than one crime, the accused may be prosecuted for each crime. He may not, however, be convicted of more than one crime if:
(1) One crime is included in the other; or
(2) The crimes differ only in that one is defined to prohibit a designated kind of conduct generally and the other to prohibit a specific instance of such conduct.
(b) If the several crimes arising from the same conduct are known to the proper prosecuting officer at the time of commencing the prosecution and are within the jurisdiction of a single court, they must be prosecuted in a single prosecution except as provided in subsection (c) of this Code section.
(c) When two or more crimes are charged as required by subsection (b) of this Code section, the court in the interest of justice may order that one or more of such charges be tried separately.

§ 16-1-8. When prosecution barred by former prosecution

(a) A prosecution is barred if the accused was formerly prosecuted for the same crime based upon the same material facts, if such former prosecution:

(1) Resulted in either a conviction or an acquittal; or

(2) Was terminated improperly after the jury was impaneled and sworn or, in a trial before a court without a jury, after the first witness was sworn but before findings were rendered by the trier of facts or after a plea of guilty was accepted by the court.

(b) A prosecution is barred if the accused was formerly prosecuted for a different crime or for the same crime based upon different facts, if such former prosecution:

(1) Resulted in either a conviction or an acquittal and the subsequent prosecution is for a crime of which the accused could have been convicted on the former prosecution, is for a crime with which the accused should have been charged on the former prosecution (unless the court ordered a separate trial of such charge), or is for a crime which involves the same conduct, unless each prosecution requires proof of a fact not required on the other prosecution or unless the crime was not consummated when the former trial began; or

(2) Was terminated improperly and the subsequent prosecution is for a crime of which the accused could have been convicted if the former prosecution had not been terminated improperly.

(c) A prosecution is barred if the accused was formerly prosecuted in a district court of the United States for a crime which is within the concurrent jurisdiction of this state if such former prosecution resulted in either a conviction or an acquittal and the subsequent prosecution is for the same conduct, unless each prosecution requires proof of a fact not required in the other prosecution or unless the crime was not consummated when the former trial began.

(d) A prosecution is not barred within the meaning of this Code section if:

(1) The former prosecution was before a court which lacked jurisdiction over the accused or the crime; or

(2) Subsequent proceedings resulted in the invalidation, setting aside, reversal, or vacating of the conviction, unless the accused was thereby adjudged not guilty or unless there was a finding that the evidence did not authorize the verdict.

(e) Termination under any of the following circumstances is not improper:

(1) The accused consents to the termination or waives by motion to dismiss or other affirmative action his right to object to the termination; or

(2) The trial court finds that the termination is necessary because:

(A) It is physically impossible to proceed with the trial;

(B) Prejudicial conduct in or out of the courtroom makes it impossible to proceed with the trial without injustice to the defendant;

(C) The jury is unable to agree upon a verdict; or

(D) False statements of a juror on voir dire prevent a fair trial.

§ 16-1-9. Application of title to crimes committed prior to enactment

This title shall govern the construction and punishment of any crime defined in this title committed on and after July 1, 1969, as well as the construction and application of any defense. This title does not apply to or govern the construction or punishment of any crime committed prior to July 1, 1969, or the construction or application of any defense. Such a crime must be construed and punished according to the law existing at the time of the commission thereof in the same manner as if this title had not been enacted.

§ 16-1-10. Punishment for crimes for which punishment not otherwise provided

Any conduct that is made criminal by this title or by another statute of this state and for which punishment is not otherwise provided, shall be punished as for a misdemeanor.

§ 16-1-11. Effect of repeal or amendment of criminal law on prosecution of prior violations

The repeal, repeal and reenactment, or amendment of any law of this state which prohibits any act or omission to act and which provides for any criminal penalty therefor, whether misdemeanor, misdemeanor of a high and aggravated nature, or felony, shall not affect or abate the status as a crime of any such act or omission which occurred prior to the effective date of the Act repealing, repealing and reenacting, or amending such law, nor shall the prosecution of such crime be abated as a result of such repeal, repeal and reenactment, or amendment unless the General Assembly expressly declares otherwise in the Act repealing, repealing and reenacting, or amending such law.

§ 16-1-12. Restrictions on contingency fee compensation of attorney appointed to represent state in forfeiture action

(a) In any forfeiture action brought pursuant to this title, an attorney appointed by the Attorney General or district attorney as a special assistant attorney general, special assistant district attorney, or other attorney appointed to represent this state in such forfeiture action shall not be compensated on a contingent basis by a percentage of assets which arise or are realized from such forfeiture action. Such attorneys shall also not be compensated on a contingent basis by an hourly, fixed fee, or other arrangement which is contingent on a successful prosecution of such forfeiture action.

(b) Nothing in this Code section shall be construed as prohibiting or otherwise restricting the Attorney General or a district attorney from appointing special assistants or other attorneys to assist in the prosecution of any action brought pursuant to this title.

CHAPTER 2. CRIMINAL LIABILITY

§ 16-2-1. "Crime" defined

(a) A "crime" is a violation of a statute of this state in which there is a joint operation of an act or omission to act and intention or criminal negligence.

(b) Criminal negligence is an act or failure to act which demonstrates a willful, wanton, or reckless disregard for the safety of others who might reasonably be expected to be injured thereby.

§ 16-2-2. Effect of misfortune or accident on guilt

A person shall not be found guilty of any crime committed by misfortune or accident where it satisfactorily appears there was no criminal scheme or undertaking, intention, or criminal negligence.

§ 16-2-3. Presumption of sound mind and discretion

Every person is presumed to be of sound mind and discretion but the presumption may be rebutted.

§ 16-2-4. Presumption that acts of sound person willful

The acts of a person of sound mind and discretion are presumed to be the product of the person's will but the presumption may be rebutted.

§ 16-2-5. Presumption that sound person intends natural and probable consequences of acts

A person of sound mind and discretion is presumed to intend the natural and probable consequences of his acts but the presumption may be rebutted.

§ 16-2-6. Intention a question of fact

A person will not be presumed to act with criminal intention but the trier of facts may find such intention upon consideration of the words, conduct, demeanor, motive, and all other circumstances connected with the act for which the accused is prosecuted.

§ 16-2-20. When a person is a party to a crime

(a) Every person concerned in the commission of a crime is a party thereto and may be charged with and convicted of commission of the crime.
(b) A person is concerned in the commission of a crime only if he:
(1) Directly commits the crime;
(2) Intentionally causes some other person to commit the crime under such circumstances that the other person is not guilty of any crime either in fact or because of legal incapacity;
(3) Intentionally aids or abets in the commission of the crime; or
(4) Intentionally advises, encourages, hires, counsels, or procures another to commit the crime.

§ 16-2-21. Prosecution of parties who did not directly commit the crime

Any party to a crime who did not directly commit the crime may be indicted, tried, convicted, and punished for commission of the crime upon proof that the crime was committed and that he was a party thereto, although the person claimed to have directly committed the crime has not been prosecuted or convicted, has been convicted of a different crime or degree of crime, or is not amenable to justice or has been acquitted.

§ 16-2-22. Criminal responsibility of corporations

(a) A corporation may be prosecuted for the act or omission constituting a crime only if:
(1) The crime is defined by a statute which clearly indicates a legislative purpose to impose liability on a corporation, and an agent of the corporation performs the conduct which is an element of the crime while acting within the scope of his office or employment and in behalf of the corporation; or
(2) The commission of the crime is authorized, requested, commanded, performed, or recklessly tolerated by the board of directors or by a managerial official who is acting within the scope of his employment in behalf of the corporation.
(b) For the purposes of this Code section, the term:
(1) "Agent" means any director, officer, servant, employee, or other person who is authorized to act in behalf of the corporation.
(2) "Managerial official" means an officer of the corporation or any other agent who has a position of comparable authority for the formulation of corporate policy or the supervision of subordinate employees.

CHAPTER 3. DEFENSES TO CRIMINAL PROSECUTIONS

§ 16-3-1. Minimum age

A person shall not be considered or found guilty of a crime unless he has attained the age of 13 years at the time of the act, omission, or negligence constituting the crime.

§ 16-3-2. Mental capacity; insanity

A person shall not be found guilty of a crime if, at the time of the act, omission, or negligence constituting the crime, the person did not have mental capacity to distinguish between right and wrong in relation to such act, omission, or negligence.

§ 16-3-3. Delusional compulsion

A person shall not be found guilty of a crime when, at the time of the act, omission, or negligence constituting the crime, the person, because of mental disease, injury, or congenital deficiency, acted as he did because of a delusional compulsion as to such act which overmastered his will to resist committing the crime.

§ 16-3-4. Intoxication

(a) A person shall not be found guilty of a crime when, at the time of the act, omission, or negligence constituting the crime, the person, because of involuntary intoxication, did not have sufficient mental capacity to distinguish between right and wrong in relation to such act.
(b) Involuntary intoxication means intoxication caused by:
(1) Consumption of a substance through excusable ignorance; or
(2) The coercion, fraud, artifice, or contrivance of another person.
(c) Voluntary intoxication shall not be an excuse for any criminal act or omission.

§ 16-3-5. Mistake of fact

A person shall not be found guilty of a crime if the act or omission to act constituting the crime was induced by a misapprehension of fact which, if true, would have justified the act or omission.

§ 16-3-6. Affirmative defenses to certain sexual crimes

(a) As used in this Code section, the term:
(1) "Coercion" shall have the same meaning as set forth in Code Section 16-5-46.
(2) "Deception" shall have the same meaning as set forth in Code Section 16-5-46.
(3) "Sexual crime" means prostitution, sodomy, solicitation of sodomy, or masturbation for hire as such offenses are proscribed in Chapter 6 of Title 16.
(4) "Sexual servitude" shall have the same meaning as set forth in Code Section 16-5-46.
(b) A person shall not be guilty of a sexual crime if the conduct upon which the alleged criminal liability is based was committed by an accused who was:
(1) Less than 18 years of age at the time of the conduct such person was being trafficked for sexual servitude in violation of subsection (c) of Code Section 16-5-46; or

(2) Acting under coercion or deception while the accused was being trafficked for sexual servitude in violation of subsection (c) of Code Section 16-5-46.

(c) A defense based upon any of the provisions of this Code section shall be an affirmative defense.

§ 16-3-20. Justification

The fact that a person's conduct is justified is a defense to prosecution for any crime based on that conduct. The defense of justification can be claimed:

(1) When the person's conduct is justified under Code Section 16-3-21, 16-3-23, 16-3-24, 16-3-25, or 16-3-26;

(2) When the person's conduct is in reasonable fulfillment of his duties as a government officer or employee;

(3) When the person's conduct is the reasonable discipline of a minor by his parent or a person in loco parentis;

(4) When the person's conduct is reasonable and is performed in the course of making a lawful arrest;

(5) When the person's conduct is justified for any other reason under the laws of this state, including as provided in Code Section 51-1-29; or

(6) In all other instances which stand upon the same footing of reason and justice as those enumerated in this article.

§ 16-3-21. Use of force in defense of self or others; evidence of belief that force was necessary in murder or manslaughter prosecution

(a) A person is justified in threatening or using force against another when and to the extent that he or she reasonably believes that such threat or force is necessary to defend himself or herself or a third person against such other's imminent use of unlawful force; however, except as provided in Code Section 16-3-23, a person is justified in using force which is intended or likely to cause death or great bodily harm only if he or she reasonably believes that such force is necessary to prevent death or great bodily injury to himself or herself or a third person or to prevent the commission of a forcible felony.

(b) A person is not justified in using force under the circumstances specified in subsection (a) of this Code section if he:

(1) Initially provokes the use of force against himself with the intent to use such force as an excuse to inflict bodily harm upon the assailant;

(2) Is attempting to commit, committing, or fleeing after the commission or attempted commission of a felony; or

(3) Was the aggressor or was engaged in a combat by agreement unless he withdraws from the encounter and effectively communicates to such other person his intent to do so and the other, notwithstanding, continues or threatens to continue the use of unlawful force.

(c) Any rule, regulation, or policy of any agency of the state or any ordinance, resolution, rule, regulation, or policy of any county, municipality, or other political subdivision of the state which is in conflict with this Code section shall be null, void, and of no force and effect.

(d) In a prosecution for murder or manslaughter, if a defendant raises as a defense a justification provided by subsection (a) of this Code section, the defendant, in order to establish the defendant's reasonable belief that the use of force or deadly force was immediately necessary, may be permitted to offer:

(1) Relevant evidence that the defendant had been the victim of acts of family violence or child abuse committed by the deceased, as such acts are described in Code Sections 19-13-1 and 19-15-1, respectively; and

(2) Relevant expert testimony regarding the condition of the mind of the defendant at the time of the offense, including those relevant facts and circumstances relating to the family violence or child abuse that are the bases of the expert's opinion.

§ 16-3-22. Immunity from criminal liability of persons rendering assistance to law enforcement officers

(a) Any person who renders assistance reasonably and in good faith to any law enforcement officer who is being hindered in the performance of his official duties or whose life is being endangered by the conduct of any other person or persons while performing his official duties shall be immune to the same extent as the law enforcement officer from any criminal liability that might otherwise be incurred or imposed as a result of rendering assistance to the law enforcement officer.

(b) The official report of the law enforcement agency shall create a rebuttable presumption of good faith and reasonableness on the part of the person who assists the law enforcement officer.

(c) The purpose of this Code section is to provide for those persons who act in good faith to assist law enforcement officers whose health and safety is being adversely affected and threatened by the conduct of any other person or persons. This Code section shall be liberally construed so as to carry out the purposes thereof.

§ 16-3-22.1. Persons who provide assistance to law enforcement officers or the Division of Family and Children Services when the health and safety of children are adversely affected and threatened

(a) Any person that in good faith has possession of materials or images in violation of Article 3 of Chapter 12 of this title and immediately notifies law enforcement officials or any person that is required by Code Section 19-7-5 to report suspected child abuse, or makes such notification within 72 hours from the time there is reasonable cause to believe such person is in possession of such materials or images, shall be immune to the same extent as a law enforcement officer would be immune from criminal liability for such possession.

(b) The official report of the law enforcement agency or the Division of Family and Children Services of the Department of Human Services shall create a rebuttable presumption of good faith and reasonableness on the part of the person that has possession.

(c) The purpose of this Code section is to provide for those persons that act in good faith to assist law enforcement officers or the Division of Family and Children Services of the Department of Human Services when the health and safety of a child are being adversely affected and threatened by the conduct of another. This Code section shall be liberally construed so as to carry out the purposes thereof.

§ 16-3-23. Use of force in defense of habitation

A person is justified in threatening or using force against another when and to the extent that he or she reasonably believes that such threat or force is necessary to prevent or terminate such other's unlawful entry into or attack upon a habitation; however, such person is justified in the use of force which is intended or likely to cause death or great bodily harm only if:

(1) The entry is made or attempted in a violent and tumultuous manner and he or she reasonably believes that the entry is attempted or made for the purpose of assaulting or offering personal violence to any person dwelling or being therein and that such force is necessary to prevent the assault or offer of personal violence;

(2) That force is used against another person who is not a member of the family or household and who unlawfully and forcibly enters or has unlawfully and forcibly entered the residence and the person using such force knew or had reason to believe that an unlawful and forcible entry occurred; or

(3) The person using such force reasonably believes that the entry is made or attempted for the purpose of committing a felony therein and that such force is necessary to prevent the commission of the felony.

§ 16-3-23.1. No duty to retreat prior to use of force in self-defense

A person who uses threats or force in accordance with Code Section 16-3-21, relating to the use of force in defense of self or others, Code Section 16-3-23, relating to the use of force in defense of a habitation, or Code Section 16-3-24, relating to the use of force in defense of property other than a habitation, has no duty to retreat and has the right to stand his or her ground and use force as provided in said Code sections, including deadly force.

§ 16-3-24. Use of force in defense of property other than a habitation

(a) A person is justified in threatening or using force against another when and to the extent that he reasonably believes that such threat or force is necessary to prevent or terminate such other's trespass on or other tortious or criminal interference with real property other than a habitation or personal property:

(1) Lawfully in his possession;
(2) Lawfully in the possession of a member of his immediate family; or
(3) Belonging to a person whose property he has a legal duty to protect.
(b) The use of force which is intended or likely to cause death or great bodily harm to prevent trespass on or other tortious or criminal interference with real property other than a habitation or personal property is not justified unless the person using such force reasonably believes that it is necessary to prevent the commission of a forcible felony.

§ 16-3-24.1. Habitation and personal property defined

As used in Code Sections 16-3-23 and 16-3-24, the term "habitation" means any dwelling, motor vehicle, or place of business, and "personal property" means personal property other than a motor vehicle.

§ 16-3-24.2. Immunity from prosecution; exception

A person who uses threats or force in accordance with Code Section 16-3-21, 16-3-23, 16-3-23.1, or 16-3-24 shall be immune from criminal prosecution therefor unless in the use of deadly force, such person utilizes a weapon the carrying or possession of which is unlawful by such person under Part 2 of Article 4 of Chapter 11 of this title.

§ 16-3-25. Entrapment

A person is not guilty of a crime if, by entrapment, his conduct is induced or solicited by a government officer or employee, or agent of either, for the purpose of obtaining evidence to be used in prosecuting the person for commission of the crime. Entrapment exists where the idea and intention of the commission of the crime originated with a government officer or employee, or with an agent of either, and he, by undue persuasion, incitement, or deceitful means, induced the accused to commit the act which the accused would not have committed except for the conduct of such officer.

§ 16-3-26. Coercion

A person is not guilty of a crime, except murder, if the act upon which the supposed criminal liability is based is performed under such coercion that the person reasonably believes that performing the act is the only way to prevent his imminent death or great bodily injury.

§ 16-3-27. Benefit of clergy

Since it is no longer needed or appropriate, the ancient device of benefit of clergy shall not exist.

§ 16-3-28. Affirmative defenses

A defense based upon any of the provisions of this article is an affirmative defense.

§ 16-3-40. Alibi

The defense of alibi involves the impossibility of the accused's presence at the scene of the offense at the time of its commission. The range of the evidence in respect to time and place must be such as reasonably to exclude the possibility of presence.

CHAPTER 4. CRIMINAL ATTEMPT, CONSPIRACY, AND SOLICITATION

§ 16-4-1. Criminal attempt

A person commits the offense of criminal attempt when, with intent to commit a specific crime, he performs any act which constitutes a substantial step toward the commission of that crime.

§ 16-4-2. Conviction for criminal attempt where crime completed

A person may be convicted of the offense of criminal attempt if the crime attempted was actually committed in pursuance of the attempt but may not be convicted of both the criminal attempt and the completed crime.

§ 16-4-3. Charge of commission of crime as including criminal attempt

A person charged with commission of a crime may be convicted of the offense of criminal attempt as to that crime without being specifically charged with the criminal attempt in the accusation, indictment, or presentment.

§ 16-4-4. Impossibility as a defense

It is no defense to a charge of criminal attempt that the crime the accused is charged with attempting was, under the attendant circumstances, factually or legally impossible of commission if such crime could have been committed had the attendant circumstances been as the accused believed them to be.

§ 16-4-5. Abandonment of effort to commit a crime as an affirmative defense

(a) When a person's conduct would otherwise constitute an attempt to commit a crime under Code Section 16-4-1, it is an affirmative defense that he abandoned his effort to commit the crime or in any other manner prevented its commission under circumstances manifesting a voluntary and complete renunciation of his criminal purpose.
(b) A renunciation of criminal purpose is not voluntary and complete if it results from:
(1) A belief that circumstances exist which increase the probability of detection or apprehension of the person or which render more difficult the accomplishment of the criminal purpose; or
(2) A decision to postpone the criminal conduct until another time.

§ 16-4-6. Penalties for criminal attempt

(a) A person convicted of the offense of criminal attempt to commit a crime punishable by death or by life imprisonment shall be punished by imprisonment for not less than one year nor more than 30 years.

(b) A person convicted of the offense of criminal attempt to commit a felony, other than a felony punishable by death or life imprisonment, shall be punished by imprisonment for not less than one year nor more than one-half the maximum period of time for which he or she could have been sentenced if he or she had been convicted of the crime attempted, by one-half the maximum fine to which he or she could have been subjected if he or she had been convicted of the crime attempted, or both.

(c) A person convicted of the offense of criminal attempt to commit a misdemeanor shall be punished as for a misdemeanor.

§ 16-4-7. Criminal solicitation

(a) A person commits the offense of criminal solicitation when, with intent that another person engage in conduct constituting a felony, he solicits, requests, commands, importunes, or otherwise attempts to cause the other person to engage in such conduct.

(b) A person convicted of the offense of criminal solicitation to commit a felony shall be punished by imprisonment for not less than one nor more than three years. A person convicted of the offense of criminal solicitation to commit a crime punishable by death or by life imprisonment shall be punished by imprisonment for not less than one nor more than five years.

(c) It is no defense to a prosecution for criminal solicitation that the person solicited could not be guilty of the crime solicited.

(d) The provisions of subsections (a) through (c) of this Code section are cumulative and shall not supersede any other penal law of this state.

§ 16-4-8. Conspiracy to commit a crime

A person commits the offense of conspiracy to commit a crime when he together with one or more persons conspires to commit any crime and any one or more of such persons does any overt act to effect the object of the conspiracy. A person convicted of the offense of criminal conspiracy to commit a felony shall be punished by imprisonment for not less than one year nor more than one-half the maximum period of time for which he could have been sentenced if he had been convicted of the crime conspired to have been committed, by one-half the maximum fine to which he could have been subjected if he had been convicted of such crime, or both. A person convicted of the offense of criminal conspiracy to commit a misdemeanor shall be punished as for a misdemeanor. A person convicted of the offense of criminal conspiracy to commit a crime punishable by death or by life imprisonment shall be punished by imprisonment for not less than one year nor more than ten years.

§ 16-4-8.1. Conviction of conspiracy even if crime completed.

A person may be convicted of the offense of conspiracy to commit a crime, as defined in Code Section 16-4-8, even if the crime which was the objective of the conspiracy was actually committed or completed in pursuance of the conspiracy, but such person may not be convicted of both conspiracy to commit a crime and the completed crime.

§ 16-4-9. Withdrawal by coconspirator from agreement to commit crime

A coconspirator may be relieved from the effects of Code Section 16-4-8 if he can show that before the overt act occurred he withdrew his agreement to commit a crime.

§ 16-4-10. Domestic terrorism; penalty

Repealed by Ga. L. 2017, p. 536, § 2-1/HB 452, effective July 1, 2017.

CHAPTER 5. CRIMES AGAINST THE PERSON

§ 16-5-1. Murder; malice murder; felony murder; murder in the second degree

(a) A person commits the offense of murder when he unlawfully and with malice aforethought, either express or implied, causes the death of another human being.

(b) Express malice is that deliberate intention unlawfully to take the life of another human being which is manifested by external circumstances capable of proof. Malice shall be implied where no considerable provocation appears and where all the circumstances of the killing show an abandoned and malignant heart.

(c) A person commits the offense of murder when, in the commission of a felony, he or she causes the death of another human being irrespective of malice.

(d) A person commits the offense of murder in the second degree when, in the commission of cruelty to children in the second degree, he or she causes the death of another human being irrespective of malice.

(e) (1) A person convicted of the offense of murder shall be punished by death, by imprisonment for life without parole, or by imprisonment for life.

(2) A person convicted of the offense of murder in the second degree shall be punished by imprisonment for not less than ten nor more than 30 years.

§ 16-5-2. Voluntary manslaughter

(a) A person commits the offense of voluntary manslaughter when he causes the death of another human being under circumstances which would otherwise be murder and if he acts solely as the result of a sudden, violent, and irresistible passion resulting from serious provocation sufficient to excite such passion in a reasonable person; however, if there should have been an interval between the provocation and the killing sufficient for the voice of reason and humanity to be heard, of which the jury in all cases shall be the judge, the killing shall be attributed to deliberate revenge and be punished as murder.

(b) A person who commits the offense of voluntary manslaughter, upon conviction thereof, shall be punished by imprisonment for not less than one nor more than 20 years.

§ 16-5-3. Involuntary manslaughter

(a) A person commits the offense of involuntary manslaughter in the commission of an unlawful act when he causes the death of another human being without any intention to do so by the commission of an unlawful act other than a felony. A person who commits the offense of involuntary manslaughter in the commission of an unlawful act, upon conviction thereof, shall be punished by imprisonment for not less than one year nor more than ten years.

(b) A person commits the offense of involuntary manslaughter in the commission of a lawful act in an unlawful manner when he causes the death of another human being without any intention to do so, by the commission of a lawful act in an unlawful manner likely to cause death or great bodily harm. A person who commits the offense of involuntary manslaughter in the commission of a lawful act in an unlawful manner, upon conviction thereof, shall be punished as for a misdemeanor.

§ 16-5-4. Time elapsed between injury and death

In order to be a homicide punishable under this article, death need not have occurred within a year and a day from the date of the injury alleged to have caused such death.

§ 16-5-5. Assisted suicide; notification of licensing board regarding violation

(a) As used in this Code section, the term:
(1) "Assists" means the act of physically helping or physically providing the means.
(2) "Health care provider" means any person licensed, certified, or registered under Chapter 9, 10A, 11, 11A, 26, 28, 30, 33, 34, 35, 39, or 44 of Title 43.
(3) "Suicide" means the intentional and willful termination of one's own life.
(b) Any person with actual knowledge that a person intends to commit suicide who knowingly and willfully assists such person in the commission of such person's suicide shall be guilty of a felony and, upon conviction thereof, shall be punished by imprisonment for not less than one nor more than ten years.
(c) The provisions of this Code section shall not apply to:
(1) Pursuant to a patient's consent, any person prescribing, dispensing, or administering medications or medical procedures when such actions are calculated or intended to relieve or prevent such patient's pain or discomfort but are not calculated or intended to cause such patient's death, even if the medication or medical procedure may have the effect of hastening or increasing the risk of death;
(2) Pursuant to a patient's consent, any person discontinuing, withholding, or withdrawing medications, medical procedures, nourishment, or hydration;
(3) Any person prescribing, dispensing, or administering medications or medical procedures pursuant to, without limitation, a living will, a durable power of attorney for health care, an advance directive for health care, a Physician Orders for Life-Sustaining Treatment form pursuant to Code Section 31-1-14, or a consent pursuant to Code Section 29-4-18 or 31-9-2 when such actions are calculated or intended to relieve or prevent a patient's pain or discomfort but are not calculated or intended to cause such patient's death, even if the medication or medical procedure may have the effect of hastening or increasing the risk of death;
(4) Any person discontinuing, withholding, or withdrawing medications, medical procedures, nourishment, or hydration pursuant to, without limitation, a living will, a durable power of attorney for health care, an advance directive for health care, a Physician Orders for Life-Sustaining Treatment form pursuant to Code Section 31-1-14, a consent pursuant to Code Section 29-4-18 or 31-9-2, or a written order not to resuscitate; or
(5) Any person advocating on behalf of a patient in accordance with this subsection.
(d) Within ten days of a conviction, a health care provider who is convicted of violating this Code section shall notify in writing the applicable licensing board for his or her licensure, certification, registration, or other authorization to conduct such health care provider's occupation. Upon being notified and notwithstanding any law, rule, or regulation to the contrary, the appropriate licensing board shall revoke the license, certification, registration, or other authorization to conduct such health care provider's occupation.

§ 16-5-19. Definitions

As used in this article, the term:
(1) "Correctional officer" means any person who is authorized to exercise the power of arrest and who is employed or appointed by the Department of Corrections or the State Board of Pardons and Paroles.
(2) "Emergency health worker" means hospital emergency department personnel and emergency medical services personnel.
(3) "Firefighter" shall have the same meaning as set forth in Code Section 25-4-2.
(4) "Highway emergency response operator" means an individual employed by the Department of Transportation who operates a towing or recovery vehicle or highway maintenance vehicle.
(5) "Jail officer" means any person who is employed or appointed by a county or a municipality and who has the responsibility of supervising inmates who are confined in a municipal or county detention facility.
(6) "Juvenile correctional officer" means any person employed or appointed by the Department of Juvenile Justice who has the primary responsibility for the supervision and control of youth confined in its programs and facilities.
(7) "Officer of the court" means a judge, attorney, clerk of court, deputy clerk of court, court reporter, or court interpreter.
(8) "Probation officer" means a community supervision officer, county or Department of Juvenile Justice juvenile probation officer, or probation officer serving pursuant to Article 6 of Chapter 8 of Title 42.
(9) "Public safety officer" means peace officer, correctional officer, emergency health worker, firefighter, highway emergency response operator, jail officer, juvenile correctional officer, or probation officer.
(10) "Public transit vehicle" shall have the same meaning as set forth in Code Section 16-5-20.
(11) "Strangulation" means impeding the normal breathing or circulation of blood of another person by applying pressure to the throat or neck of such person or by obstructing the nose and mouth of such person.

§ 16-5-20. Simple assault

(a) A person commits the offense of simple assault when he or she either:
(1) Attempts to commit a violent injury to the person of another; or
(2) Commits an act which places another in reasonable apprehension of immediately receiving a violent injury.
(b) Except as provided in subsections (c) through (h) of this Code section, a person who commits the offense of simple assault shall be guilty of a misdemeanor.
(c) Any person who commits the offense of simple assault in a public transit vehicle or station shall, upon conviction thereof, be punished for a misdemeanor of a high and aggravated nature. For purposes of this Code section, "public transit vehicle" means a bus, van, or rail car used for the transportation of passengers within a system which receives a subsidy from tax revenues or is operated under a franchise contract with a county or municipality of this state.
(d) If the offense of simple assault is committed between past or present spouses, persons who are parents of the same child, parents and children, stepparents and stepchildren, foster parents and foster children, or other persons excluding siblings living or formerly living in the same household, the defendant shall be punished for a misdemeanor of a high and aggravated nature. In no event shall this subsection be applicable to corporal punishment administered by a parent or guardian to a child or administered by a person acting in loco parentis.
(e) Any person who commits the offense of simple assault against a person who is 65 years of age or older shall, upon conviction thereof, be punished for a misdemeanor of a high and aggravated nature.
(f) Any person who commits the offense of simple assault against an employee of a public school system of this state while such employee is engaged in official duties or on school property shall, upon conviction of such offense, be punished for a misdemeanor of a high and aggravated nature. For purposes of this Code section, "school property" shall include public school buses and stops for public school buses as designated by local school boards of education.
(g) Any person who commits the offense of simple assault against a female who is pregnant at the time of the offense shall, upon conviction thereof, be punished for a misdemeanor of a high and aggravated nature.
(h) Nothing in this Code section shall be construed to permit the prosecution of:
(1) Any person for conduct relating to an abortion for which the consent of the pregnant woman, or person authorized by law to act on her behalf, has been obtained or for which such consent is implied by law;
(2) Any person for any medical treatment of the pregnant woman or her unborn child; or
(3) Any woman with respect to her unborn child.
For the purposes of this subsection, the term "unborn child" means a member of the species homo sapiens at any stage of development who is carried in the womb.

§ 16-5-21. Aggravated assault

(a) A person commits the offense of aggravated assault when he or she assaults:

(1) With intent to murder, to rape, or to rob;

(2) With a deadly weapon or with any object, device, or instrument which, when used offensively against a person, is likely to or actually does result in serious bodily injury;

(3) With any object, device, or instrument which, when used offensively against a person, is likely to or actually does result in strangulation; or

(4) A person or persons without legal justification by discharging a firearm from within a motor vehicle toward a person or persons.

(b) Except as provided in subsections (c) through (k) of this Code section, a person convicted of the offense of aggravated assault shall be punished by imprisonment for not less than one nor more than 20 years.

(c)

(1) A person who knowingly commits the offense of aggravated assault upon a public safety officer while he or she is engaged in, or on account of the performance of, his or her official duties shall, upon conviction thereof, be punished as follows:

(A) When such assault occurs by the discharge of a firearm by a person who is at least 17 years of age, such person shall be punished by imprisonment for not less than ten nor more than 20 years and shall be sentenced to a mandatory minimum term of imprisonment of ten years and no portion of the mandatory minimum sentence imposed shall be suspended, stayed, probated, deferred, or withheld by the sentencing court; provided, however, that in the court's discretion, the court may depart from such mandatory minimum sentence when the prosecuting attorney and defendant have agreed to a sentence that is below such mandatory minimum;

(B) When such assault does not involve the discharge of a firearm by a person who is at least 17 years of age, and does not involve only the use of the person's body, such person shall be punished by imprisonment for not less than five nor more than 20 years and, for persons who are at least 17 years of age, shall be sentenced to a mandatory minimum term of imprisonment of three years and no portion of the mandatory minimum sentence imposed shall be suspended, stayed, probated, deferred, or withheld by the sentencing court; provided, however, that in the court's discretion, the court may depart from such mandatory minimum sentence when the prosecuting attorney and defendant have agreed to a sentence that is below such mandatory minimum; or

(C) When such assault occurs only involving the use of the person's body, by imprisonment for not less than five nor more than 20 years.

(2) A person convicted under this subsection shall be punished, in addition to any term of imprisonment imposed, by a fine as provided by law which shall be at least $2,000.00. With respect to $2,000.00 of the fine imposed, after distributing the surcharges and deductions required by Chapter 21 of Title 15, Code Sections 36-15-9 and 42-8-34, and Title 47, it shall be earmarked for the Georgia State Indemnification Fund for purposes of payment of indemnification for death or disability as provided for in Part 1 of Article 5 of Chapter 9 of Title 45.

(3) As used in this subsection, the term "firearm" means any handgun, rifle, shotgun, or similar device or weapon which will or can be converted to expel a projectile by the action of an explosive or electrical charge.

(d) Any person who commits the offense of aggravated assault against a person who is 65 years of age or older shall, upon conviction thereof, be punished by imprisonment for not less than three nor more than 20 years.

(e) Any person who commits the offense of aggravated assault in a public transit vehicle or station shall, upon conviction thereof, be punished by imprisonment for not less than three nor more than 20 years.

(f) Any person who commits the offense of aggravated assault upon a person in the course of violating Code Section 16-8-2 where the property that was the subject of the theft was a vehicle engaged in commercial transportation of cargo or any appurtenance thereto, including without limitation any such trailer, semitrailer, container, or other associated equipment, or the cargo being transported therein or thereon, shall upon conviction be punished by imprisonment for not less than five nor more than 20 years, a fine not less than $50,000.00 nor more than $200,000.00, or both such fine and imprisonment. For purposes of this subsection, the term "vehicle" includes without limitation any railcar.

(g) Except as provided in subsection (c) of this Code section, a person convicted of an offense described in paragraph (4) of subsection (a) of this Code section shall be punished by imprisonment for not less than five nor more than 20 years.

(h) Any person who commits the offense of aggravated assault involving the use of a firearm upon a student or teacher or other school personnel within a school safety zone as defined in Code Section 16-11-127.1 shall, upon conviction thereof, be punished by imprisonment for not less than five nor more than 20 years.

(i) If the offense of aggravated assault is committed between past or present spouses, persons who are parents of the same child, parents and children, stepparents and stepchildren, foster parents and foster children, or other persons excluding siblings living or formerly living in the same household, the defendant shall be punished by imprisonment for not less than three nor more than 20 years.

(j) Any person who commits the offense of aggravated assault with intent to rape against a child under the age of 14 years shall be punished by imprisonment for not less than 25 nor more than 50 years. Any person convicted under this subsection shall, in addition, be subject to the sentencing and punishment provisions of Code Section 17-10-6.2.

(k) A person who knowingly commits the offense of aggravated assault upon an officer of the court while such officer is engaged in, or on account of the performance of, his or her official duties shall, upon conviction thereof, be punished by imprisonment for not less than five nor more than 20 years.

§ 16-5-22. Conviction of assault with intent to commit a crime if intended crime actually committed

A person may be convicted of the offense of assault with intent to commit a crime if the crime intended was actually committed as a result of the assault but may not be convicted of both the assault and completed crime.

§ 16-5-23. Simple battery

(a) A person commits the offense of simple battery when he or she either:

(1) Intentionally makes physical contact of an insulting or provoking nature with the person of another; or

(2) Intentionally causes physical harm to another.

(b) Except as otherwise provided in subsections (c) through (i) of this Code section, a person convicted of the offense of simple battery shall be punished as for a misdemeanor.

(c) Any person who commits the offense of simple battery against a person who is 65 years of age or older or against a female who is pregnant at the time of the offense shall, upon conviction thereof, be punished for a misdemeanor of a high and aggravated nature.

(d) Any person who commits the offense of simple battery in a public transit vehicle or station shall, upon conviction thereof, be punished for a misdemeanor of a high and aggravated nature. For purposes of this Code section, "public transit vehicle" has the same meaning as in subsection (c) of Code Section 16-5-20.

(e) Any person who commits the offense of simple battery against a police officer, correction officer, or detention officer engaged in carrying out official duties shall, upon conviction thereof, be punished for a misdemeanor of a high and aggravated nature.

(f) If the offense of simple battery is committed between past or present spouses, persons who are parents of the same child, parents and children, stepparents and stepchildren, foster parents and foster children, or other persons excluding siblings living or formerly living in the same household, the defendant shall be punished for a misdemeanor of a high and aggravated nature. In no event shall this subsection be applicable to corporal punishment administered by a parent or guardian to a child or administered by a person acting in loco parentis.

(g) A person who is an employee, agent, or volunteer at any facility licensed or required to be licensed under Code Section 31-7-3, relating to long-term care facilities, or Code Section 31-7-12.2, relating to assisted living communities, or Code Section 31-7-12, relating to personal care homes, or who is required to be licensed pursuant to Code Section 31-7-151 or 31-7-173, relating to home health care and hospices, who commits the offense of simple battery against a person who is admitted to or receiving services from such facility, person, or entity shall be punished for a misdemeanor of a high and aggravated nature.

(h) Any person who commits the offense of simple battery against a sports official while such sports official is officiating an amateur contest or while such sports official is on or exiting the property where he or she will officiate or has completed officiating an amateur contest shall, upon conviction thereof, be punished for a misdemeanor of a high and aggravated nature. For the purposes of this Code section, the term "sports official" means any person who officiates, umpires, or referees an amateur contest at the collegiate, elementary or secondary school, or recreational level.

(i) Any person who commits the offense of simple battery against an employee of a public school system of this state while such employee is engaged in official duties or on school property shall, upon conviction of such offense, be punished for a misdemeanor of a high and aggravated nature. For purposes of this Code section, "school property" shall include public school buses and stops for public school buses as designated by local school boards of education.

§ 16-5-23.1. Battery

(a) A person commits the offense of battery when he or she intentionally causes substantial physical harm or visible bodily harm to another.

(b) As used in this Code section, the term "visible bodily harm" means bodily harm capable of being perceived by a person other than the victim and may include, but is not limited to, substantially blackened eyes, substantially swollen lips or other facial or body parts, or substantial bruises to body parts.

(c) Except as provided in subsections (d) through (l) of this Code section, a person who commits the offense of battery is guilty of a misdemeanor.

(d) Upon the second conviction for battery against the same victim, the defendant shall be punished by imprisonment for not less than ten days nor more than 12 months, by a fine not to exceed $1,000.00, or both. The minimum sentence of ten days for a second offense shall not be suspended, probated, deferred, stayed, or withheld; provided, however, that it is within the authority and discretion of the sentencing judge to:

(1) Allow the sentence to be served on weekends by weekend confinement or during the nonworking hours of the defendant. A weekend shall commence and shall end in the discretion of the sentencing judge, and the nonworking hours of the defendant shall be determined in the discretion of the sentencing judge; or

(2) Suspend, probate, defer, stay, or withhold the minimum sentence where there exists clear and convincing evidence that imposition of the minimum sentence would either create an undue hardship upon the defendant or result in a failure of justice.

(e) Upon a third or subsequent conviction for battery against the same victim, the defendant shall be guilty of a felony and shall be punished by imprisonment for not less than one nor more than five years. The minimum sentence provisions contained in subsection (d) of this Code section shall apply to sentences imposed pursuant to this subsection.

(f) (1) As used in this subsection, the term "household member" means past or present spouses, persons who are parents of the same child, parents and children, stepparents and stepchildren, foster parents and foster children, or other persons living or formerly living in the same household.

(2) If the offense of battery is committed between household members, it shall constitute the offense of family violence battery and shall be punished as follows:

(A) Upon a first conviction of family violence battery, the defendant shall be guilty of and punished for a misdemeanor; provided, however, that if the defendant has previously been convicted of a forcible felony committed between household members under the laws of this state, of the United States, including the laws of its territories, possessions, or dominions, or any of the several states, or of any foreign nation recognized by the United States, which if committed in this state would have constituted a forcible felony committed between household members, he or she shall be guilty of a felony and shall be punished by imprisonment for not less than one nor more than five years; and

(B) Upon a second or subsequent conviction of family violence battery against the same or another victim, the defendant shall be guilty of a felony and shall be punished by imprisonment for not less than one nor more than five years.

(3) In no event shall this subsection be applicable to reasonable corporal punishment administered by parent to child.

(g) Any person who commits the offense of battery in a public transit vehicle or station shall, upon conviction thereof, be punished for a misdemeanor of a high and aggravated nature. For purposes of this Code section, "public transit vehicle" has the same meaning as in subsection (c) of Code Section 16-5-20.

(h) Any person who commits the offense of battery against a female who is pregnant at the time of the offense shall, upon conviction thereof, be punished for a misdemeanor of a high and aggravated nature.

(i) Any person who commits the offense of battery against a teacher or other school personnel engaged in the performance of official duties or while on school property shall, upon conviction thereof, be punished by imprisonment for not less than one nor more than five years or a fine of not more than $10,000.00, or both. For purposes of this Code section, "school property" shall include public school buses and public school bus stops as designated by local school boards of education.

(j) Except as otherwise provided in subsection (e) and paragraph (2) of subsection (f) of this Code section, any person who commits the offense of battery against a person who is 65 years of age or older shall, upon conviction thereof, be punished for a misdemeanor of a high and aggravated nature.

(k) A person who is an employee, agent, or volunteer at any facility licensed or required to be licensed under Code Section 31-7-3, relating to long-term care facilities, or Code Section 31-7-12.2, relating to assisted living communities, or Code Section 31-7-12, relating to personal care homes, or who is required to be licensed pursuant to Code Section 31-7-151 or 31-7-173, relating to home health care and hospices, who commits the offense of battery against a person who is admitted to or receiving services from such facility, person, or entity shall, upon conviction thereof, be punished by imprisonment for not less than one nor more than five years, or a fine of not more than $2,000.00, or both.

(l) Any person who commits the offense of battery against a sports official while such sports official is officiating an amateur contest or while such sports official is on or exiting the property where he or she will officiate or has completed officiating an amateur contest shall, upon conviction thereof, be punished for a misdemeanor of a high and aggravated nature. For purposes of this Code section, the term "sports official" means any person who officiates, umpires, or referees an amateur contest at the collegiate, elementary or secondary school, or recreational level.

§ 16-5-24. Aggravated battery

(a) A person commits the offense of aggravated battery when he or she maliciously causes bodily harm to another by depriving him or her of a member of his or her body, by rendering a member of his or her body useless, or by seriously disfiguring his or her body or a member thereof.

(b) Except as provided in subsections (c) through (g) of this Code section, a person convicted of the offense of aggravated battery shall be punished by imprisonment for not less than one nor more than 20 years.

(c) (1) A person who knowingly commits the offense of aggravated battery upon a public safety officer while the public safety officer is engaged in, or on account of the performance of, his or her official duties shall, upon conviction thereof, be punished by imprisonment for not less than ten nor more than 20 years; provided, however, that for persons who are at least 17 years of age, a mandatory minimum term of imprisonment of three years shall be imposed and no portion of the mandatory minimum sentence shall be suspended, stayed, probated, deferred, or otherwise withheld by the sentencing court; provided, however, that in the court's discretion, the court may depart from such mandatory minimum sentence when the prosecuting attorney and defendant have agreed to a sentence that is below such mandatory minimum.

(2) A person convicted under this subsection shall be punished, in addition to any term of imprisonment imposed, by a fine as provided by law which shall be at least $2,000.00. With respect to $2,000.00 of the fine imposed, after distributing the surcharges and deductions required by Chapter 21 of Title 15, Code Sections 36-15-9 and 42-8-34, and Title 47, it shall be earmarked for the Georgia State Indemnification Fund for purposes of payment of indemnification for death or disability as provided for in Part 1 of Article 5 of Chapter 9 of Title 45.

(d) Any person who commits the offense of aggravated battery against a person who is 65 years of age or older shall, upon conviction thereof, be punished by imprisonment for not less than five nor more than 20 years.

(e) Any person who commits the offense of aggravated battery in a public transit vehicle or station shall, upon conviction thereof, be punished by imprisonment for not less than five nor more than 20 years.

(f) Any person who commits the offense of aggravated battery upon a student or teacher or other school personnel within a school safety zone as defined in Code Section 16-11-127.1 shall, upon conviction thereof, be punished by imprisonment for not less than five nor more than 20 years.

(g) If the offense of aggravated battery is committed between past or present spouses, persons who are parents of the same child, parents and children, stepparents and stepchildren, foster parents and foster children, or other persons excluding siblings living or formerly living in the same household, the defendant shall be punished by imprisonment for not less than three nor more than 20 years.

§ 16-5-25. Opprobrious or abusive language as justification for simple assault or simple battery

A person charged with the offense of simple assault or simple battery may introduce in evidence any opprobrious or abusive language used by the person against whom force was threatened or used; and the trier of facts may, in its discretion, find that the words used were justification for simple assault or simple battery.

§ 16-5-26. Publication of second or subsequent conviction of simple assault, simple battery, or battery; cost of publication; good faith publications immune from liability

(a) The clerk of the court in which a person is convicted of a second or subsequent violation of Code Section 16-5-20 and is sentenced pursuant to subsection (d) of such Code section, Code Section 16-5-23 and is sentenced pursuant to subsection (f) of such Code section, or Code Section 16-5-23.1 shall cause to be published a notice of conviction for such person. Such notice of conviction shall be published in the manner of legal notices in the legal organ of the county in which such person resides or, in the case of nonresidents, in the legal organ of the county in which the person was convicted. Such notice of conviction shall be one column wide by two inches long and shall contain the photograph taken by the arresting law enforcement agency at the time of arrest; the name and address of the convicted person; the date, time, and place of arrest; and the disposition of the case and shall be published once in the legal organ of the appropriate county in the second week following such conviction or as soon thereafter as publication may be made.
(b) The convicted person for which a notice of conviction is published pursuant to this Code section shall be assessed $25.00 for the cost of publication of such notice and such assessment shall be imposed at the time of conviction in addition to any other fine imposed.
(c) The clerk of the court, the publisher of any legal organ which publishes a notice of conviction, and any other person involved in the publication of an erroneous notice of conviction shall be immune from civil or criminal liability for such erroneous publication, provided that such publication was made in good faith.

§ 16-5-27. Female genital mutilation

(a) Any person:
(1) Who knowingly circumcises, excises, or infibulates, in whole or in part, the labia majora, labia minora, or clitoris of a female under 18 years of age;
(2) Who is a parent, guardian, or has immediate custody or control of a female under 18 years of age and knowingly consents to or permits the circumcision, excision, or infibulation, in whole or in part, of the labia majora, labia minora, or clitoris of such female; or
(3) Who knowingly removes or causes or permits the removal of a female under 18 years of age from this state for the purpose of circumcising, excising, or infibulating, in whole or in part, the labia majora, labia minora, or clitoris of such female
shall be guilty of female genital mutilation.
(b) A person convicted of female genital mutilation shall be punished by imprisonment for not less than five nor more than 20 years.
(c) This Code section shall not apply to procedures performed by or under the direction of a physician, a registered professional nurse, a certified nurse midwife, or a licensed practical nurse licensed pursuant to Chapter 34 or 26, respectively, of Title 43 when necessary to preserve the physical health of the female. This Code section shall also not apply to any autopsy or limited dissection as defined by Code Section 45-16-21 which is conducted in accordance with Article 2 of Chapter 16 of Title 45.
(d) Consent of the female under 18 years of age or the parent, guardian, or custodian of the female under 18 years of age shall not be a defense to the offense of female genital mutilation. Religion, ritual, custom, or standard practice shall not be a defense to the offense of female genital mutilation.
(e) The statutory privileges provided by Chapter 5 of Title 24 shall not apply to proceedings in which one of the parties to the privilege is charged with a crime against a female under 18 years of age, but such person shall be compellable to give evidence only on the specific act for which the accused is charged.

§ 16-5-28. Assault on an unborn child

(a) For the purposes of this Code section, the term "unborn child" means a member of the species homo sapiens at any stage of development who is carried in the womb.
(b) A person commits the offense of assault of an unborn child when such person, without legal justification, attempts to inflict violent injury to an unborn child.
(c) Any person convicted of the offense of assault of an unborn child shall be guilty of a misdemeanor.
(d) Nothing in this Code section shall be construed to permit the prosecution of:
(1) Any person for conduct relating to an abortion for which the consent of the pregnant woman, or person authorized by law to act on her behalf, has been obtained or for which such consent is implied by law;
(2) Any person for any medical treatment of the pregnant woman or her unborn child; or
(3) Any woman with respect to her unborn child.

§ 16-5-29. Battery of an unborn child

(a) For the purposes of this Code section, the term "unborn child" means a member of the species homo sapiens at any stage of development who is carried in the womb.
(b) A person commits the offense of battery of an unborn child when such person, without legal justification, intentionally inflicts physical harm upon an unborn child.
(c) A person convicted of the offense of battery of an unborn child shall be guilty of a misdemeanor.
(d) Nothing in this Code section shall be construed to permit the prosecution of:
(1) Any person for conduct relating to an abortion for which the consent of the pregnant woman, or person authorized by law to act on her behalf, has been obtained or for which such consent is implied by law;
(2) Any person for any medical treatment of the pregnant woman or her unborn child; or
(3) Any woman with respect to her unborn child.

§ 16-5-40. Kidnapping

(a) A person commits the offense of kidnapping when such person abducts or steals away another person without lawful authority or warrant and holds such other person against his or her will.
(b) (1) For the offense of kidnapping to occur, slight movement shall be sufficient; provided, however, that any such slight movement of another person which occurs while in the commission of any other offense shall not constitute the offense of kidnapping if such movement is merely incidental to such other offense.
(2) Movement shall not be considered merely incidental to another offense if it:
(A) Conceals or isolates the victim;
(B) Makes the commission of the other offense substantially easier;
(C) Lessens the risk of detection; or
(D) Is for the purpose of avoiding apprehension.
(c) The offense of kidnapping shall be considered a separate offense and shall not merge with any other offense.
(d) A person convicted of the offense of kidnapping shall be punished by:
(1) Imprisonment for not less than ten nor more than 20 years if the kidnapping involved a victim who was 14 years of age or older;
(2) Imprisonment for life or by a split sentence that is a term of imprisonment for not less than 25 years and not exceeding life imprisonment, followed by probation for life, if the kidnapping involved a victim who is less than 14 years of age;
(3) Life imprisonment or death if the kidnapping was for ransom; or
(4) Life imprisonment or death if the person kidnapped received bodily injury.
(e) Any person convicted under this Code section shall, in addition, be subject to the sentencing and punishment provisions of Code Sections 17-10-6.1 and 17-10-7.
(f) The offense of kidnapping is declared to be a continuous offense, and venue may be in any county where the accused exercises dominion or control over the person of another.

§ 16-5-41. False imprisonment

(a) A person commits the offense of false imprisonment when, in violation of the personal liberty of another, he arrests, confines, or detains such person without legal authority.

(b) A person convicted of the offense of false imprisonment shall be punished by imprisonment for not less than one nor more than ten years.

(c) Any person convicted under this Code section wherein the victim is not the child of the defendant and the victim is less than 14 years of age shall, in addition, be subject to the sentencing and punishment provisions of Code Section 17-10-6.2.

§ 16-5-42. False imprisonment under color of legal process

When the arrest, confinement, or detention of a person by warrant, mandate, or process is manifestly illegal and shows malice and oppression, an officer issuing or knowingly and maliciously executing the same shall, upon conviction thereof, be removed from office and punished by imprisonment for not less than one nor more than ten years.

§ 16-5-43. Malicious confinement of sane person in an asylum

A person who maliciously causes the confinement of a sane person, knowing such person to be sane, in any asylum, public or private, shall, upon conviction thereof, be punished by imprisonment for not less than one nor more than ten years.

§ 16-5-44. Hijacking an aircraft

(a) A person commits the offense of hijacking an aircraft when he (1) by use of force or (2) by intimidation by the use of threats or coercion places the pilot of an aircraft in fear of immediate serious bodily injury to himself or to another and causes the diverting of an aircraft from its intended destination to a destination dictated by such person.

(b) The offense of hijacking is declared to be a continuing offense from the point of beginning, and jurisdiction to try a person accused of the offense of hijacking shall be in any county of this state over which the aircraft is operated.

(c) A person convicted of the offense of hijacking an aircraft shall be punished by death or life imprisonment.

§ 16-5-44.1. Hijacking a motor vehicle

(a) As used in this Code section:

(1) "Firearm" means any handgun, rifle, shotgun, or similar device or weapon which will or can be converted to expel a projectile by the action of an explosive or electrical charge and includes stun guns and tasers as defined by subsection (a) of Code Section 16-11-106, as amended, and any replica, article, or device having the appearance of a firearm.

(2) "Motor vehicle" means any vehicle which is self-propelled.

(3) "Weapon" means an object, device, or instrument which when used against a person is likely to or actually does result in serious bodily injury or death or any replica, article, or device having the appearance of such a weapon including, but not limited to, any object defined as a hazardous object by Code Section 20-2-751 or as a dangerous weapon by Code Section 16-11-121.

(b) (1) A person commits the offense of hijacking a motor vehicle in the first degree when such person while in possession of a firearm or weapon obtains a motor vehicle from an individual or the presence of another individual by force and violence or intimidation or attempts or conspires to do so.

(2) A person commits the offense of hijacking a motor vehicle in the second degree when such person obtains a motor vehicle from an individual without his or her consent or from the immediate presence of another individual without his or her consent or attempts or conspires to do so.

(c) (1) A person convicted of the offense of hijacking a motor vehicle in the first degree shall be punished by imprisonment for not less than ten nor more than 20 years and a fine of not less than $10,000.00 nor more than $100,000.00, provided that any person who has previously committed an offense under the laws of the United States or of Georgia or of any of the several states or of any foreign nation recognized by the United States which if committed in Georgia would have constituted the offense of hijacking a motor vehicle shall be punished by imprisonment for life and a fine of not less than $100,000.00 nor more than $500,000.00. The punishment imposed pursuant to this paragraph shall not be deferred, suspended, or probated. For purposes of this paragraph, the term "state" shall include the District of Columbia and any territory, possession, or dominion of the United States.

(2) A person convicted of the offense of hijacking a motor vehicle in the second degree shall be punished upon a first conviction by imprisonment for not less than one nor more than ten years and a fine of not more than $5,000.00. Upon a second conviction for hijacking a motor vehicle in the second degree, a person shall be punished by imprisonment for not less than three nor more than 15 years and a fine of not more than $5,000.00. Upon a third or subsequent conviction of hijacking a motor vehicle in the second degree, a person shall be punished by imprisonment for not less than five nor more than 20 years and a fine of not more than $5,000.00.

(d) The offense of hijacking a motor vehicle in the first degree shall be considered a separate offense and shall not merge with any other offense.

(e) (1) As used in this subsection, the terms "proceeds" and "property" shall have the same meanings as set forth in Code Section 9-16-2.

(2) Any property which is, directly or indirectly, used or intended for use in any manner to facilitate a violation of this Code section and any proceeds are declared to be contraband and no person shall have a property right in them.

(3) Any property subject to forfeiture pursuant to paragraph (2) of this subsection shall be forfeited in accordance with the procedures set forth in Chapter 16 of Title 9.

§ 16-5-45. Interference with custody

(a) As used in this Code section, the term:

(1) "Child" means any individual who is under the age of 17 years or any individual who is under the age of 18 years who is alleged to be a dependent child or a child in need of services as such terms are defined in Code Section 15-11-2.

(2) "Committed person" means any child or other person whose custody is entrusted to another individual by authority of law.

(3) "Lawful custody" means that custody inherent in the natural parents, that custody awarded by proper authority as provided in Code Section 15-11-133, or that custody awarded to a parent, guardian, or other person by a court of competent jurisdiction.

(4) "Service provider" means an entity that is registered with the Department of Human Services pursuant to Article 7 of Chapter 5 of Title 49 or a child welfare agency as defined in Code Section 49-5-12 or an agent or employee acting on behalf of such entity or child welfare agency.

(b) (1) A person commits the offense of interference with custody when without lawful authority to do so, the person:

(A) Knowingly or recklessly takes or entices any child or committed person away from the individual who has lawful custody of such child or committed person;

(B) Knowingly harbors any child or committed person who has absconded; provided, however, that this subparagraph shall not apply to a service provider that notifies the child's parent, guardian, or legal custodian of the child's location and general state of well being as soon as possible but not later than 72 hours after the child's acceptance of services; provided, further, that such notification shall not be required if:

(i) The service provider has reasonable cause to believe that the minor has been abused or neglected and makes a child abuse report pursuant to Code Section 19-7-5;

(ii) The child will not disclose the name of the child's parent, guardian, or legal custodian, and the Division of Family and Children Services within the Department of Human Services is notified within 72 hours of the child's acceptance of services; or

(iii) The child's parent, guardian, or legal custodian cannot be reached, and the Division of Family and Children Services within the Department of Human Services is notified within 72 hours of the child's acceptance of services; or

(C) Intentionally and willfully retains possession within this state of the child or committed person upon the expiration of a lawful period of visitation with the child or committed person.

(2) A person convicted of the offense of interference with custody shall be punished as follows:

(A) Upon conviction of the first offense, the defendant shall be guilty of a misdemeanor and shall be fined not less than $200.00 nor more than $500.00 or shall be imprisoned for not less than one month nor more than five months, or both fined and imprisoned;

(B) Upon conviction of the second offense, the defendant shall be guilty of a misdemeanor and shall be fined not less than $400.00 nor more than $1,000.00 or shall be imprisoned for not less than three months nor more than 12 months, or both fined and imprisoned; and

(C) Upon the conviction of the third or subsequent offense, the defendant shall be guilty of a felony and shall be punished by imprisonment for not less than one nor more than five years.

(c)(1) A person commits the offense of interstate interference with custody when without lawful authority to do so the person knowingly or recklessly takes or entices any minor or committed person away from the individual who has lawful custody of such minor or committed person and in so doing brings such minor or committed person into this state or removes such minor or committed person from this state.

(2) A person also commits the offense of interstate interference with custody when the person removes a minor or committed person from this state in the lawful exercise of a visitation right and, upon the expiration of the period of lawful visitation, intentionally retains possession of the minor or committed person in another state for the purpose of keeping the minor or committed person away from the individual having lawful custody of the minor or committed person. The offense is deemed to be committed in the county to which the minor or committed person was to have been returned upon expiration of the period of lawful visitation.

(3) A person convicted of the offense of interstate interference with custody shall be guilty of a felony and shall be imprisoned for not less than one year nor more than five years.

§ 16-5-46. Trafficking of persons for labor or sexual servitude

(a) As used in this Code section, the term:
(1) "Coercion" means:
(A) Causing or threatening to cause bodily harm to any individual, physically restraining or confining any individual, or threatening to physically restrain or confine any individual;
(B) Exposing or threatening to expose any fact or information or disseminating or threatening to disseminate any fact or information that would tend to subject an individual to criminal or immigration proceedings, hatred, contempt, or ridicule;
(C) Destroying, concealing, removing, confiscating, or possessing any actual or purported passport or other immigration document, or any other actual or purported government identification document, of any individual;
(D) Providing a controlled substance to such individual for the purpose of compelling such individual to engage in labor or sexual servitude against his or her will; or
(E) Causing or threatening to cause financial harm to any individual or using financial control over any individual.
(2) "Controlled substance" shall have the same meaning as set forth in Code Section 16-13-21.
(3) "Deception" means:
(A) Creating or confirming another's impression of an existing fact or past event which is false and which the accused knows or believes to be false;
(B) Maintaining the status or condition of an individual arising from a pledge by such individual of his or her personal services as security for a debt, if the value of those services as reasonably assessed is not applied toward the liquidation of the debt or the length and nature of those services are not respectively limited and defined, or preventing an individual from acquiring information pertinent to the disposition of such debt; or
(C) Promising benefits or the performance of services which the accused does not intend to deliver or perform or knows will not be delivered or performed. Evidence of failure to deliver benefits or perform services standing alone shall not be sufficient to authorize a conviction under this Code section.
(4) "Developmental disability" shall have the same meaning as set forth in Code Section 37-1-1.
(5) "Labor servitude" means work or service of economic or financial value which is performed or provided by another individual and is induced or obtained by coercion or deception.
(6) "Performance" shall have the same meaning as set forth in Code Section 16-12-100.
(7) "Sexually explicit conduct" shall have the same meaning as set forth in Code Section 16-12-100.
(8) "Sexual servitude" means any sexually explicit conduct or performance involving sexually explicit conduct for which anything of value is directly or indirectly given, promised to, or received by any individual, which conduct is induced or obtained:
(A) By coercion or deception;
(B) From an individual who is under the age of 18 years;
(C) From an individual whom the accused believes to be under the age of 18 years;
(D) From an individual who has a developmental disability; or
(E) From an individual whom the accused believes to have a developmental disability.
(b) A person commits the offense of trafficking a person for labor servitude when that person knowingly subjects another person to or maintains another person in labor servitude or knowingly recruits, entices, harbors, transports, provides, or obtains by any means another person for the purpose of labor servitude.
(c) A person commits the offense of trafficking an individual for sexual servitude when that person knowingly:
(1) Subjects an individual to or maintains an individual in sexual servitude;
(2) Recruits, entices, harbors, transports, provides, or obtains by any means an individual for the purpose of sexual servitude; or
(3) Solicits by any means an individual to perform sexually explicit conduct on behalf of such person when such individual is the subject of sexual servitude.
(d) The age of consent for sexual activity or the accused's lack of knowledge of the age or developmental disability of the individual being trafficked shall not constitute a defense in a prosecution for a violation of this Code section.
(e) The sexual history or history of commercial sexual activity of a person alleged to have been trafficked or such person's connection by blood or marriage to an accused in the case or to anyone involved in such person's trafficking shall be excluded from evidence if the court finds at a hearing outside the presence of the jury that the probative value of the evidence is substantially outweighed by the danger of unfair prejudice, confusion of the issues, or misleading the jury.
(f) (1) Except as provided in paragraph (2) of this subsection, any person who commits the offense of trafficking an individual for labor servitude shall be guilty of a felony, and upon conviction thereof, shall be punished by imprisonment for not less than ten nor more than 20 years and a fine not to exceed $100,000.00.
(2) Any person who commits the offense of trafficking an individual for labor servitude against an individual who is under 18 years of age and such individual under the age of 18 years was coerced or deceived into being trafficked for labor or if the offense is committed against an individual who has a developmental disability, the person shall be guilty of a felony, and upon conviction thereof, shall be punished by imprisonment for not less than 25 nor more than 50 years or life imprisonment and a fine not to exceed $100,000.00.
(3) Except as provided in paragraph (4) of this subsection, any person who violates paragraph (1) or (2) of subsection (c) of this Code section shall be guilty of a felony, and upon conviction thereof, shall be punished by imprisonment for not less than ten nor more than 20 years.
(4) Any person who violates paragraph (1) or (2) of subsection (c) of this Code section committed against an individual under 18 years of age and such individual under the age of 18 years was coerced or deceived into such violation or if such violation is committed against an individual who has a developmental disability, such person shall be guilty of a felony, and upon conviction thereof, shall be punished by imprisonment for not less than 25 nor more than 50 years or life imprisonment.
(5) Any person who violates paragraph (3) of subsection (c) of this Code section shall be guilty of a felony. When such offense is committed against an individual who is 16 or 17 years of age, upon conviction, such person shall be punished by imprisonment for not less than five nor more than 20 years. When such offense is committed against an individual who is younger than 16 years of age or an individual known to have a developmental disability, upon conviction, such person shall be punished by imprisonment for not less than ten nor more than 20 years.
(g) (1) As used in this subsection, the terms "civil forfeiture proceedings," "proceeds," and "property" shall have the same meanings as set forth in Code Section 9-16-2.
(2) Any property which is, directly or indirectly, used or intended for use in any manner to facilitate a violation of this Code section and any proceeds are declared to be contraband and no person shall have a property right in them.
(3) Any property subject to forfeiture pursuant to paragraph (2) of this subsection shall be forfeited in accordance with the procedures set forth in Chapter 16 of Title 9.
(4) The Attorney General shall be specifically authorized to commence civil forfeiture proceedings under this Code section.
(h) Prosecuting attorneys and the Attorney General shall have concurrent authority to prosecute any criminal cases arising under the provisions of this Code section and to perform any duty that necessarily appertains thereto.
(i) Each violation of this Code section shall constitute a separate offense and shall not merge with any other offense.

(j) A corporation may be prosecuted under this Code section for an act or omission constituting a crime under this Code section only if an agent of the corporation performs the conduct which is an element of the crime while acting within the scope of his or her office or employment and on behalf of the corporation and the commission of the crime was either authorized, requested, commanded, performed, or within the scope of his or her employment on behalf of the corporation or constituted a pattern of illegal activity that an agent of the company knew or should have known was occurring.

(k) The sole fact that an undercover operative or law enforcement officer was involved in the detection and investigation of an offense under this Code section shall not constitute a defense to prosecution under this Code section; provided, however, that Code Section 16-3-25 may still provide an absolute defense.

§ 16-5-47. Posting model notice with human trafficking hotline information in businesses and on Internet

(a) As used in this Code section, the term:

(1) "Adult entertainment establishment" means any place of business or commercial establishment wherein:

(A) The entertainment or activity therein consists of nude or substantially nude persons dancing with or without music or engaged in movements of a sexual nature or movements simulating sexual intercourse, oral copulation, sodomy, or masturbation;

(B) The patron directly or indirectly is charged a fee or required to make a purchase in order to view entertainment or activity which consists of persons exhibiting or modeling lingerie or similar undergarments; or

(C) The patron directly or indirectly is charged a fee to engage in personal contact by employees, devices, or equipment, or by personnel provided by the establishment.

Such term shall include, but shall not be limited to, bathhouses, lingerie modeling studios, and related or similar activities. Such term shall not include businesses or commercial establishments which have as their sole purpose the improvement of health and physical fitness through special equipment and facilities, rather than entertainment.

(2) "Agricultural products" means raising, growing, harvesting, or storing crops; feeding, breeding, or managing livestock, equine, or poultry; producing or storing feed for use in the production of livestock, including, but not limited to, cattle, calves, swine, hogs, goats, sheep, equine, and rabbits, or for use in the production of poultry, including, but not limited to, chickens, hens, ratites, and turkeys; producing plants, trees, Christmas trees, fowl, equine, or animals; or producing aquacultural, horticultural, viticultural, silvicultural, grass sod, dairy, livestock, poultry, egg, and apiarian products.

(3) "Bar" means an establishment that is devoted to the serving of alcoholic beverages for consumption by guests on the premises and in which the serving of food is only incidental to the consumption of those beverages, including, but not limited to, taverns, nightclubs, cocktail lounges, and cabarets.

(4) "Day hauler" means any person who is employed by a farm labor contractor to transport, or who for a fee transports, by motor vehicle, workers to render personal services in connection with the production of any farm products to, for, or under the direction of a third person; provided, however, that such term shall not include a person who produces agricultural products.

(5) "Farm labor contractor" means any person who, for a fee, employs workers to render personal services in connection with the production of any farm products to, for, or under the direction of a third person, or who recruits, solicits, supplies, or hires workers on behalf of an employer engaged in the growing or producing of farm products, and who, for a fee, provides in connection therewith one or more of the following services: furnishes board, lodging, or transportation for those workers; supervises, times, checks, counts, weighs, or otherwise directs or measures their work; or disburses wage payments to such persons; provided, however, that such term shall not include a person who produces agricultural products.

(5.1) "Government building with public access" means a building or portion of a building owned or leased by a government entity.

(5.2) "Government entity" means an office, agency, authority, department, commission, board, body, division, instrumentality, or institution of the executive, legislative, or judicial branch of the state government and any county, municipal corporation, or consolidated government within this state.

(6) "Hotel" means any hotel, inn, or other establishment which offers overnight accommodations to the public for hire.

(7) "Massage therapist" means a person licensed pursuant to Chapter 24A of Title 43.

(8) "Primary airport" shall have the same meaning as set forth in 49 U.S.C. Section 47102(16).

(9) "Substantially nude" means dressed in a manner so as to display any portion of the female breast below the top of the areola or displaying any portion of any person's pubic hair, anus, cleft of the buttocks, vulva, or genitals.

(10) "Truck stop" means a privately owned and operated facility that provides food, fuel, shower or other sanitary facilities, and lawful overnight truck parking.

(b) Effective September 15, 2013, the following businesses and other establishments shall post the notice described in subsection (c) of this Code section, or a substantially similar notice, in English, Spanish, and any other language deemed appropriate by the director of the Georgia Bureau of Investigation, in each public restroom for the business or establishment and either in a conspicuous place near the public entrance of the business or establishment or in another conspicuous location in clear view of the public and employees where similar notices are customarily posted:

(1) Adult entertainment establishments;

(2) Bars;

(3) Primary airports;

(4) Passenger rail or light rail stations;

(5) Bus stations;

(6) Truck stops;

(7) Emergency rooms within general acute care hospitals;

(8) Urgent care centers;

(9) Farm labor contractors and day haulers;

(10) Privately operated job recruitment centers;

(11) Safety rest areas located along interstate highways in this state;

(12) Hotels;

(13) Businesses and establishments that offer massage or bodywork services by a person who is not a massage therapist; and

(14) Government buildings; provided, however, that in the case of leased property, this paragraph shall only apply to public restrooms that are a part of such lease for exclusive use by the government entity.

(c) The Georgia Bureau of Investigation shall develop a model notice that is available for download from its Internet website. Such notice shall be at least 8 1/2 inches by 11 inches in size and printed in a 16 point font in English, Spanish, and any other language deemed appropriate by the director of the Georgia Bureau of Investigation. Such model notice shall provide information giving individuals a method to contact the National Human Trafficking Hotline and the Statewide Georgia Hotline for Domestic Minor Trafficking.

(c.1) Every government entity shall, on the homepage of its website, provide an identified hyperlink to the model notice that is on the Georgia Bureau of Investigation website as provided for in subsection (c) of this Code section.

(d) (1) A law enforcement officer shall notify, in writing, any business or establishment that has failed to comply with this Code section that it has failed to comply with the requirements of this Code section and if it does not correct the violation within 30 days from the date of receipt of the notice, the owner of such business or establishment shall be charged with a violation of this Code section and upon conviction shall be guilty of the misdemeanor offense of failure to post the National Human Trafficking Resource Center hotline number and may be punished by a fine of not more than $500.00; but the provisions of Chapter 11 of Title 17 and any other provision of law to the contrary notwithstanding, the costs of such prosecution shall not be taxed nor shall any additional penalty, fee, or surcharge to a fine for such offense be assessed against an owner for conviction thereof. Upon a second or subsequent conviction, the owner shall be guilty of a high and aggravated misdemeanor and shall be punished by a fine not to exceed $5,000.00. The notice required by this subsection may be hand delivered to the noncomplying business or establishment or mailed to it at the address of such business or establishment.

(2) This subsection shall not apply to government entities.

§ 16-5-60. Reckless conduct causing harm to or endangering the bodily safety of another; conduct by HIV infected persons; assault by HIV infected persons or hepatitis infected persons

(a) Any term used in this Code section and defined in Code Section 31-22-9.1 shall have the meaning provided for such term in Code Section 31-22-9.1.

(b) A person who causes bodily harm to or endangers the bodily safety of another person by consciously disregarding a substantial and unjustifiable risk that his act or omission will cause harm or endanger the safety of the other person and the disregard constitutes a gross deviation from the standard of care which a reasonable person would exercise in the situation is guilty of a misdemeanor.

(c) A person who is an HIV infected person who, after obtaining knowledge of being infected with HIV:

(1) Knowingly engages in sexual intercourse or performs or submits to any sexual act involving the sex organs of one person and the mouth or anus of another person and the HIV infected person does not disclose to the other person the fact of that infected person's being an HIV infected person prior to that intercourse or sexual act;

(2) Knowingly allows another person to use a hypodermic needle, syringe, or both for the introduction of drugs or any other substance into or for the withdrawal of body fluids from the other person's body and the needle or syringe so used had been previously used by the HIV infected person for the introduction of drugs or any other substance into or for the withdrawal of body fluids from the HIV infected person's body and where that infected person does not disclose to the other person the fact of that infected person's being an HIV infected person prior to such use;

(3) Offers or consents to perform with another person an act of sexual intercourse for money without disclosing to that other person the fact of that infected person's being an HIV infected person prior to offering or consenting to perform that act of sexual intercourse;

(4) Solicits another person to perform or submit to an act of sodomy for money without disclosing to that other person the fact of that infected person's being an HIV infected person prior to soliciting that act of sodomy; or

(5) Donates blood, blood products, other body fluids, or any body organ or body part without previously disclosing the fact of that infected person's being an HIV infected person to the person drawing the blood or blood products or the person or entity collecting or storing the other body fluids, body organ, or body part,

is guilty of a felony and, upon conviction thereof, shall be punished by imprisonment for not more than ten years.

(d) A person who is an HIV infected person or hepatitis infected person and who, after obtaining knowledge of being infected with HIV or hepatitis, commits an assault with the intent to transmit HIV or hepatitis, using his or her body fluids (blood, semen, or vaginal secretions), saliva, urine, or feces upon:

(1) A peace officer while the peace officer is engaged in the performance of his or her official duties or on account of the peace officer's performance of his or her official duties; or

(2) A correctional officer while the correctional officer is engaged in the performance of his or her official duties or on account of the correctional officer's performance of his or her official duties

is guilty of a felony and, upon conviction thereof, shall be punished by imprisonment for not less than five nor more than 20 years.

§ 16-5-61. Hazing

(a) As used in this Code section, the term:

(1) "Haze" means to subject a student to an activity which endangers or is likely to endanger the physical health of a student, regardless of a student's willingness to participate in such activity.

(2) "School" means any school, college, or university in this state.

(3) "School organization" means any club, society, fraternity, sorority, or a group living together which has students as its principal members.

(4) "Student" means any person enrolled in a school in this state.

(b) It shall be unlawful for any person to haze any student in connection with or as a condition or precondition of gaining acceptance, membership, office, or other status in a school organization.

(c) Any person who violates this Code section shall be guilty of a misdemeanor of a high and aggravated nature.

CHAPTER 6. SEXUAL OFFENSES

§ 16-6-1. Rape

(a) A person commits the offense of rape when he has carnal knowledge of:

(1) A female forcibly and against her will; or

(2) A female who is less than ten years of age.

Carnal knowledge in rape occurs when there is any penetration of the female sex organ by the male sex organ. The fact that the person allegedly raped is the wife of the defendant shall not be a defense to a charge of rape.

(b) A person convicted of the offense of rape shall be punished by death, by imprisonment for life without parole, by imprisonment for life, or by a split sentence that is a term of imprisonment for not less than 25 years and not exceeding life imprisonment, followed by probation for life. Any person convicted under this Code section shall, in addition, be subject to the sentencing and punishment provisions of Code Sections 17-10-6.1 and 17-10-7.

(c) When evidence relating to an allegation of rape is collected in the course of a medical examination of the person who is the victim of the alleged crime, the Georgia Crime Victims Emergency Fund, as provided for in Chapter 15 of Title 17, shall be responsible for the cost of the medical examination to the extent that expense is incurred for the limited purpose of collecting evidence.

§ 16-6-2. Sodomy; aggravated sodomy; medical expenses

(a) (1) A person commits the offense of sodomy when he or she performs or submits to any sexual act involving the sex organs of one person and the mouth or anus of another.

(2) A person commits the offense of aggravated sodomy when he or she commits sodomy with force and against the will of the other person or when he or she commits sodomy with a person who is less than ten years of age. The fact that the person allegedly sodomized is the spouse of a defendant shall not be a defense to a charge of aggravated sodomy.

(b) (1) Except as provided in subsection (d) of this Code section, a person convicted of the offense of sodomy shall be punished by imprisonment for not less than one nor more than 20 years and shall be subject to the sentencing and punishment provisions of Code Section 17-10-6.2.

(2) A person convicted of the offense of aggravated sodomy shall be punished by imprisonment for life or by a split sentence that is a term of imprisonment for not less than 25 years and not exceeding life imprisonment, followed by probation for life. Any person convicted under this Code section of the offense of aggravated sodomy shall, in addition, be subject to the sentencing and punishment provisions of Code Sections 17-10-6.1 and 17-10-7.

(c) When evidence relating to an allegation of aggravated sodomy is collected in the course of a medical examination of the person who is the victim of the alleged crime, the Georgia Crime Victims Emergency Fund, as provided for in Chapter 15 of Title 17, shall be financially responsible for the cost of the medical examination to the extent that expense is incurred for the limited purpose of collecting evidence.

(d) If the victim is at least 13 but less than 16 years of age and the person convicted of sodomy is 18 years of age or younger and is no more than four years older than the victim, such person shall be guilty of a misdemeanor and shall not be subject to the sentencing and punishment provisions of Code Section 17-10-6.2.

§ 16-6-3. Statutory rape

(a) A person commits the offense of statutory rape when he or she engages in sexual intercourse with any person under the age of 16 years and not his or her spouse, provided that no conviction shall be had for this offense on the unsupported testimony of the victim.

(b) Except as provided in subsection (c) of this Code section, a person convicted of the offense of statutory rape shall be punished by imprisonment for not less than one nor more than 20 years; provided, however, that if the person so convicted is 21 years of age or older, such person shall be punished by imprisonment for not less than ten nor more than 20 years. Any person convicted under this subsection of the offense of statutory rape shall, in addition, be subject to the sentencing and punishment provisions of Code Section 17-10-6.2.

(c) If the victim is at least 14 but less than 16 years of age and the person convicted of statutory rape is 18 years of age or younger and is no more than four years older than the victim, such person shall be guilty of a misdemeanor.

§ 16-6-4. Child molestation; aggravated child molestation

(a) A person commits the offense of child molestation when such person:
(1) Does any immoral or indecent act to or in the presence of or with any child under the age of 16 years with the intent to arouse or satisfy the sexual desires of either the child or the person; or
(2) By means of an electronic device, transmits images of a person engaging in, inducing, or otherwise participating in any immoral or indecent act to a child under the age of 16 years with the intent to arouse or satisfy the sexual desires of either the child or the person.
(b) (1) Except as provided in paragraph (2) of this subsection, a person convicted of a first offense of child molestation shall be punished by imprisonment for not less than five nor more than 20 years and shall be subject to the sentencing and punishment provisions of Code Sections 17-10-6.2 and 17-10-7. Upon a defendant being incarcerated on a conviction for a first offense, the Department of Corrections shall provide counseling to such defendant. Except as provided in paragraph (2) of this subsection, upon a second or subsequent conviction of an offense of child molestation, the defendant shall be punished by imprisonment for not less than ten years nor more than 30 years or by imprisonment for life and shall be subject to the sentencing and punishment provisions of Code Sections 17-10-6.2 and 17-10-7; provided, however, that prior to trial, a defendant shall be given notice, in writing, that the state intends to seek a punishment of life imprisonment.
(2) If the victim is at least 14 but less than 16 years of age and the person convicted of child molestation is 18 years of age or younger and is no more than four years older than the victim, such person shall be guilty of a misdemeanor and shall not be subject to the sentencing and punishment provisions of Code Section 17-10-6.2.
(c) A person commits the offense of aggravated child molestation when such person commits an offense of child molestation which act physically injures the child or involves an act of sodomy.
(d) (1) Except as provided in paragraph (2) of this subsection, a person convicted of the offense of aggravated child molestation shall be punished by imprisonment for life or by a split sentence that is a term of imprisonment for not less than 25 years and not exceeding life imprisonment, followed by probation for life, and shall be subject to the sentencing and punishment provisions of Code Sections 17-10-6.1 and 17-10-7.
(2) A person convicted of the offense of aggravated child molestation when:
(A) The victim is at least 13 but less than 16 years of age;
(B) The person convicted of aggravated child molestation is 18 years of age or younger and is no more than four years older than the victim; and
(C) The basis of the charge of aggravated child molestation involves an act of sodomy
shall be guilty of a misdemeanor and shall not be subject to the sentencing and punishment provisions of Code Section 17-10-6.1.
(e) A person shall be subject to prosecution in this state pursuant to Code Section 17-2-1 for any conduct made unlawful by paragraph (2) of subsection (a) of this Code section which the person engages in while:
(1) Either within or outside of this state if, by such conduct, the person commits a violation of paragraph (2) of subsection (a) of this Code section which involves a child who resides in this state; or
(2) Within this state if, by such conduct, the person commits a violation of paragraph (2) of subsection (a) of this Code section which involves a child who resides within or outside this state.

§ 16-6-5. Enticing a child for indecent purposes

(a) A person commits the offense of enticing a child for indecent purposes when he or she solicits, entices, or takes any child under the age of 16 years to any place whatsoever for the purpose of child molestation or indecent acts.
(b) Except as provided in subsection (c) of this Code section, a person convicted of the offense of enticing a child for indecent purposes shall be punished by imprisonment for not less than ten nor more than 30 years. Any person convicted under this Code section of the offense of enticing a child for indecent purposes shall, in addition, be subject to the sentencing and punishment provisions of Code Section 17-10-6.2.
(c) If the victim is at least 14 but less than 16 years of age and the person convicted of enticing a child for indecent purposes is 18 years of age or younger and is no more than four years older than the victim, such person shall be guilty of a misdemeanor and shall not be subject to the sentencing and punishment provisions of Code Section 17-10-6.2.

§ 16-6-5.1. Sexual assault by persons with supervisory or disciplinary authority; sexual assault by practitioner of psychotherapy against patient; consent not a defense; penalty upon conviction for sexual assault

(a) As used in this Code section, the term:
(1) "Actor" means a person accused of sexual assault.
(2) "Intimate parts" means the genital area, groin, inner thighs, buttocks, or breasts of a person.
(3) "Psychotherapy" means the professional treatment or counseling of a mental or emotional illness, symptom, or condition.
(4) "Sexual contact" means any contact between the actor and a person not married to the actor involving the intimate parts of either person for the purpose of sexual gratification of the actor.
(5) "School" means any educational program or institution instructing children at any level, pre-kindergarten through twelfth grade, or the equivalent thereof if grade divisions are not used.
(b) A person who has supervisory or disciplinary authority over another individual commits sexual assault when that person:
(1) Is a teacher, principal, assistant principal, or other administrator of any school and engages in sexual contact with such other individual who the actor knew or should have known is enrolled at the same school; provided, however, that such contact shall not be prohibited when the actor is married to such other individual;
(2) Is an employee or agent of any community supervision office, county juvenile probation office, Department of Juvenile Justice juvenile probation office, or probation office under Article 6 of Chapter 8 of Title 42 and engages in sexual contact with such other individual who the actor knew or should have known is a probationer or parolee under the supervision of any such office;
(3) Is an employee or agent of a law enforcement agency and engages in sexual contact with such other individual who the actor knew or should have known is being detained by or is in the custody of any law enforcement agency;
(4) Is an employee or agent of a hospital and engages in sexual contact with such other individual who the actor knew or should have known is a patient or is being detained in the same hospital; or
(5) Is an employee or agent of a correctional facility, juvenile detention facility, facility providing services to a person with a disability, as such term is defined in Code Section 37-1-1, or a facility providing child welfare and youth services, as such term is defined in Code Section 49-5-3, who engages in sexual contact with such other individual who the actor knew or should have known is in the custody of such facility.
(c) A person who is an actual or purported practitioner of psychotherapy commits sexual assault when he or she engages in sexual contact with another individual who the actor knew or should have known is the subject of the actor's actual or purported treatment or counseling or the actor uses the treatment or counseling relationship to facilitate sexual contact between the actor and such individual.
(d) A person who is an employee, agent, or volunteer at any facility licensed or required to be licensed under Code Section 31-7-3, 31-7-12, or 31-7-12.2 or who is required to be licensed pursuant to Code Section 31-7-151 or 31-7-173 commits sexual assault when he or she engages in sexual contact with another individual who the actor knew or should have known had been admitted to or is receiving services from such facility or the actor.
(e) Consent of the victim shall not be a defense to a prosecution under this Code section.
(f) A person convicted of sexual assault shall be punished by imprisonment for not less than one nor more than 25 years or by a fine not to exceed $100,000.00, or both; provided, however, that:
(1) Except as provided in paragraph (2) of this subsection, any person convicted of the offense of sexual assault of a child under the age of 16 years shall be punished by imprisonment for not less than 25 nor more than 50 years and shall, in addition, be subject to the sentencing and punishment provisions of Code Section 17-10-6.2; and
(2) If at the time of the offense the victim of the offense is at least 14 years of age but less than 16 years of age and the actor is 18 years of age or younger and is no more than four years older than the victim, such person shall be guilty of a misdemeanor and shall not be subject to the sentencing and punishment provisions of Code Section 17-10-6.2.

§ 16-6-6. Bestiality

(a) A person commits the offense of bestiality when he performs or submits to any sexual act with an animal involving the sex organs of the one and the mouth, anus, penis, or vagina of the other.
(b) A person convicted of the offense of bestiality shall be punished by imprisonment for not less than one nor more than five years.

§ 16-6-7. Necrophilia

(a) A person commits the offense of necrophilia when he performs any sexual act with a dead human body involving the sex organs of the one and the mouth, anus, penis, or vagina of the other.
(b) A person convicted of the offense of necrophilia shall be punished by imprisonment for not less than one nor more than ten years.

§ 16-6-8. Public indecency

(a) A person commits the offense of public indecency when he or she performs any of the following acts in a public place:
(1) An act of sexual intercourse;
(2) A lewd exposure of the sexual organs;
(3) A lewd appearance in a state of partial or complete nudity; or
(4) A lewd caress or indecent fondling of the body of another person.
(b) A person convicted of the offense of public indecency as provided in subsection (a) of this Code section shall be punished as for a misdemeanor except as provided in subsection (c) of this Code section.
(c) Upon a third or subsequent conviction for public indecency for the violation of paragraph (2), (3), or (4) of subsection (a) of this Code section, a person shall be guilty of a felony and shall be punished by imprisonment for not less than one nor more than five years.
(d) For the purposes of this Code section only, "public place" shall include jails and penal and correctional institutions of the state and its political subdivisions.
(e) This Code section shall be cumulative to and shall not prohibit the enactment of any other general and local laws, rules, and regulations of state and local authorities or agencies and local ordinances prohibiting such activities which are more restrictive than this Code section.

§ 16-6-9. Prostitution

A person commits the offense of prostitution when he or she performs or offers or consents to perform a sexual act, including but not limited to sexual intercourse or sodomy, for money or other items of value.

§ 16-6-10. Keeping a place of prostitution

A person having or exercising control over the use of any place or conveyance which would offer seclusion or shelter for the practice of prostitution commits the offense of keeping a place of prostitution when he knowingly grants or permits the use of such place for the purpose of prostitution.

§ 16-6-11. Pimping

A person commits the offense of pimping when he or she performs any of the following acts:
(1) Offers or agrees to procure a prostitute for another;
(2) Offers or agrees to arrange a meeting of persons for the purpose of prostitution;
(3) Directs or transports another person to a place when he or she knows or should know that the direction or transportation is for the purpose of prostitution;
(4) Receives money or other thing of value from a prostitute, without lawful consideration, knowing it was earned in whole or in part from prostitution; or
(5) Aids or abets, counsels, or commands another in the commission of prostitution or aids or assists in prostitution where the proceeds or profits derived therefrom are to be divided on a pro rata basis.

§ 16-6-12. Pandering

A person commits the offense of pandering when he or she solicits a person to perform an act of prostitution in his or her own behalf or in behalf of a third person or when he or she knowingly assembles persons at a fixed place for the purpose of being solicited by others to perform an act of prostitution.

§ 16-6-13. Penalties for violating Code Sections 16-6-9 through 16-6-12

(a) Except as otherwise provided in subsection (b) of this Code section, a person convicted of violating:
(1) Code Section 16-6-10 shall be punished as for a misdemeanor of a high and aggravated nature, and at the sole discretion of the judge, all but 24 hours of any term of imprisonment imposed may be suspended, stayed, or probated;
(2) Code Section 16-6-9 shall be punished as for a misdemeanor;
(3) Code Section 16-6-11 shall be punished as for a misdemeanor of a high and aggravated nature, and at the sole discretion of the judge, all but 24 hours of any term of imprisonment imposed may be suspended, stayed, or probated; or
(4) Code Section 16-6-12 shall be punished as for a misdemeanor of a high and aggravated nature, and at the sole discretion of the judge, all but 24 hours of any term of imprisonment imposed may be suspended, stayed, or probated.
(b) (1) A person convicted of any of the offenses enumerated in Code Sections 16-6-10 through 16-6-12 when such offense involves the conduct of a person who is at least 16 but less than 18 years of age shall be guilty of a felony and shall be punished by imprisonment for a period of not less than five nor more than 20 years, a fine of not less than $2,500.00 nor more than $10,000.00, or both.
(2) A person convicted of any of the offenses enumerated in Code Sections 16-6-10 through 16-6-12 when such offense involves the conduct of a person under the age of 16 years shall be guilty of a felony and shall be punished by imprisonment for a period of not less than ten nor more than 30 years, a fine of not more than $100,000.00, or both.
(3) Adjudication of guilt or imposition of a sentence for a conviction of a second or subsequent offense pursuant to this subsection, including a plea of nolo contendere, shall not be suspended, probated, deferred, or withheld.
(c)(1) The clerk of the court in which a person is convicted of pandering shall cause to be published a notice of conviction for each such person convicted. Such notices of conviction shall be published in the manner of legal notices in the legal organ of the county in which such person resides or, in the case of nonresidents, in the legal organ of the county in which the person was convicted. Such notice of conviction shall be one column wide by two inches long and shall contain the photograph taken by the arresting law enforcement agency at the time of arrest, name, and address of the convicted person and the date, time, place of arrest, and disposition of the case and shall be published once in the legal organ of the appropriate county in the second week following such conviction or as soon thereafter as publication may be made.
(2) The convicted person for which a notice of conviction is published pursuant to this subsection shall be assessed the cost of publication of such notice and such assessment shall be imposed at the time of conviction in addition to any other fine imposed pursuant to this Code section.

(3) The clerk of the court, the publisher of any legal organ which publishes a notice of conviction, and any other person involved in the publication of an erroneous notice of conviction shall be immune from civil or criminal liability for such erroneous publication, provided such publication was made in good faith.

(d) In addition to any other penalty authorized under subsections (a) and (b) of this Code section, a person convicted of an offense enumerated in Code Sections 16-6-9 through 16-6-12 shall be fined $2,500.00 if such offense was committed within 1,000 feet of any school building, school grounds, public place of worship, or playground or recreation center which is used primarily by persons under the age of 17 years.

§ 16-6-13.1. Testing for sexually transmitted diseases required

(a) Any term used in this Code section and defined in Code Section 31-22-9.1 shall have the meaning provided for such term in Code Section 31-22-9.1.

(b) Upon a verdict or plea of guilty or a plea of nolo contendere to the offense of pandering, the court in which that verdict is returned or plea entered shall as a condition of probation or a suspended sentence require the defendant in such case to submit to testing for sexually transmitted diseases within 45 days following the date of the verdict or plea and to consent to release of the test results to the defendant's spouse if the defendant is married; provided, however, that a defendant who is not a resident of this state shall, upon a verdict or plea of guilty or a plea of nolo contendere, be ordered by the court to undergo immediate testing for sexually transmitted diseases and shall remain in the custody of the court until such testing is completed. The clerk of the court, in the case of a defendant who is a resident of this state, shall mail, within three days following the date of that verdict or plea, a copy of that verdict or plea to the Department of Public Health. The tests for sexually transmitted diseases required under this subsection shall be limited to the eight most common sexually transmitted diseases as determined by the Department of Public Health.

(c) The Department of Public Health, within 30 days following the notification under subsection (b) of this Code section, shall arrange for the tests for the person required to submit thereto. Such person shall bear the costs of such tests.

(d) Any person required under this Code section to submit to testing for sexually transmitted diseases who fails or refuses to submit to the tests arranged pursuant to subsection (c) of this Code section shall be subject to such measures deemed necessary by the court in which the verdict was returned or plea entered to require voluntary submission to the tests.

§ 16-6-13.2. Civil forfeiture of motor vehicle

(a) As used in this Code section, the term "motor vehicle" shall have the same meaning as set forth in Code Section 40-1-1.

(b) Any motor vehicle used by a person to facilitate a violation of Code Section 16-6-10, 16-6-11 when the offense involved the pimping of a person to perform an act of prostitution, 16-6-12, or 16-6-14 is declared to be contraband and no person shall have a property right in it.

(c) Any property subject to forfeiture pursuant to subsection (b) of this Code section shall be forfeited in accordance with the procedures set forth in Chapter 16 of Title 9.

§ 16-6-13.3. Civil forfeiture of proceeds and property.

(a) As used in this Code section, the terms "proceeds" and "property" shall have the same meanings as set forth in Code Section 9-16-2.

(b) Any property which is, directly or indirectly, used or intended for use in any manner to facilitate a violation of Code Section 16-6-10, 16-6-11, 16-6-12, or 16-6-14 and any proceeds are declared to be contraband and no person shall have a property right in them.

(c) Any property subject to forfeiture pursuant to subsection (b) of this Code section shall be forfeited in accordance with the procedures set forth in Chapter 16 of Title 9.

§ 16-6-14. Pandering by compulsion

A person commits the offense of pandering by compulsion when he or she by duress or coercion causes a person to perform an act of prostitution and, upon conviction thereof, shall be punished by imprisonment for not less than one nor more than ten years.

§ 16-6-15. Solicitation of sodomy

(a) A person commits the offense of solicitation of sodomy when he solicits another to perform or submit to an act of sodomy. Except as provided in subsection (b) of this Code section, a person convicted of solicitation of sodomy shall be punished as for a misdemeanor.

(b) A person convicted of solicitation of sodomy when such offense involves the solicitation of a person or persons under the age of 18 years to perform or submit to an act of sodomy for money shall be guilty of a felony and shall be punished by imprisonment for a period of not less than five nor more than 20 years and shall be fined not less than $2,500.00 nor more than $10,000.00.

§ 16-6-16. Masturbation for hire

(a) A person, including a masseur or masseuse, commits the offense of masturbation for hire when he erotically stimulates the genital organs of another, whether resulting in orgasm or not, by manual or other bodily contact exclusive of sexual intercourse or by instrumental manipulation for money or the substantial equivalent thereof.

(b) A person committing the offense of masturbation for hire shall be guilty of a misdemeanor.

§ 16-6-17. Giving massages in place used for lewdness, prostitution, assignation, or masturbation for hire

(a) It shall be unlawful for any masseur or masseuse to massage any person in any building, structure, or place used for the purpose of lewdness, assignation, prostitution, or masturbation for hire.

(b) As used in this Code section, the term:

(1) "Masseur" means a male who practices massage or physiotherapy, or both.

(2) "Masseuse" means a female who practices massage or physiotherapy, or both.

(c) Any person who violates this Code section shall be guilty of a misdemeanor.

§ 16-6-18. Fornication

An unmarried person commits the offense of fornication when he voluntarily has sexual intercourse with another person and, upon conviction thereof, shall be punished as for a misdemeanor.

§ 16-6-19. Adultery

A married person commits the offense of adultery when he voluntarily has sexual intercourse with a person other than his spouse and, upon conviction thereof, shall be punished as for a misdemeanor.

§ 16-6-20. Bigamy

(a) A person commits the offense of bigamy when he, being married and knowing that his lawful spouse is living, marries another person or carries on a bigamous cohabitation with another person.

(b) It shall be an affirmative defense that the prior spouse has been continually absent for a period of seven years, during which time the accused did not know the prior spouse to be alive, or that the accused reasonably believed he was eligible to remarry.

(c) A person convicted of the offense of bigamy shall be punished by imprisonment for not less than one nor more than ten years.

§ 16-6-21. Marrying a bigamist

(a) An unmarried man or woman commits the offense of marrying a bigamist when he marries a person whom he knows to be the wife or husband of another.

(b) It shall be an affirmative defense that the prior spouse of the bigamist has been continually absent for a period of seven years, during which time the accused did not know the prior spouse of the bigamist to be alive, or that the accused reasonably believed the bigamist was eligible to remarry.

(c) A person convicted of the offense of marrying a bigamist shall be punished by imprisonment for not less than one nor more than ten years.

§ 16-6-22. Incest

(a) A person commits the offense of incest when such person engages in sexual intercourse or sodomy, as such term is defined in Code Section 16-6-2, with a person whom he or she knows he or she is related to either by blood or by marriage as follows:

(1) Father and child or stepchild;
(2) Mother and child or stepchild;
(3) Siblings of the whole blood or of the half blood;
(4) Grandparent and grandchild of the whole blood or of the half blood;
(5) Aunt and niece or nephew of the whole blood or of the half blood; or
(6) Uncle and niece or nephew of the whole blood or of the half blood.

(b) A person convicted of the offense of incest shall be punished by imprisonment for not less than ten nor more than 30 years; provided, however, that any person convicted of the offense of incest under this subsection with a child under the age of 14 years shall be punished by imprisonment for not less than 25 nor more than 50 years. Any person convicted under this Code section of the offense of incest shall, in addition, be subject to the sentencing and punishment provisions of Code Section 17-10-6.2.

§ 16-6-22.1. Sexual battery

(a) For the purposes of this Code section, the term "intimate parts" means the primary genital area, anus, groin, inner thighs, or buttocks of a male or female and the breasts of a female.

(b) A person commits the offense of sexual battery when he or she intentionally makes physical contact with the intimate parts of the body of another person without the consent of that person.

(c) Except as otherwise provided in this Code section, a person convicted of the offense of sexual battery shall be punished as for a misdemeanor of a high and aggravated nature.

(d) A person convicted of the offense of sexual battery against any child under the age of 16 years shall be guilty of a felony and, upon conviction thereof, shall be punished by imprisonment for not less than one nor more than five years.

(e) Upon a second or subsequent conviction under subsection (b) of this Code section, a person shall be guilty of a felony and, upon conviction thereof, shall be imprisoned for not less than one nor more than five years and, in addition, shall be subject to the sentencing and punishment provisions of Code Section 17-10-6.2.

§ 16-6-22.2. Aggravated sexual battery

(a) For the purposes of this Code section, the term "foreign object" means any article or instrument other than the sexual organ of a person.

(b) A person commits the offense of aggravated sexual battery when he or she intentionally penetrates with a foreign object the sexual organ or anus of another person without the consent of that person.

(c) A person convicted of the offense of aggravated sexual battery shall be punished by imprisonment for life or by a split sentence that is a term of imprisonment for not less than 25 years and not exceeding life imprisonment, followed by probation for life, and shall be subject to the sentencing and punishment provisions of Code Sections 17-10-6.1 and 17-10-7.

§ 16-6-23. Publication of name or identity of female raped or assaulted with intent to commit rape

(a) It shall be unlawful for any news media or any other person to print and publish, broadcast, televise, or disseminate through any other medium of public dissemination or cause to be printed and published, broadcast, televised, or disseminated in any newspaper, magazine, periodical, or other publication published in this state or through any radio or television broadcast originating in the state the name or identity of any female who may have been raped or upon whom an assault with intent to commit the offense of rape may have been made.

(b) This Code section does not apply to truthful information disclosed in public court documents open to public inspection.

(c) Any person or corporation violating this Code section shall be guilty of a misdemeanor.

§ 16-6-24. Adoption of ordinances by counties and municipalities which proscribe loitering or related activities

Nothing contained in this chapter shall prevent any county or municipality from adopting ordinances which proscribe loitering or related activities in public for the purpose of procuring others to engage in any sexual acts for hire.

§ 16-6-25. Harboring, concealing, or withholding information concerning a sexual offender; penalties

(a) As used in this Code section, the term "law enforcement unit" means any agency, organ, or department of this state, or a subdivision or municipality thereof, whose primary functions include the enforcement of criminal or traffic laws; the preservation of public order; the protection of life and property; or the prevention, detection, or investigation of crime. Such term shall also include the Department of Corrections, the Department of Community Supervision, and the State Board of Pardons and Paroles.

(b) Any person who knows or reasonably believes that a sexual offender, as defined in Code Section 42-1-12, is not complying, or has not complied, with the requirements of Code Section 42-1-12 and who, with the intent to assist such sexual offender in eluding a law enforcement unit that is seeking such sexual offender to question him or her about, or to arrest him or her for, his or her noncompliance with the requirements of Code Section 42-1-12:

(1) Harbors, attempts to harbor, or assists another person in harboring or attempting to harbor such sexual offender;
(2) Conceals, attempts to conceal, or assists another person in concealing or attempting to conceal such sexual offender; or
(3) Provides information to the law enforcement unit regarding such sexual offender which the person knows to be false information
commits a felony and shall be punished by imprisonment for not less than five nor more than 20 years.

CHAPTER 7. DAMAGE TO AND INTRUSION UPON PROPERTY

§ 16-7-1. Burglary

(a) As used in this Code section, the term:

(1) "Dwelling" means any building, structure, or portion thereof which is designed or intended for occupancy for residential use.

(2) "Railroad car" shall also include trailers on flatcars, containers on flatcars, trailers on railroad property, or containers on railroad property.

(b) A person commits the offense of burglary in the first degree when, without authority and with the intent to commit a felony or theft therein, he or she enters or remains within an occupied, unoccupied, or vacant dwelling house of another or any building, vehicle, railroad car, watercraft, aircraft, or other such structure designed for use as the dwelling of another. A person who commits the offense of burglary in the first degree shall be guilty of a felony and, upon conviction thereof, shall be punished by imprisonment for not less than one nor more than 20 years. Upon the second conviction for burglary in the first degree, the defendant shall be guilty of a felony and shall be punished by imprisonment for not less than two nor more than 20 years. Upon the third and all subsequent convictions for burglary in the first degree, the defendant shall be guilty of a felony and shall be punished by imprisonment for not less than five nor more than 25 years.

(c) A person commits the offense of burglary in the second degree when, without authority and with the intent to commit a felony or theft therein, he or she enters or remains within an occupied, unoccupied, or vacant building, structure, railroad car, watercraft, or aircraft. A person who commits the offense of burglary in the second degree shall be guilty of a felony and, upon conviction thereof, shall be punished by imprisonment for not less than one nor more than five years. Upon the second and all subsequent convictions for burglary in the second degree, the defendant shall be guilty of a felony and shall be punished by imprisonment for not less than one nor more than eight years.

(d) Upon a fourth and all subsequent convictions for a crime of burglary in any degree, adjudication of guilt or imposition of sentence shall not be suspended, probated, deferred, or withheld.

§ 16-7-2. Smash and grab burglary; "retail establishment" defined; penalty

(a) As used in this Code section, the term "retail establishment" means an establishment that sells goods or merchandise from a fixed location for direct consumption by a purchaser and includes establishments that prepare and sell meals or other edible products either for carry out or service within the establishment.

(b) A person commits the offense of smash and grab burglary when he or she intentionally and without authority enters a retail establishment with the intent to commit a theft and causes damage in excess of $500.00 to such establishment without the owner's consent.

(c) A person convicted of smash and grab burglary shall be guilty of a felony and, upon conviction, shall be punished by imprisonment for not less than two nor more than 20 years, by a fine of not more than $100,000.00, or both; provided, however, that upon a second or subsequent conviction, he or she shall be punished by imprisonment for not less than five nor more than 20 years, by a fine of not more than $100,000.00, or both.

§ 16-7-5. Home invasion in the first and second degree

(a) As used in this Code section, the term "dwelling" shall have the same meaning as provided in Code Section 16-7-1.

(b) A person commits the offense of home invasion in the first degree when, without authority and with intent to commit a forcible felony therein and while in possession of a deadly weapon or instrument which, when used offensively against a person, is likely to or actually does result in serious bodily injury, he or she enters the dwelling house of another while such dwelling house is occupied by any person with authority to be present therein.

(c) A person commits the offense of home invasion in the second degree when, without authority and with intent to commit a forcible misdemeanor therein and while in possession of a deadly weapon or instrument which, when used offensively against a person, is likely to or actually does result in serious bodily injury, he or she enters the dwelling house of another while such dwelling house is occupied by any person with authority to be present therein.

(d) A person convicted of the offense of home invasion in the first degree shall be guilty of a felony and, upon conviction thereof, shall be punished by imprisonment for life or imprisonment for not less than ten nor more than 20 years and by a fine of not more than $100,000.00. A person convicted of the offense of home invasion in the second degree shall be guilty of a felony and, upon conviction thereof, shall be punished by imprisonment for not less than five nor more than 20 years and by a fine of not more than $100,000.00.

(e) Adjudication of guilt or imposition of sentence for home invasion in any degree may be probated at the discretion of the judge; provided, however, that such sentence shall not be suspended, deferred, or withheld.

(f) A sentence imposed under this Code section may be imposed separately from and consecutive to a sentence for any other offense related to the act or acts establishing the offense under this Code section.

§ 16-7-20. Possession of tools for the commission of crime

(a) A person commits the offense of possession of tools for the commission of crime when he has in his possession any tool, explosive, or other device commonly used in the commission of burglary, theft, or other crime with the intent to make use thereof in the commission of a crime.

(b) A person convicted of the offense of possession of tools for the commission of crime shall be punished by imprisonment for not less than one nor more than five years.

§ 16-7-21. Criminal trespass

(a) A person commits the offense of criminal trespass when he or she intentionally damages any property of another without consent of that other person and the damage thereto is $500.00 or less or knowingly and maliciously interferes with the possession or use of the property of another person without consent of that person.

(b) A person commits the offense of criminal trespass when he or she knowingly and without authority:

(1) Enters upon the land or premises of another person or into any part of any vehicle, railroad car, aircraft, or watercraft of another person for an unlawful purpose;

(2) Enters upon the land or premises of another person or into any part of any vehicle, railroad car, aircraft, or watercraft of another person after receiving, prior to such entry, notice from the owner, rightful occupant, or, upon proper identification, an authorized representative of the owner or rightful occupant that such entry is forbidden; or

(3) Remains upon the land or premises of another person or within the vehicle, railroad car, aircraft, or watercraft of another person after receiving notice from the owner, rightful occupant, or, upon proper identification, an authorized representative of the owner or rightful occupant to depart.

(c) For the purposes of subsection (b) of this Code section, permission to enter or invitation to enter given by a minor who is or is not present on or in the property of the minor's parent or guardian is not sufficient to allow lawful entry of another person upon the land, premises, vehicle, railroad car, aircraft, or watercraft owned or rightfully occupied by such minor's parent or guardian if such parent or guardian has previously given notice that such entry is forbidden or notice to depart.

(d) A person who commits the offense of criminal trespass shall be guilty of a misdemeanor.

(e) A person commits the offense of criminal trespass when he or she intentionally defaces, mutilates, or defiles any grave marker, monument, or memorial to one or more deceased persons who served in the military service of this state, the United States of America or any of the states thereof, or the Confederate States of America or any of the states thereof, or a monument, plaque, marker, or memorial which is dedicated to, honors, or recounts the military service of any past or present military personnel of this state, the United States of America or any of the states thereof, or the Confederate States of America or any of the states thereof if such grave marker, monument, memorial, plaque, or marker is privately owned or located on land which is privately owned.

§ 16-7-22. Criminal damage to property in the first degree

(a) A person commits the offense of criminal damage to property in the first degree when he:

(1) Knowingly and without authority interferes with any property in a manner so as to endanger human life; or

(2) Knowingly and without authority and by force or violence interferes with the operation of any system of public communication, public transportation, sewerage, drainage, water supply, gas, power, or other public utility service or with any constituent property thereof.

(b) A person convicted of the offense of criminal damage to property in the first degree shall be punished by imprisonment for not less than one nor more than ten years.

§ 16-7-23. Criminal damage to property in the second degree

(a) A person commits the offense of criminal damage to property in the second degree when he:
(1) Intentionally damages any property of another person without his consent and the damage thereto exceeds $500.00; or
(2) Recklessly or intentionally, by means of fire or explosive, damages property of another person.
(b) A person convicted of the offense of criminal damage to property in the second degree shall be punished by imprisonment for not less than one nor more than five years.

§ 16-7-24. Interference with government property

(a) A person commits the offense of interference with government property when he destroys, damages, or defaces government property and, upon conviction thereof, shall be punished by imprisonment for not less than one nor more than five years.
(b) A person commits the offense of interference with government property when he forcibly interferes with or obstructs the passage into or from government property and, upon conviction thereof, shall be punished as for a misdemeanor.

§ 16-7-25. Damaging, injuring, or interfering with property of public utility companies, municipalities, or political subdivisions

(a) It shall be unlawful for any person intentionally and without authority to injure or destroy any meter, pipe, conduit, wire, line, post, lamp, or other apparatus belonging to a company, municipality, or political subdivision engaged in the manufacture or sale of electricity, gas, water, telephone, or other public services; intentionally and without authority to prevent a meter from properly registering the quantity of such service supplied; in any way to interfere with the proper action of such company, municipality, or political subdivision; intentionally to divert any services of such company, municipality, or political subdivision; or otherwise intentionally and without authority to use or cause to be used, without the consent of the company, municipality, or political subdivision, any service manufactured, sold, or distributed by the company, municipality, or political subdivision.
(b) Where there is no evidence to the contrary, the person performing any of the illegal acts set forth in subsection (a) of this Code section and the person who with knowledge of such violation receives the benefit of such service without proper charge as a result of the improper action shall be presumed to be responsible for the act of tampering or diversion.
(c) This Code section shall be cumulative to and shall not prohibit the enactment of any other general and local laws, rules, and regulations of state or local authorities or agencies and local ordinances prohibiting such activities which are more restrictive than this Code section.
(d) Any person who violates this Code section shall be guilty of a misdemeanor.

§ 16-7-26. Vandalism to a place of worship

(a) A person commits the offense of vandalism to a place of worship when he maliciously defaces or desecrates a church, synagogue, or other place of public religious worship.
(b) A person convicted of the offense of vandalism to a place of worship shall be punished by imprisonment for not less than one nor more than five years.

§ 16-7-27. Injuring, tearing down, or destroying mailboxes; injuring, defacing, or destroying mail

(a) It shall be unlawful for any person willfully or maliciously to injure, tear down, or destroy any mailbox or receptacle intended or used for the receipt or delivery of mail or willfully or maliciously to injure, deface, or destroy any mail deposited therein.
(b) Any person who violates this Code section shall be guilty of a misdemeanor.

§ 16-7-28. Redesignated

§ 16-7-29. Interference with electronic monitoring devices; "electronic monitoring device" defined; penalty

(a) For purposes of this Code section, the term "electronic monitoring device" shall include any device that is utilized to track the location of a person.
(b) It shall be unlawful for any person to knowingly and without authority remove, destroy, or circumvent the operation of an electronic monitoring device which is being used for the purpose of monitoring a person who is:
(1) Complying with a home arrest program as set forth in Code Section 42-1-8;
(2) Wearing an electronic monitoring device as a condition of bond or pretrial release;
(3) Wearing an electronic monitoring device as a condition of probation;
(4) Wearing an electronic monitoring device as a condition of parole; or
(5) Wearing an electronic monitoring device as required in Code Section 42-1-14.
(c) It shall be unlawful for any person to knowingly and without authority request or solicit any other person to remove, destroy, or circumvent the operation of an electronic monitoring device which is being used for the purposes described in subsection (b) of this Code section.
(d) Any person who violates this Code section shall be guilty of the offense of tampering with the operation of an electronic monitoring device and shall be punished by imprisonment for not less than one nor more than five years.

§ 16-7-40. Short title

Reserved. Repealed by Ga. L. 2006, p. 275, § 2-1, effective July 1, 2006.

§ 16-7-41. Legislative intent
Reserved. Repealed by Ga. L. 2006, p. 275, § 2-1, effective July 1, 2006

§ 16-7-42. Definitions

As used in this part, the term:
(1) "Litter" means any discarded or abandoned:
(A) Refuse, rubbish, junk, or other waste material; or
(B) Dead animals that are not subject to the provisions of Code Section 4-5-4.
(2) "Public or private property" means the right of way of any road or highway; any body of water or watercourse or the shores or beaches thereof; any park, playground, building, refuge, or conservation or recreation area; residential or farm properties, timberlands, or forests; or any commercial or industrial property.

§ 16-7-43. Littering public or private property or waters; enforcing personnel

(a) It shall be unlawful for any person or persons to dump, deposit, throw, or leave or to cause or permit the dumping, depositing, placing, throwing, or leaving of litter on any public or private property in this state or any waters in this state, unless:
(1) The area is designated by the state or by any of its agencies or political subdivisions for the disposal of litter and the person is authorized by the proper public authority to so use such area;
(2) The litter is placed into a nondisposable litter receptacle or container designed for the temporary storage of litter and located in an area designated by the owner or tenant in lawful possession of the property; or
(3) The person is the owner or tenant in lawful possession of such property or has first obtained consent of the owner or tenant in lawful possession or unless the act is done under the personal direction of the owner or tenant, all in a manner consistent with the public welfare.
(b) (1) Any person who violates subsection (a) of this Code section shall be guilty of a misdemeanor.
(2) In addition to the punishment provided under paragraph (1) of this subsection:
(A) In the sound discretion of the court, the person may be directed to pick up and remove from any public street or highway or public right of way for a distance not to exceed one mile any litter the person has deposited and any and all litter deposited thereon by anyone else prior to the date of execution of sentence; or
(B) In the sound discretion of the judge of the court, the person may be directed to pick up and remove from any public beach, public park, private right of way, or, with the prior permission of the legal owner or tenant in lawful possession of such property, any private property upon which it can be established by competent evidence that the person has deposited litter, any and all litter deposited thereon by anyone prior to the date of execution of sentence.
(c) The court may publish the names of persons convicted of violating subsection (a) of this Code section.
(d) Any county, municipality, consolidated government, or law enforcement agency thereof of this state which is empowered by Code Section 16-7-45 or other law to enforce the provisions of this Code section or local littering ordinances may, in its discretion, appoint any person who is a citizen of the United States, is of good moral character, and has not previously been convicted of a felony to enforce the provisions of this Code section or local littering ordinances within the county, municipality, or consolidated government in which the appointing agency exercises jurisdiction. Each person appointed pursuant to this Code section shall take and subscribe an oath of office as prescribed by the appointing authority. Any person appointed and sworn pursuant to this subsection shall be authorized to enforce the provisions of this Code section or local littering ordinances in the same manner as any employee or law enforcement officer of this state or any county, municipality, or consolidated government of this state subject to the limitations provided in subsections (e) and (f) of this Code section.
(e) No person appointed pursuant to subsection (d) of this Code section shall be deemed a peace officer under the laws of this state or:
(1) Be deemed to be an employee of or receive any compensation from the state, county, municipality, consolidated government, or appointing law enforcement agency;
(2) Be required to complete any training or be certified pursuant to the requirements of Chapter 8 of Title 35;
(3) Have the power or duty to enforce any traffic or other criminal laws of the state, county, municipality, or consolidated government;
(4) Have the power to possess and carry firearms and other weapons for the purpose of enforcing the littering laws; or
(5) Be entitled to any indemnification from the state, county, municipality, or consolidated government for any injury or property damage sustained by such person as a result of attempting to enforce the littering laws of this state or any local government.
(f) Notwithstanding any law to the contrary, neither the state nor any county, municipality, or consolidated government of this state or any department, agency, board, or officer of this state or any county, municipality, or consolidated government of this state shall be liable or accountable for or on account of any act or omission of any person appointed pursuant to this Code section in connection with such person's enforcement of the provisions of this Code section or local littering ordinances.
(g) It shall be unlawful for any person willfully to obstruct, resist, impede, or interfere with any person appointed pursuant to this Code section in connection with such person's enforcement of this Code section or local littering ordinances or to retaliate or discriminate in any manner against such person as a reprisal for any act or omission of such person. Any violation of this subsection shall be punishable as a misdemeanor.

§ 16-7-44. Prima-facie evidence; rebuttable presumption

(a) Whenever litter is thrown, deposited, dropped, or dumped from any motor vehicle, boat, airplane, or other conveyance in violation of Code Section 16-7-43, the trier of fact may in its discretion and in consideration of the totality of the circumstances infer that the operator of the conveyance has violated this part.
(b) Except as provided in subsection (a) of this Code section, whenever any litter which is dumped, deposited, thrown, or left on public or private property in violation of Code Section 16-7-43 is discovered to contain any article or articles, including but not limited to letters, bills, publications, or other writings which display the name of a person thereon in such a manner as to indicate that the article belongs or belonged to such person, the trier of fact may in its discretion and in consideration of the totality of the circumstances infer that such person has violated this part.

§ 16-7-45. Enforcement of this part

All law enforcement agencies, officers, and officials of this state or any political subdivision thereof or any enforcement agency, officer, or any official of any commission or authority of this state or any political subdivision thereof is authorized, empowered, and directed to enforce compliance with this part.

§ 16-7-46. Receptacles to be provided; notice to public

All public authorities and agencies having supervision of properties of this state are authorized, empowered, and instructed to establish and maintain receptacles for the deposit of litter at appropriate locations where the property is frequented by the public, to post signs directing persons to the receptacles and serving notice of the provisions of this part, and to otherwise publicize the availability of litter receptacles and requirements of this part.

§ 16-7-47. Designation of containers for household garbage; misuse or vandalization of container

(a) As used in this Code section, the term "household garbage" means animal, vegetable, and fruit refuse matter and other refuse matter ordinarily generated as by-products of a household or restaurant, such as tin cans, bottles, paper, cardboard, plastics, and wrapping or packaging materials.
(b) The governing authority of each county, municipality, or consolidated government of this state which provides containers for the dumping of trash or garbage therein shall be authorized to designate any or all such containers as being suitable for the dumping therein of household garbage only. If a container is clearly marked "household garbage only," it shall be unlawful for any person to dump any refuse or other material into the container other than household garbage.
(c) It shall be unlawful for any person to set fire to the contents of, indiscriminately scatter or disperse the contents of, or otherwise vandalize any containers provided by any county, municipality, or consolidated government for the dumping of trash or garbage.

(d) Any person who violates subsection (b) or (c) of this Code section shall be guilty of a misdemeanor.

§ 16-7-48. Local ordinances regulating and controlling litter

(a) Nothing in this part shall limit the authority of any state agency, county, municipality, or consolidated government to enforce any other laws, rules, or regulations relating to litter.

(b) Nothing within this part shall be construed to prohibit the adoption of local ordinances regulating and controlling litter within the jurisdiction of any county, municipality, or consolidated government. Violation of such ordinances shall be punished as provided in the municipal charter or local ordinances.

§ 16-7-50. Short title

Reserved. Repealed by Ga. L. 2006, p. 275, § 2-2, effective July 1, 2006.

§ 16-7-51. Definitions

As used in this part, the term:

(1) "Biomedical waste" means that term as defined in paragraph (1.1) of Code Section 12-8-22.

(2) "Commercial purpose" means for the purpose of economic gain.

(3) "Dump" means to throw, discard, place, deposit, discharge, burn, or dispose of a substance.

(4) "Egregious litter" means all litter, as such term is defined in paragraph (1) of Code Section 16-7-42, exceeding ten pounds in weight or 15 cubic feet in volume; any discarded or abandoned substance in any weight or volume if biomedical waste, hazardous waste, or a hazardous substance; or any substance or material dumped for commercial purposes.

(5) "Hazardous substance" means that term as defined in paragraph (4) of Code Section 12-8-92.

(6) "Hazardous waste" means that term as defined in paragraph (10) of Code Section 12-8-62.

§ 16-7-52. Unlawful dumping

It shall be unlawful for any person to intentionally dump egregious litter unless authorized to do so by law or by a duly issued permit:

(1) In or on any public highway, road, street, alley, or thoroughfare, including any portion of the right of way thereof, or on any other public lands except in containers or areas lawfully provided for such dumping;

(2) In or on any fresh-water lake, river, canal, or stream or tidal or coastal water of the state; or

(3) In or on any private property, unless prior consent of the owner has been given and unless such dumping will not adversely affect the public health and is not in violation of any other state law, rule, or regulation.

§ 16-7-53. Penalties for unlawful dumping

(a) Any person who intentionally dumps egregious litter in violation of Code Section 16-7-52 in an amount not exceeding 500 pounds in weight or 100 cubic feet in volume which is not biomedical waste, hazardous waste, or a hazardous substance and not for commercial purposes shall be guilty of a misdemeanor of a high and aggravated nature. For purposes of this subsection, each day a continuing violation occurs shall constitute a separate violation.

(b) Any person who intentionally dumps egregious litter in violation of Code Section 16-7-52 in an amount exceeding 500 pounds in weight or 100 cubic feet in volume which is not biomedical waste, hazardous waste, or a hazardous substance and not for commercial purposes shall upon the first offense be guilty of a misdemeanor of a high and aggravated nature. Upon the second and each subsequent offense such person shall be guilty of a felony and, upon conviction thereof, shall be fined not more than $25,000.00 for each violation or imprisoned for not more than five years, or both; provided, however, that the portion of any term of imprisonment exceeding two years shall be probated conditioned upon payment of a fine imposed under this subsection. For purposes of this subsection, each day a continuing violation occurs shall constitute a separate violation.

(c) Any person who intentionally dumps egregious litter in violation of Code Section 16-7-52 in any quantity if the substance is biomedical waste, hazardous waste, or a hazardous substance or if the dumping is for commercial purposes shall be guilty of a felony and, upon conviction thereof, shall be fined not more than $25,000.00 for each violation or imprisoned for not more than five years, or both; provided, however, that the portion of any term of imprisonment exceeding two years shall be probated conditioned upon payment of a fine imposed under this subsection. For purposes of this subsection, each day a continuing violation occurs shall constitute a separate violation.

(d) In addition to the penalties provided in subsections (a) and (b) of this Code section, the court may order the violator to remove or render harmless any egregious litter dumped in violation of Code Section 16-7-52, repair or restore property damaged by or pay damages resulting from such dumping, or perform public service related to the removal of illegally dumped egregious litter or to the restoration of an area polluted by such substance.

(e) (1) The court shall cause to be published a notice of conviction for each person convicted of violating any provision of this Code section. Such notices of conviction shall be published in the manner of legal notices in the legal organ of the county in which such person resides or, in the case of a nonresident, in the legal organ of the county in which the person was convicted. Such notice of conviction shall contain the name and address of the convicted person; date, time, and place of arrest; and disposition of the case and shall be published once in the legal organ of the appropriate county in the second week following such conviction or as soon thereafter as publication may be made.

(2) The convicted person for which a notice of conviction is published pursuant to this subsection shall be assessed the cost of publication of such notice, and such assessment shall be imposed at the time of conviction in addition to any other fine imposed pursuant to this Code section.

(3) The clerk of the court, the publisher of any legal organ which publishes a notice of conviction, and any other person involved in the publication of an erroneous notice of conviction shall be immune from civil or criminal liability for such erroneous publication, provided such publication was made in good faith.

§ 16-7-53.1. Vehicle impoundment for intentionally dumping egregious litter

(a) Whenever a person has been arrested for a violation of Code Section 16-7-52 committed while driving, moving, or operating a vehicle, the arresting law enforcement agency may impound the vehicle that the person was driving, moving, or operating at the time of arrest until such time as the arrestee claiming the vehicle meets the conditions for release in subsection (b) of this Code section or a person other than the arrestee meets the conditions for release in subsection (c) of this Code section.

(b) A vehicle impounded pursuant to this Code section shall not be released unless the person claiming the vehicle:

(1) Presents a valid driver's license, proof of ownership or lawful authority to operate the motor vehicle, and proof of valid motor vehicle insurance for that vehicle; and

(2) Is able to operate the vehicle in a safe manner and would not be in violation of Title 40.

(c) A vehicle impounded pursuant to this Code section may be released to a person other than the arrestee only if:

(1) The vehicle is not owned or leased by the person under arrest and the person who owns or leases the vehicle claims the vehicle and meets the conditions for release in subsection (b) of this Code section; or

(2) The vehicle is owned or leased by the arrestee, the arrestee gives written permission to another person to operate the vehicle, and the conditions for release in subsection (b) of this Code section are met.

(d) A law enforcement agency impounding a vehicle pursuant to this Code section may charge a reasonable fee for towing and storage of the vehicle. The law enforcement agency may retain custody of the vehicle until that fee is paid.

§ 16-7-54. Evidence of identity of violator

Whenever any egregious litter which is dumped in violation of Code Section 16-7-52 is discovered to contain any article or articles, including but not limited to letters, bills, publications, or other writings which display the name of a person thereon, addressed to such person or in any other manner indicating that the article belongs or belonged to such person, the trier of fact may in its discretion and in consideration of the totality of the circumstances infer that such person has violated this part.

§ 16-7-55. Enforcement of other laws, rules, or regulations not limited

(a) Nothing in this part shall limit the authority of any state agency, county, municipality, or consolidated government to enforce any other laws, rules, or regulations relating to egregious litter or the management of solid, biomedical, or hazardous waste.
(b) Nothing within this part shall be construed to prohibit the adoption of local ordinances regulating and controlling egregious litter within the jurisdiction of any county, municipality, or consolidated government. Violation of such ordinances shall be punished as provided in the municipal charter or local ordinances.

§ 16-7-56. Title 12 provisions not affected

Nothing in this part shall be construed so as to repeal, supersede, amend, or modify any provision of Title 12.

§ 16-7-58. Prohibited placements of posters, signs, and advertisements

(a) It shall be unlawful for any person to place posters, signs, or advertisements:
(1) On any public property or building, unless the owner thereof or the occupier as authorized by such owner has given permission to place such posters, signs, or advertisements on such property; provided, however, that signs within the rights of way of public roads shall be governed by Code Section 32-6-51;
(2) On any private property unless the owner thereof or the occupier as authorized by such owner has given permission to place such posters, signs, or advertisements on such property; and, provided, further that no municipal, county, or consolidated government may restrict by regulation or other means the length of time a political campaign sign may be displayed or the number of signs which may be displayed on private property for which permission has been granted; or
(3) On any property zoned for commercial or industrial uses if the placement of such posters, signs, or advertisements conflicts with any zoning laws or ordinances.
(b) Any poster, sign, or advertisement placed in violation of paragraph (1) of subsection (a) of this Code section is declared to be a public nuisance, and the officials having jurisdiction of the public property or building, including without limitation law enforcement officers, may remove or direct the removal of the same.
(c) Each poster, sign, or advertisement placed in violation of this Code section shall constitute a separate offense.
(d) Any person who violates this Code section shall be punished the same as for littering under Code Section 16-7-43.

§ 16-7-60. Arson in the first degree

(a) A person commits the offense of arson in the first degree when, by means of fire or explosive, he or she knowingly damages or knowingly causes, aids, abets, advises, encourages, hires, counsels, or procures another to damage:
(1) Any dwelling house of another without his or her consent or in which another has a security interest, including but not limited to a mortgage, a lien, or a conveyance to secure debt, without the consent of both, whether it is occupied, unoccupied, or vacant;
(2) Any building, vehicle, railroad car, watercraft, or other structure of another without his or her consent or in which another has a security interest, including but not limited to a mortgage, a lien, or a conveyance to secure debt, without the consent of both, if such structure is designed for use as a dwelling, whether it is occupied, unoccupied, or vacant;
(3) Any dwelling house, building, vehicle, railroad car, watercraft, aircraft, or other structure whether it is occupied, unoccupied, or vacant and when such is insured against loss or damage by fire or explosive and such loss or damage is accomplished without the consent of both the insurer and the insured;
(4) Any dwelling house, building, vehicle, railroad car, watercraft, aircraft, or other structure whether it is occupied, unoccupied, or vacant with the intent to defeat, prejudice, or defraud the rights of a spouse or co-owner; or
(5) Any building, vehicle, railroad car, watercraft, aircraft, or other structure under such circumstances that it is reasonably foreseeable that human life might be endangered.
(b) A person also commits the offense of arson in the first degree when, in the commission of a felony, by means of fire or explosive, he or she knowingly damages or knowingly causes, aids, abets, advises, encourages, hires, counsels, or procures another to damage anything included or described in subsection (a) of this Code section.
(c) A person convicted of the offense of arson in the first degree shall be punished by a fine of not more than $50,000.00 or by imprisonment for not less than one nor more than 20 years, or both.

§ 16-7-61. Arson in the second degree

(a) A person commits the offense of arson in the second degree as to any building, vehicle, railroad car, watercraft, aircraft, or other structure not included or described in Code Section 16-7-60 when, by means of fire or explosive, he or she knowingly damages or knowingly causes, aids, abets, advises, encourages, hires, counsels, or procures another to damage any building, vehicle, railroad car, watercraft, aircraft, or other structure of another without his or her consent or in which another has a security interest, including but not limited to a mortgage, a lien, or a conveyance to secure debt, without the consent of both.
(b) A person also commits the offense of arson in the second degree as to any building, vehicle, railroad car, watercraft, aircraft, or other structure not included or described in Code Section 16-7-60 when, in the commission of a felony, by means of fire or explosive, he or she knowingly damages or knowingly causes, aids, abets, advises, encourages, hires, counsels, or procures another to damage any building, vehicle, railroad car, watercraft, aircraft, or other structure of another without his or her consent or in which another has a security interest, including but not limited to a mortgage, a lien, or a conveyance to secure debt, without the consent of both.
(c) A person convicted of the offense of arson in the second degree shall be punished by a fine of not more than $25,000.00 or by imprisonment for not less than one nor more than ten years, or both.

§ 16-7-62. Arson in the third degree

(a) A person commits the offense of arson in the third degree when, by means of fire or explosive, he or she knowingly damages or knowingly causes, aids, abets, advises, encourages, hires, counsels, or procures another to damage:
(1) Any personal property of another without his or her consent or in which another has a security interest, including but not limited to a lien, without the consent of both and the value of the property is $25.00 or more;
(2) Any personal property when such is insured against loss or damage by fire or explosive and the loss or damage is accomplished without the consent of both the insurer and insured and the value of the property is $25.00 or more; or
(3) Any personal property with the intent to defeat, prejudice, or defraud the rights of a spouse or co-owner and the value of the property is $25.00 or more.
(b) A person also commits the offense of arson in the third degree when, in the commission of a felony, by means of fire or explosive, he or she knowingly damages or knowingly causes, aids, abets, advises, encourages, hires, counsels, or procures another to damage anything included or described in subsection (a) of this Code section.
(c) A person convicted of the offense of arson in the third degree shall be punished by a fine not to exceed $10,000.00 or by imprisonment for not less than one nor more than five years, or both.

§ 16-7-63. Burning of woodlands, brush, fields, or other lands; arson of lands; destruction of or damage to material or device used in detection or suppression of wildfires; penalties for violations

(a) It shall be unlawful:

(1) To, with intent to damage, start, cause, or procure another to start or cause a fire in any woodlands, brush, field, or other lands that are not one's own and without the permission of the owner or the lessee having control of such property;

(2) To burn any brush, field, forest land, campfire, or debris, whether on one's own land or the lands of another, without taking the necessary precautions before, during, and after the fire to prevent the escape of such fire onto the lands of another. The escape of such fire shall be prima-facie evidence that necessary precautions were not taken;

(3) For any person to cause a fire by discarding any lighted cigarette, cigar, debris, or any other flaming or smoldering material that may cause a forest fire; or

(4) To destroy or damage any material or device used in the detection or suppression of wildfires.

(b) This Code section shall not apply to fire resulting from the operation of transportation machinery or equipment used in its normal or accustomed manner.

(c) (1) Any person who violates paragraph (2), (3), or (4) of subsection (a) of this Code section shall be guilty of a misdemeanor.

(2) Any person who violates paragraph (1) of subsection (a) of this Code section shall be guilty of arson of lands in the third degree and shall be punished the same as provided by subsection (c) of Code Section 16-7-62 for arson in the third degree.

(3) Any person whose violation of paragraph (1) of subsection (a) of this Code section results in a fire that burns more than five acres that are not one's own shall be guilty of arson of lands in the second degree and shall be punished the same as provided by subsection (c) of Code Section 16-7-61 for arson in the second degree.

(4) Any person who violates paragraph (1) of subsection (a) of this Code section under such circumstances that it was reasonably foreseeable that human life might be endangered shall be guilty of arson of lands in the first degree and shall be punished the same as provided by subsection (c) of Code Section 16-7-60 for arson in the first degree.

§ 16-7-64. Criminal possession of an explosive device

Repealed by Ga. L. 1996, p. 416, § 2, effective May 1, 1996.

§ 16-7-80. Definitions

As used in this article, the term:

(1) "Bacteriological weapon" or "biological weapon" means:

(A) The following toxic chemicals:

(i) O-Alkyl (less than or equal to C10, including cycloalkyl) alkyl (Me, Et, n-Pr or i-Pr)-phosphonofluoridates; e.g., Sarin: O-Isopropyl methylphosphonofluoridate, Soman: O-Pinacolyl methylphosphonofluoridate;

(ii) O-Alkyl (less than or equal to C10, including cycloalkyl) N,N-dialkyl (Me, Et, n-Pr or i-Pr) phosphoramidocyanidates; e.g., Tabun: O-Ethyl N,N-dimethyl phosphoramidocyanidate;

(iii) O-Alkyl (H or less than or equal to C10, including cycloalkyl) S-2-dialkyl (Me, Et, n-Pr or i-Pr)-aminoethyl alkyl (Me, Et, n-Pr or i-Pr) phosphonothiolates and corresponding alkylated or protonated salts; e.g., VX: O-Ethyl S-2-diisopropylaminoethyl methyl phosphonothiolate;

(B) Sulfur mustards:

(i) 2-Chloroethylchloromethylsulfide;

(ii) Mustard gas: Bis(2-chloroethyl)sulfide;

(iii) Bis(2-chloroethylthio)methane;

(iv) Sesquimustard: 1,2-Bis(2-chloroethylthio)ethane;

(v) 1,3-Bis(2-chloroethylthio)-n-propane;

(vi) 1,4-Bis(2-chloroethylthio)-n-butane;

(vii) 1,5 Bis(2-chloroethylthio)-n-pentane;

(viii) Bis(2-chloroethylthiomethyl)ether;

(ix) O-Mustard: Bis(2-chloroethylthioethyl)ether;

(C) Lewisites:

(i) Lewisite 1: 2-Chlorovinyldichloroarsine;

(ii) Lewisite 2: Bis(2-chlorovinyl)chloroarsine;

(iii) Lewisite 3: Tris(2-chlorovinyl)arsine;

(D) Nitrogen mustards:

(i) HN1: Bis(2-chloroethyl)ethylamine;

(ii) HN2: Bis(2-chloroethyl)methylamine;

(iii) HN3: Tris(2-chloroethyl)amine;

(E) Saxitoxin;

(F) Ricin;

(G) Precursors:

(i) Alkyl (Me, Et, n-Pr or i-Pr) phosphonyldifluorides; e.g., DF: Methylphosphonyldifluoride;

(ii) O-Alkyl (H or less than or equal to C10, including cycloalkyl) O-2-dialkyl (Me, Et, n-Pr or i-Pr)-aminoethyl alkyl (Me, Et, n-Pr or i-Pr) phosphonites and corresponding alkylated or protonated salts; e.g., QL: O-Ethyl O-2-diisopropylaminoethyl methylphosphonite;

(iii) Chlorosarin: O-Isopropyl methylphosphonochloridate;

(iv) Chlorosoman: O-Pinacolyl methylphosphonochloridate; or

(H) Any device which is designed in such a manner as to permit the intentional release into the population or environment of microbial or other biological agents or toxins or vectors whatever their origin or method of production in a manner not otherwise authorized by law.

(1.1) "Biological agent" means any microorganism, including, but not limited to, bacteria, viruses, fungi, rickettsiae or protozoa, or infectious substance, or any naturally occurring, bioengineered or synthesized component of any such microorganism or infectious substance, capable of causing:

(A) Death, disease, or other biological malfunction in a human, an animal, a plant, or another living organism;

(B) Deterioration of food, water, equipment, supplies, or material of any kind; or

(C) Deleterious alteration of the environment.

(2) "Commissioner" means the Safety Fire Commissioner.

(3) "Conviction" means an adjudication of guilt of or a plea of guilty or nolo contendere to the commission of an offense against the laws of this state, any other state or territory, the United States, or a foreign nation recognized by the United States. Such term includes any such conviction or plea notwithstanding the fact that sentence was imposed pursuant to Article 3 of Chapter 8 of Title 42. Such term also includes the adjudication or plea of a juvenile to the commission of an act which if committed by an adult would constitute a crime under the laws of this state.

(4) "Destructive device" means:

(A) Any explosive, incendiary, or over-pressure device or poison gas which has been configured as a bomb; a grenade; a rocket with a propellant charge of more than four ounces; a missile having an explosive or incendiary charge of more than one-quarter ounce; a poison gas; a mine; a Molotov cocktail; or any other device which is substantially similar to such devices;

(B) Any type of weapon by whatever name known which will or may be readily converted to expel a projectile by the action of an explosive or other propellant, through a barrel which has a bore diameter of more than one-half inch in diameter; provided, however, that such term shall not include a pistol, rifle, or shotgun suitable for sporting or personal safety purposes or ammunition; a device which is neither designed or redesigned for use as a weapon; a device which, although originally designed for use as a weapon, is redesigned for use as a signaling, pyrotechnic, line throwing, safety, or similar device; or surplus military ordnance sold, loaned, or given by authority of the appropriate official of the United States Department of Defense;

(C) A weapon of mass destruction;

(D) A bacteriological weapon or biological weapon; or

(E) Any combination of parts either designed or intended for use in converting any device into a destructive device as otherwise defined in this paragraph.

(5) "Detonator" means a device containing a detonating charge that is used to initiate detonation in an explosive, including but not limited to electric blasting caps, blasting caps for use with safety fuses, and detonating cord delay connectors.

(6) "Director" means the director of the Georgia Bureau of Investigation.

(7) "Distribute" means the actual, constructive, or attempted transfer from one person to another.

(8) "Explosive" means any chemical compound or other substance or mechanical system intended for the purpose of producing an explosion capable of causing injury to persons or damage to property or containing oxidizing and combustible units or other ingredients in such proportions or quantities that ignition, fire, friction, concussion, percussion, or detonator may produce an explosion capable of causing injury to persons or damage to property, including but not limited to the substances designated in Code Section 16-7-81; provided, however, that the term explosive shall not include common fireworks as defined by Code Section 25-10-1, model rockets and model rocket engines designed, sold, and used for the purpose of propelling recoverable aero models, or toy pistol paper caps in which the explosive content does not average more than 0.25 grains of explosive mixture per paper cap for toy pistols, toy cannons, toy canes, toy guns, or other devices using such paper caps unless such devices are used as a component of a destructive device.

(9) "Explosive ordnance disposal technician" or "EOD technician" means:

(A) A law enforcement officer, fire official, emergency management official, or an employee of this state or its political subdivisions or an authority of the state or a political subdivision who is certified in accordance with Code Section 35-8-13 and members of the Georgia National Guard who are qualified as explosive ordnance disposal technicians under the appropriate laws and regulations when acting in the performance of their official duties; and

(B) An official or employee of the United States, including but not limited to a member of the armed forces of the United States, who is qualified as an explosive ordnance disposal technician under the appropriate laws and regulations when acting in the performance of his or her official duties.

(10) "Felony" means any offense punishable by imprisonment for a term of one year or more, and includes conviction by a court-martial under the Uniform Code of Military Justice for an offense which would constitute a felony under the laws of the United States. A conviction of an offense under the laws of a foreign nation shall be considered a felony for the purposes of this article if the conduct giving rise to such conviction would have constituted a felony under the laws of this state or of the United States if committed within the jurisdiction of this state or the United States at the time of such conduct.

(11) "Hoax device" or "replica" means a device or article which has the appearance of a destructive device.

(12) "Incendiary" means a flammable liquid or compound with a flash point of 150 degrees Fahrenheit or less as determined by Tagliabue or equivalent closed-cup device, including but not limited to, gasoline, kerosene, fuel oil, or a derivative of such substances.

(13) "Over-pressure device" means a frangible container filled with an explosive gas or expanding gas which is designed or constructed so as to cause the container to break or fracture in a manner which is capable of causing death, bodily harm, or property damage.

(14) "Poison gas" means any toxic chemical or its precursors that through its chemical action or properties on life processes causes death or permanent injury to human beings; provided, however, that such term shall not include:

(A) Riot control agents, smoke, and obscuration materials or medical products which are manufactured, possessed, transported, or used in accordance with the laws of the United States and of this state;

(B) Tear gas devices designed to be carried on or about the person which contain not more than one-half ounce of the chemical;

(C) Pesticides, as provided in paragraph (12) of Code Section 16-7-93.

(15) "Property" means any real or personal property of any kind including money, choses in action, and other similar interests in property.

(16) "Public building" means any structure which is generally open to members of the public with or without the payment of an admission fee or membership dues including, but not limited to structures owned, operated, or leased by the state, the United States, any of the several states, or any foreign nation or any political subdivision or authority thereof; any religious organization; any medical facility; any college, school, or university; or any corporation, partnership, or association.

(16.1) "Toxin" means the toxic material or product of plants, animals, microorganisms, including, but not limited to, bacteria, viruses, fungi, rickettsiae or protozoa, or infectious substances, or a recombinant or synthesized molecule, whatever their origin and method of production, and includes:

(A) Any poisonous substance or biological product that may be engineered as a result of biotechnology produced by a living organism; or

(B) Any poisonous isomer or biological product, homologue, or derivative of such a substance.

(16.2) "Vector" means a living organism, or molecule, including a recombinant or synthesized molecule, capable of carrying a biological agent or toxin to a host.

(17) "Weapon of mass destruction" means any device which is designed in such a way as to release radiation or radioactivity at a level which will result in internal or external bodily injury or death to any person.

§ 16-7-81. Explosive materials

The following materials are explosives within the meaning of this article:

(1) Acetylides of heavy metals;

(2) Aluminum containing polymeric propellant;

(3) Aluminum ophorite explosive;

(4) Amatex;

(5) Amatol;

(6) Ammonal;

(7) Ammonium nitrate explosive mixtures, cap sensitive;

(8) Ammonium nitrate explosive mixtures, noncap sensitive;

(9) Aromatic nitro-compound explosive mixtures;

(10) Ammonium perchlorate explosive mixtures;

(11) Ammonium perchlorate composite propellant;

(12) Ammonium picrate (picrate of ammonia, Explosive D);

(13) Ammonium salt lattice with isomorphously substituted inorganic salts;

(14) Ammonium tri-iodide;

(15) ANFO (ammonium nitrate-fuel oil);

(16) Baratol;

(17) Baronol;

(18) BEAF (1,2-bis (2,2-difluoro-2-nitroacetoxyethane));

(19) Black powder;

(20) Black powder based explosive mixtures;

(21) Blasting agents, nitro-carbo-nitrates, including noncap sensitive slurry and water-gel explosives;

(22) Blasting caps;

(23) Blasting gelatin;

(24) Blasting powder;

(25) BTNEC (bis (trinitroethyl) carbonate);

(26) Bulk salutes;

(27) BTNEN (bis (trinitroethyl) nitramine);

(28) BTTN (1,2,4 butanetriol trinitrate);

(29) Butyl tetryl;

(30) Calcium nitrate explosive mixture;

(31) Cellulose hexanitrate explosive mixture;

(32) Chlorate explosive mixtures;

(33) Composition A and variations;

(34) Composition B and variations;

(35) Composition C and variations;

(36) Copper acetylide;

(37) Cyanuric triazide;

(38) Cyclotrimethylenetrinitramine (RDX);

(39) Cyclotetramethylenetetranitramine (HMX);

(40) Cyclonite (RDX);

(41) Cyclotol;

(42) DATB (diaminotrinitrobenzene);

(43) DDNP (diazodinitrophenol);

(44) DEGDN (diethyleneglycol dinitrate);

(45) Detonating cord;

(46) Detonators;

(47) Dimethylol dimethyl methane dinitrate composition;

(48) Dinitroethyleneurea;

(49) Dinitroglycerine (glycerol dinitrate);

(50) Dinitrophenol;

(51) Dinitrophenolates;

(52) Dinitrophenyl hydrazine;

(53) Dinitroresorcinol;

(54) Dinitrotoluene-sodium nitrate explosive mixtures;

(55) DIPAM;

(56) Dipicryl sulfone;

(57) Dipicrylamine;

(58) Display fireworks;

(59) DNDP (dinitropentano nitrile);

(60) DNPA (2,2-dinitropropyl acrylate);

(61) Dynamite;

(62) EDDN (ethylene diamine dinitrate);

(63) EDNA;

(64) Ednatol;

(65) EDNP (ethyl 4,4-dinitropentanoate);

(66) Erythritol tetranitrate explosives;

(67) Esters of nitro-substituted alcohols;

(68) EGDN (ethylene glycol dinitrate);

(69) Ethyl-tetryl;

(70) Explosive conitrates;

(71) Explosive gelatins;

(72) Explosive mixtures containing oxygen-releasing inorganic salts and hydrocarbons;

(73) Explosive mixtures containing oxygen-releasing inorganic salts and nitro bodies;

(74) Explosive mixtures containing oxygen-releasing inorganic salts and water insoluble fuels;

(75) Explosive mixtures containing oxygen-releasing inorganic salts and water soluble fuels;

(76) Explosive mixtures containing sensitized nitromethane;

(77) Explosive mixtures containing tetranitromethane (nitroform);

(78) Explosive nitro compounds of aromatic hydrocarbons;

(79) Explosive organic nitrate mixtures;

(80) Explosive liquids;

(81) Explosive powders;

(82) Flash powder;

(83) Fulminate of mercury;

(84) Fulminate of silver;

(85) Fulminating gold;

(86) Fulminating mercury;

(87) Fulminating platinum;

(88) Fulminating silver;

(89) Gelatinized nitrocellulose;

(90) Gem-dinitro aliphatic explosive mixtures;

(91) Guanyl nitrosamino guanyl tetrazene;

(92) Guanyl nitrosamino guanylidene hydrazine;

(92.1) Guncotton;

(92.2) Heavy metal azides;

(92.3) Hexamitrostrilbene;

(92.4) Hexanite;

(92.5) Hexanitrodiphenylamine;

(92.6) Hexogen;

(93) Hexogene or octogene and a nitrated N-methylaniline;

(94) Hexolites;

(95) HMX (cyclo-l,3,5,7-tetramethylene-2,4,6,8-tetranitramine; Octogen);

(96) Hydrazinium nitrate/hydrazine/aluminum explosive system;

(97) Hydrazoic acid;

(98) Igniter cord;

(99) Igniters;

(100) Initiating tube systems;

(101) KDNBF (potassium dinitrobenzo-furoxane);

(102) Lead azide;

(103) Lead mannite;

(104) Lead mononitroresorcinate;

(105) Lead picrate;

(106) Lead salts, explosive;

(107) Lead styphnate (styphnate of lead, lead trinitroresorcinate);

(108) Liquid nitrated polyol and trimethylolethane;

(109) Liquid oxygen explosives;

(110) Magnesium ophorite explosives;

(111) Mannitol hexanitrate;

(112) MDNP (methyl 4,4-dinitropentanoate);

(113) MEAN (monoethanolamine nitrate);

(114) Mercuric fulminate;

(115) Mercury oxalate;

(116) Mercury tartrate;

(117) Metriol trinitrate;

(118) Minol-2 (40% TNT, 40% ammonium nitrate, 20% aluminum);

(119) MMAN (monomethylamine nitrate); methylamine nitrate;

(120) Mononitrotoluene-nitroglycerin mixture;

(121) Monopropellants;

(122) NIBTN (nitroisobutametriol trinitrate);

(123) Nitrate sensitized with gelled nitroparaffin;

(124) Nitrated carbohydrate explosive;

(125) Nitrated glucoside explosive;

(126) Nitrated polyhydric alcohol explosives;

(127) Nitrates of soda explosive mixtures;

(128) Nitric acid and a nitro aromatic compound explosive;

(129) Nitric acid and carboxylic fuel explosive;

(130) Nitric acid explosive mixtures;

(131) Nitro aromatic explosive mixtures;

(132) Nitro compounds of furane explosive mixtures;

(133) Nitrocellulose explosive;

(134) Nitroderivative of urea explosive mixture;

(135) Nitrogelatin explosive;

(136) Nitrogen trichloride;

(137) Nitrogen tri-iodide;

(138) Nitroglycerine (NG, RNG, nitro, glyceryl trinitrate, trinitroglycerine);

(139) Nitroglycide;

(140) Nitroglycol (ethylene glycol dinitrate, EGDN);

(141) Nitroguanidine explosives;

(142) Nitroparaffins Explosive Grade and ammonium nitrate mixtures;

(143) Nitronium perchlorate propellant mixtures;

(144) Nitrostarch;

(145) Nitro-substituted carboxylic acids;

(146) Nitrourea;

(147) Octogen (HMX);

(148) Octol (75% HMX, 25% TNT);

(149) Organic amine nitrates;

(150) Organic nitramines;

(151) PBX (RDX and plasticizer);

(152) Pellet powder;

(153) Penthrinite composition;

(154) Pentolite;

(155) Perchlorate explosive mixtures;

(156) Peroxide based explosive mixtures;

(157) PETN (nitropentaerythrite, pentaerythrite tetranitrate, pentaerythritol tetranitrate);

(158) Picramic acid and its salts;

(159) Picramide;

(160) Picrate of potassium explosive mixtures;

(161) Picratol;

(162) Picric acid (manufactured as an explosive);

(163) Picryl chloride;

(164) Picryl fluoride;

(165) PLX (95% nitromethane, 5% ethylenediamine);

(166) Polynitro aliphatic compounds;

(167) Polyolpolynitrate-nitrocellulose explosive gels;

(168) Potassium chlorate and lead sulfocyanate explosive;

(169) Potassium nitrate explosive mixtures;

(170) Potassium nitroaminotetrazole;

(171) Pyrotechnic compositions;
(172) PYX (2,6-bis(picrylamino)-3,5-dinitropyridine);
(173) RDX (cyclonite, hexogen, T4,cyclo-l,3,5,-trimethylene-2,4,6,-rinitramine; hexahydro-l,3,5-trinitro-S-triazine);
(174) Safety fuse;
(175) Salutes, (bulk);
(176) Salts of organic amino sulfonic acid explosive mixture;
(177) Silver acetylide;
(178) Silver azide;
(179) Silver fulminate;
(180) Silver oxalate explosive mixtures;
(181) Silver styphnate;
(182) Silver tartrate explosive mixtures;
(183) Silver tetrazene;
(184) Slurried explosive mixtures of water, inorganic oxidizing salt, gelling agent, fuel, and sensitizer, cap sensitive;
(185) Smokeless powder;
(186) Sodatol;
(187) Sodium amatol;
(188) Sodium azide explosive mixture;
(189) Sodium dinitro-ortho-cresolate;
(190) Sodium nitrate-potassium nitrate explosive mixture;
(191) Sodium picramate;
(192) Special fireworks;
(193) Squibs;
(194) Styphnic acid explosives;
(195) Tacot (tetranitro-2,3,5,6-dibenzo-l,3a,4,6a tetrazapentalene);
(196) TATB (triaminotrinitrobenzene);
(197) TATP (triacetone triperoxide);
(198) TEGDN (triethylene glycol dinitrate);
(199) Tetrazene (tetracene, tetrazine, I(5-tetrazolyl)-4-guanyl tetrazene hydrate);
(200) Tetranitrocarbazole;
(201) Tetryl (2,4,6 tetranitro-N-methylaniline);
(202) Tetrytol;
(203) Thickened inorganic oxidizer salt slurried explosive mixture;
(204) TMETN (trimethylolethane trinitrate);
(205) TNEF (trinitroethyl formal);
(206) TNEOC (trinitroethylorthocarbonate);
(207) TNEOF (trinitroethylorthoformate);
(208) TNT (trinitrotoluene, trotyl, trilite, triton);
(209) Torpex;
(210) Tridite;
(211) Trimethylol ethyl methane trinitrate composition;
(212) Trimethylolthane trinitrate-nitrocellulose;
(213) Trimonite;
(214) Trinitroanisole;
(215) Trinitrobenzene;
(216) Trinitrobenzoic acid;
(217) Trinitrocresol;
(218) Trinitro-meta-cresol;
(219) Trinitronaphthalene;
(220) Trinitrophenetol;
(221) Trinitrophloroglucinol;
(222) Trinitroresorcinol;
(223) Tritonal;
(224) Urea nitrate;
(225) Water bearing explosives having salts of oxidizing acids and nitrogen bases, sulfates, or sulfamates, cap sensitive;
(226) Water-in-oil emulsion explosive compositions;
(227) Xanthamonas hydrophilic colloid explosive mixture.

§ 16-7-82. Manufacturing, transporting, distributing, possessing with intent to distribute, and offering to distribute an explosive device

(a) It shall be unlawful for any person to possess, manufacture, transport, distribute, possess with the intent to distribute, or offer to distribute a destructive device except as provided in this article.
(b) Any person convicted of a violation of this Code section shall be punished by imprisonment for not less than three nor more than 20 years or, by a fine of not more than $25,000.00 or both or, if the defendant is a corporation, by a fine of not less than $25,000.00 nor more than $100,000.00 or not fewer than 5,000 nor more than 10,000 hours of community service or both.

§ 16-7-83. Persons convicted or under indictment for certain offenses

(a) It shall be unlawful for any person who is under indictment for or who has been convicted of a felony by a court of this state, any other state, the United States including its territories, possessions, and dominions, or a foreign nation to possess, manufacture, transport, distribute, possess with the intent to distribute, or offer to distribute a destructive device, detonator, explosive, poison gas, or hoax device.
(b) It shall be unlawful for any person knowingly to distribute a destructive device, detonator, explosive, poison gas, or hoax device to any person:
(1) Who he or she knows or should know is under indictment for or has been convicted of a felony by a court of this state, any other state, the United States including its territories, possessions, and dominions, or a foreign nation; or
(2) Who he or she knows or should know has been adjudicated to be mentally incompetent or mentally ill by a court of this state, any other state, or the United States including its territories, possessions, and dominions.

(c) Any person convicted of a violation of this Code section shall be punished, in the case of an individual, by imprisonment for not less than one nor more than 15 years or by a fine of not more than $25,000.00 or both or, if the defendant is a corporation, by a fine of not less than $10,000.00 nor more than $75,000.00 or not fewer than 1,000 nor more than 5,000 hours of community service or both.

(d) Notwithstanding any other provision of law, the Department of Behavioral Health and Developmental Disabilities shall make available to any law enforcement agency or district attorney of this state such information as may be necessary to establish that a person has been adjudicated by any court to be mentally incompetent or mentally ill.

(e) The provisions of this Code section shall not apply to:

(1) Any person who has been pardoned for a felony by the President of the United States, the State Board of Pardons and Paroles, or the person or agency empowered to grant pardons under the constitution or laws of any other state or of a foreign nation and, by the terms of the pardon, has expressly been authorized to receive, possess, distribute, or transport a destructive device, explosive, poison gas, or detonator; or

(2) A person who has been convicted of a felony, but who has been granted relief from the disabilities imposed by the laws of the United States with respect to the acquisition, receipt, transfer, shipment, or possession of explosives by the secretary of the United States Department of the Treasury pursuant to 18 U.S.C. 845, may apply to the Board of Public Safety for relief from the disabilities imposed by this Code section in the same manner as is provided in subsection (d) of Code Section 16-11-131. The board may grant such relief under the same standards and conditions as apply to firearms.

§ 16-7-84. Distribution of certain materials to persons under 21 years of age

(a) It shall be unlawful for any person to distribute or to offer to distribute a destructive device, explosive, poison gas, or detonator to any person who is under 21 years of age.

(b) Any person convicted of a violation of this Code section shall be punished, in the case of an individual, by imprisonment for not less than one nor more than three years or by a fine of not more than $10,000.00 or both or, if the defendant is a corporation, by a fine of not more than $20,000.00 or not fewer than 3,000 hours of community service or both.

§ 16-7-85. Hoax devices

(a) It shall be unlawful for any person to manufacture, possess, transport, distribute, or use a hoax device or replica of a destructive device or detonator with the intent to cause another to believe that such hoax device or replica is a destructive device or detonator.

(b) Any person convicted of a violation of this Code section shall be punished by imprisonment for not more than one year or by a fine of not more than $10,000.00 or both or, if the defendant is a corporation, a fine of not less than $1,000.00 or not fewer than 500 hours of community service or both for each such hoax device or replica; provided, however, that if such person communicates or transmits to another that such hoax device or replica is a destructive device or detonator with the intent to obtain the property of another person or to interfere with the ability of another person to conduct or carry on the ordinary course of business, trade, education, or government, such violation shall be punished by imprisonment for not less than one year nor more than five years or by a fine of not more than $25,000.00 or both or, if the defendant is a corporation, a fine of not less than $50,000.00 or not fewer than 1,000 nor more than 10,000 hours of community service or both for each such hoax device or replica.

§ 16-7-86. Attempt or conspiracy

It shall be unlawful for any person to attempt or conspire to commit any offense prohibited by this article. Any person convicted of a violation of this Code section shall be punished by imprisonment or community service; by a fine; or by both such punishments not to exceed the maximum punishment prescribed for the offense the commission of which was the object of the attempt or conspiracy.

§ 16-7-87. Interference with officers

It shall be unlawful for any person knowingly to hinder or obstruct any explosive ordnance technician, law enforcement officer, fire official, emergency management official, animal trained to detect destructive devices, or any robot or mechanical device designed or utilized by a law enforcement officer, fire official, or emergency management official of this state or of the United States in the detection, disarming, or destruction of a destructive device. Any person convicted of a violation of this Code section shall be punished as provided in subsection (b) of Code Section 16-10-24.

§ 16-7-88. Possessing, transporting, or receiving explosives, destructive devices, bacteriological weapon, or biological weapon with intent to kill, injure, or intimidate individuals or destroy public buildings; sentencing; enhanced penalties

(a) Any person who possesses, transports, or receives or attempts to possess, transport, or receive any destructive device, explosive, bacteriological weapon, or biological weapon with the knowledge or intent that it will be used to kill, injure, or intimidate any individual or to destroy any public building shall be punished by imprisonment for not less than ten nor more than 20 years or by a fine of not more than $125,000.00 or both or, if the defendant is a corporation, by a fine of not less than $125,000.00 nor more than $200,000.00 or sentenced to perform not fewer than 10,000 nor more than 20,000 hours of community service or both.

(b) In addition to any other penalty imposed under the laws of this state or of the United States, any person who shall use or attempt to use any destructive device or explosive to kill or injure any individual, including any public safety officer performing duties as a direct or proximate result of a violation of this subsection, or to destroy any public building shall be imprisoned for not less than 20 nor more than 40 years or fined the greater of the cost of replacing any property that is destroyed or $250,000.00 or both or, if the defendant is a corporation, fined the greater of the cost of replacing any property which is destroyed or $1 million or sentenced to perform not fewer than 20,000 nor more than 40,000 hours of community service or both.

(c) Any other provision of law to the contrary notwithstanding, no part of any sentence imposed pursuant to subsection (a) or (b) of this Code section shall be probated, deferred, suspended, or withheld and no person sentenced pursuant to subsection (a) or (b) of this Code section shall be eligible for early release, leave, work release, earned time, good time, or any other program administered by any agency of the executive or judicial branches of this state which would have the effect of reducing or mitigating such sentence until the defendant has completed the minimum sentence as provided by subsection (a) or (b) of this Code section.

§ 16-7-89. Separate offenses

Each violation of the provisions of this article shall be considered a separate offense.

§ 16-7-90. Records and reports

It shall be the duty of any person authorized by paragraph (1) or (2) of Code Section 16-7-93 to manufacture, possess, transport, distribute, or use a destructive device, detonator, explosive, or hoax device within the state:

(1) To maintain such records as may be required pursuant to Title 25. Such records may be inspected by the Commissioner or the director or such officers' designees or any law enforcement officer or fire official during normal business hours; and

(2) To report promptly the loss or theft of any destructive device, detonator, explosive, or hoax device to the Georgia Bureau of Investigation.

§ 16-7-91. Searches and inspections

The Commissioner or director or such officers' designees or any law enforcement officer or fire official may obtain an inspection warrant as provided in Code Section 25-2-22.1 to conduct a search or inspection of:

(1) Any person licensed pursuant to Title 25 to manufacture, possess, transport, sell, distribute, or use a destructive device or detonator within the state;

(2) Any person licensed pursuant to Chapter 7 of Title 2 to manufacture, possess, transport, sell, or distribute or use pesticides; or

(3) Any property where such pesticide, destructive device, or detonator is manufactured, possessed, transported, distributed, or used.

§ 16-7-92. Compelling attendance of witnesses and production of evidence

In any case where there is reason to believe that a destructive device, detonator, explosive, or hoax device has been manufactured, possessed, transported, distributed, or used in violation of this article or Title 25 or that there has been an attempt or a conspiracy to commit such a violation, the Attorney General, any district attorney, the director, or such persons as may be designated in writing by such officials shall have the same power to compel the attendance of witnesses and the production of evidence before such official in the same manner as the state fire marshal as provided in Code Sections 25-2-27, 25-2-28, and 25-2-29.

§ 16-7-93. Exceptions to applicability of provisions

The provisions of Code Sections 16-7-82, 16-7-84, 16-7-85, and 16-7-86 shall not apply to:

(1) Any person authorized to manufacture, possess, transport, distribute, or use a destructive device or detonator pursuant to the laws of the United States, as amended, or pursuant to Title 25 when such person is acting in accordance with such laws and any regulations issued pursuant thereto;

(2) Any person licensed as a blaster by the Commissioner pursuant to Chapter 8 of Title 25, when such blaster is acting in accordance with the laws of the state and any regulations promulgated thereunder and any ordinances and regulations of the political subdivision or authority of the state where blasting operations are being performed;

(3) Fireworks, as defined by Code Section 25-10-1 and any person authorized by the laws of this state and of the United States to manufacture, possess, distribute, transport, store, exhibit, display, or use fireworks;

(4) A law enforcement, fire service, or emergency management agency of this state, any agency or authority of a political subdivision of this state, or the United States and any employee or authorized agent thereof while in performance of official duties and any law enforcement officer, fire official, or emergency management official of the United States or any other state while attending training in this state;

(5) The armed forces of the United States or of this state;

(6) Research or educational programs conducted by or on behalf of a college, university, or secondary school which have been authorized by the chief executive officer of such educational institution or his or her designee and which is conducted in accordance with the laws of the United States and of this state;

(7) The use of explosive materials in medicines and medicinal agents in forms prescribed by the most recent published edition of the official United States Pharmacopoeia or the National Formulary;

(8) Small arms ammunition and reloading components thereof;

(9) Commercially manufactured black powder in quantities not to exceed 50 pounds, percussion caps, safety and pyrotechnic fuses, quills, quick and slow matches, and friction primers intended to be used solely for sporting, recreational, or cultural purposes in antique firearms or antique devices; or

(10) An explosive which is lawfully possessed in accordance with the rules adopted pursuant to Code Section 16-7-94.

§ 16-7-94. Agricultural activities

After consultation with the Commissioner of Agriculture or his or her designee, the Board of Public Safety may except by rule any explosive or quantity of explosive for use in legitimate agricultural activities. A copy of any such rule shall be furnished to the Commissioner of Agriculture.

§ 16-7-95. Civil forfeiture for violations of article; special provisions for destructive material

(a) As used in this Code section, the terms "proceeds" and "property" shall have the same meanings as set forth in Code Section 9-16-2.

(b) Any property which is, directly or indirectly, used or intended for use in any manner to facilitate a violation of this article and any proceeds are declared to be contraband and no person shall have a property right in them.

(c) Any property subject to forfeiture pursuant to subsection (b) of this Code section shall be forfeited in accordance with the procedures set forth in Chapter 16 of Title 9.

(d) On application of the seizing law enforcement agency, the superior court may authorize the seizing law enforcement agency to destroy or transfer to any agency of this state or of the United States which can safely store or render harmless any destructive device, explosive, poison gas, or detonator which is subject to forfeiture pursuant to this Code section if the court finds that it is impractical or unsafe for the seizing law enforcement agency to store such destructive device, explosive, poison gas, or detonator. Such application may be made at any time after seizure. Any destruction authorized pursuant to this subsection shall be made in the presence of at least one credible witness or shall be recorded on film, videotape, or other electronic imaging method. Any such film, videotape, or other electronic imaging method shall be admissible as evidence in lieu of such destructive device, explosive, poison gas, or detonator. The court may also direct the seizing agency or an agency to which such destructive device, explosive, poison gas, or detonator is transferred to make a report of the destruction, take samples, or both.

(e) The provisions of subsection (d) of this Code section shall not prohibit an explosive ordnance technician, other law enforcement officer, or fire service personnel from taking action which will render safe an explosive, destructive device, poison gas, or detonator or any object which is suspected of being an explosive, destructive device, poison gas, or detonator without the prior approval of a court when such action is intended to protect lives or property.

§ 16-7-96. Admissible evidence

(a) Photographs, videotapes, or other identification or analysis of a destructive device, explosive, poison gas, or detonator duly identified by an explosive ordnance disposal technician or a person qualified as a forensic expert in the area of destructive devices shall be admissible in any civil or criminal trial in lieu of the destructive device or detonator.

(b) If a destructive device, explosive, poison gas, or detonator which has been rendered safe is introduced into evidence in any criminal or civil action, it shall be the duty of the clerk of court immediately to photograph the same and to transfer custody of the destructive device or detonator to the director or his or her designee or an explosive ordnance disposal technician.

§ 16-7-97. Fertilizers and pesticides

The provisions of this article shall not apply to:

(1) Fertilizers, propellant actuated devices, or propellant activated industrial tools manufactured, imported, distributed, or used for their intended purposes; or

(2) A pesticide which is manufactured, stored, transported, distributed, possessed, or used in accordance with Chapter 7 of Title 2, the federal Insecticide, Fungicide, and Rodenticide Act, 61 Stat. 163, as amended, and the federal Environmental Pesticide Control Act of 1972, Pub. L. 92-516, as amended.

CHAPTER 8. OFFENSES INVOLVING THEFT

§ 16-8-1. Definitions

As used in this article, the term:

(1) "Deprive" means, without justification:

(A) To withhold property of another permanently or temporarily; or

(B) To dispose of the property so as to make it unlikely that the owner will recover it.

(2) "Financial institution" means a bank, insurance company, credit union, building and loan association, investment trust, or other organization held out to the public as a place of deposit of funds or medium of savings or collective investment.

(3) "Property of another" includes property in which any person other than the accused has an interest but does not include property belonging to the spouse of an accused or to them jointly.

§ 16-8-2. Theft by taking

A person commits the offense of theft by taking when he unlawfully takes or, being in lawful possession thereof, unlawfully appropriates any property of another with the intention of depriving him of the property, regardless of the manner in which the property is taken or appropriated.

§ 16-8-3. Theft by deception

(a) A person commits the offense of theft by deception when he obtains property by any deceitful means or artful practice with the intention of depriving the owner of the property.

(b) A person deceives if he intentionally:

(1) Creates or confirms another's impression of an existing fact or past event which is false and which the accused knows or believes to be false;

(2) Fails to correct a false impression of an existing fact or past event which he has previously created or confirmed;

(3) Prevents another from acquiring information pertinent to the disposition of the property involved;

(4) Sells or otherwise transfers or encumbers property intentionally failing to disclose a substantial and valid known lien, adverse claim, or other legal impediment to the enjoyment of the property, whether such impediment is or is not a matter of official record; or

(5) Promises performance of services which he does not intend to perform or knows will not be performed. Evidence of failure to perform standing alone shall not be sufficient to authorize a conviction under this subsection.

(c) "Deceitful means" and "artful practice" do not, however, include falsity as to matters having no pecuniary significance, or exaggeration by statements unlikely to deceive ordinary persons in the group addressed.

§ 16-8-4. Theft by conversion

(a) A person commits the offense of theft by conversion when, having lawfully obtained funds or other property of another including, but not limited to, leased or rented personal property, under an agreement or other known legal obligation to make a specified application of such funds or a specified disposition of such property, he knowingly converts the funds or property to his own use in violation of the agreement or legal obligation. This Code section applies whether the application or disposition is to be made from the funds or property of another or from the accused's own funds or property in equivalent amount when the agreement contemplates that the accused may deal with the funds or property of another as his own.

(b) When, under subsection (a) of this Code section, an officer or employee of a government or of a financial institution fails to pay on an account, upon lawful demand, from the funds or property of another held by him, he is presumed to have intended to convert the funds or property to his own use.

(c)(1) As used in this subsection, the term "personal property" means personal property having a replacement cost value greater than $100.00, excluding any late fees and penalties, and includes heavy equipment as defined in paragraph (2) of Code Section 10-1-731 and tractors and farm equipment primarily designed for use in agriculture.

(2) Any person having any personal property in such person's possession or under such person's control by virtue of a lease or rental agreement who fails to return the personal property within five days, Saturdays, Sundays, and holidays excluded, after a letter demanding return of the personal property has been mailed to such person by certified or registered mail or statutory overnight delivery, return receipt requested, at such person's last known address by the owner of the personal property or by the owner's agent shall be presumed to have knowingly converted such personal property to such person's own use in violation of such lease or agreement.

(3) In the event that any personal property is not returned as provided for in the lease or rental agreement and the court orders the lessor or renter to pay replacement costs, replacement costs shall include but not be limited to:

(A) The market value of the personal property. The market value shall be established by the owner of the property by providing from a supplier of such or reasonably similar personal property a current quotation of the value of the personal property which is of like quality, make, and model of the personal property being replaced. The value to be awarded shall be the higher of:

(i) The value on the date when the conversion occurred; or

(ii) The value on the date of the trial;

(B) All rental charges from the date the rental agreement was executed until the date of the trial or the date that the property was recovered, if recovered; and

(C) Interest on the unpaid balance each month at the current legal rate from the date the court orders the lessor or renter to pay replacement costs until the date the judgment is satisfied in full.

(4) If as a part of the order of the court the lessor or renter is placed on probation, supervision of said probation shall not be terminated until all replacement costs, fees, charges, penalties, interest, and other charges are paid in full. All payments relative to this Code section shall be made to the appropriate court of jurisdiction and the court shall make distribution to the owner within 30 days of receipt thereof.

(5) In the event that the owner incurs any expenses in the process of locating a lessor or renter who did not return any personal property according to the lease or rental agreement, the court shall provide that the lessor or renter reimburse the owner for those expenses which may include, but not be limited to, credit reports, private detective fees, investigation fees, fees charged by a law enforcement agency for such services as police reports, background checks, fees involved with swearing out a warrant for incarceration, and any other bona fide expenses.

§ 16-8-5. Theft of services

A person commits the offense of theft of services when by deception and with the intent to avoid payment he knowingly obtains services, accommodations, entertainment, or the use of personal property which is available only for compensation.

§ 16-8-5.1. Circumstances permitting inference of intent to avoid payment; exceptions

The trier of fact may infer that the accused intended to avoid payment due for the rental or lease of any personal property in any prosecution pursuant to Code Section 16-8-2, relating to theft by taking; 16-8-3, relating to theft by deception; 16-8-4, relating to theft by conversion; or 16-8-5, relating to theft of services; if a person knowingly:

(1) Used false identification;

(2) Provided false information on a written contract;

(3) Made, drew, uttered, executed, or delivered an instrument for the payment of money on any bank or other depository in exchange for present consideration, knowing that it would not be honored by the drawee;

(4) Abandoned any property at a location that is not the location agreed upon for return and that would not be reasonably known to the owner;

(5) Returned any property to a location that would not reasonably be known to the owner without notifying the owner; or

(6) Returned any property at a time beyond posted business hours of the owner.

No person shall be convicted under Code Section 16-8-2, relating to theft by taking; 16-8-3, relating to theft by deception; 16-8-4, relating to theft by conversion; or 16-8-5, relating to theft of services; where there was an agreement to delay payment for such property or services or the accused makes payment in full within two business days after returning the property or obtaining the services.

§ 16-8-5.2. Retail property fencing; civil forfeiture; related matters

(a) As used in this Code section, the term:
(1) "Retail property" means any new article, product, commodity, item, or component intended to be sold in retail commerce.
(2) "Retail property fence" means a person or entity that buys, sells, transfers, or possesses with the intent to sell or transfer retail property that such person knows or should have known was stolen.
(3) "Value" means the retail value of the item as stated or advertised by the affected retail establishment, to include applicable taxes.
(b) A person commits the offense of retail property fencing when such persons receives, disposes of, or retains retail property which was unlawfully taken or shoplifted over a period not to exceed 180 days with the intent to:
(1) Transfer, sell, or distribute such retail property to a retail property fence; or
(2) Attempt or cause such retail property to be offered for sale, transfer, or distribution for money or other things of value.
(c) Whoever knowingly receives, possesses, conceals, stores, barters, sells, or disposes of retail property with the intent to distribute any retail property which is known or should be known to have been taken or stolen in violation of this subsection with the intent to distribute the proceeds, or to otherwise promote, manage, carry on, or facilitate an offense described in this subsection, shall have committed the offense of retail property fencing.
(d) (1) It shall not be necessary in any prosecution under this Code section for the state to prove that any intended profit was actually realized. The trier of fact may infer that a particular scheme or course of conduct was undertaken for profit from all of the attending circumstances.
(2) It shall not be a defense to violating this Code section that the property was obtained by means other than through the commission of a theft offense if the property was explicitly represented to the accused as being obtained through the commission of a theft.
(e) (1) As used in this subsection, the terms "proceeds" and "property" shall have the same meanings as set forth in Code Section 9-16-2.
(2) Any property which is, directly or indirectly, used or intended for use in any manner to facilitate a violation of this Code section and any proceeds are declared to be contraband and no person shall have a property right in them; provided, however, that notwithstanding paragraph (2) of subsection (a) of Code Section 9-16-17, no property of any owner shall be forfeited under this subsection, to the extent of the interest of such owner, by reason of an act or omission established by such owner to have been committed or omitted without knowledge or consent of such owner.
(3) Any property subject to forfeiture pursuant to paragraph (2) of this subsection shall be forfeited in accordance with the procedures set forth in Chapter 16 of Title 9.
(f) Each violation of this Code section shall constitute a separate offense.

§ 16-8-6. Theft of lost or mislaid property

A person commits the offense of theft of lost or mislaid property when he comes into control of property that he knows or learns to have been lost or mislaid and appropriates the property to his own use without first taking reasonable measures to restore the property to the owner.

§ 16-8-7. Theft by receiving stolen property

(a) A person commits the offense of theft by receiving stolen property when he receives, disposes of, or retains stolen property which he knows or should know was stolen unless the property is received, disposed of, or retained with intent to restore it to the owner. "Receiving" means acquiring possession or control or lending on the security of the property.
(b) In any prosecution under this Code section it shall not be necessary to show a conviction of the principal thief.

§ 16-8-8. Theft by receiving property stolen in another state

A person commits the offense of theft by receiving property stolen in another state when he receives, disposes of, or retains stolen property which he knows or should know was stolen in another state, unless the property is received, disposed of, or retained with intent to restore it to the owner.

§ 16-8-9. Theft by bringing stolen property into state

A person commits the offense of theft by bringing stolen property into this state when he brings into this state any property which he knows or should know has been stolen in another state.

§ 16-8-10. Affirmative defenses to prosecution for violation of Code Sections 16-8-2 through 16-8-9

It is an affirmative defense to a prosecution for violation of Code Sections 16-8-2 through 16-8-9 that the person:
(1) Was unaware that the property or service was that of another;
(2) Acted under an honest claim of right to the property or service involved;
(3) Acted under a right to acquire or dispose of the property as he or she did; provided, however, that the use of a power of attorney as provided in Chapter 6B of Title 10 shall not, in and of itself, absolve a person from criminal responsibility; or
(4) Took property or service exposed for sale intending to purchase and pay for it promptly or reasonably believing that the owner, if present, would have consented.

§ 16-8-11. Venue for purposes of Code Sections 16-8-2 through 16-8-9 and 16-8-13 through 16-8-15

In a prosecution under Code Sections 16-8-2 through 16-8-9 and 16-8-13 through 16-8-15, the crime shall be considered as having been committed in any county in which the accused exercised control over the property which was the subject of the theft. In addition, in any prosecution under Code Section 16-8-4 in which there is a written rental agreement for personal property, the crime shall also be considered to have been committed in the county in which the accused signed the rental agreement.

§ 16-8-12. Penalties for theft in violation of Code Sections 16-8-2 through 16-8-9

(a) A person convicted of a violation of Code Sections 16-8-2 through 16-8-9 shall be punished as for a misdemeanor except:
(1) (A) If the property which was the subject of the theft exceeded $24,999.99 in value, by imprisonment for not less than two nor more than 20 years;
(B) If the property which was the subject of the theft was at least $5,000.00 in value but was less than $25,000.00 in value, by imprisonment for not less than one nor more than ten years and, in the discretion of the trial judge, as for a misdemeanor;
(C) If the property which was the subject of the theft was at least $1,500.01 in value but was less than $5,000.00 in value, by imprisonment for not less than one nor more than five years and, in the discretion of the trial judge, as for a misdemeanor; and
(D) If the defendant has two prior convictions for a violation of Code Sections 16-8-2 through 16-8-9, upon a third conviction or subsequent conviction, such defendant shall be guilty of a felony and shall be punished by imprisonment for not less than one nor more than five years and, in the discretion of the trial judge, as for a misdemeanor;
(2) If the property was any amount of anhydrous ammonia, as defined in Code Section 16-11-111, by imprisonment for not less than one nor more than ten years, a fine not to exceed the amount provided by Code Section 17-10-8, or both;

(3) If the property was taken by a fiduciary in breach of a fiduciary obligation or by an officer or employee of a government or a financial institution in breach of his or her duties as such officer or employee, by imprisonment for not less than one nor more than 15 years, a fine not to exceed the amount provided by Code Section 17-10-8, or both;

(4) If the crime committed was a violation of Code Section 16-8-2 and if the property which was the subject of the theft was a memorial to the dead or any ornamentation, flower, tree, or shrub placed on, adjacent to, or within any enclosure of a memorial to the dead, by imprisonment for not less than one nor more than three years. Nothing in this paragraph shall be construed as to cause action taken by a cemetery, cemetery owner, lessee, trustee, church, religious or fraternal organization, corporation, civic organization, or club legitimately attempting to clean, maintain, care for, upgrade, or beautify a grave, gravesite, tomb, monument, gravestone, or other structure or thing placed or designed for a memorial of the dead to be a criminal act;

(5) (A) The provisions of paragraph (1) of this subsection notwithstanding, if the theft or unlawful activity was committed in violation of subsection (b) of Code Section 10-1-393.5 or in violation of subsection (b) of Code Section 10-1-393.6 or while engaged in telemarketing conduct in violation of Chapter 5B of Title 10, by imprisonment for not less than one nor more than ten years or, in the discretion of the trial judge, as for a misdemeanor; provided, however, that any person who is convicted of a second or subsequent offense under this paragraph shall be punished by imprisonment for not less than one year nor more than 20 years.

(B) Subsequent offenses committed under this paragraph, including those which may have been committed after prior felony convictions unrelated to this paragraph, shall be punished as provided in Code Section 17-10-7;

(6) (A) As used in this paragraph, the term:

(i) "Destructive device" means a destructive device as such term is defined by Code Section 16-7-80.

(ii) "Explosive" means an explosive as such term is defined by Code Section 16-7-80.

(iii) "Firearm" means any rifle, shotgun, pistol, or similar device which propels a projectile or projectiles through the energy of an explosive.

(B) If the property which was the subject of the theft offense was a destructive device, explosive, or firearm, by imprisonment for not less than one nor more than ten years;

(7) If the property which was the subject of the theft is a grave marker, monument, or memorial to one or more deceased persons who served in the military service of this state, the United States of America or any of the states thereof, or the Confederate States of America or any of the states thereof, or a monument, plaque, marker, or memorial which is dedicated to, honors, or recounts the military service of any past or present military personnel of this state, the United States of America or any of the states thereof, or the Confederate States of America or any of the states thereof, and if such grave marker, monument, memorial, plaque, or marker is privately owned or located on privately owned land, by imprisonment for not less than one nor more than three years if the value of the property which was the subject of the theft is $1,000.00 or less, and by imprisonment for not less than three years and not more than five years if the value of the property which was the subject of the theft is more than $1,000.00;

(8) Reserved; or

(9) Notwithstanding the provisions of paragraph (1) of this subsection, if the property of the theft was regulated metal property, as such term is defined in Code Section 10-1-350, and the sum of the aggregate amount of such property, in its original and undamaged condition, plus any reasonable costs which are or would be incurred in the repair or the attempt to recover any property damaged in the theft or removal of such regulated metal property, exceeds $500.00, by imprisonment for not less than one nor more than five years, a fine of not more than $5,000.00, or both.

(b) Except as otherwise provided in paragraph (5) of subsection (a) of this Code section, any person who commits the offense of theft by deception when the property which was the subject of the theft exceeded $500.00 in value and the offense was committed against a person who is 65 years of age or older shall, upon conviction thereof, be punished by imprisonment for not less than five nor more than ten years.

(c) Where a violation of Code Sections 16-8-2 through 16-8-9 involves the theft of a growing or otherwise unharvested commercial agricultural product which is being grown or produced as a crop, such offense shall be punished by a fine of not less than $1,000.00 and not more than the maximum fine otherwise authorized by law. This minimum fine shall not in any such case be subject to suspension, stay, or probation. This minimum fine shall not be required in any case in which a sentence of confinement is imposed and such sentence of confinement is not suspended, stayed, or probated; but this subsection shall not prohibit imposition of any otherwise authorized fine in such a case.

§ 16-8-13. Theft of trade secrets

(a) As used in this Code section, the term:

(1) "Article" means any object, material, device, substance, or copy thereof, including any writing, record, recording, drawing, sample, specimen, prototype, model, photograph, microorganism, blueprint, or map.

(2) "Copy" means any facsimile, replica, photograph, or other reproduction of an article and any note, drawing, or sketch made of or from an article.

(3) "Representing" means describing, depicting, containing, constituting, reflecting, or recording.

(4) "Trade secret" means information, without regard to form, including, but not limited to, technical or nontechnical data, a formula, a pattern, a compilation, a program, a device, a method, a technique, a drawing, a process, financial data, financial plans, product plans, or a list of actual or potential customers or suppliers which is not commonly known by or available to the public and which information:

(A) Derives economic value, actual or potential, from not being generally known to, and not being readily ascertainable by proper means by, other persons who can obtain economic value from its disclosure or use; and

(B) Is the subject of efforts that are reasonable under the circumstances to maintain its secrecy.

(b) Any person who, with the intent to deprive or withhold from the owner thereof the exclusive use of a trade secret, or with an intent to appropriate a trade secret to his or her own use or to the use of another, does any of the following:

(1) Takes, uses, or discloses such trade secret to an unauthorized person;

(2) Acquires knowledge of such trade secret by deceitful means or artful practice; or

(3) Without authority, makes or causes to be made a copy of an article representing such trade secret

commits the offense of theft of a trade secret and, upon conviction thereof, shall be punished by imprisonment for not less than one nor more than five years and by a fine of not more than $50,000.00, provided that, if the value of such trade secret, and any article representing such trade secret that is taken, is not more than $100.00 such person shall be punished as for a misdemeanor.

(c) In a prosecution for any violation of this Code section, a court shall preserve the secrecy of an alleged trade secret by reasonable means, which may include granting protective orders in connection with discovery proceedings, holding in camera hearings, sealing the records of the action, and ordering any person involved in the litigation not to disclose an alleged trade secret without prior court approval.

(d) For the purposes of this Code section, a continuing theft by any person constitutes a single claim against that person, but this Code section shall be applied separately to the claim against each person who receives a trade secret from another person who committed the theft.

(e) This Code section shall not affect:

(1) Contractual duties or remedies, whether or not based on theft of a trade secret; or

(2) The provisions of Code Sections 10-1-761 through 10-1-767, pertaining to civil offenses and remedies involving the misappropriation of a trade secret, or other civil or criminal laws that presently apply or in the future may apply to any transaction or course of conduct that violates this Code section.

§ 16-8-14. Theft by shoplifting

(a) A person commits the offense of theft by shoplifting when such person alone or in concert with another person, with the intent of appropriating merchandise to his or her own use without paying for the same or to deprive the owner of possession thereof or of the value thereof, in whole or in part, does any of the following:

(1) Conceals or takes possession of the goods or merchandise of any store or retail establishment;

(2) Alters the price tag or other price marking on goods or merchandise of any store or retail establishment;

(3) Transfers the goods or merchandise of any store or retail establishment from one container to another;

(4) Interchanges the label or price tag from one item of merchandise with a label or price tag for another item of merchandise; or

(5) Wrongfully causes the amount paid to be less than the merchant's stated price for the merchandise.

(b) (1) A person convicted of the offense of theft by shoplifting, as provided in subsection (a) of this Code section, when the property which was the subject of the theft is $500.00 or less in value shall be punished as for a misdemeanor; provided, however, that:

(A) Upon conviction of a second offense for shoplifting, where the first offense is either a felony or a misdemeanor, as defined by this Code section, in addition to or in lieu of any imprisonment which might be imposed, the defendant shall be fined not less than $500.00, and the fine shall not be suspended or probated;

(B) Upon conviction of a third offense for shoplifting, when the first two offenses are either felonies or misdemeanors, or a combination of a felony and a misdemeanor, as defined by this Code section, in addition to or in lieu of any fine which might be imposed, the defendant shall be punished by imprisonment for not less than 30 days or confinement in a "special alternative incarceration-probation boot camp," probation detention center, or other community correctional facility of the Department of Corrections for a period of 120 days or shall be sentenced to monitored house arrest for a period of 120 days and, in addition to such types of confinement, may be required to undergo psychological evaluation and treatment to be paid for by the defendant; and such sentence of imprisonment or confinement shall not be suspended, probated, deferred, or withheld; and

(C) Upon conviction of a fourth or subsequent offense for shoplifting, where the prior convictions are either felonies or misdemeanors, or any combination of felonies and misdemeanors, as defined by this Code section, the defendant commits a felony and shall be punished by imprisonment for not less than one nor more than ten years; and the first year of such sentence shall not be suspended, probated, deferred, or withheld.

(2) A person convicted of the offense of theft by shoplifting, as provided in subsection (a) of this Code section, when the property which was the subject of the theft exceeds $500.00 in value commits a felony and shall be punished by imprisonment for not less than one nor more than ten years.

(3) A person convicted of the offense of theft by shoplifting, as provided in subsection (a) of this Code section, when the property which was the subject of the theft is taken from three separate stores or retail establishments within one county during a period of seven days or less and when the aggregate value of the property which was the subject of each theft exceeds $500.00 in value, commits a felony and shall be punished by imprisonment for not less than one nor more than ten years.

(4) A person convicted of the offense of theft by shoplifting, as provided in subsection (a) of this Code section, when the property which was the subject of the theft is taken during a period of 180 days and when the aggregate value of the property which was the subject of each theft exceeds $500.00 in value, commits a felony and shall be punished by imprisonment for not less than one nor more than ten years.

(c) In all cases involving theft by shoplifting, the term "value" means the actual retail price of the property at the time and place of the offense. The unaltered price tag or other marking on property, or duly identified photographs thereof, shall be prima-facie evidence of value and ownership of the property.

(d) Subsection (b) of this Code section shall in no way affect the authority of a sentencing judge to provide for a sentence to be served on weekends or during the nonworking hours of the defendant as provided in Code Section 17-10-3, relative to punishment for misdemeanors.

§ 16-8-14.1. Refund fraud

(a) (1) It shall be unlawful for a person to give a false or fictitious name or address or to give the name or address of another person without that person's approval or permission for the purpose of obtaining a refund from a store or retail establishment for merchandise.

(2) It shall be unlawful for a person to obtain a refund in the form of cash, check, credit on a credit or debit card, a merchant gift card, or credit in any other form from a store or retail establishment using a driver's license not issued to such person, a driver's license containing false information, an identification card containing false information, an altered identification card, or an identification card not issued to such person.

(b) A person who violates subsection (a) of this Code section shall be guilty of refund fraud and, upon conviction, except as provided in subsection (c) of this Code section, shall:

(1) When the property which was the subject of the fraud is $500.00 or less in value, be punished as for a misdemeanor;

(2) When the property which was the subject of the fraud exceeds $500.00 in value, be guilty of a felony and shall be punished by imprisonment for not less than one nor more than ten years;

(3) When the property which was the subject of the fraud is taken from three separate stores or retail establishments within one county during a period of seven days or less and when the aggregate value of the property which was the subject of each fraud exceeds $500.00 in value, be guilty of a felony and shall be punished by imprisonment for not less than one nor more than ten years; and

(4) When the property which was the subject of the fraud is taken during a period of 180 days and when the aggregate value of the property which was the subject of each fraud exceeds $500.00 in value, be guilty of a felony and shall be punished by imprisonment for not less than one nor more than ten years.

(c) (1) Upon conviction of a second offense for a violation of any provision of this Code section, in addition to or in lieu of any imprisonment which might be imposed, the defendant shall be fined not less than $500.00, and the fine shall not be suspended or probated.

(2) Upon conviction of a third offense for a violation of any provision of this Code section, the defendant shall be guilty of a felony and, in addition to or in lieu of any fine which might be imposed, the defendant shall be punished by imprisonment for not less than 30 days or confinement in a "special alternative incarceration-probation boot camp," probation detention center, or other community correctional facility of the Department of Corrections for a period of 120 days or shall be sentenced to monitored house arrest for a period of 120 days and, in addition to such types of confinement, may be required to undergo psychological evaluation and treatment to be paid for by the defendant; and such sentence of imprisonment or confinement shall not be suspended, probated, deferred, or withheld.

(3) Upon conviction of a fourth or subsequent offense for a violation of any provision of this Code section, the defendant shall be guilty of a felony and shall be punished by imprisonment for not less than one nor more than ten years; and the first year of such sentence shall not be suspended, probated, deferred, or withheld.

(d) In all cases involving refund fraud, the term "value" means the actual retail price of the property at the time and place of the offense. The unaltered price tag or other marking on property, or duly identified photographs thereof, shall be prima-facie evidence of value and ownership of the property.

(e) Subsection (b) of this Code section shall not affect the authority of a judge to provide for a sentence to be served on weekends or during the nonworking hours of the defendant as provided in Code Section 17-10-3, relative to punishment for misdemeanors.

§ 16-8-15. Conversion of payments for real property improvements

(a) Any architect, landscape architect, engineer, contractor, subcontractor, or other person who with intent to defraud shall use the proceeds of any payment made to him on account of improving certain real property for any other purpose than to pay for labor or service performed on or materials furnished by his order for this specific improvement while any amount for which he may be or become liable for such labor, services, or materials remains unpaid commits a felony and, upon conviction thereof, shall be punished by imprisonment for not less than one year nor more than five years or upon the recommendation of the jury or in the discretion of the trial judge, punished for a misdemeanor, provided that, in addition to the above sanctions, where a corporation's agent acts within the scope of his office or employment and on behalf of the corporation and with intent to defraud uses such proceeds for purposes other than for property improvements or where a corporation's board of directors or managerial official, the latter acting within the scope of his employment and on behalf of the corporation recklessly tolerates or, with intent to defraud, authorizes, requests, or commands the use of such proceeds for purposes other than for property improvements, the corporation commits a felony and, upon conviction thereof, shall be punished by a fine of not less than $1,000.00 nor more than $5,000.00.

(b) A failure to pay for material or labor furnished for such property improvements shall be prima-facie evidence of intent to defraud.

§ 16-8-16. Theft by extortion

(a) A person commits the offense of theft by extortion when he unlawfully obtains property of or from another person by threatening to:

(1) Inflict bodily injury on anyone or commit any other criminal offense;

(2) Accuse anyone of a criminal offense;

(3) Disseminate any information tending to subject any person to hatred, contempt, or ridicule or to impair his credit or business repute;

(4) Take or withhold action as a public official or cause an official to take or withhold action;

(5) Bring about or continue a strike, boycott, or other collective unofficial action if the property is not demanded or received for the benefit of the group in whose interest the actor purports to act; or

(6) Testify or provide information or withhold testimony or information with respect to another's legal claim or defense.

(b) In a prosecution under this Code section, the crime shall be considered as having been committed in the county in which the threat was made or received or in the county in which the property was unlawfully obtained.

(c) It is an affirmative defense to prosecution based on paragraph (2), (3), (4), or (6) of subsection (a) of this Code section that the property obtained by threat of accusation, exposure, legal action, or other invocation of official action was honestly claimed as restitution or indemnification for harm done in the circumstance to which such accusation, exposure, legal action, or other official action relates or as compensation for property or lawful services.

(d) A person convicted of the offense of theft by extortion shall be punished by imprisonment for not less than one nor more than ten years.

§ 16-8-17. Misuse of Universal Product Code labels

(a) (1) Except as provided in paragraph (2) of this subsection, a person who, with intent to cheat or defraud a retailer, possesses, uses, utters, transfers, makes, alters, counterfeits, or reproduces a retail sales receipt or a Universal Product Code label which results in a theft of property which exceeds $500.00 in value commits a felony and shall be punished by imprisonment for not less than one nor more than three years or by a fine or both.

(2) A person convicted of a violation of paragraph (1) of this subsection, when the property which was the subject of the theft resulting from the unlawful use of retail sales receipts or Universal Product Code labels is taken from three separate stores or retail establishments within one county during a period of seven days or less and when the aggregate value of the property which was the subject of each theft exceeds $500.00 in value, commits a felony and shall be punished by imprisonment for not less than one nor more than ten years.

(b) A person who, with intent to cheat or defraud a retailer, possesses 15 or more fraudulent retail sales receipts or Universal Product Code labels or possesses a device the purpose of which is to manufacture fraudulent retail sales receipts or Universal Product Code labels shall be guilty of a felony and punished by imprisonment for not less than one nor more than ten years.

§ 16-8-18. Entering automobile or other motor vehicle with intent to commit theft or felony

If any person shall enter any automobile or other motor vehicle with the intent to commit a theft or a felony, he shall be guilty of a felony and, upon conviction thereof, shall be punished by imprisonment for not less than one nor more than five years, or, in the discretion of the trial judge, as for a misdemeanor.

§ 16-8-19. Conversion of leased personal property

Reserved. Repealed by Ga. L. 1988, p. 763, § 2, effective July 1, 1988.

§ 16-8-20. Livestock theft

(a) A person commits the offense of livestock theft when he unlawfully takes or, being in lawful possession thereof, unlawfully appropriates any livestock of another with the intention of depriving the owner of such livestock.

(b) For the purposes of this Code section, the term "livestock" means horses, cattle, swine, sheep, goats, rabbits, and any domestic animal produced as food for human consumption.

(c) Any person committing the offense of livestock theft commits a felony and, upon conviction thereof, shall be punished by imprisonment for not less than one nor more than ten years and by a fine of $1,000.00; provided, however, that, if the fair market value of the livestock taken or appropriated is $100.00 or less, the person shall be guilty of a misdemeanor.

(d) For the purposes of this Code section, if any livestock is killed or mutilated and a portion thereof taken, the value of the whole animal while alive or his entire carcass, whichever is greater, shall be considered for the purpose of distinguishing between a misdemeanor offense and a felony offense.

§ 16-8-21. Removal or abandonment of shopping carts

(a) As used in this Code section, the term "shopping cart" means those pushcarts of the type which are commonly provided by grocery stores, drugstores, or other merchant stores or markets for the use of the public in transporting commodities in stores and markets and incidentally from the store to a place outside the store.

(b) It shall be unlawful for any person to remove a shopping cart from the premises of the owner of such shopping cart without the consent, given at the time of such removal, of the owner or of his or her agent, servant, or employee. For the purpose of this Code section, the premises shall include all the parking area set aside by the owner or on behalf of the owner for the parking of cars for the convenience of the patrons of the owner.

(c) It shall be unlawful for any person to abandon a shopping cart upon any public street, sidewalk, way, or parking lot other than a parking lot on the premises of the owner.

(d) Any person who violates this Code section shall be guilty of a misdemeanor.

§ 16-8-22. Cargo theft

(a) For purposes of this Code section, the term "vehicle" includes, without limitation, any railcar.

(b) Notwithstanding any provision of this article to the contrary, a person commits the offense of cargo theft when he or she unlawfully takes or, being in lawful possession thereof, unlawfully appropriates:

(1) Any vehicle engaged in commercial transportation of cargo or any appurtenance thereto, including, without limitation, any trailer, semitrailer, container, or other associated equipment, or the cargo being transported therein or thereon, which is the property of another with the intention of depriving such other person of the property, regardless of the manner in which the property is taken or appropriated; or

(2) Any trailer, semitrailer, container, or other associated equipment, or the cargo being transported therein or thereon, which is deployed by or used by a law enforcement agency, which is the property of another with the intention of depriving such other person of the property, regardless of the manner in which the property is taken or appropriated.

(c) The value of a vehicle engaged in commercial transportation of cargo and any appurtenance thereto and the cargo being transported which is taken or unlawfully appropriated shall be based on the fair market value of such vehicle, appurtenances, and cargo taken or unlawfully appropriated.

(d) (1) If the property taken is one or more controlled substances as defined in Code Section 16-13-21 with a collective value of less than $10,000.00, a person convicted of a violation of this Code section shall be punished by imprisonment for not less than one nor more than ten years, a fine of not less than $10,000.00 nor more than $100,000.00, or both.

(2) If the property taken is one or more controlled substances as defined in Code Section 16-13-21 with a collective value of at least $10,000.00 but less than $1 million, a person convicted of a violation of this Code section shall be punished by imprisonment for not less than five nor more than 25 years, a fine of not less than $50,000.00 nor more than $1 million, or both.

(3) If the property taken is one or more controlled substances as defined in Code Section 16-13-21 with a collective value of $1 million or more, a person convicted of a violation of this Code section shall be punished by imprisonment for not less than ten nor more than 30 years, a fine of not less than $100,000.00 nor more than $1 million, or both.

(e) (1) Except as otherwise provided in subsection (d) of this Code section, if the property taken has a collective value of $1,500.00 or less, a person convicted of a violation of this Code section shall be punished as for a misdemeanor.

(2) Except as otherwise provided in subsection (d) of this Code section, if the property taken has a collective value of more than $1,500.00 but less than $10,000.00, a person convicted of a violation of this Code section shall be punished by imprisonment for not less than one nor more than ten years, a fine of not less than $10,000.00 nor more than $100,000.00, or both.

(3) Except as otherwise provided in subsection (d) of this Code section, if the property taken has a collective value of at least $10,000.00 but less than $1 million, a person convicted of a violation of this Code section shall be punished by imprisonment for not less than five nor more than 20 years, a fine of not less than $50,000.00 nor more than $1 million, or both.

(4) Except as otherwise provided in subsection (d) of this Code section, if the property taken has a collective value of $1 million or more, a person convicted of a violation of this Code section shall be punished by imprisonment for not less than ten nor more than 20 years, a fine of not less than $100,000.00 nor more than $1 million, or both.

(f) Notwithstanding subsections (d) and (e) of this Code section, if the property taken is a trailer, semitrailer, container, or other associated equipment, or the cargo being transported therein or thereon, which is deployed by or used by a law enforcement agency, regardless of its value, a person convicted of a violation of this Code section shall be punished by imprisonment for not less than one nor more than ten years, a fine of not less than $10,000.00 nor more than $100,000.00, or both.

(g) A person convicted of a violation of this Code section may also be punished by, if applicable, the revocation of the defendant's commercial driver's license in accordance with Code Section 40-5-151.

§ 16-8-23. Prohibited uses of fifth wheel

(a) For the purposes of this Code section, the term "fifth wheel" means a device mounted on a truck tractor or similar towing vehicle, including, but not limited to, a converter dolly, which interfaces with and couples to the upper coupler assembly of a semitrailer.

(b) It shall be unlawful for any person to modify, alter, attempt to alter, and, if altered, sell, possess, offer for sale, move, or cause to be moved on the highways of this state a device known as a fifth wheel or the antitheft locking device attached to the fifth wheel with the intent to use the fifth wheel to commit or attempt to commit cargo theft as defined in Code Section 16-8-22.

(c) A person convicted of a violation of this Code section shall be punished by imprisonment for not less than one nor more than ten years, a fine of not less than $10,000.00 nor more than $100,000.00, or both.

§ 16-8-40. Robbery

(a) A person commits the offense of robbery when, with intent to commit theft, he takes property of another from the person or the immediate presence of another:

(1) By use of force;

(2) By intimidation, by the use of threat or coercion, or by placing such person in fear of immediate serious bodily injury to himself or to another; or

(3) By sudden snatching.

(b) A person convicted of the offense of robbery shall be punished by imprisonment for not less than one nor more than 20 years.

(c) Notwithstanding any other provision of this Code section, any person who commits the offense of robbery against a person who is 65 years of age or older shall, upon conviction thereof, be punished by imprisonment for not less than five nor more than 20 years.

§ 16-8-41. Armed robbery; robbery by intimidation; taking controlled substance from pharmacy in course of committing offense

(a) A person commits the offense of armed robbery when, with intent to commit theft, he or she takes property of another from the person or the immediate presence of another by use of an offensive weapon, or any replica, article, or device having the appearance of such weapon. The offense of robbery by intimidation shall be a lesser included offense in the offense of armed robbery.

(b) A person convicted of the offense of armed robbery shall be punished by death or imprisonment for life or by imprisonment for not less than ten nor more than 20 years.

(c)(1) The preceding provisions of this Code section notwithstanding, in any case in which the defendant commits armed robbery and in the course of the commission of the offense such person unlawfully takes a controlled substance from a pharmacy or a wholesale druggist and intentionally inflicts bodily injury upon any person, such facts shall be charged in the indictment or accusation and, if found to be true by the court or if admitted by the defendant, the defendant shall be punished by imprisonment for not less than 15 years.

(2) As used in this subsection, the term:

(A) "Controlled substance" means a drug, substance, or immediate precursor in Schedules I through V of Code Sections 16-13-25 through 16-13-29.

(B) "Pharmacy" means any place licensed in accordance with Chapter 4 of Title 26 wherein the possessing, displaying, compounding, dispensing, or retailing of drugs may be conducted, including any and all portions of any building or structure leased, used, or controlled by the licensee in the conduct of the business licensed by the State Board of Pharmacy at the address for which the license was issued. The term pharmacy shall also include any building, warehouse, physician's office, or hospital used in whole or in part for the sale, storage, or dispensing of any controlled substance.

(C) "Wholesale druggist" means an individual, partnership, corporation, or association registered with the State Board of Pharmacy under Chapter 4 of Title 26.

(d) Any person convicted under this Code section shall, in addition, be subject to the sentencing and punishment provisions of Code Sections 17-10-6.1 and 17-10-7.

§ 16-8-60. Reproduction of recorded material; transfer, sale, distribution, circulation; civil forfeiture; restitution

(a) It is unlawful for any person, firm, partnership, corporation, or association knowingly to:

(1) Transfer or cause to be transferred any sounds or visual images recorded on a phonograph record, disc, wire, tape, videotape, film, or other article on which sounds or visual images are recorded onto any other phonograph record, disc, wire, tape, videotape, film, or article without the consent of the person who owns the master phonograph record, master disc, master tape, master videotape, master film, or other device or article from which the sounds or visual images are derived; or

(2) Sell; distribute; circulate; offer for sale, distribution, or circulation; possess for the purpose of sale, distribution, or circulation; cause to be sold, distributed, or circulated; cause to be offered for sale, distribution, or circulation; or cause to be possessed for sale, distribution, or circulation any article or device on which sounds or visual images have been transferred, knowing it to have been made without the consent of the person who owns the master phonograph record, master disc, master tape, master videotape, master film, or other device or article from which the sounds or visual images are derived.

(b) It is unlawful for any person, firm, partnership, corporation, or association to sell; distribute; circulate; offer for sale, distribution, or circulation; or possess for the purposes of sale, distribution, or circulation any phonograph record, disc, wire, tape, videotape, film, or other article on which sounds or visual images have been transferred unless such phonograph record, disc, wire, tape, videotape, film, or other article bears the actual name and address of the transferor of the sounds or visual images in a prominent place on its outside face or package.

(c) This Code section shall not apply to any person who transfers or causes to be transferred any such sounds or visual images:

(1) Intended for or in connection with radio or television broadcast transmission or related uses;

(2) For archival purposes; or

(3) Solely for the personal use of the person transferring or causing the transfer and without any profit being derived by the person from the transfer.

(d) Every person convicted of violating this Code section shall be guilty of a felony and shall be punished as follows:

(1) Upon the first conviction of violating this Code section, by a fine of not less than $500.00 nor more than $25,000.00, by imprisonment for not less than one year nor more than two years, or both such fine and imprisonment;

(2) Upon the second conviction of violating this Code section, by a fine of not less than $1,000.00 nor more than $100,000.00, by imprisonment for not less than one year nor more than three years and the judge may suspend, stay, or probate all but 48 hours of any term of imprisonment, or both such fine and imprisonment; or

(3) Upon the third or subsequent conviction of violating this Code section, by a fine of not less than $2,000.00 nor more than $250,000.00, by imprisonment for not less than two nor more than five years and the judge may suspend, stay, or probate all but six days of any term of imprisonment, or both such fine and imprisonment.

(e) This Code section shall neither enlarge nor diminish the right of parties to enter into a private contract.

(f) (1) Any phonograph record, disc, wire, tape, videotape, film, or other article onto which sounds or visual images have been transferred in violation of this Code section are declared to be contraband and no person shall have a property right in them; provided, however, that notwithstanding paragraph (2) of subsection (a) of Code Section 9-16-17, no property of any owner shall be forfeited under this paragraph, to the extent of the interest of such owner, by reason of an act or omission established by such owner to have been committed or omitted without knowledge or consent of such owner.

(2) Any property subject to forfeiture pursuant to paragraph (1) of this subsection shall be forfeited in accordance with the procedures set forth in Chapter 16 of Title 9.

(g) For purposes of imposing restitution pursuant to Chapter 14 of Title 17 when a person is convicted pursuant to this Code section, the court shall consider damages to any owner or lawful producer of a master phonograph record, master disc, master tape, master videotape, master film, or other device or article from which sounds or visual images are derived. Restitution shall be based upon the aggregate wholesale value of lawfully manufactured and authorized recorded devices corresponding to the nonconforming recorded devices involved in the violation of this Code section and shall also include reasonable investigative costs related to the detection of the violation of this Code section.

§ 16-8-61. Display of official rating on video movies

(a) As used in this Code section, the term:
(1) "Official rating" means the official rating of a motion picture by the Classification and Rating Administration of the Motion Picture Association of America.
(2) "Video movie" means a videotape, video cassette, video disc, any prerecorded video display or visual depiction, any prerecorded device that can be converted to a visual depiction, or other reproduction or reconstruction of a motion picture.
(b) No person may sell, rent, loan, or otherwise disseminate or distribute for monetary consideration a video movie unless the official rating of the motion picture from which the video movie is copied is clearly and prominently displayed in boldface type on the outside of the cassette, case, jacket, or other covering containing the video movie. Such video movie shall be clearly and prominently marked as "not rated" if:
(1) The motion picture from which the video movie is copied has no official rating;
(2) The official rating of the motion picture from which the video movie is copied is not readily available to such person; or
(3) The video movie has been altered so that its content materially differs from the motion picture.
(c) Any person who violates subsection (b) of this Code section shall, upon conviction thereof, be punished by a fine of not more than $100.00.

§ 16-8-62. Film piracy prohibited; exceptions; penalty for violation

(a) As used in this Code section, the term:
(1) "Audiovisual recording device" means any device capable of recording or transmitting a motion picture, or any part thereof, using any technology now known or later developed.
(2) "Facility" shall not include a personal residence.
(b) Any person who knowingly operates the recording function of an audiovisual recording device while a motion picture is being exhibited, without the consent of the owner, operator, or lessee of the exhibition facility and of the licensor of the motion picture being exhibited, shall be guilty of film piracy.
(c) The provisions of this Code section shall not be construed to prevent any lawfully authorized investigative, law enforcement, or intelligence personnel of the state or federal government from operating any audiovisual recording device in a facility where a motion picture is being exhibited as part of their official duties or activities.
(d) This Code section is not applicable to a person who operates an audiovisual recording device in a retail establishment solely to demonstrate the use of the device for sales purposes.
(e) A prosecution under this Code section shall not preclude obtaining any other civil or criminal remedy under any other provision of law.
(f) Violation of this Code section is a misdemeanor of a high and aggravated nature and punishable upon conviction as provided in Code Section 17-10-4. A second or subsequent conviction for violation of this Code section shall be punishable as a felony.

§ 16-8-80. Short title

This article shall be known and may be cited as the "Motor Vehicle Chop Shop and Stolen and Altered Property Act."

§ 16-8-81. Legislative findings

(a) The General Assembly finds and declares the following:
(1) The annual number of reported motor vehicle thefts has exceeded 1 million. Approximately 50 percent of all larcenies reported to law enforcement authorities in the United States are directed against motor vehicles. The recovery rate of stolen motor vehicles has decreased significantly during the most recent decade;
(2) Thefts of motor vehicles and the disposition of stolen motor vehicles and motor vehicle parts are becoming more professional in nature. Such theft and disposition activities have attracted criminal elements which have used intimidation and violence as a means of obtaining increased control of such activities;
(3) The theft of motor vehicles has brought increased and unnecessary burdens to motor vehicle users and taxpayers, as the national financial cost of motor vehicle related theft offenses currently approaches $5 billion annually;
(4) Prosecutors should give increased emphasis to the prosecution of persons committing motor vehicle thefts, with particular emphasis given to professional motor vehicle theft operations and to persons engaged in the dismantling of stolen motor vehicles for the purpose of trafficking in stolen motor vehicle parts; and
(5) Traditional law enforcement strategies and techniques that concentrate on bringing criminal penalties to bear on motor vehicle thieves, but do not focus on chop shops that are heavily involved in the dismantling of stolen motor vehicles or the distribution of motor vehicle parts and that do not enlist the assistance of private enforcement and use civil sanctions, are inadequate to control motor vehicle theft, as well as related offenses. Comprehensive strategies must be formulated; more effective law enforcement techniques must be developed; evidentiary, procedural, and substantive laws must be strengthened; and criminal penalties and civil sanctions must be enhanced.
(b) The General Assembly, therefore, concludes that for the protection of the general public interest, the "Motor Vehicle Chop Shop and Stolen and Altered Property Act" shall be enacted.

§ 16-8-82. Definitions

As used in this article, the term:
(1) "Chop shop" means any building, lot, or other premise where one or more persons knowingly engage in altering, destroying, disassembling, dismantling, reassembling, or storing any motor vehicle or motor vehicle part known to be illegally obtained by theft, fraud, or conspiracy to defraud in order to either:
(A) Alter, counterfeit, deface, destroy, disguise, falsify, forge, obliterate, or remove the identification, including the vehicle identification number of such motor vehicle or motor vehicle part, in order to misrepresent the identity of such motor vehicle or motor vehicle part or to prevent the identification of such motor vehicle or motor vehicle part; or
(B) Sell or dispose of such motor vehicle or motor vehicle part.
(2) "Motor vehicle" includes every device in, upon, or by which any person or property is or may be transported or drawn upon a highway which is self-propelled or which may be connected to and towed by a self-propelled device and also includes any and all other land based devices which are self-propelled but which are not designed for use upon a highway, including, but not limited to, farm machinery and construction equipment.
(3) "Person" includes a natural person, company, corporation, unincorporated association, partnership, professional corporation, and any other legal entity.
(4) "Unidentifiable" means that the uniqueness of a motor vehicle or motor vehicle part cannot be established by either expert law enforcement investigative personnel specially trained and experienced in motor vehicle theft investigative procedures and motor vehicle identification examination techniques or by expert employees of not for profit motor vehicle theft prevention agencies specially trained and experienced in motor vehicle theft investigation procedures and motor vehicle identification examination techniques.
(5) "Vehicle identification number" includes, but is not limited to, a number or numbers, a letter or letters, a character or characters, a datum or data, a derivative or derivatives, or a combination or combinations thereof, used by the manufacturer or the Department of Revenue for the purpose of uniquely identifying a motor vehicle or motor vehicle part.

§ 16-8-83. Owning, operating, or conducting a chop shop; penalty

(a) Any person who knowingly and with intent:
(1) Owns, operates, or conducts a chop shop;
(2) Transports any motor vehicle or motor vehicle part to or from a location knowing it to be a chop shop; or

(3) Sells, transfers, purchases, or receives any motor vehicle or motor vehicle part either to or from a location knowing it to be a chop shop

shall be guilty of a felony and, upon conviction thereof, shall be punished by imprisonment for not less than three years nor more than ten years, by a fine of not more than $100,000.00, or by both such fine and imprisonment.

(b) Any person who knowingly alters, counterfeits, defaces, destroys, disguises, falsifies, forges, obliterates, or removes a vehicle identification number with the intent to misrepresent the identity or prevent the identification of a motor vehicle or motor vehicle part shall be guilty of a felony and, upon conviction thereof, shall be punished by imprisonment for not less than one year nor more than ten years, by a fine of not more than $50,000.00, or by both such fine and imprisonment.

(c)(1) Any person who buys, disposes, sells, transfers, or possesses a motor vehicle or motor vehicle part with knowledge that the vehicle identification number of the motor vehicle or motor vehicle part has been altered, counterfeited, defaced, destroyed, disguised, falsified, forged, obliterated, or removed shall be guilty of a felony and, upon conviction thereof, shall be punished by imprisonment for not less than one year nor more than ten years, by a fine of not more than $50,000.00, or by both such fine and imprisonment.

(2) The provisions of paragraph (1) of this subsection shall not apply to a motor vehicle scrap processor who, in the normal legal course of business and in good faith, processes a motor vehicle or motor vehicle part by crushing, compacting, or other similar methods, provided that any vehicle identification number is not removed from the motor vehicle or motor vehicle part prior to or during any such processing.

(3) The provisions of paragraph (1) of this subsection shall not apply to any owner or authorized possessor of a motor vehicle recovered by law enforcement authorities after having been stolen or where the condition of the vehicle identification number of the motor vehicle or motor vehicle part is known to or has been reported to law enforcement authorities. It shall be presumed that law enforcement authorities have knowledge of all vehicle identification numbers on a motor vehicle or motor vehicle part which are altered, counterfeited, defaced, disguised, falsified, forged, obliterated, or removed when law enforcement authorities deliver or return the motor vehicle or motor vehicle part to its owner or authorized possessor after it has been recovered by law enforcement authorities after having been reported stolen.

(d) A person commits the offense of attempted operation of a chop shop when, with the intent to commit a violation proscribed by subsection (a), (b), or (c) of this Code section, the person does any act which constitutes a substantial step toward the commission of a violation proscribed by subsection (a), (b), or (c) of this Code section; and such person shall be guilty of a felony and, upon conviction thereof, shall be punished by imprisonment for not less than one year nor more than five years, by a fine of not more than $25,000.00, or by both such fine and imprisonment.

(e) A person commits the offense of conspiracy when, with the intent that a violation proscribed by subsection (a), (b), or (c) of this Code section be committed, the person agrees with another to the commission of a violation proscribed by subsection (a), (b), or (c) of this Code section; and such person shall be guilty of a felony and, upon conviction thereof, shall be punished by imprisonment for not less than one year nor more than five years, by a fine of not more than $25,000.00, or by both such fine and imprisonment. No person may be convicted of conspiracy under this subsection unless an act in furtherance of such agreement is alleged and proved to have been committed by that person or a coconspirator.

(f) A person commits the offense of solicitation when, with the intent that a violation proscribed by subsection (a), (b), or (c) of this Code section be committed, the person commands, encourages, or requests another to commit a violation proscribed by subsection (a), (b), or (c) of this Code section; and such person shall be guilty of a felony and, upon conviction thereof, shall be punished by imprisonment for not less than one year nor more than five years, by a fine of not more than $25,000.00, or by both such fine and imprisonment.

(g) A person commits the offense of aiding and abetting when, either before or during the commission of a violation proscribed by subsection (a), (b), or (c) of this Code section and with the intent to promote or facilitate such commission, the person aids, abets, agrees, or attempts to aid another in the planning or commission of a violation proscribed by subsection (a), (b), or (c) of this Code section; and such person shall be guilty of a felony and, upon conviction thereof, shall be punished by imprisonment for not less than one year nor more than five years, by a fine of not more than $25,000.00, or by both such fine and imprisonment.

(h) A person is an accessory after the fact who maintains, assists, or gives any other aid to an offender while knowing or having reasonable grounds to believe the offender has committed a violation under subsection (a), (b), or (c) of this Code section; and such person shall be guilty of a felony and, upon conviction thereof, shall be punished by imprisonment for not less than one year nor more than five years, by a fine of not more than $25,000.00, or by both such fine and imprisonment.

(i) No prosecution shall be brought and no person shall be convicted of any violation under this Code section where the acts of such person otherwise constituting a violation were done in good faith in order to comply with the laws or regulations of any state or territory of the United States or of the United States government.

(j) The sentence imposed upon a person convicted of any violation of this Code section shall not be reduced to less than one year of imprisonment for a second conviction or less than five years for a third or subsequent conviction, and no sentence imposed upon a person for a second or subsequent conviction of any violation of this Code section shall be suspended or reduced until such person shall have served the minimum period of imprisonment provided for in this Code section. A person convicted of a second or subsequent violation of this Code section shall not be eligible for probation, parole, furlough, or work release.

(k)(1) In addition to any other punishment, a person who violates this Code section shall be ordered to make restitution to the lawful owner or owners of the stolen motor vehicle or vehicles or the stolen motor vehicle part or parts, to the owner's insurer to the extent that the owner has been compensated by the insurer, and to any other person for any financial loss sustained as a result of a violation of this Code section.

(2) For purposes of this Code section, the term:

(A) "Financial loss" shall include, but not be limited to, loss of earnings, out-of-pocket and other expenses, repair and replacement costs, and claims payments.

(B) "Lawful owner" shall include an innocent bona fide purchaser for value of a stolen motor vehicle or motor vehicle part who does not know that the motor vehicle or part is stolen or an insurer to the extent that such insurer has compensated a bona fide purchaser for value.

(3) The court shall determine the extent and method of restitution required under this subsection. In an extraordinary case, the court may determine that the best interests of the victim and justice would not be served by ordering restitution. In any such case, the court shall make and enter specific written findings on the record concerning the extraordinary circumstances presented which mitigated against restitution.

§ 16-8-84. Seizure of personal property used or possessed in connection with violation of Code Section 16-8-83

(a) Any tool, implement, or instrumentality, including, but not limited to, a motor vehicle or motor vehicle part, used or possessed in connection with any violation of Code Section 16-8-83 may be seized by a member of a state or local law enforcement agency upon process issued by any court of competent jurisdiction.

(b) Seizure of property described in subsection (a) of this Code section may be made by a member of a state or local law enforcement agency without process if:

(1) The seizure is made in accordance with any applicable law or regulation;

(2) The seizure is incident to inspection under an administrative inspection warrant;

(3) The seizure is incident to a search made under a search warrant;

(4) The seizure is incident to a lawful arrest;

(5) The seizure is made pursuant to a valid consent to search;

(6) The property seized has been the subject of a prior judgment in favor of the state in a criminal proceeding or in an injunction or forfeiture proceeding under Code Section 16-8-86; or

(7) There are reasonable grounds to believe that the property is directly or indirectly dangerous to the health or safety of the public.

(c) When property is seized pursuant to this Code section, the seizing agency may:

(1) Place the property under seal; or

(2) Remove the property to a place selected and designated by the seizing agency.

§ 16-8-85. Civil forfeiture of personal property seized

(a) The following are subject to forfeiture unless obtained by theft, fraud, or conspiracy to defraud and the rightful owner is known or can be identified and located:

(1) Any tool;

(2) Any implement; or

(3) Any instrumentality, including, but not limited to, any motor vehicle or motor vehicle part, whether or not owned by the person from whose possession or control it was seized, which is used or possessed either in violation of Code Section 16-8-83 or to promote or facilitate a violation of Code Section 16-8-83.

(b) Any motor vehicle, other conveyance, or motor vehicle part used by any person as a common carrier is subject to forfeiture under this Code section where the owner or other person in charge of the motor vehicle, other conveyance, or motor vehicle part is a consenting party to a violation of Code Section 16-8-83.

(c) If a motor vehicle part has an apparent value in excess of $1,000.00:

(1) The seizing agency shall consult with an expert of the type specified in paragraph (4) of Code Section 16-8-82; and

(2) The seizing agency shall also request searches of the online and offline files of the National Crime Information Center and the National Automobile Theft Bureau when the Georgia Bureau of Investigation and Georgia Crime Information Center files have been searched with negative results.

(d) Any property subject to forfeiture pursuant to this Code section shall be forfeited in accordance with the procedures set forth in Chapter 16 of Title 9, except as specifically set forth in subsections (g) through (j) of this Code section.

(e) A copy of a forfeiture order shall be filed with the sheriff of the county in which the forfeiture occurs and with each federal or state department or agency with which such property is required to be registered. Such order, when filed, constitutes authority for the issuance to the agency to whom the property is delivered and retained for use or to any purchaser of the property of a certificate of title, registration certificate, or other special certificate as may be required by law in consideration of the condition of the property.

(f) No motor vehicle, either seized under Code Section 16-8-84 or forfeited under this Code section, shall be released by the seizing agency or used or sold by an agency designated by the court unless any altered, counterfeited, defaced, destroyed, disguised, falsified, forged, obliterated, or removed vehicle identification number is corrected by the issuance and affixing of either an assigned or replacement vehicle identification number plate as may be appropriate under laws or regulations of this state.

(g) No motor vehicle part having any altered, counterfeited, defaced, destroyed, disguised, falsified, forged, obliterated, or removed vehicle identification number may be disposed of upon forfeiture except by destruction thereof, except that this subsection shall not apply to any such motor vehicle part which is assembled with and constitutes part of a motor vehicle.

(h) No motor vehicle or motor vehicle part shall be forfeited under this Code section solely on the basis that it is unidentifiable. Instead of forfeiture, any seized motor vehicle or motor vehicle part which is unidentifiable shall be the subject of a written report sent by the seizing agency to the Department of Revenue which shall include a description of the motor vehicle or motor vehicle part, including its color, if any; the date, time, and place of its seizure; the name of the person from whose possession or control it was seized; the grounds for its seizure; and the location where the same is held or stored.

(i) When a seized unidentifiable motor vehicle or motor vehicle part has been held for 60 days or more after the notice to the Department of Revenue specified in subsection (h) of this Code section has been given, the seizing agency, or its agent, shall cause the motor vehicle or motor vehicle part to be sold at a public sale to the highest bidder. Notice of the time and place of sale shall be posted in a conspicuous place for at least 30 days prior to the sale on the premises where the motor vehicle or motor vehicle part has been stored.

(j) (1) When a seized unidentifiable motor vehicle or motor vehicle part has an apparent value of $1,000.00 or less, the seizing agency shall authorize the disposal of the motor vehicle or motor vehicle part, provided that no such disposition shall be made sooner than 60 days after the date of seizure.

(2) The proceeds of the public sale of an unidentifiable motor vehicle or motor vehicle part shall be deposited into the general fund of the state, county, or municipal corporation employing the seizing agency after deduction of any reasonable and necessary towing and storage charges.

(k) Seizing agencies shall utilize their best efforts to arrange for the towing and storing of motor vehicles and motor vehicle parts in the most economical manner possible. In no event shall the owner of a motor vehicle or a motor vehicle part be required to pay more than the minimum reasonable costs of towing and storage.

(l) A seized motor vehicle or motor vehicle part that is neither forfeited nor unidentifiable shall be held subject to the order of the court in which the criminal action is pending or, if a request for its release from such custody is made, until the prosecutor has notified the defendant or the defendant's attorney of such request and both the prosecution and defense have been afforded a reasonable opportunity for an examination of the property to determine its true value and to produce or reproduce, by photographs or other identifying techniques, legally sufficient evidence for introduction at trial or other criminal proceedings. Upon expiration of a reasonable time for the completion of the examination, which in no event shall exceed 14 days from the date of service upon the defense of the notice of request for return of property as provided in this subsection, the property shall be released to the person making such request after satisfactory proof of such person's entitlement to the possession thereof. Notwithstanding the foregoing, upon application by either party with notice to the other, the court may order retention of the property if it determines that retention is necessary in the furtherance of justice.

(m) When a seized vehicle is forfeited, restored to its owner, or disposed of as unidentifiable, the seizing agency shall retain a report of the transaction for a period of at least one year from the date of the transaction.

(n) When an applicant for a certificate of title or salvage certificate of title presents to the Department of Revenue proof that the applicant purchased or acquired a motor vehicle at public sale conducted pursuant to this Code section and such fact is attested to by the seizing agency, the Department of Revenue shall issue a certificate of title or a salvage certificate of title, as determined by the state revenue commissioner, for such motor vehicle upon receipt of the statutory fee, a properly executed application for a certificate of title or other certificate of ownership, and the affidavit of the seizing agency that a state assigned number was applied for and affixed to the motor vehicle prior to the time that the motor vehicle was released by the seizing agency to the purchaser.

§ 16-8-86. Civil action for violation of this article

(a) The Attorney General, any prosecutor, or any aggrieved person may institute a civil action against any person in a court of competent jurisdiction seeking relief from conduct constituting a violation of any provision of this article. If the plaintiff in such action proves the alleged violation, or its threat, by a preponderance of the evidence, any court of competent jurisdiction after due provision for the rights of innocent persons shall grant relief by entering any appropriate order or judgment, including, but not limited to:

(1) Ordering any defendant to be divested of any interest in any property;

(2) Imposing reasonable restrictions upon the future activities or investments of any defendant, including prohibiting any defendant from engaging in the same type of endeavor as the defendant was engaged in previously;

(3) Ordering the suspension or revocation of a license, permit, or prior approval granted by any public agency or any other public authority; or

(4) Ordering the surrender of the charter of a corporation organized under the laws of this state or the revocation of a certificate authorizing a foreign corporation to conduct business within this state upon a finding that the board of directors or a managerial agent acting on behalf of the corporation, in conducting the affairs of the corporation, has authorized or engaged in conduct made unlawful by this article and that, for the prevention of future criminal conduct, the public interest requires the charter of the corporation be surrendered and the corporation dissolved or the certificate to conduct business in this state revoked.

(b) In a proceeding under this Code section, injunctive relief shall be granted in conformity with the principles that govern the granting of relief from injury or threatened injury in other cases, but no showing of special or irreparable injury shall have to be made. Pending final determination of a proceeding under this Code section, a temporary restraining order or a preliminary injunction may be issued upon a showing of immediate danger of significant injury, including the possibility that any judgment for money damages might be difficult to execute, and, in a proceeding initiated by an aggrieved person, upon the execution of proper bond against injury for an injunction improvidently granted.

(c) Any person injured, directly or indirectly, by conduct constituting a violation by any person of Code Section 16-8-83 shall, in addition to any other relief, have a cause of action for threefold the actual damages sustained by the person.

(d) A final judgment or decree rendered against the defendant in any civil or criminal proceeding shall estop the defendant in any subsequent civil action or proceeding brought by any person as to all matters to which the judgment or decree would be an estoppel as between the parties to the civil or criminal proceeding.

(e) Notwithstanding any other provision of law providing for a shorter period of limitations, a civil action under this Code section may be commenced at any time within five years after the conduct made unlawful under Code Section 16-8-83 terminates or the cause of action accrues or within any longer statutory period that may be applicable. If any action is brought by a prosecutor to punish, prevent, or restrain any activity made unlawful under Code Section 16-8-83, the running of the period of limitations shall be suspended during the pendency of such action and for two years following its termination.

(f) Personal service of any process in an action under this Code section may be made upon any person outside the state if the person has engaged in any conduct constituting a violation of Code Section 16-8-83 in this state. The person shall be deemed to have thereby submitted to the jurisdiction of the courts of this state for the purposes of this subsection.

(g) Obtaining any civil remedy under this Code section shall not preclude obtaining any other civil or criminal remedy under this article or any other provision of law. Civil remedies under this Code section are supplemental and not exclusive.

§ 16-8-100. Short title

This article shall be known and may be cited as the "Georgia Residential Mortgage Fraud Act."

§ 16-8-101. Definitions

As used in this article, the term:
(1) "Mortgage lending process" means the process through which a person seeks or obtains a residential mortgage loan including, but not limited to, solicitation, application, or origination, negotiation of terms, third-party provider services, underwriting, signing and closing, and funding of the loan. Such term shall also include the execution of deeds under power of sale that are required to be recorded pursuant to Code Section 44-14-160 and the execution of assignments that are required to be recorded pursuant to subsection (b) of Code Section 44-14-162. Documents involved in the mortgage lending process include, but shall not be limited to, uniform residential loan applications or other loan applications; appraisal reports; HUD-1 settlement statements; supporting personal documentation for loan applications such as W-2 forms, verifications of income and employment, bank statements, tax returns, and payroll stubs; and any required disclosures.
(2) "Pattern of residential mortgage fraud" means one or more misstatements, misrepresentations, or omissions made during the mortgage lending process that involve two or more residential properties, which have the same or similar intents, results, accomplices, victims, or methods of commission or otherwise are interrelated by distinguishing characteristics.
(3) "Person" means a natural person, corporation, company, limited liability company, partnership, trustee, association, or any other entity.
(4) "Residential mortgage loan" means a loan or agreement to extend credit made to a person, which loan is secured by a deed to secure debt, security deed, mortgage, security interest, deed of trust, or other document representing a security interest or lien upon any interest in one-to-four family residential property located in Georgia including the renewal or refinancing of any such loan.

§ 16-8-102. Residential mortgage fraud

A person commits the offense of residential mortgage fraud when, with the intent to defraud, such person:
(1) Knowingly makes any deliberate misstatement, misrepresentation, or omission during the mortgage lending process with the intention that it be relied on by a mortgage lender, borrower, or any other party to the mortgage lending process;
(2) Knowingly uses or facilitates the use of any deliberate misstatement, misrepresentation, or omission, knowing the same to contain a misstatement, misrepresentation, or omission, during the mortgage lending process with the intention that it be relied on by a mortgage lender, borrower, or any other party to the mortgage lending process;
(3) Receives any proceeds or any other funds in connection with a residential mortgage closing that such person knew resulted from a violation of paragraph (1) or (2) of this Code section;
(4) Conspires to violate any of the provisions of paragraph (1), (2), or (3) of this Code section; or
(5) Files or causes to be filed with the official registrar of deeds of any county of this state any document such person knows to contain a deliberate misstatement, misrepresentation, or omission. An offense of residential mortgage fraud shall not be predicated solely upon information lawfully disclosed under federal disclosure laws, regulations, and interpretations related to the mortgage lending process nor upon truthful information contained in documents filed with the official registrar of deeds of any county of this state for the stated purpose of correcting scrivener's errors, mistakes, inadvertent misstatements, or omissions contained in previously filed documents.

§ 16-8-103. Venue

For the purpose of venue under this article, any violation of this article shall be considered to have been committed:
(1) In the county in which the residential property for which a mortgage loan is being sought is located;
(2) In any county in which any act was performed in furtherance of the violation;
(3) In any county in which any person alleged to have violated this article had control or possession of any proceeds of the violation;
(4) If a closing occurred, in any county in which the closing occurred; or
(5) In any county in which a document containing a deliberate misstatement, misrepresentation, or omission is filed with the official registrar of deeds.

§ 16-8-104. Authority to investigate and prosecute for residential mortgage fraud

District attorneys and the Attorney General shall have the authority to conduct the criminal investigation and prosecution of all cases of residential mortgage fraud under this article or under any other provision of this title. Nothing in this Code section shall be construed to preclude otherwise authorized law enforcement agencies from conducting investigations of offenses related to residential mortgage fraud.

§ 16-8-105. Penalties

(a) Any person violating this article shall be guilty of a felony and, upon conviction, shall be punished by imprisonment for not less than one year nor more than ten years, by a fine not to exceed $5,000.00, or both.
(b) If a violation of this article involves engaging or participating in a pattern of residential mortgage fraud or a conspiracy or endeavor to engage or participate in a pattern of residential mortgage fraud, said violation shall be punishable by imprisonment for not less than three years nor more than 20 years, by a fine not to exceed $100,000.00, or both.
(c) Each residential property transaction subject to a violation of this article shall constitute a separate offense and shall not merge with any other crimes set forth in this title.

§ 16-8-106. Civil forfeiture

(a) As used in this Code section, the terms "civil forfeiture proceedings," "proceeds," and "property" shall have the same meanings as set forth in Code Section 9-16-2.
(b) Any property which is, directly or indirectly, used or intended for use in any manner to facilitate a violation of this article and any proceeds are declared to be contraband and no person shall have a property right in them.
(c) Any property subject to forfeiture pursuant to subsection (b) of this Code section shall be forfeited in accordance with the procedures set forth in Chapter 16 of Title 9.
(d) The Attorney General shall be specifically authorized to commence civil forfeiture proceedings under this Code section.

CHAPTER 9. FORGERY AND FRAUDULENT PRACTICES

§ 16-9-1. Forgery; classification of forgery offenses

(a) As used in this Code section, the term:
(1) "Bank" means incorporated banks, savings banks, banking companies, trust companies, credit unions, and other corporations doing a banking business.
(2) "Check" means any instrument for the payment or transmission of money payable on demand and drawn on a bank.

(3) "Writing" includes, but shall not be limited to, printing or any other method of recording information, money, coins, tokens, stamps, seals, credit cards, badges, trademarks, and other symbols of value, right, privilege, or identification.

(b) A person commits the offense of forgery in the first degree when with the intent to defraud he or she knowingly makes, alters, or possesses any writing, other than a check, in a fictitious name or in such manner that the writing as made or altered purports to have been made by another person, at another time, with different provisions, or by authority of one who did not give such authority and utters or delivers such writing.

(c) A person commits the offense of forgery in the second degree when with the intent to defraud he or she knowingly makes, alters, or possesses any writing, other than a check, in a fictitious name or in such manner that the writing as made or altered purports to have been made by another person, at another time, with different provisions, or by authority of one who did not give such authority.

(d) A person commits the offense of forgery in the third degree when with the intent to defraud he or she knowingly:

(1) Makes, alters, possesses, utters, or delivers any check written in the amount of $1,500.00 or more in a fictitious name or in such manner that the check as made or altered purports to have been made by another person, at another time, with different provisions, or by authority of one who did not give such authority; or

(2) Possesses ten or more checks written without a specified amount in a fictitious name or in such manner that the checks as made or altered purport to have been made by another person, at another time, with different provisions, or by authority of one who did not give such authority.

(e) A person commits the offense of forgery in the fourth degree when with the intent to defraud he or she knowingly:

(1) Makes, alters, possesses, utters, or delivers any check written in the amount of less than $1,500.00 in a fictitious name or in such manner that the check as made or altered purports to have been made by another person, at another time, with different provisions, or by authority of one who did not give such authority; or

(2) Possesses less than ten checks written without a specified amount in a fictitious name or in such manner that the checks as made or altered purport to have been made by another person, at another time, with different provisions, or by authority of one who did not give such authority.

§ 16-9-2. Penalties for forgery

(a) A person who commits the offense of forgery in the first degree shall be guilty of a felony and, upon conviction thereof, shall be punished by imprisonment for not less than one nor more than 15 years.

(b) A person who commits the offense of forgery in the second degree shall be guilty of a felony and, upon conviction thereof, shall be punished by imprisonment for not less than one nor more than five years.

(c) A person who commits the offense of forgery in the third degree shall be guilty of a felony and, upon conviction thereof, shall be punished by imprisonment for not less than one nor more than five years.

(d) A person who commits the offense of forgery in the fourth degree shall be guilty of a misdemeanor; provided, however, that upon the third and all subsequent convictions for such offense, the defendant shall be guilty of a felony and shall be punished by imprisonment for not less than one nor more than five years.

§ 16-9-3. "Writing" defined

Reserved. Repealed by Ga. L. 2012, p. 899, § 3-5/HB 1176, effective July 1, 2012.

§ 16-9-4. Manufacturing, selling, or distributing false identification document; civil forfeiture; penalty

(a) As used in this Code section, the term:

(1) "Access device" means a unique electronic identification number, address, description, or routing code or a device containing a unique electronic identification number, address, description, or routing code issued to an individual which permits or facilitates entry into a facility or computer or provides access to the financial resources, including, but not limited, to the credit resources of the individual to whom the device or card is issued.

(2) "Description" means any identifying information about a person, including, but not limited to, date of birth, place of birth, address, social security number, height, weight, hair or eye color, or unique biometric data such as fingerprint, voice print, retina or iris image, DNA profile, or other unique physical representation.

(3) "Government agency" means any agency of the executive, legislative, or judicial branch of government or political subdivision or authority thereof of this state, any other state, the United States, or any foreign government or international governmental or quasi-governmental agency recognized by the United States or by any of the several states.

(4) "Identification document" means:

(A) Any document or card issued to an individual by a government agency or by the authority of a government agency containing the name of a person and a description of the person or such person's photograph, or both, and includes, without being limited to, a passport, visa, military identification card, driver's license, or an identification card;

(B) Any document issued to an individual for the purpose of identification by or with the authority of the holder of a trademark or trade name of another, as these terms are defined in Code Section 10-1-371, that contains the trademark or trade name and the name of the person to whom the document is issued and a description of the person or the person's photograph, or both; or

(C) Any access device.

(b)(1) It shall be unlawful for any person to knowingly possess, display, or use any false, fictitious, fraudulent, or altered identification document.

(2) It shall be unlawful for any person to knowingly manufacture, alter, sell, distribute, deliver, possess with intent to sell, deliver, or distribute, or offer for sale, delivery, or distribution a false, fraudulent, or fictitious identification document or any identification document which contains any false, fictitious, or fraudulent statement or entry.

(3) It shall be unlawful for any person to knowingly manufacture, alter, sell, distribute, deliver, possess with the intent to sell, deliver, or distribute, or offer for sale, delivery, or distribution any identification document containing the trademark or trade name of another without the written consent of the owner of the trademark or trade name.

(4) It shall be unlawful for any person to knowingly possess, display, or use any false, fictitious, fraudulent, or altered identification document containing the logo or legal or official seal of a government agency or any colorable imitation thereof in furtherance of a conspiracy or attempt to commit a violation of the criminal laws of this state or of the United States or any of the several states which is punishable by imprisonment for one year or more.

(5) It shall be unlawful for any person to knowingly manufacture, alter, sell, distribute, deliver, possess with the intent to sell, deliver, or distribute, or offer for sale or distribution any other identification document containing the logo or legal or official seal of a government agency or any colorable imitation thereof without the written consent of the government agency.

(6) It shall be unlawful for any person to knowingly possess, display, or use an identification document issued to or on behalf of another person without the permission or consent of the other person for a lawful purpose, unless the identification document is possessed, displayed, or used with the intent to restore it to the other person or government agency or other entity that issued the identification document to the person.

(c) (1) Except as provided in paragraph (2) or (3) of this subsection, any person who violates the provisions of paragraph (1), (3), or (6) of subsection (b) of this Code section shall be guilty of a misdemeanor.

(2) Except as provided in paragraph (3) of this subsection, any person who violates the provisions of paragraph (1), (3), or (6) of subsection (b) of this Code section for the second or any subsequent offense shall be guilty of a felony and shall be punished by a fine of not more than $25,000.00 or by imprisonment for not more than three years, or both.

(3) Except as provided in paragraph (5) of this subsection, any person who manufactures, alters, sells, distributes, delivers, receives, possesses, or offers for sale or distribution three or more identification documents in violation of the provisions of subsection (b) of this Code section shall be punished by imprisonment for not less than three nor more than ten years, a fine not to exceed $100,000.00, or both.

(4) Except as provided in paragraph (3) or (5) of this subsection, any person who violates the provisions of paragraph (2), (4), or (5) of subsection (b) of this Code section shall be punished by imprisonment for not less than one nor more than five years, a fine not to exceed $100,000.00, or both.

(5) Any person who is under 21 years of age and violates the provisions of subsection (b) of this Code section for the purpose of the identification being used to obtain entry into an age restricted facility or being used to purchase a consumable good that is age restricted, shall, upon a first conviction thereof, be guilty of a misdemeanor and upon a second or subsequent conviction shall be punished as for a misdemeanor of a high and aggravated nature.

(6) Any person convicted of an attempt or conspiracy to violate the provisions of subsection (b) of this Code section shall be punished by imprisonment, by a fine, or by both such punishments not to exceed the maximum punishment prescribed for the offense the commission of which was the object of the attempt or conspiracy.

(d) Each violation of this Code section shall constitute a separate offense.

(e) Any violation of this Code section shall be considered to have been committed in any county of this state in which the evidence shows that the identification document was manufactured, altered, sold, displayed, distributed, delivered, received, offered for sale or distribution, or possessed.

(f) The provisions of this Code section shall not apply to any lawfully authorized investigative, protective, or intelligence activity of an agency of the United States, this state, or any of the several states or their political subdivisions or any activity authorized under Chapter 224 of Title 18 of the United States Code or any similar such law relating to witness protection.

(g) It shall not be a defense to a violation of this Code section that a false, fictitious, fraudulent, or altered identification document contained words indicating that it is not an identification document.

(h) (1) As used in this subsection, the terms "proceeds" and "property" shall have the same meanings as set forth in Code Section 9-16-2.

(2) Any property which is, directly or indirectly, used or intended for use in any manner to facilitate a violation of this Code section and any proceeds are declared to be contraband and no person shall have a property right in them.

(3) Any property subject to forfeiture pursuant to paragraph (2) of this subsection shall be forfeited in accordance with the procedures set forth in Chapter 16 of Title 9.

(i) It shall be an affirmative defense to the manufacturing, selling, or distributing of identification documents that contain false, fictitious, or altered information that the person manufacturing, selling, or distributing the documents used due diligence to ascertain the truth of the information contained in the identification document.

§ 16-9-5. Counterfeit or false proof of insurance document

(a) As used in this Code section, the term "proof of insurance document" means any document issued by, on behalf of, or purportedly on behalf of an insurer to a motor vehicle policyholder or applicant for motor vehicle coverage, which document is designed to constitute proof or evidence of the minimum motor vehicle liability insurance required by law for the purposes of Code Section 40-6-10.

(b) (1) It shall be unlawful for any person knowingly to manufacture, sell, or distribute a counterfeit or false proof of insurance document.

(2) It shall be unlawful for any person to possess a counterfeit or false proof of insurance document that he or she knows to be a counterfeit or false proof of insurance document.

(3) A proof of insurance document shall be deemed counterfeit or false if the proof of insurance document has been altered, modified, or originally issued in any manner which contains false information concerning the insurer, the owner, the motor vehicle, or the insurance thereon.

(c) (1) Any person who violates paragraph (1) of subsection (b) of this Code section shall be guilty of a felony and upon conviction shall be punished by a fine of not more than $10,000.00 or by imprisonment for not less than two nor more than ten years, or both.

(2) Any person who violates paragraph (2) of subsection (b) of this Code section shall upon conviction be guilty of and be punished as for a misdemeanor.

§ 16-9-6. Punishment for fiduciary in violation of chapter

Unless a greater penalty is specifically provided in this chapter, any violation of this chapter by a fiduciary in breach of a fiduciary obligation against a person who is 65 years of age or older shall be punished by imprisonment for not less than one nor more than 15 years, a fine not to exceed the amount provided by Code Section 17-10-8, or both.

§ 16-9-20. Deposit account fraud

(a) A person commits the offense of deposit account fraud when such person makes, draws, utters, executes, or delivers an instrument for the payment of money on any bank or other depository in exchange for a present consideration or wages, knowing that it will not be honored by the drawee. For the purposes of this Code section, it is prima-facie evidence that the accused knew that the instrument would not be honored if:

(1) The accused had no account with the drawee at the time the instrument was made, drawn, uttered, or delivered;

(2) Payment was refused by the drawee for lack of funds upon presentation within 30 days after delivery and the accused or someone for him or her shall not have tendered the holder thereof the amount due thereon, together with a service charge, within ten days after receiving written notice that payment was refused upon such instrument. For purposes of this paragraph:

(A) Notice mailed by certified or registered mail or statutory overnight delivery evidenced by return receipt to the person at the address printed on the instrument or given at the time of issuance shall be deemed sufficient and equivalent to notice having been received as of the date on the return receipt by the person making, drawing, uttering, executing, or delivering the instrument. A single notice as provided in subparagraph (B) of this paragraph shall be sufficient to cover all instruments on which payment was refused and which were delivered within a ten-day period by the accused to a single entity, provided that the form of notice lists and identifies each instrument; and

(B) The form of notice shall be substantially as follows:
"You are hereby notified that the following instrument(s)

Name

of
Number   Date   Amount   Ban

drawn upon   and payable to   , (has) (have) been
dishonored. Pursuant to Georgia law, you have ten days from
receipt of this notice to tender payment of the total amount of
the instrument(s) plus the applicable service charge(s) of $
and any fee charged to the holder of the instrument(s) by a bank
or financial institution as a result of the instrument(s) not
being honored, the total amount due being   dollars and
cents. Unless this amount is paid in full within the
specified time above, a presumption in law arises that you
delivered the instrument(s) with the intent to defraud and the
dishonored instrument(s) and all other available information
relating to this incident may be submitted to the magistrate for
the issuance of a criminal warrant or citation or to the district
attorney or solicitor-general for criminal prosecution."; or

(3) Notice mailed by certified or registered mail or statutory overnight delivery is returned undelivered to the sender when such notice was mailed within 90 days of dishonor to the person at the address printed on the instrument or given by the accused at the time of issuance of the instrument.

(b) (1) Except as provided in paragraphs (2) and (3) of this subsection and subsection (c) of this Code section, a person convicted of the offense of deposit account fraud shall be guilty of a misdemeanor and, upon conviction thereof, shall be punished as follows:

(A) When the instrument is for less than $500.00, a fine of not more than $500.00 or imprisonment not to exceed 12 months, or both;

(B) When the instrument is for $500.00 or more but less than $1,000.00, a fine of not more than $1,000.00 or imprisonment not to exceed 12 months, or both; or

(C) When more than one instrument is involved and such instruments were drawn within 90 days of one another and each is in an amount less than $500.00, the amounts of such separate instruments may be added together to arrive at and be punishable under subparagraph (B) of this paragraph.

(2) Except as provided in paragraph (3) of this subsection and subsection (c) of this Code section, a person convicted of the offense of deposit account fraud, when the instrument is for an amount of not less than $1,000.00 nor more than $1,499.99, shall be guilty of a misdemeanor of a high and aggravated nature. When more than one instrument is involved and such instruments were given to the same entity within a 15 day period and the cumulative total of such instruments is not less than $1,000.00 nor more than $1,499.00, the person drawing and giving such instruments shall upon conviction be guilty of a misdemeanor of a high and aggravated nature.

(3) Except as provided in subsection (c) of this Code section, a person convicted of the offense of deposit account fraud, when the instrument is for $1,500.00 or more, shall be guilty of a felony and, upon conviction thereof, shall be punished by a fine of not less than $500.00 nor more than $5,000.00 or by imprisonment for not more than three years, or both.

(4) Upon conviction of a first or any subsequent offense under this subsection or subsection (c) of this Code section, in addition to any other punishment provided by this Code section, the defendant shall be required to make restitution of the amount of the instrument, together with all costs of bringing a complaint under this Code section. The court may require the defendant to pay as interest a monthly payment equal to 1 percent of the amount of the instrument. Such amount shall be paid each month in addition to any payments on the principal until the entire balance, including the principal and any unpaid interest payments, is paid in full. Such amount shall be paid without regard to any reduction in the principal balance owed. Costs shall be determined by the court from competent evidence of costs provided by the party causing the criminal warrant or citation to issue; provided, however, that the minimum costs shall not be less than $25.00. Restitution may be made while the defendant is serving a probated or suspended sentence.

(c) A person who commits the offense of deposit account fraud by the making, drawing, uttering, executing, or delivering of an instrument on a bank of another state shall be guilty of a felony and, upon conviction thereof, shall be punished by imprisonment for not less than one nor more than five years or by a fine in an amount of up to $1,000.00, or both.

(d) The prosecuting authority of the court with jurisdiction over a violation of subsection (c) of this Code section may seek extradition for criminal prosecution of any person not within this state who flees the state to avoid prosecution under this Code section.

(e) In any prosecution or action under this Code section, an instrument for which the information required in this subsection is available at the time of issuance shall constitute prima-facie evidence of the identity of the party issuing or executing the instrument and that the person was a party authorized to draw upon the named account. To establish this prima-facie evidence, the following information regarding the identity of the party presenting the instrument shall be obtained by the party receiving such instrument: the full name, residence address, and home phone number.

(1) Such information may be provided by either of two methods:

(A) The information may be recorded upon the instrument itself; or

(B) The number of a check-cashing identification card issued by the receiving party may be recorded on the instrument. The check-cashing identification card shall be issued only after the information required in this subsection has been placed on file by the receiving party.

(2) In addition to the information required in this subsection, the party receiving an instrument shall witness the signature or endorsement of the party presenting such instrument and as evidence of such the receiving party shall initial the instrument.

(f) As used in this Code section, the term:

(1) "Bank" shall include a financial institution as defined in this Code section.

(2) "Conviction" shall include the entering of a guilty plea, the entering of a plea of nolo contendere, or the forfeiting of bail.

(3) "Financial institution" shall have the same meaning as defined in paragraph (21) of Code Section 7-1-4 and shall also include a national bank, a state or federal savings bank, a state or federal credit union, and a state or federal savings and loan association.

(4) "Holder in due course" shall have the same meaning as in Code Section 11-3-302.

(5) "Instrument" means a check, draft, debit card sales draft, or order for the payment of money.

(6) "Present consideration" shall include without limitation:

(A) An obligation or debt of rent which is past due or presently due;

(B) An obligation or debt of state taxes which is past due or presently due;

(C) An obligation or debt which is past due or presently due for child support when made for the support of such minor child and which is given pursuant to an order of court or written agreement signed by the person making the payment;

(D) A simultaneous agreement for the extension of additional credit where additional credit is being denied; and

(E) A written waiver of mechanic's or materialmen's lien rights.

(7) "State taxes" shall include payments made to the Georgia Department of Labor as required by Chapter 8 of Title 34.

(g) This Code section shall in no way affect the authority of a sentencing judge to provide for a sentence to be served on weekends or during the nonworking hours of the defendant as provided in Code Section 17-10-3.

(h) (1) Any party holding a worthless instrument and giving notice in substantially similar form to that provided in subparagraph (a)(2)(B) of this Code section shall be immune from civil liability for the giving of such notice and for proceeding as required under the forms of such notice; provided, however, that, if any person shall be arrested or prosecuted for violation of this Code section and payment of any instrument shall have been refused because the maker or drawer had no account with the bank or other depository on which such instrument was drawn, the one causing the arrest or prosecution shall be deemed to have acted with reasonable or probable cause even though he, she, or it has not mailed the written notice or waited for the ten-day period to elapse. In any civil action for damages which may be brought by the person who made, drew, uttered, executed, or delivered such instrument, no evidence of statements or representations as to the status of the instrument involved or of any collateral agreement with reference to the instrument shall be admissible unless such statements, representations, or collateral agreement shall be written simultaneously with or upon the instrument at the time it is delivered by the maker thereof.

(2) Except as otherwise provided by law, any party who holds a worthless instrument, who complies with the requirements of subsection (a) of this Code section, and who causes a criminal warrant or citation to be issued shall not forfeit his or her right to continue or pursue civil remedies authorized by law for the collection of the worthless instrument; provided, however, that if interest is awarded and collected on any amount ordered by the court as restitution in the criminal case, interest shall not be collectable in any civil action on the same amount. It shall be deemed conclusive evidence that any action is brought upon probable cause and without malice where such party holding a worthless instrument has complied with the provisions of subsection (a) of this Code section regardless of whether the criminal charges are dismissed by a court due to payment in full of the face value of the instrument and applicable service charges subsequent to the date that affidavit for the warrant or citation is made. In any civil action for damages which may be brought by the person who made, drew, uttered, executed, or delivered such instrument, no evidence of statements or representations as to the status of the instrument involved or of any collateral agreement with reference to the instrument shall be admissible unless such statements, representations, or collateral agreement shall be written simultaneously with or upon the instrument at the time it is delivered by the maker thereof.

(i) Notwithstanding paragraph (2) of subsection (a) of this Code section or any other law on usury, charges, or fees on loans or credit extensions, any lender of money or extender of other credit who receives an instrument drawn on a bank or other depository institution given by any person in full or partial repayment of a loan, installment payment, or other extension of credit may, if such instrument is not paid or is dishonored by such institution, charge and collect from the borrower or person to whom the credit was extended a bad instrument charge. This charge shall not be deemed interest or a finance or other charge made as an incident to or as a condition to the granting of the loan or other extension of credit and shall not be included in determining the limit on charges which may be made in connection with the loan or extension of credit or any other law of this state.

(j) For purposes of this Code section, no service charge or bad instrument charge shall exceed $30.00 or 5 percent of the face amount of the instrument, whichever is greater, except that the holder of the instrument may also charge the maker an additional fee in an amount equal to that charged to the holder by the bank or financial institution as a result of the instrument not being honored.

(k) An action under this Code section may be prosecuted by the party initially receiving a worthless instrument or by any subsequent holder in due course of any such worthless instrument.

§ 16-9-21. Printing, executing, or negotiating checks, drafts, orders, or debit card sales drafts knowing information thereon to be in error, fictitious, or assigned to another account holder

(a) It shall be unlawful for any person to print or cause to be printed checks, drafts, orders, or debit card sales drafts, drawn upon any financial institution or to execute or negotiate any check, draft, order, or debit card sales draft knowing that the account number, routing number, or other information printed on such check, draft, order, or debit card sales draft is in error, fictitious, or assigned to another account holder or financial institution.

(b) Any person who violates subsection (a) of this Code section shall be punished by a fine of not more than $5,000.00 or by imprisonment for not less than one year nor more than five years, or both.

§ 16-9-30. Definitions

As used in this article, the term:

(1) "Acquirer" means a business organization, government, financial institution, or an agent of a business organization, government, or financial institution that authorizes a merchant to accept payment by financial transaction card for money, goods, services, or anything else of value.

(2) "Automated banking device" means any machine which when properly activated by a financial transaction card and personal identification code may be used for any of the purposes for which a financial transaction card may be used.

(3) "Cardholder" means the person, government, or organization to whom or for whose benefit the financial transaction card is issued by an issuer.

(4) "Expired financial transaction card" means a financial transaction card which is no longer valid because the term for which it was issued has elapsed.

(5) "Financial transaction card" or "FTC" means any instrument or device, whether known as a credit card, credit plate, bank services card, banking card, check guarantee card, debit card, or by any other name, issued with or without fee by an issuer for the use of the cardholder:

(A) In obtaining money, goods, services, or anything else of value;

(B) In certifying or guaranteeing to a person or business the availability to the cardholder of funds on deposit that are equal to or greater than the amount necessary to honor a draft or check payable to the order of such person or business; or

(C) In providing the cardholder access to a demand deposit account, savings account, or time deposit account for the purpose of:

(i) Making deposits of money or checks therein;

(ii) Withdrawing funds in the form of money, money orders, or traveler's checks therefrom;

(iii) Transferring funds from any demand deposit account, savings account, or time deposit account to any other demand deposit account, savings account, or time deposit account;

(iv) Transferring funds from any demand deposit account, savings account, or time deposit account to any credit card accounts, overdraft privilege accounts, loan accounts, or any other credit accounts in full or partial satisfaction of any outstanding balance owed existing therein;

(v) For the purchase of goods, services, or anything else of value; or

(vi) Obtaining information pertaining to any demand deposit account, savings account, or time deposit account.

(5.1) "Financial transaction card account number" means a number, numerical code, alphabetical code, or alphanumeric code assigned by the issuer to a particular financial transaction card and which identifies the cardholder's account with the issuer.

(5.2) "Government" means:

(A) Every state department, agency, board, bureau, commission, and authority;

(B) Every county, municipal corporation, school system, or other political subdivision of this state;

(C) Every department, agency, board, bureau, commission, authority, or similar body of each such county, municipal corporation, school system, or other political subdivision of this state;

(D) Every city, county, regional, or other authority established pursuant to the laws of this state; and

(E) Every locally elected clerk of superior court, judge of the probate court, sheriff, tax receiver, tax collector, or tax commissioner.

(6) "Issuer" means the business organization or financial institution or its duly authorized agent which issues a financial transaction card.

(7) "Personal identification code" means a numeric or alphabetical code, signature, photograph, fingerprint, or any other means of electronic or mechanical confirmation used by the cardholder of a financial transaction card to permit authorized electronic use of that financial transaction card.

(8) "Presenting" means those actions taken by a cardholder or any person to introduce a financial transaction card into an automated banking device with or without utilization of a personal identification code or merely displaying or showing, with intent to defraud, a financial transaction card to the issuer or to any person or organization providing money, goods, services, or anything else of value or to any other entity.

(8.1) "Purchasing card," "PCard," or "P-Card" means a type of financial transaction card allowing persons, governments, or business organizations to use financial transaction infrastructure.

(9) "Receives" or "receiving" means acquiring possession of or control of or accepting a financial transaction card as security for a loan.

(10) "Revoked financial transaction card" means a financial transaction card which is no longer valid because permission to use it has been suspended or terminated by the issuer.

§ 16-9-31. Financial transaction card theft

(a) A person commits the offense of financial transaction card theft when:

(1) He takes, obtains, or withholds a financial transaction card from the person, possession, custody, or control of another without the cardholder's consent; or who, with knowledge that it has been so taken, obtained, or withheld, receives the financial transaction card with intent to use it or to sell it or to transfer it to a person other than the issuer or the cardholder;

(2) He receives a financial transaction card that he knows to have been lost, mislaid, or delivered under a mistake as to the identity or address of the cardholder and he retains possession with intent to use it or sell it or to transfer it to a person other than the issuer or the cardholder;

(3) He, not being the issuer, sells a financial transaction card or buys a financial transaction card from a person other than the issuer; or

(4) He, not being the issuer, during any 12 month period receives two or more financial transaction cards in the names of persons which he has reason to know were taken or retained under circumstances which constitute a violation of paragraph (3) of subsection (a) of Code Section 16-9-33 and paragraph (3) of this subsection.

(b) Taking, obtaining, or withholding a financial transaction card without consent of the cardholder or issuer is included in conduct defined in Code Section 16-8-2 as the offense of theft by taking.

(c) Conviction of the offense of financial transaction card theft is punishable as provided in subsection (b) of Code Section 16-9-38.

(d) When a person has in his possession or under his control two or more financial transaction cards issued in the names of persons other than members of his immediate family or without the consent of the cardholder, such possession shall be prima-facie evidence that the financial transaction cards have been obtained in violation of subsection (a) of this Code section.

§ 16-9-32. Forgery of financial transaction card

(a) A person commits the offense of financial transaction card forgery when:

(1) With intent to defraud a purported issuer; a person or organization providing money, goods, services, or anything else of value; or any other person, he falsely makes or falsely embosses a purported financial transaction card;

(2) With intent to defraud a purported issuer; a person or organization providing money, goods, services, or anything else of value; or any other person, he falsely encodes, duplicates, or alters existing encoded information on a financial transaction card or utters such a financial transaction card; or

(3) He, not being the cardholder or a person authorized by him, with intent to defraud the issuer; a person or organization providing money, goods, services, or anything else of value; or any other person, signs a financial transaction card.

(b) A person falsely makes a financial transaction card when he makes or draws in whole or in part a device or instrument which purports to be the financial transaction card of a named issuer but which is not such a financial transaction card because the issuer did not authorize the making or drawing or when he alters a financial transaction card which was validly issued.

(c) A person falsely embosses a financial transaction card when without authorization of the named issuer he completes a financial transaction card by adding any of the matter other than the signature of the cardholder, which an issuer requires to appear on the financial transaction card before it can be used by a cardholder.

(d) A person falsely encodes a financial transaction card when without authorization of the purported issuer he records, erases, or otherwise alters magnetically, electronically, electromagnetically, or by any other means whatsoever information on a financial transaction card which will permit acceptance of that card by any automated banking device.

(e) Conviction of the offense of financial transaction card forgery shall be punishable as provided in subsection (b) of Code Section 16-9-38.

(f) When a person other than the purported issuer possesses two or more financial transaction cards which are falsely made, falsely encoded, or falsely embossed, such possession shall be prima-facie evidence that said cards were obtained in violation of paragraph (1) or (2) of subsection (a) of this Code section.

§ 16-9-33. Financial transaction card fraud

(a) A person commits the offense of financial transaction card fraud when, with intent to defraud the issuer; a person or organization providing money, goods, services, or anything else of value; or any other person; or cardholder, such person:

(1) Uses for the purpose of obtaining money, goods, services, or anything else of value:

(A) A financial transaction card obtained or retained or which was received with knowledge that it was obtained or retained in violation of Code Section 16-9-31 or 16-9-32;

(B) A financial transaction card which he or she knows is forged, altered, expired, revoked, or was obtained as a result of a fraudulent application in violation of subsection (d) of this Code section; or

(C) The financial transaction card account number of a financial transaction card which he or she knows has not in fact been issued or is forged, altered, expired, revoked, or was obtained as a result of a fraudulent application in violation of subsection (d) of this Code section;

(2) Obtains money, goods, services, or anything else of value by:

(A) Representing without the consent of the cardholder that he or she is the holder of a specified card;

(B) Presenting the financial transaction card without the authorization or permission of the cardholder or issuer;

(C) Falsely representing that he or she is the holder of a card and such card has not in fact been issued; or

(D) Giving, orally or in writing, a financial transaction card account number to the provider of the money, goods, services, or other thing of value for billing purposes without the authorization or permission of the cardholder or issuer for such use;

(3) Obtains control over a financial transaction card as security for debt;

(4) Deposits into his or her account or any account by means of an automated banking device a false, fictitious, forged, altered, or counterfeit check, draft, money order, or any other such document not his or her lawful or legal property; or

(5) Receives money, goods, services, or anything else of value as a result of a false, fictitious, forged, altered, or counterfeit check, draft, money order, or any other such document having been deposited into an account via an automated banking device, knowing at the time of receipt of the money, goods, services, or item of value that the document so deposited was false, fictitious, forged, altered, or counterfeit or that the above-deposited item was not his lawful or legal property.

(b) A person who is authorized by an issuer to furnish money, goods, services, or anything else of value upon presentation of a financial transaction card by the cardholder or any agent or employee of such person commits the offense of financial transaction card fraud when, with intent to defraud the issuer or the cardholder, he or she:

(1) Furnishes money, goods, services, or anything else of value upon presentation of a financial transaction card obtained or retained in violation of Code Section 16-9-31 or a financial transaction card which he or she knows is forged, expired, or revoked;

(2) Alters a charge ticket or purchase ticket to reflect a larger amount than that approved by the cardholder; or

(3) Fails to furnish money, goods, services, or anything else of value which he or she represents in writing to the issuer that he or she has furnished.

(c) Conviction of the offense of financial transaction card fraud as provided in subsection (a) or (b) of this Code section is punishable as provided in subsection (a) of Code Section 16-9-38 if the value of all money, goods, services, and other things of value furnished in violation of this Code section or if the difference between the value actually furnished and the value represented to the issuer to have been furnished in violation of this Code section does not exceed $100.00 in any six-month period. Conviction of the offense of financial transaction card fraud as provided in subsection (a) or (b) of this Code section is punishable as provided in subsection (b) of Code Section 16-9-38 if such value exceeds $100.00 in any six-month period.

(d) A person commits the offense of financial transaction card fraud when, upon application for a financial transaction card to an issuer, he or she knowingly makes or causes to be made a false statement or report relative to his or her name, occupation, employer, financial condition, assets, or liabilities or willfully and substantially overvalues any assets or willfully omits or substantially undervalues any indebtedness for the purpose of influencing the issuer to issue a financial transaction card. Financial transaction card fraud as provided in this subsection is punishable as provided in subsection (b) of Code Section 16-9-38.

(e) A cardholder commits the offense of financial transaction card fraud when he or she willfully, knowingly, and with an intent to defraud the issuer; a person or organization providing money, goods, services, or anything else of value; or any other person submits verbally or in writing to the issuer or any other person any false notice or report of the theft, loss, disappearance, or nonreceipt of his or her financial transaction card and personal identification code. Conviction of the offense of financial transaction card fraud as provided in this subsection is punishable as provided in subsection (b) of Code Section 16-9-38.

(f) A person authorized by an acquirer to furnish money, goods, services, or anything else of value upon presentation of a financial transaction card or a financial transaction card account number by a cardholder or any agent or employee of such person, who, with intent to defraud the issuer, acquirer, or cardholder, remits to an issuer or acquirer, for payment, a financial transaction card record of a sale, which sale was not made by such person, agent, or employee, commits the offense of financial transaction card fraud. Conviction of the offense of financial transaction card fraud as provided in this subsection shall be punishable as provided in subsection (b) of Code Section 16-9-38.

(g) Reserved.

(h) For purposes of this Code section, revocation shall be construed to include either notice given in person or notice given in writing to the person to whom the financial transaction card and personal identification code was issued. Notice of revocation shall be immediate when notice is given in person. The sending of a notice in writing by registered or certified mail or statutory overnight delivery in the United States mail, duly stamped and addressed to such person at his or her last address known to the issuer, shall be prima-facie evidence that such notice was duly received after seven days from the date of deposit in the mail. If the address is located outside the United States, Puerto Rico, the Virgin Islands, the Canal Zone, and Canada, notice shall be presumed to have been received ten days after mailing by registered or certified mail or statutory overnight delivery.

§ 16-9-34. Criminal possession of financial transaction card forgery devices

(a) A person commits the offense of criminal possession of financial transaction card forgery devices when:

(1) He is a person other than the cardholder and possesses two or more incomplete financial transaction cards with intent to complete them without the consent of the issuer; or

(2) With knowledge of its character, he possesses machinery, plates, or any other contrivance designed to reproduce instruments purporting to be financial transaction cards of an issuer who has not consented to the preparation of such financial transaction cards.

(b) A financial transaction card is incomplete if part of the matter, other than the signature of the cardholder, which an issuer requires to appear on the financial transaction card before it can be used by a cardholder has not yet been stamped, embossed, imprinted, encoded, or written upon.

(c) Conviction of the offense of criminal possession of financial transaction card forgery devices is punishable as provided in subsection (b) of Code Section 16-9-38.

§ 16-9-35. Criminal receipt of goods and services fraudulently obtained

A person commits the offense of criminally receiving goods and services fraudulently obtained when he receives money, goods, services, or anything else of value obtained in violation of subsection (a) of Code Section 16-9-33 with the knowledge or belief that the same were obtained in violation of subsection (a) of Code Section 16-9-33. Conviction of the offense of criminal receipt of goods and services fraudulently obtained is punishable as provided in subsection (a) of Code Section 16-9-38 if the value of all money, goods, services, and anything else of value obtained in violation of this Code section does not exceed $100.00 in any six-month period. Conviction of the offense of criminal receipt of goods and services fraudulently obtained is punishable as provided in subsection (b) of Code Section 16-9-38 if such value exceeds $100.00 in any six-month period.

§ 16-9-36. Rebuttable presumption of criminal receipt of goods and services fraudulently obtained

A person who obtains at a discount price a ticket issued by an airline, railroad, steamship, or other transportation company from other than an authorized agent of such company, which ticket was acquired in violation of subsection (a) of Code Section 16-9-33 without reasonable inquiry to ascertain that the person from whom it was obtained had a legal right to possess it shall be rebuttably presumed to know that such ticket was acquired under circumstances constituting a violation of subsection (a) of Code Section 16-9-33 if the ticket shows on its face that it was issued through the use of a financial transaction card or that it is otherwise nonrefundable.

§ 16-9-36.1. Criminal factoring of financial transaction card records

Any person who, without the acquirer's express authorization, employs or solicits an authorized merchant or any agent or employee of such merchant to remit to an issuer or acquirer, for payment, a financial transaction card record of a sale, which sale was not made by such merchant, agent, or employee, commits the offense of criminal factoring of financial transaction card records. Conviction of criminal factoring of financial transaction card records shall be punishable as provided in subsection (b) of Code Section 16-9-38.

§ 16-9-37. Unauthorized use of financial transaction card; misuse of government issued cards

(a) Any person who has been issued or entrusted with a financial transaction card for specifically authorized purposes, provided such authorization is in writing stating a maximum amount charges that can be made with the financial transaction card, and who uses the financial transaction card in a manner and for purposes not authorized in order to obtain or purchase money, goods, services, or anything else of value shall be punished as provided in subsection (a) of Code Section 16-9-38.
(b) Any person who has been issued or entrusted with a financial transaction card by a government for specifically limited and specifically authorized purposes, provided such limitations and authorizations are in writing, and who uses the financial transaction card in a manner and for purposes not authorized shall be punished as provided in subsection (b) of Code Section 16-9-38.

§ 16-9-38. Punishment and penalties

(a) A person who is subject to the punishment and penalties of this subsection shall be fined not more than $1,000.00 or imprisoned not less than one year nor more than two years, or both.
(b) A person subject to punishment under this subsection shall be guilty of a felony and shall be punished by a fine of not more than $5,000.00 or imprisonment for not less than one year nor · more than three years, or both.

§ 16-9-39. Publication of information regarding schemes, devices, means, or methods for financial transaction card fraud or theft of telecommunication services

(a) As used in this Code section, "publish" means the communication or dissemination of information to any one or more persons either orally, in person, by telephone, radio or television, or in a writing of any kind, including without limitation a letter, memorandum, circular, handbill, newspaper or magazine article, or book.
(b) A person who publishes the number or code of any existing, canceled, revoked, or nonexistent telephone number, credit number, or other credit device, or method of numbering or coding which is employed in the issuance of telephone numbers, credit numbers, or other credit devices with knowledge or reason to believe that it may be used to avoid the payment of any lawful telephone or telegraph toll charge under circumstances evidencing an intent to have such telephone number, credit number, credit device, or method of numbering or coding so used shall be punished as provided in subsection (a) of Code Section 16-9-38.
(c) An offense under this Code section may be deemed to have been committed at either the place at which the publication was initiated, at which publication was received, or at which the information so published was utilized to avoid or attempt to avoid payment of any lawful telephone or telegraph charge.

§ 16-9-40. Venue determinations

(a) In any prosecution for a violation of this article, the state is not required to establish that all of the acts constituting the crime occurred in this state or within one city, county, or local jurisdiction, and it is no defense that some of the acts constituting the crime did not occur in this state or within one city, county, or local jurisdiction. Except as otherwise provided by Code Section 17-2-2, for purposes of venue, the crime defined by this Code section shall be considered as having been committed in the county where the commission of the crime commenced.
(b) In any prosecution for a violation of this article by a public official or government employee, using government funds or a financial transaction card issued to such official or government employee by or on behalf of government, the crime shall be considered to have been committed in the county in which such public official holds office or such government employee is employed.

§ 16-9-50. Deceptive business practices

(a) A person commits the offense of using a deceptive business practice when in the regular course of business he knowingly:
(1) Uses or possesses for use a false weight or measure or any other device for falsely determining or recording any quality or quantity;
(2) Sells, offers, or exposes for sale or delivers less than the represented quality or quantity of any commodity; or
(3) Takes or attempts to take more than the represented quantity of any commodity when as buyer he furnishes the weight or measure.
(b) Any person who commits the offense of using a deceptive business practice shall be guilty of a misdemeanor.

§ 16-9-51. Destruction, removal, concealment, encumbrance, or transfer of property subject to security interest

(a) Except as provided in subsection (b) of this Code section, a person who destroys, removes, conceals, encumbers, transfers, or otherwise deals with property subject to a security interest with intent to hinder enforcement of that interest shall be guilty of a misdemeanor.
(b) A person who destroys, removes, conceals, encumbers, transfers, or otherwise deals with property subject to a security interest with intent to hinder enforcement of that security interest and in so doing does damage to such property in an amount greater than $500.00 shall be guilty of a misdemeanor of a high and aggravated nature.
(c) In a prosecution under this Code section the crime shall be considered as having been committed in any county where any act in furtherance of the criminal scheme was done or caused to be done.

§ 16-9-52. Improper solicitation of money

(a) A person commits the offense of improper solicitation of money when he solicits payment of money by another by means of a statement or invoice or any writing that could reasonably be interpreted as a statement or invoice for goods not yet ordered or for services not yet performed and not yet ordered, unless there appears on the face of the statement or invoice or writing in 30 point boldface type the following warning:
"This is a solicitation for the order of goods or services and you are under no obligation to make payment unless you accept the offer contained herein."
(b) Any person who violates subsection (a) of this Code section shall be guilty of a misdemeanor.
(c) In addition to other remedies, any person damaged by noncompliance with subsection (a) of this Code section is entitled to damages in the amount equal to three times the sum solicited.

§ 16-9-53. Damaging, destroying, or secreting property to defraud another

(a) A person commits the offense of damaging, destroying, or secreting property to defraud another person when he knowingly and with intent to defraud another person damages, destroys, or secretes any property of whatever class or character, whether the property of himself or of another person.

(b) A person convicted of the offense of damaging, destroying, or secreting property to defraud another person shall be punished by imprisonment for not less than one nor more than five years.

§ 16-9-54. False statements by telephone solicitors

(a) In making a telephone solicitation for the purpose of the sale of goods or services or for the purpose of seeking charitable contributions, it shall be unlawful for any person to make false statements regarding the purpose of the solicitation, the person or persons represented by the solicitor, or the person or persons benefiting from the solicitation.

(b) Any person who violates subsection (a) of this Code section shall be guilty of a misdemeanor.

§ 16-9-55. Fraudulently obtaining or attempting to obtain public housing or reduction in public housing rent

(a) Any person who obtains or attempts to obtain or who establishes or attempts to establish eligibility for, and any person who knowingly or intentionally aids or abets such person in obtaining or attempting to obtain or in establishing or attempting to establish eligibility for, any public housing or a reduction in public housing rental charges or any rent subsidy or payment from a tenant in connection with public housing to which such person would not otherwise be entitled, by means of a false statement, failure to disclose information, impersonation, or other fraudulent scheme or device shall be guilty of a misdemeanor.

(b) As used in this Code section, "public housing" means housing which is constructed, operated, maintained, financed, or subsidized by the state, a county, a municipal corporation, the Georgia Housing and Finance Authority, a housing authority, or by any other political subdivision or public corporation of the state or its subdivisions.

(c) Notice of subsection (a) of this Code section shall be printed on the application form for public housing and shall be displayed in the office where such application is made.

§ 16-9-56. Fraudulent attempts to obtain refunds

(a) It shall be unlawful for any person to give a false or fictitious name, address, or telephone number as that person's own or to give the name, address, or telephone number of any other person without that other person's knowledge and approval for the purpose of obtaining or attempting to obtain a refund for merchandise returned to a business establishment or a refund on a ticket or other document which is evidence of a service purchased from a business establishment, which service is yet to be performed.

(b) Any person who violates this Code section shall be guilty of a misdemeanor.

§ 16-9-57. False representation as representative of peace officer organization or fire service organization

(a) It shall be unlawful for any person to solicit or accept a fee, consideration, or donation or to offer for sale or to sell advertising as a representative of a peace officer organization or fire service organization or under the guise of representing a peace officer organization or fire service organization unless such person is employed by, is acting pursuant to the authority of, or is a member of such organization.

(b) As used in this Code section, the term:

(1) "Fire service" shall include any person duly elected, appointed, or employed to engage in fire fighting.

(2) "Peace officer" shall include any person duly elected, appointed, or employed to engage in public law enforcement work.

(c) Any person, firm, association, or corporation violating subsection (a) of this Code section shall be guilty of a misdemeanor and, upon conviction thereof, shall be punished by a fine of not more than $500.00 or by imprisonment for not more than 30 days, or both.

(d) Any person, firm, association, or corporation violating subsection (a) of this Code section through the use of some form of communication across the boundaries of the state, whether such communication is by mail, by the use of any electronic device including but not limited to the use of a telephone or telegraph, or by any other means, shall be guilty of a felony and, upon conviction thereof, shall be punished by imprisonment for not less than one year nor more than three years or by a fine of not less than $1,000.00 nor more than $5,000.00, or both.

§ 16-9-58. Failing to pay for natural products or chattels

Any person, either on his or her own account or for others, who with fraudulent intent shall buy cotton, corn, rice, crude turpentine, spirits of turpentine, rosin, pitch, tar, timber, pulpwood, Christmas trees, pine needles, horticultural crops, poultry and poultry products, cattle, hogs, sheep, goats, ratites, horses, mules, pecans, peaches, apples, watermelons, cantaloupes, or other products or chattels and fail or refuse to pay therefor within 20 days following receipt of such products or chattels or by such other payment due date explicitly stated in a written contract agreed to by the buyer and seller, whichever is later, shall be guilty of a misdemeanor; except that if the value of the products or chattels exceeded $500.00 such person shall be guilty of a felony and, upon conviction thereof, shall be imprisoned for not less than one year nor more than five years.

§ 16-9-59. Operation of credit repair services organization

(a) As used in this Code section, the term:

(1) "Buyer" means any individual who is solicited to purchase or who purchases the services of a credit repair services organization.

(2)(A) "Credit repair services organization" means any person who, with respect to the extension of credit to a buyer by others, sells, provides, or performs, or represents that he can or will sell, provide, or perform, in return for the payment of money or other valuable consideration any of the following services:

(i) Improving a buyer's credit record, history, or rating;

(ii) Obtaining an extension of credit for a buyer;

(iii) Providing advice or assistance to a buyer with regard to either division (i) or (ii) of this subparagraph.

(B) "Credit repair services organization" does not include:

(i) Any person authorized to make loans or extensions of credit under the laws of this state or the United States who is subject to regulation and supervision by this state or the United States;

(ii) Any bank or savings and loan institution whose deposits or accounts are eligible for insurance by the Federal Deposit Insurance Corporation or the Savings Association Insurance Fund of the Federal Deposit Insurance Corporation;

(iii) Any nonprofit organization exempt from taxation under Section 501(c)(3) of the Internal Revenue Code of 1986;

(iv) Any person licensed as a real estate broker by this state if the person is acting within the course and scope of that license;

(v) Any person licensed to practice law in this state if the person renders services within the course and scope of his or her practice as an attorney;

(vi) Any broker-dealer registered with the Securities and Exchange Commission or the Commodity Futures Trading Commission if the broker-dealer is acting within the course and scope of those regulatory agencies; or

(vii) Any consumer reporting agency as defined in the federal Fair Credit Reporting Act (15 U.S.C. 1681-1681t).

(3) "Extension of credit" means the right to defer payment of debt or to incur debt and defer its payment, offered or granted primarily for personal, family, or household purposes.

(b) A person commits the offense of operating a credit repair services organization when he or she owns, operates, or is affiliated with a credit repair services organization.

(c) Any person who commits the offense of operating a credit repair services organization shall be guilty of a misdemeanor.

§ 16-9-60. "Foreclosure fraud" construed; penalty

(a) For purposes of this Code section, the term "foreclosure fraud" shall include any of the following: knowingly or willfully representing that moneys provided to or on behalf of a debtor, as defined in Code Section 44-14-162.1 in connection with property used as a dwelling place by said debtor, are a loan if in fact they are used to purchase said property or such debtor's interest therein; or knowingly or willfully making fraudulent representation to a debtor about assisting the debtor in connection with said property.

(b) Any person who by foreclosure fraud purchases or attempts to purchase residential property by means of such fraudulent scheme shall be guilty of a felony.

(c) A person who violates subsection (b) of this Code section shall be punished by imprisonment for not less than one year nor more than three years or by a fine of not less than $1,000.00 nor more than $5,000.00, or both.

§ 16-9-61. Misrepresenting the origin or ownership of timber or agricultural commodities

(a) A person commits the crime of misrepresenting the origin or ownership of timber or agricultural commodities when, in the course of a sale, attempted sale, delivery, or other completed or attempted transaction regarding timber or agricultural commodities, he or she knowingly, willfully, and with criminal intent to defraud makes a false statement or knowingly, willfully, and with criminal intent to defraud causes a false statement to be made with regard to any specific ownership of the timber or agricultural commodities or with regard to the location or ownership of the land where the timber was cut or the agricultural commodities were harvested.

(b) Misrepresenting the origin of timber or agricultural commodities shall be punished, upon conviction, as for a misdemeanor; except that if the property which was the subject of the misrepresentation exceeded $500.00 in value, it shall be a felony offense punishable upon conviction by a sentence of imprisonment of not less than one year and not exceeding five years.

§ 16-9-62. Crimes utilizing automated sales suppression devices, zapper, or phantom-ware; penalties

(a) As used in this Code section, the term:

(1) "Automated sales suppression device" or "zapper" means a software program, carried on a memory stick or removable compact disc, accessed through an Internet link, or accessed through any other means, that falsifies the electronic records of electronic cash registers and other point-of-sale systems, including, but not limited to, transaction data and transaction reports.

(2) "Electronic cash register" means a device that keeps a register or supporting documents through the means of an electronic device or computer system designed to record transaction data for the purpose of computing, compiling, or processing retail sales transaction data in whatever manner.

(3) "Phantom-ware" means a hidden, preinstalled, or installed at a later time programming option embedded in the operating system of an electronic cash register or hardwired into the electronic cash register that can be used to create a virtual second till or may eliminate or manipulate transaction records that may or may not be preserved in digital formats to represent the true or manipulated record of transactions in the electronic cash register.

(4) "Transaction data" includes items purchased by a customer, the price for each item, a taxability determination for each item, a segregated tax amount for each of the taxed items, the amount of cash or credit tendered, the net amount returned to the customer in change, the date and time of the purchase, the name, address, and identification number of the vendor, and the receipt or invoice number of the transaction.

(5) "Transaction reports" means a report documenting, but not limited to, the sales, taxes collected, media totals, and discount voids at an electronic cash register that is printed on cash register tape at the end of a day or shift, or a report documenting every action at an electronic cash register that is stored electronically.

(b) It shall be unlawful to willfully and knowingly sell, purchase, install, transfer, or possess in this state any automated sales suppression device or zapper or phantom-ware.

(c) Any person convicted of a violation of subsection (b) of this Code section shall be guilty of a felony and shall be punished by imprisonment of not less than one nor more than five years, a fine not to exceed $100,000.00, or both.

(d) Any person violating subsection (b) of this Code section shall be liable for all taxes and penalties due the state as the result of the fraudulent use of an automated sales suppression device or phantom-ware and shall disgorge all profits associated with the sale or use of an automated sales suppression device or phantom-ware.

(e) An automated sales suppression device or phantom-ware and any device containing such device or software shall be contraband.

§ 16-9-63. False representation as veteran

(a) As used in this Code section, the term:

(1) "Armed forces of the United States" means the army, navy, air force, marine corps, or coast guard and the reserve components thereof and the uniformed components of the Public Health Service or the National Oceanic and Atmospheric Administration.

(2) "Military decoration" means:

(A) A medal, decoration, badge, or ribbon authorized by law, executive order, or regulation to be awarded to a member of the armed forces of the United States by the President of the United States, Congress, the United States Department of Defense, or the United States Department of Homeland Security;

(B) A medal, decoration, badge, or ribbon authorized by law, executive order, or regulation to be awarded to members of the organized militia; or

(C) A rosette or metal lapel button depicting a medal, decoration, badge, or ribbon described in subparagraph (A) or (B) of this paragraph which is authorized by law, executive order, or regulation to be worn on civilian clothing.

(3) "Military medal award" shall have the same meaning as provided for under Code Section 40-2-85.1.

(4) "Military veteran" means a current, former, or retired member of the armed forces of the United States, the organized militia, or a state military force of another state.

(5) "Organized militia" means the Army National Guard, the Air National Guard, the Georgia Naval Militia, and the State Defense Force.

(6) "Tangible benefit" means:

(A) A benefit, preference, service, or other thing of value offered to a military veteran which is enhanced or offered at a reduced rate or free of charge by an agency of this state, or any political subdivision or authority thereof, based on such military veteran's service or the award of a military decoration;

(B) Employment or promotion in an individual's employment; or

(C) Election to public office.

(b) It shall be unlawful for any individual, with the intent to secure a tangible benefit for himself or herself, to make a false, fictitious, or fraudulent statement or representation that such individual is a military veteran or recipient of a military decoration.

(c) It shall be unlawful for any individual, with the intent to deceive, to appear in a court of this state while wearing:

(1) The uniform of the armed forces of the United States or of the organized militia of this state if such individual is not authorized to wear such uniform; or

(2) Any military decoration which such individual has not, in fact, been awarded.

(d) Any person who violates this Code section shall be guilty of a misdemeanor; provided, however, that if such violation involves a military medal award, such person shall be guilty of a misdemeanor of a high and aggravated nature.

(e) Any violation of this Code section shall be considered a separate offense and shall not merge with any other offense. If an individual is convicted of a violation of Code Section 16-10-20 and this Code section arising out of the same incident, any penalty imposed for a violation of this Code section shall be served consecutively to any sentence that may be imposed for a violation of Code Section 16-10-20.

§ 16-9-70. Criminal use of an article with an altered identification mark

(a) A person commits the offense of criminal use of an article with an altered identification mark when he or she buys, sells, receives, disposes of, conceals, or has in his or her possession a radio, piano, phonograph, sewing machine, washing machine, typewriter, adding machine, comptometer, bicycle, firearm, safe, vacuum cleaner, dictaphone, watch, watch movement, watch case, or any other mechanical or electrical device, appliance, contrivance, material, vessel as defined in Code Section 52-7-3, or other piece of apparatus or equipment, other than a motor vehicle as defined in Code Section 40-1-1, from which he or she knows the manufacturer's name plate, serial number, or any other distinguishing number or identification mark has been removed for the purpose of concealing or destroying the identity of such article.

(b) A person convicted of the offense of criminal use of an article with an altered identification mark shall be punished by imprisonment for not less than one nor more than five years.

(c) This Code section does not apply to those cases or instances where any of the changes or alterations enumerated in subsection (a) of this Code section have been customarily made or done as an established practice in the ordinary and regular conduct of business by the original manufacturer or by his duly appointed direct representative or under specific authorization from the original manufacturer.

§ 16-9-71. Removal of collars or identifying items or marks on animals

(a) It shall be unlawful for any person without the express permission of the owner or lessee of an animal to remove a collar, tag, tattoo, or any identification mark artificially attached to or imprinted on an animal for the purposes of identification which causes or is likely to cause the loss of the animal to the owner thereof.

(b) Any person who violates subsection (a) of this Code section shall be guilty of a misdemeanor.

§ 16-9-90. Short title

This article shall be known and may be cited as the "Georgia Computer Systems Protection Act."

§ 16-9-91. Legislative findings

The General Assembly finds that:

(1) Computer related crime is a growing problem in the government and in the private sector;

(2) Such crime occurs at great cost to the public, since losses for each incident of computer crime tend to be far greater than the losses associated with each incident of other white collar crime;

(3) The opportunities for computer related crimes in state programs, and in other entities which operate within the state, through the introduction of fraudulent records into a computer system, unauthorized use of computer facilities, alteration or destruction of computerized information files, and stealing of financial instruments, data, or other assets are great;

(4) Computer related crime operations have a direct effect on state commerce;

(5) Liability for computer crimes should be imposed on all persons, as that term is defined in this title; and

(6) The prosecution of persons engaged in computer related crime is difficult under previously existing Georgia criminal statutes.

§ 16-9-92. Definitions

As used in this article, the term:

(1) "Computer" means an electronic, magnetic, optical, hydraulic, electrochemical, or organic device or group of devices which, pursuant to a computer program, to human instruction, or to permanent instructions contained in the device or group of devices, can automatically perform computer operations with or on computer data and can communicate the results to another computer or to a person. The term includes any connected or directly related device, equipment, or facility which enables the computer to store, retrieve, or communicate computer programs, computer data, or the results of computer operations to or from a person, another computer, or another device. This term specifically includes, but is not limited to, mail servers and e-mail networks. This term does not include a device that is not used to communicate with or to manipulate any other computer.

(2) "Computer network" means a set of related, remotely connected computers and any communications facilities with the function and purpose of transmitting data among them through the communications facilities.

(3) "Computer operation" means computing, classifying, transmitting, receiving, retrieving, originating, switching, storing, displaying, manifesting, measuring, detecting, recording, reproducing, handling, or utilizing any form of data for business, scientific, control, or other purposes.

(4) "Computer program" means one or more statements or instructions composed and structured in a form acceptable to a computer that, when executed by a computer in actual or modified form, cause the computer to perform one or more computer operations. The term "computer program" shall include all associated procedures and documentation, whether or not such procedures and documentation are in human readable form.

(5) "Data" includes any representation of information, intelligence, or data in any fixed medium, including documentation, computer printouts, magnetic storage media, punched cards, storage in a computer, or transmission by a computer network.

(6) "Electronic communication" means any transfer of signs, signals, writing, images, sounds, data, or intelligence of any nature transmitted in whole or in part by a wire, radio, electromagnetic, photoelectronic, or photo-optical system that affects interstate or foreign commerce, but does not include:

(A) Any wire or oral communication;

(B) Any communication made through a tone-only paging device;

(C) Any communication from a tracking device; or

(D) Electronic funds transfer information stored by a financial institution in a communications system used for the electronic storage and transfer of funds.

(7) "Electronic communication service" means any service which provides to its users the ability to send or receive wire or electronic communications.

(8) "Electronic communications system" means any wire, radio, electromagnetic, photoelectronic, photo-optical, or facilities for the transmission of wire or electronic communications, and any computer facilities or related electronic equipment for the electronic storage of such communications.

(9) "Electronic means" is any device or apparatus which can be used to intercept a wire, oral, or electronic communication other than:

(A) Any telephone or telegraph instrument, equipment, or facility, or any component thereof,

(i) Furnished to the subscriber or user by a provider of electronic communication service in the ordinary course of its business and used by the subscriber or user in the ordinary course of its business or furnished by such subscriber or user for connection to the facilities of such service and used in the ordinary course of its business; or

(ii) Used by a provider of electronic communication service in the ordinary course of its business or by an investigative or law enforcement officer in the ordinary course of his or her duties; or

(B) A hearing aid or similar device being used to correct subnormal hearing to better than normal.

(10) "Electronic storage" means:

(A) Any temporary, intermediate storage of wire or electronic communication incidental to its electronic transmission; and

(B) Any storage of such communication by an electronic communication service for purposes of backup protection of such communication.

(11) "Financial instruments" includes any check, draft, money order, note, certificate of deposit, letter of credit, bill of exchange, credit or debit card, transaction-authorizing mechanism, or marketable security, or any computer representation thereof.

(12) "Law enforcement unit" means any law enforcement officer charged with the duty of enforcing the criminal laws and ordinances of the state or of the counties or municipalities of the state who is employed by and compensated by the state or any county or municipality of the state or who is elected and compensated on a fee basis. The term shall include, but not be limited to, members of the Department of Public Safety, municipal police, county police, sheriffs, deputy sheriffs, and agents and investigators of the Georgia Bureau of Investigation.

(13) "Property" includes computers, computer networks, computer programs, data, financial instruments, and services.

(14) "Remote computing service" means the provision to the public of computer storage or processing services by means of an electronic communications system.

(15) "Services" includes computer time or services or data processing services.

(16) "Use" includes causing or attempting to cause:

(A) A computer or computer network to perform or to stop performing computer operations;

(B) The obstruction, interruption, malfunction, or denial of the use of a computer, computer network, computer program, or data; or

(C) A person to put false information into a computer.

(17) "Victim expenditure" means any expenditure reasonably and necessarily incurred by the owner to verify that a computer, computer network, computer program, or data was or was not altered, deleted, damaged, or destroyed by unauthorized use.

(18) "Without authority" includes the use of a computer or computer network in a manner that exceeds any right or permission granted by the owner of the computer or computer network.

§ 16-9-93. Computer crimes defined; exclusivity of article; civil remedies; criminal penalties

(a) Computer theft. Any person who uses a computer or computer network with knowledge that such use is without authority and with the intention of:
(1) Taking or appropriating any property of another, whether or not with the intention of depriving the owner of possession;
(2) Obtaining property by any deceitful means or artful practice; or
(3) Converting property to such person's use in violation of an agreement or other known legal obligation to make a specified application or disposition of such property
shall be guilty of the crime of computer theft.
(b) Computer Trespass. Any person who uses a computer or computer network with knowledge that such use is without authority and with the intention of:
(1) Deleting or in any way removing, either temporarily or permanently, any computer program or data from a computer or computer network;
(2) Obstructing, interrupting, or in any way interfering with the use of a computer program or data; or
(3) Altering, damaging, or in any way causing the malfunction of a computer, computer network, or computer program, regardless of how long the alteration, damage, or malfunction persists
shall be guilty of the crime of computer trespass.
(c) Computer Invasion of Privacy. Any person who uses a computer or computer network with the intention of examining any employment, medical, salary, credit, or any other financial or personal data relating to any other person with knowledge that such examination is without authority shall be guilty of the crime of computer invasion of privacy.
(d) Computer Forgery. Any person who creates, alters, or deletes any data contained in any computer or computer network, who, if such person had created, altered, or deleted a tangible document or instrument would have committed forgery under Article 1 of this chapter, shall be guilty of the crime of computer forgery. The absence of a tangible writing directly created or altered by the offender shall not be a defense to the crime of computer forgery if a creation, alteration, or deletion of data was involved in lieu of a tangible document or instrument.
(e) Computer Password Disclosure. Any person who discloses a number, code, password, or other means of access to a computer or computer network knowing that such disclosure is without authority and which results in damages (including the fair market value of any services used and victim expenditure) to the owner of the computer or computer network in excess of $500.00 shall be guilty of the crime of computer password disclosure.
(f) Article not Exclusive. The provisions of this article shall not be construed to preclude the applicability of any other law which presently applies or may in the future apply to any transaction or course of conduct which violates this article.
(g) Civil Relief; Damages.
(1) Any person whose property or person is injured by reason of a violation of any provision of this article may sue therefor and recover for any damages sustained and the costs of suit. Without limiting the generality of the term, "damages" shall include loss of profits and victim expenditure.
(2) At the request of any party to an action brought pursuant to this Code section, the court shall by reasonable means conduct all legal proceedings in such a way as to protect the secrecy and security of any computer, computer network, data, or computer program involved in order to prevent possible recurrence of the same or a similar act by another person and to protect any trade secrets of any party.
(3) The provisions of this article shall not be construed to limit any person's right to pursue any additional civil remedy otherwise allowed by law.
(4) A civil action under this Code section must be brought within four years after the violation is discovered or by exercise of reasonable diligence should have been discovered. For purposes of this article, a continuing violation of any one subsection of this Code section by any person constitutes a single violation by such person.
(h) Criminal Penalties.
(1) Any person convicted of the crime of computer theft, computer trespass, computer invasion of privacy, or computer forgery shall be fined not more than $50,000.00 or imprisoned not more than 15 years, or both.
(2) Any person convicted of computer password disclosure shall be fined not more than $5,000.00 or incarcerated for a period not to exceed one year, or both.

§ 16-9-93.1. Misleading transmittal and use of individual name, trade name, registered trademark, logo, legal or official seal, or copyrighted symbol over computer or telephone network; criminal penalty; civil remedies

(a) It shall be unlawful for any person, any organization, or any representative of any organization knowingly to transmit any data through a computer network or over the transmission facilities or through the network facilities of a local telephone network for the purpose of setting up, maintaining, operating, or exchanging data with an electronic mailbox, home page, or any other electronic information storage bank or point of access to electronic information if such data uses any individual name, trade name, registered trademark, logo, legal or official seal, or copyrighted symbol to falsely identify the person, organization, or representative transmitting such data or which would falsely state or imply that such person, organization, or representative has permission or is legally authorized to use such trade name, registered trademark, logo, legal or official seal, or copyrighted symbol for such purpose when such permission or authorization has not been obtained; provided, however, that no telecommunications company or Internet access provider shall violate this Code section solely as a result of carrying or transmitting such data for its customers.
(b) Any person violating subsection (a) of this Code section shall be guilty of a misdemeanor.
(c) Nothing in this Code section shall be construed to limit an aggrieved party's right to pursue a civil action for equitable or monetary relief, or both, for actions which violate this Code section.

§ 16-9-94. Venue

For the purpose of venue under this article, any violation of this article shall be considered to have been committed:
(1) In the county of the principal place of business in this state of the owner of a computer, computer network, or any part thereof;
(2) In any county in which any person alleged to have violated any provision of this article had control or possession of any proceeds of the violation or of any books, records, documents, or property which were used in furtherance of the violation;
(3) In any county in which any act was performed in furtherance of any transaction which violated this article; and
(4) In any county from which, to which, or through which any use of a computer or computer network was made, whether by wires, electromagnetic waves, microwaves, or any other means of communication.

§ 16-9-100. Definitions

As used in this part, the term:
(1) "Advertiser" means a person or entity that advertises through the use of commercial e-mail.
(2) "Automatic technical process" means the actions performed by an e-mail service provider's or telecommunications carrier's computers or computer network while acting as an intermediary between the sender and the recipient of an e-mail.
(3) "Commercial e-mail" means any e-mail message initiated for the purpose of advertising or promoting the lease, sale, rental, gift, offer, or other disposition of any property, services, or extension of credit.
(4) "Direct consent" means that the recipient has expressly consented to receive e-mail advertisements from the advertiser or initiator, either in response to a clear and conspicuous request for direct consent or at the recipient's own initiative.
(5) "Domain" means any alphanumeric designation which is registered with or assigned by any domain name registrar, domain name registry, or other domain name registration authority as part of an electronic address on the Internet.
(6) "Domain owner" means, in relation to an e-mail address, the actual owner at the time an e-mail is received at that address of a domain that appears in or comprises a portion of the e-mail address. The registrant of a domain is presumed to be the actual owner of that domain.

(7) "E-mail" means an electronic message that is sent to an e-mail address and transmitted between two or more telecommunications devices, computers, or electronic devices capable of receiving electronic messages, whether or not the message is converted to hard copy format after receipt, viewed upon transmission, or stored for later retrieval. The term includes electronic messages that are transmitted through a local, regional, or global computer network.

(8) "E-mail address" means a destination, commonly expressed as a string of characters, to which e-mail can be sent or delivered. An e-mail address consists of a user name or mailbox, the "@" symbol, and reference to a domain.

(9) "E-mail service provider" means any person, including an Internet service provider, that is an intermediary in sending or receiving e-mail or that provides to end-users of the e-mail service the ability to send or receive e-mail.

(10) "False or misleading," when used in relation to a commercial e-mail, means that:

(A) The header information includes an originating or intermediate e-mail address, domain name, or Internet protocol address which was obtained by means of false or fraudulent pretenses or representations;

(B) The header information fails to accurately identify the computer used to initiate the e-mail;

(C) The subject line of the e-mail is intended to mislead a recipient about a material fact regarding the content or subject matter of the e-mail;

(D) The header information is altered or modified in a manner that impedes or precludes the recipient of the e-mail or an e-mail service provider from identifying, locating, or contacting the person who initiated the e-mail;

(E) The header information or content of the commercial e-mail, without authorization and with intent to mislead, references a personal name, entity name, trade name, mark, domain, address, phone number, or other personally identifying information belonging to a third party in such manner as would cause a recipient to believe that the third party authorized, endorsed, sponsored, sent, or was otherwise involved in the transmission of the commercial e-mail;

(F) The header information or content of the commercial e-mail contains false or fraudulent information regarding the identity, location, or means of contacting the initiator of the commercial e-mail; or

(G) The commercial e-mail falsely or erroneously states or represents that the transmission of the e-mail was authorized on the basis of:

(i) The recipient's prior direct consent to receive the commercial e-mail; or

(ii) A preexisting or current business relationship between the recipient and either the initiator or advertiser.

(11) "Header information" means those portions of an e-mail message which designate or otherwise identify:

(A) The sender;

(B) All recipients;

(C) An alternative return e-mail address, if any; and

(D) The names or Internet protocol addresses of the computers, systems, or other means used to send, transmit, route, or receive the e-mail message.

The term does not include either the subject line or the content of an e-mail message.

(12) "Incident" means the contemporaneous initiation in violation of this part of one or more commercial e-mails containing substantially similar content.

(13) "Initiate" or "initiator" means to transmit or cause to be transmitted a commercial e-mail, but does not include the routine transmission of the commercial e-mail through the network or system of a telecommunications utility or an e-mail service provider.

(14) "Internet protocol address" means the unique numerical address assigned to and used to identify a specific computer or computer network that is directly connected to the Internet.

(15) "Minor" means any person under the age of 18 years.

(16) "Person" means a person as defined by Code Section 16-1-3 and specifically includes any limited liability company, trust, joint venture, or other legally cognizable entity.

(17) "Preexisting or current business relationship," as used in connection with the sending of a commercial e-mail, means that the recipient has made an inquiry and has provided his or her e-mail address, or has made an application, purchase, or transaction, with or without consideration, regarding products or services offered by the advertiser.

(18) "Protected computer" means any computer that, at the time of an alleged violation of any provision of this part involving that computer, was located within the geographic boundaries of the State of Georgia.

(19) "Recipient" means any addressee of a commercial e-mail advertisement. If an addressee of a commercial e-mail has one or more e-mail addresses to which a commercial e-mail is sent, the addressee shall be deemed to be a separate recipient for each e-mail address to which the e-mail is sent.

(20) "Routine transmission" means the forwarding, routing, relaying, handling, or storing of an e-mail message through an automatic technical process. The term shall not include the sending, or the knowing participation in the sending, of commercial e-mail advertisements.

§ 16-9-101. Initiation of deceptive commercial e-mail

Any person who initiates a commercial e-mail that the person knew or should have known to be false or misleading that is sent from, passes through, or is received by a protected computer shall be guilty of the crime of initiation of deceptive commercial e-mail.

§ 16-9-102. Penalties

(a) Any person convicted of a violation of Code Section 16-9-101 shall be guilty of a misdemeanor and punished by a fine of not more than $1,000.00 or by imprisonment of not more than 12 months, or both, except:

(1) Where the volume of commercial e-mail transmitted exceeded 10,000 attempted recipients in any 24 hour period;

(2) Where the volume of commercial e-mail transmitted exceeded 100,000 attempted recipients in any 30 day period;

(3) Where the volume of commercial e-mail transmitted exceeded one million attempted recipients in any one-year period;

(4) Where the revenue generated from a specific commercial e-mail exceeded $1,000.00;

(5) Where the total revenue generated from all commercial e-mail transmitted to any e-mail service provider or its subscribers exceeded $50,000.00; or

(6) Where any person knowingly hires, employs, uses, or permits any minor to assist in the transmission of commercial e-mail in violation of Code Section 16-9-101,

the person shall be guilty of a felony and punished by a fine of not more than $50,000.00 or by imprisonment of not more than five years, or both.

(b) For the second conviction of Code Section 16-9-101 within a five-year period, as measured from the dates of previous arrests for which convictions were obtained to the date of the current arrest for which a conviction is obtained, the person shall be guilty of a felony and punished by a fine of not more than $50,000.00 or by imprisonment of not more than five years, or both. For the purpose of this subsection, the term "conviction" shall include a plea of nolo contendere.

§ 16-9-103. Venue

For the purpose of venue under this part, any violation of this part shall be considered to have been committed:

(1) In the county of the principal place of business in this state of the owner of an involved protected computer, computer network, or any part thereof;

(2) In any county in which any person alleged to have violated any provision of this part had control or possession of any proceeds of the violation or of any books, records, documents, or property which were used in furtherance of the violation;

(3) In any county in which any act was performed in furtherance of any transaction which violated this part; and

(4) In any county from which, to which, or through which any use of an involved protected computer or computer network was made, whether by wires, electromagnetic waves, microwaves, or any other means of communication.

§ 16-9-104. Jurisdiction for prosecutions

The Attorney General shall have concurrent jurisdiction with the district attorneys and solicitors-general to conduct the criminal prosecution of violations of this part.

§ 16-9-105. Civil actions

(a) The following persons shall have standing to assert a civil action under this part:
(1) Any e-mail service provider whose protected computer was used to send, receive, or transmit an e-mail that was sent in violation of this part; and
(2) A domain owner of any e-mail address to which a deceptive commercial e-mail is sent in violation of this part, provided that the domain owner also owns a protected computer at which the e-mail was received.
(b) Any person who has standing and who suffers personal, property, or economic damage by reason of a violation of any provision of this part may initiate a civil action for and recover the greater of:
(1) Five thousand dollars plus expenses of litigation and reasonable attorney's fees;
(2) Liquidated damages of $1,000.00 for each offending commercial e-mail, up to a limit of $2 million per incident, plus expenses of litigation and reasonable attorney's fees; or
(3) Actual damages, plus expenses of litigation and reasonable attorney's fees.

§ 16-9-106. Violations as separate offenses; construction with other laws; e-mail policies of service providers not limited or restricted

(a) Any crime committed in violation of this part shall be considered a separate offense.
(b) The provisions of this part shall not be construed as limiting or precluding the application of any other provision of law which applies to any transaction or course of conduct which violates this part.
(c) Nothing in this part shall be construed to limit or restrict the adoption, implementation, or enforcement by an e-mail service provider or Internet service provider of a policy of declining to transmit, receive, route, relay, handle, or store certain types of e-mail.

§ 16-9-107. No cause of action against service providers

There shall be no cause of action under this part against an e-mail service provider on the basis of its routine transmission of any commercial e-mail over its computer network.

§ 16-9-108. Investigative and subpoena powers of district attorneys and the Attorney General

(a) In any investigation of a violation of this article or any investigation of a violation of Code Section 16-12-100, 16-12-100.1, 16-12-100.2, 16-5-90, Article 8 of Chapter 5 of this title, or Article 8 of this chapter involving the use of a computer in furtherance of the act, the Attorney General or any district attorney shall have the power to administer oaths; to call any party to testify under oath at such investigation; to require the attendance of witnesses and the production of books, records, and papers; and to take the depositions of witnesses. The Attorney General or any such district attorney is authorized to issue a subpoena for any witness or a subpoena to compel the production of any books, records, or papers.
(b) In case of refusal to obey a subpoena issued under this Code section to any person and upon application by the Attorney General or district attorney, the superior court in whose jurisdiction the witness is to appear or in which the books, records, or papers are to be produced may issue to that person an order requiring him or her to appear before the court to show cause why he or she should not be held in contempt for refusal to obey the subpoena. Failure to obey a subpoena may be punished by the court as contempt of court.

§ 16-9-109. Disclosures by service providers pursuant to investigations

(a) Any law enforcement unit, the Attorney General, or any district attorney who is conducting an investigation of a violation of this article or an investigation of a violation of Code Section 16-12-100, 16-12-100.1, 16-12-100.2, 16-5-90, or 16-11-221, Article 8 of Chapter 5 of this title, or Article 8 of this chapter involving the use of a computer, cellular telephone, or any other electronic device used in furtherance of the act may require the disclosure by a provider of electronic communication service or remote computing service of the contents of a wire or electronic communication that is in electronic storage in an electronic communications system for 180 days or less pursuant to a search warrant issued under the provisions of Article 2 of Chapter 5 of Title 17 by a court with jurisdiction over the offense under investigation. Such court may require the disclosure by a provider of electronic communication service or remote computing service of the contents of a wire or electronic communication that has been in electronic storage in an electronic communications system for more than 180 days as set forth in subsection (b) of this Code section.
(b) (1) Any law enforcement unit, the Attorney General, or any district attorney may require a provider of electronic communication service or remote computing service to disclose a record or other information pertaining to a subscriber to or customer of such service, exclusive of the contents of communications, only when any law enforcement unit, the Attorney General, or any district attorney:
(A) Obtains a search warrant as provided in Article 2 of Chapter 5 of Title 17;
(B) Obtains a court order for such disclosure under subsection (c) of this Code section; or
(C) Has the consent of the subscriber or customer to such disclosure.
(2) A provider of electronic communication service or remote computing service shall disclose to any law enforcement unit, the Attorney General, or any district attorney the:
(A) Name;
(B) Address;
(C) Local and long-distance telephone connection records, or records of session times and durations;
(D) Length of service, including the start date, and types of service utilized;
(E) Telephone or instrument number or other subscriber number or identity, including any temporarily assigned network address; and
(F) Means and source of payment for such service, including any credit card or bank account number of a subscriber to or customer of such service when any law enforcement unit, the Attorney General, or any district attorney uses a subpoena authorized by Code Section 16-9-108, 35-3-4.1, or 45-15-17 or a grand jury or trial subpoena when any law enforcement unit, the Attorney General, or any district attorney complies with paragraph (1) of this subsection.
(3) Any law enforcement unit, the Attorney General, or any district attorney receiving records or information under this subsection shall not be required to provide notice to a subscriber or customer. A provider of electronic communication service or remote computing service shall not disclose to a subscriber or customer the existence of any search warrant or subpoena issued pursuant to this article nor shall a provider of electronic communication service or remote computing service disclose to a subscriber or customer that any records have been requested by or disclosed to any law enforcement unit, the Attorney General, or any district attorney pursuant to this article.
(c) A court order for disclosure issued pursuant to subsection (b) of this Code section may be issued by any superior court with jurisdiction over the offense under investigation and shall only issue such court order for disclosure if any law enforcement unit, the Attorney General, or any district attorney offers specific and articulable facts showing that there are reasonable grounds to believe that the contents of an electronic communication, or the records or other information sought, are relevant and material to an ongoing criminal investigation. A court issuing an order pursuant to this Code section, on a motion made promptly by a provider of electronic communication service or remote computing service, may quash or modify such order, if compliance with such order would be unduly burdensome or oppressive on such provider.
(d) (1) Any records supplied pursuant to this part shall be accompanied by the affidavit of the custodian or other qualified witness, stating in substance each of the following:
(A) The affiant is the duly authorized custodian of the records or other qualified witness and has authority to certify the records;
(B) The copy is a true copy of all the records described in the subpoena, court order, or search warrant and the records were delivered to the attorney, the attorney's representative, or the director of the Georgia Bureau of Investigation or the director's designee;
(C) The records were prepared by the personnel of the business in the ordinary course of business at or near the time of the act, condition, or event;
(D) The sources of information and method and time of preparation were such as to indicate its trustworthiness;

(E) The identity of the records; and

(F) A description of the mode of preparation of the records.

(2) If the business has none or only part of the records described, the custodian or other qualified witness shall so state in the affidavit.

(3) If the original records would be admissible in evidence if the custodian or other qualified witness had been present and testified to the matters stated in the affidavit, the copy of the records shall be admissible in evidence. When more than one person has knowledge of the facts, more than one affidavit shall be attached to the records produced.

(4) No later than 30 days prior to trial, a party intending to offer such evidence produced in compliance with this subsection shall provide written notice of such intentions to the opposing party or parties. A motion opposing the admission of such evidence shall be filed within ten days of the filing of such notice, and the court shall hold a hearing and rule on such motion no later than ten days prior to trial. Failure of a party to file such motion opposing admission prior to trial shall constitute a waiver of objection to such records and affidavit. However, the court, for good cause shown, may grant relief from such waiver.

§ 16-9-109.1. Fraudulent business practices using Internet or e-mail; definitions; penalties and sanctions; immunity

(a) As used in this part, the term:

(1) "E-mail message" means a message sent to a unique destination, commonly expressed as a string of characters, consisting of a unique user name or mailbox, commonly referred to as the "local part," and a reference to an Internet domain, commonly referred to as the "domain part," whether or not displayed, to which an electronic message can be sent or delivered.

(2) "Employer" includes a business entity's officers, directors, parent corporation, subsidiaries, affiliates, and other corporate entities under common ownership or control within a business enterprise.

(3) "Identifying information" means, with respect to an individual, any of the following:

(A) Social security number;

(B) Driver's license number;

(C) Bank account number;

(D) Credit card or debit card number;

(E) Personal identification number or PIN;

(F) Automated or electronic signature;

(G) Unique biometric data;

(H) Account password; or

(I) Any other piece of information that can be used to access an individual's financial accounts or to obtain goods or services.

(4) "Internet" shall have the meaning set forth in paragraph (10) of Code Section 16-9-151.

(5) "Web page" means a location that has a single uniform resource locator or other single location with respect to the Internet.

(b) (1) It shall be unlawful for any person with intent to defraud, by means of a web page, e-mail message, or otherwise through use of the Internet, to solicit, request, or take any action to induce another person to provide identifying information by representing himself, herself, or itself to be a business without the authority or approval of such business.

(2) It shall be unlawful for any person, with actual knowledge, conscious avoidance of actual knowledge, or willfully, to possess with intent to use in a fraudulent manner, sell, or distribute any identifying information obtained in violation of paragraph (1) of this subsection.

(c) Any person who intentionally violates subsection (b) of this Code section shall be guilty of a felony and shall be punished by imprisonment for not less than one nor more than 20 years, a fine of not less than $1,000.00 nor more than $500,000.00, or both.

(d) (1) No employer shall be held criminally liable under this Code section as a result of any actions taken:

(A) With respect to computer equipment used by its employees, contractors, subcontractors, agents, leased employees, or other staff which the employer owns, leases, or otherwise makes available or allows to be connected to the employer's network or other computer facilities when such equipment is used for an illegal purpose without the employer's knowledge, consent, or approval; or

(B) By employees, contractors, subcontractors, agents, leased employees, or other staff who misuse an employer's computer equipment for an illegal purpose without the employer's knowledge, consent, or approval.

(2) No person shall be held criminally liable under this Code section when its protected computers, computer equipment, or software product has been used by unauthorized users to violate this Code section without such person's knowledge, consent, or approval.

(e) This Code section shall not apply to a telecommunications provider's or Internet service provider's good faith transmission or routing of, or intermediate temporary storing or caching of, identifying information.

(f) No provider of an interactive computer service may be held liable in a civil action under any law of this state, or any of its political subdivisions, for removing or disabling access to content on an Internet website or other online location controlled or operated by such provider, when such provider believes in good faith that such content has been used to engage in a violation of this part.

§ 16-9-110. Sale or transfer of new motor vehicles not manufactured in compliance with federal standards

(a) It shall be unlawful for any person, firm, or corporation knowingly to sell, transfer, or otherwise convey any motor vehicle which was not manufactured to comply with federal emission and safety standards applicable to new motor vehicles as required by 42 U.S.C. Section 7401 through Section 7642, known as the federal Clean Air Act, as amended, and as required by 15 U.S.C. Section 1381 through Section 1431, known as the National Traffic and Motor Vehicle Safety Act of 1966, as amended, unless and until the United States Customs Service or the United States Department of Transportation and the United States Environmental Protection Agency have certified that the motor vehicle complies with such applicable federal standards.

(b) Any person convicted of violating subsection (a) of this Code section shall be guilty of a misdemeanor.

§ 16-9-111. Importation, manufacture, selling, offering for sale, installation, or reinstallation of counterfeit, nonfunctional, and such other types of air bags

(a) As used in this Code section, the term:

(1) "Air bag" means a device that is part of a motor vehicle inflatable occupant restraint system, and all component parts, that operate in the event of a collision and is designed in accordance with federal motor vehicle safety standards for the specific make, model, and year of the motor vehicle, including, but not limited to, the cushion material, cover, sensors, controllers, inflators, wiring, and seat belt systems.

(2) "Counterfeit air bag" means a replacement device that is part of a motor vehicle inflatable occupant restraint system, and any replacement component parts, that are intended to operate in the event of a collision, including, but not limited to, the cushion material, cover, sensors, controllers, inflators, wiring, and seat belt systems that bear, without authorization, a mark identical or substantially similar to the genuine mark of the manufacturer for the specific motor vehicle or a supplier of parts to the manufacturer of the specific motor vehicle.

(3) "Nonfunctional air bag" means a replacement device that is part of a motor vehicle inflatable occupant restraint system, and any replacement component parts, including, but not limited to, the cushion material, cover, sensors, controllers, inflators, wiring, and seat belt systems that:

(A) Has been deployed or damaged;

(B) Has an electric fault that is detected by the vehicle's diagnostic system after the installation procedure is completed; or

(C) Includes any object, including, but not limited to, a counterfeit air bag or repaired air bag, air bag component, or other component intended to deceive a vehicle owner or operator into believing that it is a functional air bag.

(b) A person shall not knowingly and intentionally:

(1) Import, manufacture, sell, offer for sale, install, or reinstall in a motor vehicle a counterfeit air bag, nonfunctional air bag, or other device intended to replace a motor vehicle inflatable occupant restraint system, or any component parts, that are intended to operate in the event of a collision, including, but not limited to, the cushion material, cover, sensors, controllers, inflators, wiring, and seat belt systems, that such person knows was not designed to comply with federal motor vehicle safety standards for the specific make, model, and year of such motor vehicle; or
(2) Sell, offer for sale, install, or reinstall in a motor vehicle any device that causes such motor vehicle's diagnostic system to inaccurately indicate that such motor vehicle is equipped with a properly functioning air bag.
(c) Any person who is convicted of violating this Code section shall be guilty of and punished as for a misdemeanor of a high and aggravated nature.

§ 16-9-120. Definitions

As used in this article, the term:
(1) "Attorney General" means the Attorney General or his or her designee.
(2) "Business victim" means any individual or entity that provided money, credit, goods, services, or anything of value to someone other than the intended recipient where the intended recipient has not given permission for the actual recipient to receive it and the individual or entity that provided money, credit, goods, services, or anything of value has suffered financial loss as a direct result of the commission or attempted commission of a violation of this article.
(3) "Consumer victim" means any individual whose personal identifying information has been obtained, compromised, used, or recorded in any manner without the permission of that individual.
(4) "Health care records" means records however maintained and in whatever form regarding an individual's health, including, but not limited to, doctors' and nurses' examinations and other notes, examination notes of other medical professionals, hospital records, rehabilitation facility records, nursing home records, assisted living facility records, results of medical tests, X-rays, CT scans, MRI scans, vision examinations, pharmacy records, prescriptions, hospital charts, surgical records, mental health treatments and counseling, dental records, and physical therapy notes and evaluations.
(5) "Identifying information" shall include, but not be limited to:
(A) Current or former names;
(B) Social security numbers;
(C) Driver's license numbers;
(D) Checking account numbers;
(E) Savings account numbers;
(F) Credit and other financial transaction card numbers;
(G) Debit card numbers;
(H) Personal identification numbers;
(I) Electronic identification numbers;
(J) Digital or electronic signatures;
(K) Medical identification numbers;
(L) Birth dates;
(M) Mother's maiden name;
(N) Selected personal identification numbers;
(O) Tax identification numbers;
(P) State identification card numbers issued by state departments;
(Q) Veteran and military medical identification numbers; and
(R) Any other numbers or information which can be used to access a person's or entity's resources or health care records.
(6) "Resources" includes, but is not limited to:
(A) A person's or entity's credit, credit history, credit profile, and credit rating;
(B) United States currency, securities, real property, and personal property of any kind;
(C) Credit, charge, and debit accounts;
(D) Loans and lines of credit;
(E) Documents of title and other forms of commercial paper recognized under Title 11;
(F) Any account, including a safety deposit box, with a financial institution as defined by Code Section 7-1-4, including a national bank, federal savings and loan association, or federal credit union or a securities dealer licensed by the Secretary of State or the federal Securities and Exchange Commission;
(G) A person's personal history, including, but not limited to, records of such person's driving records; criminal, medical, or insurance history; education; or employment; and
(H) A person's health insurance, health savings accounts, health spending accounts, flexible spending accounts, medicare accounts, Medicaid accounts, dental insurance, vision insurance, and other forms of health insurance and health benefit plans.

§ 16-9-121. Elements of offense

(a) A person commits the offense of identity fraud when he or she willfully and fraudulently:
(1) Without authorization or consent, uses or possesses with intent to fraudulently use identifying information concerning a person;
(2) Uses identifying information of an individual under 18 years old over whom he or she exercises custodial authority;
(3) Uses or possesses with intent to fraudulently use identifying information concerning a deceased individual;
(4) Creates, uses, or possesses with intent to fraudulently use any counterfeit or fictitious identifying information concerning a fictitious person with intent to use such counterfeit or fictitious identification information for the purpose of committing or facilitating the commission of a crime or fraud on another person; or
(5) Without authorization or consent, creates, uses, or possesses with intent to fraudulently use any counterfeit or fictitious identifying information concerning a real person with intent to use such counterfeit or fictitious identification information for the purpose of committing or facilitating the commission of a crime or fraud on another person.
(b) A person commits the offense of identity fraud by receipt of fraudulent identification information when he or she willingly accepts for identification purposes identifying information which he or she knows to be fraudulent, stolen, counterfeit, or fictitious. In any prosecution under this subsection it shall not be necessary to show a conviction of the principal thief, counterfeiter, or fraudulent user.
(c) The offenses created by this Code section shall not merge with any other offense.
(d) This Code section shall not apply to a person under the age of 21 who uses a fraudulent, counterfeit, or other false identification card for the purpose of obtaining entry into a business establishment or for purchasing items which he or she is not of legal age to purchase.

§ 16-9-121.1. Offense of aggravated identity fraud

(a) A person commits the offense of aggravated identity fraud when he or she willfully and fraudulently uses any counterfeit or fictitious identifying information concerning a real, fictitious, or deceased person with intent to use such counterfeit or fictitious identifying information for the purpose of obtaining employment.
(b) The offense created by this Code section shall not merge with any other offense.

§ 16-9-122. Attempting or conspiring to commit offense; penalty

It shall be unlawful for any person to attempt or conspire to commit any offense prohibited by this article. Any person convicted of a violation of this Code section shall be punished by imprisonment or community service, by a fine, or by both such punishments not to exceed the maximum punishment prescribed for the offense the commission of which was the object of the attempt or conspiracy.

§ 16-9-123. Investigations

The Attorney General shall have the authority to investigate any complaints of consumer victims regarding identity fraud. In conducting such investigations the Attorney General shall have all investigative powers which are available to the Attorney General under Part 2 of Article 15 of Chapter 1 of Title 10, the "Fair Business Practices Act of 1975." If, after such investigation, the Attorney General determines that a person has been a consumer victim of identity fraud in this state, the Attorney General shall, at the request of the consumer victim, provide the consumer victim with certification of the findings of such investigation. Copies of any and all complaints received by any law enforcement agency of this state regarding potential violations of this article shall be transmitted to the Georgia Bureau of Investigation. The Georgia Bureau of Investigation shall maintain a repository for all complaints in the State of Georgia regarding identity fraud. Information contained in such repository shall not be subject to public disclosure. The information in the repository may be transmitted to any other appropriate investigatory agency or entity. Consumer victims of identity fraud may file complaints directly with the office of the Attorney General, the Georgia Bureau of Investigation, or with local law enforcement. Any and all transmissions authorized under this Code section may be transmitted electronically, provided that such transmissions are made through a secure channel for the transmission of such electronic communications or information, the sufficiency of which is acceptable to the Attorney General. Nothing in this Code section shall be construed to preclude any otherwise authorized law enforcement or prosecutorial agencies from conducting investigations and prosecuting offenses of identity fraud.

§ 16-9-124. Prosecutions

The Attorney General and prosecuting attorneys shall have the authority to conduct the criminal prosecution of all cases of identity fraud.

§ 16-9-125. County of offense

The General Assembly finds that identity fraud involves the use of identifying information which is uniquely personal to the consumer or business victim of that identity fraud and which information is considered to be in the lawful possession of the consumer or business victim wherever the consumer or business victim currently resides or is found. Accordingly, the fraudulent use of that information involves the fraudulent use of information that is, for the purposes of this article, found within the county where the consumer or business victim of the identity fraud resides or is found. Accordingly, in a proceeding under this article, the crime will be considered to have been committed in any county where the person whose means of identification or financial information was appropriated resides or is found, or in any county in which any other part of the offense took place, regardless of whether the defendant was ever actually in such county.

§ 16-9-125.1. Victim's right to file report

(a) A person who has learned or reasonably believes that he or she has been the victim of identity fraud may contact the local law enforcement agency with jurisdiction over his or her actual residence for the purpose of making an incident report. The law enforcement agency having jurisdiction over the complainant's residence shall make a report of the complaint and provide the complainant with a copy of the report. Where jurisdiction for the investigation and prosecution of the complaint lies with another agency, the law enforcement agency making the report shall forward a copy to the agency having such jurisdiction and shall advise the complainant that the report has been so forwarded.
(b) Nothing in this Code section shall be construed so as to interfere with the discretion of a law enforcement agency to allocate resources for the investigation of crimes. A report created pursuant to this Code section is not required to be counted as an open case file.

§ 16-9-126. Penalty for violations

(a) A violation of this article, other than a violation of Code Section 16-9-121.1 or 16-9-122, shall be punishable by imprisonment for not less than one nor more than ten years or a fine not to exceed $100,000.00, or both. Any person who commits such a violation for the second or any subsequent offense shall be punished by imprisonment for not less than three nor more than 15 years, a fine not to exceed $250,000.00, or both.
(a.1) A violation of Code Section 16-9-121.1 shall be punishable by imprisonment for not less than one nor more than 15 years, a fine not to exceed $250,000.00, or both, and such sentence shall run consecutively to any other sentence which the person has received.
(b) A violation of this article which does not involve the intent to commit theft or appropriation of any property, resource, or other thing of value that is committed by a person who is less than 21 years of age shall be punishable by imprisonment for not less than one nor more than three years or a fine not to exceed $5,000.00, or both.
(c) Any person found guilty of a violation of this article may be ordered by the court to make restitution to any consumer victim or any business victim of such fraud.
(d) Each violation of this article shall constitute a separate offense.
(e) Upon a conviction of a violation of this article, the court may issue any order necessary to correct a public record that contains false information resulting from the actions which resulted in the conviction.

§ 16-9-127. Authority of Attorney General

The Attorney General shall have authority to initiate any proceedings and to exercise any power or authority in the same manner as if he or she were acting under Part 2 of Article 15 of Chapter 1 of Title 10, as regards violations or potential violations of this article.

§ 16-9-128. Exemptions

(a) The prohibitions set forth in Code Sections 16-9-121, 16-9-121.1, and 16-9-122 shall not apply to nor shall any cause of action arise under Code Sections 16-9-129 and 16-9-131 for:
(1) The lawful obtaining of credit information in the course of a bona fide consumer or commercial transaction;
(2) The lawful, good faith exercise of a security interest or a right to offset by a creditor or a financial institution;
(3) The lawful, good faith compliance by any party when required by any warrant, levy, garnishment, attachment, court order, or other judicial or administrative order, decree, or directive; or
(4) The good faith use of identifying information with the permission of the affected person.
(b) The exemptions provided in subsection (a) of this Code section shall not apply to a person intending to further a scheme to violate Code Section 16-9-121, 16-9-121.1, or 16-9-122.
(c) It shall not be necessary for the state to negate any exemption or exception in this article in any complaint, accusation, indictment, or other pleading or in any trial, hearing, or other proceeding under this article involving a business victim. In such cases, the burden of proof of any exemption or exception is upon the business victim claiming it.

§ 16-9-129. Actual and punitive damages available to business victim

Any business victim who is injured by reason of any violation of this article shall have a cause of action for the actual damages sustained and, where appropriate, punitive damages. Such business victim may also recover attorney's fees in the trial and appellate courts and the costs of investigation and litigation reasonably incurred.

§ 16-9-130. Damages available to consumer victim; no defense that others engage in comparable practices; service of complaint

(a) Any consumer victim who suffers injury or damages as a result of a violation of this article may bring an action individually or as a representative of a class against the person or persons engaged in such violations under the rules of civil procedure to seek equitable injunctive relief and to recover general and punitive damages sustained as a consequence thereof in any court having jurisdiction over the defendant; provided, however, that punitive damages shall be awarded only in cases of intentional violation. A claim under this article may also be asserted as a defense, setoff, cross-claim, or counterclaim or third-party claim against such person.

(b) A court shall award three times actual damages for an intentional violation.

(c) If the court finds in any action that there has been a violation of this article, the consumer victim injured by such violation shall, in addition to other relief provided for in this Code section and irrespective of the amount in controversy, be awarded reasonable attorney's fees and expenses of litigation incurred in connection with said action.

(d) It shall not be a defense in any action under this article that others were, are, or will be engaged in like practices.

(e) In any action brought under this article the Attorney General shall be served by certified or registered mail or statutory overnight delivery with a copy of the initial complaint and any amended complaint within 20 days of the filing of such complaint. The Attorney General shall be entitled to be heard in any such action, and the court where such action is filed may enter an order requiring any of the parties to serve a copy of any other pleadings in an action upon the Attorney General.

§ 16-9-131. Criminal prosecution

Whenever an investigation has been conducted by the Attorney General under this article and such investigation reveals conduct which constitutes a criminal offense, the Attorney General shall have the authority to prosecute such cases or forward the results of such investigation to any other prosecuting attorney of this state who shall commence any criminal prosecution that he or she deems appropriate.

§ 16-9-132. Article cumulative and not exclusive

This article is cumulative with other laws and is not exclusive. The rights or remedies provided for in this article shall be in addition to any other procedures, rights, remedies, or duties provided for in any other law or in decisions of the courts of this state dealing with the same subject matter.

§ 16-9-150. Short title

This article shall be known and may be cited as the "Georgia Computer Security Act of 2005."

§ 16-9-151. Definitions

As used in this article, the term:

(1) "Advertisement" means a communication, the primary purpose of which is the commercial promotion of a commercial product or service, including content on an Internet website operated for a commercial purpose.

(2) "Authorized user," with respect to a computer, means a person who owns or is authorized by the owner or lessee to use the computer.

(3) "Cause to be copied" means to distribute or transfer computer software or any component thereof. Such term shall not include providing:

(A) Transmission, routing, provision of intermediate temporary storage, or caching of software;

(B) A storage medium, such as a compact disk, website, or computer server, through which the software was distributed by a third party; or

(C) An information location tool, such as a directory, index, reference, pointer, or hypertext link, through which the user of the computer located the software.

(4) "Computer software" means a sequence of instructions written in any programming language that is executed on a computer. Such term shall not include a text or data file, a web page, or a data component of a web page that is not executable independently of the web page.

(5) "Computer virus" means a computer program or other set of instructions that is designed to degrade the performance of or disable a computer or computer network and is designed to have the ability to replicate itself on other computers or computer networks without the authorization of the owners of those computers or computer networks.

(6) "Consumer" means an individual who resides in this state and who uses the computer in question primarily for personal, family, or household purposes.

(6.1) "Covered file-sharing program" means a computer program, application, or software that enables the computer on which such program, application, or software is installed to designate files as available for searching by and copying to one or more other computers, to transmit such designated files directly to one or more other computers, and to request the transmission of such designated files directly from one or more other computers. Covered file-sharing program does not mean a program, application, or software designed primarily to operate as a server that is accessible over the Internet using the Internet Domain Name System, to transmit or receive e-mail messages, instant messaging, real-time audio or video communications, or real-time voice communications, to provide network or computer security, network management, hosting and backup services, maintenance, diagnostics, or technical support or repair, or to detect or prevent fraudulent activities.

(7) "Damage" means any significant impairment to the integrity or availability of data, software, a system, or information.

(8) "Execute," when used with respect to computer software, means the performance of the functions or the carrying out of the instructions of the computer software.

(9) "Intentionally deceptive" means any of the following:

(A) By means of an intentionally and materially false or fraudulent statement;

(B) By means of a statement or description that intentionally omits or misrepresents material information in order to deceive the consumer; or

(C) By means of an intentional and material failure to provide any notice to an authorized user regarding the download or installation of software in order to deceive the consumer.

(10) "Internet" means the global information system that is logically linked together by a globally unique address space based on the Internet Protocol or its subsequent extensions; that is able to support communications using the Transmission Control Protocol/Internet Protocol suite, its subsequent extensions, or other Internet Protocol compatible protocols; and that provides, uses, or makes accessible, either publicly or privately, high level services layered on the communications and related infrastructure described in this paragraph.

(11) "Person" means any individual, partnership, corporation, limited liability company, or other organization, or any combination thereof.

(12) "Personally identifiable information" means any of the following:

(A) A first name or first initial in combination with a last name;

(B) Credit or debit card numbers or other financial account numbers;

(C) A password or personal identification number required to access an identified financial account;

(D) A social security number; or

(E) Any of the following information in a form that personally identifies an authorized user:

(i) Account balances;

(ii) Overdraft history;

(iii) Payment history;

(iv) A history of websites visited;

(v) A home address;

(vi) A work address; or

(vii) A record of a purchase or purchases.

§ 16-9-152. Spyware, browsers, hijacks, and other software prohibited

(a) It shall be illegal for a person or entity that is not an authorized user, as defined in Code Section 16-9-151, of a computer in this state to knowingly, willfully, or with conscious indifference or disregard cause computer software to be copied onto such computer and use the software to do any of the following:

(1) Modify, through intentionally deceptive means, any of the following settings related to the computer's access to, or use of, the Internet:

(A) The page that appears when an authorized user launches an Internet browser or similar software program used to access and navigate the Internet;

(B) The default provider or web proxy the authorized user uses to access or search the Internet; or

(C) The authorized user's list of bookmarks used to access web pages;

(2) Collect, through intentionally deceptive means, personally identifiable information that meets any of the following criteria:

(A) It is collected through the use of a keystroke-logging function that records all keystrokes made by an authorized user who uses the computer and transfers that information from the computer to another person;

(B) It includes all or substantially all of the websites visited by an authorized user, other than websites of the provider of the software, if the computer software was installed in a manner designed to conceal from all authorized users of the computer the fact that the software is being installed; or

(C) It is a data element described in subparagraph (B), (C), or (D) of paragraph (12) of Code Section 16-9-151, or in division (12)(E)(i) or (12)(E)(ii) of Code Section 16-9-151, that is extracted from the consumer's or business entity's computer hard drive for a purpose wholly unrelated to any of the purposes of the software or service described to an authorized user;

(3) Prevent, without the authorization of an authorized user, through intentionally deceptive means, an authorized user's reasonable efforts to block the installation of, or to disable, software, by causing software that the authorized user has properly removed or disabled to automatically reinstall or reactivate on the computer without the authorization of an authorized user;

(4) Intentionally misrepresent that software will be uninstalled or disabled by an authorized user's action, with knowledge that the software will not be so uninstalled or disabled; or

(5) Through intentionally deceptive means, remove, disable, or render inoperative security, antispyware, or antivirus software installed on the computer.

(b) Nothing in this Code section shall apply to any monitoring of, or interaction with, a user's Internet or other network connection or service, or a protected computer, by a telecommunications carrier, cable operator, computer hardware or software provider, or provider of information service or interactive computer service for network or computer security purposes, diagnostics, technical support, repair, network management, network maintenance, authorized updates of software or system firmware, authorized remote system management, or detection or prevention of the unauthorized use of or fraudulent or other illegal activities in connection with a network, service, or computer software, including scanning for and removing software proscribed under this article.

§ 16-9-153. E-mail virus distribution, denial of service attacks, and other conduct prohibited

(a) It shall be illegal for a person or entity that is not an authorized user, as defined in Code Section 16-9-151, of a computer in this state to knowingly, willfully, or with conscious indifference or disregard cause computer software to be copied onto such computer and use the software to do any of the following:

(1) Take control of the consumer's or business entity's computer by doing any of the following:

(A) Transmitting or relaying commercial e-mail or a computer virus from the consumer's or business entity's computer, where the transmission or relaying is initiated by a person other than the authorized user and without the authorization of an authorized user;

(B) Accessing or using the consumer's or business entity's modem or Internet service for the purpose of causing damage to the consumer's or business entity's computer or of causing an authorized user or a third party affected by such conduct to incur financial charges for a service that is not authorized by an authorized user;

(C) Using the consumer's or business entity's computer as part of an activity performed by a group of computers for the purpose of causing damage to another computer, including, but not limited to, launching a denial of service attack; or

(D) Opening multiple, sequential, stand-alone advertisements in the consumer's or business entity's Internet browser without the authorization of an authorized user and with knowledge that a reasonable computer user cannot close the advertisements without turning off the computer or closing the consumer's or business entity's Internet browser;

(2) Modify any of the following settings related to the computer's access to, or use of, the Internet:

(A) An authorized user's security or other settings that protect information about the authorized user for the purpose of stealing personal information of an authorized user; or

(B) The security settings of the computer for the purpose of causing damage to one or more computers; or

(3) Prevent, without the authorization of an authorized user, an authorized user's reasonable efforts to block the installation of, or to disable, software, by doing any of the following:

(A) Presenting the authorized user with an option to decline installation of software with knowledge that, when the option is selected by the authorized user, the installation nevertheless proceeds; or

(B) Falsely representing that software has been disabled.

(b) Nothing in this Code section shall apply to any monitoring of, or interaction with, a user's Internet or other network connection or service, or a protected computer, by a telecommunications carrier, cable operator, computer hardware or software provider, or provider of information service or interactive computer service for network or computer security purposes, diagnostics, technical support, repair, network management, network maintenance, authorized updates of software or system firmware, authorized remote system management, or detection or prevention of the unauthorized use of or fraudulent or other illegal activities in connection with a network, service, or computer software, including scanning for and removing software proscribed under this article.

§ 16-9-154. Inducement to install, copy, or execute software through misrepresentation prohibited

(a) It shall be illegal for a person or entity that is not an authorized user, as defined in Code Section 16-9-151, of a computer in this state to do any of the following with regard to such computer:

(1) Induce an authorized user to install a software component onto the computer by intentionally misrepresenting that installing software is necessary for security or privacy reasons or in order to open, view, or play a particular type of content;

(2) Deceptively causing the copying and execution on the computer of a computer software component with the intent of causing an authorized user to use the component in a way that violates any other provision of this Code section;

(3) Prevent reasonable efforts to block the installation, execution, or disabling of a covered file-sharing program on the computer; or

(4) Install, offer to install, or make available for installation, reinstallation, or update a covered file-sharing program on the computer without first providing clear and conspicuous notice to the authorized user of the computer showing which files on that computer will be made available to the public, obtaining consent from the authorized user to install the covered file-sharing program, and requiring affirmative steps by the authorized user to activate any feature on the covered file-sharing program that will make files on that computer available to the public. Such notice shall be redisplayed each time a change occurs in the list of files that will be made available to the public.

(b) Nothing in this Code section shall apply to any monitoring of, or interaction with, a user's Internet or other network connection or service, or a protected computer, by a telecommunications carrier, cable operator, computer hardware or software provider, or provider of information service or interactive computer service for network or computer security purposes, diagnostics, technical support, repair, network management, network maintenance, authorized updates of software or system firmware, authorized remote system management, or detection or prevention of the unauthorized use of or fraudulent or other illegal activities in connection with a network, service, or computer software, including scanning for and removing software proscribed under this article.

§ 16-9-155. Penalties

(a) Any person who violates the provisions of paragraph (2) of Code Section 16-9-152, subparagraph (a)(1)(A), (a)(1)(B), or (a)(1)(C) of Code Section 16-9-153, or paragraph (2) of subsection (a) of Code Section 16-9-153 shall be guilty of a felony and, upon conviction thereof, shall be sentenced to imprisonment for not less than one nor more than ten years or a fine of not more than $3 million, or both.

(b) The Attorney General may bring a civil action against any person violating this article to enforce the penalties for the violation and may recover any or all of the following:

(1) A civil penalty of up to $100.00 per violation of this article, or up to $100,000.00 for a pattern or practice of such violations;

(2) Costs and reasonable attorney's fees; and

(3) An order to enjoin the violation.

(c) In the case of a violation of subparagraph (a)(1)(B) of Code Section 16-9-153 that causes a telecommunications carrier to incur costs for the origination, transport, or termination of a call triggered using the modem of a customer of such telecommunications carrier as a result of such violation, the telecommunications carrier may bring a civil action against the violator to recover any or all of the following:

(1) The charges such carrier is obligated to pay to another carrier or to an information service provider as a result of the violation, including, but not limited to, charges for the origination, transport, or termination of the call;

(2) Costs of handling customer inquiries or complaints with respect to amounts billed for such calls;

(3) Costs and reasonable attorney's fees; and

(4) An order to enjoin the violation.

(d) An Internet service provider or software company that expends resources in good faith assisting consumers or business entities harmed by a violation of this chapter, or a trademark owner whose mark is used to deceive consumers or business entities in violation of this chapter, may enforce the violation and may recover any or all of the following:

(1) Statutory damages of not more than $100.00 per violation of this article, or up to $1 million for a pattern or practice of such violations;

(2) Costs and reasonable attorney's fees; and

(3) An order to enjoin the violation.

§ 16-9-156. Exceptions

(a) For the purposes of this Code section, the term "employer" includes a business entity's officers, directors, parent corporation, subsidiaries, affiliates, and other corporate entities under common ownership or control within a business enterprise. No employer may be held criminally or civilly liable under this article as a result of any actions taken:

(1) With respect to computer equipment used by its employees, contractors, subcontractors, agents, leased employees, or other staff which the employer owns, leases, or otherwise makes available or allows to be connected to the employer's network or other computer facilities; or

(2) By employees, contractors, subcontractors, agents, leased employees, or other staff who misuse an employer's computer equipment for an illegal purpose without the employer's knowledge, consent, or approval.

(b) No person shall be held criminally or civilly liable under this article when its protected computers have been used by unauthorized users to violate this article or other laws without such person's knowledge, consent, or approval.

(c) A manufacturer or retailer of computer equipment shall not be liable under this Code section, criminally or civilly, to the extent that the manufacturer or retailer is providing third-party branded software that is installed on the computer equipment that the manufacturer or retailer is manufacturing or selling.

§ 16-9-157. Legislative findings and preemption

The General Assembly finds that this article is a matter of state-wide concern. This article supersedes and preempts all rules, regulations, codes, ordinances, and other laws adopted by any county, municipality, consolidated government, or other local governmental agency regarding spyware and notices to consumers from computer software providers regarding information collection.

CHAPTER 10. OFFENSES AGAINST PUBLIC ADMINISTRATION

§ 16-10-1. Violation of oath by public officer

Any public officer who willfully and intentionally violates the terms of his oath as prescribed by law shall, upon conviction thereof, be punished by imprisonment for not less than one nor more than five years.

§ 16-10-2. Bribery

(a) A person commits the offense of bribery when:

(1) He or she gives or offers to give to any person acting for or on behalf of the state or any political subdivision thereof, or of any agency of either, any benefit, reward, or consideration to which he or she is not entitled with the purpose of influencing him or her in the performance of any act related to the functions of his or her office or employment; or

(2) A public official, elected or appointed, or an employee of this state or any agency, authority, or entity of the state, or any county or municipality or any agency, authority, or entity thereof, directly or indirectly solicits, receives, accepts, or agrees to receive a thing of value by inducing the reasonable belief that the giving of the thing will influence his or her performance or failure to perform any official action. A thing of value shall not include:

(A) Food or beverage consumed at a single meal or event;

(B) Legitimate salary, benefits, fees, commissions, or expenses associated with a recipient's nonpublic business, employment, trade, or profession;

(C) An award, plaque, certificate, memento, or similar item given in recognition of the recipient's civic, charitable, political, professional, or public service;

(D) Food, beverages, and registration at group events to which all members of an agency, as defined in paragraph (1) of subsection (a) of Code Section 21-5-30.2, are invited. An agency shall include the Georgia House of Representatives, the Georgia Senate, committees and subcommittees of such bodies, and the governing body of each political subdivision of this state;

(E) Actual and reasonable expenses for food, beverages, travel, lodging, and registration for a meeting which are provided to permit participation or speaking at the meeting;

(F) A commercially reasonable loan made in the ordinary course of business;

(G) Any gift with a value less than $100.00;

(H) Promotional items generally distributed to the general public or to public officers;

(I) A gift from a member of the public officer's immediate family; or

(J) Food, beverage, or expenses afforded public officers, members of their immediate families, or others that are associated with normal and customary business or social functions or activities; provided, however, that receiving, accepting, or agreeing to receive anything not enumerated in subparagraphs (A) through (J) of this paragraph shall not create the presumption that the offense of bribery has been committed.

(b) A person convicted of the offense of bribery shall be punished by a fine of not more than $5,000.00 or by imprisonment for not less than one nor more than 20 years, or both.

§ 16-10-3. Using private funds for law enforcement; off-duty employment of law enforcement officers

(a) Except as otherwise provided in this Code section, any officer or employee of the state or any agency thereof who receives from any private person, firm, or corporation funds or other things of value to be used in the enforcement of the penal laws or regulations of the state is guilty of a misdemeanor.

(b) Except as otherwise provided in this Code section, any officer or employee of a political subdivision who receives from any private person, firm, or corporation funds or other things of value to be used in the enforcement of the penal laws or regulations of the political subdivision of which he is an officer or employee is guilty of a misdemeanor.

(c) Nothing contained within this Code section shall be deemed or construed so as to prohibit any law enforcement officer of the state or any political subdivision thereof:

(1) From being employed by private persons, firms, or corporations during his off-duty hours when such employment is approved in writing by the chief or head, or his duly designated agent, of the law enforcement agency by which such law enforcement officer is employed; or

(2) From soliciting for or accepting contributions of equipment or of funds to be used solely for the purchase of equipment to be used in the enforcement of the penal laws or regulations of this state or any political subdivision thereof when such acceptance is approved in writing by the chief or head, or his duly designated agent, of the law enforcement agency by which such law enforcement officer is employed.

§ 16-10-4. Influencing of legislative action by state and local government officers or employees

(a) Any officer or employee of the state or any agency thereof who asks for or receives anything of value to which he or she is not entitled in return for an agreement to procure or attempt to procure the passage or defeat the passage of any legislation by the General Assembly, or procure or attempt to procure the approval or disapproval of the same by the Governor, shall be guilty of a felony and, upon conviction thereof, shall be punished by a fine of not more than $100,000.00 or by imprisonment for not less than one nor more than five years, or both.

(b) Any officer or employee of a political subdivision who asks for or receives anything of value to which he or she is not entitled in return for an agreement to procure or attempt to procure the passage or defeat the passage of any legislation by the legislative body of the political subdivision of which he or she is an officer or employee shall be guilty of a felony and, upon conviction thereof, shall be punished by a fine of not more than $100,000.00 or by imprisonment for not less than one nor more than five years, or both.

§ 16-10-5. Influencing of officer or employee of state or political subdivision by another officer or employee

(a) Any officer or employee of the state or any agency thereof who asks for or receives anything of value to which he or she is not entitled in return for an agreement to influence or attempt to influence official action by any other officer or employee of the state or any agency thereof shall be guilty of a felony and, upon conviction thereof, shall be punished by a fine of not more than $100,000.00 or by imprisonment for not less than one nor more than five years, or both.

(b) Any officer or employee of a political subdivision who asks for or receives anything of value to which he or she is not entitled in return for an agreement to influence or attempt to influence official action by any other officer or employee of that political subdivision shall be guilty of a felony and, upon conviction thereof, shall be punished by a fine of not more than $100,000.00 or by imprisonment for not less than one nor more than five years, or both.

§ 16-10-6. Sale of real or personal property to political subdivision by local officer or employee; exceptions; limitation of civil liability

(a) As used in this Code section, the term "employing local authority" means a local authority or board created by a local Act of the General Assembly or a local constitutional amendment or created by general law and requiring activation by an ordinance or resolution of a local governing authority.

(b) Any employee, appointed officer, or elected officer of a political subdivision, hereafter referred to as "employing political subdivision," or agency thereof or any employee or appointed officer of an employing local authority who for himself or herself or in behalf of any business entity sells any real or personal property to:

(1) The employing political subdivision or employing local authority;

(2) An agency of the employing political subdivision;

(3) A political subdivision for which local taxes for education are levied by the employing political subdivision; or

(4) A political subdivision which levies local taxes for education for the employing political subdivision

shall, upon conviction thereof, be punished by imprisonment for not less than one nor more than five years.

(c) Subsection (b) of this Code section shall not apply to:

(1) Sales of personal property of less than $800.00 per calendar quarter;

(2) Sales of personal property made pursuant to sealed competitive bids made by the employee, appointed officer, or elected officer, either for himself or herself or on behalf of any business entity; or

(3) Sales of real property in which a disclosure has been made:

(A) To the judge of the probate court of the county in which the purchasing political subdivision or local authority is wholly included or, if not wholly included in any one county, to the judge of the probate court of any county in which the purchasing political subdivision or local authority is partially included and which shall have been designated by the purchasing political subdivision or local authority to receive such disclosures, provided that if the sale is made by the judge of the probate court, a copy of such disclosure shall also be filed with any superior court judge of the superior court of the county;

(B) At least 15 days prior to the date the contract or agreement for such sale will become final and binding on the parties thereto; and

(C) Which shows that an employee, appointed officer, or elected officer of an employing political subdivision or agency thereof or of an employing local authority has a personal interest in such sale, which interest includes, without being limited to, any commission, fee, profit, or similar benefit and which gives the name of such person, his or her position in the political subdivision or agency or local authority, the purchase price, and location of the property.

(d) Any contract or transaction for a sale made in accordance with subsection (c) of this Code section shall be valid and no employee, appointed officer, or elected officer shall be subject to civil liability for any such sale.

§ 16-10-7. False acknowledgments, certificates, or statements of appearance or oath by officer authorized to do same

Any officer authorized to administer oaths or to take and certify acknowledgments who knowingly makes a false acknowledgment, certificate, or statement concerning the appearance before him or the taking of an oath or affirmation by any person is guilty of a misdemeanor.

§ 16-10-8. False official certificates or writings by officers or employees of state and political subdivisions

An officer or employee of the state or any political subdivision thereof or other person authorized by law to make or give a certificate or other writing who knowingly makes and delivers such a certificate or writing containing any statement which he knows to be false shall, upon conviction thereof, be punished by imprisonment for not less than one nor more than five years.

§ 16-10-9. Acceptance of office or employment in more than one branch of government

(a) It shall be unlawful for:

(1) Members of the General Assembly to accept or hold office or employment in the executive branch of the state government or any agency thereof or in the judicial branch of the state government;

(2) Judges of courts of record or their clerks and assistants to accept or hold office or employment in the executive branch of the state government or any agency thereof or in the legislative branch of the state government; or

(3) Officers or employees of the executive branch of the state government to accept or hold office or employment in the legislative or judicial branches of the state government.

(b) A person who knowingly disburses or receives any compensation or money in violation of this Code section is guilty of a misdemeanor.

(c) Nothing in this Code section shall be construed to apply to any officer or employee of the executive branch who has taken a leave of absence without pay from his post for temporary service as an employee of the legislative branch while it is in session and during the authorized stay-over period.

§ 16-10-20. False statements and writings, concealment of facts, and fraudulent documents in matters within jurisdiction of state or political subdivisions

A person who knowingly and willfully falsifies, conceals, or covers up by any trick, scheme, or device a material fact; makes a false, fictitious, or fraudulent statement or representation; or makes or uses any false writing or document, knowing the same to contain any false, fictitious, or fraudulent statement or entry, in any matter within the jurisdiction of any department or agency of state government or of the government of any county, city, or other political subdivision of this state shall, upon conviction thereof, be punished by a fine of not more than $1,000.00 or by imprisonment for not less than one nor more than five years, or both.

§ 16-10-20.1. Filing false documents

(a) As used in this Code section, the term "document" means information that is inscribed on a tangible medium or that is stored in an electronic or other medium and is retrievable in perceivable form and shall include, but shall not be limited to, liens, encumbrances, documents of title, instruments relating to a security interest in or title to real or personal property, or other records, statements, or representations of fact, law, right, or opinion.
(b) Notwithstanding Code Sections 16-10-20 and 16-10-71, it shall be unlawful for any person to:
(1) Knowingly file, enter, or record any document in a public record or court of this state or of the United States knowing or having reason to know that such document is false or contains a materially false, fictitious, or fraudulent statement or representation; or
(2) Knowingly alter, conceal, cover up, or create a document and file, enter, or record it in a public record or court of this state or of the United States knowing or having reason to know that such document has been altered or contains a materially false, fictitious, or fraudulent statement or representation.
(c) Any person who violates subsection (b) of this Code section shall be guilty of a felony and, upon conviction thereof, shall be punished by imprisonment of not less than one nor more than ten years, a fine not to exceed $10,000.00, or both.
(d) This Code section shall not apply to a court clerk, registrar of deeds, or any other government employee who is acting in the course of his or her official duties.

§ 16-10-21. Conspiracy to defraud state or political subdivision

(a) A person commits the offense of conspiracy to defraud the state when he conspires or agrees with another to commit theft of any property which belongs to the state or to any agency thereof or which is under the control or possession of a state officer or employee in his official capacity. The crime shall be complete when the conspiracy or agreement is effected and an overt act in furtherance thereof has been committed, regardless of whether the theft is consummated. A person convicted of the offense of conspiracy to defraud the state shall be punished by imprisonment for not less than one nor more than five years.
(b) A person commits the offense of conspiracy to defraud a political subdivision when he conspires or agrees with another to commit theft of any property which belongs to a political subdivision or to any agency thereof or which is under the control or possession of an officer or employee of a political subdivision in his official capacity. The crime shall be complete when the conspiracy or agreement is effected and an overt act in furtherance thereof has been committed, regardless of whether the theft is consummated. A person convicted of the offense of conspiracy to defraud a political subdivision shall be punished by imprisonment for not less than one nor more than five years.

§ 16-10-22. Conspiracy in restraint of free and open competition in transactions with state or political subdivisions; forfeiture of right to bid on or enter into contracts

(a) A person who enters into a contract, combination, or conspiracy in restraint of trade or in restraint of free and open competition in any transaction with the state or any agency thereof, whether the transaction is for goods, materials, or services, shall, upon conviction thereof, be punished by imprisonment for not less than one nor more than five years. The crime of conspiracy in restraint of free and open competition in transactions with the state shall be complete when the contract, combination, or conspiracy is effected and an overt act in furtherance thereof has been committed.
(b) A person who enters into a contract, combination, or conspiracy in restraint of trade or in restraint of free and open competition in any transaction with a political subdivision or any agency thereof, whether the transaction is for goods, materials, or services, shall, upon conviction thereof, be punished by imprisonment for not less than one nor more than five years. The crime of conspiracy in restraint of free and open competition in transactions with political subdivisions shall be complete when the contract, combination, or conspiracy is effected and an overt act in furtherance thereof has been committed.
(c) A person who is convicted of or who pleads guilty to a violation of subsection (a) or (b) of this Code section as a result of any contract, combination, or conspiracy in restraint of trade or in restraint of free and open competition in any transaction which was entered into or carried out, in whole or in part, on or after July 1, 1985, shall be ineligible to submit a bid on, enter into, or participate in any contract with any department, agency, branch, board, or authority of the state or any county, municipality, board of education, or other political subdivision thereof for a period of five years following the date of the conviction or entry of the plea.

§ 16-10-23. Impersonating a public officer or employee

A person who falsely holds himself out as a peace officer or other public officer or employee with intent to mislead another into believing that he is actually such officer commits the offense of impersonating an officer and, upon conviction thereof, shall be punished by a fine of not more than $1,000.00 or by imprisonment for not less than one nor more than five years, or both.

§ 16-10-24. Obstructing or hindering law enforcement officers; penalty

(a) Except as otherwise provided in subsection (b) of this Code section, a person who knowingly and willfully obstructs or hinders any law enforcement officer, prison guard, jailer, correctional officer, community supervision officer, county or Department of Juvenile Justice juvenile probation officer, probation officer serving pursuant to Article 6 of Chapter 8 of Title 42, or conservation ranger in the lawful discharge of his or her official duties shall be guilty of a misdemeanor.
(b) Whoever knowingly and willfully resists, obstructs, or opposes any law enforcement officer, prison guard, jailer, correctional officer, community supervision officer, county or Department of Juvenile Justice juvenile probation officer, probation officer serving pursuant to Article 6 of Chapter 8 of Title 42, or conservation ranger in the lawful discharge of his or her official duties by offering or doing violence to the person of such officer or legally authorized person shall be guilty of a felony and shall, upon a first conviction thereof, be punished by imprisonment for not less than one year nor more than five years. Upon a second conviction for a violation of this subsection, such person shall be punished by imprisonment for not less than two years nor more than ten years. Upon a third or subsequent conviction for a violation of this subsection, such person shall be punished by imprisonment for not less than three years nor more than 15 years.
(c) Whoever knowingly and willfully resists, obstructs, or opposes any law enforcement officer, prison guard, jailer, correctional officer, community supervision officer, county or Department of Juvenile Justice juvenile probation officer, probation officer serving pursuant to Article 6 of Chapter 8 of Title 42, or conservation ranger in the lawful discharge of his or her official duties by knowingly and willfully throwing, projecting, or expelling human or animal blood, urine, feces, vomitus, or seminal fluid on or at such individual shall be guilty of a felony and shall, upon conviction thereof, be punished by imprisonment for not less than one year nor more than five years.
(d) A person convicted under this Code section shall be punished, in addition to any term of imprisonment imposed, by a fine as provided by law which shall be at least $300.00. With respect to $300.00 of the fine imposed, after distributing the surcharges and deductions required by Chapter 21 of Title 15, Code Sections 36-15-9 and 42-8-34, and Title 47, it shall be earmarked for the Georgia State Indemnification Fund for purposes of payment of indemnification for death or disability as provided for in Part 1 of Article 5 of Chapter 9 of Title 45.

§ 16-10-24.1. Obstructing or hindering firefighters

(a) As used in this Code section, the term "firefighter" means:
(1) Any person who is employed as a professional firefighter on a full-time basis for at least 40 hours per week by any county, municipal, or state fire department when such person has responsibility for preventing and suppressing fires, protecting life and property, enforcing municipal, county, or state fire prevention codes, or enforcing any law or ordinance pertaining to the prevention or control of fires;
(2) Any volunteer firefighter as the term "volunteer firefighter" is defined by paragraph (7) of Code Section 47-7-1 as said paragraph (7) exists on January 1, 1988; or

(3) Any person employed as a professional firefighter on a full-time basis for at least 40 hours per week by a person or corporation which has a contract with a municipality or county to provide fire prevention and fire-fighting services for such municipality or county when such person has responsibility for preventing and suppressing fires, protecting life and property, enforcing municipal or county fire prevention codes, or enforcing any municipal or county ordinances pertaining to the prevention and control of fires.

(b) Except as otherwise provided in subsection (c) of this Code section, a person who knowingly and willfully obstructs or hinders any firefighter in the lawful discharge of the firefighter's official duties is guilty of a misdemeanor.

(c) Whoever knowingly and willfully resists, obstructs, or opposes any firefighter in the lawful discharge of the firefighter's official duties by offering or doing violence to the person of such firefighter is guilty of a felony and shall, upon conviction thereof, be punished by imprisonment for not less than one nor more than five years.

§ 16-10-24.2. Obstructing or hindering emergency medical technicians or emergency medical professionals; criminal penalty

(a) As used in this Code section, the term:

(1) "Emergency medical professional" means any person performing emergency medical services who is licensed or certified to provide health care in accordance with the provisions of Chapter 11, Chapter 26, or Chapter 34 of Title 43.

(2) "Emergency medical technician" means any person who has been certified as an emergency medical technician, cardiac technician, paramedic, or first responder pursuant to Chapter 11 of Title 31.

(b) Except as otherwise provided in subsection (c) of this Code section, a person who knowingly and willfully obstructs or hinders any emergency medical technician, any emergency medical professional, or any properly identified person working under the direction of an emergency medical professional in the lawful discharge of the official duties of such emergency medical technician, emergency medical professional, or properly identified person working under the direction of an emergency medical professional is guilty of a misdemeanor.

(c) Whoever knowingly and willfully resists or obstructs any emergency medical technician, any emergency medical professional, or any properly identified person working under the direction of an emergency medical professional in the lawful discharge of the official duties of the emergency medical technician, emergency medical professional, or properly identified person working under the direction of an emergency medical professional by threatening or doing violence to the person of such emergency medical technician, emergency medical professional, or properly identified person working under the direction of an emergency medical professional is guilty of a felony and shall, upon conviction thereof, be punished by imprisonment for not less than one nor more than five years.

§ 16-10-24.3. Obstructing or hindering persons making emergency telephone calls

Any person who verbally or physically obstructs, prevents, or hinders another person with intent to cause or allow physical harm or injury to another person from making or completing a 9-1-1 telephone call or a call to any law enforcement agency to request police protection or to report the commission of a crime is guilty of a misdemeanor and shall, upon conviction thereof, be punished by a fine not to exceed $1,000.00 or imprisonment not to exceed 12 months, or both.

§ 16-10-24.4. Obstructing or hindering park ranger

(a) As used in this Code section, the term "park ranger" means any person, other than a law enforcement officer and other individuals covered under Code Section 16-10-24, however designated, who is employed by the state, any political subdivision of the state, or the United States for the enforcement of park rules and regulations.

(b) Except as otherwise provided in subsection (c) of this Code section, a person who knowingly and willfully obstructs or hinders any park ranger in the lawful discharge of his or her official duties shall be guilty of a misdemeanor.

(c) Whoever knowingly and willfully resists, obstructs, or opposes any park ranger in the lawful discharge of his or her official duties by offering or doing violence to the person of such park ranger shall be guilty of a felony and, upon conviction thereof, be punished by imprisonment for not less than one nor more than five years.

§ 16-10-25. Giving false name, address, or birthdate to law enforcement officer

A person who gives a false name, address, or date of birth to a law enforcement officer in the lawful discharge of his official duties with the intent of misleading the officer as to his identity or birthdate is guilty of a misdemeanor.

§ 16-10-26. False report of a crime

A person who willfully and knowingly gives or causes a false report of a crime to be given to any law enforcement officer or agency of this state is guilty of a misdemeanor.

§ 16-10-27. Transmitting false report of fire

A person who transmits in any manner to a fire department, public or private, or to any other group which is organized for the purpose of preventing or controlling fires a false report of a fire, knowing at the time that there is no reasonable ground for believing that such fire exists, is guilty of a misdemeanor.

§ 16-10-28. Transmitting a false public alarm; restitution

(a) As used in this Code section, the term:

(1) "Critical infrastructure" means any building, place of assembly, or facility that is located in this state and necessary for national or public security, education, or public safety.

(2) "Destructive device" means a destructive device as such term is defined by Code Section 16-7-80.

(3) "Hazardous substance" means a hazardous substance as such term is defined by Code Section 12-8-92.

(b) A person commits the offense of transmitting a false public alarm when he or she knowingly and intentionally transmits in any manner a report or warning knowing at the time of the transmission that there is no reasonable ground for believing such report or warning and when the report or warning relates to:

(1) A destructive device or hazardous substance is located in such a place that its explosion, detonation, or release would endanger human life or cause injury or damage to property; or

(2) An individual who has caused or threatened to cause physical harm to himself or herself or another individual by using a deadly weapon or with any object, device, or instrument which, when used offensively against a person, is likely to result in serious bodily injury.

(c) (1) Except as provided in paragraph (2) of this subsection, a person convicted of a violation of subsection (b) of this Code section shall be punished as for a misdemeanor of a high and aggravated nature and upon conviction for a second or subsequent violation of subsection (b) of this Code section shall be guilty of a felony and punished by imprisonment for not less than one nor more than ten years, by a fine of not less than $5,000.00, or both.

(2) If the location of the violation of paragraph (1) of subsection (b) of this Code section is critical infrastructure, such person shall be guilty of a felony and upon conviction shall be punished by imprisonment for not less than five nor more than ten years, a fine of not more than $100,000.00, or both.

(d) In addition to any other penalty imposed by law for a violation of this Code section, the court may require the defendant to make restitution to any affected public or private entity for the reasonable costs or damages associated with the offense including, without limitation, the actual value of any goods, services, or income lost as a result of such violation. Restitution made pursuant to this subsection shall not preclude any party from obtaining any other civil or criminal remedy available under any other provision of law. The restitution authorized by this subsection is supplemental and not exclusive.

§ 16-10-29. Request for ambulance service when not reasonably needed

(a) It shall be unlawful for any person to transmit in any manner a request for ambulance service to any person, firm, or corporation furnishing ambulance service, public or private, knowing at the time of making the request for ambulance service that there exists no reasonable need for such ambulance service.

(b) Any person who violates subsection (a) of this Code section shall be guilty of a misdemeanor.

§ 16-10-30. Refusal to obey official request at fire or other emergency

A person in a gathering who refuses to obey the reasonable official request or order of a peace officer or firefighter to move, for the purpose of promoting the public safety by dispersing those gathered in dangerous proximity to a fire or other emergency, is guilty of a misdemeanor.

§ 16-10-31. Concealing death of another person

A person who, by concealing the death of any other person, hinders a discovery of whether or not such person was unlawfully killed is guilty of a felony and upon conviction shall be punished by imprisonment for not less than one nor more than ten years, a fine of not less than $1,000.00 nor more than $5,000.00, or both.

§ 16-10-32. Attempted murder or threatening of witnesses in official proceedings

(a) Any person who attempts to kill another person with intent to:

(1) Prevent the attendance or testimony of any person in an official proceeding;

(2) Prevent the production of a record, document, or other object, in an official proceeding; or

(3) Prevent the communication by any person to a law enforcement officer, prosecuting attorney, or judge of this state of information relating to the commission or possible commission of a criminal offense or a violation of conditions of probation, parole, or release pending judicial proceedings

shall be guilty of a felony and, upon conviction thereof, shall be punished by imprisonment for not less than ten nor more than 20 years.

(b) Any person who threatens or causes physical or economic harm to another person or a member of such person's family or household, threatens to damage or damages the property of another person or a member of such person's family or household, or attempts to cause physical or economic harm to another person or a member of such person's family or household with the intent to hinder, delay, prevent, or dissuade any person from:

(1) Attending or testifying in an official proceeding;

(2) Reporting in good faith to a law enforcement officer, prosecuting attorney, or judge of a court of this state, or its political subdivisions or authorities, the commission or possible commission of an offense under the laws of this state or a violation of conditions of probation, parole, or release pending judicial proceedings;

(3) Arresting or seeking the arrest of another person in connection with a criminal offense; or

(4) Causing a criminal prosecution, or a parole or probation revocation proceeding, to be sought or instituted, or assisting in such prosecution or proceeding

shall be guilty of a felony and, upon conviction thereof, shall be punished by imprisonment for not less than two years nor more than ten years or by a fine of not less than $10,000.00 nor more than $25,000.00, or both.

(c)(1) For the purposes of this Code section, the term "official proceeding" means any hearing or trial conducted by a court of this state or its political subdivisions, a grand jury, or an agency of the executive, legislative, or judicial branches of government of this state or its political subdivisions or authorities.

(2) An official proceeding need not be pending or about to be instituted at the time of any offense defined in this Code section.

(3) The testimony, record, document, or other object which is prevented or impeded or attempted to be prevented or impeded in an official proceeding in violation of this Code section need not be admissible in evidence or free of a claim of privilege.

(4) In a prosecution for an offense under this Code section, no state of mind need be proved with respect to the circumstance:

(A) That the official proceeding before a judge, court, magistrate, grand jury, or government agency is before a judge or court of this state, a magistrate, a grand jury, or an agency of state or local government; or

(B) That the judge is a judge of this state or its political subdivisions or that the law enforcement officer is an officer or employee of the State of Georgia or a political subdivision or authority of the state or a person authorized to act for or on behalf of the State of Georgia or a political subdivision or authority of the state.

(5) A prosecution under this Code section may be brought in the county in which the official proceeding, whether or not pending or about to be instituted, was intended to be affected or in the county in which the conduct constituting the alleged offense occurred.

(d) Any crime committed in violation of subsection (a) or (b) of this Code section shall be considered a separate offense.

§ 16-10-33. Removal or attempted removal of weapon from public official; punishment

(a) For the purposes of this Code section, the term "firearm" shall include stun guns and tasers. A stun gun or taser is any device that is powered by electrical charging units such as batteries and emits an electrical charge in excess of 20,000 volts or is otherwise capable of incapacitating a person by an electrical charge.

(b) It shall be unlawful for any person knowingly to remove or attempt to remove a firearm, chemical spray, or baton from the possession of another person if:

(1) The other person is lawfully acting within the course and scope of employment; and

(2) The person has knowledge or reason to know that the other person is employed as:

(A) A peace officer as defined in paragraph (8) of Code Section 35-8-2;

(B) An employee with the power of arrest by the Department of Corrections;

(C) An employee with the power of arrest by the State Board of Pardons and Paroles;

(D) A community supervision officer or other employee with the power of arrest by the Department of Community Supervision;

(E) A jail officer or guard by a county or municipality and has the responsibility of supervising inmates who are confined in a county or municipal jail or other detention facility; or

(F) A juvenile correctional officer by the Department of Juvenile Justice and has the primary responsibility for the supervision and control of youth confined in such department's programs and facilities.

(c) Any person who violates subsection (b) of this Code section shall, upon conviction thereof, be punished by imprisonment for not less than one nor more than five years or a fine of not more than $10,000.00, or both.

(d) A violation of this Code section shall constitute a separate offense. A sentence imposed under this Code section may be imposed separately from and consecutive to or concurrent with a sentence for any other offense related to the act or acts establishing the offense under this Code section.

§ 16-10-34. Use of laser devices against law enforcement officer

(a) For purposes of this Code section, the term "laser device" means a device designed to amplify electromagnetic radiation by stimulated emission that emits a beam designed to be used by the operator as a pointer or highlighter to indicate, mark, or identify a specific position, place, item, or object. Such term also means a device that projects a beam or point of light by means of light amplification by stimulated emission of radiation or other means or that emits light which simulates the appearance of a beam of light.

(b) It shall be unlawful for any person to knowingly and intentionally project upon a law enforcement officer any laser device without such officer's permission if:

(1) The law enforcement officer is lawfully acting within the course and scope of employment; and

(2) The person has knowledge or reason to know that the law enforcement officer is employed as:

(A) A peace officer as defined in paragraph (8) of Code Section 35-8-2;

(B) An employee with the power of arrest by the Department of Corrections;

(C) An employee with the power of arrest by the State Board of Pardons and Paroles;

(D) A community supervision officer or other employee with the power of arrest by the Department of Community Supervision;

(E) A jail officer or guard by a county or municipality and has the responsibility of supervising inmates who are confined in a county or municipal jail or other detention facility; or

(F) A juvenile correctional officer or juvenile probation officer by the Department of Juvenile Justice and has the primary responsibility for the supervision and control of youth confined in such department's programs and facilities.

(c) Any person who violates subsection (b) of this Code section shall be guilty of a high and aggravated misdemeanor.

(d) It shall not be a defense to a prosecution for a violation of this Code section that the laser device was pointed at such officer through a glass, window, or other transparent or translucent object.

(e) Each violation of this Code section shall constitute a separate offense. A sentence imposed under this Code section may be imposed separately from and consecutive to or concurrent with a sentence for any other offense related to the act or acts establishing the offense under this Code section.

§ 16-10-50. Hindering apprehension or punishment of criminal

(a) A person commits the offense of hindering the apprehension or punishment of a criminal when, with intention to hinder the apprehension or punishment of a person whom he knows or has reasonable grounds to believe has committed a felony or to be an escaped inmate or prisoner, he:

(1) Harbors or conceals such person; or

(2) Conceals or destroys evidence of the crime.

(b) A person convicted of the offense of hindering apprehension or punishment of a criminal shall be punished by imprisonment for not less than one nor more than five years.

§ 16-10-51. Bail jumping

(a) Any person who has been charged with or convicted of the commission of a felony under the laws of this state and has been set at liberty on bail or on his own recognizance upon the condition that he will subsequently appear at a specified time and place commits the offense of felony-bail jumping if, after actual notice to the defendant in open court or notice to the person by mailing to his last known address or otherwise being notified personally in writing by a court official or officer of the court, he fails without sufficient excuse to appear at that time and place. A person convicted of the offense of felony-bail jumping shall be punished by imprisonment for not less than one nor more than five years or by a fine of not more than $5,000.00, or both.

(b) Any person who has been charged with or convicted of the commission of a misdemeanor and has been set at liberty on bail or on his own recognizance upon the condition that he will subsequently appear at a specified time and place commits the offense of misdemeanor-bail jumping if, after actual notice to the defendant in open court or notice to the person by mailing to his last known address or otherwise being notified personally in writing by a court official or officer of the court, he fails without sufficient excuse to appear at that time and place. A person convicted of the offense of misdemeanor-bail jumping shall be guilty of a misdemeanor.

(c)(1) Any person who has been charged with or convicted of the commission of any of the misdemeanors listed in paragraph (2) of this subsection and has been set at liberty on bail or on his or her own recognizance upon the condition that he or she will subsequently appear at a specified time and place and who, after actual notice to the defendant in open court or notice to the defendant by mailing to the defendant's last known address or otherwise being notified personally in writing by a court official or officer of the court, leaves the state to avoid appearing in court at such time commits the offense of out-of-state-bail jumping. A person convicted of the offense of out-of-state-bail jumping shall be guilty of a felony and shall be punished by imprisonment for not less than one year nor more than five years or by a fine of not less than $1,000.00 nor more than $5,000.00, or both.

(2) Paragraph (1) of this subsection shall apply only to the following misdemeanors:

(A) Abandonment, as provided in Code Sections 19-10-1 and 19-10-2;

(B) Simple assault, as provided in Code Section 16-5-20;

(C) Carrying a weapon or long gun in an unauthorized location, as provided in Code Section 16-11-127;

(D) Bad checks, as provided in Code Section 16-9-20;

(E) Simple battery, as provided in Code Section 16-5-23;

(F) Bribery, as provided in Code Section 16-10-3;

(G) Failure to report child abuse, as provided in Code Section 19-7-5;

(H) Criminal trespass, as provided in Code Section 16-7-21;

(I) Contributing to the delinquency of a minor, as provided in Code Section 16-12-1;

(J) Escape, as provided in Code Sections 16-10-52 and 16-10-53;

(K) Tampering with evidence, as provided in Code Section 16-10-94;

(L) Family violence, as provided in Code Section 19-13-6;

(M) Deceptive business practices, as provided in Code Section 16-9-50;

(N) Reserved;

(O) Fraud in obtaining public assistance, food stamps, or Medicaid, as provided in Code Section 49-4-15;

(P) Reckless conduct, as provided in Code Section 16-5-60;

(Q) Any offense under Chapter 8 of this title which is a misdemeanor;

(R) Any offense under Chapter 13 of this title which is a misdemeanor;

(S) Driving under the influence of alcohol or drugs, as provided in Code Section 40-6-391;

(T) Driving without a license in violation of Code Section 40-5-20 or driving while a license is suspended or revoked as provided in Code Section 40-5-121; and

(U) Any offense under Code Section 40-6-10, relating to requirement of the operator or owner of a motor vehicle to have proof of insurance.

(d) Subsections (b) and (c) of this Code section shall not apply to any person who has been charged or convicted of the commission of a misdemeanor under the laws of this state and has been set at liberty after posting a cash bond and fails to appear in court at the specified time and place where such failure to appear, in accordance with the rules of the court having jurisdiction over such misdemeanor, is construed as an admission of guilt and the cash bond is forfeited without the need for any further statutory procedures and the proceeds of the cash bond are applied and distributed as any fine imposed by the court would be.

§ 16-10-52. Escape

(a) A person commits the offense of escape when he or she:

(1) Having been convicted of a felony or misdemeanor or of the violation of a municipal ordinance, intentionally escapes from lawful custody or from any place of lawful confinement;

(2) Being in lawful custody or lawful confinement prior to conviction, intentionally escapes from such custody or confinement;

(3) Having been adjudicated of a delinquent act or a juvenile traffic offense, or as a child in need of services subject to lawful custody or lawful confinement, intentionally escapes from lawful custody or from any place of lawful confinement;

(4) Being in lawful custody or lawful confinement prior to adjudication, intentionally escapes from such custody or confinement; or

(5) Intentionally fails to return as instructed to lawful custody or lawful confinement or to any residential facility operated by the Georgia Department of Corrections after having been released on the condition that he or she will so return; provided, however, such person shall be allowed a grace period of eight hours from the exact time specified for return if such person can prove he or she did not intentionally fail to return.

(a.1) Revocation of probation for conduct in violation of any provision of subsection (a) of this Code section shall not preclude an independent criminal prosecution under this Code section based on the same conduct.

66

(b)(1) A person who, having been convicted of a felony, is convicted of the offense of escape shall be punished by imprisonment for not less than one nor more than ten years.

(2) Any person charged with a felony who is in lawful confinement prior to conviction or adjudication who is convicted of the offense of escape shall be punished by imprisonment for not less than one nor more than five years.

(3) Notwithstanding paragraphs (1) and (2) of this subsection, a person who commits the offense of escape while armed with a dangerous weapon shall, upon conviction thereof, be punished by imprisonment for not less than one nor more than 20 years.

(4) Any other person convicted of the offense of escape shall be punished as for a misdemeanor.

§ 16-10-53. Aiding or permitting another to escape lawful custody or confinement

(a) A person who knowingly aids another in escaping from lawful custody or from any place of lawful confinement shall, upon conviction thereof, be punished by imprisonment for not less than one nor more than five years.

(b) A peace officer or employee of any place of lawful confinement who recklessly permits any person in his custody to escape is guilty of a misdemeanor.

§ 16-10-54. Assailing, opposing, or resisting officer of the law in a penal institution

A person in the lawful custody of any penal institution of the state or of a political subdivision of the state who assails, opposes, or resists an officer of the law or of such penal institution or a member of the guard with intent to cause serious bodily injury commits the offense of mutiny and, upon conviction thereof, shall be punished by imprisonment for not less than one nor more than five years.

§ 16-10-55. Persuading, enticing, instigating, aiding, or abetting person in a penal institution to commit mutiny

A person who persuades, entices, instigates, counsels, aids, or abets a person in the lawful custody of any penal institution to commit the offense of mutiny shall, upon conviction thereof, be punished by imprisonment for not less than one nor more than five years.

§ 16-10-56. Unlawful acts of violence in a penal institution

(a) As used in this Code section, the term "penal institution" means any place of confinement for persons accused of or convicted of violating a law of this state or an ordinance of a municipality or political subdivision of this state.

(b) No person legally confined to a penal institution shall commit an unlawful act of violence or any other act in a violent or tumultuous manner in a penal institution.

(c) Any person who violates this Code section shall be guilty of a felony and, upon conviction thereof, shall be punished by imprisonment of not less than one year nor more than 20 years.

§ 16-10-70. Perjury

(a) A person to whom a lawful oath or affirmation has been administered commits the offense of perjury when, in a judicial proceeding, he knowingly and willfully makes a false statement material to the issue or point in question.

(b) A person convicted of the offense of perjury shall be punished by a fine of not more than $1,000.00 or by imprisonment for not less than one nor more than ten years, or both. A person convicted of the offense of perjury that was a cause of another's being imprisoned shall be sentenced to a term not to exceed the sentence provided for the crime for which the other person was convicted. A person convicted of the offense of perjury that was a cause of another's being punished by death shall be punished by life imprisonment.

§ 16-10-71. False swearing

(a) A person to whom a lawful oath or affirmation has been administered or who executes a document knowing that it purports to be an acknowledgment of a lawful oath or affirmation commits the offense of false swearing when, in any matter or thing other than a judicial proceeding, he knowingly and willfully makes a false statement.

(b) A person convicted of the offense of false swearing shall be punished by a fine of not more than $1,000.00 or by imprisonment for not less than one nor more than five years, or both.

§ 16-10-72. Subornation of perjury or false swearing

A person commits the offense of subornation of perjury or false swearing when he procures or induces another to commit the offense of perjury or the offense of false swearing and, upon conviction thereof, shall be punished by a fine of not more than $1,000.00 or by imprisonment for not less than one nor more than ten years, or both.

§ 16-10-73. Impersonating another in the acknowledgment of recognizance, bail, or judgment

Any person except an attorney of record who shall acknowledge or cause to be acknowledged, in any of the courts of the state or before any authorized officer, any recognizance, bail, or judgment in the name of any person not privy or consenting thereto commits the offense of impersonating in a legal proceeding and, upon conviction thereof, shall be punished by a fine of not more than $1,000.00 or by imprisonment for not less than one nor more than five years, or both.

§ 16-10-90. Compounding a crime

(a) A person commits the offense of compounding a crime when, after institution of criminal proceedings and without leave of the court or of the prosecuting attorney of the court where the criminal proceedings are pending, he accepts or agrees to accept any benefit in consideration of a promise, express or implied, not to prosecute or aid in the prosecution of a criminal offense.

(b) A person convicted of the offense of compounding a crime which is a felony shall be punished by a fine of not more than $1,000.00 or by imprisonment for not less than one nor more than five years, or both. A person convicted of the offense of compounding a crime which is a misdemeanor is guilty of a misdemeanor.

§ 16-10-91. Embracery

(a) A person commits the offense of embracery when he:

(1) With intent to influence a person summoned or serving as a juror, communicates with him otherwise than is authorized by law in an attempt to influence his action as a juror; or

(2) Summoned as a juror, accepts anything of value offered to him with the understanding that it is given with the intent of influencing his action as a juror.

(b) A person convicted of the offense of embracery shall be punished by a fine of not more than $1,000.00 or by imprisonment for not less than one nor more than five years, or both.

§ 16-10-92. Acceptance of benefit, reward, or consideration by witness for changing testimony or being absent from trial, hearing, or other proceeding

A person who is or may be a witness at a trial, hearing, or other proceeding before any court or any officer authorized by the law to hear evidence or take testimony and who receives or agrees or offers to receive any benefit, reward, or consideration to which he is not entitled, pursuant to an agreement or understanding that his testimony will be influenced thereby or that he will absent himself from the trial, hearing, or other proceeding, shall, upon conviction thereof, be punished by imprisonment for not less than one nor more than five years.

§ 16-10-93. Influencing witnesses

(a) A person who, with intent to deter a witness from testifying freely, fully, and truthfully to any matter pending in any court, in any administrative proceeding, or before a grand jury, communicates, directly or indirectly, to such witness any threat of injury or damage to the person, property, or employment of the witness or to the person, property, or employment of any relative or associate of the witness or who offers or delivers any benefit, reward, or consideration to such witness or to a relative or associate of the witness shall, upon conviction thereof, be punished by imprisonment for not less than one nor more than five years.
(b)(1) It shall be unlawful for any person knowingly to use intimidation, physical force, or threats; to persuade another person by means of corruption or to attempt to do so; or to engage in misleading conduct toward another person with intent to:
(A) Influence, delay, or prevent the testimony of any person in an official proceeding;
(B) Cause or induce any person to:
(i) Withhold testimony or a record, document, or other object from an official proceeding;
(ii) Alter, destroy, mutilate, or conceal an object with intent to impair the object's integrity or availability for use in an official proceeding;
(iii) Evade legal process summoning that person to appear as a witness or to produce a record, document, or other object in an official proceeding; or
(iv) Be absent from an official proceeding to which such person has been summoned by legal process; or
(C) Hinder, delay, or prevent the communication to a law enforcement officer, prosecuting attorney, or judge of this state of information relating to the commission or possible commission of a criminal offense or a violation of conditions of probation, parole, or release pending judicial proceedings.
(2) Any person convicted of a violation of this subsection shall be guilty of a felony and, upon conviction thereof, shall be punished by imprisonment for not less than two nor more than ten years or by a fine of not less than $10,000.00 nor more than $20,000.00, or both.
(3)(A) For the purposes of this Code section, the term "official proceeding" means any hearing or trial conducted by a court of this state or its political subdivisions, a grand jury, or an agency of the executive, legislative, or judicial branches of government of this state or its political subdivisions or authorities.
(B) An official proceeding need not be pending or about to be instituted at the time of any offense defined in this subsection.
(C) The testimony, record, document, or other object which is prevented or impeded or attempted to be prevented or impeded in an official proceeding in violation of this Code section need not be admissible in evidence or free of a claim of privilege.
(D) In a prosecution for an offense under this Code section, no state of mind need be proved with respect to the circumstance:
(i) That the official proceeding before a judge, court, magistrate, grand jury, or government agency is before a judge or court of this state, a magistrate, a grand jury, or an agency of state or local government; or
(ii) That the judge is a judge of this state or its political subdivisions or that the law enforcement officer is an officer or employee of the State of Georgia or a political subdivision or authority of the state or a person authorized to act for or on behalf of the State of Georgia or a political subdivision or authority of the state.
(E) A prosecution under this Code section may be brought in the county in which the official proceeding, whether or not pending or about to be instituted, was intended to be affected or in the county in which the conduct constituting the alleged offense occurred.
(c) Any crime committed in violation of subsection (a) or (b) of this Code section shall be considered a separate offense.

§ 16-10-94. Tampering with evidence

(a) A person commits the offense of tampering with evidence when, with the intent to prevent the apprehension or cause the wrongful apprehension of any person or to obstruct the prosecution or defense of any person, he knowingly destroys, alters, conceals, or disguises physical evidence or makes, devises, prepares, or plants false evidence.
(b) Nothing in this Code section shall be deemed to abrogate or alter any privilege which any person is entitled to claim under existing laws.
(c) Except as otherwise provided in this subsection, any person who violates subsection (a) of this Code section involving the prosecution or defense of a felony and involving another person shall be guilty of a felony and, upon conviction thereof, shall be punished by imprisonment for not less than one nor more than three years; provided, however, that any person who violates subsection (a) of this Code section involving the prosecution or defense of a serious violent felony as defined in subsection (a) of Code Section 17-10-6.1 and involving another person shall be guilty of a felony and, upon conviction thereof, shall be punished by imprisonment for not less than one nor more than ten years. Except as otherwise provided in this subsection, any person who violates subsection (a) of this Code section involving the prosecution or defense of a misdemeanor shall be guilty of a misdemeanor.

§ 16-10-94.1. Willful destruction, alteration, or falsification of medical records

(a) As used in this Code section, the term:
(1) "Patient" means any person who has received health care services from a provider.
(2) "Provider" means all hospitals, including public, private, osteopathic, and tuberculosis hospitals; other special care units, including podiatric facilities, skilled nursing facilities, and kidney disease treatment centers, including freestanding hemodialysis units; intermediate care facilities; ambulatory surgical or obstetrical facilities; health maintenance organizations; and home health agencies. Such term shall also mean any person licensed to practice under Chapter 9, 11, 26, 34, 35, or 39 of Title 43.
(3) "Record" means a patient's health record, including, but not limited to, evaluations, diagnoses, prognoses, laboratory reports, X-rays, prescriptions, and other technical information used in assessing the patient's condition, or the pertinent portion of the record relating to a specific condition or a summary of the record.
(b) Any person who, with intent to conceal any material fact relating to a potential claim or cause of action, knowingly and willfully destroys, alters, or falsifies any record shall be guilty of a misdemeanor.

§ 16-10-95. Barratry; penalty

Reserved. Repealed by Ga. L. 2006, p. 69, § 1/HB 804, effective July 1, 2006.

§ 16-10-96. Impersonating another in the course of an action, proceeding, or prosecution

Any person who shall falsely represent or impersonate another and in such assumed character answer as a witness to interrogatories or do any other act in the course of any action, proceeding, or prosecution or in any other way, matter, or thing, whereby the person so impersonated or represented, or any other person, might suffer damage, loss, or injury shall, upon conviction thereof, be punished by confinement for not less than one year nor more than five years.

§ 16-10-97. Intimidation or injury of any officer in or of any court

(a) A person who by threat or force or by any threatening action, letter, or communication:
(1) Endeavors to intimidate or impede any grand juror or trial juror or any officer in or of any court of this state or any court of any county or municipality of this state or any officer who may be serving at any proceeding in any such court while in the discharge of such juror's or officer's duties;

(2) Injures any grand juror or trial juror in his or her person or property on account of any indictment or verdict assented to by him or her or on account of his or her being or having been such juror; or

(3) Injures any officer in or of any court of this state or any court of any county or municipality of this state or any officer who may be serving at any proceeding in any such court in his or her person or property on account of the performance of his or her official duties

shall, upon conviction thereof, be punished by a fine of not more than $5,000.00 or by imprisonment for not more than 20 years, or both.

(b) As used in this Code section, the term "any officer in or of any court" means a judge, attorney, clerk of court, deputy clerk of court, court reporter, community supervision officer, county or Department of Juvenile Justice juvenile probation officer, or probation officer serving pursuant to Article 6 of Chapter 8 of Title 42.

(c) A person who by threat or force or by any threatening action, letter, or communication endeavors to intimidate any law enforcement officer, outside the scope and course of his or her employment, or his or her immediate family member in retaliation or response to the discharge of such officer's official duties shall be guilty of a felony and, upon conviction thereof, shall be punished by imprisonment for not less than one nor more than five years, a fine not to exceed $5,000.00, or both.

§ 16-10-98. Illegal remuneration of judges and law enforcement officials

(a) It shall be unlawful for a judge, prosecuting attorney, investigating officer, or law enforcement officer who is a witness in a case to receive or agree to receive remuneration during the period of time between indictment and the completion of direct appeal in any criminal case in which the judge, prosecuting attorney, or law enforcement officer is involved for any of the following activities:
(1) Publishing a book or article concerning the case;
(2) Making a public appearance concerning the case; or
(3) Participating in any commercial activity concerning the case.
(b) A person convicted of a violation of subsection (a) of this Code section shall be guilty of a misdemeanor.
(c) For purposes of this Code section remuneration shall not be deemed to include customary and ordinary salary and benefits of the individual or customary and ordinary expenses paid for public appearances.

CHAPTER 11. OFFENSES AGAINST PUBLIC ORDER AND SAFETY

§ 16-11-1. Treason

(a) A person owing allegiance to the state commits the offense of treason when he knowingly levies war against the state, adheres to her enemies, or gives them aid and comfort. No person shall be convicted of the offense of treason except on the testimony of two witnesses to the same overt act or on confession in open court. When the overt act of treason is committed outside this state, the person charged therewith may be tried in any county in this state.
(b) A person convicted of the offense of treason shall be punished by death or by imprisonment for life or for not less than 15 years.

§ 16-11-2. Insurrection

(a) A person commits the offense of insurrection when he combines with others to overthrow or attempt to overthrow the representative and constitutional form of government of the state or any political subdivision thereof when the same is manifested by acts of violence.
(b) A person convicted of the offense of insurrection shall be punished by imprisonment for not less than one nor more than ten years. Insurrection shall be bailable only in the discretion of a judge of the superior court.

§ 16-11-3. Inciting to insurrection

(a) A person commits the offense of inciting to insurrection when he incites others to overthrow or attempt to overthrow the representative and constitutional form of government of the state or any political subdivision thereof and he or they commit any violent act in furtherance thereof.
(b) A person convicted of the offense of inciting to insurrection shall be punished by imprisonment for not less than one nor more than ten years. Inciting to insurrection shall be bailable only in the discretion of a judge of the superior court.

§ 16-11-4. Advocating overthrow of government

(a) As used in this Code section, the term:
(1) "Organization" means any corporation, company, partnership, association, trust, foundation, fund, club, society, committee, political party, or any group of persons, whether or not incorporated, permanently or temporarily associated together for joint action or advancement of views on any subject.
(2) "Subversive organization" means any organization which engages in or advocates, abets, advises, or teaches, or which has a purpose of engaging in or advocating, abetting, advising, or teaching activities intended to overthrow, to destroy, or to assist in the overthrow or destruction of the government of the state or of any political subdivision thereof by force or violence.
(b) A person commits the offense of advocating the overthrow of the government if he knowingly and willfully commits any of the following acts:
(1) Advocates, abets, advises, or teaches the duty, necessity, desirability, or propriety of overthrowing or destroying the government of the state or any political subdivision thereof by force or violence;
(2) Prints, publishes, edits, issues, circulates, sells, distributes, exhibits, or displays any written or printed matter advocating, advising, or teaching the duty, necessity, desirability, or propriety of overthrowing or destroying the government of the state or of any political subdivision thereof by force or violence;
(3) Assists in the formation, participates in the management, or contributes to the support of any subversive organization, knowing the purpose thereof;
(4) Becomes a member or continues to be a member of a subversive organization, knowing the purpose thereof;
(5) Destroys any books, records, or files or secretes any funds in this state of a subversive organization, knowing the organization to be such; or
(6) Conspires with one or more persons to commit any of the acts prohibited by this Code section.
(c) A person convicted of violating any provision of this Code section shall be punished by a fine of not more than $20,000.00 or by imprisonment for not less than one nor more than 20 years, or both.

§ 16-11-5. Short title

This part may be cited as the "Sedition and Subversive Activities Act of 1953."

§ 16-11-6. Definitions

As used in this part, the term:
(1) "Foreign government" means the government of any country, nation, or group of nations other than the government of the United States of America or of one of the states thereof.

(2) "Foreign subversive organizations" means any organization directed, dominated, or controlled directly or indirectly by a foreign government which engages in or advocates, abets, advises, or teaches, or a purpose of which is to engage in or to advocate, abet, advise, or teach activities intended to overthrow, to destroy, or to assist in the overthrow or destruction of the government of the United States or of this state or of any political subdivision of either of them and to establish in place thereof any form of government the direction and control of which is to be vested in, or exercised by or under, the domination or control of any foreign government, organization, or individual.

(3) "Organization" means an organization, corporation, company, partnership, association, trust, foundation, fund, club, society, committee, political party, or any group of persons, whether or not incorporated, permanently or temporarily associated together for joint action or advancement of views on any subject or subjects.

(4) "Subversive organization" means an organization which engages in or advocates, abets, advises, or teaches, or a purpose for which is to engage in or advocate, abet, advise, or teach activities intended to overthrow, to destroy, or to assist in the overthrow or destruction of the government of the United States, government of this state, or of any political subdivision of either of them by revolution, force, or violence.

(5) "Subversive person" means any person who commits, attempts to commit, or aids in the commission or advocates, abets, advises, or teaches by any means any person to commit, attempt to commit, or aid in the commission of any act intended to overthrow, to destroy, or to assist in the overthrow or destruction of the government of the United States or of this state or any political subdivision of either of them by revolution, force, or violence; or who is a knowing member of a subversive organization or a foreign subversive organization.

§ 16-11-7. Special assistant attorney general for investigation and prosecution of subversive activities

The Governor, with the concurrence of the Attorney General, is authorized and directed to appoint a special assistant attorney general for investigating and prosecuting subversive activities, whose responsibility it shall be, under the supervision of the Attorney General, to assemble, arrange, and deliver to the district attorney of any county, together with a list of necessary witnesses for presentation to the next grand jury in the county, all information and evidence of matters within the county which have come to his or her attention relating in any manner to the acts prohibited by this part and relating generally to the purpose, processes, and activities of subversive organizations, associations, groups, or persons. Such evidence may be presented by the Attorney General or the special assistant attorney general to the grand jury of any county directly, and he or she may represent the state on the trial of such a case, should he or she feel the ends of justice would be best served thereby, and the special assistant attorney general may testify before any grand jury as to matters referred to in this part as to which he or she may have information.

§ 16-11-8. Duties imposed on prosecuting attorneys, commissioner of public safety, sheriffs, and police to furnish information and assistance; establishment of special enforcement agencies

For the collection of any evidence and information referred to in this part, the Governor and the Attorney General are authorized and directed to call upon all prosecuting attorneys, the commissioner of public safety, sheriffs, and county and municipal police authorities to furnish to the special assistant, provided for in Code Section 16-11-7, such assistance as may from time to time be required. Such police authorities are directed to furnish information and assistance as may be from time to time so requested. The police authorities shall transmit immediately to the special assistant attorney general any information coming to their notice and attention regarding the activities of any subversive persons, subversive organizations, or foreign subversive organizations. The Governor by executive order is authorized to establish within existing departments such special enforcement agencies, designate such personnel, and fix such duties as may from time to time be required to perform any of the functions and duties required by this part.

§ 16-11-9. Maintenance of records by special assistant; classification of records

The Attorney General shall require the special assistant to maintain complete records of all information received by him and all matters handled by him under the requirements of this part. Such records as may reflect on the loyalty of any resident of this state shall not be made public or divulged to any person except with permission of the Governor or the Attorney General to effectuate the purposes of this part. All such records shall be classified as confidential state secrets until declassified by the Governor or the Attorney General.

§ 16-11-10. Grand jury investigations

The judge of any court exercising general criminal jurisdiction, when in his or her discretion it appears appropriate or when informed by the Attorney General or district attorney that there is information or evidence of the character described in Code Section 16-11-7 to be considered by the grand jury, shall charge the grand jury to inquire into violations of this part for the purpose of proper action and further to inquire generally into the purposes, processes, and activities, and any other matters affecting subversive organizations, associations, groups, or persons.

§ 16-11-11. Dissolution of subversive organizations; revocation of charter, funds, books, and records

It shall be unlawful for any subversive organization or foreign subversive organization to exist or function in this state. Any organization which by a court of competent jurisdiction is found to have violated this Code section shall be dissolved and, if it is a corporation organized and existing under the laws of this state, a finding by a court of competent jurisdiction that it has violated this Code section shall constitute legal cause for revocation of its charter and its charter shall be revoked. All funds, books, records, and files of every kind and all other property of any organization found to have violated this Code section shall be seized by and for this state, the funds to be deposited in the state treasury and the books, records, files, and other property to be turned over to the Attorney General.

§ 16-11-12. Eligibility of subversive persons to hold office or position in government

No subversive person shall be eligible for employment in or appointment to any office or any position of trust or profit in the government of this state or in the administration of the business of this state or of any county, municipality, or other political subdivision thereof.

§ 16-11-13. Investigation of all state employees prior to appointment or employment; questionnaire; promulgation of orders, rules, and regulations

(a) Every person and every board, commission, council, department, or other agency of the state or any political subdivision thereof which appoints, employs, or supervises in any manner the appointment or employment of public officials or employees shall establish, by rules, regulations, or otherwise, procedures designated to ascertain before any person, including teachers and other employees of any public educational institution in this state, is appointed or employed, that he is not a subversive person and that there are no reasonable grounds to believe such person is a subversive person. In the event such reasonable grounds exist, he shall not be appointed or employed. In securing any facts necessary to ascertain the information required by this Code section, all applicants and employees shall be required to sign a written statement or questionnaire containing answers to such inquiries as may be material and containing the following questions:

(1) Full name including maiden name, names of former marriages, former names changed legally or otherwise, aliases, and nicknames, and the dates used;
(2) Address;
(3)(A) Are you now or have you been within the last ten years a member of any organization which to your knowledge at the time of membership advocates or has as one of its objectives the overthrow of the government of the United States or of the government of the State of Georgia by force or violence? Yes   No . If "Yes," state the name of the organization and your past and present membership status including any offices held therein.
(B) If the answer to (A) is "Yes" and the employing authority deems further inquiry necessary, you will be notified of such determination. No action adverse to your application will be taken because of an affirmative answer until after such an inquiry, with notice to you and an opportunity for you to present evidence, and only if the result of such inquiry brings your application within the prohibition within the "Sedition and Subversive Activities Act of 1953."

70

(4)(A) Have you ever been convicted or are any charges now pending against you by federal, state, or other law enforcement authorities, for any violation of any federal law, state law, county or municipal law, regulation, or ordinance? (Do not include anything that happened before your sixteenth birthday. Do not include minor traffic violations for which a fine of $35.00 or less was imposed. All other convictions must be included even if they were pardoned.) Yes   No   .
(B) If the answer to (A) is "Yes," state the reason convicted, the date convicted, and the place where convicted.
(b) The written statement or questionnaire shall contain notice that it is subject to the penalties of false swearing.
(c) The Governor is authorized to make appropriate orders, rules, and regulations to effectuate the purposes of Code Section 16-11-12, this Code section, and Code Section 16-11-14.

§ 16-11-14. False swearing in written statement

(a) Every written statement made pursuant to this part by an applicant for appointment or employment or by any employee shall be deemed to have been made under oath if it contains a declaration preceding the signature of the maker to the effect that it is made under the penalties of false swearing. Any person who makes a material misstatement of fact in any such written statement, in any affidavit made pursuant to this part, under oath in any hearing conducted by any agency of this state or of any of its political subdivisions pursuant to this part, or in any written statement by an applicant for appointment or employment or by an employee in any state-aided or private institution of learning in this state intended to determine whether or not such applicant or employee is a subversive person, which statement contains notice that it is subject to the penalties of false swearing, shall be subject to the penalties of false swearing as prescribed in Code Section 16-10-71.
(b) Nothing contained in subsection (a) of this Code section shall be construed to repeal in any way the laws of this state dealing with perjury and false swearing.

§ 16-11-15. Information concerning membership of relative in a subversive organization

No person giving any information, whether by answering a questionnaire or otherwise, as provided in Code Section 16-11-13 shall be required to give any information or answer any questions relative to the membership in any organization of any relative of such person.

§ 16-11-16. Filing written statement

Any questionnaires or statements prepared as provided in Code Section 16-11-13 shall be filed at the place of employment rather than with a central state agency.

§ 16-11-30. Riot

(a) Any two or more persons who shall do an unlawful act of violence or any other act in a violent and tumultuous manner commit the offense of riot.
(b) Any persons who violate subsection (a) of this Code section are guilty of a misdemeanor.

§ 16-11-31. Inciting to riot

(a) A person who with intent to riot does an act or engages in conduct which urges, counsels, or advises others to riot, at a time and place and under circumstances which produce a clear and present danger of a riot, commits the offense of inciting to riot.
(b) Any person who violates subsection (a) of this Code section is guilty of a misdemeanor.

§ 16-11-32. Affray

(a) An affray is the fighting by two or more persons in some public place to the disturbance of the public tranquility.
(b) A person who commits the offense of affray is guilty of a misdemeanor.

§ 16-11-33. Unlawful assembly

A person who knowingly participates in either of the following acts or occurrences is guilty of a misdemeanor:
(1) The assembly of two or more persons for the purpose of committing an unlawful act and the failure to withdraw from the assembly on being lawfully commanded to do so by a peace officer and before any member of the assembly has inflicted injury to the person or property of another; or
(2) The assembly of two or more persons, without authority of law, for the purpose of doing violence to the person or property of one supposed by the accused to have been guilty of a violation of the law, or for the purpose of exercising correctional or regulative powers over any person by violence; provided, however, that it shall be an affirmative defense to a prosecution under this paragraph that the accused withdrew from the assembly on being lawfully commanded to do so by a peace officer or before any member of the assembly had inflicted injury to the person or property of another.

§ 16-11-34. Preventing or disrupting lawful meetings, gatherings, or processions

(a) A person who recklessly or knowingly commits any act which may reasonably be expected to prevent or disrupt a lawful meeting, gathering, or procession is guilty of a misdemeanor.
(b) This Code section shall not be construed to affect the powers delegated to counties or to municipal corporations to pass laws to punish disorderly conduct within their respective limits.

§ 16-11-34.1. Preventing or disrupting General Assembly sessions or other meetings of members; unlawful activities within the state capitol or certain Capitol Square buildings

(a) It shall be unlawful for any person recklessly or knowingly to commit any act which may reasonably be expected to prevent or disrupt a session or meeting of the Senate or House of Representatives, a joint session thereof, or any meeting of any standing or interim committee, commission, or caucus of members thereof.
(b) It shall be unlawful for any person, other than those persons who are exempt from the provisions of Code Sections 16-11-126 through 16-11-127.2, to enter, occupy, or remain within the state capitol building or any building housing committee offices, committee rooms, or offices of members, officials, or employees of the General Assembly or either house thereof while in the possession of any firearm; knife, as such term is defined in Code Section 16-11-125.1; explosive or incendiary device or compound; bludgeon; knuckles, whether made from metal, thermoplastic, wood, or other similar material; or any other dangerous or deadly weapon, instrument, or device.
(c) It shall be unlawful for any person purposely or recklessly and without authority of law to obstruct any street, sidewalk, hallway, office, or other passageway in that area designated as Capitol Square by Code Section 50-2-28 in such a manner as to render it impassable without unreasonable inconvenience or hazard or to fail or refuse to remove such obstruction after receiving a reasonable official request or the order of a peace officer to do so.
(d) It shall be unlawful for any person willfully and knowingly to enter or to remain upon the floor of the Senate or the floor of the House of Representatives or within any cloakroom, lobby, or anteroom adjacent to such floor unless such person is authorized, pursuant to the rules of the Senate or House of Representatives or pursuant to authorization given by the Senate or House of Representatives, to enter or remain upon the floor or within such area.
(e) It shall be unlawful for any person willfully and knowingly to enter or to remain in the gallery of the Senate or the gallery of the House of Representatives in violation of rules governing admission to such gallery adopted by the Senate or the House of Representatives or pursuant to authorization given by such body.

(f) It shall be unlawful for any person willfully and knowingly to enter or to remain in any room, chamber, office, or hallway within the state capitol building or any building housing committee offices, committee rooms, or offices of members, officials, or employees of the General Assembly or either house thereof with intent to disrupt the orderly conduct of official business or to utter loud, threatening, or abusive language or engage in any disorderly or disruptive conduct in such buildings or areas.

(g) It shall be unlawful for any person to parade, demonstrate, or picket within the state capitol building or any building housing committee offices, committee rooms, or offices of members, officials, or employees of the General Assembly or either house thereof with intent to disrupt the orderly conduct of official business or to utter loud, threatening, or abusive language or engage in any disorderly or disruptive conduct in such buildings or areas.

(h)(1) Any person violating this Code section for the first time shall be guilty of a misdemeanor.

(2) Any person violating this Code section for the second time shall be guilty of a misdemeanor of a high and aggravated nature.

(3) Any person violating this Code section for the third or any subsequent time shall be guilty of a felony and, upon conviction thereof, shall be punished by imprisonment for not less than one nor more than three years.

(i) The enactment of this Code section shall not repeal any other provision of law proscribing or regulating any conduct otherwise prohibited by this Code section.

§ 16-11-34.2. Disorderly or disruptive conduct at any funeral or memorial service

(a) The General Assembly declares that the interest of persons in planning, participating in, and attending a funeral or memorial service for a deceased relative or loved one without unwanted impediment, disruption, disturbance, or interference is a substantial interest and the General Assembly further recognizes the need to impose content neutral time, place, and manner restrictions on unwanted acts carried out with the intent to impede, disrupt, disturb, or interfere with such funeral or memorial service.

(b) It shall be unlawful to engage in any disorderly or disruptive conduct with the intent to impede, disrupt, disturb, or interfere with the orderly conduct of any funeral or memorial service or with the normal activities and functions carried on in the facilities or buildings where such funeral or memorial service is taking place. Any or all of the following shall constitute such disorderly or disruptive conduct:

(1) Displaying any visual images that convey fighting words or actual or imminent threats of harm directed to any person or property associated with said funeral or memorial service within 500 feet of the ceremonial site or location being used for the funeral or memorial service at any time one hour prior to, during, or one hour after the posted time for said funeral or memorial service;

(2) Uttering loud, threatening, or abusive language or singing, chanting, whistling, or yelling with or without noise amplification including, but not limited to, bullhorns, automobile horns, and microphones, such as would tend to impede, disrupt, disturb, or interfere with a funeral or memorial service within 500 feet of the ceremonial site or location being used for the funeral or memorial service;

(3) Attempting to block or blocking pedestrian or vehicular access to the ceremonial site or location being used for a funeral or memorial service at any time one hour prior to, during, or one hour after the posted time for said funeral or memorial service; or

(4) Conducting a public assembly, parade, demonstration, or other like event, either fixed or processional, within 500 feet of the ceremonial site or location being used for a funeral or memorial service at any time one hour prior to, during, or one hour after the posted time for said funeral or memorial service.

(c) Any person who violates any provision of subsection (b) of this Code section shall be guilty of a misdemeanor.

§ 16-11-35. Removal from campus or facility of unit of university system or school; failure to leave

(a) As used in this Code section, the term:

(1) "Chief administrative officer," in the case of a public school, means the principal of the school or an officer designated by the superintendent or board of education having jurisdiction of the school to be the officer in charge of the public school.

(2) "Chief administrative officer," in the case of a unit of the university system, means the president of the unit of the university system or the officer designated by the Board of Regents of the University System of Georgia to administer and be the officer in charge of a campus or other facility of a unit of the university system.

(3) "Public school" means any school under the control and management of a county, independent, or area board of education supported by public funds and any school under the control and management of the State Board of Education or department or agency thereof supported by public funds.

(4) "Unit of the university system" means any college or university under the government, control, and management of the Board of Regents of the University System of Georgia.

(b) In any case in which a person who is not a student or officer or employee of a unit of the university system or of a public school and who is not required by his or her employment to be on the campus or any other facility of any such unit or of any public school enters the campus or facility, and it reasonably appears to the chief administrative officer of the campus or facility, or to any officer or employee designated by him or her to maintain order on the campus or facility, that such person is committing any act likely to interfere with the peaceful conduct of the activities of the campus or facility, or has entered the campus or facility for the purpose of committing any such act, the chief administrative officer or the officers or employees designated by him or her to maintain order on the campus or facility may direct the person to leave the campus or facility, and, if the person fails to do so, he or she shall be guilty of a misdemeanor of a high and aggravated nature.

§ 16-11-36. Loitering or prowling

(a) A person commits the offense of loitering or prowling when he is in a place at a time or in a manner not usual for law-abiding individuals under circumstances that warrant a justifiable and reasonable alarm or immediate concern for the safety of persons or property in the vicinity.

(b) Among the circumstances which may be considered in determining whether alarm is warranted is the fact that the person takes flight upon the appearance of a law enforcement officer, refuses to identify himself, or manifestly endeavors to conceal himself or any object. Unless flight by the person or other circumstances make it impracticable, a law enforcement officer shall, prior to any arrest for an offense under this Code section, afford the person an opportunity to dispel any alarm or immediate concern which would otherwise be warranted by requesting the person to identify himself and explain his presence and conduct. No person shall be convicted of an offense under this Code section if the law enforcement officer failed to comply with the foregoing procedure or if it appears at trial that the explanation given by the person was true and would have dispelled the alarm or immediate concern.

(c) A person committing the offense of loitering or prowling shall be guilty of a misdemeanor.

(d) This Code section shall not be deemed or construed to affect or limit the powers of counties or municipal corporations to adopt ordinances or resolutions prohibiting loitering or prowling within their respective limits.

§ 16-11-37. Terroristic threats and acts; penalties

(a) As used in this Code section, the term "hazardous substance" shall have the same meaning as set forth in Code Section 12-8-92.

(b) (1) A person commits the offense of a terroristic threat when he or she threatens to:

(A) Commit any crime of violence;

(B) Release any hazardous substance; or

(C) Burn or damage property.

(2) Such terroristic threat shall be made:

(A) With the purpose of terrorizing another;

(B) With the purpose of causing the evacuation of a building, place of assembly, or facility of public transportation;

(C) With the purpose of otherwise causing serious public inconvenience; or

(D) In reckless disregard of the risk of causing the terror, evacuation, or inconvenience described in subparagraph (A), (B), or (C) of this paragraph.

(3) No person shall be convicted under this subsection on the uncorroborated testimony of the party to whom the threat is communicated.

(c) A person commits the offense of a terroristic act when:

(1) He or she uses a burning or flaming cross or other burning or flaming symbol or flambeau with the intent to terrorize another or another's household;

(2) While not in the commission of a lawful act, he or she shoots at or throws an object at a conveyance which is being operated or which is occupied by passengers; or

(3) He or she releases any hazardous substance or any simulated hazardous substance under the guise of a hazardous substance:

(A) For the purpose of terrorizing another;

(B) For the purpose of causing the evacuation of a building, place of assembly, or facility of public transportation;

(C) For the purpose of otherwise causing serious public inconvenience; or

(D) In reckless disregard of the risk of causing the terror, evacuation, or inconvenience described in subparagraph (A), (B), or (C) of this paragraph.

(d) (1) A person convicted of the offense of a terroristic threat shall be punished as a misdemeanor; provided, however, that if the threat suggested the death of the threatened individual, the person convicted shall be guilty of a felony and shall be punished by a fine of not more than $1,000.00, imprisonment for not less than one nor more than five years, or both.

(2) A person convicted of the offense of a terroristic act shall be punished by a fine of not more than $5,000.00, imprisonment for not less than one nor more than ten years, or both; provided, however, that if any person suffers a serious physical injury as a direct result of an act giving rise to a conviction under subsection (b) of this Code section, the person so convicted shall be punished by a fine of not more than $250,000.00, imprisonment for not less than five nor more than 40 years, or both.

(e) A person who commits or attempts to commit a violation of subsection (b) or (c) of this Code section shall, upon conviction thereof, be punished by a fine of not less than $50,000.00, imprisonment for not less than five nor more than 20 years, or both, when such act is done with the intent to retaliate against any person for or intimidate or threaten any person from:

(1) Attending a judicial or administrative proceeding as a witness, attorney, judge, clerk of court, deputy clerk of court, court reporter, community supervision officer, county or Department of Juvenile Justice juvenile probation officer, probation officer serving pursuant to Article 6 of Chapter 8 of Title 42, or party or producing any record, document, or other object in a judicial or official proceeding; or

(2) Providing to a law enforcement officer, community supervision officer, county or Department of Juvenile Justice juvenile probation officer, probation officer serving pursuant to Article 6 of Chapter 8 of Title 42, prosecuting attorney, or judge any information relating to the commission or possible commission of an offense under the laws of this state or of the United States or a violation of conditions of bail, pretrial release, probation, or parole.

§ 16-11-37.1. Dissemination of information relating to terroristic acts

It shall be unlawful for any person knowingly to furnish or disseminate through a computer or computer network any picture, photograph, drawing, or similar visual representation or verbal description of any information designed to encourage, solicit, or otherwise promote terroristic acts as defined in Code Section 16-11-37. Any person convicted for violation of this Code section shall be guilty of a misdemeanor of a high and aggravated nature; provided, however, that if such act is in violation of paragraph (1) of subsection (e) of Code Section 16-11-37, the person convicted shall be guilty of a felony and shall be punished by imprisonment for not less than one nor more than ten years or by a fine not to exceed $100,000.00 or both.

§ 16-11-38. Wearing mask, hood, or device which conceals identity of wearer

(a) A person is guilty of a misdemeanor when he wears a mask, hood, or device by which any portion of the face is so hidden, concealed, or covered as to conceal the identity of the wearer and is upon any public way or public property or upon the private property of another without the written permission of the owner or occupier of the property to do so.

(b) This Code section shall not apply to:

(1) A person wearing a traditional holiday costume on the occasion of the holiday;

(2) A person lawfully engaged in trade and employment or in a sporting activity where a mask is worn for the purpose of ensuring the physical safety of the wearer, or because of the nature of the occupation, trade, or profession, or sporting activity;

(3) A person using a mask in a theatrical production including use in Mardi gras celebrations and masquerade balls; or

(4) A person wearing a gas mask prescribed in emergency management drills and exercises or emergencies.

§ 16-11-39. Disorderly conduct

(a) A person commits the offense of disorderly conduct when such person commits any of the following:

(1) Acts in a violent or tumultuous manner toward another person whereby such person is placed in reasonable fear of the safety of such person's life, limb, or health;

(2) Acts in a violent or tumultuous manner toward another person whereby the property of such person is placed in danger of being damaged or destroyed;

(3) Without provocation, uses to or of another person in such other person's presence, opprobrious or abusive words which by their very utterance tend to incite to an immediate breach of the peace, that is to say, words which as a matter of common knowledge and under ordinary circumstances will, when used to or of another person in such other person's presence, naturally tend to provoke violent resentment, that is, words commonly called "fighting words"; or

(4) Without provocation, uses obscene and vulgar or profane language in the presence of or by telephone to a person under the age of 14 years which threatens an immediate breach of the peace.

(b) Any person who commits the offense of disorderly conduct shall be guilty of a misdemeanor.

(c) This Code section shall not be deemed or construed to affect or limit the powers of counties or municipal corporations to adopt ordinances or resolutions prohibiting disorderly conduct within their respective limits.

§ 16-11-39.1. Harassing communications; venue; separate offenses; impact on free speech

(a) A person commits the offense of harassing communications if such person:

(1) Contacts another person repeatedly via telecommunication, e-mail, text messaging, or any other form of electronic communication for the purpose of harassing, molesting, threatening, or intimidating such person or the family of such person;

(2) Threatens bodily harm via telecommunication, e-mail, text messaging, or any other form of electronic communication;

(3) Telephones another person and intentionally fails to hang up or disengage the connection; or

(4) Knowingly permits any device used for telecommunication, e-mail, text messaging, or any other form of electronic communication under such person's control to be used for any purpose prohibited by this subsection.

(b) Any person who commits the offense of harassing communications shall be guilty of a misdemeanor.

(c) The offense of harassing communications shall be considered to have been committed in the county where:

(1) The defendant was located when he or she placed the telephone call or transmitted, sent, or posted an electronic communication; or

(2) The telephone call or electronic communication was received.

(d) Any violation of this Code section shall constitute a separate offense and shall not merge with any other crimes set forth in this title.

(e) This Code section shall not apply to constitutionally protected speech.

§ 16-11-39.2. Unlawful conduct during 9-1-1 call

(a) As used in this Code section, the term:

(1) "Call" shall have the same meaning as set forth in paragraph (2.1) of Code Section 46-5-122.

(2) "False report" means the fabrication of an incident or crime or of material information relating to an incident or crime which the person making the report knows to be false at the time of making the report.

(3) "Harass" means to knowingly and willingly engage in any conduct directed toward a communications officer that is likely to impede or interfere with such communications officer's duties, that threatens such communication officer or any member of his or her family, or that places any member of the public served or to be served by 9-1-1 service in danger of injury or delayed assistance.

(4) "Harassing" means the willful use of opprobrious and abusive language which has no legitimate purpose in relation to imparting information relevant to an emergency call.

(5) "9-1-1" means a public safety answering point as defined in paragraph (15) of Code Section 46-5-122. The term "9-1-1" also means the digits, address, Internet Protocol address, or other information used to access or initiate a call to a public safety answering point.

(b) A person commits the offense of unlawful conduct during a 9-1-1 telephone call if he or she:

(1) Without provocation, uses obscene, vulgar, or profane language with the intent to intimidate or harass a 9-1-1 communications officer;

(2) Calls or otherwise contacts 9-1-1, whether or not conversation ensues, for the purpose of annoying, harassing, or molesting a 9-1-1 communications officer or for the purpose of interfering with or disrupting emergency telephone service;

(3) Calls or otherwise contacts 9-1-1 and fails to hang up or disengage the connection for the intended purpose of interfering with or disrupting emergency service;

(4) Calls or otherwise contacts 9-1-1 with the intention to harass a communications officer; or

(5) Calls or otherwise contacts 9-1-1 and makes a false report.

(c) Any person who violates subsection (b) of this Code section shall be guilty of a misdemeanor and, upon conviction thereof, shall be punished by a fine of not more than $500.00 or 12 months in jail, or both.

(d) Any violation of subsection (b) of this Code section shall be considered to have been committed in any county where such call to or contact with 9-1-1 originated or in any county where the call to or contact with 9-1-1 was received.

§ 16-11-40. Criminal defamation

Reserved. Repealed by Ga. L. 2015, p. 385, § 3-1/HB 252, effective July 1, 2015.

§ 16-11-40.1. Definitions; identification of minors; criminal offense

(a) As used in this Code section, the term:

(1) "Minor" means an individual who is under the age of 18 years.

(2) "Nudity" shall have the same meaning as set forth in Code Section 16-11-90.

(3) "Obscene depiction" means a visual depiction of an individual displaying nudity or sexually explicit conduct.

(4) "Sexually explicit conduct" shall have the same meaning as set forth in Code Section 16-12-100.

(b) No person shall intentionally cause a minor to be identified as the individual in an obscene depiction in such a manner that a reasonable person would conclude that the image depicted was that of such minor. Such identification shall include, without limitation, the minor's name, address, telephone number, e-mail address, username, or other electronic identification. Such identification shall also include the electronic imposing of the facial image of a minor onto an obscene depiction.

(c) Any person convicted of violating this Code section shall be guilty of a misdemeanor; provided, however, that upon a second or subsequent violation of this Code section, he or she shall be guilty of a felony and, upon conviction thereof, shall be punished by imprisonment of not less than one nor more than five years, a fine of not more than $100,000.00, or both.

(d) A person shall be subject to prosecution in this state pursuant to Code Section 17-2-1 for any conduct made unlawful by this Code section in which such person engages while:

(1) Either within or outside of this state if, by such conduct, the person commits a violation of this Code section which involves an individual who resides in this state; or

(2) Within this state if, by such conduct, the person commits a violation of this Code section which involves an individual who resides within or outside this state.

(e) The provisions of subsection (b) of this Code section shall not apply to:

(1) The activities of law enforcement and prosecution agencies in the investigation and prosecution of criminal offenses; or

(2) An image and identification made pursuant to or in anticipation of a civil action.

(f) Any violation of this Code section shall constitute a separate offense and shall not merge with any other crimes set forth in this title.

§ 16-11-41. Public drunkenness

(a) A person who shall be and appear in an intoxicated condition in any public place or within the curtilage of any private residence not his own other than by invitation of the owner or lawful occupant, which condition is made manifest by boisterousness, by indecent condition or act, or by vulgar, profane, loud, or unbecoming language, is guilty of a misdemeanor.

(b) This Code section shall not be construed to affect the powers delegated to counties or to municipal corporations to pass laws to punish drunkenness or disorderly conduct within their respective limits.

§ 16-11-42. Refusal to relinquish telephone party line in case of emergency; false request on party line as to emergency; warning printed in telephone books

(a) A person is guilty of a misdemeanor when he fails to relinquish a telephone party line consisting of subscriber line telephone circuit with two or more main telephone stations connected therewith, each having a distinctive ring or telephone number, after he has been requested to do so to permit another to place a call in an emergency, in which property or human life is in jeopardy and the prompt summoning of aid is essential, to a fire or police department or for medical aid or ambulance service, if the party line at the time of the request is not being used for any such other emergency call. Any person who shall request the use of the party line by falsely stating that the same is needed for any of such purposes, knowing the statement to be false, is guilty of a misdemeanor.

(b) In every telephone directory distributed to the general public in this state, in which is listed the call numbers of any telephones located within this state, except such as are distributed solely for business advertising purposes, commonly known as classified telephone directories, there shall be printed in type not smaller than the smallest type appearing on the same page, a notice setting forth the substance of subsection (a) of this Code section preceded by the word "warning" printed in boldface type.

§ 16-11-43. Obstructing highways, streets, sidewalks, or other public passages

A person who, without authority of law, purposely or recklessly obstructs any highway, street, sidewalk, or other public passage in such a way as to render it impassable without unreasonable inconvenience or hazard and fails or refuses to remove the obstruction after receiving a reasonable official request or the order of a peace officer that he do so, is guilty of a misdemeanor.

§ 16-11-44. Maintaining a disorderly house

A person who keeps and maintains, either by himself or others, a common, ill-governed, and disorderly house, to the encouragement of gaming, drinking, or other misbehavior, or to the common disturbance of the neighborhood or orderly citizens, is guilty of a misdemeanor.

§ 16-11-45. Use of laser against aircraft

(a) As used in this Code section, the term:

(1) "Laser" means any device that projects a beam or point of light by means of light amplification by stimulated emission of radiation or a device that emits light which simulates the appearance of a laser.

(2) "Laser pointer" means any device designed or used to amplify electromagnetic radiation by stimulated emission that emits a beam designed to be used by the operator as a pointer or highlighter to indicate, mark, or identify a specific position, place, item, or object.
(b) Except as otherwise provided in subsection (c) of this Code section, whoever knowingly and intentionally aims the beam of a laser pointer, or projects a laser, at an aircraft or at the flight path of an aircraft shall be guilty of a misdemeanor.
(c) Laser or laser pointer airspace uses that have been reviewed and approved by the Federal Aviation Administration are exempt from the provisions of this Code section.

§ 16-11-60. Definitions

As used within this part, the term:
(1) "Device" means an instrument or apparatus used for overhearing, recording, intercepting, or transmitting sounds or for observing, photographing, videotaping, recording, or transmitting visual images and which involves in its operation electricity, electronics, or infrared, laser, or similar beams. Without limiting the generality of the foregoing, the term "device" shall specifically include any camera, photographic equipment, video equipment, or other similar equipment or any electronic, mechanical, or other apparatus which can be used to intercept a wire, oral, or electronic communication other than:
(A) Any telephone or telegraph instrument, equipment, or facility or any component thereof:
(i) Furnished to the subscriber or user by a provider of wire or electronic communication service in the ordinary course of its business and being used by the subscriber or user in the ordinary course of its business or furnished by such subscriber or user for connection to the facilities of such service and used in the ordinary course of its business; or
(ii) Being used by a provider of wire or electronic communication service in the ordinary course of its business or by an investigative or law enforcement officer in the ordinary course of his or her duties; or
(B) A hearing aid or similar device being used to correct subnormal hearing to not better than normal;
(C) Focusing, lighting, or illuminating equipment, optical magnifying equipment; and
(D) A "pen register" or "trap and trace device" as defined in this Code section.
(2) "Pen register" means a device or process which records or decodes dialing, routing, addressing, or signaling information transmitted by an instrument or facility from which a wire or electronic communication is transmitted; provided, however, that such information shall not include the contents of any communication; but such term does not include any device or process used by a provider or customer of a wire or electronic communication service for billing, or recording as an incident to billing, for communications services provided by such provider or any device or process used by a provider or customer of a wire communication service for cost accounting or other like purposes in the ordinary course its business.
(3) "Private place" means a place where there is a reasonable expectation of privacy.
(4) "Trap and trace device" means a device or process which captures the incoming electronic or other impulses which identify the originating number or other dialing, routing, addressing, and signaling information reasonably likely to identify the source of a wire or electronic communication; provided, however, that such information shall not include the contents of any communication.

§ 16-11-61. Peeping Toms

(a) It shall be unlawful for any person to be a "peeping Tom" on or about the premises of another or to go about or upon the premises of another for the purpose of becoming a "peeping Tom."
(b) As used in this Code section, the term "peeping Tom" means a person who peeps through windows or doors, or other like places, on or about the premises of another for the purpose of spying upon or invading the privacy of the persons spied upon and the doing of any other acts of a similar nature which invade the privacy of such persons.

§ 16-11-62. Eavesdropping, surveillance, or intercepting communication which invades privacy of another; divulging private message

It shall be unlawful for:
(1) Any person in a clandestine manner intentionally to overhear, transmit, or record or attempt to overhear, transmit, or record the private conversation of another which shall originate in any private place;
(2) Any person, through the use of any device, without the consent of all persons observed, to observe, photograph, or record the activities of another which occur in any private place and out of public view; provided, however, that it shall not be unlawful:
(A) To use any device to observe, photograph, or record the activities of persons incarcerated in any jail, correctional institution, or other facility in which persons who are charged with or who have been convicted of the commission of a crime are incarcerated, provided that such equipment shall not be used while the prisoner is discussing his or her case with his or her attorney;
(B) For an owner or occupier of real property to use for security purposes, crime prevention, or crime detection any device to observe, photograph, or record the activities of persons who are on the property or an approach thereto in areas where there is no reasonable expectation of privacy;
(C) To use for security purposes, crime prevention, or crime detection any device to observe, photograph, or record the activities of persons who are within the curtilage of the residence of the person using such device. A photograph, videotape, or record made in accordance with this subparagraph, or a copy thereof, may be disclosed by such resident to the district attorney or a law enforcement officer and shall be admissible in a judicial proceeding, without the consent of any person observed, photographed, or recorded; or
(D) For a law enforcement officer or his or her agent to use a device in the lawful performance of his or her official duties to observe, photograph, videotape, or record the activities of persons that occur in the presence of such officer or his or her agent;
(3) Any person to go on or about the premises of another or any private place, except as otherwise provided by law, for the purpose of invading the privacy of others by eavesdropping upon their conversations or secretly observing their activities;
(4) Any person intentionally and secretly to intercept by the use of any device, instrument, or apparatus the contents of a message sent by telephone, telegraph, letter, or by any other means of private communication;
(5) Any person to divulge to any unauthorized person or authority the content or substance of any private message intercepted lawfully in the manner provided for in Code Section 16-11-65;
(6) Any person to sell, give, or distribute, without legal authority, to any person or entity any photograph, videotape, or record, or copies thereof, of the activities of another which occur in any private place and out of public view without the consent of all persons observed; or
(7) Any person to commit any other acts of a nature similar to those set out in paragraphs (1) through (6) of this Code section which invade the privacy of another.

§ 16-11-63. Possession, sale, or distribution of eavesdropping devices

(a) Other than law enforcement officers permitted by this part to employ such devices, it shall be unlawful for any person to possess, sell, offer for sale, or distribute any eavesdropping device.
(b) An "eavesdropping device" shall mean any instrument or apparatus which by virtue of its size, design, and method of operation has no normal or customary function or purpose other than to permit the user thereof secretly to intercept, transmit, listen to, or record private conversations of others.

§ 16-11-64. Interception of wire or oral transmissions by law enforcement officers

(a) Application of part to law enforcement officers. Except only as provided in subsection (b) of this Code section, nothing in this part shall apply to a duly constituted law enforcement officer in the performance of his official duties in ferreting out offenders or suspected offenders of the law or in secretly watching a person suspected of violating the laws of the United States or of this state, or any subdivision thereof, for the purpose of apprehending such suspected violator.
(b) When in the course of his or her official duties, a law enforcement officer desiring to make use of any device, but only as such term is defined in Code Section 16-11-60, and such use would otherwise constitute a violation of Code Section 16-11-62, the law enforcement official shall act in compliance with the provisions provided for in this part.
(c) Upon written application, under oath, of the district attorney having jurisdiction over prosecution of the crime under investigation or the Attorney General made before a judge of superior court having jurisdiction over the crime under investigation, such court may issue an investigation warrant permitting the use of a device for the surveillance of a person or place to the extent the same

is consistent with and subject to the terms, conditions, and procedures provided for by 18 U.S.C. Chapter 119. Such warrant shall have state-wide application and interception of communications shall be permitted in any location in this state.

(d) Evidence obtained in conformity with this part shall be admissible only in the courts of this state having felony and misdemeanor jurisdiction.

(e) Defenses. A good faith reliance on a court order or legislative authorization shall constitute a complete defense to any civil or criminal action brought under this part or under any other law.

§ 16-11-64.1. Application and issuance of order authorizing installation and use of pen register or trap and trace device

Any district attorney having jurisdiction over the prosecution of the crime under investigation or the Attorney General is authorized to make application for an order or an extension of an order authorizing or approving the installation and use of a pen register or a trap and trace device to a judge of the superior court of the same judicial circuit as the district attorney, or, in the case of the Attorney General, in any judicial circuit; and such court shall be authorized to enter an order authorizing the use of a pen register or a trap and trace device, to the extent the same is consistent with and permitted by the laws of the United States. Such order shall have state-wide application and the interception by use of a pen register or trap and trace device shall be permitted in any location in this state.

§ 16-11-64.2. Emergency situation and other grounds authorizing installation and use of pen register or trap and trace device prior to order; time for order approving installation or use

Any investigative or law enforcement officer, specially designated in writing for such purpose by the Attorney General or by a district attorney, who reasonably determines that:

(1) An emergency situation exists that involves:

(A) Immediate danger of death or serious bodily injury to any person; or

(B) Conspiratorial activities characteristic of organized crime

that requires the installation and use of a pen register or a trap and trace device before an order authorizing such installation and use can, with due diligence, be obtained; and

(2) There are grounds upon which an order could be entered under the laws of the United States to authorize such installation and use

may have installed and use a pen register or trap and trace device if, within 48 hours of the time the pen register or trap and trace device is installed, an order approving the installation or use is issued in accordance with Code Section 16-11-64.1.

§ 16-11-64.3. Emergency situation; application for an investigation warrant

(a) Notwithstanding any other provision of this part, in the event that the Attorney General or a district attorney of the judicial circuit having jurisdiction over the emergency situation described herein or where the observation, monitoring, or recording of the activities of any person may occur as provided in this subsection determines that:

(1) An emergency situation exists involving the immediate danger of death or serious physical injury to any person;

(2) The said emergency situation requires the immediate interception of a wire, oral, or electronic communications or the immediate observation, monitoring, or recording of the activities of any person involved in said emergency situation in violation of the provisions of Code Section 16-11-62 before an order authorizing such interception or surveillance can, with due diligence, be obtained; and

(3) There are grounds upon which an investigation warrant pursuant to Code Section 16-11-64 could be issued,

then any investigative or law enforcement officer specifically designated by the prosecuting official making such determination may utilize any device as defined in Code Section 16-11-60 to intercept the wire, oral, or electronic communications or to observe, monitor, or record the activities of the person or persons involved in said emergency situation, provided that an application for an investigation warrant is made pursuant to Code Section 16-11-64 within 48 hours after said interception or surveillance commences.

(b) In the event that an application for an investigation warrant made pursuant to this Code section is granted, then the interception or surveillance shall be conducted in accordance with the provisions of Code Section 16-11-64, except that said interception or surveillance shall continue only so long as the emergency situation exists.

(c) In the event that an application for an investigation warrant made pursuant to this Code section is denied or in any event where the interception or surveillance is terminated without an investigation warrant having been issued, the contents of any intercepted communications or other surveillance effected pursuant to this Code section shall not be admissible in any court of this state except to prove violations of this part. The contents of any such intercepted communications or other surveillance effected pursuant to this Code section without an investigation warrant having been issued shall be confidential and shall not be disclosed except to prove violations of this part.

§ 16-11-65. License to intercept telephonic communications for business service improvement; regulatory powers of Georgia Public Service Commission

(a) Nothing contained within Code Section 16-11-62 shall prohibit the employment and use of any equipment or device which is owned by any person or is furnished by any telephone company authorized to do business in this state under proper tariffs filed with and approved by the Georgia Public Service Commission which may be attached to any telephonic equipment of any user of or subscriber to such equipment which permits the interception of telephonic communications solely for the purposes of business service improvement when the user of or subscriber to such facilities and equipment has duly applied for and obtained from the Georgia Public Service Commission a license for the employment and installation of the equipment. No license shall be issued until the applicant has demonstrated to the commission a clear, apparent, and logically reasonable need for the use of the equipment in connection with a legitimate business activity of the user or subscriber and demonstrated to the satisfaction of the commission that it will be operated by persons of good moral character and that the equipment will be used in a lawful manner and in conformity with the tariffs filed for the equipment. The commission is authorized to establish the necessary procedures to be employed and followed in applying for such permits and to require from the user or subscriber of such equipment the furnishing of any reasonable information required by the commission in regard to the intended and actual use of the equipment.

(b) The Georgia Public Service Commission is authorized to revoke any license and to order any owner of such equipment or any telephone company supplying such equipment to remove from the premises of the licensee the equipment when it is established to the satisfaction of the commission that the equipment is being used in an unlawful manner contrary to the tariff applicable to the equipment or in a manner contrary to the purposes and uses for which the license had been issued. Such licenses may also be revoked by the commission if it is subsequently discovered that a material misrepresentation of fact has been made in applying for the license. The commission is authorized to promulgate such rules and regulations in connection with the licensing and revocation thereof of such users of such equipment as will enable it to carry out the purposes, duties, and responsibilities imposed upon the commission by this Code section. Such rules and regulations shall afford to any aggrieved licensee an opportunity to a full and impartial hearing before the commission. The commission shall further have the authority to adopt any and all appropriate rules and regulations of any sort to ensure the privacy of telephonic and telegraphic communications. A violation of such rules and regulations shall be a violation of this part.

(c) All telephone companies shall have printed in a conspicuously accessible location within their directories a notice to the public that there is available without cost at the business office of the telephone company served by the directory a list of subscribers of such equipment which will be made available to any member of the general public requesting the same from such companies.

(d) The provisions of this part shall not apply to acts by duly authorized employees of any telephone company regulated by the Georgia Public Service Commission, with regard to the reasonable and limited intercepting of telephone communications under circumstances reasonably calculated to assure the privacy of telephone communications when such interception is accomplished solely for the purpose of maintaining the quality of service furnished to the public or for the purpose of preventing the unlawful use of telephone service. All such telephone companies shall adopt regulations and procedures consistent with the requirements of this Code section governing the use of equipment which permits the interception of telephone messages by their employees and file the same with the commission. After being filed with the commission, such regulations and procedures shall be public records.

§ 16-11-66. Interception of wire, oral, or electronic communication by party thereto; consent requirements for recording and divulging conversations to which child under 18 years is a party; parental exception

(a) Nothing in Code Section 16-11-62 shall prohibit a person from intercepting a wire, oral, or electronic communication where such person is a party to the communication or one of the parties to the communication has given prior consent to such interception.

(b) After obtaining the consent required by this subsection, the telephonic conversations or electronic communications to which a child under the age of 18 years is a party may be recorded and divulged, and such recording and dissemination may be done by a private citizen, law enforcement agency, or prosecutor's office. Nothing in this subsection shall be construed to require that the recording device be activated by the child. Consent for the recording or divulging of the conversations of a child under the age of 18 years conducted by telephone or electronic communication shall be given only by order of a judge of a superior court upon written application, as provided in subsection (c) of this Code section, or by a parent or guardian of said child as provided in subsection (d) of this Code section. Said recording shall not be used in any prosecution of the child in any delinquency or criminal proceeding. An application to a judge of the superior court made pursuant to this Code section need not comply with the procedures set out in Code Section 16-11-64.

(c) A judge to whom a written application has been made shall issue the order provided by subsection (b) of this Code section only:

(1) Upon finding probable cause that a crime has been committed;

(2) Upon finding that the child understands that the conversation is to be recorded and that such child agrees to participate; and

(3) Upon determining that participation is not harmful to such child.

A true and correct copy of the recording provided for in subsection (b) of this Code section shall be returned to the superior court judge who issued the order and such copy of the recording shall be kept under seal until further order of the court.

(d) The provisions of this article shall not be construed to prohibit a parent or guardian of a child under 18 years of age, with or without the consent of such minor child, from monitoring or intercepting telephonic conversations of such minor child with another person by use of an extension phone located within the family home, or electronic or other communications of such minor child from within the family home, for the purpose of ensuring the welfare of such minor child. If the parent or guardian has a reasonable or good faith belief that such conversation or communication is evidence of criminal conduct involving such child as a victim or an attempt, conspiracy, or solicitation to involve such child in criminal activity affecting the welfare or best interest of such child, the parent or guardian may disclose the content of such telephonic conversation or electronic communication to the district attorney or a law enforcement officer. A recording or other record of any such conversation or communication made by a parent or guardian in accordance with this subsection that contains evidence of criminal conduct involving such child as a victim or an attempt, conspiracy, or solicitation to involve such child in criminal activity shall be admissible in a judicial proceeding except as otherwise provided in subsection (b) of this Code section.

§ 16-11-66.1. Disclosure of stored wire or electronic communications; records; search warrants; issuance of subpoena; violation

(a) A law enforcement officer, a prosecuting attorney, or the Attorney General may require the disclosure of stored wire or electronic communications, as well as transactional records pertaining thereto, to the extent and under the procedures and conditions provided for by the laws of the United States.

(b) A provider of electronic communication service or remote computing service shall provide the contents of, and transactional records pertaining to, wire and electronic communications in its possession or reasonably accessible thereto when a requesting law enforcement officer, a prosecuting attorney, or the Attorney General complies with the provisions for access thereto set forth by the laws of the United States.

(c) Search warrants for production of stored wire or electronic communications and transactional records pertaining thereto shall have state-wide application or application as provided by the laws of the United States when issued by a judge with jurisdiction over the criminal offense under investigation and to which such records relate.

(d) A subpoena for the production of stored wire or electronic communications and transactional records pertaining thereto may be issued at any time upon a showing by a law enforcement official, a prosecuting attorney, or the Attorney General that the subpoenaed material relates to a pending criminal investigation.

(e) Violation of this Code section shall be punishable as contempt.

§ 16-11-67. Admissibility of evidence obtained in violation of part

No evidence obtained in a manner which violates any of the provisions of this part shall be admissible in any court of this state except to prove violations of this part.

§ 16-11-68. Admissibility of privileged communications

Nothing contained within this part shall permit the introduction into evidence of any communication which is privileged by the laws of this state or by the decisions of the appellate courts thereof.

§ 16-11-69. Penalty for violations of part

Except as otherwise provided in subsection (d) of Code Section 16-11-66.1, any person violating any of the provisions of this part shall be guilty of a felony and, upon conviction thereof, shall be punished by imprisonment for not less than one nor more than five years or a fine not to exceed $10,000.00, or both.

§ 16-11-70. Telephone records privacy protection

(a) As used in this Code section, the term:

(1) "End user" means any person, corporation, partnership, firm, municipality, cooperative, organization, governmental agency, building owner, or other entity provided with a telecommunications service for its own consumption and not for resale.

(2) "Telephone record" means information retained by a telecommunications company that relates to the telephone number dialed by the customer, the number of telephone calls directed to a customer, or other data related to the telephone calls typically contained on a customer telephone bill, such as the time the calls started and ended, the duration of the calls, the time of day the calls were made, and any charges applied. For purposes of this Code section, any information collected and retained by, or on behalf of, customers utilizing caller identification or other similar technology does not constitute a telephone record.

(3) "Telephone records broker" means any person or organization that is neither a telecommunications company nor a vendor or supplier for a telecommunications company obligated by contract to protect the confidentiality of telephone records and that purchases, acquires, sells, or releases the telephone record of any third party with whom it has no prior or existing business relationship or that attempts to purchase, acquire, sell, or release the telephone record of any party with whom it has no prior or existing business relationship.

(b) It is unlawful for any telephone records broker to purchase, acquire, sell, or release the telephone records of any person who is a Georgia resident or to attempt to purchase, acquire, sell, or release the telephone record of any third party who is a Georgia resident. This Code section applies whether the customer's telephone record is obtained by the telephone records broker directly from a telecommunications company or from any other third-party source. For purposes of this Code section, a person is a Georgia resident if the individual has a Georgia billing address.

(c) A violation of any provision of this Code section shall be punishable by a civil fine in an amount not to exceed $10,000.00 for each violation. The prosecuting attorney or the Attorney General shall be authorized to prosecute the civil case. Each telephone record purchased, acquired, sold, or released and each attempt to purchase, acquire, sell, or release a telephone record constitutes a separate violation of this Code section.

(d) Any violation of this Code section shall constitute a tort and shall create a right of action in the person or entity whose telephone records have been purchased, acquired, sold, or released for which damages may be recovered. Special damages may be inferred by the violation. Reasonable attorney's fees shall be awarded to the plaintiff where the plaintiff has prevailed in the underlying action.

(e) No provision of this Code section shall be construed to prevent any action by a law enforcement agency or any officer, employee, or agent of a law enforcement agency to obtain the telephone records or personal identifying information of any third party who is a Georgia resident in connection with the performance of the official duties of the agency, officer, employee, or agent.

§ 16-11-80. "Business of preparing federal or state income tax returns or assisting taxpayers in preparing such returns" defined

For the purposes of this part, a person is engaged in the business of preparing federal or state income tax returns or assisting taxpayers in preparing such returns if he does either of the following:

(1) Advertises or gives publicity to the effect that he prepares or assists others in the preparation of state or federal income tax returns; or

(2) Prepares or assists others in the preparation of state or federal income tax returns for compensation.

§ 16-11-81. Disclosure of information obtained in business of preparing federal or state income tax returns or assisting in preparation

It shall be unlawful for any person, including an individual, firm, corporation, association, partnership, joint venture, or any employee or agent thereof, to disclose any information obtained in the business of preparing federal or state income tax returns or assisting taxpayers in preparing such returns unless such disclosure is within any of the following:
(1) Consented to in writing by the taxpayer in a separate document;
(2) Expressly authorized by state or federal law;
(3) Necessary to the preparation of the return;
(4) Pursuant to court order; or
(5) Transmitted to a computer center for preparation.

§ 16-11-82. Contacting taxpayer to obtain written consent

Contacting a taxpayer to obtain his written consent to disclosure does not constitute a violation of this part.

§ 16-11-83. Penalty for violations of part

Any person violating the provisions of this part shall be guilty of a misdemeanor.

§ 16-11-90. Prohibition on nude or sexually explicit electronic transmissions

(a) As used in this Code section, the term:
(1) "Harassment" means engaging in conduct directed at a depicted person that is intended to cause substantial emotional harm to the depicted person.
(2) "Nudity" means:
(A) The showing of the human male or female genitals, pubic area, or buttocks without any covering or with less than a full opaque covering;
(B) The showing of the female breasts without any covering or with less than a full opaque covering; or
(C) The depiction of covered male genitals in a discernibly turgid state.
(3) "Sexually explicit conduct" shall have the same meaning as set forth in Code Section 16-12-100.
(b) A person violates this Code section if he or she, knowing the content of a transmission or post, knowingly and without the consent of the depicted person:
(1) Electronically transmits or posts, in one or more transmissions or posts, a photograph or video which depicts nudity or sexually explicit conduct of an adult when the transmission or post is harassment or causes financial loss to the depicted person and serves no legitimate purpose to the depicted person; or
(2) Causes the electronic transmission or posting, in one or more transmissions or posts, of a photograph or video which depicts nudity or sexually explicit conduct of an adult when the transmission or post is harassment or causes financial loss to the depicted person and serves no legitimate purpose to the depicted person.
(c) Any person who violates this Code section shall be guilty of a misdemeanor of a high and aggravated nature; provided, however, that upon a second or subsequent violation of this Code section, he or she shall be guilty of a felony and, upon conviction thereof, shall be punished by imprisonment of not less than one nor more than five years, a fine of not more than $100,000.00, or both.
(d) A person shall be subject to prosecution in this state pursuant to Code Section 17-2-1 for any conduct made unlawful by this Code section which the person engages in while:
(1) Either within or outside of this state if, by such conduct, the person commits a violation of this Code section which involves an individual who resides in this state; or
(2) Within this state if, by such conduct, the person commits a violation of this Code section which involves an individual who resides within or outside this state.
(e) The provisions of subsection (b) of this Code section shall not apply to:
(1) The activities of law enforcement and prosecution agencies in the investigation and prosecution of criminal offenses;
(2) Legitimate medical, scientific, or educational activities;
(3) Any person who transmits or posts a photograph or video depicting only himself or herself engaged in nudity or sexually explicit conduct;
(4) The transmission or posting of a photograph or video that was originally made for commercial purposes;
(5) Any person who transmits or posts a photograph or video depicting a person voluntarily engaged in nudity or sexually explicit conduct in a public setting; or
(6) A transmission that is made pursuant to or in anticipation of a civil action.
(f) There shall be a rebuttable presumption that an information service, system, or access software provider that provides or enables computer access by multiple users to a computer server, including specifically a service or system that provides access to the Internet, for content provided by another person, does not know the content of an electronic transmission or post.
(g) Any violation of this Code section shall constitute a separate offense and shall not merge with any other crimes set forth in this title.

§ 16-11-91. Use or installation of device to film underneath or through an individual's clothing under certain circumstances

(a) As used in this Code section, the term:
(1) "Device" means an instrument or apparatus used for observing, photographing, videotaping, recording, or transmitting visual images, including but not limited to a camera, photographic equipment, video equipment, mobile phone, or other similar equipment.
(2) "Intimate parts" shall have the same meaning as set forth in Code Section 16-6-22.1.
(b) (1) Notwithstanding Code Section 16-11-90, it shall be unlawful for any person to, knowingly and without the consent of the individual observed, use or install a device for the purpose of surreptitiously observing, photographing, videotaping, filming, or video recording such individual underneath or through such individual's clothing, for the purpose of viewing the intimate parts of the body of or the undergarments worn by such individual, under circumstances in which such individual has a reasonable expectation of privacy, regardless of whether it occurs in a public place.
(2) It shall be unlawful to disseminate any image or recording with knowledge that it was taken or obtained in violation of paragraph (1) of this subsection.
(c) Any person convicted of violating this Code section shall be guilty of a felony and, upon conviction thereof, shall be punished by imprisonment of not less than one year nor more than five years, a fine of not more than $10,000.00, or both, or in the discretion of the court, as for a misdemeanor.
(d) Subsection (b) of this Code section shall not apply to:
(1) The lawful activities of law enforcement and prosecution agencies; or
(2) A business's or entity's surveillance device used in the ordinary course of its business, provided that signage conspicuously warns of such surveillance and the use of such device is primarily designed to detect unlawful activity.
(e) Any violation of this Code section shall constitute a separate offense and shall not merge with any other crimes set forth in this title.

§ 16-11-100. Abandoning, discarding, or leaving unattended containers which lock or fasten automatically; abandoning or discarding motor vehicle which does not have door or window removed

(a) A person is guilty of a misdemeanor when that person leaves in any place accessible to children any abandoned, unattended, or discarded container which has a compartment of more than 1 1/2 cubic feet capacity and a door or lid which locks or fastens automatically when closed and which cannot easily be opened from the inside, without first removing the lid, door, or locking device from such container.
(b) A person is guilty of a misdemeanor when that person leaves in any place accessible to children any abandoned or discarded motor vehicle which does not have at least one door which can easily be opened from the inside or one door or window which has been removed.

§ 16-11-101. Furnishing knuckles or a knife to person under the age of 18 years

A person is guilty of a misdemeanor of a high and aggravated nature when he or she knowingly sells to or furnishes to a person under the age of 18 years knuckles, whether made from metal, thermoplastic, wood, or other similar material, or a knife designed for the purpose of offense and defense.

§ 16-11-101.1. Furnishing pistol or revolver to person under the age of 18 years

(a) For the purposes of this Code section, the term:
(1) "Minor" means any person under the age of 18 years.
(2) "Pistol or revolver" means a handgun as defined in subsection (a) of Code Section 16-11-125.1.
(b) It shall be unlawful for a person intentionally, knowingly, or recklessly to sell or furnish a pistol or revolver to a minor, except that it shall be lawful for a parent or legal guardian to permit possession of a pistol or revolver by a minor for the purposes specified in subsection (c) of Code Section 16-11-132 unless otherwise expressly limited by subsection (c) of this Code section.
(c)(1) It shall be unlawful for a parent or legal guardian to permit possession of a pistol or revolver by a minor if the parent or legal guardian knows of a minor's conduct which violates the provisions of Code Section 16-11-132 and fails to make reasonable efforts to prevent any such violation of Code Section 16-11-132.
(2) Notwithstanding any provisions of subsection (c) of Code Section 16-11-132 or any other law to the contrary, it shall be unlawful for any parent or legal guardian intentionally, knowingly, or recklessly to furnish to or permit a minor to possess a pistol or revolver if such parent or legal guardian is aware of a substantial risk that such minor will use a pistol or revolver to commit a felony offense or if such parent or legal guardian who is aware of such substantial risk fails to make reasonable efforts to prevent commission of the offense by the minor.
(3) In addition to any other act which violates this subsection, a parent or legal guardian shall be deemed to have violated this subsection if such parent or legal guardian furnishes to or permits possession of a pistol or revolver by any minor who has been convicted of a forcible felony or forcible misdemeanor, as defined in Code Section 16-1-3, or who has been adjudicated for committing a delinquent act under the provisions of Article 6 of Chapter 11 of Title 15 for an offense which would constitute a forcible felony or forcible misdemeanor, as defined in Code Section 16-1-3, if such minor were an adult.
(d) Upon conviction of a violation of subsection (b) or (c) of this Code section, a person shall be guilty of a felony and punished by a fine not to exceed $5,000.00 or by imprisonment for not less than three nor more than five years, or both.

§ 16-11-102. Pointing or aiming gun or pistol at another

A person is guilty of a misdemeanor when he intentionally and without legal justification points or aims a gun or pistol at another, whether the gun or pistol is loaded or unloaded.

§ 16-11-103. Discharge of gun or pistol near public highway; penalty

(a) As used in this Code section, the term:
(1) "Firearm" means any handgun, rifle, or shotgun.
(2) "Public highway" means every public street, road, and highway in this state.
(3) "Sport shooting range" means an area designated and operated by a person or entity for the sport shooting of firearms, target practice, trapshooting, skeet shooting, or shooting sporting clays and not available for such use by the general public without payment of a fee, membership contribution, or dues or without the invitation of an authorized person, or any area so designated and operated by a unit of government, regardless of the terms of admission thereto.
(4) "Unit of government" means any of the departments, agencies, authorities, or political subdivisions of the state, cities, municipal corporations, townships, or villages and any of their respective departments, agencies, or authorities.
(b) Except as provided in subsection (c) of this Code section, it shall be unlawful for any person, without legal justification, to discharge a firearm on or within 50 yards of a public highway.
(c) This Code section shall not apply to a discharge of a firearm which occurs within 50 yards of a public highway if such discharge is shielded from the view of a traveler on the public highway and occurs at:
(1) An indoor or outdoor sport shooting range;
(2) Facilities used for firearm or hunting safety courses sponsored by a unit of government, nonprofit corporation, or commercial enterprise; or
(3) The business location of any person, firm, retail dealer, wholesale dealer, pawnbroker, or corporation licensed as a firearm dealer.
(d) Any person who violates subsection (b) of the Code section shall be guilty of a misdemeanor.

§ 16-11-104. Discharge of firearms on property of another

(a) It shall be unlawful for any person to fire or discharge a firearm on the property of another person, firm, or corporation without having first obtained permission from the owner or lessee of the property. This Code section shall not apply to:
(1) Persons who fire or discharge a firearm in defense of person or property; and
(2) Law enforcement officers.
(b) Any person who violates subsection (a) of this Code section is guilty of a misdemeanor.

§ 16-11-105. Discharge of firearm on Sunday; exceptions; penalty

Reserved. Repealed by Ga. L. 2005, p. 641, § 2/SB 259, effective July 1, 2005.

§ 16-11-106. Possession of firearm or knife during commission of or attempt to commit certain crimes

(a) For the purposes of this Code section, the term "firearm" shall include stun guns and tasers. A stun gun or taser is any device that is powered by electrical charging units such as batteries and emits an electrical charge in excess of 20,000 volts or is otherwise capable of incapacitating a person by an electrical charge.
(b) Any person who shall have on or within arm's reach of his or her person a firearm or a knife having a blade of three or more inches in length during the commission of, or the attempt to commit:
(1) Any crime against or involving the person of another;
(2) The unlawful entry into a building or vehicle;
(3) A theft from a building or theft of a vehicle;
(4) Any crime involving the possession, manufacture, delivery, distribution, dispensing, administering, selling, or possession with intent to distribute any controlled substance or marijuana as provided in Code Section 16-13-30, any counterfeit substance as defined in Code Section 16-13-21, or any noncontrolled substance as provided in Code Section 16-13-30.1; or
(5) Any crime involving the trafficking of cocaine, marijuana, or illegal drugs as provided in Code Section 16-13-31,
and which crime is a felony, commits a felony and, upon conviction thereof, shall be punished by confinement for a period of five years, such sentence to run consecutively to any other sentence which the person has received.

(c) Upon the second or subsequent conviction of a person under this Code section, the person shall be punished by confinement for a period of ten years. Notwithstanding any other law to the contrary, the sentence of any person which is imposed for violating this Code section a second or subsequent time shall not be suspended by the court and probationary sentence imposed in lieu thereof.

(d) The punishment prescribed for the violation of subsections (b) and (c) of this Code section shall not be reducible to misdemeanor punishment as is provided by Code Section 17-10-5.

(e) Any crime committed in violation of subsections (b) and (c) of this Code section shall be considered a separate offense.

§ 16-11-107. Harming a law enforcement animal

(a) As used in this Code section, the term:

(1) "Accelerant detection dog" means a dog trained to detect hydrocarbon substances.

(2) "Bomb detection dog" means a dog trained to locate bombs or explosives by scent.

(2.1) "Dangerous weapon" shall have the same meaning as provided for in Code Section 16-11-121.

(2.2) "Firearm" means any handgun, rifle, shotgun, stun gun, taser, or dangerous weapon.

(3) "Firearms detection dog" means a dog trained to locate firearms by scent.

(3.1) "Knowingly" means having knowledge that an animal is a law enforcement animal.

(3.2) "Law enforcement animal" means a police dog, police horse, or any other animal trained to support a peace officer, fire department, or the state fire marshal in performance of law enforcement duties.

(4) "Narcotic detection dog" means a dog trained to locate narcotics by scent.

(5) "Narcotics" means any controlled substance as defined in paragraph (4) of Code Section 16-13-21 and shall include marijuana as defined by paragraph (16) of Code Section 16-13-21.

(6) "Patrol dog" means a dog trained to protect a peace officer and to apprehend or hold without excessive force a person in violation of the criminal statutes of this state.

(6.1) "Performance of its duties" means performing law enforcement, fire department, or state fire marshal duties as trained.

(7) "Police dog" means a bomb detection dog, a firearms detection dog, a narcotic detection dog, a patrol dog, an accelerant detection dog, or a tracking dog used by a law enforcement agency. Such term also means a search and rescue dog.

(8) "Police horse" means a horse trained to transport, carry, or be ridden by a law enforcement officer and used by a law enforcement agency.

(8.1) "Search and rescue dog" means any dog that is owned or the services of which are employed by a fire department or the state fire marshal for the principal purpose of aiding in the detection of missing persons, including but not limited to persons who are lost, who are trapped under debris as a result of a natural or manmade disaster, or who are drowning victims.

(9) "Tracking dog" means a dog trained to track and find a missing person, escaped inmate, or fleeing felon.

(b) A person commits the offense of harming a law enforcement animal in the fourth degree when he or she knowingly and intentionally causes physical harm to such law enforcement animal while such law enforcement animal is in performance of its duties or because of such law enforcement animal's performance of its duties. Any person convicted of a violation of this subsection shall be guilty of a misdemeanor of a high and aggravated nature and, upon conviction thereof, shall be punished by imprisonment not to exceed 12 months, a fine not to exceed $5,000.00, or both.

(c) A person commits the offense of harming a law enforcement animal in the third degree when he or she knowingly and intentionally and with a deadly weapon causes, or with any object, device, instrument, or body part which, when used offensively against such law enforcement animal, is likely to or actually does cause, serious physical injury to such law enforcement animal while such law enforcement animal is in performance of its duties or because of such law enforcement animal's performance of its duties. Any person convicted of a violation of this subsection shall be guilty of a misdemeanor of a high and aggravated nature and, upon conviction thereof, shall be punished by imprisonment for not less than six nor more than 12 months, a fine not to exceed $5,000.00, or both.

(d) A person commits the offense of harming a law enforcement animal in the second degree when he or she knowingly and intentionally shoots a law enforcement animal with a firearm or causes debilitating physical injury to a law enforcement animal while such law enforcement animal is in performance of its duties or because of such law enforcement animal's performance of its duties. Any person convicted of a violation of this subsection shall be guilty of a felony and, upon conviction thereof, shall be punished by imprisonment for not less than one nor more than five years, a fine not to exceed $25,000.00, or both.

(e) A person commits the offense of harming a law enforcement animal in the first degree when he or she knowingly and intentionally causes the death of a law enforcement animal while such law enforcement animal is in performance of its duties or because of such law enforcement animal's performance of its duties. Any person convicted of a violation of this subsection shall be guilty of a felony and, upon conviction thereof, shall be punished by imprisonment for not less than 18 months nor more than five years, a fine not to exceed $50,000.00, or both.

(f) In addition to any other penalty provided for under this Code section, any person convicted of a violation under this Code section shall pay restitution to the law enforcement agency, fire department, or the state fire marshal which is the owner of, or which owned, such law enforcement animal in the amount of associated veterinary expenses incurred in the treatment of such law enforcement animal pursuant to Article 1 of Chapter 14 of Title 17; provided, however, that if such law enforcement animal died or is no longer able to engage in performance of its duties as a result of a violation of this Code section, the amount paid in restitution shall additionally include the amount of the actual replacement value of the law enforcement animal, which shall include the value of an animal to replace the law enforcement animal and all costs associated with training such animal and its handler or handlers.

(g) Nothing in this Code section shall prohibit the killing or euthanasia of a law enforcement animal for humane purposes.

(h) Nothing in this Code section shall prohibit the defense of a person against a law enforcement animal that attacks such person without or in spite of commands given by its handler.

(i) The Division of Forensic Sciences of the Georgia Bureau of Investigation shall perform forensic pathology services upon any law enforcement animal whose death occurred while in performance of its duties or because of such law enforcement animal's performance of its duties.

§ 16-11-107.1. Harassment of assistance dog by humans or other dogs; penalty

(a) As used in this Code section, the term:

(1) "Assistance dog" means a dog that is or has been trained by a licensed or certified person, organization, or agency to perform physical tasks for a physically challenged person. Assistance dogs include guide or leader dogs that guide individuals who are legally blind; hearing dogs that alert individuals who are deaf or hard of hearing to specific sounds; and service dogs for individuals with disabilities other than blindness or deafness, which are trained to perform a variety of physical tasks, including, but not limited to, pulling a wheelchair, lending balance support, picking up dropped objects, or providing assistance in a medical crisis.

(2) "Harass" means to engage in any conduct directed toward an assistance dog that is knowingly likely to impede or interfere with the assistance dog's performance of its duties or that places the blind, deaf, or physically limited person being served or assisted by the dog in danger of injury.

(3) "Notice" means an oral or otherwise communicated warning proscribing the behavior of another person and a request that the person stop the particular behavior.

(b) Any person who knowingly and intentionally harasses or attempts to harass an assistance dog, knowing the dog to be an assistance dog, shall be guilty of a misdemeanor and, upon conviction thereof, shall be punished by imprisonment for not less than 90 days or a fine not to exceed $500.00, or both.

(c) Any person who has received notice that his or her behavior is interfering with the use of an assistance dog who continues to knowingly and intentionally harass an assistance dog, knowing the dog to be an assistance dog, shall be guilty of a misdemeanor and, upon conviction thereof, shall be punished by imprisonment for not less than 90 days or a fine not to exceed $500.00, or both, provided that any person who is convicted of a second or subsequent violation of this subsection shall be punished as for a misdemeanor of a high and aggravated nature.

(d) Any person who knowingly and intentionally allows his or her dog to harass an assistance dog, knowing the dog to be an assistance dog, shall be guilty of a misdemeanor and, upon conviction thereof, shall be punished by imprisonment for not less than 90 days or a fine not to exceed $500.00, or both, provided that any person who is convicted of a second or subsequent violation of this subsection shall be punished as for a misdemeanor of a high and aggravated nature.

(e) Any person who knowingly and intentionally allows his or her dog to cause death or physical harm to an assistance dog by rendering a part of the assistance dog's body useless or by seriously disfiguring the assistance dog, knowing the dog to be an assistance dog, shall be punished as for a misdemeanor of a high and aggravated nature.

§ 16-11-108. Misuse of firearm or archery tackle while hunting

(a) Any person who while hunting wildlife uses a firearm or archery tackle in a manner to endanger the bodily safety of another person by consciously disregarding a substantial and unjustifiable risk that his act or omission will cause harm to or endanger the safety of another person and the disregard constitutes a gross deviation from the standard of care which a reasonable person would exercise in the situation is guilty of a misdemeanor; provided, however, if such conduct results in serious bodily harm to another person, the person engaging in such conduct shall be guilty of a felony and, upon conviction thereof, shall be punished by a fine of not more than $5,000.00 or by imprisonment for not less than one nor more than ten years, or both.

(b) Whenever a person is charged with violating subsection (a) of this Code section, the arresting law enforcement officer shall take the hunting license of the person so charged. The hunting license shall be attached to the court's copy of the citation, warrant, accusation, or indictment and shall be forwarded to the court having jurisdiction of the offense. A copy of the citation, warrant, accusation, or indictment shall be forwarded, within 15 days of its issuance, to the Game and Fish Division of the Department of Natural Resources.

(c) In order to obtain a temporary hunting license, a person charged with violating subsection (a) of this Code section must present to the director of the Game and Fish Division of the Department of Natural Resources a certificate of satisfactory completion, after the date of the incident for which the person was charged and regardless of the person's age or date of birth, of a hunter education course prescribed by the Board of Natural Resources. A temporary hunting license issued under such circumstances shall be valid until the next March 31 or until suspended or revoked under any provision of this title or of Title 27. The director of the Game and Fish Division of the Department of Natural Resources may renew the temporary hunting license during the pendency of charges.

(d)(1) If the person is convicted of violating subsection (a) of this Code section, the court shall, within 15 days of such conviction, forward the person's hunting license and a copy of the record of the disposition of the case to the Game and Fish Division of the Department of Natural Resources. At this time, the court shall also require the person to surrender any temporary hunting licenses issued pursuant to the provisions of subsection (c) of this Code section.

(2) If the person is not convicted of violating subsection (a) of this Code section, the court shall return the hunting license to the person.

§ 16-11-109. Activities prohibited to person charged with violation of subsection (a) of Code Section 16-11-108; penalty for violation of Code section; surrender of hunting license

(a) It shall be unlawful during the pendency of such charges and any period of license revocation and ineligibility pursuant to Code Section 16-11-110 for any person charged with or convicted of a violation of subsection (a) of Code Section 16-11-108 to either:

(1) Hunt without a license in violation of Code Section 27-2-1; or

(2) Possess a Georgia hunting license other than a temporary hunting license issued by the director of the Game and Fish Division of the Department of Natural Resources pursuant to the provisions of subsection (c) of Code Section 16-11-108.

(b) Any person who violates subsection (a) of this Code section shall be guilty of a felony and, upon conviction thereof, shall be punished by a fine of not more than $5,000.00 or by imprisonment for not less than one nor more than five years, or both.

(c) Upon conviction of a violation of subsection (a) of this Code section, the court shall, within 15 days of such conviction, forward any hunting license found in the possession of the convicted person and a copy of the record of the disposition of the case to the Game and Fish Division of the Department of Natural Resources.

§ 16-11-110. Revocation of hunting license for violation of subsection (a) of Code Section 16-11-108 or subsection (a) of Code Section 16-11-109

(a) Any hunting license of any person convicted of violating subsection (a) of Code Section 16-11-108 or subsection (a) of Code Section 16-11-109 shall by operation of law be revoked.

(b) Any person convicted of violating subsection (a) of Code Section 16-11-108 or subsection (a) of Code Section 16-11-109 shall be ineligible for a hunting license for a period of five years from the date of conviction.

(c) If a person's hunting license is revoked by operation of law as provided in subsection (a) of this Code section, the fact that the person's hunting license was not surrendered to the law enforcement officer at the time the person was charged with violating subsection (a) of Code Section 16-11-108 or the fact that the person's hunting license was not retained by the court and forwarded to the Game and Fish Division of the Department of Natural Resources as provided in subsection (d) of Code Section 16-11-108 or in subsection (c) of Code Section 16-11-109 shall not affect such revocation.

§ 16-11-111. "Anhydrous ammonia" defined; crime for possession

(a)(1) As used in this Code section, the term "anhydrous ammonia" means any substance identified to contain the compound ammonia which is capable of being utilized in the production of methamphetamine or any other controlled substance.

(2) A person commits the crime of unlawful possession of anhydrous ammonia if the person:

(A) Purchases, possesses, transfers, or distributes any amount of anhydrous ammonia knowing that the anhydrous ammonia will be used unlawfully to manufacture a controlled substance;

(B) Possesses, maintains, or transports any quantity of anhydrous ammonia in a container or receptacle other than a tank truck, tank trailer, rail tank car, bulk storage tank, field (nurse) tank, field applicator, or any container approved for anhydrous ammonia by the Department of Agriculture or the United States Department of Transportation; or

(C) Tampers with equipment manufactured to hold, apply, or transport anhydrous ammonia without the express consent of the owner of the equipment.

(3) A person who violates subparagraph (B) of paragraph (2) of this subsection shall be subject to civil penalties in accordance with Code Section 40-1-23.

(b) Any person who violates this Code section shall, upon conviction thereof, be punished by imprisonment for not less than one year nor more than ten years and by a fine not to exceed $100,000.00.

§ 16-11-112. Vehicles with false or secret compartments

(a) As used in this Code section, the term:

(1) (A) "False or secret compartment" means any enclosure which is integrated into or attached to a vehicle and the purpose of the compartment is to conceal, hide, or prevent discovery by law enforcement officers of:

(i) A person concealed for an unlawful purpose;

(ii) Controlled substances possessed in violation of Article 2 of Chapter 13 of this title; or

(iii) Other contraband.

(B) Examples of "false or secret compartment" may include, but are not limited to:

(i) False, altered, or modified fuel tanks;

(ii) Original factory equipment on a vehicle that has been modified; or

(iii) Any compartment, space, or box that is added or attached to existing compartments, spaces, or boxes of the vehicle.

(2) "Vehicle" includes, but is not limited to, cars, trucks, buses, motorcycles, bicycles, aircraft, helicopters, boats, ships, yachts, and other vessels.

(b) It may be inferred that the accused intended to use a false or secret compartment if a person knowingly has a false or secret compartment which:

(1) Is concealing a person for an unlawful purpose;

(2) Is concealing a controlled substance in violation of Article 2 of Chapter 13 of this title;

(3) Is concealing other contraband;

(4) Shows evidence of the previous concealment of a person for an unlawful purpose;

(5) Shows evidence of the previous concealment of controlled substances in violation of Article 2 of Chapter 13 of this title; or

(6) Shows evidence of the previous concealment of other contraband.

(c) (1) It is unlawful for any person to knowingly own or operate any vehicle containing a false or secret compartment.

(2) It is unlawful for any person to knowingly install, create, build, or fabricate in any vehicle a false or secret compartment.

(3) It is unlawful for any person to knowingly sell, trade, or otherwise dispose of a vehicle which is in violation of this Code section.

(d) Any person who violates this Code section shall, upon conviction thereof, be punished by imprisonment for not less than one nor more than two years, by a fine not to exceed $10,000.00, or both.

(e) Upon the arrest of a person who owns or is operating a vehicle which is in violation of this Code section, if the vehicle is not otherwise subject to forfeiture under other provisions of law, or not determined to be needed to be held as evidence, the law enforcement officer shall seize the license plate and registration for such vehicle and shall issue a citation for violation of this Code section and a temporary license plate for the vehicle. The temporary license plate shall be on a form as prescribed by the state revenue commissioner. The temporary license plate shall be valid for 30 days or until the owner of the vehicle provides verification that such vehicle has been repaired so as to eliminate any violation of this Code section, whichever occurs first. Such vehicle shall be subject to inspection by law enforcement and if it is determined that such vehicle has been repaired, the license plate and registration shall be returned to the owner at such time.

§ 16-11-113. Offense of transferring firearm to individual other than actual buyer

Any person who attempts to solicit, persuade, encourage, or entice any dealer to transfer or otherwise convey a firearm other than to the actual buyer, as well as any other person who willfully and intentionally aids or abets such person, shall be guilty of a felony. This Code section shall not apply to a federal law enforcement officer or a peace officer, as defined in Code Section 16-1-3, in the performance of his or her official duties or other person under such officer's direct supervision.

§ 16-11-120. Short title

This part shall be known and may be cited as the "Georgia Firearms and Weapons Act."

§ 16-11-121. Definitions

As used in this part, the term:

(1) "Dangerous weapon" means any weapon commonly known as a "rocket launcher," "bazooka," or "recoilless rifle" which fires explosive or nonexplosive rockets designed to injure or kill personnel or destroy heavy armor, or similar weapon used for such purpose. The term shall also mean a weapon commonly known as a "mortar" which fires high explosive from a metallic cylinder and which is commonly used by the armed forces as an antipersonnel weapon or similar weapon used for such purpose. The term shall also mean a weapon commonly known as a "hand grenade" or other similar weapon which is designed to explode and injure personnel or similar weapon used for such purpose.

(2) "Machine gun" means any weapon which shoots or is designed to shoot, automatically, more than six shots, without manual reloading, by a single function of the trigger.

(3) "Person" means any individual, partnership, company, association, or corporation.

(4) "Sawed-off rifle" means a weapon designed or redesigned, made or remade, and intended to be fired from the shoulder; and designed or redesigned, made or remade, to use the energy of the explosive in a fixed metallic cartridge to fire only a single projectile through a rifle bore for each single pull of the trigger; and which has a barrel or barrels of less than 16 inches in length or has an overall length of less than 26 inches.

(5) "Sawed-off shotgun" means a shotgun or any weapon made from a shotgun whether by alteration, modification, or otherwise having one or more barrels less than 18 inches in length or if such weapon as modified has an overall length of less than 26 inches.

(6) "Shotgun" means a weapon designed or redesigned, made or remade, and intended to be fired from the shoulder; and designed or redesigned, and made or remade, to use the energy of the explosive in a fixed shotgun shell to fire through a smooth bore either a number of ball shot or a single projectile for each single pull of the trigger.

(7) "Silencer" means any device for silencing or diminishing the report of any portable weapon such as a rifle, carbine, pistol, revolver, machine gun, shotgun, fowling piece, or other device from which a shot, bullet, or projectile may be discharged by an explosive.

§ 16-11-122. Possession of sawed-off shotgun or rifle, machine gun, silencer, or dangerous weapon prohibited

No person shall have in his possession any sawed-off shotgun, sawed-off rifle, machine gun, dangerous weapon, or silencer except as provided in Code Section 16-11-124.

§ 16-11-123. Unlawful possession of firearms or weapons

A person commits the offense of unlawful possession of firearms or weapons when he or she knowingly has in his or her possession any sawed-off shotgun, sawed-off rifle, machine gun, dangerous weapon, or silencer, and, upon conviction thereof, he or she shall be punished by imprisonment for a period of five years.

§ 16-11-124. Exemptions from application of part

This part shall not apply to:

(1) A peace officer of any duly authorized police agency of this state or of any political subdivision thereof, or a law enforcement officer of any department or agency of the United States who is regularly employed and paid by the United States, this state, or any such political subdivision, or an employee of the Department of Corrections of this state who is authorized in writing by the commissioner of corrections to transfer or possess such firearms while in the official performance of his duties;

(2) A member of the National Guard or of the armed forces of the United States to wit: the army, navy, marine corps, air force, or coast guard who, while serving therein, possesses such firearm in the line of duty;

(3) Any sawed-off shotgun, sawed-off rifle, machine gun, dangerous weapon, or silencer which has been modified or changed to the extent that it is inoperative. Examples of the requisite modification include weapons with their barrel or barrels filled with lead, hand grenades filled with sand, or other nonexplosive materials;

(4) Possession of a sawed-off shotgun, sawed-off rifle, machine gun, dangerous weapon, or silencer by a person who is authorized to possess the same because he has registered the sawed-off shotgun, sawed-off rifle, machine gun, dangerous weapon, or silencer in accordance with the dictates of the National Firearms Act, 68A Stat. 725 (26 U.S.C. Sections 5841-5862); and

(5) A security officer employed by a federally licensed nuclear power facility or a licensee of such facility, including a contract security officer, who is trained and qualified under a security plan approved by the United States Nuclear Regulatory Commission or other federal agency authorized to regulate nuclear facility security; provided, however, that this exemption shall apply only while such security officer is acting in connection with his or her official duties on the premises of such nuclear power facility or on properties outside the facility property pursuant to a written agreement entered into with the local law enforcement agency having jurisdiction over the facility. The exemption under this paragraph does not include the possession of silencers.

§ 16-11-125. Burden of proof as to exemptions

In any complaint, accusation, or indictment and in any action or proceeding brought for the enforcement of this part it shall not be necessary to negative any exception, excuse, proviso, or exemption contained in this part, and the burden of proof of any such exception, excuse, proviso, or exemption shall be upon the defendant.

§ 16-11-125.1. Definitions

As used in this part, the term:

(1) "Handgun" means a firearm of any description, loaded or unloaded, from which any shot, bullet, or other missile can be discharged by an action of an explosive where the length of the barrel, not including any revolving, detachable, or magazine breech, does not exceed 12 inches; provided, however, that the term "handgun" shall not include a gun which discharges a single shot of .46 centimeters or less in diameter.

(2) "Knife" means a cutting instrument designed for the purpose of offense and defense consisting of a blade that is greater than 12 inches in length which is fastened to a handle.

(3) "License holder" means a person who holds a valid weapons carry license.

(4) "Long gun" means a firearm with a barrel length of at least 18 inches and overall length of at least 26 inches designed or made and intended to be fired from the shoulder and designed or made to use the energy of the explosive in a fixed:

(A) Shotgun shell to fire through a smooth bore either a number of ball shot or a single projectile for each single pull of the trigger or from which any shot, bullet, or other missile can be discharged; or

(B) Metallic cartridge to fire only a single projectile through a rifle bore for each single pull of the trigger;

provided, however, that the term "long gun" shall not include a gun which discharges a single shot of .46 centimeters or less in diameter.

(5) "Weapon" means a knife or handgun.

(6) "Weapons carry license" or "license" means a license issued pursuant to Code Section 16-11-129.

§ 16-11-126. Having or carrying handguns, long guns, or other weapons; license requirement; exceptions for homes, motor vehicles, private property, and other locations and conditions

(a) Any person who is not prohibited by law from possessing a handgun or long gun may have or carry on his or her person a weapon or long gun on his or her property or inside his or her home, motor vehicle, or place of business without a valid weapons carry license.

(b) Any person who is not prohibited by law from possessing a handgun or long gun may have or carry on his or her person a long gun without a valid weapons carry license, provided that if the long gun is loaded, it shall only be carried in an open and fully exposed manner.

(c) Any person who is not prohibited by law from possessing a handgun or long gun may have or carry any handgun provided that it is enclosed in a case and unloaded.

(d) Any person who is not prohibited by law from possessing a handgun or long gun who is eligible for a weapons carry license may transport a handgun or long gun in any private passenger motor vehicle; provided, however, that private property owners or persons in legal control of private property through a lease, rental agreement, licensing agreement, contract, or any other agreement to control access to such private property shall have the right to exclude or eject a person who is in possession of a weapon or long gun on their private property in accordance with paragraph (3) of subsection (b) of Code Section 16-7-21, except as provided in Code Section 16-11-135.

(e) (1) (A) Any person licensed to carry a weapon in any other state whose laws recognize and give effect to a license issued pursuant to this part shall be authorized to carry a weapon in this state, but only while the licensee is not a resident of this state; provided, however, that:

(i) Such licensee licensed to carry a weapon in any other state shall carry the weapon in compliance with the laws of this state; and

(ii) No other state shall be required to recognize and give effect to a license issued pursuant to this part that is held by a person who is younger than 21 years of age.

(B) The Attorney General shall create and maintain on the Department of Law's website a list of states whose laws recognize and give effect to a license issued pursuant to this part.

(2) Any person who is not a weapons carry license holder in this state and who is licensed to carry a weapon in any other state whose laws recognize and give effect to a license issued pursuant to this part shall be authorized to carry a weapon in this state for 90 days after he or she becomes a resident of this state; provided, however, that such person shall carry the weapon in compliance with the laws of this state, shall as soon as practicable submit a weapons carry license application as provided for under Code Section 16-11-129, and shall remain licensed in such other state for the duration of time that he or she is a resident of this state but not a weapons carry license holder in this state.

(f) (1) Any person with a valid hunting or fishing license on his or her person, or any person not required by law to have a hunting or fishing license, who is engaged in legal hunting, fishing, or sport shooting when the person has the permission of the owner of the land on which the activities are being conducted may have or carry on his or her person a weapon or long gun without a valid weapons carry license while hunting, fishing, or engaging in sport shooting.

(2) Any person with a valid hunting or fishing license on his or her person, or any person not required by law to have a hunting or fishing license, who is otherwise engaged in legal hunting, fishing, or sport shooting on recreational or wildlife management areas owned by this state may have or carry on his or her person a knife without a valid weapons carry license while engaging in such hunting, fishing, or sport shooting.

(g) Notwithstanding Code Sections 12-3-10, 27-3-1.1, 27-3-6, and 16-12-122 through 16-12-127, any person with a valid weapons carry license may carry a weapon in all parks, historic sites, or recreational areas, as such term is defined in Code Section 12-3-10, including all publicly owned buildings located in such parks, historic sites, and recreational areas, in wildlife management areas, and on public transportation; provided, however, that a person shall not carry a handgun into a place where it is prohibited by federal law.

(h) (1) No person shall carry a weapon without a valid weapons carry license unless he or she meets one of the exceptions to having such license as provided in subsections (a) through (g) of this Code section.

(2) A person commits the offense of carrying a weapon without a license when he or she violates the provisions of paragraph (1) of this subsection.

(i) Upon conviction of the offense of carrying a weapon without a valid weapons carry license, a person shall be punished as follows:

(1) For the first offense, he or she shall be guilty of a misdemeanor; and

(2) For the second offense within five years, as measured from the dates of previous arrests for which convictions were obtained to the date of the current arrest for which a conviction is obtained, and for any subsequent offense, he or she shall be guilty of a felony and, upon conviction thereof, shall be imprisoned for not less than two years and not more than five years.

(j) Nothing in this Code section shall in any way operate or be construed to affect, repeal, or limit the exemptions provided for under Code Section 16-11-130.

§ 16-11-127. Carrying weapons in unauthorized locations

(a) As used in this Code section, the term:

(1) "Courthouse" means a building occupied by judicial courts and containing rooms in which judicial proceedings are held.

(2) "Government building" means:

(A) The building in which a government entity is housed;

(B) The building where a government entity meets in its official capacity; provided, however, that if such building is not a publicly owned building, such building shall be considered a government building for the purposes of this Code section only during the time such government entity is meeting at such building; or

(C) The portion of any building that is not a publicly owned building that is occupied by a government entity.

(3) "Government entity" means an office, agency, authority, department, commission, board, body, division, instrumentality, or institution of the state or any county, municipal corporation, consolidated government, or local board of education within this state.

(4) "Parking facility" means real property owned or leased by a government entity, courthouse, jail, prison, or place of worship that has been designated by such government entity, courthouse, jail, prison, or place of worship for the parking of motor vehicles at a government building or at such courthouse, jail, prison, or place of worship.

(b) Except as provided in Code Section 16-11-127.1 and subsection (d) or (e) of this Code section, a person shall be guilty of carrying a weapon or long gun in an unauthorized location and punished as for a misdemeanor when he or she carries a weapon or long gun while:

(1) In a government building as a nonlicense holder;

(2) In a courthouse;

(3) In a jail or prison;

(4) In a place of worship, unless the governing body or authority of the place of worship permits the carrying of weapons or long guns by license holders;

(5) In a state mental health facility as defined in Code Section 37-1-1 which admits individuals on an involuntary basis for treatment of mental illness, developmental disability, or addictive disease; provided, however, that carrying a weapon or long gun in such location in a manner in compliance with paragraph (3) of subsection (d) of this Code section shall not constitute a violation of this subsection;

(6) On the premises of a nuclear power facility, except as provided in Code Section 16-11-127.2, and the punishment provisions of Code Section 16-11-127.2 shall supersede the punishment provisions of this Code section; or

(7) Within 150 feet of any polling place when elections are being conducted and such polling place is being used as a polling place as provided for in paragraph (27) of Code Section 21-2-2, except as provided in subsection (i) of Code Section 21-2-413.

(c) A license holder or person recognized under subsection (e) of Code Section 16-11-126 shall be authorized to carry a weapon as provided in Code Section 16-11-135 and in every location in this state not listed in subsection (b) or prohibited by subsection (e) of this Code section; provided, however, that private property owners or persons in legal control of private property through a lease, rental agreement, licensing agreement, contract, or any other agreement to control access to such private property shall have the right to exclude or eject a person who is in possession of a weapon or long gun on their private property in accordance with paragraph (3) of subsection (b) of Code Section 16-7-21, except as provided in Code Section 16-11-135. A violation of subsection (b) of this Code section shall not create or give rise to a civil action for damages.

(d) Subsection (b) of this Code section shall not apply:

(1) To the use of weapons or long guns as exhibits in a legal proceeding, provided such weapons or long guns are secured and handled as directed by the personnel providing courtroom security or the judge hearing the case;

(2) To a license holder who approaches security or management personnel upon arrival at a location described in subsection (b) of this Code section and notifies such security or management personnel of the presence of the weapon or long gun and explicitly follows the security or management personnel's direction for removing, securing, storing, or temporarily surrendering such weapon or long gun; and

(3) To a weapon or long gun possessed by a license holder which is under the possessor's control in a motor vehicle or is in a locked compartment of a motor vehicle or one which is in a locked container in or a locked firearms rack which is on a motor vehicle and such vehicle is parked in a parking facility.

(e) (1) A license holder shall be authorized to carry a weapon in a government building when the government building is open for business and where ingress into such building is not restricted or screened by security personnel. A license holder who enters or attempts to enter a government building carrying a weapon where ingress is restricted or screened by security personnel shall be guilty of a misdemeanor if at least one member of such security personnel is certified as a peace officer pursuant to Chapter 8 of Title 35; provided, however, that a license holder who immediately exits such building or immediately leaves such location upon notification of his or her failure to clear security due to the carrying of a weapon shall not be guilty of violating this subsection or paragraph (1) of subsection (b) of this Code section. A person who is not a license holder and who attempts to enter a government building carrying a weapon shall be guilty of a misdemeanor.

(2) Any license holder who violates subsection (b) of this Code section in a place of worship shall not be arrested but shall be fined not more than $100.00. Any person who is not a license holder who violates subsection (b) of this Code section in a place of worship shall be punished as for a misdemeanor.

(f) Nothing in this Code section shall in any way operate or be construed to affect, repeal, or limit the exemptions provided for under Code Section 16-11-130.

§ 16-11-127.1. Carrying weapons within school safety zones, at school functions, or on a bus or other transportation furnished by a school

(a) As used in this Code section, the term:

(1) "Bus or other transportation furnished by a school" means a bus or other transportation furnished by a public or private elementary or secondary school.

(2) "School function" means a school function or related activity that occurs outside of a school safety zone and is for a public or private elementary or secondary school.

(3) "School safety zone" means in or on any real property or building owned by or leased to:

(A) Any public or private elementary school, secondary school, or local board of education and used for elementary or secondary education; and

(B) Any public or private technical school, vocational school, college, university, or other institution of postsecondary education.

(4) "Weapon" means and includes any pistol, revolver, or any weapon designed or intended to propel a missile of any kind, or any dirk, bowie knife, switchblade knife, ballistic knife, any other knife having a blade of two or more inches, straight-edge razor, razor blade, spring stick, knuckles, whether made from metal, thermoplastic, wood, or other similar material, blackjack, any bat, club, or other bludgeon-type weapon, or any flailing instrument consisting of two or more rigid parts connected in such a manner as to allow them to swing freely, which may be known as a nun chahka, nun chuck, nunchaku, shuriken, or fighting chain, or any disc, of whatever configuration, having at least two points or pointed blades which is designed to be thrown or propelled and which may be known as a throwing star or oriental dart, or any weapon of like kind, and any stun gun or taser as defined in subsection (a) of Code Section 16-11-106. This paragraph excludes any of these instruments used for classroom work authorized by the teacher.

(b) (1) Except as otherwise provided in subsection (c) of this Code section, it shall be unlawful for any person to carry to or to possess or have under such person's control while within a school safety zone, at a school function, or on a bus or other transportation furnished by a school any weapon or explosive compound, other than fireworks or consumer fireworks the possession of which is regulated by Chapter 10 of Title 25.

(2) Except as provided for in paragraph (20) of subsection (c) of this Code section, any license holder who violates this subsection shall be guilty of a misdemeanor. Any person who is not a license holder who violates this subsection shall be guilty of a felony and, upon conviction thereof, be punished by a fine of not more than $10,000.00, by imprisonment for not less than two nor more than ten years, or both.

(3) Any person convicted of a violation of this subsection involving a dangerous weapon or machine gun, as such terms are defined in Code Section 16-11-121, shall be punished by a fine of not more than $10,000.00 or by imprisonment for a period of not less than five nor more than ten years, or both.

(4) A child who violates this subsection may be subject to the provisions of Code Section 15-11-601.

(c) The provisions of this Code section shall not apply to:

(1) Baseball bats, hockey sticks, or other sports equipment possessed by competitors for legitimate athletic purposes;

(2) Participants in organized sport shooting events or firearm training courses;

(3) Persons participating in military training programs conducted by or on behalf of the armed forces of the United States or the Georgia Department of Defense;

(4) Persons participating in law enforcement training conducted by a police academy certified by the Georgia Peace Officer Standards and Training Council or by a law enforcement agency of the state or the United States or any political subdivision thereof;

(5) The following persons, when acting in the performance of their official duties or when en route to or from their official duties:

(A) A peace officer as defined by Code Section 35-8-2;

(B) A law enforcement officer of the United States government;

(C) A prosecuting attorney of this state or of the United States;

(D) An employee of the Department of Corrections or a correctional facility operated by a political subdivision of this state or the United States who is authorized by the head of such department or correctional agency or facility to carry a firearm;

(E) An employee of the Department of Community Supervision who is authorized by the commissioner of community supervision to carry a firearm;

(F) A person employed as a campus police officer or school security officer who is authorized to carry a weapon in accordance with Chapter 8 of Title 20; and

(G) Medical examiners, coroners, and their investigators who are employed by the state or any political subdivision thereof;

provided, however, that this Code section shall not apply to any extent to persons who are provided for under Code Section 16-11-130;

(6) A person who has been authorized in writing by a duly authorized official of a public or private elementary or secondary school or a public or private technical school, vocational school, college, university, or other institution of postsecondary education or a local board of education as provided in Code Section 16-11-130.1 to have in such person's possession or use within a school safety zone, at a school function, or on a bus or other transportation furnished by a school a weapon which would otherwise be prohibited by this Code section. Such authorization shall specify the weapon or weapons which have been authorized and the time period during which the authorization is valid;

(7) A person who is licensed in accordance with Code Section 16-11-129 or issued a permit pursuant to Code Section 43-38-10, when such person carries or picks up a student within a school safety zone, at a school function, or on a bus or other transportation furnished by a school or a person who is licensed in accordance with Code Section 16-11-129 or issued a permit pursuant to Code Section 43-38-10 when he or she has any weapon legally kept within a vehicle when such vehicle is parked within a school safety zone or is in transit through a designated school safety zone;

(8) A weapon possessed by a license holder which is under the possessor's control in a motor vehicle or which is in a locked compartment of a motor vehicle or one which is in a locked container in or a locked firearms rack which is on a motor vehicle which is being used by an adult over 21 years of age to bring to or pick up a student within a school safety zone, at a school function, or on a bus or other transportation furnished by a school, or when such vehicle is used to transport someone to an activity being conducted within a school safety zone which has been authorized by a duly authorized official or local board of education as provided by paragraph (6) of this subsection; provided, however, that this exception shall not apply to a student attending a public or private elementary or secondary school;

(9) Persons employed in fulfilling defense contracts with the government of the United States or agencies thereof when possession of the weapon is necessary for manufacture, transport, installation, and testing under the requirements of such contract;

(10) Those employees of the State Board of Pardons and Paroles when specifically designated and authorized in writing by the members of the State Board of Pardons and Paroles to carry a weapon;

(11) The Attorney General and those members of his or her staff whom he or she specifically authorizes in writing to carry a weapon;

(12) Community supervision officers employed by and under the authority of the Department of Community Supervision when specifically designated and authorized in writing by the commissioner of community supervision;

(13) Public safety directors of municipal corporations;

(14) State and federal trial and appellate judges;

(15) United States attorneys and assistant United States attorneys;

(16) Clerks of the superior courts;

(17) Teachers and other personnel who are otherwise authorized to possess or carry weapons, provided that any such weapon is in a locked compartment of a motor vehicle or one which is in a locked container in or a locked firearms rack which is on a motor vehicle;

(18) Constables of any county of this state;

(19) Any person who is 18 years of age or older or currently enrolled in classes on the campus in question and carrying, possessing, or having under such person's control an electroshock weapon while in or on any building or real property owned by or leased to such public technical school, vocational school, college or university or other public institution of postsecondary education; provided, however, that, if such person makes use of such electroshock weapon, such use shall be in defense of self or others. The exemption under this paragraph shall apply only to such person in regard to such electroshock weapon. As used in this paragraph, the term "electroshock weapon" means any commercially available device that is powered by electrical charging units and designed exclusively to be capable of incapacitating a person by electrical charge, including, but not limited to, a stun gun or taser as defined in subsection (a) of Code Section 16-11-106; or

(20) (A) Any weapons carry license holder when he or she is in any building or on real property owned by or leased to any public technical school, vocational school, college, or university, or other public institution of postsecondary education; provided, however, that such exception shall:

(i) Not apply to buildings or property used for athletic sporting events or student housing, including, but not limited to, fraternity and sorority houses;

(ii) Not apply to any preschool or childcare space located within such buildings or real property;

(iii) Not apply to any room or space being used for classes related to a college and career academy or other specialized school as provided for under Code Section 20-4-37;

(iv) Not apply to any room or space being used for classes in which high school students are enrolled through a dual enrollment program, including, but not limited to, classes related to the "Move on When Ready Act" as provided for under Code Section 20-2-161.3;

(v) Not apply to faculty, staff, or administrative offices or rooms where disciplinary proceedings are conducted;

(vi) Only apply to the carrying of handguns which a licensee is licensed to carry pursuant to subsection (e) of Code Section 16-11-126 and pursuant to Code Section 16-11-129; and

(vii) Only apply to the carrying of handguns which are concealed.

(B) Any weapons carry license holder who carries a handgun in a manner or in a building, property, room, or space in violation of this paragraph shall be guilty of a misdemeanor; provided, however, that for a conviction of a first offense, such weapons carry license holder shall be punished by a fine of $25.00 and not be sentenced to serve any term of confinement.

(C) As used in this paragraph, the term:

(i) "Concealed" means carried in such a fashion that does not actively solicit the attention of others and is not prominently, openly, and intentionally displayed except for purposes of defense of self or others. Such term shall include, but not be limited to, carrying on one's person while such handgun is substantially, but not necessarily completely, covered by an article of clothing which is worn by such person, carrying within a bag of a nondescript nature which is being carried about by such person, or carrying in any other fashion as to not be clearly discernible by the passive observation of others.

(ii) "Preschool or childcare space" means any room or continuous collection of rooms or any enclosed outdoor facilities which are separated from other spaces by an electronic mechanism or human-staffed point of controlled access and designated for the provision of preschool or childcare services, including, but not limited to, preschool or childcare services licensed or regulated under Article 1 of Chapter 1A of Title 20.

(d) (1) This Code section shall not prohibit any person who resides or works in a business or is in the ordinary course transacting lawful business or any person who is a visitor of such resident located within a school safety zone from carrying, possessing, or having under such person's control a weapon within a school safety zone; provided, however, that it shall be unlawful for any such person to carry, possess, or have under such person's control while at a school building or school function or on school property or a bus or other transportation furnished by a school any weapon or explosive compound, other than fireworks the possession of which is regulated by Chapter 10 of Title 25.

(2) Any person who violates this subsection shall be subject to the penalties specified in subsection (b) of this Code section.

(e) It shall be no defense to a prosecution for a violation of this Code section that:

(1) School was or was not in session at the time of the offense;

(2) The real property was being used for other purposes besides school purposes at the time of the offense; or

(3) The offense took place on a bus or other transportation furnished by a school.

(f) In a prosecution under this Code section, a map produced or reproduced by any municipal or county agency or department for the purpose of depicting the location and boundaries of the area of the real property of a school board or a private or public elementary or secondary school that is used for school purposes or the area of any public or private technical school, vocational school, college, university, or other institution of postsecondary education, or a true copy of the map, shall, if certified as a true copy by the custodian of the record, be admissible and shall constitute prima-facie evidence of the location and boundaries of the area, if the governing body of the municipality or county has approved the map as an official record of the location and boundaries of the area. A map approved under this Code section may be revised from time to time by the governing body of the municipality or county. The original of every map approved or revised under this subsection or a true copy of such original map shall be filed with the municipality or county and shall be maintained as an official record of the municipality or county. This subsection shall not preclude the prosecution from introducing or relying upon any other evidence or testimony to establish any element of this offense. This subsection shall not preclude the use or admissibility of a map or diagram other than the one which has been approved by the municipality or county.

(g) A county school board may adopt regulations requiring the posting of signs designating the areas of school boards and private or public elementary and secondary schools as "Weapon-free and Violence-free School Safety Zones."

(h) Nothing in this Code section shall in any way operate or be construed to affect, repeal, or limit the exemptions provided for under Code Section 16-11-130.

§ 16-11-127.2. Weapons on premises of nuclear power facility

(a) Except as provided in subsection (c) of this Code section, it shall be unlawful for any person to carry, possess, or have under such person's control while on the premises of a nuclear power facility a weapon or long gun. Any person who violates this subsection shall be guilty of a misdemeanor.

(b) Any person who violates subsection (a) of this Code section with the intent to do bodily harm on the premises of a nuclear power facility shall be guilty of a felony and, upon conviction thereof, shall be punished by a fine of not more than $10,000.00, by imprisonment for not less than two nor more than 20 years, or both.

(c) This Code section shall not apply to a security officer authorized to carry dangerous weapons pursuant to Code Section 16-11-124 who is acting in connection with his or her official duties on the premises of a federally licensed nuclear power facility; nor shall this Code section apply to persons designated in paragraph (2), (3), (4), or (8) of subsection (c) of Code Section 16-11-127.1.

(d) Nothing in this Code section shall in any way operate or be construed to affect, repeal, or limit the exemptions provided for under Code Section 16-11-130.

§ 16-11-128. Carrying pistol without license

Reserved. Repealed by Ga. L. 2010, p. 963, § 1-6, effective June 4, 2010.

85

§ 16-11-129. Weapons carry license; gun safety information; temporary renewal permit; mandamus; verification of license

(a) Application for weapons carry license or renewal license; term. The judge of the probate court of each county shall, on application under oath, on payment of a fee of $30.00, and on investigation of applicant pursuant to subsections (b) and (d) of this Code section, issue a weapons carry license or renewal license valid for a period of five years to any person whose domicile is in that county or who is on active duty with the United States armed forces and who is not a domiciliary of this state but who either resides in that county or on a military reservation located in whole or in part in that county at the time of such application. Such license or renewal license shall authorize that person to carry any weapon in any county of this state notwithstanding any change in that person's county of residence or state of domicile. Applicants shall submit the application for a weapons carry license or renewal license to the judge of the probate court on forms prescribed and furnished free of charge to persons wishing to apply for the license or renewal license. An application shall be considered to be for a renewal license if the applicant has a weapons carry license or renewal license with 90 or fewer days remaining before the expiration of such weapons carry license or renewal license or 30 or fewer days since the expiration of such weapons carry license or renewal license regardless of the county of issuance of the applicant's expired or expiring weapons carry license or renewal license. An applicant who is not a United States citizen shall provide sufficient personal identifying data, including without limitation his or her place of birth and United States issued alien or admission number, as the Georgia Bureau of Investigation may prescribe by rule or regulation. An applicant who is in nonimmigrant status shall provide proof of his or her qualifications for an exception to the federal firearm prohibition pursuant to 18 U.S.C. Section 922(y). Forms shall be designed to elicit information from the applicant pertinent to his or her eligibility under this Code section, including citizenship, but shall not require data which is nonpertinent or irrelevant, such as serial numbers or other identification capable of being used as a de facto registration of firearms owned by the applicant. The Department of Public Safety shall furnish application forms and license forms required by this Code section. The forms shall be furnished to each judge of each probate court within this state at no cost.

(a.1) Gun safety information.

(1) Upon receipt of an application for a weapons carry license or renewal license, the judge of the probate court may provide applicants printed information on gun safety that is produced by any person or organization that, in the discretion of the judge of the probate court, offers practical advice for gun safety. The source of such printed information shall be prominently displayed on such printed information.

(2) The Department of Natural Resources shall maintain on its principal, public website information, or a hyperlink to information, which provides resources for information on hunter education and classes and courses in this state that render instruction in gun safety. No person shall be required to take such classes or courses for purposes of this Code section where such information shall be provided solely for the convenience of the citizens of this state.

(3) Neither the judge of the probate court nor the Department of Natural Resources shall be liable to any person for personal injuries or damage to property arising from conformance to this subsection.

(b) Licensing exceptions.

(1) As used in this subsection, the term:

(A) "Armed forces" means active duty or a reserve component of the United States Army, United States Navy, United States Marine Corps, United States Coast Guard, United States Air Force, United States National Guard, Georgia Army National Guard, or Georgia Air National Guard.

(B) "Controlled substance" means any drug, substance, or immediate precursor included in the definition of controlled substances in paragraph (4) of Code Section 16-13-21.

(C) "Convicted" means an adjudication of guilt. Such term shall not include an order of discharge and exoneration pursuant to Article 3 of Chapter 8 of Title 42.

(D) "Dangerous drug" means any drug defined as such in Code Section 16-13-71.

(2) No weapons carry license shall be issued to:

(A) Any person younger than 21 years of age unless he or she:

(i) Is at least 18 years of age;

(ii) Provides proof that he or she has completed basic training in the armed forces of the United States; and

(iii) Provides proof that he or she is actively serving in the armed forces of the United States or has been honorably discharged from such service;

(B) Any person who has been convicted of a felony by a court of this state or any other state; by a court of the United States, including its territories, possessions, and dominions; or by a court of any foreign nation and has not been pardoned for such felony by the President of the United States, the State Board of Pardons and Paroles, or the person or agency empowered to grant pardons under the constitution or laws of such state or nation;

(C) Any person against whom proceedings are pending for any felony;

(D) Any person who is a fugitive from justice;

(E) Any person who is prohibited from possessing or shipping a firearm in interstate commerce pursuant to subsections (g) and (n) of 18 U.S.C. Section 922;

(F) Any person who has been convicted of an offense arising out of the unlawful manufacture or distribution of a controlled substance or other dangerous drug;

(G) Any person who has had his or her weapons carry license revoked pursuant to subsection (e) of this Code section within three years of the date of his or her application;

(H) Any person who has been convicted of any of the following:

(i) Carrying a weapon without a weapons carry license in violation of Code Section 16-11-126; or

(ii) Carrying a weapon or long gun in an unauthorized location in violation of Code Section 16-11-127

and has not been free of all restraint or supervision in connection therewith and free of any other conviction for at least five years immediately preceding the date of the application;

(I) Any person who has been convicted of any misdemeanor involving the use or possession of a controlled substance and has not been free of all restraint or supervision in connection therewith or free of:

(i) A second conviction of any misdemeanor involving the use or possession of a controlled substance; or

(ii) Any conviction under subparagraphs (E) through (G) of this paragraph

for at least five years immediately preceding the date of the application;

(J) Except as provided for in subsection (b.1) of this Code section, any person who has been hospitalized as an inpatient in any mental hospital or alcohol or drug treatment center within the five years immediately preceding the application. The judge of the probate court may require any applicant to sign a waiver authorizing any mental hospital or treatment center to inform the judge whether or not the applicant has been an inpatient in any such facility in the last five years and authorizing the superintendent of such facility to make to the judge a recommendation regarding whether the applicant is a threat to the safety of others and whether a license to carry a weapon should be issued. When such a waiver is required by the judge, the applicant shall pay a fee of $3.00 for reimbursement of the cost of making such a report by the mental health hospital, alcohol or drug treatment center, or the Department of Behavioral Health and Developmental Disabilities, which the judge shall remit to the hospital, center, or department. The judge shall keep any such hospitalization or treatment information confidential. It shall be at the discretion of the judge, considering the circumstances surrounding the hospitalization and the recommendation of the superintendent of the hospital or treatment center where the individual was a patient, to issue the weapons carry license or renewal license;

(K) Except as provided for in subsection (b.1) of this Code section, any person who has been adjudicated mentally incompetent to stand trial; or

(L) Except as provided for in subsection (b.1) of this Code section, any person who has been adjudicated not guilty by reason of insanity at the time of the crime pursuant to Part 2 of Article 6 of Chapter 7 of Title 17.

(b.1) Petitions for relief from certain licensing exceptions.

(1) Persons provided for under subparagraphs (b)(2)(J), (b)(2)(K), and (b)(2)(L) of this Code section may petition the court in which such adjudication, hospitalization, or treatment proceedings, if any, under Chapter 3 or 7 of Title 37 occurred for relief. A copy of such petition for relief shall be served as notice upon the opposing civil party or the prosecuting attorney for the state, as the case may be, or their successors, who appeared in the underlying case. Within 30 days of the receipt of such petition, such court shall hold a hearing on such petition for relief. Such prosecuting attorney for the state may represent the interests of the state at such hearing.

(2) At the hearing provided for under paragraph (1) of this subsection, the court shall receive and consider evidence in a closed proceeding concerning:

(A) The circumstances which caused the person to be subject to subparagraph (b)(2)(J), (b)(2)(K), or (b)(2)(L) of this Code section;

(B) The person's mental health and criminal history records, if any. The judge of such court may require any such person to sign a waiver authorizing the superintendent of any mental hospital or treatment center to make to the judge a recommendation regarding whether such person is a threat to the safety of others. When such a waiver is required by the judge, the applicant shall pay a

86

fee of $3.00 for reimbursement of the cost of making such a report by the mental health hospital, alcohol or drug treatment center, or the Department of Behavioral Health and Developmental Disabilities, which the judge shall remit to the hospital, center, or department;

(C) The person's reputation which shall be established through character witness statements, testimony, or other character evidence; and

(D) Changes in the person's condition or circumstances since such adjudication, hospitalization, or treatment proceedings under Chapter 3 or 7 of Title 37.

The judge shall issue an order of his or her decision no later than 30 days after the hearing.

(3) The court shall grant the petition for relief if such court finds by a preponderance of the evidence that the person will not likely act in a manner dangerous to public safety in carrying a weapon and that granting the relief will not be contrary to the public interest. A record shall be kept of the hearing; provided, however, that such records shall remain confidential and be disclosed only to a court or to the parties in the event of an appeal. Any appeal of the court's ruling on the petition for relief shall be de novo review.

(4) If the court grants such person's petition for relief, the applicable subparagraph (b)(2)(J), (b)(2)(K), or (b)(2)(L) of this Code section shall not apply to such person in his or her application for a weapons carry license or renewal; provided, however, that such person shall comply with all other requirements for the issuance of a weapons carry license or renewal license. The clerk of such court shall report such order to the Georgia Crime Information Center immediately, but in no case later than ten business days after the date of such order.

(5) A person may petition for relief under this subsection not more than once every two years. In the case of a person who has been hospitalized as an inpatient, such person shall not petition for relief prior to being discharged from such treatment.

(c) Fingerprinting. Following completion of the application for a weapons carry license, the judge of the probate court shall require the applicant to proceed to an appropriate law enforcement agency in the county or to any vendor approved by the Georgia Bureau of Investigation for fingerprint submission services with the completed application so that such agency or vendor can capture the fingerprints of the applicant. The law enforcement agency shall be entitled to a fee of $5.00 from the applicant for its services in connection with fingerprinting and processing of an application. Fingerprinting shall not be required for applicants seeking temporary renewal licenses or renewal licenses.

(d) Investigation of applicant; issuance of weapons carry license; renewal.

(1) (A) For weapons carry license applications, the judge of the probate court shall within five business days following the receipt of the application or request direct the law enforcement agency to request a fingerprint based criminal history records check from the Georgia Crime Information Center and Federal Bureau of Investigation for purposes of determining the suitability of the applicant and return an appropriate report to the judge of the probate court. Fingerprints shall be in such form and of such quality as prescribed by the Georgia Crime Information Center and under standards adopted by the Federal Bureau of Investigation. The Georgia Bureau of Investigation may charge such fee as is necessary to cover the cost of the records search.

(B) For requests for license renewals, the presentation of a weapons carry license issued by any probate judge in this state shall be evidence to the judge of the probate court to whom a request for license renewal is made that the fingerprints of the weapons carry license holder are on file with the judge of the probate court who issued the weapons carry license, and the judge of the probate court to whom a request for license renewal is made shall, within five business days following the receipt of the request, direct the law enforcement agency to request a nonfingerprint based criminal history records check from the Georgia Crime Information Center and Federal Bureau of Investigation for purposes of determining the suitability of the applicant and return an appropriate report to the judge of the probate court to whom a request for license renewal is made.

(2) For both weapons carry license applications and requests for license renewals, the judge of the probate court shall within five business days following the receipt of the application or request also direct the law enforcement agency, in the same manner as provided for in subparagraph (B) of paragraph (1) of this subsection, to conduct a background check using the Federal Bureau of Investigation's National Instant Criminal Background Check System and return an appropriate report to the probate judge.

(3) When a person who is not a United States citizen applies for a weapons carry license or renewal of a license under this Code section, the judge of the probate court shall direct the law enforcement agency to conduct a search of the records maintained by United States Immigration and Customs Enforcement and return an appropriate report to the probate judge. As a condition to the issuance of a license or the renewal of a license, an applicant who is in nonimmigrant status shall provide proof of his or her qualifications for an exception to the federal firearm prohibition pursuant to 18 U.S.C. Section 922(y).

(4) The law enforcement agency shall report to the judge of the probate court within 20 days, by telephone and in writing, of any findings relating to the applicant which may bear on his or her eligibility for a weapons carry license or renewal license under the terms of this Code section. When no derogatory information is found on the applicant bearing on his or her eligibility to obtain a license or renewal license, a report shall not be required. The law enforcement agency shall return the application directly to the judge of the probate court within such time period. Not later than ten days after the judge of the probate court receives the report from the law enforcement agency concerning the suitability of the applicant for a license, the judge of the probate court shall issue such applicant a license or renewal license to carry any weapon unless facts establishing ineligibility have been reported or unless the judge determines such applicant has not met all the qualifications, is not of good moral character, or has failed to comply with any of the requirements contained in this Code section. The judge of the probate court shall date stamp the report from the law enforcement agency to show the date on which the report was received by the judge of the probate court. The judge of the probate court shall not suspend the processing of the application or extend, delay, or avoid any time requirements provided for under this paragraph.

(e) Revocation, loss, or damage to license.

(1) If, at any time during the period for which the weapons carry license was issued, the judge of the probate court of the county in which the license was issued shall learn or have brought to his or her attention in any manner any reasonable ground to believe the licensee is not eligible to retain the license, the judge may, after notice and hearing, revoke the license of the person upon a finding that such person is not eligible for a weapons carry license pursuant to subsection (b) of this Code section or an adjudication of falsification of application, mental incompetency, or chronic alcohol or narcotic usage. The judge of the probate court shall report such revocation to the Georgia Crime Information Center immediately but in no case later than ten days after such revocation. It shall be unlawful for any person to possess a license which has been revoked pursuant to this paragraph, and any person found in possession of any such revoked license, except in the performance of his or her official duties, shall be guilty of a misdemeanor.

(2) If a person is convicted of any crime or otherwise adjudicated in a matter which would make the maintenance of a weapons carry license by such person unlawful pursuant to subsection (b) of this Code section, the judge of the superior court or state court hearing such case or presiding over such matter shall inquire whether such person is the holder of a weapons carry license. If such person is the holder of a weapons carry license, then the judge of the superior court or state court shall inquire of such person the county of the probate court which issued such weapons carry license, or if such person has ever had his or her weapons carry license renewed, then of the county of the probate court which most recently issued such person a renewal license. The judge of the superior court or state court shall notify the judge of the probate court of such county of the matter which makes the maintenance of a weapons carry license by such person to be unlawful pursuant to subsection (b) of this Code section. The Council of Superior Court Judges of Georgia and The Council of State Court Judges of Georgia shall provide by rule for the procedures which judges of the superior court and the judges of the state courts, respectively, are to follow for the purposes of this paragraph.

(3) Loss of any license issued in accordance with this Code section or damage to the license in any manner which shall render it illegible shall be reported to the judge of the probate court of the county in which it was issued within 48 hours of the time the loss or damage becomes known to the license holder. The judge of the probate court shall thereupon issue a replacement for and shall take custody of and destroy a damaged license; and in any case in which a license has been lost, he or she shall issue a cancellation order. The judge shall charge the fee specified in subsection (k) of Code Section 15-9-60 for such services.

(4) Any person, upon petition to the judge of the probate court, who has a weapons carry license or renewal license with more than 90 days remaining before the expiration of such weapons carry license or renewal license and who has had a legal name change, including, but not limited to, on account of marriage or divorce, or an address change shall be issued a replacement weapons carry license for the same time period of the weapons carry license or renewal license being replaced. Upon issuance and receipt of such replacement weapons carry license, the license holder shall surrender the weapons carry license being replaced to the judge of the probate court and such judge shall take custody of and destroy the weapons carry license being replaced. The judge of the probate court shall provide for the updating of any records as necessary to account for the license holder's change of name or address. The judge of the probate court shall charge the fee specified in paragraph (13) of subsection (k) of Code Section 15-9-60 for services provided under this paragraph.

(f) (1) Weapons carry license specifications. Weapons carry licenses issued prior to January 1, 2012, shall be in the format specified by the former provisions of this paragraph as they existed on June 30, 2013.

(2) On and after January 1, 2012, newly issued or renewal weapons carry licenses shall incorporate overt and covert security features which shall be blended with the personal data printed on the license to form a significant barrier to imitation, replication, and duplication. There shall be a minimum of three different ultraviolet colors used to enhance the security of the license incorporating variable data, color shifting characteristics, and front edge only perimeter visibility. The weapons carry license shall have a color photograph viewable under ambient light on both the front and back of the license. The license shall incorporate custom optical variable devices featuring the great seal of the State of Georgia as well as matching demetalized optical variable devices viewable under ambient light from the front and back of the license incorporating microtext and unique alphanumeric serialization specific to the license holder. The license shall be of similar material, size, and thickness of a credit card and have a holographic laminate to secure and protect the license for the duration of the license period.

(3) Using the physical characteristics of the license set forth in paragraph (2) of this subsection, The Council of Probate Court Judges of Georgia shall create specifications for the probate courts so that all weapons carry licenses in this state shall be uniform and so that probate courts can petition the Department of Administrative Services to purchase the equipment and supplies necessary for producing such licenses. The department shall follow the competitive bidding procedure set forth in Code Section 50-5-102.

(g) Alteration or counterfeiting of license; penalty. A person who deliberately alters or counterfeits a weapons carry license or who possesses an altered or counterfeit weapons carry license with the intent to misrepresent any information contained in such license shall be guilty of a felony and, upon conviction thereof, shall be punished by imprisonment for a period of not less than one nor more than five years.

(h) (1) Licenses for former law enforcement officers. Except as otherwise provided in Code Section 16-11-130, any person who has served as a law enforcement officer for at least:

(A) Ten of the 12 years immediately preceding the retirement of such person as a law enforcement officer; or

(B) Ten years and left such employment as a result of a disability arising in the line of duty; and

retired or left such employment in good standing with a state or federal certifying agency and receives benefits under the Peace Officers' Annuity and Benefit Fund provided for under Chapter 17 of Title 47 or from a county, municipal, State of Georgia, state authority, federal, private sector, individual, or educational institution retirement system or program shall be entitled to be issued a weapons carry license as provided for in this Code section without the payment of any of the fees provided for in this Code section.

(2) Such person as provided for in paragraph (1) of this subsection shall comply with all the other provisions of this Code section relative to the issuance of such licenses, including, but not limited to the requirements under paragraph (2) of subsection (b) of this Code section. Any person seeking to be issued a license pursuant to this subsection shall state his or her qualifications for eligibility under this subsection on his or her application under oath as provided for in subsection (a) of this Code section.

(3) As used in this subsection, the term "law enforcement officer" means any peace officer who is employed by the United States government or by the State of Georgia or any political subdivision thereof and who is required by the terms of his or her employment, whether by election or appointment, to give his or her full time to the preservation of public order or the protection of life and property or the prevention of crime. Such term shall include conservation rangers.

(i) Temporary renewal licenses.

(1) Any person who holds a weapons carry license under this Code section may, at the time he or she applies for a renewal of the license, also apply for a temporary renewal license if less than 90 days remain before expiration of the license he or she then holds or if the previous license has expired within the last 30 days.

(2) Unless the judge of the probate court knows or is made aware of any fact which would make the applicant ineligible for a five-year renewal license, the judge shall at the time of application issue a temporary renewal license to the applicant.

(3) Such a temporary renewal license shall be in the form of a paper receipt indicating the date on which the court received the renewal application and shall show the name, address, sex, age, and race of the applicant and that the temporary renewal license expires 90 days from the date of issue.

(4) During its period of validity the temporary renewal license, if carried on or about the holder's person together with the holder's previous license, shall be valid in the same manner and for the same purposes as a five-year license.

(5) A $1.00 fee shall be charged by the probate court for issuance of a temporary renewal license.

(6) A temporary renewal license may be revoked in the same manner as a five-year license.

(j) Applicant may seek relief. When an eligible applicant fails to receive a license, temporary renewal license, or renewal license within the time period required by this Code section and the application or request has been properly filed, the applicant may bring an action in mandamus or other legal proceeding in order to obtain a license, temporary renewal license, or renewal license. When an applicant is otherwise denied a license, temporary renewal license, or renewal license and contends that he or she is qualified to be issued a license, temporary renewal license, or renewal license, the applicant may bring an action in mandamus or other legal proceeding in order to obtain such license. Additionally, the applicant may request a hearing before the judge of the probate court relative to the applicant's fitness to be issued such license. Upon the issuance of a denial, the judge of the probate court shall inform the applicant of his or her rights pursuant to this subsection. If such applicant is the prevailing party, he or she shall be entitled to recover his or her costs in such action, including reasonable attorney's fees.

(k) Data base prohibition. A person or entity shall not create or maintain a multijurisdictional data base of information regarding persons issued weapons carry licenses.

(l) Verification of license. The judge of a probate court or his or her designee shall be authorized to verify the legitimacy and validity of a weapons carry license of a license holder pursuant to a subpoena or court order, for public safety purposes to law enforcement agencies pursuant to paragraph (40) of subsection (a) of Code Section 50-18-72, and for licensing to a judge of a probate court or his or her designee pursuant to paragraph (40) of subsection (a) of Code Section 50-18-72; provided, however, that the judge of a probate court or his or her designee shall not be authorized to provide any further information regarding license holders.

§ 16-11-130. Exemptions from Code Sections 16-11-126 through 16-11-127.2

(a) Except to the extent provided for in subsection (c.1) of this Code section, Code Sections 16-11-126 through 16-11-127.2 shall not apply to or affect any of the following persons if such persons are employed in the offices listed below or when authorized by federal or state law, regulations, or order:

(1) Peace officers, as such term is defined in paragraph (11) of Code Section 16-1-3, and retired peace officers so long as they remain certified whether employed by the state or a political subdivision of the state or another state or a political subdivision of another state but only if such other state provides a similar privilege for the peace officers of this state;

(2) Wardens, superintendents, and keepers of correctional institutions, jails, or other institutions for the detention of persons accused or convicted of an offense;

(3) Persons in the military service of the state or of the United States;

(4) Persons employed in fulfilling defense contracts with the government of the United States or agencies thereof when possession of the weapon or long gun is necessary for manufacture, transport, installation, and testing under the requirements of such contract;

(5) District attorneys, investigators employed by and assigned to a district attorney's office, assistant district attorneys, attorneys or investigators employed by the Prosecuting Attorneys' Council of the State of Georgia, and any retired district attorney, assistant district attorney, district attorney's investigator, or attorney or investigator retired from the Prosecuting Attorneys' Council of the State of Georgia, if such employee is retired in good standing and is receiving benefits under Title 47 or is retired in good standing and receiving benefits from a county or municipal retirement system;

(6) State court solicitors-general; investigators employed by and assigned to a state court solicitor-general's office; assistant state court solicitors-general; the corresponding personnel of any city court expressly continued in existence as a city court pursuant to Article VI, Section X, Paragraph I, subparagraph (5) of the Constitution; and the corresponding personnel of any civil court expressly continued as a civil court pursuant to said provision of the Constitution;

(7) Those employees of the State Board of Pardons and Paroles when specifically designated and authorized in writing by the members of the State Board of Pardons and Paroles to carry a weapon or long gun;

(8) The Attorney General and those members of his or her staff whom he or she specifically authorizes in writing to carry a weapon or long gun;

(9) Community supervision officers employed by and under the authority of the Department of Community Supervision when specifically designated and authorized in writing by the commissioner of community supervision;

(10) Public safety directors of municipal corporations;

(11) Explosive ordnance disposal technicians, as such term is defined by Code Section 16-7-80, and persons certified as provided in Code Section 35-8-13 to handle animals trained to detect explosives, while in the performance of their duties;

(12) Federal judges, Justices of the Supreme Court, Judges of the Court of Appeals, judges of superior, state, probate, juvenile, and magistrate courts, full-time judges of municipal and city courts, permanent part-time judges of municipal and city courts, and administrative law judges;

(12.1) Former federal judges, Justices of the Supreme Court, Judges of the Court of Appeals, judges of superior, state, probate, juvenile, and magistrate courts, full-time judges of municipal and city courts, permanent part-time judges of municipal courts, and administrative law judges who are retired from their respective offices, provided that such judge or Justice would otherwise be qualified to be issued a weapons carry license;

(12.2) Former federal judges, Justices of the Supreme Court, Judges of the Court of Appeals, judges of superior, state, probate, juvenile, and magistrate courts, full-time judges of municipal and city courts, permanent part-time judges of municipal courts, and administrative law judges who are no longer serving in their respective office, provided that he or she served as such judge or Justice for more than 24 months; and provided, further, that such judge or Justice would otherwise be qualified to be issued a weapons carry license;

(13) United States Attorneys and Assistant United States Attorneys;

(14) County medical examiners and coroners and their sworn officers employed by county government;

(15) Clerks of the superior courts; and

(16) Constables employed by a magistrate court of this state.

(b) Except to the extent provided for in subsection (c.1) of this Code section, Code Sections 16-11-126 through 16-11-127.2 shall not apply to or affect persons who at the time of their retirement from service with the Department of Community Supervision were community supervision officers, when specifically designated and authorized in writing by the commissioner of community supervision.

(c) (1) As used in this subsection, the term "courthouse" means a building or annex occupied by judicial courts and containing rooms in which judicial proceedings are held.

(2) Except to the extent provided for in subsection (c.1) of this Code section, Code Sections 16-11-126 through 16-11-127.2 shall not apply to or affect any:

(A) Sheriff, retired sheriff, deputy sheriff, or retired deputy sheriff if such retired sheriff or deputy sheriff is eligible to receive or is receiving benefits under the Peace Officers' Annuity and Benefit Fund provided under Chapter 17 of Title 47, the Sheriffs' Retirement Fund of Georgia provided under Chapter 16 of Title 47, or any other public retirement system established under the laws of this state for service as a law enforcement officer;

(B) Member of the Georgia State Patrol, agent of the Georgia Bureau of Investigation, retired member of the Georgia State Patrol, or retired agent of the Georgia Bureau of Investigation if such retired member or agent is receiving benefits under the Employees' Retirement System;

(C) Full-time law enforcement chief executive engaging in the management of a county, municipal, state, state authority, or federal law enforcement agency in the State of Georgia, including any college or university law enforcement chief executive who is registered or certified by the Georgia Peace Officer Standards and Training Council; or retired law enforcement chief executive who formerly managed a county, municipal, state, state authority, or federal law enforcement agency in the State of Georgia, including any college or university law enforcement chief executive who was registered or certified at the time of his or her retirement by the Georgia Peace Officer Standards and Training Council, if such retired law enforcement chief executive is receiving benefits under the Peace Officers' Annuity and Benefit Fund provided under Chapter 17 of Title 47 or is retired in good standing and receiving benefits from a county, municipal, State of Georgia, state authority, or federal retirement system;

(D) Police officer of any county, municipal, state, state authority, or federal law enforcement agency in the State of Georgia, including any college or university police officer who is registered or certified by the Georgia Peace Officer Standards and Training Council, or retired police officer of any county, municipal, state, state authority, or federal law enforcement agency in the State of Georgia, including any college or university police officer who was registered or certified at the time of his or her retirement by the Georgia Peace Officer Standards and Training Council, if such retired police officer is receiving benefits under the Peace Officers' Annuity and Benefit Fund provided under Chapter 17 of Title 47 or is retired in good standing and receiving benefits from a county, municipal, State of Georgia, state authority, or federal retirement system; or

(E) Person who is a citizen of this state and:

(i) Has retired with at least ten years of aggregate service as a law enforcement officer with powers of arrest under the laws of any state of the United States or of the United States;

(ii) Separated from service in good standing, as determined by criteria established by the Georgia Peace Officer Standards and Training Council, from employment with his or her most recent law enforcement agency; and

(iii) Possesses on his or her person an identification card for retired law enforcement officers as issued by the Georgia Peace Officer Standards and Training Council; provided, however, that such person meets the standards for the issuance of such card as provided for by the council, including, but not limited to, maintenance of qualification in firearms training.

In addition, any such sheriff, retired sheriff, deputy sheriff, retired deputy sheriff, member or retired member of the Georgia State Patrol, agent or retired agent of the Georgia Bureau of Investigation, officer or retired officer of the Department of Natural Resources, active or retired law enforcement chief executive, person who is a retired law enforcement officer as provided for in paragraph (2) of this subsection, or other law enforcement officer referred to in this subsection shall be authorized to carry a handgun on or off duty anywhere within this state, including, but not limited to, in a courthouse except to the extent provided for in subsection (c.1) of this Code section, and Code Sections 16-11-126 through 16-11-127.2 shall not apply to the carrying of such firearms.

(c.1) (1) As used in the subsection, the term:

(A) "Active" means nonretired.

(B) "Courthouse" means a building or annex occupied by judicial courts and containing rooms in which judicial proceedings are held.

(C) "Law enforcement agency" means sheriffs or any unit, organ, or department of this state, or a subdivision or municipality thereof, whose functions by law include the enforcement of criminal or traffic laws; the preservation of public order; the protection of life and property; the prevention, detection, or investigation of crime; or court security that is providing security for a courthouse.

(D) "Law enforcement personnel" means sheriffs or deputy sheriffs or peace officers employed by a law enforcement agency.

(2) (A) Pursuant to a security plan implemented by law enforcement personnel, including as provided for under a comprehensive plan as provided for in subsection (a) of Code Section 15-16-10, the law enforcement agency with jurisdiction over a courthouse may provide for facilities or the means for the holding of weapons carried by persons enumerated under this Code section, except as provided for in paragraph (3) of this subsection, provided that ingress to such courthouse is actively restricted or screened by law enforcement personnel and such facilities or means are located in the immediate proximity of the area which is restricted or screened by such law enforcement personnel.

(B) If the requirements of this paragraph are met, the persons enumerated under this Code section shall, except as provided for in paragraph (3) of this subsection, upon request of law enforcement personnel place his or her weapons in such holding with law enforcement personnel while such persons are within the restricted or screened area. Upon request of any person enumerated under this Code section, in preparation for his or her exit from the restricted or screened area, law enforcement personnel shall immediately provide for the return of the person's weapons which are in holding.

(3) Notwithstanding a security plan implemented by law enforcement personnel, including as provided for under a comprehensive plan as provided for in subsection (a) of Code Section 15-16-10, active law enforcement officers referred to in subsection (c) of this Code section shall be authorized to carry their service handguns and weapons in any courthouse if they are wearing the assigned uniform of their law enforcement office or have the official badge and identification credentials issued to them by their law enforcement office displayed and plainly visible on their person while in the performance of their official duties.

(d) A prosecution based upon a violation of Code Section 16-11-126 or 16-11-127 need not negative any exemptions.

§ 16-11-130.1. Allowing personnel to carry weapons within certain school safety zones and at school functions

(a) As used in this Code section, the term:

(1) "Bus or other transportation furnished by a school" means a bus or other transportation furnished by a public or private elementary or secondary school.

(2) "School function" means a school function or related activity that occurs outside of a school safety zone for a public or private elementary or secondary school.

(3) "School safety zone" means in or on any real property or building owned by or leased to any public or private elementary or secondary school or local board of education and used for elementary or secondary education.

(4) "Weapon" shall have the same meaning as set forth in Code Section 16-11-127.1.

(b) This Code section shall not be construed to require or otherwise mandate that any local board of education or school administrator adopt or implement a practice or program for the approval of personnel to possess or carry weapons within a school safety zone, at a school function, or on a bus or other transportation furnished by a school nor shall this Code section create any liability for adopting or declining to adopt such practice or program. Such decision shall rest with each individual local board of education. If a local board of education adopts a policy to allow certain personnel to possess or carry weapons as provided in paragraph (6) of subsection (c) of Code Section 16-11-127.1, such policy shall include approval of personnel to possess or carry weapons and provide for:

(1) Training of approved personnel prior to authorizing such personnel to carry weapons. The training shall at a minimum include training on judgment pistol shooting, marksmanship, and a review of current laws relating to the use of force for the defense of self and others; provided, however, that the local board of education training policy may substitute for certain training requirements the personnel's prior military or law enforcement service if the approved personnel has previously served as a certified law enforcement officer or has had military service which involved similar weapons training;

(2) An approved list of the types of weapons and ammunition and the quantity of weapons and ammunition authorized to be possessed or carried;

(3) The exclusion from approval of any personnel who has had an employment or other history indicating any type of mental or emotional instability as determined by the local board of education; and

(4) A mandatory method of securing weapons which shall include at a minimum a requirement that the weapon, if permitted to be carried concealed by personnel, shall be carried on the person and not in a purse, briefcase, bag, or similar other accessory which is not secured on the body of the person and, if maintained separate from the person, shall be maintained in a secured lock safe or similar lock box that cannot be easily accessed by students.

(c) Any personnel selected to possess or carry weapons within a school safety zone, at a school function, or on a bus or other transportation furnished by a school shall be a license holder, and the local board of education shall be responsible for conducting a criminal history background check of such personnel annually to determine whether such personnel remains qualified to be a license holder.

(d) The selection of approved personnel to possess or carry a weapon within a school safety zone, at a school function, or on a bus or other transportation furnished by a school shall be done strictly on a voluntary basis. No personnel shall be required to possess or carry a weapon within a school safety zone, at a school function, or on a bus or other transportation furnished by a school and shall not be terminated or otherwise retaliated against for refusing to possess or carry a weapon.

(e) The local board of education shall be responsible for any costs associated with approving personnel to carry or possess weapons within a school safety zone, at a school function, or on a bus or other transportation furnished by a school; provided, however, that nothing contained in this Code section shall prohibit any approved personnel from paying for part or all of such costs or using any other funding mechanism available, including donations or grants from private persons or entities.

(f) Documents and meetings pertaining to personnel approved to carry or possess weapons within a school safety zone, at a school function, or on a bus or other transportation furnished by a school shall be considered employment and public safety security records and shall be exempt from disclosure under Article 4 of Chapter 18 of Title 50.

§ 16-11-130.2. Carrying a weapon or long gun at a commercial service airport

(a) No person shall enter the restricted access area of a commercial service airport, in or beyond the airport security screening checkpoint, knowingly possessing or knowingly having under his or her control a weapon or long gun. Such area shall not include an airport drive, general parking area, walkway, or shops and areas of the terminal that are outside the screening checkpoint and that are normally open to unscreened passengers or visitors to the airport. Any restricted access area shall be clearly indicated by prominent signs indicating that weapons are prohibited in such area.

(a.1) As used in this Code section, the term:

(1) "Commercial service airport" means an airport that receives scheduled passenger aircraft service from any major airline carrier.

(2) "Major airline carrier" means an airline that has more than $1 billion in annual operating revenue during a fiscal year.

(b) A person who is not a license holder and who violates this Code section shall be guilty of a misdemeanor. A license holder who violates this Code section shall be guilty of a misdemeanor; provided, however, that a license holder who is notified at the screening checkpoint for the restricted access area that he or she is in possession of a weapon or long gun and who immediately leaves the restricted access area following such notification and completion of federally required transportation security screening procedures shall not be guilty of violating this Code section.

(c) Any person who violates this Code section with the intent to commit a separate felony offense shall be guilty of a felony and, upon conviction thereof, shall be punished by a fine of not less than $1,000.00 nor more than $15,000.00, imprisonment for not less than one nor more than ten years, or both.

(d) Any ordinance, resolution, regulation, or policy of any county, municipality, or other political subdivision of this state which is in conflict with this Code section shall be null, void, and of no force and effect, and this Code section shall preempt any such ordinance, resolution, regulation, or policy.

§ 16-11-131. Possession of firearms by convicted felons and first offender probationers

(a) As used in this Code section, the term:

(1) "Felony" means any offense punishable by imprisonment for a term of one year or more and includes conviction by a court-martial under the Uniform Code of Military Justice for an offense which would constitute a felony under the laws of the United States.

(2) "Firearm" includes any handgun, rifle, shotgun, or other weapon which will or can be converted to expel a projectile by the action of an explosive or electrical charge.

(b) Any person who is on probation as a felony first offender pursuant to Article 3 of Chapter 8 of Title 42 or who has been convicted of a felony by a court of this state or any other state; by a court of the United States including its territories, possessions, and dominions; or by a court of any foreign nation and who receives, possesses, or transports any firearm commits a felony and, upon conviction thereof, shall be imprisoned for not less than one nor more than five years; provided, however, that if the felony as to which the person is on probation or has been previously convicted is a forcible felony, then upon conviction of receiving, possessing, or transporting a firearm, such person shall be imprisoned for a period of five years.

(b.1) Any person who is prohibited by this Code section from possessing a firearm because of conviction of a forcible felony or because of being on probation as a first offender for a forcible felony pursuant to this Code section and who attempts to purchase or obtain transfer of a firearm shall be guilty of a felony and shall be punished by imprisonment for not less than one nor more than five years.

(c) This Code section shall not apply to any person who has been pardoned for the felony by the President of the United States, the State Board of Pardons and Paroles, or the person or agency empowered to grant pardons under the constitutions or laws of the several states or of a foreign nation and, by the terms of the pardon, has expressly been authorized to receive, possess, or transport a firearm.

(d) A person who has been convicted of a felony, but who has been granted relief from the disabilities imposed by the laws of the United States with respect to the acquisition, receipt, transfer, shipment, or possession of firearms by the secretary of the United States Department of the Treasury pursuant to 18 U.S.C. Section 925, shall, upon presenting to the Board of Public Safety proof that the relief has been granted and it being established from proof submitted by the applicant to the satisfaction of the Board of Public Safety that the circumstances regarding the conviction and the applicant's record and reputation are such that the acquisition, receipt, transfer, shipment, or possession of firearms by the person would not present a threat to the safety of the citizens of Georgia and that the granting of the relief sought would not be contrary to the public interest, be granted relief from the disabilities imposed by this Code section. A person who has been convicted under federal or state law of a felony pertaining to antitrust violations, unfair trade practices, or restraint of trade shall, upon presenting to the Board of Public Safety proof, and it being established from said proof, submitted by the applicant to the satisfaction of the Board of Public Safety that the circumstances regarding the conviction and the applicant's record and reputation are such that the acquisition, receipt, transfer, shipment, or possession of firearms by the person would not present a threat to the safety of the citizens of Georgia and that the granting of the relief sought would not be contrary to the public interest, be granted relief from the disabilities imposed by this Code section. A record that the relief has been granted by the board shall be entered upon the criminal history of the person maintained by the Georgia Crime Information Center and the board shall maintain a list of the names of such persons which shall be open for public inspection.

(e) As used in this Code section, the term "forcible felony" means any felony which involves the use or threat of physical force or violence against any person and further includes, without limitation, murder; murder in the second degree; burglary in any degree; robbery; armed robbery; home invasion in any degree; kidnapping; hijacking of an aircraft or hijacking a motor vehicle in the first degree; aggravated stalking; rape; aggravated child molestation; aggravated sexual battery; arson in the first degree; the manufacturing, transporting, distribution, or possession of explosives with intent to kill, injure, or intimidate individuals or destroy a public building; terroristic threats; or acts of treason or insurrection.

(f) Any person placed on probation as a first offender pursuant to Article 3 of Chapter 8 of Title 42 and subsequently discharged without court adjudication of guilt as a matter of law pursuant to Code Section 42-8-60 shall, upon such discharge, be relieved from the disabilities imposed by this Code section.

§ 16-11-132. Possession of handgun by person under the age of 18 years

(a) For the purposes of this Code section, a handgun is considered loaded if there is a cartridge in the chamber or cylinder of the handgun.

(b) Notwithstanding any other provisions of this part and except as otherwise provided in this Code section, it shall be unlawful for any person under the age of 18 years to possess or have under such person's control a handgun. A person convicted of a first violation of this subsection shall be guilty of a misdemeanor and shall be punished by a fine not to exceed $1,000.00 or by imprisonment for not more than 12 months, or both. A person convicted of a second or subsequent violation of this subsection shall be guilty of a felony and shall be punished by a fine of $5,000.00 or by imprisonment for a period of three years, or both.

(c) Except as otherwise provided in subsection (d) of this Code section, the provisions of subsection (b) of this Code section shall not apply to:

(1) Any person under the age of 18 years who is:

(A) Attending a hunter education course or a firearms safety course;

(B) Engaging in practice in the use of a firearm or target shooting at an established range authorized by the governing body of the jurisdiction where such range is located;

(C) Engaging in an organized competition involving the use of a firearm or participating in or practicing for a performance by an organized group under 26 U.S.C. Section 501(c)(3) which uses firearms as a part of such performance;

(D) Hunting or fishing pursuant to a valid license if such person has in his or her possession such a valid hunting or fishing license if required; is engaged in legal hunting or fishing; has permission of the owner of the land on which the activities are being conducted; and the handgun, whenever loaded, is carried only in an open and fully exposed manner; or

(E) Traveling to or from any activity described in subparagraphs (A) through (D) of this paragraph if the handgun in such person's possession is not loaded;

(2) Any person under the age of 18 years who is on real property under the control of such person's parent, legal guardian, or grandparent and who has the permission of such person's parent or legal guardian to possess a handgun; or

(3) Any person under the age of 18 years who is at such person's residence and who, with the permission of such person's parent or legal guardian, possesses a handgun for the purpose of exercising the rights authorized in Code Section 16-3-21 or 16-3-23.

(d) Subsection (c) of this Code section shall not apply to any person under the age of 18 years who has been convicted of a forcible felony or forcible misdemeanor, as defined in Code Section 16-1-3, or who has been adjudicated for committing a delinquent act under the provisions of Article 6 of Chapter 11 of Title 15 for an offense which would constitute a forcible felony or forcible misdemeanor, as defined in Code Section 16-1-3, if such person were an adult.

§ 16-11-133. Minimum periods of confinement for persons convicted who have prior convictions

(a) As used in this Code section, the term:

(1) "Felony" means any offense punishable by imprisonment for a term of one year or more and includes conviction by a court-martial under the Uniform Code of Military Justice for an offense which would constitute a felony under the laws of the United States.

(2) "Firearm" includes any handgun, rifle, shotgun, stun gun, taser, or other weapon which will or can be converted to expel a projectile by the action of an explosive or electrical charge.

(b) Any person who has previously been convicted of or who has previously entered a guilty plea to the offense of murder, murder in the second degree, armed robbery, home invasion in any degree, kidnapping, rape, aggravated child molestation, aggravated sodomy, aggravated sexual battery, or any felony involving the use or possession of a firearm and who shall have on or within arm's reach of his or her person a firearm during the commission of, or the attempt to commit:

(1) Any crime against or involving the person of another;

(2) The unlawful entry into a building or vehicle;

(3) A theft from a building or theft of a vehicle;

(4) Any crime involving the possession, manufacture, delivery, distribution, dispensing, administering, selling, or possession with intent to distribute any controlled substance as provided in Code Section 16-13-30; or

(5) Any crime involving the trafficking of cocaine, marijuana, or illegal drugs as provided in Code Section 16-13-31,

and which crime is a felony, commits a felony and, upon conviction thereof, shall be punished by confinement for a period of 15 years, such sentence to run consecutively to any other sentence which the person has received.

(c) Upon the second or subsequent conviction of a convicted felon under this Code section, such convicted felon shall be punished by confinement for life. Notwithstanding any other law to the contrary, the sentence of any convicted felon which is imposed for violating this Code section a second or subsequent time shall not be suspended by the court and probationary sentence imposed in lieu thereof.

(d) Any crime committed in violation of subsections (b) and (c) of this Code section shall be considered a separate offense.

§ 16-11-134. Discharging firearm while under the influence of alcohol or drugs

(a) It shall be unlawful for any person to discharge a firearm while:

(1) Under the influence of alcohol or any drug or any combination of alcohol and any drug to the extent that it is unsafe for the person to discharge such firearm except in the defense of life, health, and property;

(2) The person's alcohol concentration is 0.08 grams or more at any time while discharging such firearm or within three hours after such discharge of such firearm from alcohol consumed before such discharge ended; or

(3) Subject to the provisions of subsection (b) of this Code section, there is any amount of marijuana or a controlled substance, as defined in Code Section 16-13-21, present in the person's blood or urine, or both, including the metabolites and derivatives of each or both without regard to whether or not any alcohol is present in the person's breath or blood.

(b) The fact that any person charged with violating this Code section is or has been legally entitled to use a drug shall not constitute a defense against any charge of violating this Code section; provided, however, that such person shall not be in violation of this Code section unless such person is rendered incapable of possessing or discharging a firearm safely as a result of using a drug other than alcohol which such person is legally entitled to use.

(c) Any person convicted of violating subsection (a) of this Code section shall be guilty of a misdemeanor of a high and aggravated nature.

§ 16-11-135. Public or private employer's parking lots; right of privacy in vehicles in employer's parking lot or invited guests on lot; severability; rights of action

(a) Except as provided in this Code section, no private or public employer, including the state and its political subdivisions, shall establish, maintain, or enforce any policy or rule that has the effect of allowing such employer or its agents to search the locked privately owned vehicles of employees or invited guests on the employer's parking lot and access thereto.

(b) Except as provided in this Code section, no private or public employer, including the state and its political subdivisions, shall condition employment upon any agreement by a prospective employee that prohibits an employee from entering the parking lot and access thereto when the employee's privately owned motor vehicle contains a firearm or ammunition, or both, that is locked out of sight within the trunk, glove box, or other enclosed compartment or area within such privately owned motor vehicle, provided that any applicable employees possess a Georgia weapons carry license.

(c) Subsection (a) of this Code section shall not apply:

(1) To searches by certified law enforcement officers pursuant to valid search warrants or valid warrantless searches based upon probable cause under exigent circumstances;

(2) To vehicles owned or leased by an employer;

(3) To any situation in which a reasonable person would believe that accessing a locked vehicle of an employee is necessary to prevent an immediate threat to human health, life, or safety; or

(4) When an employee consents to a search of his or her locked privately owned vehicle by licensed private security officers for loss prevention purposes based on probable cause that the employee unlawfully possesses employer property.

(d) Subsections (a) and (b) of this Code section shall not apply:

(1) To an employer providing applicable employees with a secure parking area which restricts general public access through the use of a gate, security station, security officers, or other similar means which limit public access into the parking area, provided that any employer policy allowing vehicle searches upon entry shall be applicable to all vehicles entering the property and applied on a uniform and frequent basis;

(2) To any penal institution, correctional institution, detention facility, jail, or similar place of confinement or confinement alternative;

(3) To facilities associated with electric generation owned or operated by a public utility;

(4) To any United States Department of Defense contractor, if such contractor operates any facility on or contiguous with a United States military base or installation or within one mile of an airport;

(5) To an employee who is restricted from carrying or possessing a firearm on the employer's premises due to a completed or pending disciplinary action;

(6) Where transport of a firearm on the premises of the employer is prohibited by state or federal law or regulation;

(7) To parking lots contiguous to facilities providing natural gas transmission, liquid petroleum transmission, water storage and supply, and law enforcement services determined to be so vital to the State of Georgia, by a written determination of the Georgia Department of Homeland Security, that the incapacity or destruction of such systems and assets would have a debilitating impact on public health or safety; or

(8) To any area used for parking on a temporary basis.

(e) No employer, property owner, or property owner's agent shall be held liable in any criminal or civil action for damages resulting from or arising out of an occurrence involving the transportation, storage, possession, or use of a firearm, including, but not limited to, the theft of a firearm from an employee's automobile, pursuant to this Code section unless such employer commits a criminal act involving the use of a firearm or unless the employer knew that the person using such firearm would commit such criminal act on the employer's premises. Nothing contained in this Code section shall create a new duty on the part of the employer, property owner, or property owner's agent. An employee at will shall have no greater interest in employment created by this Code section and shall remain an employee at will.

(f) In any action relating to the enforcement of any right or obligation under this Code section, an employer, property owner, or property owner's agent's efforts to comply with other applicable federal, state, or local safety laws, regulations, guidelines, or ordinances shall be a complete defense to any employer, property owner, or property owner's agent's liability.

(g) In any action brought against an employer, employer's agent, property owner, or property owner's agent relating to the criminal use of firearms in the workplace, the plaintiff shall be liable for all legal costs of such employer, employer's agent, property owner, or property owner's agent if such action is concluded in such employer, employer's agent, property owner, or property owner's agent's favor.

(h) This Code section shall not be construed so as to require an employer, property owner, or property owner's agent to implement any additional security measures for the protection of employees, customers, or other persons. Implementation of remedial security measures to provide protection to employees, customers, or other persons shall not be admissible in evidence to show prior negligence or breach of duty of an employer, property owner, or property owner's agent in any action against such employer, its officers or shareholders, or property owners.

(i) All actions brought based upon a violation of subsection (a) of this Code section shall be brought exclusively by the Attorney General.

(j) In the event that subsection (e) of this Code section is declared or adjudged by any court to be invalid or unconstitutional for any reason, the remaining portions of this Code section shall be invalid and of no further force or effect. The General Assembly declares that it would not have enacted the remaining provisions of this Code section if it had known that such portion hereof would be declared or adjudged invalid or unconstitutional.

(k) Nothing in this Code section shall restrict the rights of private property owners or persons in legal control of property through a lease, a rental agreement, a contract, or any other agreement to control access to such property. When a private property owner or person in legal control of property through a lease, a rental agreement, a contract, or any other agreement is also an employer, his or her rights as a private property owner or person in legal control of property shall govern.

§ 16-11-136. Restrictions on possession, manufacture, sale, or transfer of knives

(a) As used in this Code section, the term:
(1) "Courthouse" shall have the same meaning as set forth in Code Section 16-11-127.
(2) "Government building" shall have the same meaning as set forth in Code Section 16-11-127.
(3) "Knife" means any cutting instrument with a blade and shall include, without limitation, a knife as such term is defined in Code Section 16-11-125.1.
(b) Except for restrictions in courthouses and government buildings, no county, municipality, or consolidated government shall, by rule or ordinance, constrain the possession, manufacture, sale, or transfer of a knife more restrictively than the provisions of this part.

§ 16-11-137. Required possession of weapons carry license or proof of exemption when carrying a weapon; detention for investigation of carrying permit

(a) Every license holder shall have his or her valid weapons carry license in his or her immediate possession at all times when carrying a weapon, or if such person is exempt from having a weapons carry license pursuant to Code Section 16-11-130 or subsection (c) of Code Section 16-11-127.1, he or she shall have proof of his or her exemption in his or her immediate possession at all times when carrying a weapon, and his or her failure to do so shall be prima-facie evidence of a violation of the applicable provision of Code Sections 16-11-126 through 16-11-127.2.
(b) A person carrying a weapon shall not be subject to detention for the sole purpose of investigating whether such person has a weapons carry license.
(c) A person convicted of a violation of this Code section shall be fined not more than $10.00 if he or she produces in court his or her weapons carry license, provided that it was valid at the time of his or her arrest, or produces proof of his or her exemption.

§ 16-11-138. Defense of self or others as absolute defense

Defense of self or others, as contemplated by and provided for under Article 2 of Chapter 3 of this title, shall be an absolute defense to any violation under this part.

§ 16-11-150. Short title

This part shall be known and may be cited as the "Georgia Antiterroristic Training Act."

§ 16-11-151. Prohibited training

(a) As used in this Code section, the term "dangerous weapon" has the same meaning as found in paragraph (1) of Code Section 16-11-121.
(b) It shall be unlawful for any person to:
(1) Teach, train, or demonstrate to any other person the use, application, or making of any illegal firearm, dangerous weapon, explosive, or incendiary device capable of causing injury or death to persons either directly or through a writing or over or through a computer or computer network if the person teaching, training, or demonstrating knows, has reason to know, or intends that such teaching, training, or demonstrating will be unlawfully employed for use in or in furtherance of a civil disorder, riot, or insurrection; or
(2) Assemble with one or more persons for the purpose of being taught, trained, or instructed in the use of any illegal firearm, dangerous weapon, explosive, or incendiary device capable of causing injury or death to persons if such person so assembling knows, has reason to know, or intends that such teaching, training, or instruction will be unlawfully employed for use in or in furtherance of a civil disorder, riot, or insurrection.
(c) Any person who violates any provision of subsection (b) of this Code section shall be guilty of a felony and, upon conviction thereof, shall be punished by a fine of not more than $5,000.00 or by imprisonment for not less than one nor more than five years, or both.

§ 16-11-152. Authorized training

This part shall not apply to:
(1) Any act of any peace officer which is performed in the lawful performance of official duties;
(2) Any training for law enforcement officers conducted by or for any police agency of the state or any political subdivision thereof or any agency of the United States;
(3) Any activities of the National Guard or of the armed forces of the United States; or
(4) Any hunter education classes taught under the auspices of the Department of Natural Resources, or other classes intended to teach the safe handling of firearms for hunting, recreation, competition, or self-defense.

§ 16-11-160. Use of machine guns, sawed-off rifles, sawed-off shotguns, or firearms with silencers during commission of certain offenses; enhanced criminal penalties

(a) (1) It shall be unlawful for any person to possess or to use a machine gun, sawed-off rifle, sawed-off shotgun, or firearm equipped with a silencer, as those terms are defined in Code Section 16-11-121, during the commission or the attempted commission of any of the following offenses:

(A) Aggravated assault as defined in Code Section 16-5-21;

(B) Aggravated battery as defined in Code Section 16-5-24;

(C) Robbery as defined in Code Section 16-8-40;

(D) Armed robbery as defined in Code Section 16-8-41;

(D.1) Home invasion in any degree as defined in Code Section 16-7-5;

(E) Murder or felony murder as defined in Code Section 16-5-1;

(F) Voluntary manslaughter as defined in Code Section 16-5-2;

(G) Involuntary manslaughter as defined in Code Section 16-5-3;

(H) Sale, possession for sale, transportation, manufacture, offer for sale, or offer to manufacture controlled substances in violation of any provision of Article 2 of Chapter 13 of this title, the "Georgia Controlled Substances Act";

(I) Terroristic threats or acts as defined in Code Section 16-11-37;

(J) Arson as defined in Code Section 16-7-60, 16-7-61, or 16-7-62 or arson of lands as defined in Code Section 16-7-63;

(K) Influencing witnesses as defined in Code Section 16-10-93; and

(L) Participation in criminal gang activity as defined in Code Section 16-15-4.

(2)(A) As used in this paragraph, the term "bulletproof vest" means a bullet-resistant soft body armor providing, as a minimum standard, the level of protection known as "threat level I," which means at least seven layers of bullet-resistant material providing protection from at least three shots of 158-grain lead ammunition fired from a .38 caliber handgun at a velocity of 850 feet per second.

(B) It shall be unlawful for any person to wear a bulletproof vest during the commission or the attempted commission of any of the following offenses:

(i) Any crime against or involving the person of another in violation of any of the provisions of this title for which a sentence of life imprisonment may be imposed;

(ii) Any felony involving the manufacture, delivery, distribution, administering, or selling of controlled substances or marijuana as provided in Code Section 16-13-30; or

(iii) Trafficking in cocaine, illegal drugs, marijuana, or methamphetamine as provided in Code Section 16-13-31.

(b) Any person who violates paragraph (1) of subsection (a) of this Code section shall be guilty of a felony, and, upon conviction thereof, shall be punished by confinement for a period of ten years, such sentence to run consecutively to any other sentence which the person has received. Any person who violates paragraph (2) of subsection (a) of this Code section shall be guilty of a felony, and, upon conviction thereof, shall be punished by confinement for a period of one to five years, such sentence to run consecutively to any other sentence which the person has received.

(c) Upon the second or subsequent conviction of a person under this Code section, the person shall be punished by life imprisonment. Notwithstanding any other law to the contrary, the sentence of any person which is imposed for violating this Code section a second or subsequent time shall not be suspended by a court or a probationary sentence imposed in lieu thereof.

(d) The punishment prescribed for the violation of subsections (a) and (c) of this Code section shall not be probated or suspended as is provided by Code Section 17-10-7.

(e) Any crime committed in violation of this Code section shall be considered a separate offense.

§ 16-11-161. Consistent local laws or ordinances authorized

Nothing in this part shall be construed to prohibit a local governing authority from adopting and enforcing laws consistent with this part relating to gangs and gang violence. Where local laws or ordinances duplicate or supplement this part, this part shall be construed as providing alternative remedies and not as preempting the field.

§ 16-11-162. Exemption for use of force in defense of others

This part shall not apply to persons who use force in defense of others as provided by Code Section 16-3-21. This part is intended to supplement not to supplant Code Section 16-11-106.

§ 16-11-170. Intent to provide state background check law; construction of part

Reserved. Repealed by Ga. L. 2005, p. 613, § 1, effective July 1, 2005.

§ 16-11-171. Definitions

As used in this part, the term:

(1) "Center" means the Georgia Crime Information Center within the Georgia Bureau of Investigation.

(2) "Dealer" means any person licensed as a dealer pursuant to 18 U.S.C. Section 921, et seq.

(3) "Firearm" means any weapon that is designed to or may readily be converted to expel a projectile by the action of an explosive or the frame or receiver of any such weapon, any firearm muffler or firearm silencer, or any destructive device as defined in 18 U.S.C. Section 921(a)(3).

(4) "Involuntarily hospitalized" means hospitalized as an inpatient in any mental health facility pursuant to Code Section 37-3-81 or hospitalized as an inpatient in any mental health facility as a result of being adjudicated mentally incompetent to stand trial or being adjudicated not guilty by reason of insanity at the time of the crime pursuant to Part 2 of Article 6 of Title 17.

(5) "NICS" means the National Instant Criminal Background Check System created by the federal "Brady Handgun Violence Prevention Act" (P. L. No. 103-159).

§ 16-11-172. Transfers or purchases of firearms subject to the NICS; information concerning persons who have been involuntarily hospitalized to be forwarded to the FBI; penalties for breach of confidentiality; exceptions

(a) All transfers or purchases of firearms conducted by a licensed importer, licensed manufacturer, or licensed dealer shall be subject to the NICS. To the extent possible, the center shall provide to the NICS all necessary criminal history information and wanted person records in order to complete an NICS check.

(b) The center shall forward to the Federal Bureau of Investigation information concerning persons who have been involuntarily hospitalized as defined in this part for the purpose of completing an NICS check.

(c) Any government official who willfully or intentionally compromises the identity, confidentiality, and security of any records and data pursuant to this part shall be guilty of a felony and fined no less than $5,000.00 and shall be subject to automatic dismissal from his or her employment.

(d) The provisions of this part shall not apply to:

(1) Any firearm, including any handgun with a matchlock, flintlock, percussion cap, or similar type of ignition system, manufactured in or before 1898;

(2) Any replica of any firearm described in paragraph (1) of this subsection if such replica is not designed or redesigned to use rimfire or conventional center-fire fixed ammunition or uses rimfire or conventional center-fire fixed ammunition which is no longer manufactured in the United States and which is not readily available in the ordinary channels of commercial trade; and

(3) Any firearm which is a curio or relic as defined by 27 C.F.R. 178.11.

§ 16-11-173. Legislative findings; preemption of local regulation and lawsuits; exceptions

(a) (1) It is declared by the General Assembly that the regulation of firearms and other weapons is properly an issue of general, state-wide concern.

(2) The General Assembly further declares that the lawful design, marketing, manufacture, and sale of firearms and ammunition and other weapons to the public is not unreasonably dangerous activity and does not constitute a nuisance per se.

(b) (1) Except as provided in subsection (c) of this Code section, no county or municipal corporation, by zoning, by ordinance or resolution, or by any other means, nor any agency, board, department, commission, political subdivision, school district, or authority of this state, other than the General Assembly, by rule or regulation or by any other means shall regulate in any manner:

(A) Gun shows;

(B) The possession, ownership, transport, carrying, transfer, sale, purchase, licensing, or registration of firearms or other weapons or components of firearms or other weapons;

(C) Firearms dealers or dealers of other weapons; or

(D) Dealers in components of firearms or other weapons.

(2) The authority to bring suit and right to recover against any weapons, firearms, or ammunition manufacturer, trade association, or dealer by or on behalf of any governmental unit created by or pursuant to an Act of the General Assembly or the Constitution, or any department, agency, or authority thereof, for damages, abatement, or injunctive relief resulting from or relating to the lawful design, manufacture, marketing, or sale of weapons, firearms, or ammunition to the public shall be reserved exclusively to the state. This paragraph shall not prohibit a political subdivision or local government authority from bringing an action against a weapons, firearms, or ammunition manufacturer or dealer for breach of contract or express warranty as to weapons, firearms, or ammunition purchased by the political subdivision or local government authority.

(c) (1) A county or municipal corporation may regulate the transport, carrying, or possession of firearms by employees of the local unit of government, or by unpaid volunteers of such local unit of government, in the course of their employment or volunteer functions with such local unit of government; provided, however, that the sheriff or chief of police shall be solely responsible for regulating and determining the possession, carrying, and transportation of firearms and other weapons by employees under his or her respective supervision so long as such regulations comport with state and federal law.

(2) The commanding officer of any law enforcement agency shall regulate and determine the possession, carrying, and transportation of firearms and other weapons by employees under his or her supervision so long as such regulations comport with state and federal law.

(3) The district attorney, and the solicitor-general in counties where there is a state court, shall regulate and determine the possession, carrying, and transportation of firearms and other weapons by county employees under his or her supervision so long as such regulations comport with state and federal law.

(d) Nothing contained in this Code section shall prohibit municipalities or counties, by ordinance or resolution, from requiring the ownership of guns by heads of households within the political subdivision.

(e) Nothing contained in this Code section shall prohibit municipalities or counties, by ordinance or resolution, from reasonably limiting or prohibiting the discharge of firearms within the boundaries of the municipal corporation or county.

(f) As used in this Code section, the term "weapon" means any device designed or intended to be used, or capable of being used, for offense or defense, including but not limited to firearms, bladed devices, clubs, electric stun devices, and defense sprays.

(g) Any person aggrieved as a result of a violation of this Code section may bring an action against the person who caused such aggrievement. The aggrieved person shall be entitled to reasonable attorney's fees and expenses of litigation and may recover or obtain against the person who caused such damages any of the following:

(1) Actual damages or $100.00, whichever is greater;

(2) Equitable relief, including, but not limited to, an injunction or restitution of money and property; and

(3) Any other relief which the court deems proper.

§§ 16-11-174 through 16-11-184

Repealed by Ga. L. 2005, p. 613, § 1/SB 175, effective July 1, 2005.

§ 16-11-200. Definitions; offense of transporting or moving illegal aliens; exceptions; penalties

(a) As used in this Code section, the term:

(1) "Illegal alien" means a person who is verified by the federal government to be present in the United States in violation of federal immigration law.

(2) "Motor vehicle" shall have the same meaning as provided in Code Section 40-1-1.

(b) A person who, while committing another criminal offense, knowingly and intentionally transports or moves an illegal alien in a motor vehicle for the purpose of furthering the illegal presence of the alien in the United States shall be guilty of the offense of transporting or moving an illegal alien.

(c) Except as provided in this subsection, a person convicted for a first offense of transporting or moving an illegal alien who moves seven or fewer illegal aliens at the same time shall be guilty of a misdemeanor and, upon conviction thereof, shall be punished by imprisonment not to exceed 12 months, a fine not to exceed $1,000.00, or both. A person convicted for a second or subsequent offense of transporting or moving an illegal alien, and a person convicted on a first offense of transporting or moving an illegal alien who moves eight or more illegal aliens at the same time, shall be guilty of a felony and, upon conviction thereof, shall be punished by imprisonment of not less than one or more than five years, a fine of not less than $5,000.00 or more than $20,000.00, or both. A person who commits the offense of transporting or moving an illegal alien who does so with the intent of making a profit or receiving anything of value shall be guilty of a felony and, upon conviction thereof, shall be punished by imprisonment of not less than one or more than five years, a fine of not less than $5,000.00 or more than $20,000.00, or both.

(d) This Code section shall not apply to:

(1) A government employee transporting or moving an illegal alien as a part of his or her official duties or to any person acting at the direction of such employee;

(2) A person who transports an illegal alien to or from a judicial or administrative proceeding when such illegal alien is required to appear pursuant to a summons, subpoena, court order, or other legal process;

(3) A person who transports an illegal alien to a law enforcement agency or a judicial officer for official government purposes;

(4) An employer transporting an employee who was lawfully hired; or

(5) A person providing privately funded social services.

§ 16-11-201. Definitions; offense of concealing, harboring, or shielding an illegal alien; penalties; exceptions

(a) As used in this Code section, the term:

(1) "Harboring" or "harbors" means any conduct that tends to substantially help an illegal alien to remain in the United States in violation of federal law but shall not include a person providing services to infants, children, or victims of a crime; a person providing privately funded social services; a person providing emergency medical service; or an attorney or his or her employees for the purpose of representing a criminal defendant.

(2) "Illegal alien" means a person who is verified by the federal government to be present in the United States in violation of federal immigration law.

(b) A person who is acting in violation of another criminal offense and who knowingly conceals, harbors, or shields an illegal alien from detection in any place in this state, including any building or means of transportation, when such person knows that the person being concealed, harbored, or shielded is an illegal alien, shall be guilty of the offense of concealing or harboring an illegal alien.

(c) Except as provided in this subsection, a person convicted of concealing or harboring an illegal alien who conceals or harbors seven or fewer illegal aliens at the same time in the same location shall be guilty of a misdemeanor and, upon conviction thereof, shall be punished by imprisonment not to exceed 12 months, a fine not to exceed $1,000.00, or both. A person convicted of concealing or harboring an illegal alien who conceals or harbors eight or more illegal aliens at the same time in the same location, or who conceals or harbors an illegal alien with the intent of making a profit or receiving anything of value, shall be guilty of a felony and, upon conviction thereof, shall be punished by imprisonment of not less than one or more than five years, a fine of not less than $5,000.00 or more than $20,000.00, or both.

(d) This Code section shall not apply to a government employee or any person acting at the express direction of a government employee who conceals, harbors, or shelters an illegal alien when such illegal alien is or has been the victim of a criminal offense or is a witness in any civil or criminal proceeding or who holds an illegal alien in a jail, prison, or other detention facility.

§ 16-11-202. Illegal alien defined; offense of inducing an illegal alien to enter state; penalties

(a) As used in this Code section, the term "illegal alien" means a person who is verified by the federal government to be present in the United States in violation of federal immigration law.

(b) A person who is acting in violation of another criminal offense and who knowingly induces, entices, or assists an illegal alien to enter into this state, when such person knows that the person being induced, enticed, or assisted to enter into this state is an illegal alien, shall be guilty of the offense of inducing an illegal alien to enter into this state.

(c) Except as provided in subsection (d) of this Code section, for a first offense, a person convicted of inducing an illegal alien to enter into this state shall be guilty of a misdemeanor and, upon conviction thereof, shall be punished by imprisonment not to exceed 12 months, a fine not to exceed $1,000.00, or both. For a second or subsequent conviction of inducing an illegal alien to enter into this state, a person shall be guilty of a felony and, upon conviction thereof, shall be punished by imprisonment of not less than one or more than five years, a fine of not less than $5,000.00 or more than $20,000.00, or both.

(d) A person who commits the offense of inducing an illegal alien to enter into this state who does so with the intent of making a profit or receiving any thing of value shall be guilty of a felony and, upon conviction thereof, shall be punished by imprisonment of not less than one or more than five years, a fine of not less than $5,000.00 or more than $20,000.00, or both.

§ 16-11-203. Authority of law enforcement officers to enforce federal immigration laws; documentation

The testimony of any officer, employee, or agent of the federal government having confirmed that a person is an illegal alien shall be admissible to prove that the federal government has verified such person to be present in the United States in violation of federal immigration law. Verification that a person is present in the United States in violation of federal immigration law may also be established by any document authorized by law to be recorded or filed and in fact recorded or filed in a public office where items of this nature are kept.

§ 16-11-220. Definitions

As used in this article, the term:

(1) "Critical infrastructure" means publicly or privately owned facilities, systems, functions, or assets, whether physical or virtual, providing or distributing services for the benefit of the public, including, but not limited to, energy, fuel, water, agriculture, health care, finance, or communication.

(2) "Domestic terrorism" means any felony violation of, or attempt to commit a felony violation of the laws of this state which, as part of a single unlawful act or a series of unlawful acts which are interrelated by distinguishing characteristics, is intended to cause serious bodily harm, kill any individual or group of individuals, or disable or destroy critical infrastructure, a state or government facility, or a public transportation system when such disability or destruction results in major economic loss, and is intended to:

(A) Intimidate the civilian population of this state or any of its political subdivisions;

(B) Alter, change, or coerce the policy of the government of this state or any of its political subdivisions by intimidation or coercion; or

(C) Affect the conduct of the government of this state or any of its political subdivisions by use of destructive devices, assassination, or kidnapping.

(3) "Public transportation system" means all facilities, conveyances, and instrumentalities, whether publicly or privately owned, that are used in or for publicly available services for the transportation of individuals or cargo.

(4) "Serious bodily harm" means harm to the body of another by depriving him or her of a member of his or her body, by rendering a member of his or her body useless, or by seriously disfiguring his or her body or a member thereof.

(5) "State or government facility" means any permanent or temporary facility or conveyance that is used or occupied by representatives of this state or any of its political subdivisions, by the legislature, by the judiciary, or by officials or employees of this state or any of its political subdivisions.

§ 16-11-221. Penalties

(a) Any person who commits domestic terrorism shall be guilty of a felony and upon conviction thereof shall be punished as follows:

(1) If death results to any individual, by death, by imprisonment for life without parole, or by imprisonment for life;

(2) If kidnapping occurs, by imprisonment for not less than 15 nor more than 35 years, or by imprisonment for life;

(3) If serious bodily harm occurs, by imprisonment for not less than 15 nor more than 35 years; or

(4) If critical infrastructure, a state or government facility, or a public transportation system is disabled or destroyed, by imprisonment for not less than five nor more than 35 years.

(b) No sentence imposed under this Code section shall be suspended, stayed, probated, deferred, or withheld by the sentencing court; provided, however, that in the court's discretion, the court may suspend, stay, probate, defer, or withhold part of such sentence when the prosecuting attorney and the defendant have agreed to such sentence.

§ 16-11-222. Persons and conduct subject to prosecution for offense of domestic terrorism

A person shall be subject to prosecution in this state pursuant to Code Section 17-2-1 for any conduct made unlawful by this article which the person engages in while:

(1) Either within or outside of this state if, by such conduct, the person commits a violation of this article which involves an individual who resides in this state or which involves critical infrastructure, a state or government facility, or a public transportation system located in this state; or

(2) Within this state if, by such conduct, the person commits a violation of this article which involves an individual who resides within or outside this state or which involves critical infrastructure, a state or government facility, or a public transportation system located in this state.

§ 16-11-223. Jurisdiction for prosecutions

The Attorney General shall have concurrent jurisdiction with district attorneys to conduct the criminal prosecution of a violation of this article.

§ 16-11-224. Construction; constitutional protections

This article shall not be construed to infringe upon constitutionally protected speech or assembly.

CHAPTER 12. OFFENSES AGAINST PUBLIC HEALTH AND MORALS

§ 16-12-1. Contributing to the delinquency or dependency of a minor

(a) As used in this Code section, the term:

(1) "Delinquent act" means a delinquent act as defined in Code Section 15-11-2.

(2) "Felony" means any act which constitutes a felony under the laws of this state, the laws of any other state of the United States, or the laws of the United States.

(3) "Minor" means any individual who is under the age of 17 years who is alleged to have committed a delinquent act or any individual under the age of 18 years.

(4) "Serious injury" means an injury involving a broken bone, the loss of a member of the body, the loss of use of a member of the body, the substantial disfigurement of the body or of a member of the body, an injury which is life threatening, or any sexual abuse of a child under 16 years of age by means of an act described in subparagraph (a)(4)(A), (a)(4)(G), or (a)(4)(I) of Code Section 16-12-100.

(5) "Service provider" means an entity that is registered with the Department of Human Services pursuant to Article 7 of Chapter 5 of Title 49 or a child welfare agency as defined in Code Section 49-5-12 or agent or employee acting on behalf of such entity or child welfare agency.

(b) A person commits the offense of contributing to the delinquency or dependency of a minor or causing a child to be a child in need of services when such person:

(1) Knowingly and willfully encourages, causes, abets, connives, or aids a minor in committing a delinquent act;

(2) Knowingly and willfully encourages, causes, abets, connives, or aids a minor in committing an act which would cause such minor to be a child in need of services as such term is defined in Code Section 15-11-2; provided, however, that this paragraph shall not apply to a service provider that notifies the minor's parent, guardian, or legal custodian of the minor's location and general state of well-being as soon as possible but not later than 72 hours after the minor's acceptance of services; provided, further, that such notification shall not be required if:

(A) The service provider has reasonable cause to believe that the minor has been abused or neglected and makes a child abuse report pursuant to Code Section 19-7-5;

(B) The minor will not disclose the name of the minor's parent, guardian, or legal custodian, and the Division of Family and Children Services within the Department of Human Services is notified within 72 hours of the minor's acceptance of services; or

(C) The minor's parent, guardian, or legal custodian cannot be reached, and the Division of Family and Children Services within the Department of Human Services is notified within 72 hours of the minor's acceptance of services;

(3) Willfully commits an act or acts or willfully fails to act when such act or omission would cause a minor to be adjudicated to be a dependent child as such term is defined in Code Section 15-11-2;

(4) Knowingly and willfully hires, solicits, engages, contracts with, conspires with, encourages, abets, or directs any minor to commit any felony which encompasses force or violence as an element of the offense or delinquent act which would constitute a felony which encompasses force or violence as an element of the offense if committed by an adult;

(5) Knowingly and willfully provides to a minor any firearm as defined in Code Section 16-11-127.1, any dangerous weapon as defined in Code Section 16-11-121, or any hazardous object as defined in Code Section 20-2-751 to commit any felony which encompasses force or violence as an element of the offense or delinquent act which would constitute a felony which encompasses force or violence as an element of the offense if committed by an adult; or

(6) Knowingly and willfully hires, solicits, engages, contracts with, conspires with, encourages, abets, or directs any minor to commit any smash and grab burglary which would constitute a felony if committed by an adult.

(c) It shall not be a defense to the offense provided for in this Code section that the minor has not been formally adjudged to have committed a delinquent act or has not been adjudged to be a dependent child or a child in need of services.

(d) A person convicted pursuant to paragraph (1) or (2) of subsection (b) of this Code section shall be punished as follows:

(1) Upon conviction of the first or second offense, the defendant shall be guilty of a misdemeanor and shall be fined not more than $1,000.00 or shall be imprisoned for not more than 12 months, or both fined and imprisoned; and

(2) Upon the conviction of the third or subsequent offense, the defendant shall be guilty of a felony and shall be fined not less than $1,000.00 nor more than $5,000.00 or shall be imprisoned for not less than one year nor more than three years, or both fined and imprisoned.

(d.1) A person convicted pursuant to paragraph (3) of subsection (b) of this Code section shall be punished as follows:

(1) Upon conviction of an offense which resulted in the serious injury or death of a child, without regard to whether such offense was a first, second, third, or subsequent offense, the defendant shall be guilty of a felony and shall be punished as provided in subsection (e) of this Code section;

(2) Upon conviction of an offense which does not result in the serious injury or death of a child and which is the first conviction, the defendant shall be guilty of a misdemeanor and shall be fined not more than $1,000.00 or shall be imprisoned for not more than 12 months, or both fined and imprisoned;

(3) Upon conviction of an offense which does not result in the serious injury or death of a child and which is the second conviction, the defendant shall be guilty of a high and aggravated misdemeanor and shall be fined not less than $1,000.00 nor more than $5,000.00 or shall be imprisoned for not less than one year, or both fined and imprisoned; and

(4) Upon the conviction of an offense which does not result in the serious injury or death of a child and which is the third or subsequent conviction, the defendant shall be guilty of a felony and shall be fined not less than $10,000.00 or shall be imprisoned for not less than one year nor more than five years, or both fined and imprisoned.

(e) A person convicted pursuant to paragraph (4), (5), or (6) of subsection (b) or paragraph (1) of subsection (d.1) of this Code section shall be guilty of a felony and punished as follows:

(1) Upon conviction of the first offense, the defendant shall be imprisoned for not less than one nor more than ten years; and

(2) Upon conviction of the second or subsequent offense, the defendant shall be imprisoned for not less than three years nor more than 20 years.

§ 16-12-1.1. Child, family, or group-care facility operators prohibited from employing or allowing to reside or be domiciled persons with certain past criminal violations

(a) As used in this Code section the term:

(1) "Facility" means any child care learning center, family child care learning home, group-care facility, or similar facility at which any child who is not a member of an operator's family is received for pay for supervision and care, without transfer of legal custody, for fewer than 24 hours per day.

(2) "Operator" means any person who applies for or holds a permit or license to operate a facility.

(b) Unless otherwise authorized as provided in Code Section 20-1A-43, it shall be unlawful for any operator of a facility to knowingly have any person reside at, be domiciled at, or be employed at any such facility if such person has been convicted of or has entered a plea of guilty or nolo contendere to or has been adjudicated a delinquent for:

(1) A violation of Code Section 16-4-1, relating to criminal attempt, when the crime attempted is any of the crimes specified in paragraphs (2) through (10) of this subsection;

(2) A violation of Code Section 16-5-23.1, relating to battery, when the victim at the time of such offense was a minor;

(3) A violation of any provision of Chapter 6 of this title, relating to sexual offenses, when the victim at the time of such offense was a minor;

(4) A violation of Code Section 16-12-1, relating to contributing to the delinquency of a minor;

(5) A violation of Code Section 16-5-1;

(6) A violation of Code Section 16-5-2, relating to voluntary manslaughter;

(7) A violation of Code Section 16-6-2, relating to aggravated sodomy;

(8) A violation of Code Section 16-6-3, relating to rape;

(9) A violation of Code Section 16-6-22.2, relating to aggravated sexual battery; or

(10) A violation of Code Section 16-8-41, relating to armed robbery, if committed with a firearm.

(c) Any person violating subsection (b) of this Code section shall be guilty of a misdemeanor.

§ 16-12-2. Smoking in public places

(a) A person smoking tobacco in violation of Chapter 12A of Title 31 shall be guilty of a misdemeanor and, if convicted, shall be punished by a fine of not less than $100.00 nor more than $500.00.

(b) This Code section shall be cumulative to and shall not prohibit the enactment of any other general and local laws, rules and regulations of state or local agencies, and local ordinances prohibiting smoking which are more restrictive than this Code section.

§ 16-12-3. Suspension of gas or electrical service for not making payments on appliances purchased from or repaired by utility company

(a) It shall be unlawful for any gas or electric utility company or electric membership corporation to cut off or suspend gas or electric service in any residence because the resident has failed to pay for or has failed to make timely payments for any appliance purchased from or any appliance repaired by such company or corporation. Payments received from a resident shall be first applied to the service, unless otherwise specified by the resident at the time of payment.

(b) Any company or corporation or any agent or employee thereof acting within the scope of his authority knowingly violating subsection (a) of this Code section shall be guilty of a misdemeanor.

§ 16-12-4. Cruelty to animals

(a) As used in this Code section, the term:

(1) "Animal" shall not include any fish nor shall such term include any pest that might be exterminated or removed from a business, residence, or other structure.

(2) "Malice" means:

(A) An actual intent, which may be shown by the circumstances connected to the act, to cause the particular harm produced without justification or excuse; or

(B) The wanton and willful doing of an act with an awareness of a plain and strong likelihood that a particular harm may result.

(b) A person commits the offense of cruelty to animals when he or she:

(1) Causes physical pain, suffering, or death to an animal by any unjustifiable act or omission; or

(2) Having intentionally exercised custody, control, possession, or ownership of an animal, fails to provide to such animal adequate food, water, sanitary conditions, or ventilation that is consistent with what a reasonable person of ordinary knowledge would believe is the normal requirement and feeding habit for such animal's size, species, breed, age, and physical condition.

(c) Any person convicted of the offense of cruelty to animals shall be guilty of a misdemeanor; provided, however, that any person who has had a prior adjudication of guilt for the offense of cruelty to animals or aggravated cruelty to animals, or an adjudication of guilt for the commission of an offense under the laws of any other state, territory, possession, or dominion of the United States, or of any foreign nation recognized by the United States, which would constitute the offense of cruelty to animals or aggravated cruelty to animals if committed in this state, including an adjudication of a juvenile for the commission of an act, whether committed in this state or in any other state, territory, possession, or dominion of the United States, or any foreign nation recognized by the United States, which if committed by an adult would constitute the offense of cruelty to animals or aggravated cruelty to animals, upon the second or subsequent conviction of cruelty to animals shall be guilty of a misdemeanor of a high and aggravated nature.

(d) A person commits the offense of aggravated cruelty to animals when he or she:

(1) Maliciously causes the death of an animal;

(2) Maliciously causes physical harm to an animal by depriving it of a member of its body, by rendering a part of such animal's body useless, or by seriously disfiguring such animal's body or a member thereof;

(3) Maliciously tortures an animal by the infliction of or subjection to severe or prolonged physical pain;

(4) Maliciously administers poison to an animal, or exposes an animal to any poisonous substance, with the intent that the substance be taken or swallowed by the animal; or

(5) Having intentionally exercised custody, control, possession, or ownership of an animal, maliciously fails to provide to such animal adequate food, water, sanitary conditions, or ventilation that is consistent with what a reasonable person of ordinary knowledge would believe is the normal requirement and feeding habit for such animal's size, species, breed, age, and physical condition to the extent that the death of such animal results or a member of its body is rendered useless or is seriously disfigured.

(e) Any person convicted of the offense of aggravated cruelty to animals shall be guilty of a felony and shall be punished by imprisonment for not less than one nor more than five years, a fine not to exceed $15,000.00, or both; provided, however, that any person who has had a prior adjudication of guilt for the offense of aggravated cruelty to animals, or an adjudication of guilt for the commission of an offense under the laws of any other state, territory, possession, or dominion of the United States, or of any foreign nation recognized by the United States, which would constitute the offense of aggravated cruelty to animals if committed in this state, including an adjudication of a juvenile for the commission of an act, whether committed in this state or in any other state, territory, possession, or dominion of the United States, or any foreign nation recognized by the United States, which if committed by an adult would constitute the offense of aggravated cruelty to animals, upon the second or subsequent conviction of aggravated cruelty to animals shall be punished by imprisonment for not less than one nor more than ten years, a fine not to exceed $100,000.00, or both.

(f) Before sentencing a defendant for any conviction under this Code section, the sentencing judge may require psychological evaluation of the offender and shall consider the entire criminal record of the offender.

(g) The provisions of this Code section shall not be construed as prohibiting conduct which is otherwise permitted under the laws of this state or of the United States, including, but not limited to, agricultural, animal husbandry, butchering, food processing, marketing, scientific research, training, medical, zoological, exhibition, competitive, hunting, trapping, fishing, wildlife management, or pest control practices or the authorized practice of veterinary medicine nor to limit in any way the authority or duty of the Department of Agriculture, Department of Natural Resources, any county board of health, any law enforcement officer, dog, animal, or rabies control officer, humane society, veterinarian, or private landowner protecting his or her property.

(h) (1) In addition to justification and excuse as provided in Article 2 of Chapter 3 of this title, a person shall be justified in injuring or killing an animal when and to the extent that he or she reasonably believes that such act is necessary to defend against an imminent threat of injury or damage to any person, other animal, or property.

(2) A person shall not be justified in injuring or killing an animal under the circumstances set forth in paragraph (1) of this subsection when:

(A) The person being threatened is attempting to commit, committing, or fleeing after the commission or attempted commission of a crime;

(B) The person or other animal being threatened is attempting to commit or committing a trespass or other tortious interference with property; or

(C) The animal being threatened is not lawfully on the property where the threat is occurring.

(3) The method used to injure or kill an animal under the circumstances set forth in paragraph (1) of this subsection shall be designed to be as humane as is possible under the circumstances. A person who humanely injures or kills an animal under the circumstances indicated in this subsection shall incur no civil liability or criminal responsibility for such injury or death.

§ 16-12-5. Tattooing

(a) As used in this Code section, the term "tattoo" means to mark or color the skin of any person by pricking in, inserting, or implanting pigments, except when performed by a physician licensed as such pursuant to Chapter 34 of Title 43.

(b) It shall be unlawful for any person to tattoo the body of any person within any area within one inch of the nearest part of the eye socket of such person. Any person who violates this Code section shall be guilty of a misdemeanor.

§ 16-12-20. Definitions

As used in this part, the term:

(1) "Bet" means an agreement that, dependent upon chance even though accompanied by some skill, one stands to win or lose something of value. A bet does not include:

(A) Contracts of indemnity or guaranty or life, health, property, or accident insurance; or

(B) An offer of a prize, award, or compensation to the actual contestants in any bona fide contest for the determination of skill, speed, strength, or endurance or to the owners of animals, vehicles, watercraft, or aircraft entered in such contest.

(2) "Gambling device" means:

(A) Any contrivance which for a consideration affords the player an opportunity to obtain money or other thing of value, the award of which is determined by chance even though accompanied by some skill, whether or not the prize is automatically paid by contrivance;

(B) Any slot machine or any simulation or variation thereof;

(C) Any matchup or lineup game machine or device, operated for any consideration, in which two or more numerals, symbols, letters, or icons align in a winning combination on one or more lines vertically, horizontally, diagonally, or otherwise, without assistance by the player. Use of skill stops shall not be considered assistance by the player; or

(D) Any video game machine or device, operated for any consideration, for the play of poker, blackjack, any other card game, or keno or any simulation or variation of any of the foregoing, including, but not limited to, any game in which numerals, numbers, or any pictures, representations, or symbols are used as an equivalent or substitute for cards in the conduct of such game. Any item described in subparagraph (B), (C), or (D) of this paragraph shall be a prohibited gambling device subject to and prohibited by this part, notwithstanding any inference to the contrary in any other law of this state.

(3) "Gambling place" means any real estate, building, room, tent, vehicle, boat, or other property whatsoever, one of the principal uses of which is the making or settling of bets; the receiving, holding, recording, or forwarding of bets or offers to bet; or the conducting of a lottery or the playing of gambling devices.

(4) "Lottery" means any scheme or procedure whereby one or more prizes are distributed by chance among persons who have paid or promised consideration for a chance to win such prize, whether such scheme or procedure is called a pool, lottery, raffle, gift, gift enterprise, sale, policy game, or by some other name. Except as otherwise provided in Code Section 16-12-35, a lottery shall also include the payment of cash or other consideration or the payment for merchandise or services and the option to participate in or play, even if others can participate or play for free, a no skill game or to participate for cash, other consideration, other evidence of winnings, or other noncash prizes by lot or in a finite pool on a computer, mechanical device, or electronic device whereby the player is able to win a cash or noncash prize, other consideration, or other evidence of winnings. A lottery shall also include the organization of chain letter or pyramid clubs as provided in Code Section 16-12-38. A lottery shall not mean a:

(A) Promotional giveaway or contest which conforms with the qualifications of a lawful promotion specified in paragraph (16) of subsection (b) of Code Section 10-1-393;

(B) Scheme whereby a business gives away prizes to persons selected by lot if such prizes are made on the following conditions:

(i) Such prizes are conducted as advertising and promotional undertakings in good faith solely for the purpose of advertising the goods, wares, and merchandise of such business;

(ii) No person to be eligible to receive such prize shall be required to:

(I) Pay any tangible consideration to the operator of such business in the form of money or other property or thing of value;

(II) Purchase any goods, wares, merchandise, or anything of value from such business; or

(III) Be present or be asked to participate in a seminar, sales presentation, or any other presentation, by whatever name denominated, in order to win such prizes; and

(iii) The prizes awarded shall be noncash prizes and cannot be awarded based upon the playing of a game on a computer, mechanical device, or electronic device at a place of business in this state;

(C) Raffle authorized under Code Section 16-12-22.1; or

(D) National or regional promotion, contest, or sweepstakes conducted by any corporation or wholly owned subsidiary or valid franchise of such corporation, either directly or through another entity, provided that, at the time of such promotion, contest, or sweepstakes, such corporation:

(i) Is registered under the federal Securities Exchange Act of 1934; and

(ii) Has total assets of not less than $100 million.

The provisions of this part shall not be applicable to games offered by the Georgia Lottery Corporation pursuant to Chapter 27 of Title 50.

§ 16-12-21. Gambling

(a) A person commits the offense of gambling when he:

(1) Makes a bet upon the partial or final result of any game or contest or upon the performance of any participant in such game or contest;

(2) Makes a bet upon the result of any political nomination, appointment, or election or upon the degree of success of any nominee, appointee, or candidate; or

(3) Plays and bets for money or other thing of value at any game played with cards, dice, or balls.

(b) A person who commits the offense of gambling shall be guilty of a misdemeanor.

§ 16-12-22. Commercial gambling

(a) A person commits the offense of commercial gambling when he intentionally does any of the following acts:

(1) Operates or participates in the earnings of a gambling place;

(2) Receives, records, or forwards a bet or offer to bet;

(3) For gain, becomes a custodian of anything of value bet or offered to be bet;

(4) Contracts to have or give himself or another the option to buy or sell or contracts to buy or sell at a future time any gain or other commodity whatsoever or any stock or security of any company, when it is at the time of making such contract intended by both parties thereto that the contract to buy or sell, the option whenever exercised or the contract resulting therefrom, shall be settled not by the receipt or delivery of such property but by the payment only of differences in prices thereof;

(5) Sells chances upon the partial or final result of or upon the margin of victory in any game or contest or upon the performance of any participant in any game or contest or upon the result of any political nomination, appointment, or election or upon the degree of success of any nominee, appointee, or candidate;

(6) Sets up or promotes any lottery, sells or offers to sell, or knowingly possesses for transfer or transfers any card, stub, ticket, check, or other device designed to serve as evidence of participation in any lottery; or

(7) Conducts, advertises, operates, sets up, or promotes a bingo game without having a valid license to operate a bingo game as provided by law.

(b) A person who commits the offense of commercial gambling shall be guilty of a felony and, upon conviction thereof, shall be punished by imprisonment for not less than one nor more than five years or by a fine not to exceed $20,000.00, or both.

§ 16-12-22.1. Raffles operated by nonprofit, tax-exempt organizations

(a) It is the intention of the General Assembly that only nonprofit, tax-exempt churches, schools, civic organizations, or related support groups; nonprofit organizations qualified under Section 501(c) of the Internal Revenue Code, as amended; or bona fide nonprofit organizations approved by the sheriff, which are properly licensed pursuant to this Code section shall be allowed to operate raffles.

(b) As used in this Code section, the term:

(1) "Nonprofit, tax-exempt organization" means churches, schools, civic organizations, or related support groups; nonprofit organizations qualified under Section 501(c) of the Internal Revenue Code, as amended; or bona fide nonprofit organizations approved by the sheriff.

(2) "Operate," "operated," or "operating" means the direction, supervision, management, operation, control, or guidance of activity.

(3) "Raffle" means any scheme or procedure whereby one or more prizes are distributed by chance among persons who have paid or promised consideration for a chance to win such prize. Such term shall also include door prizes which are awarded to persons attending meetings or activities provided that the cost of admission to such meetings or activities does not exceed the usual cost of similar activities where such prizes are not awarded.

(4) "Sheriff" means the sheriff of the county in which the nonprofit tax-exempt organization is located.

(c) Any other law to the contrary notwithstanding, no nonprofit, tax-exempt organization shall be permitted to operate a raffle until the sheriff issues a license to the organization authorizing it to do so. The license described in this subsection is in addition to and not in lieu of any other licenses which may be required by this state or any political subdivision thereof, and no raffle shall be operated until such time as all requisite licenses have been obtained. In the event a nonprofit, tax-exempt organization desires to conduct a raffle in more than one county, such organization shall not be required to obtain a license under this Code section in each county in which such raffle is to be conducted and shall only be required to obtain such license from the sheriff of the county in which the state headquarters of such organization are located.

(d)(1) Any nonprofit, tax-exempt organization desiring to obtain a license to operate raffles shall make application to the sheriff on forms prescribed by the sheriff. The sheriff may require the payment of an annual fee not to exceed $100.00. No license shall be issued to any nonprofit, tax-exempt organization unless the organization has been in existence for 24 months immediately prior to the issuance of the license. The license will expire at 12:00 Midnight on December 31 following the granting of the license. Renewal applications for each calendar year shall be filed with the sheriff prior to January 1 of each year and shall be on a form prescribed by the sheriff.

(2) Each application for a license and each application for renewal of a license shall contain the following information:

(A) The name and home address of the applicant and, if the applicant is a corporation, association, or other similar legal entity, the names and home addresses of each of the officers of the organization as well as the names and addresses of the directors, or other persons similarly situated, of the organization;

(B) The names and home addresses of each of the persons who will be operating, advertising, or promoting the raffle;

(C) The names and home addresses of any persons, organizations, or other legal entities that will act as surety for the applicant or to which the applicant is financially indebted or to which any financial obligation is owed by the applicant;

(D) A determination letter from the Internal Revenue Service certifying that the applicant is an organization exempt under federal tax law;

(E) A statement affirming that the applicant is exempt under the income tax laws of this state under Code Section 48-7-25;

(F) The location at which the applicant will conduct the raffles and, if the premises on which the raffles are to be conducted is to be leased, a copy of the lease or rental agreement; and

(G) A statement showing the convictions, if any, for criminal offenses other than minor traffic offenses of each of the persons listed in subparagraphs (A), (B), and (C) of this paragraph.

(3) The sheriff shall refuse to grant a raffle license to any applicant who fails to provide fully the information required by this Code section.

(4) When a nonprofit, tax-exempt organization which operates or intends to operate raffles for residents and patients of a retirement home, nursing home, or hospital operated by that organization at which gross receipts are or will be limited to $100.00 or less during each raffle and pays or will pay prizes having a value of $100.00 or less during each raffle, then, notwithstanding any other provision of this Code section or any rule or regulation promulgated by the sheriff pursuant to the provisions of subsection (I) of this Code section, neither the applicant nor any of the persons whose names and addresses are required under subparagraphs (A) and (B) of paragraph (2) of this subsection shall be required to submit or provide fingerprints or photographs as a condition of being granted a license.

(e)(1) The sheriff shall have the specific authority to suspend or revoke any license for any violation of this Code section. Any licensee accused of violating any provision of this Code section shall be entitled, unless waived, to a hearing on the matter of the alleged violation conducted in accordance with Chapter 13 of Title 50, the "Georgia Administrative Procedure Act."

(2) By making application for a license under this Code section, every applicant consents that the sheriff, as well as any of his agents, together with any prosecuting attorney, as well as any of his agents, may come upon the premises of any licensee or upon any premises on which any licensee is conducting a raffle for the purpose of examining the accounts and records of the licensee to determine if a violation of this Code section has occurred.

(f) The sheriff shall, upon the request of any prosecuting attorney or such prosecuting attorney's designee, certify the status of any organization as to that organization's exemption from payment of state income taxes as a nonprofit organization. The sheriff shall also upon request issue a certificate indicating whether any particular organization holds a currently valid license to operate a raffle. Such certificates properly executed shall be admissible in evidence in any prosecution, and Code Section 48-7-60, relative to the disclosure of income tax information, shall not apply to the furnishing of such certificate.

(g) Notwithstanding the other provisions of this Code section, the sheriff, upon receiving written evidence of the bona fide nonprofit, tax-exempt status of the applicant organization, shall be authorized to issue a special limited license to a nonprofit, tax-exempt organization which will allow it to operate up to three raffles during a calendar year. In such cases, the sheriff shall waive the application and license fee provided for in subsection (d) of this Code section and the annual report provided for in subsection (j) of this Code section.

(h) Raffles shall be operated only on premises owned by the nonprofit, tax-exempt organization operating the raffle, on property leased by the nonprofit, tax-exempt organization and used regularly by that organization for purposes other than the operation of a raffle, or on property leased by the nonprofit, tax-exempt organization operating the raffle from another nonprofit, tax-exempt organization.

(i) No person under the age of 18 years shall be permitted to play any raffle conducted pursuant to any license issued under this Code section unless accompanied by an adult.

(j) On or before April 15 of each year, every nonprofit, tax-exempt organization engaged in operating raffles shall file with the sheriff a report disclosing all receipts and expenditures relating to the operation of raffles in the previous year. The report shall be in addition to all other reports required by law. The report shall be prepared and signed by a certified public accountant competent to prepare such a report and shall be deemed a public record subject to public inspection.

(k)(1) A licensee that conducts or operates a raffle shall maintain the following records for at least three years from the date on which the raffle is conducted:

(A) An itemized list of the gross receipts for each raffle;

(B) An itemized list of all expenses other than prizes that are incurred in the conducting of the raffle as well as the name of each person to whom the expenses are paid and a receipt for all of the expenses;

(C) A list of all prizes awarded during the raffle and the name and address of all persons who are winners of prizes of $50.00 or more in value;

(D) An itemized list of the recipients other than the licensee of the proceeds of the raffle, including the name and address of each recipient to whom such funds are distributed; and

(E) A record of the number of persons who participate in any raffle conducted by the licensee.

(2) A licensee shall:

(A) Own all the equipment used to conduct a raffle or lease such equipment from an organization that is also licensed to conduct a raffle;

(B) Display its raffle license conspicuously at the location where the raffle is conducted;

(C) Conduct raffles only as specified in the licensee's application; and

(D) Not conduct more than one raffle during any one calendar day.

(3) No nonprofit, tax-exempt organization shall enter into any contract with any individual, firm, association, or corporation to have such individual, firm, association, or corporation operate raffles or concessions on behalf of the nonprofit, tax-exempt organization.

(4) A nonprofit, tax-exempt organization shall not lend its name nor allow its identity to be used by any individual, firm, association, or corporation in the operating or advertising of a raffle in which said nonprofit, tax-exempt organization is not directly and solely operating the raffle.

(5) No person shall pay consulting fees to any person for any services performed in relation to the operation or conduct of a raffle.

(6) A person who is a member of more than one nonprofit, tax-exempt organization shall be permitted to participate in the raffle operations of only two organizations of which such person is a member; provided, however, that such person shall not receive more than $30.00 per day for assisting in the conduct of raffles regardless of whether such person assists both organizations in the same day.

(l) The sheriff is authorized to promulgate rules and regulations which the sheriff deems necessary for the proper administration and enforcement of this Code section which are not in conflict with any provision of this Code section.

(m) Any person who operates a raffle without a valid license issued by the sheriff as provided in this Code section commits the offense of commercial gambling as defined in Code Section 16-12-22 and, upon conviction thereof, shall be punished accordingly. Any person who knowingly aids, abets, or otherwise assists in the operation of a raffle for which a license has not been obtained as provided in this Code section similarly commits the offense of commercial gambling. Any person who violates any other provision of this Code section shall be guilty of a misdemeanor of a high and aggravated nature. Any person who commits any such violation after having previously been convicted of any violations of this Code section shall be guilty of a felony and, upon conviction thereof, shall be punished by imprisonment for not less than one nor more than five years or by a fine not to exceed $10,000.00, or both.

§ 16-12-23. Keeping a gambling place

(a) A person who knowingly permits any real estate, building, room, tent, vehicle, boat, or other property whatsoever owned by him or under his control to be used as a gambling place or who rents or lets any such property with a view or expectation that it be so used commits the offense of keeping a gambling place.

(b) A person who commits the offense of keeping a gambling place shall be guilty of a misdemeanor of a high and aggravated nature.

§ 16-12-24. Possession, manufacture, or transfer of gambling device or parts; possession of antique slot machines

(a) A person who knowingly owns, manufactures, transfers commercially, or possesses any device which he knows is designed for gambling purposes or anything which he knows is designed as a subassembly or essential part of such device is guilty of a misdemeanor of a high and aggravated nature.

(b)(1) As used in this subsection, the term:

(A) "Antique slot machine" means a coin operated, nonelectronic mechanical gambling device that pays off according to the matching of symbols on wheels spun by a handle and was manufactured in its entirety, except for identical replacement parts, prior to January 1, 1950.

(B) "Conviction" includes a plea of nolo contendere to a felony.

(2) It shall be a defense to any action or prosecution under this Code section for possession of a gambling device that the device is an antique slot machine and that said device was not being used for gambling; provided, however, the defense shall not be available to any person who has been convicted of a felony in this or any other state or under federal law and provided, further, that this defense shall not be available if the antique slot machine is on the premises of a private or public club or in an establishment where alcoholic beverages are sold.

(3) Any antique slot machine seized as a result of a violation of this Code section shall be contraband and subject to seizure and destruction as provided in Code Section 16-12-32. An antique slot machine seized for a violation of this Code section shall not be destroyed, altered, or sold until the owner has been afforded a reasonable opportunity to present evidence that the device was not operated for unlawful gambling or in violation of this Code section. If the court determines that the device is an antique slot machine and was not operated or possessed in violation of this or any other Code section, such device shall be returned to its owner.

§ 16-12-25. Solicitation of another to gamble with intent to defraud or deceive

(a) Any person who solicits another person to commit any of the following acts with the intent to defraud or deceive such person on or adjacent to the premises of any business operated for pecuniary gain shall be guilty of a felony and, upon conviction thereof, shall be punished by imprisonment for not less than one nor more than five years:
(1) Keeps, maintains, employs, or carries on a game for the hazarding of money or other thing of value;
(2) Permits the playing for money or other thing of value of a game or device for the hazarding of money or other thing of value;
(3) Keeps or employs a device or equipment for the purpose of carrying on or operating a game or device for the hazarding of money or other thing of value;
(4) Permits the betting or wagering of money or other thing of value;
(5) Sells or offers to sell to a person a ticket number or combination or chance or anything representing a chance in a lottery or other similar scheme;
(6) Keeps, maintains, employs, or carries on a lottery or scheme or device for the hazarding of money or other thing of value;
(7) Keeps, maintains, or employs a lottery ticket, lottery book, lottery ribbon, or other article used in keeping, maintaining, or carrying on a lottery or other scheme, game, or device for the hazarding of money or other thing of value;
(8) Solicits a person to engage in a game or to operate a device for the hazarding of money or other thing of value; or
(9) Solicits a person to engage in a lottery or other scheme or device for the hazarding of money or other thing of value.
(b) This Code section is cumulative of and supplemental to any laws making any of the activities prohibited by this Code section unlawful and punishable as a misdemeanor; and nothing in this Code section shall be construed to repeal, amend, alter, or supersede any such laws.

§ 16-12-26. Advertising commercial gambling

(a) A person who knowingly prints, publishes, or advertises any lottery or other scheme for commercial gambling or who knowingly prints or publishes any lottery ticket, policy ticket, or other similar device designed to serve as evidence of participation in a lottery commits the offense of advertising commercial gambling.
(b) A person who commits the offense of advertising commercial gambling shall be guilty of a misdemeanor of a high and aggravated nature.

§ 16-12-27. Advertisement or solicitation for participation in lotteries

(a) It shall be unlawful for any person, partnership, firm, corporation, or other entity to sell, distribute, televise, broadcast, or disseminate any advertisement, television or radio commercial, or any book, magazine, periodical, newspaper, or other written or printed matter containing an advertisement or solicitation for participation in any lottery declared to be unlawful by the laws of this state unless such advertisement, commercial, or solicitation contains or includes the words "void in Georgia" printed or spoken so as to be clearly legible or audible to persons viewing or hearing such advertisement, commercial, or solicitation.
(b) Any person, partnership, firm, corporation, or other entity violating subsection (a) of this Code section shall be guilty of a misdemeanor.

§ 16-12-28. Communicating gambling information

(a) A person who knowingly communicates information as to bets, betting odds, or changes in betting odds or who knowingly installs or maintains equipment for the transmission or receipt of such information with the intent to further gambling commits the offense of communicating gambling information.
(b) A person who commits the offense of communicating gambling information, upon conviction thereof, shall be punished by imprisonment for not less than one nor more than five years or by a fine not to exceed $5,000.00, or both.

§ 16-12-29. Competent witnesses

On the trial of any person for violating Code Section 16-12-21, 16-12-22, 16-12-23, or 16-12-24, any other person who may have played and bet at the same time or table shall be a competent witness.

§ 16-12-30. Seizure and destruction of gambling devices

Reserved. Repealed by Ga. L. 2015, p. 693, § 2-13/HB 233, effective July 1, 2015.

§ 16-12-32. Civil forfeiture

(a) As used in this Code section, the terms "proceeds," "property," and "United States" shall have the same meanings as set forth in Code Section 9-16-2, and "enterprise" means any person, sole proprietorship, partnership, corporation, trust, association, or other legal entity created under the laws the United States or any foreign nation or a group of individuals associated in fact although not a legal entity and includes illicit as well as licit enterprises and governmental as well as other entities.
(b) The following are declared to be contraband, and no person shall have a property right in them:
(1) Every gambling device except antique slot machines as provided for in subsection (b) of Code Section 16-12-24;
(2) Any property which is, directly or indirectly, used or intended for use in any manner to facilitate a violation of this article and any proceeds;
(3) Any property located in this state which was, directly or indirectly, used or intended for use in any manner to facilitate a violation of this article or of the laws of the United States relating to gambling and any proceeds;
(4) Any interest, security, claim, or property or contractual right of any kind affording a source of influence over any enterprise that a person has established, operated, controlled, conducted, or participated in the conduct of in violation of this article or any of the laws of the United States relating to gambling and any proceeds; and
(5) Any property found in close proximity to any gambling device or other property subject to forfeiture under this Code section.
(c) Any property declared as contraband pursuant to subsection (b) of this Code section shall be forfeited in accordance with the procedures set forth in Chapter 16 of Title 9.

§ 16-12-33. Bribery of a contestant

A person who gives, offers, or promises any reward, money, or other thing of value to anyone who participates or expects to participate in any amateur or professional athletic contest, sporting event, or exhibition or to any coach, trainer, manager or official in such athletic contest, sporting event, or exhibition with intent to influence such person to lose, try to lose, or cause to be lost or to affect the margin of victory or defeat in such athletic contest, sporting event, or exhibition commits the offense of bribery of a contestant and, upon conviction thereof, shall be punished by a fine of not less than $1,000.00 nor more than $5,000.00 or by imprisonment for not less than one nor more than five years, or both.

§ 16-12-34. Soliciting or accepting a bribe to influence outcome of athletic contests, sporting events, or exhibitions

A person participating or expecting to participate or any coach, trainer, manager, or official in any amateur or professional athletic contest, sporting event, or exhibition who solicits or accepts any reward, money, or other thing of value with the intent, understanding, or agreement that it influence him to lose, try to lose, or cause to be lost or to limit the margin of victory or defeat in such athletic contest, sporting event, or exhibition by failing to exert his best efforts or to exercise his best judgment commits the offense of soliciting or accepting a bribe and, upon conviction thereof, shall be punished by a fine of not less than $1,000.00 nor more than $5,000.00 or by imprisonment for not less than one nor more than five years, or both.

§ 16-12-35. Applicability of part; penalty for violation

(a) As used in this Code section, the term "some skill" means any presence of the following factors, alone or in combination with one another:

(1) A learned power of doing a thing competently;

(2) A particular craft, art, ability, strategy, or tactic;

(3) A developed or acquired aptitude or ability;

(4) A coordinated set of actions, including, but not limited to, eye-hand coordination;

(5) Dexterity, fluency, or coordination in the execution of learned physical or mental tasks or both;

(6) Technical proficiency or expertise;

(7) Development or implementation of strategy or tactics in order to achieve a goal; or

(8) Knowledge of the means or methods of accomplishing a task.

The term some skill refers to a particular craft, coordinated effort, art, ability, strategy, or tactic employed by the player to affect in some way the outcome of the game played on a bona fide coin operated amusement machine as defined in paragraph (2) of Code Section 50-27-70. If a player can take no action to affect the outcome of the game, the bona fide coin operated amusement machine does not meet the "some skill" requirement of this Code section.

(b) Nothing in this part shall apply to a coin operated game or device designed and manufactured for bona fide amusement purposes only which may by application of some skill entitle the player to earn replays of the game or device at no additional cost and to discharge the accumulated free replays only by reactivating the game or device for each accumulated free replay or by reactivating the game or device for a portion or all of the accumulated free plays in a single play. This subsection shall not apply, however, to any game or device classified by the United States government as requiring a federal gaming tax stamp under applicable provisions of the Internal Revenue Code or any item described as a gambling device in subparagraph (B), (C), or (D) of paragraph (2) of Code Section 16-12-20.

(c)(1) Nothing in this part shall apply to a crane game machine or device meeting the requirements of paragraph (2) of this subsection.

(2) A crane game machine or device acceptable for the purposes of paragraph (1) of this subsection shall meet the following requirements:

(A) The machine or device must be designed and manufactured only for bona fide amusement purposes and must involve at least some skill in its operation;

(B) The machine or device must reward a winning player exclusively with free replays or merchandise contained within the machine itself and such merchandise must be limited to noncash merchandise, prizes, toys, gift certificates, or novelties, each of which has a wholesale value not exceeding $5.00. A player may be rewarded with both free replays and noncash merchandise, prizes, toys, or novelties for a single play of the game or device as provided in this Code section;

(C) The player of the machine or device must be able to control the timing of the use of the claw or grasping device to attempt to pick up or grasp a prize, toy, or novelty;

(D) The player of the machine or device must be made aware of the total time which the machine or device allows during a game for the player to maneuver the claw or grasping device into a position to attempt to pick up or grasp a prize, toy, or novelty;

(E) The claw or grasping device must not be of a size, design, or shape that prohibits picking up or grasping a prize, toy, or novelty contained within the machine or device; and

(F) The machine or device must not be classified by the United States government as requiring a federal gaming stamp under applicable provisions of the Internal Revenue Code.

(d)(1) Nothing in this part shall apply to a coin operated game or device designed and manufactured only for bona fide amusement purposes which involves some skill in its operation if it rewards the player exclusively with:

(A) Free replays;

(B) Merchandise limited to noncash merchandise, prizes, toys, gift certificates, or novelties, each of which has a wholesale value of not more than $5.00 received for a single play of the game or device;

(C) Points, tokens, vouchers, tickets, or other evidence of winnings which may be exchanged for rewards set out in subparagraph (A) of this paragraph or subparagraph (B) of this paragraph or a combination of rewards set out in subparagraph (A) and subparagraph (B) of this paragraph; or

(D) Any combination of rewards set out in two or more of subparagraph (A), (B), or (C) of this paragraph.

This subsection shall not apply, however, to any game or device classified by the United States government as requiring a federal gaming stamp under applicable provisions of the Internal Revenue Code or any item described as a gambling device in subparagraph (B), (C), or (D) of paragraph (2) of Code Section 16-12-20.

(2) A player of bona fide coin operated amusement games or devices described in paragraph (1) of this subsection may accumulate winnings for the successful play of such bona fide coin operated amusement games or devices through tokens, vouchers, points, or tickets. Points may be accrued on the machine or device. A player may carry over points on one play to subsequent plays. A player may redeem accumulated tokens, vouchers, or tickets for noncash merchandise, prizes, toys, gift certificates, or novelties so long as the amount of tokens, vouchers, or tickets received does not exceed $5.00 for a single play.

(e) Any person who gives to any other person money for free replays on coin operated games or devices described in subsection (b), (c), or (d) of this Code section shall be guilty of a misdemeanor.

(f) Any person owning or possessing an amusement game or device described in subsection (c) or (d) of this Code section or any person employed by or acting on behalf of any such person who gives to any other person money for any noncash merchandise, prize, toy, gift certificate, or novelty received as a reward in playing any such amusement game or device shall be guilty of a misdemeanor.

(g) Any person owning or possessing an amusement game or device described in subsection (b), (c), or (d) of this Code section or any person employed by or acting on behalf of any such person who gives to any other person money as a reward for the successful play or winning of any such amusement game or device shall be guilty of a misdemeanor of a high and aggravated nature.

(g.1) Any location owner or location operator or person employed by a location owner or location operator who violates subsection (h) or (i) of this Code section for the second separate offense shall be guilty of a felony and, upon conviction, shall be punished by imprisonment for not less than one nor more than five years, a fine not to exceed $25,000.00, or both, as well as loss of location license and all other state licenses.

(h) Any gift certificates, tokens, vouchers, tickets, or other evidence of winnings awarded under subsection (c) or (d) of this Code section must be redeemable only at the premises on which the game or device is located. It shall be unlawful for any person to provide to any other person as a reward for play on any such game or device any gift certificate, token, voucher, ticket, or other evidence of winning which is redeemable or exchangeable for any thing of value at any other premises. It shall be unlawful for any person at any premises other than those on which the game or device is located to give any thing of value to any other person for any gift certificate, token, voucher, ticket, or other evidence of winning received by such other person from play on such game or device. Any person who violates this subsection shall be guilty of a misdemeanor of a high and aggravated nature. This subsection shall not apply to any ticket or product of the Georgia Lottery Corporation.

(i) The merchandise, prizes, toys, gift certificates, novelties, or rewards which may be awarded under subsection (c) or (d) of this Code section may not include or be redeemable or exchangeable for any firearms, alcohol, or tobacco. Any person who violates this subsection shall be guilty of a misdemeanor of a high and aggravated nature.

(j) Any other laws to the contrary notwithstanding, this part shall not be applicable to the manufacturing, processing, selling, possessing, or transporting of any printed materials, equipment, devices, or other materials used or designated for use in a legally authorized lottery nor shall it be applicable to the manufacturing, processing, selling, possessing, or transporting of any gaming equipment, devices, or other materials used or designated for use only in jurisdictions in which the use of such items is legal. This part shall in no way prohibit communications between persons in this state and persons involved with such legal lotteries or gaming devices relative to such printed materials, equipment, devices, or other materials or prohibit demonstrations of same within this state.

(k) Any person, location owner, or location operator who places, provides, or displays a bona fide coin operated amusement machine and offers it to play for consideration in Georgia in an establishment for which the location owner or location operator is not licensed or in a private residence shall be guilty of a felony and, upon conviction, shall be punished by imprisonment for not less than one nor more than five years, a fine not to exceed $25,000.00, or both.

§ 16-12-36. Lawful promotional and giveaway contests

(a) A promotional or giveaway contest which conforms with the qualifications of a lawful promotion specified in paragraph (16) of subsection (b) of Code Section 10-1-393 shall not be a lottery.
(b) Except as provided in subsection (a) of this Code section, all promotions or promotional contests involving an element of chance in the distribution of prizes, gifts, awards, or other items which otherwise meet the definition of a "lottery" in this article shall be included within the definition of the term "lottery" for purposes of this article, unless specifically exempted by some other statute or law.

§ 16-12-37. Dogfighting

(a) As used in this Code section, the term "dog" means any domestic canine.
(b) Any person who:
(1) Owns, possesses, trains, transports, or sells any dog with the intent that such dog shall be engaged in fighting with another dog;
(2) For amusement or gain, causes any dog to fight with another dog or for amusement or gain, causes any dogs to injure each other;
(3) Wagers money or anything of value on the result of such dogfighting;
(4) Knowingly permits any act in violation of paragraph (1) or (2) of this subsection on any premises under the ownership or control of such person or knowingly aids or abets any such act; or
(5) Knowingly promotes or advertises an exhibition of fighting with another dog
shall be guilty of a felony and, upon the first conviction thereof, shall be punished by imprisonment of not less than one nor more than five years, a fine of not less than $5,000.00, or both such fine and imprisonment. On a second or subsequent conviction, such person shall be punished by imprisonment of not less than one nor more than ten years, a fine of not less than $15,000.00, or both such fine and imprisonment. Each act or omission in violation of this subsection shall constitute a separate offense.
(c) Any person who is knowingly present only as a spectator at any place for the fighting of dogs shall, upon a first conviction thereof, be guilty of a misdemeanor of a high and aggravated nature. On a second conviction, such person shall be guilty of a felony and shall be punished by imprisonment of not less than one nor more than five years, a fine of not less than $5,000.00, or both such fine and imprisonment. On a third or subsequent conviction, such person shall be punished by imprisonment of not less than one nor more than ten years, a fine of not less than $15,000.00, or both such fine and imprisonment. Each act in violation of this subsection shall constitute a separate offense.
(d) Any dog subject to fighting may be impounded pursuant to the provisions of Code Sections 4-11-9.2 through 4-11-9.6.
(e) This Code section shall not prohibit, impede, or otherwise interfere with animal husbandry, training techniques, competition, events, shows, or practices not otherwise specifically prohibited by law and shall not apply to the following activities:
(1) Owning, using, breeding, training, or equipping any animal to pursue, take, hunt, or recover wildlife or any animal lawfully hunted under Title 27 or participating in hunting or fishing in accordance with the provisions of Title 27 and rules and regulations promulgated pursuant thereto as such rules and regulations existed on the date specified in Code Section 27-1-39;
(2) Owning, using, breeding, training, or equipping dogs to work livestock for agricultural purposes in accordance with the rules and regulations of the Commissioner of Agriculture as such rules and regulations existed on January 1, 2008;
(3) Owning, using, breeding, training, or equipping dogs for law enforcement purposes; or
(4) Owning, using, breeding, training, or equipping any animal to control damage from nuisance or pest species in and around structures or agricultural operations.

§ 16-12-38. Pyramid promotional schemes; exceptions; penalties

(a) As used in this Code section, the term:
(1) "Compensation" means a payment of any money, thing of value, or financial benefit.
(2) "Consideration" means the payment of cash or the purchase of goods, services, or intangible property, and does not include the purchase of goods or services furnished at cost to be used in making sales and not for resale, or time and effort spent in pursuit of sales or recruiting activities.
(3) "Inventory" includes both goods and services, including company produced promotional materials, sales aids, and sales kits that the plan or operation requires independent salespersons to purchase.
(4) "Inventory loading" means that the plan or operation requires or encourages its independent salespersons to purchase inventory in an amount which unreasonably exceeds that which the salesperson can expect to resell for ultimate consumption or to use or consume in a reasonable time period.
(5) "Participant" means a person who joins a plan or operation.
(6) "Person" means an individual, a corporation, a partnership, or any association or unincorporated organization.
(7) "Promote" means to contrive, prepare, establish, plan, operate, advertise, or to otherwise induce or attempt to induce another person to be a participant.
(8) "Pyramid promotional scheme" means any plan or operation in which a participant gives consideration for the right to receive compensation that is derived primarily from the recruitment of other persons as participants into the plan or operation rather than from the sale of goods, services, or intangible property to participants or by participants to others.
(b)(1) No person may establish, promote, operate, or participate in any pyramid promotional scheme. A limitation as to the number of persons who may participate or the presence of additional conditions affecting eligibility for the opportunity to receive compensation under the plan does not change the identity of the plan as a pyramid promotional scheme. It is not a defense under this subsection that a person, on giving consideration, obtains goods, services, or intangible property in addition to the right to receive compensation.
(2) Nothing in this Code section may be construed to prohibit a plan or operation, or to define a plan or operation as a pyramid promotional scheme, based on the fact that participants in the plan or operation give consideration in return for the right to receive compensation based upon purchases of goods, services, or intangible property by participants for personal use, consumption, or resale so long as the plan or operation does not promote or induce inventory loading and complies with the cancellation requirements of subsection (d) of Code Section 10-1-415.
(3) Any person who participates in a pyramid promotional scheme shall be guilty of a misdemeanor of a high and aggravated nature. Any person who establishes, promotes, or operates a pyramid promotional scheme shall be guilty of a felony and, upon conviction thereof, shall be punished by imprisonment for not less than one nor more than five years.
(4) Nothing in this Code section shall be construed so as to include a "multilevel distribution company," as defined in paragraph (6) of Code Section 10-1-410, which is operating in compliance with Part 3 of Article 15 of Chapter 1 of Title 10.

§ 16-12-50. Legislative intent

It is the intention of the General Assembly that, except for recreational bingo, only nonprofit, tax-exempt organizations which are properly licensed pursuant to this part shall be allowed to operate bingo games.

§ 16-12-51. Definitions

As used in this part, the term:
(1) "Bingo game" or "nonprofit bingo game" means a game of chance played on cards with numbered squares in which counters or indicators are placed on numbers chosen by lot and won by covering a previously specified number or order of numbered squares. A bingo game may be played manually or with an electronic or computer device that stores the numbers from a player's card or cards, tracks the numbers chosen by lot when such numbers are entered by the player, and notifies the player of a winning combination; provided, however, that the numbers chosen by

lot shall be chosen by a natural person who is physically located on the premises or property described in Code Section 16-12-57 on which the game is operated. Such words, terms, or phrases, as used in this paragraph, shall be strictly construed to include only the series of acts generally defined as bingo and shall exclude all other activity.

(2) "Bingo session" means a time period during which bingo games are played.

(3) "Director" means the director of the Georgia Bureau of Investigation.

(3.1) "Nonprofit, tax-exempt organization" means an organization, association, corporation, or other legal entity which has been determined by the federal Internal Revenue Service to be exempt from taxation under federal tax law and which is exempt from taxation under the income tax laws of this state under Code Section 48-7-25; which is organized or incorporated in this state or authorized to do business in this state; and which uses the proceeds from any bingo games conducted by such organization solely within this state.

(4) "Operate," "operated," or "operating" means the direction, supervision, management, operation, control, or guidance of activity.

(5) "Recreational bingo" means a bingo session operated by any person or entity at no charge to participants in which the prizes for each bingo game during the bingo session shall be noncash prizes and the total of such prizes for each such game shall not exceed the amount established pursuant to regulations established by the director. No such noncash prize awarded in recreational bingo shall be exchanged or redeemed for money or for any other prize with a value in excess of the amount established pursuant to regulations established by the director. Recreational bingo shall also include a bingo session operated by a nonprofit, tax-exempt licensed operator of bingo games at no charge to participants in which the participants are senior citizens attending a function at a facility of the tax-exempt licensed organization or are residents of nursing homes, retirement homes, senior centers, or hospitals and in which the prizes for each bingo game during the bingo session shall be nominal cash prizes not to exceed $5.00 for any single prize and the total of such prizes for each such game shall not exceed the amount established pursuant to regulations established by the director. Recreational bingo shall also include a bingo session operated by an employer with ten or more full-time employees for the purposes of providing a safe workplace incentive and in which the prizes are determined by the employer; provided, however, that no monetary consideration is required by any participant other than the employer and the employer expressly prohibits any monetary consideration from any employee. Recreational bingo shall not be considered a lottery as defined in paragraph (4) of Code Section 16-12-20 or a form of gambling as defined in Code Section 16-12-21.

§ 16-12-52. License required to operate bingo game; recreational bingo exception

(a) Any other law to the contrary notwithstanding except for subsection (b) of this Code section, no nonprofit, tax-exempt organization shall be permitted to operate a bingo game until the director issues a license to the organization authorizing it to do so. In the event of any controversy concerning whether or not certain activity constitutes bingo for which a license may be issued, the decision of the director shall control. The license described in this Code section is in addition to and not in lieu of any other licenses which may be required by this state or any political subdivision thereof, and no bingo game shall be operated until such time as all requisite licenses have been obtained.

(b) Recreational bingo is a nonprofit bingo game or a bingo game operated by an employer with ten or more full-time employees for the purpose of providing a safe workplace incentive and shall not be subject to the licensing requirements and regulations provided in this part applicable to bingo games not considered recreational bingo and operated by nonprofit, tax-exempt organizations.

§ 16-12-53. Licensing procedure; fee; renewal

(a) Any nonprofit, tax-exempt organization desiring to obtain a license to operate bingo games shall make application to the director on forms prescribed by the Georgia Bureau of Investigation and shall pay an annual fee of $100.00. No license shall be issued to any nonprofit, tax-exempt organization unless the organization has been in existence for 12 months immediately prior to the issuance of the license. The license will expire at 12:00 Midnight on December 31 following the granting of the license. Renewal applications for each calendar year shall be filed with the director prior to January 1 of each year and shall be on a form prescribed by the Georgia Bureau of Investigation.

(b) Each application for a license and each application for renewal of a license shall contain the following information:

(1) The name and home address of the applicant and, if the applicant is a corporation, association, or other similar legal entity, the names and home addresses of each of the officers of the organization as well as the names and addresses of the directors, or other persons similarly situated, of the organization;

(2) The names and home addresses of each of the persons who will be operating, advertising, or promoting the bingo game;

(3) The names and home addresses of any persons, organizations, or other legal entities that will act as surety for the applicant or to which the applicant is financially indebted or to which any financial obligation is owed by the applicant;

(4) A determination letter from the Internal Revenue Service certifying that the applicant is an organization exempt under federal tax law;

(5) A statement affirming that the applicant is exempt under the income tax laws of this state under Code Section 48-7-25;

(6) The location at which the applicant will conduct the bingo games and, if the premises on which the games are to be conducted is to be leased, a copy of the lease or rental agreement;

(7) A statement showing the convictions, if any, for criminal offenses other than minor traffic offenses of each of the persons listed in paragraphs (1), (2), and (3) of this subsection; and

(8) Any other necessary and reasonable information which the director may require.

(c) The director shall refuse to grant a bingo license to any applicant who fails to provide fully the information required by this Code section.

(d) When a nonprofit, tax-exempt organization which operates or intends to operate bingo games for residents and patients of a retirement home, nursing home, or hospital operated by that organization at which gross receipts are or will be limited to $100.00 or less during each bingo session and pays or will pay prizes having a value of $100.00 or less during each bingo session, then, notwithstanding any other provision of this part or any rule or regulation promulgated by the director pursuant to the provisions of Code Section 16-12-61, neither the applicant nor any of the persons whose names and addresses are required under paragraphs (1) and (2) of subsection (b) of this Code section shall be required to submit or provide fingerprints or photographs as a condition of being granted a license.

(e) If the director determines that an organization has one or more auxiliaries, the members of any such auxiliary may assist in such organization's bingo operations, even if such auxiliary holds a license under this part, and the members of the main organization may assist in the bingo operations of any such licensed auxiliary.

§ 16-12-54. Revocation of licenses; access to premises by law enforcement agencies

(a) The director shall have the specific authority to suspend or revoke any license for any violation of this part or for any violation of any rule or regulation promulgated under this part. Any licensee accused of violating any provision of this part or of any rule or regulation promulgated hereunder shall be entitled, unless waived, to a hearing on the matter of the alleged violation conducted in accordance with Chapter 13 of Title 50, the "Georgia Administrative Procedure Act."

(b) By making application for a license under this part, every applicant consents that the director, as well as any of his agents, together with any prosecuting attorney, as well as any of his agents, may come upon the premises of any licensee or upon any premises on which any licensee is conducting a bingo game for the purpose of examining the accounts and records of the licensee to determine if a violation of this part has occurred.

§ 16-12-55. Certification of tax-exempt status of organization; issuance of certificate of licensure.

The director shall upon the request of any prosecuting attorney or his or her designee certify the status of any organization as to that organization's exemption from payment of state income taxes as a nonprofit organization. The director shall also upon request issue a certificate indicating whether any particular organization holds a currently valid license to operate a bingo game. Code Section 48-7-60, relative to the disclosure of income tax information, shall not apply to the furnishing of such certificate.

§ 16-12-56. Issuance of annual one-day license to nonprofit, tax-exempt school; application

Notwithstanding the other provisions of this part, the director upon receiving written application therefor shall be authorized to issue a one-time license to a nonprofit, tax-exempt school which will allow it to operate a bingo game one day annually. In such cases, the director shall have the power to waive the license fee provided for in Code Section 16-12-53, to waive the annual report provided for in Code Section 16-12-59, and otherwise promulgate rules and regulations to carry out this Code section.

§ 16-12-57. Restrictions as to ownership of premises utilized

Bingo games shall be operated only on premises owned by the nonprofit, tax-exempt organization operating the bingo game, on property leased by the nonprofit, tax-exempt organization and used regularly by that organization for purposes other than the operation of a bingo game, or on property leased by the nonprofit, tax-exempt organization operating the bingo game from another nonprofit, tax-exempt organization.

§ 16-12-58. Age restrictions

No person under the age of 18 years shall be permitted to play any game or games of bingo conducted pursuant to any license issued under this part unless accompanied by an adult. No person under the age of 18 years shall be permitted to conduct or assist in the conducting of any game of bingo conducted pursuant to any license issued under this part.

§ 16-12-59. Annual report to be filed with the director

On or before April 15 of each year, every nonprofit, tax-exempt organization engaged in operating bingo games shall file with the director a report disclosing all receipts and expenditures relating to the operation of bingo games in the previous year. The report shall be in addition to all other reports required by law. The report shall be prepared and signed by a certified public accountant competent to prepare such a report and shall be deemed a public record subject to public inspection.

§ 16-12-60. Rules and regulations

(a) A licensee that conducts or operates a bingo session shall maintain the following records for at least three years from the date on which the bingo session is conducted:
(1) An itemized list of the gross receipts for each session;
(2) An itemized list of all expenses other than prizes that are incurred in the conducting of the bingo session as well as the name of each person to whom the expenses are paid and a receipt for all of the expenses;
(3) A list of all prizes awarded during the bingo session and the name and address of all persons who are winners of prizes of $50.00 or more in value;
(4) An itemized list of the recipients other than the licensee of the proceeds of the bingo game, including the name and address of each recipient to whom such funds are distributed; and
(5) A record of the number of persons who participate in any bingo session conducted by the licensee.
(b) A licensee shall:
(1) Own all the equipment used to conduct a bingo game or lease such equipment;
(2) Display its bingo license conspicuously at the location where the bingo game is conducted;
(3) Conduct bingo games only at the single location specified in the licensee's application; and
(4) Not conduct more than one bingo session during any one calendar day, which session shall not exceed five hours.
(c) No nonprofit, tax-exempt organization shall enter into any contract with any individual, firm, association, or corporation to have such individual, firm, association, or corporation operate bingo games or concessions on behalf of the nonprofit, tax-exempt organization.
(d) A nonprofit, tax-exempt organization shall not lend its name nor allow its identity to be used by any individual, firm, association, or corporation in the operating or advertising of a bingo game in which said nonprofit, tax-exempt organization is not directly and solely operating the bingo game.
(e) It shall be unlawful for two or more nonprofit, tax-exempt organizations which are properly licensed pursuant to this part to operate bingo games jointly or to operate bingo games upon the same premises during any 18 hour period.
(f) It shall be unlawful to award prizes in excess of $3,000.00 in cash or gifts of equivalent value during any calendar week. It shall be unlawful to exceed such limitation at any combination of locations operated by a single licensee or such licensee's agents or employees. It shall be unlawful for two or more licensees to pyramid the valuation of prizes in such manner as to exceed the limitation contained in this Code section. The term "equivalent value" shall mean the fair market value of the gift on the date the gift is given as the prize in a bingo game.
(g) No person or organization by whatever name or composition thereof shall take any salary, expense money, or fees for the operation of any bingo game, except that not more than $30.00 per day may be paid to one or more individuals for assisting in the conduct of such games on such day.
(h) No person shall pay consulting fees to any person for any services performed in relation to the operation or conduct of a bingo game.
(i) A person who is a member of more than one nonprofit, tax-exempt organization shall be permitted to participate in the bingo operations of only two organizations of which such person is a member; provided, however, that such person shall not receive more than $30.00 per day for assisting in the conduct of bingo games regardless of whether such person assists both organizations in the same day.

§ 16-12-61. Promulgation of necessary rules and regulations by director authorized

The director is authorized to promulgate rules and regulations which he deems necessary for the proper administration and enforcement of this part.

§ 16-12-62. Penalties

Any person who operates a bingo game for which a license is required without a valid license issued by the director as provided in this part commits the offense of commercial gambling as defined in Code Section 16-12-22 and, upon conviction thereof, shall be punished accordingly. Any person who knowingly aids, abets, or otherwise assists in the operation of a bingo game for which a license is required and has not been obtained as provided in this part similarly commits the offense of commercial gambling. Any person who violates any other provision of this part, including the provisions relating to recreational bingo, shall be guilty of a misdemeanor of a high and aggravated nature. Any person who commits any such violation after having previously been convicted of any violations of this part shall be guilty of a felony and, upon conviction thereof, shall be punished by imprisonment for not less than one nor more than five years or by a fine not to exceed $10,000.00, or both.

§ 16-12-80. Distributing obscene material; obscene material defined; penalty

(a) A person commits the offense of distributing obscene material when he sells, lends, rents, leases, gives, advertises, publishes, exhibits, or otherwise disseminates to any person any obscene material of any description, knowing the obscene nature thereof, or offers to do so, or possesses such material with the intent to do so, provided that the word "knowing," as used in this Code section, shall be deemed to be either actual or constructive knowledge of the obscene contents of the subject matter; and a person has constructive knowledge of the obscene contents if he has knowledge of facts which would put a reasonable and prudent person on notice as to the suspect nature of the material; provided, however, that the character and reputation of the individual charged with an offense under this law, and, if a commercial dissemination of obscene material is involved, the character and reputation of the business establishment involved may be placed in evidence by the defendant on the question of intent to violate this law. Undeveloped photographs, molds, printing plates, and the like shall be deemed obscene notwithstanding that processing or other acts may be required to make the obscenity patent or to disseminate it.
(b) Material is obscene if:
(1) To the average person, applying contemporary community standards, taken as a whole, it predominantly appeals to the prurient interest, that is, a shameful or morbid interest in nudity, sex, or excretion;
(2) The material taken as a whole lacks serious literary, artistic, political, or scientific value; and
(3) The material depicts or describes, in a patently offensive way, sexual conduct specifically defined in subparagraphs (A) through (E) of this paragraph:

(A) Acts of sexual intercourse, heterosexual or homosexual, normal or perverted, actual or simulated;

(B) Acts of masturbation;

(C) Acts involving excretory functions or lewd exhibition of the genitals;

(D) Acts of bestiality or the fondling of sex organs of animals; or

(E) Sexual acts of flagellation, torture, or other violence indicating a sadomasochistic sexual relationship.

(c) Any device designed or marketed as useful primarily for the stimulation of human genital organs is obscene material under this Code section.

(d) Material not otherwise obscene may be obscene under this Code section if the distribution thereof, the offer to do so, or the possession with the intent to do so is a commercial exploitation of erotica solely for the sake of their prurient appeal.

(e) It is an affirmative defense under this Code section that dissemination of the material was restricted to:

(1) A person associated with an institution of higher learning, either as a member of the faculty or a matriculated student, teaching or pursuing a course of study related to such material; or

(2) A person whose receipt of such material was authorized in writing by a licensed medical practitioner or psychiatrist.

(f) A person who commits the offense of distributing obscene material shall be guilty of a misdemeanor of a high and aggravated nature.

§ 16-12-81. Distribution of material depicting nudity or sexual conduct; penalty

(a) A person commits the offense of distributing material depicting nudity or sexual conduct when he sends unsolicited through the mail or otherwise unsolicited causes to be delivered material depicting nudity or sexual conduct to any person or residence or office unless there is imprinted upon the envelope or container of such material in not less than eight-point boldface type the following notice:

"Notice -- The material contained herein depicts nudity or sexual conduct. If the viewing of such material could be offensive to the addressee, this container should not be opened but returned to the sender."

(b) As used within this Code section, the term:

(1) "Nudity" means the showing of the human male or female genitals, pubic area, or buttocks with less than a full opaque covering or the depiction of covered male genitals in a discernibly turgid state.

(2) "Sexual conduct" means acts of masturbation, homosexuality, sodomy, sexual intercourse, or physical contact with a person's clothed or unclothed genitals, pubic area, buttocks, or, if the person is female, breast.

(c) A person who commits the offense of distributing material depicting nudity or sexual conduct, upon conviction thereof, shall be punished by imprisonment for not less than one nor more than three years or by a fine not to exceed $10,000.00, or both.

§ 16-12-82. Public nuisances

The use of any premises in violation of any of the provisions of this part shall constitute a public nuisance.

§ 16-12-83. Contraband

Any materials declared to be obscene by this part and advertisements for such materials are declared to be contraband.

§ 16-12-84. Public indecency in plays, nightclub acts, and motion pictures

Reserved. Repealed by Ga. L. 1981, p. 915, § 1, effective April 9, 1981.

§ 16-12-85. Display of restricted film previews to general audiences

(a) It shall be unlawful for any motion picture theater owner, operator, or projectionist to display to the audience within the theater scenes from a film to be shown at the theater at some future time when the viewing of that film from which the scenes are taken is restricted to adults or requires minors to be accompanied by a parent or guardian. Scenes of such restricted films may be shown within a theater if the audience has been similarly restricted as to viewing age and conditions.

(b) This Code section shall not apply to motion pictures which are not rated as to viewing audience nor to the first display of a preview trailer from any motion picture.

(c) Any person who violates subsection (a) of this Code section shall be guilty of a misdemeanor.

§ 16-12-100. Sexual exploitation of children; reporting violation; civil forfeiture; penalties

(a) As used in this Code section, the term:

(1) "Minor" means any person under the age of 18 years.

(2) "Performance" means any play, dance, or exhibit to be shown to or viewed by an audience.

(3) "Producing" means producing, directing, manufacturing, issuing, or publishing.

(4) "Sexually explicit conduct" means actual or simulated:

(A) Sexual intercourse, including genital-genital, oral-genital, anal-genital, or oral-anal, whether between persons of the same or opposite sex;

(B) Bestiality;

(C) Masturbation;

(D) Lewd exhibition of the genitals or pubic area of any person;

(E) Flagellation or torture by or upon a person who is nude;

(F) Condition of being fettered, bound, or otherwise physically restrained on the part of a person who is nude;

(G) Physical contact in an act of apparent sexual stimulation or gratification with any person's unclothed genitals, pubic area, or buttocks or with a female's nude breasts;

(H) Defecation or urination for the purpose of sexual stimulation of the viewer; or

(I) Penetration of the vagina or rectum by any object except when done as part of a recognized medical procedure.

(5) "Visual medium" means any film, photograph, negative, slide, magazine, or other visual medium.

(b) (1) It is unlawful for any person knowingly to employ, use, persuade, induce, entice, or coerce any minor to engage in or assist any other person to engage in any sexually explicit conduct for the purpose of producing any visual medium depicting such conduct.

(2) It is unlawful for any parent, legal guardian, or person having custody or control of a minor knowingly to permit the minor to engage in or to assist any other person to engage in sexually explicit conduct for the purpose of producing any visual medium depicting such conduct.

(3) It is unlawful for any person knowingly to employ, use, persuade, induce, entice, or coerce any minor to engage in or assist any other person to engage in any sexually explicit conduct for the purpose of any performance.

(4) It is unlawful for any parent, legal guardian, or person having custody or control of a minor knowingly to permit the minor to engage in or to assist any other person to engage in sexually explicit conduct for the purpose of any performance.

(5) It is unlawful for any person knowingly to create, reproduce, publish, promote, sell, distribute, give, exhibit, or possess with intent to sell or distribute any visual medium which depicts a minor or a portion of a minor's body engaged in any sexually explicit conduct.

(6) It is unlawful for any person knowingly to advertise, sell, purchase, barter, or exchange any medium which provides information as to where any visual medium which depicts a minor or a portion of a minor's body engaged in any sexually explicit conduct can be found or purchased.

(7) It is unlawful for any person knowingly to bring or cause to be brought into this state any material which depicts a minor or a portion of a minor's body engaged in any sexually explicit conduct.

(8) It is unlawful for any person knowingly to possess or control any material which depicts a minor or a portion of a minor's body engaged in any sexually explicit conduct.

(c) A person who, in the course of processing or producing visual or printed matter either privately or commercially, has reasonable cause to believe that the visual or printed matter submitted for processing or producing depicts a minor engaged in sexually explicit conduct shall immediately report such incident, or cause a report to be made, to the Georgia Bureau of Investigation or the law enforcement agency for the county in which such matter is submitted. Any person participating in the making of a report or causing a report to be made pursuant to this subsection or participating in any judicial proceeding or any other proceeding resulting therefrom shall in so doing be immune from any civil or criminal liability that might otherwise be incurred or imposed, providing such participation pursuant to this subsection is made in good faith.

(d) The provisions of subsection (b) of this Code section shall not apply to:

(1) The activities of law enforcement and prosecution agencies in the investigation and prosecution of criminal offenses;

(2) Legitimate medical, scientific, or educational activities; or

(3) Any person who creates or possesses a visual medium depicting only himself or herself engaged in sexually explicit conduct.

(e) (1) As used in this subsection, the terms "proceeds" and "property" shall have the same meaning as set forth in Code Section 9-16-2.

(2) Any property which is, directly or indirectly, used or intended to be used in any manner to facilitate a violation of this Code section and any proceeds are declared to be contraband and no person shall have a property right in them.

(3) Any property subject to forfeiture pursuant to paragraph (2) of this subsection shall be forfeited in accordance with the procedures set forth in Chapter 16 of Title 9.

(f) (1) Except as otherwise provided in paragraphs (2) and (3) of this subsection, any person who violates a provision of this Code section shall be guilty of a felony and, upon conviction thereof, shall be punished by imprisonment for not less than five nor more than 20 years and by a fine of not more than $100,000.00; provided, however, that if the person so convicted is a member of the immediate family of the victim, no fine shall be imposed. Any person punished as provided in this paragraph shall, in addition, be subject to the sentencing and punishment provisions of Code Section 17-10-6.2.

(2) Any person who violates subsection (c) of this Code section shall be guilty of a misdemeanor.

(3) Any person who violates paragraph (1), (5), (7), or (8) of subsection (b) of this Code section shall be guilty of a misdemeanor if:

(A) The minor depicted was at least 14 years of age at the time the visual medium was created;

(B) The visual medium was created with the permission of the minor depicted; and

(C) The defendant was 18 years of age or younger at the time of the offense and:

(i) The defendant's violation of such paragraphs did not involve the distribution of such visual medium to another person; or

(ii) In the court's discretion, and when the prosecuting attorney and the defendant have agreed, if the defendant's violation of such paragraphs involved the distribution of such visual medium to another person but such distribution was not for the purpose of:

(I) Harassing, intimidating, or embarrassing the minor depicted; or

(II) For any commercial purpose.

§ 16-12-100.1. Electronically furnishing obscene material to minors

(a) As used in this Code section, the term:

(1) "Bulletin board system" means a computer data and file service that is accessed wirelessly or by physical connection to store and transmit information.

(2) "CD-ROM" means a compact disc with read only memory which has the capacity to store audio, video, and written materials and is used by computers to reveal the above-said material.

(3) "Electronically furnishes" means:

(A) To make available by electronic storage device, including floppy disks and other magnetic storage devices, or by CD-ROM; or

(B) To make available by allowing access to information stored in a computer, including making material available by operating a computer bulletin board system.

(4) "Harmful to minors" means that quality of description or representation, in whatever form, of nudity, sexual conduct, sexual excitement, or sadomasochistic abuse, when it:

(A) Taken as a whole, predominantly appeals to the prurient, shameful, or morbid interest of minors;

(B) Is patently offensive to prevailing standards in the adult community as a whole with respect to what is suitable material for minors; and

(C) Is, when taken as a whole, lacking in serious literary, artistic, political, or scientific value for minors.

(5) "Minor" means an unmarried person younger than 18 years of age.

(6) "Sadomasochistic abuse" means flagellation or torture by or upon a person who is nude or clad in undergarments or in revealing or bizarre costume or the condition of being fettered, bound, or otherwise physically restrained on the part of one so clothed.

(7) "Sexual conduct" means human masturbation, sexual intercourse, or any touching of the genitals, pubic areas, or buttocks of the human male or female or the breasts of the female, whether alone or between members of the same or opposite sex or between humans and animals in an act of apparent sexual stimulation or gratification.

(8) "Sexual excitement" means the condition of human male or female genitals or the breasts of the female when in a state of sexual stimulation.

(b) A person commits the crime of electronically furnishing obscene materials to minors if:

(1) Knowing or having good reason to know the character of the material furnished, the person electronically furnishes to an individual whom the person knows or should have known is a minor:

(A) Any picture, photograph, drawing, or similar visual representation or image of a person or portion of a human body which depicts sexually explicit nudity, sexual conduct, or sadomasochistic abuse and which is harmful to minors; or

(B) Any written or aural matter that contains material of the nature described in subparagraph (A) of this paragraph or contains explicit verbal descriptions or narrative accounts of sexual conduct, sexual excitement, or sadomasochistic abuse;

(2) The offensive portions of the material electronically furnished to the minor are not merely an incidental part of an otherwise nonoffending whole;

(3) The material furnished to the minor, taken as a whole, lacks serious literary, artistic, political, or scientific value; and

(4) The material furnished to the minor, taken as a whole, is harmful to minors in that it appeals to and incites prurient interest.

(c) Except as provided in subsection (d) of this Code section, any person who violates this Code section shall be guilty of a misdemeanor of a high and aggravated nature.

(d) Any person who violates this Code section shall be guilty of a misdemeanor if:

(1) At the time of the offense, the minor receiving the obscene materials was at least 14 years of age;

(2) The receipt of the materials was with the permission of the minor; and

(3) The defendant was 18 years of age or younger.

§ 16-12-100.2. Computer or electronic pornography and child exploitation prevention

(a) This Code section shall be known and may be cited as the "Computer or Electronic Pornography and Child Exploitation Prevention Act of 2007."

(b) As used in this Code section, the term:

(1) "Child" means any person under the age of 16 years.

(2) "Electronic device" means any device used for the purpose of communicating with a child for sexual purposes or any device used to visually depict a child engaged in sexually explicit conduct, store any image or audio of a child engaged in sexually explicit conduct, or transmit any audio or visual image of a child for sexual purposes. Such term may include, but shall not be limited to, a computer, cellular phone, thumb drive, video game system, or any other electronic device that can be used in furtherance of exploiting a child for sexual purposes;

(3) "Identifiable child" means a person:

(A) Who was a child at the time the visual depiction was created, adapted, or modified or whose image as a child was used in creating, adapting, or modifying the visual depiction; and

(B) Who is recognizable as an actual person by the person's face, likeness, or other distinguishing characteristic, such as a unique birthmark or other recognizable feature or by electronic or scientific means as may be available.

The term shall not be construed to require proof of the actual identity of the child.

(4) "Sadomasochistic abuse" has the same meaning as provided in Code Section 16-12-100.1.

(5) "Sexual conduct" has the same meaning as provided in Code Section 16-12-100.1.

(6) "Sexual excitement" has the same meaning as provided in Code Section 16-12-100.1.

(7) "Sexually explicit nudity" has the same meaning as provided in Code Section 16-12-102.

(8) "Visual depiction" means any image and includes undeveloped film and video tape and data stored on computer disk or by electronic means which is capable of conversion into a visual image or which has been created, adapted, or modified to show an identifiable child engaged in sexually explicit conduct.

(c) (1) A person commits the offense of computer or electronic pornography if such person intentionally or willfully:

(A) Compiles, enters into, or transmits by computer or other electronic device;

(B) Makes, prints, publishes, or reproduces by other computer or other electronic device;

(C) Causes or allows to be entered into or transmitted by computer or other electronic device; or

(D) Buys, sells, receives, exchanges, or disseminates

any notice, statement, or advertisement, or any child's name, telephone number, place of residence, physical characteristics, or other descriptive or identifying information for the purpose of offering or soliciting sexual conduct of or with an identifiable child or the visual depiction of such conduct.

(2) Except as provided in paragraphs (3) and (4) of this subsection, any person convicted of violating paragraph (1) of this subsection shall be punished by a fine of not more than $10,000.00 and by imprisonment for not less than one nor more than 20 years.

(3) Any person who violates paragraph (1) of this subsection shall be guilty of a misdemeanor if:

(A) At the time of the offense, any identifiable child visually depicted was at least 14 years of age when the visual depiction was created;

(B) The visual depiction was created with the permission of such child;

(C) The defendant possessed the visual depiction with the permission of such child; and

(D) The defendant was 18 years of age or younger at the time of the offense and:

(i) The defendant did not distribute the visual depiction to another person; or

(ii) In the court's discretion, and when the prosecuting attorney and the defendant have agreed, if the defendant's violation involved the distribution of such visual depiction to another person but such distribution was not for the purpose of:

(I) Harassing, intimidating, or embarrassing the minor depicted; or

(II) For any commercial purpose.

(4) The prohibition contained in paragraph (1) of this subsection shall not apply to any person who creates or possesses a visual depiction of only himself or herself.

(d) (1) It shall be unlawful for any person intentionally or willfully to utilize a computer wireless service or Internet service, including, but not limited to, a local bulletin board service, Internet chat room, e-mail, instant messaging service, or other electronic device, to seduce, solicit, lure, or entice, or attempt to seduce, solicit, lure, or entice a child, another person believed by such person to be a child, any person having custody or control of a child, or another person believed by such person to have custody or control of a child to commit any illegal act by, with, or against a child as described in Code Section 16-6-2, relating to the offense of sodomy or aggravated sodomy; Code Section 16-6-4, relating to the offense of child molestation or aggravated child molestation; Code Section 16-6-5, relating to the offense of enticing a child for indecent purposes; or Code Section 16-6-8, relating to the offense of public indecency, or to engage in any conduct that by its nature is an unlawful sexual offense against a child.

(2) Any person who violates paragraph (1) of this subsection shall be guilty of a felony and, upon conviction thereof, shall be punished by imprisonment for not less than one nor more than 20 years and by a fine of not more than $25,000.00; provided, however, that if at the time of the offense the victim was at least 14 years of age and the defendant was 18 years of age or younger, then the defendant shall be guilty of a misdemeanor.

(e) (1) A person commits the offense of obscene Internet contact with a child if he or she has contact with someone he or she knows to be a child or with someone he or she believes to be a child via a computer wireless service or Internet service, including, but not limited to, a local bulletin board service, Internet chat room, e-mail, or instant messaging service, and the contact involves any matter containing explicit verbal descriptions or narrative accounts of sexually explicit nudity, sexual conduct, sexual excitement, or sadomasochistic abuse that is intended to arouse or satisfy the sexual desire of either the child or the person, provided that no conviction shall be had for a violation of this subsection on the unsupported testimony of a child.

(2) Any person who violates paragraph (1) of this subsection shall be guilty of a felony and, upon conviction thereof, shall be punished by imprisonment for not less than one nor more than ten years or by a fine of not more than $10,000.00; provided, however, that if at the time of the offense the victim was at least 14 years of age and the defendant was 18 years of age or younger, then the defendant shall be guilty of a misdemeanor.

(f) (1) It shall be unlawful for any owner or operator of a computer online service, Internet service, local bulletin board service, or other electronic device that is in the business of providing a service that may be used to sexually exploit a child to intentionally or willfully to permit a subscriber to utilize the service to commit a violation of this Code section, knowing that such person intended to utilize such service to violate this Code section. No owner or operator of a public computer online service, Internet service, local bulletin board service, or other electronic device that is in the business of providing a service that may be used to sexually exploit a child shall be held liable on account of any action taken in good faith in providing the aforementioned services.

(2) Any person who violates paragraph (1) of this subsection shall be guilty of a misdemeanor of a high and aggravated nature.

(g) The sole fact that an undercover operative or law enforcement officer was involved in the detection and investigation of an offense under this Code section shall not constitute a defense to prosecution under this Code section.

(h) A person is subject to prosecution in this state pursuant to Code Section 17-2-1, relating to jurisdiction over crimes and persons charged with commission of crimes generally, for any conduct made unlawful by this Code section which the person engages in while:

(1) Either within or outside of this state if, by such conduct, the person commits a violation of this Code section which involves a child who resides in this state or another person believed by such person to be a child residing in this state; or

(2) Within this state if, by such conduct, the person commits a violation of this Code section which involves a child who resides within or outside this state or another person believed by such person to be a child residing within or outside this state.

(i) Any violation of this Code section shall constitute a separate offense.

§ 16-12-100.3. Obscene telephone contact; conviction; penalties

(a) As used in this Code section, the terms "sexual conduct," "sexual excitement," and "sadomasochistic abuse" have the same meanings as provided for those terms in Code Section 16-12-100.1, relating to electronically furnishing obscene materials to minors; the term "sexually explicit nudity" has the same meaning as provided for that term in Code Section 16-12-102, relating to distributing harmful materials to minors; and the term "child" means a person under 14 years of age.

(b) A person 17 years of age or over commits the offense of obscene telephone contact with a child if that person has telephone contact with an individual whom that person knows or should have known is a child, and that contact involves any aural matter containing explicit verbal descriptions or narrative accounts of sexually explicit nudity, sexual conduct, sexual excitement, or sadomasochistic abuse which is intended to arouse or satisfy the sexual desire of either the child or the person, provided that no conviction shall be had for this offense on the unsupported testimony of the victim.

(c)(1) Except as otherwise provided in other paragraphs of this subsection, a person convicted of the offense of obscene telephone contact with a child shall be guilty of a misdemeanor of a high and aggravated nature.

(2) Upon the first conviction of the offense of obscene telephone contact with a child:

(A) If the person convicted is less than 21 years of age, such person shall be guilty of a misdemeanor; or

(B) The judge may probate the sentence without regard to the age of the convicted person, and such probation may be upon the special condition that the defendant undergo a mandatory period of counseling administered by a licensed psychiatrist or a licensed psychologist. However, if the judge finds that such probation should not be imposed, the judge shall sentence the defendant to imprisonment; provided, further, that upon a defendant's being incarcerated on a conviction for such first offense, the place of incarceration shall provide counseling to such defendant.

(3) Upon a second or subsequent conviction of such offense, the defendant shall be guilty of a felony and punished by imprisonment for not less than one nor more than five years.

§ 16-12-101. Legislative purpose

The General Assembly finds that the sale, loan, and exhibition of harmful materials to minors has become a matter of increasingly grave concern to the people of this state. The elimination of such sales, loans, and exhibition and the consequent protection of minors from harmful materials are in the best interest of the morals and general welfare of the citizens of this state in general and of minors in this state in particular. The accomplishment of these ends can best be achieved by providing public prosecutors with an effective power to commence criminal proceedings against persons who engage in the sale, loan, or exhibition of harmful materials to minors.

§ 16-12-102. Definitions

As used in this part, the term:

(1) "Harmful to minors" means that quality of description or representation, in whatever form, of nudity, sexual conduct, sexual excitement, or sadomasochistic abuse, when it:

(A) Taken as a whole, predominantly appeals to the prurient, shameful, or morbid interest of minors;

(B) Is patently offensive to prevailing standards in the adult community as a whole with respect to what is suitable material for minors; and

(C) Is, when taken as a whole, lacking in serious literary, artistic, political, or scientific value for minors.

(2) "Knowingly" means having a general knowledge of, or reason to know, or a belief or ground for belief which warrants further inspection or inquiry of both:

(A) The character and content of any material described in this part which is reasonably susceptible to examination by the defendant; and

(B) The age of the minor; provided, however, that an honest mistake shall constitute an excuse from liability in this part if the defendant made a reasonable, bona fide attempt to ascertain the true age of such minor.

(3) "Minor" means a person less than 18 years of age.

(4) "Sadomasochistic abuse" means actual or simulated flagellation or torture by or upon a person who is nude, clad in undergarments, a mask or bizarre costume, or the condition of being fettered, bound, or otherwise physically restrained by one so clothed or nude.

(5) "Sexual conduct" means actual or simulated acts of masturbation, homosexuality, sexual intercourse, or physical contact in an act of apparent sexual stimulation or gratification with a person's clothed or unclothed genitals, pubic area, buttocks, or, if such person is female, breasts.

(6) "Sexual excitement" means the condition of human male or female genitals when in a state of sexual stimulation or arousal.

(7) "Sexually explicit nudity" means a state of undress so as to expose the human male or female genitals, pubic area, or buttocks with less than a full opaque covering, or the showing of the female breast with less than a fully opaque covering of any portion thereof below the top of the nipple, or the depiction of covered or uncovered male genitals in a discernibly turgid state.

§ 16-12-103. Selling, loaning, distributing, or exhibiting; duties of video game retailers

(a) It shall be unlawful for any person knowingly to sell or loan for monetary consideration or otherwise furnish or disseminate to a minor:

(1) Any picture, photograph, drawing, sculpture, motion picture film, or similar visual representation or image of a person or portion of the human body which depicts sexually explicit nudity, sexual conduct, or sadomasochistic abuse and which is harmful to minors; or

(2) Any book, pamphlet, magazine, printed matter however reproduced, or sound recording which contains any matter enumerated in paragraph (1) of this subsection, or explicit and detailed verbal descriptions or narrative accounts of sexual excitement, sexual conduct, or sadomasochistic abuse and which, taken as a whole, is harmful to minors.

(b)(1) It shall be unlawful for any person knowingly to sell or furnish to a minor an admission ticket or pass or knowingly to admit a minor to premises whereon there is exhibited a motion picture, show, or other presentation which, in whole or in part, depicts sexually explicit nudity, sexual conduct, or sadomasochistic abuse and which is harmful to minors or exhibit any such motion picture at any such premises which are not designed to prevent viewing from any public way of such motion picture by minors not admitted to any such premises.

(2) It shall be unlawful for any person knowingly to sell or to furnish to a person under the age of 21 an admission ticket or pass or knowingly to admit a person under the age of 21 to premises whereon there is exhibited a show or performance which is harmful to minors and which, in whole or in part, consists of sexually explicit nudity on the part of one or more live performers; sexual conduct on the part of one or more live performers; or sadomasochistic abuse on the part of one or more live performers.

(c) It shall be unlawful for any person to falsely represent his or her age to any person mentioned in subsection (a) or subsection (b) of this Code section or to his or her agent with the intent to unlawfully procure any material set forth in subsection (a) of this Code section or with the intent to unlawfully procure such person's admission to any motion picture, show, or other presentation, as set forth in subsection (b) of this Code section.

(d) It shall be unlawful for any person knowingly to make a false representation to any person mentioned in subsection (a) or subsection (b) of this Code section or to his or her agent that he or she is the parent or guardian of any minor or knowingly to make a false representation with respect to the age of another person with the intent to unlawfully procure for such other person any material set forth in subsection (a) of this Code section or with the intent to unlawfully procure such other person's admission to any motion picture, show, or other presentation, as set forth in subsection (b) of this Code section.

(e) It shall be unlawful for any person knowingly to exhibit, expose, or display in public at newsstands or any other business or commercial establishment or at any other public place frequented by minors or where minors are or may be invited as part of the general public:

(1) Any picture, photograph, drawing, sculpture, motion picture film, or similar visual representation or image of a person or portion of the human body which depicts sexually explicit nudity, sexual conduct, or sadomasochistic abuse and which is harmful to minors; or

(2) Any book, pamphlet, magazine, printed matter however reproduced, or sound recording which contains any matter enumerated in paragraph (1) of this subsection, or explicit and detailed verbal descriptions or narrative accounts of sexual excitement, sexual conduct, or sadomasochistic abuse and which, taken as a whole, is harmful to minors.

(f)(1) As used in this subsection, the term:

(A) "Video game" means an object or device that stores recorded data or instructions, receives data or instructions generated by a person who uses it, and, by processing the data or instructions, creates an interactive game capable of being played, viewed, or experienced on or through a computer, gaming system, console, or other technology.

(B) "Video game retailer" means a person who sells or rents video games to the public.

(2) Every video game retailer shall post a sign providing information to consumers about any video game rating system which appears on a video game offered by such retailer. The sign shall be posted in a conspicuous place within the portion of the establishment dedicated to the display or advertisement of video games. Each video game retailer shall make available to consumers, upon request, written information explaining each such rating system.

(3) A person violating the provisions of this subsection shall be punished with a civil fine in an amount not less than $250.00 and not more than $500.00 for each violation. Each day in violation of this subsection shall constitute a separate offense.

§ 16-12-104. Library exception

The provisions of Code Section 16-12-103 shall not apply to any public library operated by the state or any of its political subdivisions nor to any library operated as a part of any school, college, or university.

§ 16-12-105. Penalty

(a) Except as provided in subsection (b) of this Code section, any person who violates any provision of Code Section 16-12-103 or 16-12-104 shall be guilty of a misdemeanor of a high and aggravated nature.

(b) Any person who violates subsection (a) of Code Section 16-12-103 shall be guilty of a misdemeanor if:

(1) The person depicted was at least 14 years of age;

(2) The items described in subsection (a) of Code Section 16-12-103 were furnished or disseminated with the permission of the minor depicted; and

(3) The defendant was 18 years of age or younger at the time of the offense.

§§ 16-12-106 through 16-12-108

Repealed by Ga. L. 1981, p. 1578, § 2, effective July 1, 1981.

§ 16-12-120. Certain acts in public transit buses, rapid rail cars, or stations; penalty

(a) A person who commits or attempts to commit any of the following acts in a public transit bus, a rapid rail car, or a rapid rail station or intermodal bus station shall be guilty of a misdemeanor:

(1) Spits, defecates, or urinates;

(2) Discards litter, except into receptacles designated for that purpose;

(3) Smokes tobacco in any form;

(4) Consumes food or beverage or possesses any open food or beverage container, provided that this paragraph shall not apply to resealable beverages in resealable plastic containers, to an operator of a public transit bus at an authorized layover point, or to a person providing food or beverage to any child under age five; provided, further, that nothing in this paragraph shall apply to a rapid rail station or intermodal bus station, unless the public transit system operating such station adopts a policy prohibiting food or beverages in such station; and provided, further, that nothing in this paragraph shall preclude a public transit system operated or funded by a county, municipality, or consolidated government from prohibiting the consumption of any beverage in a public transit bus;

(5) Plays any radio; cassette, cartridge, or tape player; or similar device unless such device is connected to an earphone that limits the sound to the hearing of the individual user;

(6) Carries or possesses any explosives, acids, other dangerous articles, or live animals, except for the following:

(A) A guide dog or service dog as described in Code Section 30-4-2, provided that such guide dog or service dog is accompanied by a physically disabled person, blind person, person with visual disabilities, deaf person, or a person who is responsible for training a guide dog or service dog; and

(B) Small pets confined to rigid pet carriers with locks or latches;

(7) Obstructs, hinders, interferes with, or otherwise disrupts or disturbs the operation, operator, or passengers of a public transit bus or rapid rail car;

(8) Boards any public transit bus through the rear exit door, unless so directed by an employee or agent of the carrier;

(9) Remains aboard any public transit bus or rapid rail car after such vehicle has completed its scheduled route and passengers have been advised to exit the vehicle or remains aboard any public transit bus or rapid rail car after having been warned and after such vehicle has entered a garage or other restricted area not open to the public;

(10) Enters, exits, or passes through any emergency door of any rapid rail car or public transit bus in the absence of a bona fide emergency; or

(11) Enters the operator's cab or driver's seat of any rapid rail car or public transit bus in the absence of a bona fide emergency.

(a.1)(1) It shall be unlawful to solicit money or sell goods or services for a fee to the operator or passengers of a public transit bus or rapid rail car within the confines of such vehicle or within the paid areas of any rapid rail station or intermodal bus station without the express permission or grant of a concession by the public transportation authority or carrier.

(2) It shall be unlawful to deliver or distribute handbills or flyers of a commercial nature to the operator or passengers of a public transit bus or rapid rail car within the confines of such vehicle or within the paid area of any rapid rail station or intermodal bus station.

(3) A person violating the provisions of this subsection shall be guilty of a misdemeanor and, upon conviction thereof, shall be punished by a fine of not less than $50.00 and not more than $100.00. Upon a second or subsequent conviction, a person shall be punished by a fine of not less than $100.00 and not more than $250.00 or by imprisonment for not more than ten days, or both.

(b) Employees of a public transportation authority or carrier while at work performing the duties of their employment shall be exempted from the restrictions of paragraphs (8), (9), (10), and (11) of subsection (a) of this Code section.

(c) A person convicted of a first offense of violating subsection (a) of this Code section shall be punished by a fine of not less than $50.00 and not more than $100.00. Upon a second or subsequent conviction, a person shall be punished by a fine of not less than $100.00 and not more than $250.00 or by imprisonment for not more than ten days, or both.

(d) This Code section shall be cumulative to and shall not prohibit the enactment of any other general and local laws, rules, and regulations of state or local authorities or agencies, and local ordinances prohibiting such activities which are more restrictive than this Code section.

§ 16-12-120.1. Altered fare coins, tokens, stored value cards, transfers, transaction cards, and tickets; sale or exchange of tokens, stored value card transfers, transaction cards, or tickets without consent

A person who commits or attempts to commit any of the following acts shall be guilty of a misdemeanor if such person:

(1) Sells, makes, or possesses any coin, token, stored value card, transfer, transaction card, ticket, or any other fare medium which has been altered from its original condition contrary to its intended use to enter or gain entry into or on any bus, rail vehicle, or station;

(2) Sells or exchanges any token, stored value card, transfer, transaction card, ticket, fare medium, or similar article which was obtained by fraudulent or illegal means and which is used or to be used as payment for entry into or on any bus, rail vehicle, or terminal without the express consent of the public transit agency owning or operating such vehicles or stations;

(3) Offers entry or provides entry into or on any bus, rapid rail car, or station to any person without the payment of the proper fare to the public transit agency owning or operating such vehicles or stations;

(4) Gains entry into or on any bus, rapid rail car, or station without the payment of the proper fare; or

(5) Gains entry into or on any bus, rapid rail car, or station through the use of a coin, token, transfer, transaction card, ticket, or any other fare medium which is the property of another person when the use of such medium is limited by its terms to a single user. This paragraph shall not apply to stored value cards or similar fare media which deduct the cost of the fare from the value stored on the card or other fare medium each time such card or other fare medium is used.

§ 16-12-121. Short title

This part shall be known and may be cited as the "Transportation Passenger Safety Act."

§ 16-12-122. Definitions

As used in this part, the term:

(1) "Aircraft" means any machine, whether heavier or lighter than air, used or designed for navigation of or flight in the air.

(2) "Avoid a security measure" means to take any action that is intended to result in any person, baggage, container, or item of any type being allowed into a secure area without being subjected to security measures or the assembly of items into an object or substance that is prohibited under the laws of this state or of the United States or any of their agencies, political subdivisions, or authorities after such items have passed through a security measure into a secure area.

(3) "Bus" means any passenger bus or coach or other motor vehicle having a seating capacity of not less than 15 passengers operated by a transportation company for the purpose of carrying passengers or freight for hire.

(4) "Charter" means a group of persons, pursuant to a common purpose and under a single contract and at a fixed charge for the vehicle in accordance with a transportation company's tariff, who have acquired the exclusive use of an aircraft, bus, or rail vehicle to travel together as a group to a specified destination.

(5) "Interfere with a security measure" means to take any action that is intended to defeat, disable, or prevent the full operation of equipment or procedures designed or intended to detect any object or substance, including, but not limited to, disabling of any device so that it cannot fully function, creation of any diversion intended to defeat a security measure, or packaging of any item or substance so as to avoid detection by a security measure.

(6) "Passenger" means any person served by the transportation company; and, in addition to the ordinary meaning of passenger, the term shall include any person accompanying or meeting another person who is transported by such company, any person shipping or receiving freight, and any person purchasing a ticket or receiving a pass.

(7) "Rail vehicle" means any railroad or rail transit car, carriage, coach, or other vehicle, whether self-propelled or not and designed to be operated upon a rail or rails or other fixed right of way by a transportation company for the purpose of carrying passengers or freight or both for hire.

(8) "Secure area" means any enclosed or unenclosed area within a terminal whereby access is restricted in any manner or the possession of items subject to security measures is prohibited. Access to a secure area may be restricted to persons specifically authorized by law, regulation, or policy of the governing authority or transportation company operating said terminal, and such access into a secure area may be conditioned on passing through security measures, and possession of items may be restricted to designated persons who are acting in the course of their official duties.

(9) "Security measure" means any process or procedure by which employees, agents, passengers, persons accompanying passengers, containers, baggage, freight, or possessions of passengers or persons accompanying passengers are screened, inspected, or examined by any means for the purpose of ensuring the safety and welfare of aircraft, bus, or rail vehicles and the employees, agents, passengers, and freight of any transportation company. The security measures may be operated by or under the authority of any governmental entity, transportation company, or any entity contracting therewith.

(10) "Terminal" means an aircraft, bus, or rail vehicle station, depot, any such transportation facility, or infrastructure relating thereto operated by a transportation company or governmental entity or authority. This term includes a reasonable area immediately adjacent to any designated stop along the route traveled by any coach or rail vehicle operated by a transportation company or governmental entity operating aircraft, bus, or rail vehicle transportation facility and parking lots or parking areas adjacent to a terminal.

(11) "Transportation company" or "company" means any person, group of persons, or corporation providing for-hire transportation to passengers or freight by aircraft, by bus upon the highways in this state, by rail vehicle upon any public or private right of way in this state, or by all, including passengers and freight in interstate or intrastate travel. This term shall also include transportation facilities owned or operated by local public bodies; by municipalities; and by public corporations, authorities, boards, and commissions established under the laws of this state, any of the several states, the United States, or any foreign nation.

§ 16-12-123. Bus or rail vehicle hijacking; boarding with concealed weapon; company use of reasonable security measures

(a)(1) A person commits the offense of bus or rail vehicle hijacking when he or she:
(A) Seizes or exercises control by force or violence or threat of force or violence of any bus or rail vehicle within the jurisdiction of this state;
(B) By force or violence or by threat of force or violence seizes or exercises control of any transportation company or all or any part of the transportation facilities owned or operated by any such company; or
(C) By force or violence or by threat of force or violence substantially obstructs, hinders, interferes with, or otherwise disrupts or disturbs the operation of any transportation company or all or any part of a transportation facility.
(2) Any person convicted of the offense of bus or rail hijacking shall be guilty of a felony and, upon conviction thereof, shall be punished by imprisonment for life or by imprisonment for not less than one nor more than 20 years.
(b) Any person who boards or attempts to board an aircraft, bus, or rail vehicle with any explosive, destructive device, or hoax device as such term is defined in Code Section 16-7-80; firearm for which such person does not have on his or her person a valid weapons carry license issued pursuant to Code Section 16-11-129 unless possessing such firearm is prohibited by federal law; hazardous substance as defined by Code Section 12-8-92; or knife or other device designed or modified for the purpose of offense and defense concealed on or about his or her person or property which is or would be accessible to such person while on the aircraft, bus, or rail vehicle shall be guilty of a felony and, upon conviction thereof, shall be sentenced to imprisonment for not less than one nor more than ten years. The prohibition of this subsection shall not apply to any law enforcement officer, peace officer retired from a state or federal law enforcement agency, person in the military service of the state or of the United States, or commercial security personnel employed by the transportation company who is in possession of weapons used within the course and scope of employment; nor shall the prohibition apply to persons transporting weapons contained in baggage which is not accessible to passengers if the presence of such weapons has been declared to the transportation company and such weapons have been secured in a manner prescribed by state or federal law or regulation for the purpose of transportation or shipment. The provisions of this subsection shall not apply to any privately owned aircraft, bus, or rail vehicle if the owner of such aircraft or vehicle has given his or her express permission to board the aircraft or vehicle with the item.
(c) The company may employ reasonable security measures, including any method or device, to detect concealed weapons, explosives, or hazardous material in baggage or freight or upon the person of the passenger. Upon the discovery of any such item or material in the possession of a person, unless the item is a weapon in the possession of a person exempted under subsection (b) of this Code section from the prohibition of that subsection (b), the company shall obtain possession and retain custody of such item or materials until they are transferred to the custody of law enforcement officers.

§ 16-12-124. Removal of baggage, freight, or other items transported by bus or stored in a terminal

(a) It shall be unlawful to remove any baggage, freight, container, or other item transported upon an aircraft, bus, or rail vehicle or stored in a terminal without consent of the owner of such property or the company or its duly authorized representative. Any person violating this Code section shall be guilty of a felony and, upon conviction thereof, shall be punished by imprisonment for not less than one nor more than five years.
(b) The actual value of an item removed in violation of this Code section shall not be material to the crime herein defined.

§ 16-12-125. Avoiding or interfering with securing measures; penalty; exemption

(a) Except as otherwise provided in this Code section, it shall be unlawful for any person to avoid or interfere with a properly functioning security measure. Any person convicted of a violation of this Code section shall be guilty of a misdemeanor of a high and aggravated nature; provided, however, that any person who violates this Code section with the intent to commit a felony within the terminal or with regard to any aircraft, bus, or rail vehicle shall be punished by imprisonment for not less than five nor more than 25 years, a fine not to exceed $100,000.00, or both.
(b) Any violation of this Code section shall be considered a separate offense.
(c) This Code section shall not apply to authorized agents of the entity owning or operating such security measure.

§ 16-12-126. Intentionally interfering with safety or traffic control devices; penalty; exemption

(a) Except as otherwise provided in this Code section, it shall be unlawful intentionally to disable or inhibit the operation or effectiveness of any properly functioning safety device of any description or to render any item or substance less safe when said item or substance is in any freight of a transportation company, in baggage or possessions of a passenger, or in a terminal.
(b) Except as otherwise provided in this Code section, it shall be unlawful to intentionally render inoperable or partially inoperable for any period of time any properly functioning device designed or operated for traffic control that is owned, operated, or maintained by or for the benefit of a transportation company.
(c) Any violation of this Code section shall be punished by imprisonment for not less than five nor more than 20 years, a fine not to exceed $100,000.00, or both.
(d) Any violation of this Code section shall be considered a separate offense.
(e) This Code section shall not apply to authorized agents of the entity owning or operating such safety device or device designed or operated for traffic control.

§ 16-12-127. Prohibition on firearms, hazardous substances, knives, or other devices; penalty; affirmative defenses

(a) It shall be unlawful for any person, with the intention of avoiding or interfering with a security measure or of introducing into a terminal any explosive, destructive device, or hoax device as defined in Code Section 16-7-80; firearm for which such person does not have on his or her person a valid weapons carry license issued pursuant to Code Section 16-11-129 unless possessing such firearm is prohibited by federal law; hazardous substance as defined by Code Section 12-8-92; or knife or other device designed or modified for the purpose of offense and defense, to:
(1) Have any such item on or about his or her person, or
(2) Place or cause to be placed or attempt to place or cause to be placed any such item:
(A) In a container or freight of a transportation company;
(B) In the baggage or possessions of any person or any transportation company without the knowledge of the passenger or transportation company; or
(C) Aboard such aircraft, bus, or rail vehicle.
(b) A person violating the provisions of this Code section shall be guilty of a felony and shall, upon conviction, be sentenced to imprisonment for not less than one year nor more than 20 years, a fine not to exceed $15,000.00, or both. A prosecution under this Code section shall not be barred by the imposition of a civil penalty imposed by any governmental entity.
(c) It is an affirmative defense to a violation of this Code section if a person notifies a law enforcement officer or other person employed to provide security for a transportation company of the presence of such item as soon as possible after learning of its presence and surrenders or secures such item as directed by the law enforcement officer or other person employed to provide security for a transportation company.

§ 16-12-128. Effect of part on other provisions of law; civil or criminal proceedings; restitution

(a) This part shall be cumulative and supplemental to any other law of this state. A conviction or acquittal under any of the criminal provisions of Code Section 16-12-123, 16-12-124, 16-12-125, or 16-12-126 shall not be a bar to any other civil or criminal proceeding.
(b) In addition to any other penalty imposed by law for a violation of this part, the court may require the defendant to make restitution to any affected public or private entity for the reasonable costs or damages associated with the offense. Restitution made pursuant to this subsection shall not preclude any party from obtaining any other civil or criminal remedy available under any other provision of law. The restitution authorized by this subsection is supplemental and not exclusive.

§ 16-12-129. Defense of self or others an absolute defense to violation under this part

Defense of self or others, as contemplated by and provided for under Article 2 of Chapter 3 of this title, shall be an absolute defense to any violation under this part.

§ 16-12-140. Criminal abortion

(a) A person commits the offense of criminal abortion when, in violation of Code Section 16-12-141, he or she administers any medicine, drugs, or other substance whatever to any woman or when he or she uses any instrument or other means whatever upon any woman with intent to produce a miscarriage or abortion.
(b) A person convicted of the offense of criminal abortion shall be punished by imprisonment for not less than one nor more than ten years.

§ 16-12-141. Restrictions on the performance of abortions; availability of records

(a) No abortion is authorized or shall be performed in violation of subsection (a) of Code Section 31-9B-2.
(b) (1) No abortion is authorized or shall be performed after the first trimester unless the abortion is performed in a licensed hospital, in a licensed ambulatory surgical center, or in a health facility licensed as an abortion facility by the Department of Community Health.
(2) An abortion shall only be performed by a physician licensed under Article 2 of Chapter 34 of Title 43.
(c) (1) No abortion is authorized or shall be performed if the probable gestational age of the unborn child has been determined in accordance with Code Section 31-9B-2 to be 20 weeks or more unless the pregnancy is diagnosed as medically futile, as such term is defined in Code Section 31-9B-1, or in reasonable medical judgment the abortion is necessary to:
(A) Avert the death of the pregnant woman or avert serious risk of substantial and irreversible physical impairment of a major bodily function of the pregnant woman. No such condition shall be deemed to exist if it is based on a diagnosis or claim of a mental or emotional condition of the pregnant woman or that the pregnant woman will purposefully engage in conduct which she intends to result in her death or in substantial and irreversible physical impairment of a major bodily function; or
(B) Preserve the life of an unborn child.
As used in this paragraph, the term "probable gestational age of the unborn child" has the meaning provided by Code Section 31-9B-1.
(2) In any case described in subparagraph (A) or (B) of paragraph (1) of this subsection, the physician shall terminate the pregnancy in the manner which, in reasonable medical judgment, provides the best opportunity for the unborn child to survive unless, in reasonable medical judgment, termination of the pregnancy in that manner would pose a greater risk either of the death of the pregnant woman or of the substantial and irreversible physical impairment of a major bodily function of the pregnant woman than would another available method. No such greater risk shall be deemed to exist if it is based on a diagnosis or claim of a mental or emotional condition of the pregnant woman or that the pregnant woman will purposefully engage in conduct which she intends to result in her death or in substantial and irreversible physical impairment of a major bodily function. If the child is capable of sustained life, medical aid then available must be rendered.
(d) Hospital or other licensed health facility records shall be available to the district attorney of the judicial circuit in which the hospital or health facility is located.

§ 16-12-141.1. Disposal of aborted fetuses; reporting requirements; penalties; public report; confidentiality of identity of physicians filing reports

(a) (1) Every hospital and clinic in which abortions are performed or occur spontaneously, and any laboratory to which the aborted fetuses are delivered, shall provide for the disposal of the aborted fetuses by cremation, interment, or other manner approved of by the commissioner of public health. The hospital, clinic, or laboratory may complete any laboratory tests necessary for the health of the woman or her future offspring prior to disposing of the aborted fetus.
(2) Each hospital, clinic, and laboratory shall report, on a form provided by the commissioner of public health, the manner in which it disposes of the aborted fetus. Such reports shall be made annually by December 31 and whenever the method of disposal changes. The commissioner of public health shall provide forms for reporting under this Code section.
(b) Any hospital, clinic, or laboratory violating the provisions of subsection (a) of this Code section shall be punished by a fine of not less than $1,000.00 nor more than $5,000.00.
(c) Within 90 days after May 10, 2005, the Department of Human Resources (now known as the Department of Public Health for these purposes) shall prepare a reporting form for physicians which shall include:
(1) The number of females whose parent or guardian was provided the notice required in paragraph (1) of subsection (a) of Code Section 15-11-682 by the physician or such physician's agent; of that number, the number of notices provided personally under subparagraphs (a)(1)(A) and (a)(1)(B) of Code Section 15-11-682 and the number of notices provided by mail under subparagraph (a)(1)(C) of Code Section 15-11-682; and, of each of those numbers, the number of females who, to the best of the reporting physician's information and belief, went on to obtain the abortion;
(2) The number of females upon whom the physician performed an abortion without providing to the parent or guardian of a minor the notice required by subsection (a) of Code Section 15-11-682; and of that number, the number of females for which subsection (b) of Code Section 15-11-682 and Code Section 15-11-686 were applicable;
(3) The number of abortions performed upon a female by the physician after receiving judicial authorization pursuant to subsection (b) of Code Section 15-11-682 and Code Section 15-11-684; and
(4) The same information described in paragraphs (1), (2), and (3) of this subsection with respect to females for whom a guardian or conservator has been appointed.
(d) The Department of Public Health shall ensure that copies of the reporting forms described in subsection (c) of this Code section, together with a reprint of this Code section, are provided:

111

(1) Within 120 days after May 10, 2005, to all health facilities licensed as an abortion facility by the Department of Human Resources (now known as the Department of Community Health for these purposes);

(2) To each physician licensed or who subsequently becomes licensed to practice medicine in this state at the same time as official notification to that physician that the physician is so licensed; and

(3) By December 1 of every year, other than the calendar year in which forms are distributed in accordance with paragraph (1) of this subsection, to all health facilities licensed as an abortion facility by the Department of Community Health.

(e) By February 28 of each year following a calendar year in any part of which this subsection was in effect, each physician who provided, or whose agent provided, the notice described in subsection (a) of Code Section 15-11-682 and any physician who knowingly performed an abortion upon a female or upon a female for whom a guardian or conservator had been appointed because of a finding of incompetency during the previous calendar year shall submit to the Department of Public Health a copy of the form described in subsection (c) of this Code section with the requested data entered accurately and completely.

(f) Reports that are submitted more than 30 days following the due date shall be subject to a late fee of $500.00 for that period and the same fee for each additional 30 day period or portion of a 30 day period in which they remain overdue. Any physician required to report in accordance with this Code section who submits an incomplete report or fails to submit a report for more than one year following the due date may, in an action brought by the Department of Public Health, be directed by a court of competent jurisdiction to submit a complete report within a period stated by court order or be subject to sanctions for civil contempt.

(g) By June 30 of each year, the Department of Public Health shall issue a public report providing statistics for the previous calendar year compiled from all the reports covering that year submitted in accordance with this Code section for each of the items listed in subsection (c) of this Code section. The report shall also include statistics which shall be obtained by the Administrative Office of the Courts giving the total number of petitions or motions filed under subsection (b) of Code Section 15-11-682 and, of that number, the number in which the court appointed a guardian ad litem, the number in which the court appointed counsel, the number in which the judge issued an order authorizing an abortion without notification, the number in which the judge denied such an order, and, of the last, the number of denials from which an appeal was filed, the number of such appeals that resulted in the denials being affirmed, and the number of such appeals that resulted in reversals of such denials. Each report shall also provide the statistics for all previous calendar years for which such a public statistical report was required to be issued, adjusted to reflect any additional information from late or corrected reports. The Department of Public Health shall ensure that none of the information included in the public reports could reasonably lead to the identification of any individual female or of any female for whom a guardian or conservator has been appointed.

(h) The Department of Public Health may by regulation alter the dates established by paragraph (3) of subsection (d) and subsections (e) and (g) of this Code section or consolidate the forms or reports to achieve administrative convenience or fiscal savings or to reduce the burden of reporting requirements so long as reporting forms are sent to all facilities licensed as an abortion facility by the Department of Community Health at least once every year and the report described in subsection (g) of this Code section is issued at least once each year.

(i) The Department of Public Health shall ensure that the names and identities of the physicians filing reports under this Code section shall remain confidential. The names and identities of such physicians shall not be subject to Article 4 of Chapter 18 of Title 50.

§ 16-12-142. Objections by medical facilities, physicians, or pharmacists to providing abortion-related services

(a) Nothing in this article shall require a hospital or other medical facility or physician to admit any patient under the provisions of this article for the purpose of performing an abortion. In addition, any person who states in writing an objection to any abortion or all abortions on moral or religious grounds shall not be required to participate in procedures which will result in such abortion; and the refusal of the person to participate therein shall not form the basis of any claim for damages on account of such refusal or for any disciplinary or recriminatory action against the person. The written objection shall remain in effect until the person revokes it or terminates his association with the facility with which it is filed.

(b) Any pharmacist who states in writing an objection to any abortion or all abortions on moral or religious grounds shall not be required to fill a prescription for a drug which purpose is to terminate a pregnancy; and the refusal of the person to fill such prescription shall not form the basis of any claim for damages on account of such refusal or for any disciplinary or recriminatory action against the person; provided, however, that the pharmacist shall make all reasonable efforts to locate another pharmacist who is willing to fill such prescription or shall immediately return the prescription to the prescription holder. The written objection shall remain in effect until the person revokes it or terminates his or her association with the facility with which it is filed. Nothing in this subsection shall be construed to authorize a pharmacist to refuse to fill a prescription for birth control medication, including any process, device, or method to prevent pregnancy and including any drug or device approved by the federal Food and Drug Administration for such purpose.

§ 16-12-143. Failure to file or maintain required written reports

A person who fails to file or maintain in complete form any of the written reports required in this article within the time set forth is guilty of a misdemeanor.

§ 16-12-144. Partial-birth abortions

(a) As used in this Code section, the term:

(1) "Fetus" means the biological offspring of human parents.

(2) "Partial-birth abortion" means an abortion in which the person performing the abortion partially vaginally delivers a living human fetus before ending the life of the fetus and completing the delivery.

(b) Any person who knowingly performs a partial-birth abortion and thereby ends the life of a human fetus shall, upon conviction thereof, be punished by a fine not to exceed $5,000.00, imprisonment for not more than five years, or both. This prohibition shall not apply to a partial-birth abortion that is necessary to save the life of the mother because her life is endangered by a physical disorder, physical illness, or physical injury, including a life-endangering condition caused by or arising from the pregnancy itself, provided that no other medical procedure will suffice to save the mother's life.

(c)(1) The father of the fetus, and the maternal grandparents of the fetus if the mother has not attained the age of 18 years of age at the time of the abortion, may obtain appropriate relief in a civil action, unless the pregnancy resulted from the plaintiff's criminal conduct or the plaintiff consented to the abortion.

(2) Such relief shall include:

(A) Money damages for all injuries, psychological and physical, occasioned by the violation of this Code section; and

(B) Statutory damages equal to three times the cost of the partial-birth abortion.

(d) A woman upon whom a partial-birth abortion is performed may not be prosecuted under this Code section for violating this Code section or any provision thereof, or for conspiracy or for an attempt to violate this Code section or any provision thereof.

§ 16-12-160. Buying or selling or offering to buy or sell the human body or parts

(a) It shall be unlawful, except as provided in subsection (b) of this Code section, for any person, firm, or corporation to buy or sell, to offer to buy or sell, or to assist another in buying or selling or offering to buy or sell a human body or any part of a human body or buy or sell a human fetus or any part thereof.

(b) The prohibition contained in subsection (a) of this Code section shall not apply to:

(1) The purchase or sale of whole blood, blood plasma, blood products, blood derivatives, other self-replicating body fluids, or hair;

(2) A gift or donation of a human body or any part of a human body or any procedure connected therewith as provided in Article 6 of Chapter 5 of Title 44 or to the payment of a fee in connection with such gift or donation pursuant to subsection (b) of Code Section 44-5-154 if such fee is paid to a procurement organization, as that term is defined in Code Section 44-5-141;

(3) The reimbursement of actual expenses, including medical costs, lost income, and travel expenses, incurred by a living person in giving or donating a part of the person's body;

(4) The payment of financial assistance under a plan of insurance or other health care coverage;

(5) The purchase or sale of human tissue, organs, or other parts of the human body for health sciences education; or

(6) The payment of reasonable costs associated with the removal, storage, or transportation of a human body or any part of a human body given or donated for medical or scientific purposes.

(c) Any person, firm, or corporation convicted of violating subsection (a) of this Code section shall be guilty of a felony and, upon conviction thereof, shall be punished by a fine not exceeding $5,000.00 or by imprisonment for not less than one year nor more than five years, or both.

§ 16-12-161. Removal of body parts from scene of death or dismemberment; criminal penalty

(a) It shall be unlawful for any person to remove from the scene of the death or dismemberment of any person any human body part; provided, however, that this Code section shall not apply to a law enforcement officer acting in the lawful discharge of his or her official duties, or to any person acting under the direction of a law enforcement officer, a physician or an emergency medical technician in the course of their professions, or in the absence of any such person to any person who transports such body part directly to a medical facility, law enforcement agency, or licensed funeral home, although all such persons remain obligated to comply with the provisions of Article 2 of Chapter 16 of Title 45 concerning death investigations.
(b) Any person violating the provisions of subsection (a) of this Code section shall be guilty of a misdemeanor of a high and aggravated nature.

§ 16-12-170. Definitions

As used in this article, the term:
(1) "Alternative nicotine product" means any noncombustible product containing nicotine that is intended for human consumption, whether chewed, absorbed, dissolved, or ingested by any other means. The term "alternative nicotine product" shall not include any tobacco product, vapor product, or any product regulated as a drug or device by the United States Food and Drug Administration under Chapter V of the Food, Drug, and Cosmetic Act.
(2) "Cigar wraps" means individual cigar wrappers, known as wraps, blunt wraps, or roll your own cigar wraps, that consist in whole or in part of reconstituted tobacco leaf or flavored tobacco leaf.
(3) "Cigarette" means roll for smoking made wholly or in part of tobacco when the cover of the roll is paper or any substance other than tobacco.
(4) "Community service" means a public service which a minor might appropriately be required to perform, as determined by the court, as punishment for certain offenses provided for in this article.
(5) "Minor" means any person who is under the age of 18 years.
(6) "Person" means any natural person or any firm, partnership, company, corporation, or other entity.
(7) "Proper identification" means any document issued by a governmental agency containing a description of the person, such person's photograph, or both, and giving such person's date of birth and includes, without being limited to, a passport, military identification card, driver's license, or an identification card authorized under Code Sections 40-5-100 through 40-5-104. Proper identification shall not include a birth certificate.
(8) "Tobacco product" means any cigars, little cigars, granulated, plug cut, crimp cut, ready rubbed, and other smoking tobacco; snuff or snuff powder; cavendish; plug and twist tobacco; fine-cut and other chewing tobaccos; shorts; refuse scraps, clippings, cuttings, and sweepings of tobacco; and other kinds and forms of tobacco, prepared in such a manner as to be suitable for chewing or smoking in a pipe or otherwise, or both for chewing and smoking. The term "tobacco product" shall not include any alternative nicotine product, vapor product, or product regulated as a drug or device by the United States Food and Drug Administration under Chapter V of the Food, Drug, and Cosmetic Act.
(9) "Tobacco related objects" means any papers, wrappers, or other products, devices, or substances, including cigar wraps, which are used for the purpose of making cigarettes or tobacco products in any form whatsoever.
(10) "Vapor product" means any noncombustible product containing nicotine that employs a heating element, power source, electronic circuit, or other electronic, chemical, or mechanical means, regardless of shape or size, that can be used to produce vapor from nicotine in a solution or other form. The term "vapor product" shall include any electronic cigarette, electronic cigar, electronic cigarillo, electronic pipe, or similar product or device and any vapor cartridge or other container of nicotine in a solution or other form that is intended to be used with or in an electronic cigarette, electronic cigar, electronic cigarillo, electronic pipe, or similar product or device. The term "vapor product" shall not include any product regulated as a drug or device by the United States Food and Drug Administration under Chapter V of the Food, Drug, and Cosmetic Act.

§ 16-12-171. Prohibited acts

(a) (1) It shall be unlawful for any person knowingly to:
(A) Sell or barter, directly or indirectly, any cigarettes, tobacco products, tobacco related objects, alternative nicotine products, or vapor products to a minor;
(B) Purchase any cigarettes, tobacco products, tobacco related objects, alternative nicotine products, or vapor products for any minor unless the minor for whom the purchase is made is the child of the purchaser; or
(C) Advise, counsel, or compel any minor to smoke, inhale, chew, or use cigarettes, tobacco products, tobacco related objects, alternative nicotine products, or vapor products.
(2) (A) The prohibition contained in paragraph (1) of this subsection shall not apply with respect to sale of cigarettes, tobacco products, tobacco related objects, alternative nicotine products, or vapor products by a person when such person has been furnished with proper identification showing that the person to whom the cigarettes, tobacco products, tobacco related objects, alternative nicotine products, or vapor products are sold is 18 years of age or older.
(B) In any case where a reasonable or prudent person could reasonably be in doubt as to whether or not the person to whom cigarettes, tobacco products, tobacco related objects, alternative nicotine products, or vapor products are to be sold or otherwise furnished is actually 18 years of age or older, it shall be the duty of the person selling or otherwise furnishing such cigarettes, tobacco products, tobacco related objects, alternative nicotine products, or vapor products to request to see and to be furnished with proper identification as provided for in subsection (b) of this Code section in order to verify the age of such person. The failure to make such request and verification in any case where the person to whom the cigarettes, tobacco products, tobacco related objects, alternative nicotine products, or vapor products are sold or otherwise furnished is less than 18 years of age may be considered by the trier of fact in determining whether the person selling or otherwise furnishing such cigarettes, tobacco products, tobacco related objects, alternative nicotine products, or vapor products did so knowingly.
(3) Any person who violates this subsection shall be guilty of a misdemeanor.
(b) (1) It shall be unlawful for any minor to:
(A) Purchase, attempt to purchase, or possess for personal use any cigarettes, tobacco products, tobacco related objects, alternative nicotine products, or vapor products. This subparagraph shall not apply to possession of cigarettes, tobacco products, tobacco related objects, alternative nicotine products, or vapor products by a minor when a parent or guardian of such minor gives the cigarettes, tobacco products, tobacco related objects, alternative nicotine products, or vapor products to the minor and possession is in the home of the parent or guardian and such parent or guardian is present; or
(B) Misrepresent such minor's identity or age or use any false identification for the purpose of purchasing or procuring any cigarettes, tobacco products, tobacco related objects, alternative nicotine products, or vapor products.
(2) A minor who commits an offense provided for in paragraph (1) of this subsection may be punished as follows:
(A) By requiring the performance of community service not exceeding 20 hours;
(B) By requiring attendance at a publicly or privately sponsored lecture or discussion on the health hazards of smoking or tobacco use, provided such lecture or discussion is offered without charge to the minor; or
(C) By a combination of the punishments described in subparagraphs (A) and (B) of this paragraph.

§ 16-12-172. Posting signs in place of business

(a) Any person owning or operating a place of business in which cigarettes, tobacco products, or tobacco related objects are sold or offered for sale shall post in a conspicuous place a sign which shall contain the following statement:
"SALE OF CIGARETTES, TOBACCO, TOBACCO PRODUCTS, TOBACCO RELATED OBJECTS, ALTERNATIVE NICOTINE PRODUCTS, OR VAPOR PRODUCTS TO PERSONS UNDER 18 YEARS OF AGE IS PROHIBITED BY LAW."
Such sign shall be printed in letters of at least one-half inch in height.

(b) Any person who fails to comply with the requirements of subsection (a) of this Code section shall be guilty of a misdemeanor.

§ 16-12-173. Sales from vending machines

(a) (1) Any person who maintains in such person's place of business a vending machine which dispenses cigarettes, tobacco products, tobacco related objects, alternative nicotine products, or vapor products shall place or cause to be placed in a conspicuous place on such vending machine a sign containing the following statement:
"THE PURCHASE OF CIGARETTES, TOBACCO PRODUCTS, TOBACCO RELATED OBJECTS, ALTERNATIVE NICOTINE PRODUCTS, OR VAPOR PRODUCTS FROM THIS VENDING MACHINE BY ANY PERSON UNDER 18 YEARS OF AGE IS PROHIBITED BY LAW."
(2) Any person who maintains in such person's place of business a vending machine which dispenses cigarettes, tobacco products, tobacco related objects, alternative nicotine products, or vapor products shall not dispense any other type of product, other than matches, in such vending machine.
(b) Any person who fails to comply with the requirements of subsection (a) of this Code section shall be guilty of a misdemeanor; provided, however, for a first offense, the sentence shall be a fine not to exceed $300.00.
(c) It shall be a violation of subsection (a) of Code Section 16-12-171 for any person knowingly to allow a minor to operate a vending machine which dispenses cigarettes, tobacco products, tobacco related objects, alternative nicotine products, or vapor products.
(d) The offenses provided for by paragraph (1) of subsection (b) of Code Section 16-12-171 shall apply to the operation by a minor of a vending machine which dispenses cigarettes, tobacco products, tobacco related objects, alternative nicotine products, or vapor products.
(e) (1) The sale or offering for sale of cigarettes, tobacco products, tobacco related objects, alternative nicotine products, or vapor products from vending machines shall not be permitted except:
(A) In locations which are not readily accessible to minors, including but not limited to:
(i) Factories, businesses, offices, and other places which are not open to the general public;
(ii) Places open to the general public which do not admit minors; and
(iii) Places where alcoholic beverages are offered for sale;
(B) In areas which are in the immediate vicinity, plain view, and under the continuous supervision of the proprietor of the establishment or an employee who will observe the purchase of cigarettes, tobacco products, tobacco related objects, alternative nicotine products, and vapor products from the vending machine; and
(C) In rest areas adjacent to roads and highways of the state.
(2) Violation of this subsection shall be punished as provided in subsection (b) of this Code section for violation of subsection (a) of this Code section.

§ 16-12-174. Distribution of tobacco product samples

(a) As used in this Code section, the term "tobacco product sample" means a cigarette, tobacco product, alternative nicotine product, or vapor product distributed to members of the general public at no cost for purposes of promoting the product.
(b) It shall be unlawful for any person to distribute any tobacco product sample to any person under the age of 18 years.
(c) A person distributing tobacco product samples shall require proof of age from a prospective recipient if an ordinary person would conclude on the basis of appearance that such prospective recipient may be under the age of 18 years.
(d) It shall be unlawful for any person who has not attained the age of 18 years to receive or attempt to receive any tobacco product sample.
(e) No person shall distribute tobacco product samples on any public street, sidewalk, or park within 500 feet of any school or playground when those facilities are being used primarily by persons under the age of 18 years.
(f) Violation of this Code section shall be punished as a misdemeanor.

§ 16-12-175. Enforcement actions; collection and report of fines; inspections by law enforcement agencies; annual report

(a) The provisions of this article, inclusive, shall be enforced through actions brought in any court of competent jurisdiction by the prosecuting attorney for the county in which the alleged violation occurred as well as through administrative citations issued by special agents or enforcement officers of the state revenue commissioner. Any fine collected for a violation of said provision shall be paid to the clerk of the court of the jurisdiction in which the violation occurred. Upon receipt of a fine for any violation of said provision, the clerk shall promptly notify the state revenue commissioner of the violation.
(b) The state revenue commissioner, acting through special agents or enforcement officers, shall annually conduct random, unannounced inspections at locations where cigarettes, tobacco products, alternative nicotine products, or vapor products are sold or distributed to ensure compliance with this article. Persons under the age of 18 years may be enlisted to test compliance with this article; provided, however, that such persons may be used to test compliance with this article only if the testing is conducted under the direct supervision of such special agents or enforcement officers and written parental consent has been provided. Any other use of persons under the age of 18 years to test compliance with this article or any other prohibition of like or similar import shall be unlawful and the person or persons responsible for such use shall be subject to the penalties prescribed in this article. The state revenue commissioner shall prepare annually for submission by the Governor to the secretary of the United States Department of Health and Human Services the report required by section 1926 of subpart I of part B of Title XIX of the federal Public Health Service Act, 42 U.S.C. 300x-26.

§ 16-12-176. Administration and enforcement

The state revenue commissioner shall administer and enforce this article and may make reasonable rules and regulations for its administration and enforcement. The state revenue commissioner may designate employees of the Department of Revenue for the purpose of administering and enforcing this article and may delegate to employees of such department any of the duties required of the state revenue commissioner pursuant to this article.

§ 16-12-190. Definition

As used in this article, the term "low THC oil" means an oil that contains an amount of cannabidiol and not more than 5 percent by weight of tetrahydrocannabinol, tetrahydrocannabinolic acid, or a combination of tetrahydrocannabinol and tetrahydrocannabinolic acid which does not contain plant material exhibiting the external morphological features of the plant of the genus Cannabis.

§ 16-12-191. Possession, manufacture, distribution, or sale of low THC oil; penalties

(a) (1) Notwithstanding any provision of Chapter 13 of this title, it shall be lawful for any person to possess or have under his or her control 20 fluid ounces or less of low THC oil if such substance is in a pharmaceutical container labeled by the manufacturer indicating the percentage of tetrahydrocannabinol therein and:
(A) Such person is registered with the Department of Public Health as set forth in Code Section 31-2A-18 and has in his or her possession a registration card issued by the Department of Public Health; or
(B) Such person has in his or her possession a registration card issued by another state that allows the same possession of low THC oil as provided by this state's law; provided, however, that such registration card shall not be lawful authority when such person has been present in this state for 45 days or more.
(2) Notwithstanding any provision of Chapter 13 of this title, any person who possesses or has under his or her control 20 fluid ounces or less of low THC oil without complying with paragraph (1) of this subsection shall be punished as for a misdemeanor.
(b) (1) Notwithstanding any provision of Chapter 13 of this title, it shall be lawful for any person to possess or have under his or her control 20 fluid ounces or less of low THC oil if:

(A) Such person is involved in a clinical research program being conducted by the Board of Regents of the University System of Georgia or any authorized clinical trial or research study in this state or their authorized agent pursuant to Chapter 51 of Title 31 as:

(i) A program participant;

(ii) A parent, guardian, or legal custodian of a program participant;

(iii) An employee of the board of regents designated to participate in the research program;

(iv) A program agent;

(v) A program collaborator and their designated employees;

(vi) A program supplier and their designated employees;

(vii) A program physician;

(viii) A program clinical researcher;

(ix) Program pharmacy personnel; or

(x) Other program medical personnel;

(B) Such person has in his or her possession a permit issued as provided in Code Section 31-51-7; and

(C) Such substance is in a pharmaceutical container labeled by the manufacturer indicating the percentage of tetrahydrocannabinol therein.

(2) Notwithstanding any provision of Chapter 13 of this title, any person who possesses or has under his or her control 20 fluid ounces or less of low THC oil without complying with subparagraphs (A), (B), and (C) of paragraph (1) of this subsection shall be punished as for a misdemeanor.

(c) Notwithstanding any provision of Chapter 13 of this title, any person having possession of or under his or her control more than 20 fluid ounces of low THC oil but less than 160 fluid ounces of low THC oil or who manufactures, distributes, dispenses, sells, or possesses with the intent to distribute low THC oil shall be guilty of a felony, and upon conviction thereof, shall be punished by imprisonment for not less than one nor more than ten years, a fine not to exceed $50,000.00, or both.

(d) Notwithstanding any provision of Chapter 13 of this title, any person who sells, manufactures, delivers, brings into this state, or has possession of 160 or more fluid ounces of low THC oil shall be guilty of the felony offense of trafficking in low THC oil and, upon conviction thereof, shall be punished as follows:

(1) If the quantity of low THC oil is at least 160 fluid ounces but less than 31,000 fluid ounces, by imprisonment for not less than five years nor more than ten years and a fine not to exceed $100,000.00;

(2) If the quantity of low THC oil is at least 31,000 fluid ounces but less than 154,000 fluid ounces, by imprisonment for not less than seven years nor more than 15 years and a fine not to exceed $250,000.00; and

(3) If the quantity of low THC oil is 154,000 or more fluid ounces, by imprisonment for not less than ten years nor more than 20 years and a fine not to exceed $1 million.

(e) Subsections (c) and (d) of this Code section shall not apply to a person involved in a research program being conducted by the Board of Regents of the University System of Georgia or its authorized agent pursuant to Chapter 51 of Title 31 as an employee of the board of regents designated to participate in such program, a program agent, a program collaborator and their designated employees, a program supplier and their designated employees, a physician, clinical researcher, pharmacy personnel, or other medical personnel, provided that such person has in his or her possession a permit issued as provided in Code Section 31-51-7 and such possession, sale, manufacturing, distribution, or dispensing is solely for the purposes set forth in Chapter 51 of Title 31.

(f) Nothing in this article shall require an employer to permit or accommodate the use, consumption, possession, transfer, display, transportation, sale, or growing of marijuana in any form, or to affect the ability of an employer to have a written zero tolerance policy prohibiting the on-duty, and off-duty, use of marijuana, or prohibiting any employee from having a detectable amount of marijuana in such employee's system while at work.

CHAPTER 13. CONTROLLED SUBSTANCES

§ 16-13-1. Drug related objects

(a) As used in this Code section, the term:

(1) "Controlled substance" shall have the same meaning as defined in Article 2 of this chapter, relating to controlled substances. For the purposes of this Code section, the term "controlled substance" shall include marijuana as defined by paragraph (16) of Code Section 16-13-21.

(2) "Dangerous drug" shall have the same meaning as defined in Article 3 of this chapter, relating to dangerous drugs.

(3) "Drug related object" means any machine, instrument, tool, equipment, contrivance, or device which an average person would reasonably conclude is intended to be used for one or more of the following purposes:

(A) To introduce into the human body any dangerous drug or controlled substance under circumstances in violation of the laws of this state;

(B) To enhance the effect on the human body of any dangerous drug or controlled substance under circumstances in violation of the laws of this state;

(C) To conceal any quantity of any dangerous drug or controlled substance under circumstances in violation of the laws of this state; or

(D) To test the strength, effectiveness, or purity of any dangerous drug or controlled substance under circumstances in violation of the laws of this state.

(4) "Knowingly" means having general knowledge that a machine, instrument, tool, item of equipment, contrivance, or device is a drug related object or having reasonable grounds to believe that any such object is or may, to an average person, appear to be a drug related object. If any such object has printed thereon or is accompanied by instructions explaining the purpose and use of such object and if following such instructions would cause a person to commit an act involving the use or possession of a dangerous drug or controlled substance in violation of the laws of this state, then such instructions shall constitute prima-facie evidence of knowledge that the object in question is a drug related object.

(5) "Minor" means any unmarried person under the age of 18 years.

(b) Except as otherwise provided by subsection (d) of this Code section, it shall be unlawful for any person knowingly to sell, deliver, distribute, display for sale, or provide to a minor or knowingly possess with intent to sell, deliver, distribute, display for sale, or provide to a minor any drug related object.

(c) It shall be unlawful for any minor falsely to represent to any person that such minor is 18 years of age or older with the intent to purchase or otherwise obtain any drug related object.

(d) No person shall be guilty of violating subsection (b) of this Code section if:

(1) The person had reasonable cause to believe that the minor involved was 18 years of age or older because the minor exhibited to such person a driver's license, birth certificate, or other official or apparently official document purporting to establish that the minor was 18 years of age or older;

(2) The person made an honest mistake in believing that the minor was 18 years of age or over after making a reasonable bona fide attempt to ascertain the true age of the minor;

(3) The person was the parent or guardian of the minor; or

(4) The person was acting in his capacity as an employee or official of any governmental agency, governmental institution, public school or other public educational institution, any bona fide private school, educational institution, health care facility, or institution; or the person was acting in his capacity as a registered pharmacist or veterinarian or under the direction of a registered pharmacist or veterinarian to sell such object for a legitimate medical purpose.

(e) Any person who violates subsection (b) of this Code section shall be guilty of a misdemeanor for the first offense. For the second or any subsequent offense, a person violating subsection (b) of this Code section shall be guilty of a felony and, upon conviction thereof, shall be punished by imprisonment for not less than one nor more than five years or by a fine of not less than $1,000.00 nor more than $5,000.00, or both. Any person violating subsection (c) of this Code section shall be guilty of a misdemeanor.

§ 16-13-2. Conditional discharge for possession of controlled substances as first offense and certain nonviolent property crimes; dismissal of charges; restitution to victims

(a) Whenever any person who has not previously been convicted of any offense under Article 2 or Article 3 of this chapter or of any statute of the United States or of any state relating to narcotic drugs, marijuana, or stimulant, depressant, or hallucinogenic drugs, pleads guilty to or is found guilty of possession of a narcotic drug, marijuana, or stimulant, depressant, or hallucinogenic drug, the court may without entering a judgment of guilt and with the consent of such person defer further proceedings and place him on probation upon such reasonable terms and conditions as the court may require, preferably terms which require the person to undergo a comprehensive rehabilitation program, including, if necessary, medical treatment, not to exceed three years, designed to acquaint him with the ill effects of drug abuse and to provide him with knowledge of the gains and benefits which can be achieved by being a good member of society. Upon violation of a term or condition, the court may enter an adjudication of guilt and proceed accordingly. Upon fulfillment of the terms and conditions, the court shall discharge the person and dismiss the proceedings against him. Discharge and dismissal under this Code section shall be without court adjudication of guilt and shall not be deemed a conviction for purposes of this Code section or for purposes of disqualifications or disabilities imposed by law upon conviction of a crime. Discharge and dismissal under this Code section may occur only once with respect to any person.

(b) Notwithstanding any law to the contrary, any person who is charged with possession of marijuana, which possession is of one ounce or less, shall be guilty of a misdemeanor and punished by imprisonment for a period not to exceed 12 months or a fine not to exceed $1,000.00, or both, or public works not to exceed 12 months.

(c) Persons charged with an offense enumerated in subsection (a) of this Code section and persons charged for the first time with nonviolent property crimes which, in the judgment of the court exercising jurisdiction over such offenses, were related to the accused's addiction to a controlled substance or alcohol who are eligible for any court approved drug treatment program may, in the discretion of the court and with the consent of the accused, be sentenced in accordance with subsection (a) of this Code section. The probated sentence imposed may be for a period of up to five years. No discharge and dismissal without court adjudication of guilt shall be entered under this subsection until the accused has made full restitution to all victims of the charged offenses. Discharge and dismissal under this Code section shall be without court adjudication of guilt and shall not be deemed a conviction for purposes of this Code section or for purposes of disqualifications or disabilities imposed by law upon conviction of a crime. Discharge and dismissal under this Code section may not be used to disqualify a person in any application for employment or appointment to office in either the public or private sector.

§ 16-13-3. Penalty for abandonment of dangerous drugs, poisons, or controlled substances

Any person who shall abandon, in a public place, any dangerous drug, poison, or controlled substance as defined by Article 2 or Article 3 of this chapter shall be guilty of a misdemeanor.

§ 16-13-4. Approval by Food and Drug Administration as prerequisite to sale of controlled substances and dangerous drugs

(a) No controlled substance or dangerous drug shall be sold for dispensing unless the controlled substance, as defined in Code Section 16-13-21, or the dangerous drug, as defined in Code Section 16-13-71:
(1) Is approved by the Food and Drug Administration for resale;
(2) Has a new approved drug application number (known as an NDA number) unless excepted by the Food and Drug Administration; or
(3) Has an approved abbreviated new drug application number (known as an ANDA number) unless excepted by the Food and Drug Administration.
(b) Any person who violates subsection (a) of this Code section shall be guilty of a felony and, upon conviction thereof, shall be punished by imprisonment of not less than one year nor more than five years.

§ 16-13-5. Immunity from arrest or prosecution for persons seeking medical assistance for drug overdose

(a) As used in this Code section, the term:
(1) "Drug overdose" means an acute condition, including, but not limited to, extreme physical illness, decreased level of consciousness, respiratory depression, coma, mania, or death, resulting from the consumption or use of a controlled substance or dangerous drug by the distressed individual in violation of this chapter or that a reasonable person would believe to be resulting from the consumption or use of a controlled substance or dangerous drug by the distressed individual.
(2) "Drug violation" means:
(A) A violation of subsection (a) of Code Section 16-13-30 for possession of a controlled substance if the aggregate weight, including any mixture, is less than four grams of a solid substance, less than one milliliter of liquid substance, or if the substance is placed onto a secondary medium with a combined weight of less than four grams;
(B) A violation of paragraph (1) of subsection (j) of Code Section 16-13-30 for possession of less than one ounce of marijuana; or
(C) A violation of Code Section 16-13-32.2, relating to possession and use of drug related objects.
(3) "Medical assistance" means aid provided to a person by a health care professional licensed, registered, or certified under the laws of this state who, acting within his or her lawful scope of practice, may provide diagnosis, treatment, or emergency medical services.
(4) "Seeks medical assistance" means accesses or assists in accessing the 9-1-1 system or otherwise contacts or assists in contacting law enforcement or a poison control center and provides care to a person while awaiting the arrival of medical assistance to aid such person.
(b) Any person who in good faith seeks medical assistance for a person experiencing or believed to be experiencing a drug overdose shall not be arrested, charged, or prosecuted for a drug violation if the evidence for the arrest, charge, or prosecution of such drug violation resulted solely from seeking such medical assistance. Any person who is experiencing a drug overdose and, in good faith, seeks medical assistance for himself or herself or is the subject of such a request shall not be arrested, charged, or prosecuted for a drug violation if the evidence for the arrest, charge, or prosecution of such drug violation resulted solely from seeking such medical assistance. Any such person shall also not be subject to, if related to the seeking of such medical assistance:
(1) Penalties for a violation of a permanent or temporary protective order or restraining order; or
(2) Sanctions for a violation of a condition of pretrial release, condition of probation, or condition of parole based on a drug violation.
(c) Nothing in this Code section shall be construed to limit the admissibility of any evidence in connection with the investigation or prosecution of a crime with regard to a defendant who does not qualify for the protections of subsection (b) of this Code section or with regard to other crimes committed by a person who otherwise qualifies for protection pursuant to subsection (b) of this Code section. Nothing in this Code section shall be construed to limit any seizure of evidence or contraband otherwise permitted by law. Nothing in this Code section shall be construed to limit or abridge the authority of a law enforcement officer to detain or take into custody a person in the course of an investigation or to effectuate an arrest for any offense except as provided in subsection (b) of this Code section.

§ 16-13-20. Short title

This article shall be known and may be cited as the "Georgia Controlled Substances Act."

§ 16-13-21. Definitions

As used in this article, the term:
(0.5) "Addiction" means a primary, chronic, neurobiologic disease with genetic, psychosocial, and environmental factors influencing its development and manifestations. It is characterized by behaviors that include the following: impaired control drug use, craving, compulsive use, and continued use despite harm. Physical dependence and tolerance are normal physiological consequences of extended opioid therapy for pain and are not the same as addiction.
(1) "Administer" means the direct application of a controlled substance, whether by injection, inhalation, ingestion, or by any other means, to the body of a patient or research subject by:
(A) A practitioner or, in his or her presence, by his or her authorized agent; or
(B) The patient or research subject at the direction and in the presence of the practitioner.
(1.1) "Agency" means the Georgia Drugs and Narcotics Agency established pursuant to Code Section 26-4-29.

(2) "Agent" of a manufacturer, distributor, or dispenser means an authorized person who acts on behalf of or at the direction of a manufacturer, distributor, or dispenser. It does not include a common or contract carrier, public warehouseman, or employee of the carrier or warehouseman.

(2.1) "Board" means the State Board of Pharmacy or its designee, so long as such designee is another state entity.

(3) "Bureau" means the Georgia Bureau of Investigation.

(4) "Controlled substance" means a drug, substance, or immediate precursor in Schedules I through V of Code Sections 16-13-25 through 16-13-29 and Schedules I through V of 21 C.F.R. Part 1308.

(5) "Conveyance" means any object, including aircraft, vehicle, or vessel, but not including a person, which may be used to carry or transport a substance or object.

(6) "Counterfeit substance" means:

(A) A controlled substance which, or the container or labeling of which, without authorization, bears the trademark, trade name, or other identifying mark, imprint, number, or device, or any likeness thereof, of a manufacturer, distributor, or dispenser other than the person who in fact manufactured, distributed, or dispensed the controlled substance;

(B) A controlled substance or noncontrolled substance, which is held out to be a controlled substance or marijuana, whether in a container or not which does not bear a label which accurately or truthfully identifies the substance contained therein; or

(C) Any substance, whether in a container or not, which bears a label falsely identifying the contents as a controlled substance.

(6.1) "Dangerous drug" means any drug, other than a controlled substance, which cannot be dispensed except upon the issuance of a prescription drug order by a practitioner authorized under this chapter.

(6.2) "DEA" means the United States Drug Enforcement Administration.

(7) "Deliver" or "delivery" means the actual, constructive, or attempted transfer from one person to another of a controlled substance, whether or not there is an agency relationship.

(8) "Dependent," "dependency," "physical dependency," "psychological dependency," or "psychic dependency" means and includes the state of adaptation that is manifested by drug class specific signs and symptoms that can be produced by abrupt cessation, rapid dose reduction, decreasing blood level of the drug, and administration of an antagonist. Physical dependence, by itself, does not equate with addiction.

(9) "Dispense" means to deliver a controlled substance to an ultimate user or research subject by or pursuant to the lawful order of a practitioner, including the prescribing, administering, packaging, labeling, or compounding necessary to prepare the substance for that delivery, or the delivery of a controlled substance by a practitioner, acting in the normal course of his or her professional practice and in accordance with this article, or to a relative or representative of the person for whom the controlled substance is prescribed.

(10) "Dispenser" means a person licensed under the laws of this state, or any other state or territory of the United States, to dispense or deliver a Schedule II, III, IV, or V controlled substance to the ultimate user in this state but shall not include:

(A) A pharmacy licensed as a hospital pharmacy by the Georgia State Board of Pharmacy pursuant to Code Section 26-4-110;

(B) An institutional pharmacy that serves only a health care facility, including, but not limited to, a nursing home, an intermediate care home, a personal care home, or a hospice program, which provides patient care and which pharmacy dispenses such substances to be administered and used by a patient on the premises of the facility;

(C) A practitioner or other authorized person who administers such a substance; or

(D) A pharmacy operated by, on behalf of, or under contract with the Department of Corrections for the sole and exclusive purpose of providing services in a secure environment to prisoners within a penal institution, penitentiary, prison, detention center, or other secure correctional institution. This shall include correctional institutions operated by private entities in this state which house inmates under the Department of Corrections.

(11) "Distribute" means to deliver a controlled substance, other than by administering or dispensing it.

(12) "Distributor" means a person who distributes.

(12.05) "FDA" means the United States Food and Drug Administration.

(12.1) "Imitation controlled substance" means:

(A) A product specifically designed or manufactured to resemble the physical appearance of a controlled substance such that a reasonable person of ordinary knowledge would not be able to distinguish the imitation from the controlled substance by outward appearances; or

(B) A product, not a controlled substance, which, by representations made and by dosage unit appearance, including color, shape, size, or markings, would lead a reasonable person to believe that, if ingested, the product would have a stimulant or depressant effect similar to or the same as that of one or more of the controlled substances included in Schedules I through V of Code Sections 16-13-25 through 16-13-29.

(13) "Immediate precursor" means a substance which the State Board of Pharmacy has found to be and by rule identifies as being the principal compound commonly used or produced primarily for use, and which is an immediate chemical intermediary used or likely to be used, in the manufacture of a controlled substance, the control of which is necessary to prevent, curtail, or limit manufacture.

(14) "Isomers" means stereoisomers (optical isomers), geometrical isomers, and structural isomers (chain and positional isomers) but shall not include functional isomers.

(15) "Manufacture" means the production, preparation, propagation, compounding, conversion, or processing of a controlled substance, either directly or indirectly by extraction from substances of natural origin, or independently by means of chemical synthesis, and includes any packaging or repackaging of the substance or labeling or relabeling of its container, except that this term does not include the preparation, compounding, packaging, or labeling of a controlled substance:

(A) By a practitioner as an incident to his or her administering or dispensing of a controlled substance in the course of his or her professional practice; or

(B) By a practitioner or by his or her authorized agent under his or her supervision for the purpose of, or as an incident to, research, teaching, or chemical analysis and not for sale.

(16) "Marijuana" means all parts of the plant of the genus Cannabis, whether growing or not, the seeds thereof, the resin extracted from any part of such plant, and every compound, manufacture, salt, derivative, mixture, or preparation of such plant, its seeds, or resin; but shall not include samples as described in subparagraph (P) of paragraph (3) of Code Section 16-13-25 and shall not include the completely defoliated mature stalks of such plant, fiber produced from such stalks, oil, or cake, or the completely sterilized samples of seeds of the plant which are incapable of germination.

(17) "Narcotic drug" means any of the following, whether produced directly or indirectly by extraction from substances of vegetable origin, or independently by means of chemical synthesis, or by a combination of extraction and chemical synthesis:

(A) Opium and opiate, and any salt, compound, derivative, or preparation of opium or opiate;

(B) Any salt, compound, isomer, derivative, or preparation thereof which is chemically equivalent or identical to any of the substances referred to in subparagraph (A) of this paragraph, but not including the isoquinoline alkaloids of opium;

(C) Opium poppy and poppy straw; or

(D) Coca leaves and any salt, compound, derivative, stereoisomers of cocaine, or preparation of coca leaves, and any salt, compound, stereoisomers of cocaine, derivative, or preparation thereof which is chemically equivalent or identical to any of these substances, but not including decocainized coca leaves or extractions of coca leaves which do not contain cocaine or ecgonine.

(17.1) "Noncontrolled substance" means any drug or other substance other than a controlled substance as defined by paragraph (4) of this Code section.

(18) "Opiate" means any substance having an addiction-forming or addiction-sustaining liability similar to morphine or being capable of conversion into a drug having addiction-forming or addiction-sustaining liability. It does not include, unless specifically designated as controlled under Code Section 16-13-22, the dextrorotatory isomer of 3-methoxy-n-methylmorphinan and its salts (dextromethorphan). It does include its racemic and levorotatory forms.

(19) "Opium poppy" means the plant of the species Papaver somniferum L., except its seeds.

(19.1) "Patient" means the person who is the intended consumer of a drug for whom a prescription is issued or for whom a drug is dispensed.

(20) "Person" means an individual, corporation, government, or governmental subdivision or agency, business trust, estate, trust, partnership, or association, or any other legal entity.

(21) "Poppy straw" means all parts, except the seeds, of the opium poppy after mowing.

(22) "Potential for abuse" means and includes a substantial potential for a substance to be used by an individual to the extent of creating hazards to the health of the user or the safety of the public, or the substantial potential of a substance to cause an individual using that substance to become dependent upon that substance.

(23) "Practitioner" means:

(A) A physician, dentist, pharmacist, podiatrist, scientific investigator, or other person licensed, registered, or otherwise authorized under the laws of this state to distribute, dispense, conduct research with respect to, or administer a controlled substance in the course of professional practice or research in this state;

(B) A pharmacy, hospital, or other institution licensed, registered, or otherwise authorized by law to distribute, dispense, conduct research with respect to, or administer a controlled substance in the course of professional practice or research in this state;

(C) An advanced practice registered nurse acting pursuant to the authority of Code Section 43-34-25. For purposes of this chapter and Code Section 43-34-25, an advanced practice registered nurse is authorized to register with the DEA and appropriate state authorities; or

(D) A physician assistant acting pursuant to the authority of subsection (e.1) of Code Section 43-34-103. For purposes of this chapter and subsection (e.1) of Code Section 43-34-103, a physician assistant is authorized to register with the DEA and appropriate state authorities.

(23.1) "Prescriber" means a physician, dentist, scientific investigator, or other person licensed, registered, or otherwise authorized under the laws of this state, or any other state or territory of the United States, to prescribe a controlled substance in the course of professional practice or research in this state.

(24) "Production" includes the manufacture, planting, cultivation, growing, or harvesting of a controlled substance.

(25) "Registered" or "register" means registration as required by this article.

(26) "Registrant" means a person who is registered under this article.

(26.1) "Schedule II, III, IV, or V controlled substance" means a controlled substance that is classified as a Schedule II, III, IV, or V controlled substance under Code Section 16-13-26, 16-13-27, 16-13-28, or 16-13-29, respectively, or under the federal Controlled Substances Act, 21 U.S.C. Section 812.

(27) "State," when applied to a part of the United States, includes any state, district, commonwealth, territory, insular possession thereof, or any area subject to the legal authority of the United States.

(27.1) "Tolerance" means a physiologic state resulting from regular use of a drug in which an increased dosage is needed to produce a specific effect or a reduced effect is observed with a constant dose over time. Tolerance may or may not be evident during opioid treatment and does not equate with addiction.

(28) "Ultimate user" means a person who lawfully possesses a controlled substance for his or her own use, for the use of a member of his or her household, or for administering to an animal owned by him or her or by a member of his or her household or an agent or representative of the person.

§ 16-13-22. Administration of article; standards and schedules

(a) The State Board of Pharmacy shall administer this article and shall add substances to or reschedule all substances enumerated in the schedules in Code Sections 16-13-25 through 16-13-29 pursuant to the procedures of Chapter 13 of Title 50, the "Georgia Administrative Procedure Act." In making a determination or identification regarding a substance, the State Board of Pharmacy shall consider the following factors:

(1) The actual or relative potential for abuse;

(2) The scientific evidence of its pharmacological effect, if known;

(3) The state of current scientific knowledge regarding the substance;

(4) The history and current pattern of abuse;

(5) The scope, duration, and significance of abuse;

(6) The risk to the public health;

(7) The potential of the substance to produce psychic or physiological dependence liability;

(8) Whether the substance is an immediate precursor of a substance already controlled under this article; and

(9) The designation, deletion, or rescheduling of a substance under federal law controlling controlled substances.

(b) After considering the factors enumerated in subsection (a) of this Code section, the State Board of Pharmacy shall make findings with respect thereto and cause the publication of such findings as a rule, in accordance with Chapter 13 of Title 50, the "Georgia Administrative Procedure Act," controlling the substance if it finds the substance has a potential for abuse.

(c) If the State Board of Pharmacy identifies a substance as an immediate precursor, substances which are precursors of the controlled substance shall not be subject to control solely because they are precursors of the controlled substance.

(d) Authority to control under this Code section does not extend to distilled spirits, wine, malt beverages, or tobacco, as those terms are defined or used in Title 3 or 48.

§ 16-13-23. Nomenclature for controlled substances

The controlled substances listed in the schedules in Code Sections 16-13-25 through 16-13-29 are included by whatever official, common, usual, chemical, or trade name designated.

§ 16-13-24. Establishment of schedules of controlled substances

(a) There are established five schedules of controlled substances, to be known as Schedules I, II, III, IV, and V. The schedules shall consist of the substances listed in Code Sections 16-13-25 through 16-13-29. The schedules so established shall be updated and republished by the State Board of Pharmacy on an annual basis.

(b) Except in the case of an immediate precursor, a drug or other substance may not be placed in any schedule unless the findings required for such schedule are made with respect to the drug or other substance. The findings for each of the schedules are as follows:

(1) Schedule I:

(A) The drug or other substance has a high potential for abuse;

(B) The drug or other substance has no currently accepted medical use in treatment in the United States; and

(C) There is a lack of accepted safety for use of the drug or other substance under medical supervision.

(2) Schedule II:

(A) The drug or other substance has a high potential for abuse;

(B) The drug or other substance has a currently accepted medical use in treatment in the United States or a currently accepted medical use with severe restrictions; and

(C) Abuse of the drug or other substance may lead to severe psychological or physical dependence.

(3) Schedule III:

(A) The drug or other substance has a potential for abuse less than the drugs or other substances in Schedules I and II;

(B) The drug or other substance has a currently accepted medical use in treatment in the United States; and

(C) Abuse of the drug or other substance may lead to moderate or low physical dependence or high psychological dependence.

(4) Schedule IV:

(A) The drug or other substance has a low potential for abuse relative to the drugs or other substances in Schedule III;

(B) The drug or other substance has a currently accepted medical use in treatment in the United States; and

(C) Abuse of the drug or other substance may lead to limited physical dependence or psychological dependence relative to the drugs or other substances in Schedule III.

(5) Schedule V:

(A) The drug or other substance has a low potential for abuse relative to the drugs or other substances in Schedule IV;

(B) The drug or other substance has a currently accepted medical use in treatment in the United States; and

(C) Abuse of the drug or other substance may lead to limited physical dependence or psychological dependence relative to the drugs or other substances in Schedule IV.

§ 16-13-25. Schedule I

The controlled substances listed in this Code section are included in Schedule I:

(1)   Any of the following opiates, including their isomers, esters, ethers, salts, and salts of isomers, esters, and ethers, unless specifically excepted, pursuant to this article, whenever the existence of these isomers, esters, ethers, and salts is possible within the specific chemical designation:

(A) Acetylmethadol;(B) Allylprodine;(C) Reserved;(D) Alphameprodine;

(E) Alphamethadol;(F) Benzethidine;(G) Betacetylmethadol;(H) Betameprodine;

(I) Betamethadol;(J) Betaprodine;(K) Clonitazene;(L) Dextromoramide;(M) Dextromorphan;

(N) Diampromide;(O) Diethylthiambutene;(P) Dimenoxadol;(Q) Dimepheptanol;

(R) Dimethylthiambutene;(S) Dioxaphetyl butyrate;(T) Dipipanone;(U) Ethylmethylthiambutene;

(V) Etonitazene;(W) Etoxeridene;(X) Furethidine;(Y) Hydroxypethidine;

(Z) Ketobemidone;(AA) Levomoramide;(BB) Levophenacylmorphan;(CC) Morpheridine;(DD) Noracymethadol;

(EE) Norlevorphanol;(FF) Normethadone;(GG) Norpipanone;(HH) Phenadoxone;

(II) Phenampromide;(JJ) Phenomorphan;(KK) Phenoperidine;(LL) Piritramide;

(MM) Proheptazine;(NN) Properidine;(OO) Propiram;(PP) Racemoramide;

(QQ) Trimeperidine;(RR) 3,4-dichloro-N-[(1-dimethylamino)cyclohexylmethyl]benzamide (AH-7921);

(SS) 3,4-dichloro-N-(2-(dimethylamino)cyclohexyl)-N-methylbenzamide (U-47700);

(2) Any of the following opium derivatives, their salts, isomers, and salts of isomers, unless specifically excepted, whenever the existence of these salts, isomers, and salts of isomers is possible within the specific chemical designation:
(A) Acetorphine;(B) Acetyldihydrocodeine;(C) Benzylmorphine;(D) Codeine methylbromide;

(E) Codeine-N-Oxide;(F) Cyprenorphine;(G) Desomorphine;(H) Dihydromorphine;

(I) Etorphine;(J) Heroin;(K) Hydromorphinol;(L) Methyldesorphine;(M) Methyldihydromorphine;

(N) Morphine methylbromide;(O) Morphine methylsulfonate;(P) Morphine-N-Oxide;(Q) Myrophine;

(R) Nicocodeine;(S) Nicomorphine;(T) Normorphine;(U) Pholcodine;(V) Thebacon;

(3) Any material, compound, mixture, or preparation which contains any quantity of the following hallucinogenic substances, their salts, isomers (whether optical, position, or geometrics), and salts of isomers, unless specifically excepted, whenever the existence of these salts, isomers, and salts of isomers is possible within the specific chemical designation:
(A) 3, 4-methylenedioxyamphetamine;
(B) 5-methoxy-3, 4-methylenedioxyamphetamine;
(C) 3, 4, 5-trimethoxyamphetamine;
(D) Bufotenine;
(E) Diethyltryptamine;
(F) Dimethyltryptamine;
(G) 4-methyl-2, 5-dimethoxyamphetamine;
(H) Ibogaine;
(I) Lysergic acid diethylamide;
(J) Mescaline;
(K) Peyote;
(L) N-ethyl-3-piperidyl benzilate;
(M) N-methyl-3-piperidyl benzilate;
(N) Psilocybin;
(O) Psilocyn (Psilocin);
(P) Tetrahydrocannabinol, tetrahydrocannabinolic acid, or a combination of tetrahydrocannabinol and tetrahydrocannabinolic acid which does not contain plant material exhibiting the external morphological features of the plant of the genus Cannabis;
(Q) 2, 5-dimethoxyamphetamine;
(R) 4-bromo-2, 5-dimethoxyamphetamine;
(S) 4-methoxyamphetamine;
(T) Cyanoethylamphetamine;
(U) (1-phenylcyclohexyl) ethylamine;
(V) 1-(1-phenylcyclohexyl) pyrrolidine;
(W) Phencyclidine;
(X) 1-piperidinocyclohexanecarbonitrile;
(Y) 1-phenyl-2-propanone (phenylacetone);
(Z) 3, 4-Methylenedioxymethamphetamine (MDMA);
(AA) 1-methyl-4-phenyl-4-propionoxypiperidine;
(BB) 1-(2-phenylethyl)-4-phenyl-4-acetyloxypiperidine;
(CC) Reserved;
(DD) N-ethyl-3, 4-methylenedioxyamphetamine;
(EE) Reserved;
(FF) 2,5-Dimethoxy-4-Ethylamphetamine;
(GG) Cathinone;
(HH) Reserved;
(II) PEPAP (1-(2-phenethyl)-4 phenyl-4-acetoxypiperide);
(JJ) Reserved;
(KK) Reserved;
(LL) Reserved;
(MM) Reserved;
(NN) Reserved;
(OO) 3,4-Methylenedioxy-N-Ethylamphetamine;
(PP) 4-Methylaminorex;
(QQ) N-Hydroxy-3,4-Methylenedioxyamphetamine;
(RR) Reserved;
(SS) Chlorophenylpiperazine (CPP);
(TT) N, N-Dimethylamphetamine;
(UU) 1-(1-(2-thienyl)cyclohexy)pyrrolidine;
(VV) 4-Bromo-2,5-Dimethoxyphenethylamine (DMPE);

(WW) Alpha-Ethyltryptamine;

(XX) Methcathinone;

(YY) Aminorex;

(ZZ) 4-iodo-2,5-dimethoxyamphetamine;

(AAA) 4-chloro-2,5-dimethoxyamphetamine;

(BBB) 3,4-Methylenedioxypyrovalerone (MDPV);

(CCC) 4-Methylmethcathinone (Mephedrone);

(DDD) 3,4-Methylenedioxymethcathinone (Methylone);

(EEE) 4-Methoxymethcathinone;

(FFF) Fluoromethcathinone;

(GGG) Fluorophenylpiperazine (FPP);

(HHH) 4-iodo-2,5-dimethoxyphenethylamine (2C-I);

(III) 4-chloro-2,5-dimethoxyphenethylamine (2C-C);

(JJJ) 4-iodo-2,5-dimethoxy-N-[(2-methoxyphenyl)methyl]-
benzeneethanamine (25I-NBOMe);

(KKK) 4-chloro-2,5-dimethoxy-N-[(2-methoxyphenyl)methyl]-
benzeneethanamine (25C-NBOMe);

(LLL) 4-bromo-2,5-dimethoxy-N-[(2-methoxyphenyl)methyl]-
benzeneethanamine (25B-NBOMe);

(MMM) N,N-Diallyl-5-Methoxytryptamine (5-MeO-DALT);

(NNN) 2-(2,5-dimethoxy-4-ethylphenyl)ethanamine (2C-E);

(OOO) 2-(2,5-Dimethoxy-4-nitrophenyl)-N-(2-methoxybenzyl)
ethanamine (25N-NBOMe);

(PPP) 4-acetoxy-N-ethyl-N-methyltryptamine (4-AcO-MET);

(QQQ) 4-nitro-2,5-dimethoxyphenethylamine (2C-N);

(RRR) 5-methoxy-N,N-methylisopropyltryptamine (5-MeO-MIPT);

(SSS) Methoxetamine;

(TTT) N-acetyl-3,4-methylenedioxymethcathinone;

(UUU) 3-(1,3-benzenodioxol-5-yl)-N,2-dimethylpropan-1-amine (3,4-methylenedioxymethamphetamine methyl homolog);

(VVV) (2-aminopropyl)-2,3-dihydrobenzofuran (APDB);

(WWW) 4-methyl-2,5-dimethoxy-N-[(2-methoxyphenyl)
methyl]-benzeneethanamine (25D-NBOMe);

(XXX) 2-chloro-4,5-methylenedioxymethamphetamine;

(YYY) 4-hydroxy-N-methyl-N-ethyltryptamine (4-HO-MET);

(ZZZ) 2-bromo-4,5-methylenedioxymethamphetamine;

(AAAA) 2-(2,5-dimethoxyphenyl)-N-(2-methoxybenzyl)ethanamine (25H-NBOMe);

(BBBB) Methoxyphencyclidine (MeO-PCP);

(CCCC) 4-hydroxy-N-methyl-N-isopropyltryptamine (4-OH-MiPT);

(DDDD) N,a-dimethyl-5-benzofuranethanamine (5-MAPB);

(EEEE) 1-(1-benzofuran-6-yl)propan-2-amine (6-APB);

(FFFF) 1-(1-benzofuran-5-yl)-N-ethylpropan-2-amine (5-EAPB);

(4) Any material, compound, mixture, or preparation which contains any of the following substances having a stimulant effect on the central nervous system, including its salts, isomers, and salts of isomers, unless specifically excepted, whenever the existence of these salts, isomers, and salts of isomers is possible within the specific chemical designation:

(A) Fenethylline;

(B) Reserved;

(C) Reserved;

(D) Para-methoxyphenylpiperazine (MeOPP);

(5) Any material, compound, mixture, or preparation which contains any quantity of the following substances, their salts, isomers (whether optical, position, or geometrics), and salts of isomers, unless specifically excepted, whenever the existence of these substances, their salts, isomers, and salts of isomers is possible within the specific chemical designation:

(A) Gamma hydroxybutyric acid (gamma hydroxy butyrate); provided, however, that this does not include any amount naturally and normally occurring in the human body; and

(B) Sodium oxybate, when the FDA approved form of this drug is not:

(i) In a container labeled in compliance with subsection (a) or (b) of Code Section 26-3-8; and

(ii) In the possession of:

(I) A registrant permitted to dispense the drug;

(II) Any person other than to whom the drug was prescribed; or

(III) Any person who attempts to or does unlawfully possess, sell, distribute, or give this drug to any other person;

(6) Notwithstanding the fact that Schedule I substances have no currently accepted medical use, the General Assembly recognizes certain of these substances which are currently accepted for certain limited medical uses in treatment in the United States but have a high potential for abuse. Accordingly, unless specifically excepted or unless listed in another schedule, any material, compound, mixture, or preparation which contains any quantity of methaqualone, including its salts, isomers, optical isomers, salts of their isomers, and salts of these optical isomers, is included in Schedule I;

(7) 2,5-Dimethoxy-4-(n)-propylthiophenethylamine (2C-T-7);

(8) 1-(3-Trifluoromethylphenyl) Piperazine (TFMPP);

(9) N-Benzylpiperazine (BZP);

(10) 5-Methoxy-N,N-Diisopropyltryptamine (5-MeO-DIPT);

(11) Alpha-Methyltryptamine (AMT);

(12) Any of the following compounds, derivatives, their salts, isomers, or salts of isomers, halogen analogues, or homologues, unless specifically utilized as part of the manufacturing process by a commercial industry of a substance or material not intended for human ingestion or consumption, as a prescription administered under medical supervision, or research at a recognized institution, whenever the existence of these salts, isomers, or salts of isomers, halogen analogues, or homologues is possible within the specific chemical designation:

(A) Naphthoylindoles;

(B) Naphthylmethylindoles;

(C) Naphthoylpyrroles;

(D) Naphthylideneindenes;

(E) Phenylacetylindoles;

(F) Cyclohexylphenols;

(G) Benzoylindoles;

(H) Tricyclic benzopyrans;

(I) Adamantoylindoles;

(J) Indazole amides;

(K) [2,3-Dihydro-5-methyl-3-(4-morpholinylmethyl)pyrrolo[1,2,3-de]-1,4-benzoxazin-6-yl]-1-naphthalenylmethanone (WIN 55,212-2);

(L) Any compound, unless specifically excepted or listed in this or another schedule, structurally derived from 2-aminopropan-1-one by substitution at the 1-position with either phenyl, naphthyl, or thiophene ring systems, whether or not the compound is further modified in any of the following ways:

(i) By substitution in the ring system to any extent with alkyl, alkylenedioxy, alkoxy, haloalkyl, hydroxyl, or halide substitutions, whether or not further substituted in the ring system;

(ii) By substitution at the 3-position with an acyclic alkyl substitution; or

(iii) By substitution at the 2-amino nitrogen atom with alkyl, dialkyl, benzyl, or methoxybenzyl groups, or by inclusion of the 2-amino nitrogen atom in a cyclic structure;

(M) Indole carboxamides;

(N) Indole carboxylates;

(O) [1,1'-biphenyl]-3-yl-carbamic acid, cyclohexyl ester (URB602);

(P) Indazole carboxylates;

(Q) [3-(3-carbamoylphenyl)phenyl] N-cyclohexylcarbamate (URB597);

(R) 6-methyl-2-[(4-methylphenyl)amino]-1-benzoxazin-4-one (URB754);

(S) Indole tetramethylcyclopropanecarbonyls;

(T) Napthoylbenzimidazoles;

(U) 1-naphthalenyl[4-(pentylox)-1-naphthalenyl]-methanone (CB-13);

(V) Naphthoylindazoles;

(13) The fentanyl analog structural class, including any of the following derivatives, their salts, isomers, or salts of isomers, unless specifically utilized as part of the manufacturing process by a commercial industry of a substance or material not intended for human ingestion or consumption, as a prescription administered under medical supervision, or for research at a recognized institution, whenever the existence of these salts, isomers, or salts of isomers is possible within the specific chemical designation or unless specifically excepted or listed in this or another schedule, structurally derived from fentanyl, and whether or not further modified in any of the following ways:

(A) Substitution anywhere on the phenethyl group with:

(i) Alkyl group;

(ii) Hydroxyl group;

(iii) Halide group;

(B) Replacement of the phenethyl group with:

(i) Thienyl ethyl group, which can be further substituted with:

(I) Alkyl group;

(II) Hydroxyl group;

(III) Halide group;

(ii) Oxotetrazol ethyl group, which can be further substituted with:

(I) Alkyl group;

(II) Hydroxyl group;

(III) Halide group;

(iii) Alkyl group;

(iv) Thienyl methyl group, which can be further substituted with:

(I) Alkyl group;

(II) Hydroxyl group;

(III) Halide group;

(v) Benzyl group, which can be further substituted with:

(I) Alkyl group;

(II) Hydroxyl group;

(III) Halide group;

(vi) Furanyl ethyl group, which can be further substituted with:

(I) Alkyl group;

(II) Hydroxyl group;

(III) Halide group;

(vii) Phenyl alkyl group, which can be further substituted with:

(I) Alkyl group;

(II) Hydroxyl group;

(III) Halide group;

(viii) Pyridinyl ethyl group, which can be further substituted with:

(I) Alkyl group;

(II) Hydroxyl group;

(III) Halide group;

(ix) Diazole ethyl group, which can be further substituted with:

(I) Alkyl group;

(II) Hydroxyl group;

(III) Halide group;

(IV) Nitro group;

(x) Thiazole ethyl group, which can be further substituted with:

(I) Alkyl group;

(II) Hydroxyl group;

(III) Halide group;

(xi) Benzoxazolinone ethyl group, which can be further substituted with:

(I) Alkyl group;

(II) Hydroxyl group;

(III) Halide group;

(C) Substitution anywhere on the piperidine ring with:

(i) Alkyl group;

(ii) Allyl group;

(iii) Phenyl group;

(iv) Ester group;

(v) Ether group;

(vi) Pyridine group, which can be further substituted with:

(I) Alkyl group;

(II) Hydroxyl group;

(III) Halide group;

(vii) Thiazole group, which can be further substituted with:

(I) Alkyl group;

(II) Hydroxyl group;

(III) Halide group;

(viii) Oxadiazole group, which can be further substituted with:

(I) Alkyl group;

(II) Hydroxyl group;

(III) Halide group;

(IV) Ether group;

(D) Substitution anywhere on the propanamide group with:

(i) Cyclic alkyl group;

(ii) Acyclic alkyl group:

(iii) Methoxy group;

(E) Replacement of the propanamide group with:

(i) Acryloyl amino group;

(ii) Acetamide group, which itself can be further substituted with a cyclic alkyl group;

(iii) Methoxy acetamide group;

(iv) Furanyl amide group;

(F) Substitution anywhere on the phenyl ring with:

(i) Halide group;

(ii) Methoxy group;

(iii) Alkyl group;

(G) Replacement of the phenyl ring with the pyrazine ring;

(14) The piperidinyl-sulfonamide structural class, including any of the following compounds, derivatives, their salts, isomers, or salts of isomers, halogen analogues, or homologues, unless specifically utilized as part of the manufacturing process by a commercial industry of a substance or material not intended for human ingestion or consumption, as a prescription administered under medical supervision, or for research at a recognized institution, whenever the existence of these salts, isomers, or salts of isomers, halogen analogues, or homologues is possible within the specific chemical designation or unless specifically excepted or listed in this or another schedule, structurally derived from piperidinyl-sulfonamide, and whether or not further modified in any of the following ways:

(A) By substitution at the 1-position of the piperidinyl ring with any of the following:

(i) Alkyl group;

(ii) Phenyl alkyl group;

(iii) Amino substituted phenyl alkyl group;

(iv) Nitro substituted phenyl alkyl group;

(v) Cycloalkyl group;

(vi) Alkenyl substituent group;

(B) By substitution at the 3-position or 4-position of the piperidinyl ring with any of the following:

(i) Halide group;

(ii) Alkyl group;

(iii) Alkoxy substituent;

(C) By substitution on the sulfonamide with any of the following:

(i) Pyridyl group;

(ii) Alkyl group;

(iii) Phenyl group;

(iv) Phenyl alkyl group;

(v) Alkoxy substituted phenyl group;

(vi) Halogen substituted phenyl group;

(vii) Nitro substituted phenyl group;

(viii) Amino substituted phenyl group;

(ix) Alkanoylamino substituted phenyl group;

(x) Amido substituted phenyl group;

(15) The 1-cyclohexyl-4-(1,2-diphenylethy)-piperazine (MT-45) structural class, including any of the following derivatives, their salts, isomers, or salts of isomers, unless specifically utilized as part of the manufacturing process by a commercial industry of a substance or material not intended for human ingestion or consumption, as a prescription administered under medical supervision, or for research at a recognized institution, whenever the existence of these salts, isomers, or salts of isomers is possible within the specific chemical designation or unless specifically excepted or listed in this or another schedule, structurally derived from 1-cyclohexyl-4-(1,2-diphenylethy)-piperazine (MT-45), and whether or not further modified in any of the following ways:

(A) Replacement of the cyclohexyl group with any of the following:

(i) Cycloheptyl group;

(ii) Cyclooctyl group;

(B) Substitution on the diphenyl groups with any of the following:

(i) Hydroxyl group;

(ii) Halide;

(iii) Alkoxy group;

(iv) Alkyl group;

(v) Ester group;

(vi) Phenyl ether group.

§ 16-13-26. Schedule II

The controlled substances listed in this Code section are included in Schedule II:

(1) Any of the following substances, or salts thereof, except those narcotic drugs specifically exempted or listed in other schedules, whether produced directly or indirectly by extraction from substances of vegetable origin, or independently by extraction from substances of vegetable origin, or independently by means of chemical synthesis, or by combination of extraction and chemical synthesis:

(A) Opium and opiate, and any salt, compound, derivative, or preparation of opium or opiate, excluding naloxone hydrochloride, but including the following:

(i) Raw opium;

(ii) Opium extracts;

(iii) Opium fluid extracts;

(iv) Powdered opium;

(v) Granulated opium;

(vi) Tincture of opium;

(vii) Codeine;

(viii) Ethylmorphine;

(ix) Hydrocodone;

(x) Hydromorphone;

(xi) Metopon;

(xii) Morphine;

(xiii) Oripavine;

(xiv) Oxycodone;

(xv) Oxymorphone;

(xvi) Thebaine;

(B) Any salt, compound, isomer, derivative, or preparation thereof which is chemically equivalent or identical with any of the substances referred to in subparagraph (A) of this paragraph, except that these substances shall not include the isoquinoline alkaloids of opium;

(C) Opium poppy and poppy straw;

(D) Cocaine, coca leaves, any salt, compound, derivative, stereoisomers of cocaine, or preparation of coca leaves, and any salt, compound, derivative, stereoisomers of cocaine, or preparation thereof which is chemically equivalent or identical with any of these substances, but not including decocainized coca leaves or extractions which do not contain cocaine or ecgonine;

(2) Any of the following opiates, including their isomers, esters, ethers, salts, and salts of isomers, whenever the existence of these isomers, esters, ethers, and salts is possible within the specific chemical designation:

(A) Alfentanil;

(A.1) Alphaprodine;

(B) Anileridine;

(C) Bezitramide;

(C.5) Carfentanil;

(D) Dihydrocodeine;

(E) Diphenoxylate;

(F) Fentanyl;

(G) Isomethadone;

(G.5) Levo-alphacetylmethadol (some other names: levomethadyl acetate, LAAM);

(H) Levomethorphan;

(I) Levorphanol;

(J) Methazocine;

(K) Methadone;

(L) Methadone-Intermediate, 4-cyano-2-dimethylamino-4, 4-di-
phenyl butane;

(M) Moramide-Intermediate, 2-methyl-3-morpholino-1, 1-diphenyl-
propane-carboxylic acid;

(N) Pethidine (meperidine);

(O) Pethidine-Intermediate-A, 4-cyano-1-methyl-4-phenylpi-
peridine;

(P) Pethidine-Intermediate-B, ethyl-4-phenylpiperidine-4-carboxylate;

(Q) Pethidine-Intermediate-C, 1-methyl-4-phenylpiperidine-4-carboxylic acid;

(R) Phenazocine;

(S) Piminodine;

(T) Racemethorphan;

(U) Racemorphan;

(U.1) Remifentanil;

(V) Sufentanil;

(V.1) Tapentadol;

(V.2) Thiafentanil;

(W) 4-anilino-N-phenethyl-4-piperidine (ANPP);

(3) Unless specifically excepted or unless listed in another schedule, any material, compound, mixture, or preparation which contains any quantity of the following substances included as having a stimulant effect on the central nervous system:

(A) Amphetamine, its salts, optical isomers, and salts of its optical isomers;

(B) Any substance which contains any quantity of methamphetamine, including its salts, isomers, and salts of isomers;

(C) Phenmetrazine and its salts;

(D) Methylphenidate, including its salts, isomers, and salts of isomers;

(E) Reserved;

(F) Nabilone;

(G) Lisdexamfetamine;

(4) Unless specifically excepted or unless listed in another schedule, any material, compound, mixture, or preparation which contains any of the following substances included as having a depressant effect on the central nervous system, including its salts, isomers, and salts of isomers whenever the existence of such salts, isomers, and salts of isomers is possible within the specific chemical designation:

(A) Amobarbital;

(A.5) Glutethimide;

(B) Secobarbital;

(C) Pentobarbital.

§ 16-13-27. Schedule III

The controlled substances listed in this Code section are included in Schedule III:

(1) Unless specifically excepted or unless listed in another schedule, any material, compound, mixture, or preparation which contains any quantity of the following substances, included as having a stimulant effect on the central nervous system, including its salts, isomers (whether optical, position, or geometric), and salts of such isomers whenever the existence of such salts, isomers, and salts of isomers is possible within the specific chemical designation:

(A) Those compounds, mixtures, or preparations in dosage unit forms containing any stimulant substances which are listed as excepted compounds by the State Board of Pharmacy pursuant to this article, and any other drug of quantitative composition so excepted or which is the same except that it contains a lesser quantity of controlled substances;

(B) Benzphetamine;

(C) Chlorphentermine;

(D) Clortermine;

(E) Phendimetrazine;

(2) Unless specifically excepted or unless listed in another schedule, any material, compound, mixture, or preparation which contains any quantity of the following substances included as having a depressant effect on the central nervous system:

(A) Any compound, mixture, or preparation containing amobarbital, secobarbital, pentobarbital, or any salts thereof and one or more active medicinal ingredients which are not listed in any schedule;

(B) Any suppository dosage form containing amobarbital, secobarbital, pentobarbital, or any salt of any of these drugs and approved by the State Board of Pharmacy for marketing only as a suppository;

(C) Any substance which contains any quantity of a derivative of barbituric acid or any salt thereof;

(D) Chlorhexadol;

(E) Reserved;

(F) Lysergic acid;

(G) Lysergic acid amide;

(H) Methyprylon;

(I) Sulfondiethylmethane;

(J) Sulfonethylmethane;

(K) Sulfonmethane;

(L) Tiletamine/Zolazepam (Telazol);

(3) Nalorphine;

(4) Unless specifically excepted or unless listed in another schedule, any material, compound, mixture, or preparation containing limited quantities of the following narcotic drugs, or any salts thereof:

(A) Not more than 1.8 grams of codeine, or any of its salts, per 100 milliliters or not more than 90 milligrams per dosage unit, with an equal or greater quantity of an isoquinoline alkaloid of opium;

(B) Not more than 1.8 grams of codeine, or any of its salts, per 100 milliliters or not more than 90 milligrams per dosage unit, with one or more active, nonnarcotic ingredients in recognized therapeutic amounts;

(C) Reserved;

(D) Reserved;

(E) Not more than 1.8 grams of dihydrocodeine, or any of its salts, per 100 milliliters or not more than 90 milligrams per dosage unit, with one or more active, nonnarcotic ingredients in recognized therapeutic amounts;

(F) Not more than 300 milligrams of ethylmorphine, or any of its salts, per 100 milliliters or not more than 15 milligrams per dosage unit, with one or more active, nonnarcotic ingredients in recognized therapeutic amounts;

(G) Not more than 500 milligrams of opium per 100 milliliters or per 100 grams, or not more than 25 milligrams per dosage unit, with one or more active, nonnarcotic ingredients in recognized therapeutic amounts;

(H) Not more than 50 milligrams of morphine, or any of its salts, per 100 milliliters or per 100 grams with one or more active, nonnarcotic ingredients in recognized therapeutic amounts;

(5) The State Board of Pharmacy may except by rule any compound, mixture, or preparation containing any stimulant or depressant substance listed in paragraphs (1) and (2) of this Code section from the application of all or any part of this article if the compound, mixture, or preparation contains one or more active, medicinal ingredients not having a stimulant or depressant effect on the central nervous system, and if the admixtures are included therein in combinations, quantity, proportion, or concentration that vitiate the potential for abuse of the substances which have a stimulant or depressant effect on the central nervous system;

(6) Any anabolic steroid or any salt, ester, or isomer of a drug or substance described or listed in this paragraph, if that salt, ester, or isomer promotes muscle growth. Such term does not include an anabolic steroid which is expressly intended for administration through implants to cattle or other nonhuman species and which has been approved by the secretary of health and human services for such administration:

(A) Boldenone;(A.5) Boldione (Androsta-1,4-diene-3,17-dione);(B) Chlorotestosterone;(C) Clostebol;

(D) Dehydrochlormethyltestosterone;(D.1) Desoxymethyltestosterone (17a-methyl-5a-androst-2-en-17-ol, madol);(E) Dihydrotestosterone;

(F) Drostanolone;(G) Ethylestrenol;(H) Fluoxymesterone;(I) Formebolone;(J) Mesterolone;(K) Methandienone;(L) Methandranone;

(M) Methandriol;(N) Methandrostenolone;(N.5) Methasterone;(O) Methenolone;(P) Methyltestosterone;(Q) Mibolerone;(R) Nandrolone;

(S) Norethandrolone;(T) Oxandrolone;(U) Oxymesterone;(V) Oxymetholone;(V.5) Prostanozol;(W) Stanolone;(X) Stanozolol;

(Y) Testolactone;(Z) Testosterone;(AA) Trenbolone;(BB) 19-nor-4,9(10)-androstadienedione (estra-4,9(10)-di-ene-3,17-dione);(7) Ketamine;

(8) Dronabinol (synthetic) in sesame oil and encapsulated in a U.S. Food and Drug Administration approved drug product also known as Marinol;

(9) Sodium oxybate, when the FDA approved form of this drug is in a container labeled in compliance with subsection (a) or (b) of Code Section 26-3-8, in the possession of a registrant permitted to dispense the drug, or in the possession of a person to whom it has been lawfully prescribed;

(10) Buprenorphine;(11) Embutramide;

(12) Any drug product in hard or soft gelatin capsule form containing natural dronabinol (derived from the cannabis plant) or synthetic dronabinol (produced from synthetic materials) in sesame oil, for which an abbreviated new drug application (ANDA) has been approved by the FDA under section 505(j) of the Federal Food, Drug, and Cosmetic Act (21 U.S.C. 355(j)) which references as its listed drug the drug product referred to in paragraph (8) of this Code section;

(13) Perampanel and its salts, isomers, and salts of isomers.

§ 16-13-27.1. Exempt anabolic steroids

The following anabolic steroid containing compounds, mixtures, or preparations have been exempted as Schedule III Controlled Substances by the United States Drug Enforcement Administration, as listed in 21 C.F.R. 1308.34, and are therefore exempted from paragraph (6) of Code Section 16-13-27:

TABLE OF EXEMPT ANABOLIC STEROID PRODUCTS

Trade Name	Company
Androgen LA St. Louis, MO	Forest Pharmaceuticals
Andro-Estro 90-4 Rockville Centre, NY	Rugby Labs
depANDROGYN St. Louis, M	Forest Pharmaceuticals
DEPO-T.E. Carmel, IN	Quality Research Pharm
depTESTROGEN Phoenix, AZ	Maroca Pharm
Duomone Pacific, MO	Winitec Pharm
DURATESTRIN Alpharetta, GA	W. E. Hauck
DUO-SPAN II Gardena, CA	Premedics Labs
Estratest Marietta, GA	Solvay Pharmaceuticals
Estratest HS Marietta, GA	Solvay Pharmaceuticals
PAN ESTRA TEST Covington, LA	Pan American Labs
Premarin 1.25mg with Methyltestosterone	Ayerst Labs, Inc. New York, NY
Premarin 0.625mg with Methyltestosterone	Ayerst Labs, Inc. New York, NY
TEST-ESTRO Cypionates Rockville Centre, NY	Rugby Labs
Testosterone Cyp 50 Estradiol Cyp 2	I.D.E. Interstate Amityville, NY
Testosterone Cypionate-Estradiol Cypionate Injection	Best Generics N. Miami Beach, FL
Testosterone Cypionate-Estradiol Cypionate Injection	Schein Pharm Port Washington, NY
Testosterone Cypionate-Estradiol Cypionate Injection	Steris Labs, Inc. Phoenix, AZ
Testosterone Cypionate-Estradiol Valerate Injection	Schein Pharm Port Washington, NY
Testosterone Enanthate-Estradiol Valerate Injection	Steris Labs, Inc. Phoenix, AZ

§ 16-13-28. Schedule IV

(a)   The controlled substances listed in this Code section are included in Schedule IV. Unless specifically excepted or unless listed in another schedule, any material, compound, mixture, or preparation which contains any quantity of the following substances, including its salts, isomers, and salts of isomers whenever the existence of such salts, isomers, and salts of isomers is possible within the specified chemical designation, included as having a stimulant or depressant effect on the central nervous system or a hallucinogenic effect:

(1) Alfaxalone;(1.5) Armodafinil;(2) Barbital;(2.1) Bromazepam;(2.15) Butorphanol;(2.25) Carisoprodol;
(2.3) Cathine;(3) Chloral betaine;(4) Chloral hydrate;
(5) Chlordiazepoxide, but not including librax (chlordiazepoxide hydrochloride and clidinium bromide) or menrium (chlordiazepoxide and water soluble esterified estrogens);
(5.1) Clobazam;(6) Reserved;(7) Clotiazepam;(8) Reserved;(8.5) Dexfenfluramine;(9) Reserved;(10) Reserved;(11) Diethylpropion;(11.05) Difenoxin;
(11.5) Eluxadoline;(12) Ethchlorvynol;(13) Ethinamate;(13.15) Etizolam;(13.2) Fencamfamin;(14) Fenfluramine;(14.2) Fenproporex;(15) Fospropofol;

(16) Indiplon;(17) Lorcaserin;(18) Mazindol;(19) Mebutamate;(19.2) Mefenorex;(20) Meprobamate;(21) Methohexital;(22) Methylphenobarbital;
(22.1) Modafinil;(23) Reserved;(24) Paraldehyde;(25) Pemoline;(26) Pentazocine;(27) Petrichloral;(28) Phenobarbital;(29) Phentermine;
(29.1) Pipradrol;(30) Propofol;(30.05) Propoxyphene (including all salts and optical isomers);(30.07) Pyrazolam;(30.1) Quazepam;
(30.2) Sibutramine;(30.3) SPA (-)-1-dimethylamino-1, 2-diphenylethane;(30.5) Suvorexant;(31) Reserved;
(31.5) Tramadol [2-((dimethylamino)methyl)-1-(3-methoxyphenyl)cyclohexanol, its salts, optical and geometric isomers, and salts of these isomers];
(32) Zaleplon;(33) Zolpidem;(34) Zopiclone.
(b) The controlled substances in the benzodiazepine structural class include any of the following compounds, derivatives, their salts, isomers, or salts of isomers, halogen analogues, or homologues, unless specifically utilized as part of the manufacturing process by a commercial industry of a substance or material not intended for human ingestion or consumption, as a prescription administered under medical supervision, or for research at a recognized institution, whenever the existence of these salts, isomers, or salts of isomers, halogen analogues, or homologues is possible within the specific chemical designation or unless specifically excepted or listed in this or another schedule, structurally derived from 1,4-benzodiazepine by substitution at the 5-position with a phenyl ring system (which may itself be further substituted), whether or not the compound is further modified in any of the following ways:
(1) By substitution at the 2-position with a ketone or a thione;
(2) By substitution at the 3-position with a hydroxyl group or ester group, which itself may be further substituted;
(3) By a fused triazole ring at the 1,2- position, which itself may be further substituted;
(4) By a fused imidazole ring at the 1,2- position, which itself may be further substituted;
(5) By a fused oxazolidine ring at the 4,5- position, which itself may be further substituted;
(6) By a fused oxazine ring at the 4,5- position, which itself may be further substituted;
(7) By substitution at the 7-position with a nitro group;
(8) By substitution at the 7-position with a halogen group; or
(9) By substitution at the 1-position with an alkyl group, which itself may be further substituted.
(c) The State Board of Pharmacy may except by rule any compound, mixture, or preparation containing any depressant, stimulant, or hallucinogenic substance listed in subsection (a) or (b) of this Code section from the application of all or any part of this article if the compound, mixture, or preparation contains one or more active, medicinal ingredients not having a depressant or stimulant effect on the central nervous system, and if the admixtures are included therein in combinations, quantity, proportion, or concentration that vitiate the potential for abuse of the substances which have a depressant or stimulant effect on the central nervous system.

§ 16-13-29. Schedule V

The controlled substances listed in this Code section are included in Schedule V:
(1) Any compound, mixture, or preparation containing limited quantities of any of the following narcotic drugs, or salts thereof, which also contains one or more nonnarcotic, active, medicinal ingredients in sufficient proportion to confer upon the compound, mixture, or preparation valuable medicinal qualities other than those possessed by the narcotic drug alone:
(A) Not more than 200 milligrams of codeine, or any of its salts, per 100 milliliters or per 100 grams;
(B) Not more than 100 milligrams of dihydrocodeine, or any of its salts, per 100 milliliters or per 100 grams;
(C) Not more than 100 milligrams of ethylmorphine, or any of its salts, per 100 milliliters or per 100 grams;
(D) Not more than 2.5 milligrams of diphenoxylate and not less than 25 micrograms of atropine sulfate per dosage unit;
(E) Not more than 100 milligrams of opium per 100 milliliters or per 100 grams;
(2) Lacosamide;
(3) Pregabalin;
(4) Pyrovalerone;
(5) Pseudoephedrine as an exempt over-the-counter Schedule V controlled substance distributed in the same manner as set forth in Code Section 16-13-29.2; provided, however, that such exemption shall take effect immediately and shall not require rulemaking by the State Board of Pharmacy; provided, further, that wholesale drug distributors located within this state and licensed by the State Board of Pharmacy and which are registered and regulated by the DEA shall not be subject to any board requirements for controlled substances for the storage, reporting, record keeping, or physical security of drug products containing pseudoephedrine which are more stringent than those included in DEA regulations;
(6) Ezogabine; or
(7) Brivaracetam.

§ 16-13-29.1. Nonnarcotic substances excluded from schedules of controlled substances

The following nonnarcotic substances which may, under the Federal Food, Drug, and Cosmetic Act (21 U.S.C. 301), be lawfully sold over the counter without a prescription, are excluded from all schedules of controlled substances under this article:

Trade name or designation (Dosage form)	Composition/Potency	Manufacturer or distributor
Amodrine (Tablet) Racephedrine/25.00 mg	Phenobarbital/8.00 mg; Aminophylline/100.00 mg;	Searle, G.D. & Co.
Amodrine E C (Enteric-coated tablet)	Phenobarbital/8.00 mg; Aminophylline/100.00 mg; Racephedrine/25.00 mg	Searle, G.D. & Co.
Anodyne (Ointment)	Chloral hydrate/0.69 g/30 g	Zemmer Co.
Anti-Asthma (Tablet) Ephedrine hydrochloride/ 25.00 mg	Phenobarbital/8.00 mg; Theophylline/130.00 mg;	Ormont Drug & Chem.
Anti-asthmatic (Tablet) 24.00 mg; Theophylline/ 130.00 mg	Phenobarbital/8.10 mg; Ephedrine hydrochloride/	Zenith Labs., Inc.
Asma-Ese (Tablet) Ephedrine hydrochloride/ 24.30 mg	Phenobarbital/8.10 mg; Theophylline/129.60 mg;	Parmed Pharm.

Product	Composition	Manufacturer
Asma-Lief (Tablet)	Phenobarbital/8.10 mg; Ephedrine hydrochloride/24.30 mg; Theophylline/129.60 mg	Columbia Medical Co.
Asma-Lief Pediatric (Suspension)	Phenobarbital/4.00 mg/05 ml; Ephedrine hydrochloride/12.00 mg/05 ml; Theophylline/65.00 mg/05 ml	Columbia Medical Co.
Asma Tuss (Syrup)	Phenobarbital/4.00 mg/05 ml; Glyceryl guaiacolate/50.00 mg/05 ml; Chlorphentramine maleate/1.00 mg/05 ml; Ephedrine sulfate/12.00 mg/05 ml; Theophylline/15.00 mg/05 ml	Halsey Drug Co.
Azma-Aid (Tablet)	Phenobarbital/8.00 mg; Theophylline/129.60 mg Ephedrine hydrochloride/24.30 mg	Rondex Labs.
Azmadrine (Tablet)	Phenobarbital/8.00 mg; Ephedrine hydrochloride/24.00 mg; Theophylline/130.00 mg	U.S. Ethicals.
Benzedrex Inhaler (Inhaler)	Propylhexedrine	Smith Kline Consumer Products.
Bet-U-Lol (Liquid)	Chloral hydrate/0.54 g/30 ml; Methyl salicylate/30.10 g/30 ml; Menthol/0.69 g/30 ml	Huxley Pharm.
Bronkolixir (Elixir)	Phenobarbital/4.00 mg/05 ml; Theophylline/15.00 mg/05 ml; Ephedrine sulfate/12.00 mg/05 ml; Glyceryl guaiacolate/50.00 mg/05 ml	Breon Labs.
Bronkotabs (Tablet)	Phenobarbital/8.00 mg; Theophylline/100.00 mg; Glyceryl guaiacolate/100.00 mg; Ephedrine sulfate/24.00 mg	Breon Labs.
Bronkotabs-Hafs (Tablet)	Phenobarbital/4.00 mg; Glyceryl guaiacolate/50.00 mg; Theophylline/50.00 mg; Ephedrine sulfate/12.00 mg	Breon Labs.
Ceepa (Tablet)	Phenobarbital/8.00 mg; Theophylline/130.00 mg; Ephedrine hydrochloride/24.00 mg	Geneva Drugs.
Chlorasal (Ointment)	Chloral hydrate/648.00 mg/30 g; Menthol/972.00 mg/30 g; Methyl salicylate/4.277 g/30 g	Wisconsin Pharmacal.
Choate's Leg Freeze (Liquid)	Chloral hydrate/7.40 g/30 ml; Ether/10.3 ml/30 ml; Menthol/6.3 g/30 ml; Camphor/8.7 g/30 ml	Bickmore, Inc.
Chloro-salicylate (Ointment)	Chloral hydrate/648.00 mg/30 g; Methyl salicylate/6.66 g/30 g; Menthol/1.13 g/30 g	Kremers-Urban Co.
Menthalgesic (Ointment)	Chloral hydrate/0.45 g/30 g; Menthol/0.45 g/30 g; Methyl salicylate/3.60 g/30 g; Camphor/0.45 g/30 g	Blue Line Chem Co.
Neoasma (Tablet)	Phenobarbital/10.00 mg; Theophylline/130.00 mg; Ephedrine hydrochloride/24.00 mg	Tarmac Products.
P.E.C.T. (Tablet)	Phenobarbital/8.10 mg; Chlorpheniramine maleate/2.00 mg; Ephedrine	Halsom Drug Co.

127

Product	Composition	Manufacturer
	sulfate/24.30 mg; Theophylline/129.60 mg	
Primatene (Tablet)	Phenobarbital/8.00 mg; Ephedrine hydrochloride/24.00 mg; Theophylline/130.00 mg	Whitehall Labs.
Rynal (Spray)	d1-methamphetamine hydrochloride/0.11 g/50 ml; Antipyrine/0.14 g/50 ml; Pyriamine maleate/0.005 g/50 ml; Hyamine 2389/0.01 g/50 ml	Blaine Co.
S-K Asthma (Tablet)	Phenobarbital/8.00 mg; Ephedrine hydrochloride/24.30 mg; Theophylline/129.60 mg	S-K Research Labs.
Tedral (Tablet)	Phenobarbital/8.00 mg; Theophylline/130.00 mg; Ephedrine hydrochloride/24.00 mg	Warner-Chilcott.
Tedral Anti H (Tablet)	Phenobarbital/8.00 mg; Chlorpheniramine maleate/2.00 mg; Theophylline/130.00 mg; Ephedrine hydrochloride/24.00 mg	Warner-Chilcott.
Tedral Antiasthmatic (Tablet)	Phenobarbital/8.00 mg; Theophylline/130.00 mg; Ephedrine hydrochloride/24.00 mg	Parke-Davis & Co.
Tedral Elixir (Elixir)	Phenobarbital/2.00 mg/05 ml; Ephedrine hydrochloride/6.00 mg/05 ml; Theophylline/32.50 mg/05 ml	Warner-Chilcott.
Tedral Pediatric (Suspension)	Phenobarbital/4.00 mg/05 ml; Ephedrine hydrochloride/12.00 mg/05 ml; Theophylline/65.00 mg/05 ml	Warner-Chilcott.
Teephen (Tablet)	Phenobarbital/8.00 mg; Ephedrine hydrochloride/24.00 mg; Theophylline/130.00 mg	Robinson Labs.
Teephen Pediatric (Suspension)	Phenobarbital/4.00 mg/05 ml; Ephedrine hydrochloride/12.00 mg/05 ml; Theophylline anhydrous/65.00 mg/05 ml	Robinson Labs.
TEP (Tablet)	Phenobarbital/8.00 mg; Theophylline/130.00 mg; Ephedrine hydrochloride/24.00 mg	Towne, Paulsen & Co., Inc.
T.E.P. Compound (Tablet)	Phenobarbital/8.10 mg; Theophylline/129.60 mg; Ephedrine hydrochloride/24.30 mg	Stanlabs, Inc.
Thedrizem (Tablet)	Phenobarbital/8.00 mg; Ephedrine hydrochloride/25.00 mg; Theophylline/100.00 mg	Zemmer Co.
Theobal (Tablet)	Phenobarbital/8.00 mg; Ephedrine hydrochloride/24.00 mg; Theophylline/130.00 mg	Halsey Drug Co.
Val-Tep (Tablet)	Phenobarbital/8.00 mg; Ephedrine hydrochloride/24.00 mg; Theophylline/130.00 mg	Vale Chemical Co.
Verequad (Suspension)	Phenobarbital/4.00 mg/05 ml; Ephedrine hydrochloride/12.00 mg/05 ml; Theophylline calcium salicylate/65.00 mg/05 ml; Glyceryl guaiacolate/50.00 mg/05 ml	Knoll Pharm.

Verequad (Tablet)	Phenobarbital/8.00 mg; Ephedrine hydrochloride/ 24.00 mg; Glyceryl guaiacolate/100.00 mg; Theophylline calcium salicylate/130.00 mg	Knoll Pharm.
Vicks Inhaler (Inhaler)	1-Desoxyephedrine/113.00 mg	Vick Chemical Co.

§ 16-13-29.2. Authority for exemption of over-the-counter Schedule V controlled substances

The State Board of Pharmacy shall have the authority to exempt and control the sale of Schedule V controlled substances by rule which shall allow the sale of such substances without the need for issuance of a prescription from a medical practitioner and shall require such substances to be sold only in a pharmacy when such substances are sold without a prescription. Such substances shall be known as Exempt Over-the-Counter (OTC) Schedule V Controlled Substances.

§ 16-13-30. Purchase, possession, manufacture, distribution, or sale of controlled substances or marijuana; penalties

(a) Except as authorized by this article, it is unlawful for any person to purchase, possess, or have under his or her control any controlled substance.

(b) Except as authorized by this article, it is unlawful for any person to manufacture, deliver, distribute, dispense, administer, sell, or possess with intent to distribute any controlled substance.

(c) Except as otherwise provided, any person who violates subsection (a) of this Code section with respect to a controlled substance in Schedule I or a narcotic drug in Schedule II shall be guilty of a felony and, upon conviction thereof, shall be punished as follows:

(1) If the aggregate weight, including any mixture, is less than one gram of a solid substance, less than one milliliter of a liquid substance, or if the substance is placed onto a secondary medium with a combined weight of less than one gram, by imprisonment for not less than one nor more than three years;

(2) If the aggregate weight, including any mixture, is at least one gram but less than four grams of a solid substance, at least one milliliter but less than four milliliters of a liquid substance, or if the substance is placed onto a secondary medium with a combined weight of at least one gram but less than four grams, by imprisonment for not less than one nor more than eight years; and

(3) (A) Except as provided in subparagraph (B) of this paragraph, if the aggregate weight, including any mixture, is at least four grams but less than 28 grams of a solid substance, at least four milliliters but less than 28 milliliters of a liquid substance, or if the substance is placed onto a secondary medium with a combined weight of at least four grams but less than 28 grams, by imprisonment for not less than one nor more than 15 years.

(B) This paragraph shall not apply to morphine, heroin, opium, or any substance identified in subparagraph (RR) or (SS) of paragraph (1) or paragraph (13), (14), or (15) of Code Section 16-13-25, or subparagraph (A), (C.5), (F), (U.1), (V), or (V.2) of paragraph (2) of Code Section 16-13-26 or any salt, isomer, or salt of an isomer; rather, the provisions of Code Section 16-13-31 shall control these substances.

(d) Except as otherwise provided, any person who violates subsection (b) of this Code section with respect to a controlled substance in Schedule I or Schedule II shall be guilty of a felony and, upon conviction thereof, shall be punished by imprisonment for not less than five years nor more than 30 years. Upon conviction of a second or subsequent offense, he or she shall be imprisoned for not less than ten years nor more than 40 years or life imprisonment. The provisions of subsection (a) of Code Section 17-10-7 shall not apply to a sentence imposed for a second such offense; provided, however, that the remaining provisions of Code Section 17-10-7 shall apply for any subsequent offense.

(e) Any person who violates subsection (a) of this Code section with respect to a controlled substance in Schedule II, other than a narcotic drug, shall be guilty of a felony and, upon conviction thereof, shall be punished as follows:

(1) If the aggregate weight, including any mixture, is less than two grams of a solid substance, less than two milliliters of a liquid substance, or if the substance is placed onto a secondary medium with a combined weight of less than two grams, by imprisonment for not less than one nor more than three years;

(2) If the aggregate weight, including any mixture, is at least two grams but less than four grams of a solid substance, at least two milliliters but less than four milliliters of a liquid substance, or if the substance is placed onto a secondary medium with a combined weight of at least two grams but less than four grams, by imprisonment for not less than one nor more than eight years; and

(3) If the aggregate weight, including any mixture, is at least four grams but less than 28 grams of a solid substance, at least four milliliters but less than 28 milliliters of a liquid substance, or if the substance is placed onto a secondary medium with a combined weight of at least four grams but less than 28 grams, by imprisonment for not less than one nor more than 15 years.

(f) Upon a third or subsequent conviction for a violation of subsection (a) of this Code section with respect to a controlled substance in Schedule I or II or subsection (i) of this Code section, such person shall be punished by imprisonment for a term not to exceed twice the length of the sentence applicable to the particular crime.

(g) Except as provided in subsection (l) of this Code section, any person who violates subsection (a) of this Code section with respect to a controlled substance in Schedule III, IV, or V shall be guilty of a felony and, upon conviction thereof, shall be punished by imprisonment for not less than one year nor more than three years. Upon conviction of a third or subsequent offense, he or she shall be imprisoned for not less than one year nor more than five years.

(h) Any person who violates subsection (b) of this Code section with respect to a controlled substance in Schedule III, IV, or V shall be guilty of a felony and, upon conviction thereof, shall be punished by imprisonment for not less than one year nor more than ten years.

(i) (1) Except as authorized by this article, it is unlawful for any person to possess or have under his or her control a counterfeit substance. Any person who violates this paragraph shall be guilty of a felony and, upon conviction thereof, shall be punished by imprisonment for not less than one year nor more than two years.

(2) Except as authorized by this article, it is unlawful for any person to manufacture, deliver, distribute, dispense, administer, purchase, sell, or possess with intent to distribute a counterfeit substance. Any person who violates this paragraph shall be guilty of a felony and, upon conviction thereof, shall be punished by imprisonment for not less than one year nor more than ten years.

(j) (1) It shall be unlawful for any person to possess, have under his or her control, manufacture, deliver, distribute, dispense, administer, purchase, sell, or possess with intent to distribute marijuana.

(2) Except as otherwise provided in subsection (c) of Code Section 16-13-31 or in Code Section 16-13-2, any person who violates this subsection shall be guilty of a felony and, upon conviction thereof, shall be punished by imprisonment for not less than one year nor more than ten years.

(k) It shall be unlawful for any person to hire, solicit, engage, or use an individual under the age of 17 years, in any manner, for the purpose of manufacturing, distributing, or dispensing, on behalf of the solicitor, any controlled substance, counterfeit substance, or marijuana unless the manufacturing, distribution, or dispensing is otherwise allowed by law. Any person who violates this subsection shall be guilty of a felony and, upon conviction thereof, shall be punished by imprisonment for not less than five years nor more than 20 years or by a fine not to exceed $20,000.00, or both.

(l) (1) Any person who violates subsection (a) of this Code section with respect to flunitrazepam, a Schedule IV controlled substance, shall be guilty of a felony and, upon conviction thereof, shall be punished as follows:

(A) If the aggregate weight, including any mixture, is less than two grams of a solid substance of flunitrazepam, less than two milliliters of liquid flunitrazepam, or if flunitrazepam is placed onto a secondary medium with a combined weight of less than two grams, by imprisonment for not less than one nor more than three years;

(B) If the aggregate weight, including any mixture, is at least two grams but less than four grams of a solid substance of flunitrazepam, at least two milliliters but less than four milliliters of liquid flunitrazepam, or if the flunitrazepam is placed onto a secondary medium with a combined weight of at least two grams but less than four grams, by imprisonment for not less than one nor more than eight years; and

(C) If the aggregate weight, including any mixture, is at least four grams of a solid substance of flunitrazepam, at least four milliliters of liquid flunitrazepam, or if the flunitrazepam is placed onto a secondary medium with a combined weight of at least four grams, by imprisonment for not less than one nor more than 15 years.

(2) Any person who violates subsection (b) of this Code section with respect to flunitrazepam, a Schedule IV controlled substance, shall be guilty of a felony and, upon conviction thereof, shall be punished by imprisonment for not less than five years nor more than 30 years. Upon conviction of a second or subsequent offense, such person shall be punished by imprisonment for not less

than ten years nor more than 40 years or life imprisonment. The provisions of subsection (a) of Code Section 17-10-7 shall not apply to a sentence imposed for a second such offense, but that subsection and the remaining provisions of Code Section 17-10-7 shall apply for any subsequent offense.

(m) As used in this Code section, the term "solid substance" means a substance that is not in a liquid or gas form. Such term shall include tablets, pills, capsules, caplets, powder, crystal, or any variant of such items.

§ 16-13-30.1. Unlawful manufacture, delivery, distribution, possession, or sale of noncontrolled substances; civil forfeiture

(a)(1) It is unlawful for any person knowingly to manufacture, deliver, distribute, dispense, possess with the intent to distribute, or sell a noncontrolled substance upon either:
(A) The express or implied representation that the substance is a narcotic or nonnarcotic controlled substance;
(B) The express or implied representation that the substance is of such nature or appearance that the recipient of said delivery will be able to distribute said substance as a controlled substance; or
(C) The express or implied representation that the substance has essentially the same pharmacological action or effect as a controlled substance.
(2) The definitions of the terms "deliver," "delivery," "distribute," "dispense," and "manufacture" provided in Code Section 16-13-21 shall not be applicable to this Code section; but such terms as used in this Code section shall have the meanings ascribed to them in the ordinary course of business.
(b) An implied representation may be shown by proof of any two of the following:
(1) The manufacture, delivery, distribution, dispensing, or sale included an exchange or a demand for money or other valuable property as consideration for delivery of the substance and the amount of such consideration was substantially in excess of the reasonable value of the noncontrolled substance;
(2) The physical appearance of the finished product containing the substance is substantially identical to a specific controlled substance;
(3) The finished product bears an imprint, identifying mark, number, or device which is substantially identical to the trademark, identifying mark, imprint, number, or device of a manufacturer licensed by the Food and Drug Administration of the United States Department of Health and Human Services.
(c) In any prosecution for unlawful manufacture, delivery, distribution, possession with intent to distribute, dispensing, or sale of a noncontrolled substance, it is no defense that the accused believed the noncontrolled substance to be actually a controlled substance.
(d) The provisions of this Code section shall not prohibit a duly licensed business establishment, acting in the usual course of business, from selling or for a practitioner, acting in the usual course of his professional practice, from dispensing a drug preparation manufactured by a manufacturer licensed by the Food and Drug Administration of the United States Department of Health and Human Services for over-the-counter sale which does not bear a label stating "Federal law prohibits dispensing without a prescription" or similar language meaning that the drug preparation requires a prescription.
(e) The unlawful manufacture, delivery, distribution, dispensing, possession with the intention to distribute, or sale of a noncontrolled substance in violation of this Code section is a felony and, upon conviction thereof, such person shall be punished by imprisonment for not less than one year nor more than ten years or by a fine not to exceed $25,000.00, or both.
(f) (1) As used in this subsection, the terms "proceeds" and "property" shall have the same meanings as set forth in Code Section 9-16-2.
(2) Any property which is, directly or indirectly, used or intended for use in any manner to facilitate a violation of this Code section, and any proceeds, and any noncontrolled substance which is manufactured, distributed, dispensed, possessed with the intent to distribute, or sold in violation of this Code section are declared to be contraband and no person shall have a property right in them.
(3) Any property or noncontrolled substance subject to forfeiture pursuant to paragraph (2) of this subsection shall be forfeited in accordance with the procedures set forth in Chapter 16 of Title 9.

§ 16-13-30.2. Unlawful manufacture, distribution, or possession with intent to distribute of imitation controlled substances; civil forfeiture

(a) Any person who knowingly manufactures, distributes, or possesses with intent to distribute an imitation controlled substance as defined in paragraph (12.1) of Code Section 16-13-21 is guilty of a misdemeanor of a high and aggravated nature.
(b) The provisions of this Code section are cumulative and shall not be construed as restricting any remedy, provisional or otherwise, provided by law for the benefit of any party.
(c) No civil or criminal liability shall be imposed by virtue of this Code section on any person registered under this article who manufactures, distributes, or possesses an imitation controlled substance for use by a practitioner, as defined in paragraph (23) of Code Section 16-13-21, in the course of lawful professional practice or research.
(d) All materials which are manufactured, distributed, or possessed in violation of this Code section and any proceeds are declared to be contraband and no person shall have a property right in them and shall be forfeited according to the procedure set forth in Chapter 16 of Title 9. As used in this subsection, the term "proceeds" shall have the same meaning as set forth in Code Section 9-16-2.

§ 16-13-30.3. Possession of substances containing ephedrine or pseudoephedrine; restrictions on sales of products containing those ingredients

(a) As used in this Code section, the term:
(1) "Ephedrine" or "pseudoephedrine" means any drug product containing ephedrine or pseudoephedrine or any of their salts, isomers, or salts of isomers, alone or in a mixture.
(2) "Georgia Meth Watch" means the program entitled Georgia Meth Watch or a similar program which has been promulgated, approved, and distributed by the Georgia Council on Substance Abuse.
(3) "Pharmacy" has the same meaning as in Code Section 26-4-5.
(4) "Real-time electronic logging system" means an electronic system approved by the Georgia Bureau of Investigation which is operated in real time and which can track required information and generate a stop sale alert to notify a pharmacy that a purchase of ephedrine or pseudoephedrine which exceeds the quantity limits set forth in this Code section is being attempted. Such system shall:
(A) Contain an override function that will not only allow a pharmacy to complete a sale in violation of this Code section when the person making the sale is in reasonable fear of imminent bodily harm if he or she does not complete the sale but also will track any override sales made;
(B) Be accessible to the state, pharmacies, and law enforcement agencies, without a charge or fee, including a transaction fee; and
(C) Have real-time interstate communicability with similar systems in other states.
(5) "Required information" means the full name and address of the purchaser; the type of government issued photographic identification presented, including the issuer and identification number; a description of the nonprescription product purchased which contains ephedrine or pseudoephedrine, including the number of grams of pseudoephedrine in the product; and the date and time of the purchase.
(b) (1) It shall be unlawful for any person, other than a person or entity described in paragraph (22), (28), (29), (30), (33), or (41) of Code Section 26-4-5, to possess any product that contains ephedrine or pseudoephedrine in an amount which exceeds 300 pills, tablets, gelcaps, capsules, or other individual units or more than 9 grams of ephedrine or pseudoephedrine or a combination of these substances, whichever is smaller.
(2) It shall be unlawful for any person to possess any product containing ephedrine or pseudoephedrine with the intent to manufacture amphetamine or methamphetamine.
(3) Any person who violates the provisions of this subsection shall be guilty of a felony and, upon conviction thereof, shall be punished by imprisonment for not less than one year nor more than ten years.
(c) (1) Products whose sole active ingredient is pseudoephedrine may be offered for retail sale only if sold in blister packaging. Nonprescription products whose sole active ingredient is ephedrine or pseudoephedrine shall only be sold in a pharmacy in a manner which complies with State Board of Pharmacy rules established pursuant to Code Section 16-13-29.2.
(2) No person shall distribute or purchase any nonprescription product containing more than 3.6 grams of ephedrine or pseudoephedrine per day in dosage form or more than 9 grams of ephedrine or pseudoephedrine per 30 day period in dosage form of any product. The limits set forth in this paragraph shall apply to the total amount of ephedrine or pseudoephedrine contained in the product and not the overall weight of such product.

(3) The pharmacy shall maintain a record of required information for each sale of a nonprescription product which contains ephedrine or pseudoephedrine for a period of two years from the date of each transaction. Except as to law enforcement agencies in this state which shall be provided immediate access by a pharmacy to all written and electronic logs or records upon request, the records maintained by a pharmacy pursuant to this Code section shall not be disclosed. Pharmacies may destroy the required information collected pursuant to this subsection after two years from the date of the transaction.

(4) (A) On and after January 1, 2017, pharmacies shall, before completing a sale of a nonprescription product which contains ephedrine or pseudoephedrine, electronically track all such sales and submit the required information to a real-time electronic logging system. A pharmacy shall not complete the sale of a nonprescription product which contains ephedrine or pseudoephedrine if the real-time electronic logging system generates a stop sale alert except as provided in subparagraph (a)(4)(A) of this Code section.

(B) If a pharmacy selling a nonprescription product which contains ephedrine or pseudoephedrine experiences mechanical or electronic failure of the real-time electronic logging system and is unable to comply with the requirements of this paragraph, the pharmacy shall maintain a written log or an alternative electronic recording mechanism until such time as the pharmacy is able to comply with the electronic logging requirement.

(C) Absent negligence, wantonness, recklessness, or deliberate misconduct, any pharmacy utilizing the real-time electronic logging system in accordance with this paragraph shall not be civilly liable as a result of any act or omission in carrying out the duties required by this paragraph and shall be immune from liability to any third party unless the pharmacy has violated any provision of this paragraph in relation to a claim brought for such violation.

(D) The Georgia Bureau of Investigation shall provide real-time access to records on such logging system through an online portal to law enforcement agencies in this state.

(5) It shall be unlawful for a pharmacy to purchase any product containing ephedrine or pseudoephedrine from any person or entity other than a manufacturer or a wholesale distributor licensed by the State Board of Pharmacy.

(6) This subsection shall preempt all local ordinances or regulations governing the retail sale of products containing ephedrine or pseudoephedrine except such local ordinances or regulations that existed on or before December 31, 2004. Effective January 1, 2006, this subsection shall preempt all local ordinances.

(7) (A) Any person convicted of a violation of paragraph (1), (2), (3), or (4) of this subsection shall be guilty of a misdemeanor which, upon the first conviction, shall be punished by a fine of not more than $500.00 and, upon the second or subsequent conviction, shall be punished by not more than six months' imprisonment or a fine of not more than $1,000.00, or both.

(B) Any person convicted of a violation of paragraph (5) of this subsection shall, upon the first conviction, be guilty of a misdemeanor and, upon the second or subsequent conviction, be guilty of a misdemeanor of a high and aggravated nature.

(C) It shall be a defense to a prosecution pursuant to this paragraph by law enforcement of a pharmacy for violation of paragraph (1), (2), (3), (4), or (5) of this subsection that, at the time of the alleged violation, all of the employees of the pharmacy had completed training complying with standards established under Georgia Meth Watch as such standards existed on June 30, 2016, and the pharmacy was in compliance with procedures established by Georgia Meth Watch as such standards existed on June 30, 2016; provided, however, that this subparagraph shall not apply to the State Board of Pharmacy or prevent it from taking disciplinary action for a violation of this subsection.

(d) This Code section shall not apply to products that the State Board of Pharmacy, upon application of a manufacturer, exempts by rule from this Code section because the product has been formulated in such a way as to prevent effectively the conversion of the active ingredient into methamphetamine or its salts or precursors.

(e) Except as authorized by this article, it is unlawful for any person to possess, have under his or her control, manufacture, deliver, distribute, dispense, administer, purchase, sell, or possess with intent to distribute any product containing any amounts of ephedrine or pseudoephedrine which have been altered from their original condition so as to be powdered, liquefied, or crushed. This subsection shall not apply to any of the substances identified within this subsection which are possessed or altered for a legitimate medical purpose. Any person who violates this subsection shall be guilty of a felony and, upon conviction thereof, shall be punished by imprisonment for not less than one year nor more than ten years.

§ 16-13-30.4. Licenses for sale, transfer, or purchase for resale of products containing pseudoephedrine; reporting and record-keeping requirements; grounds for denial, suspension, or revocation of licenses; civil forfeiture; penalties

(a) As used in this Code section and unless otherwise specified, the term "board" or "board of pharmacy" shall mean the State Board of Pharmacy.

(b)(1) A wholesale distributor who sells, transfers, purchases for resale, or otherwise furnishes any product containing pseudoephedrine must first obtain a license from the board of pharmacy; provided, however, that a wholesale distributor that has a valid license as a wholesale distributor under Code Section 26-4-113 shall not be required to obtain an additional license under this Code section.

(2) Wholesale distributors licensed under Code Section 26-4-113 shall be subject to the provisions of this Code section in the same manner as wholesale distributors licensed under this Code section.

(3) Every wholesale distributor licensed as provided in this Code section shall:

(A) Submit reports, upon verbal or written request from the Georgia Drugs and Narcotics Agency, the Georgia Bureau of Investigation, or the sheriff of a county or the police chief of a municipality located in this state, to account for all transactions with persons or firms located within this state; such reportable transactions shall include all sales, distribution, or transactions dealing with products containing pseudoephedrine; and

(B) Within seven days, notify the Georgia Drugs and Narcotics Agency of any purchases of products containing pseudoephedrine from the wholesale distributor which the wholesaler judges to be excessive.

(4) Whenever any firm or person located in this state receives, purchases, or otherwise gains access to products containing pseudoephedrine from any wholesale distributor, whether located in or outside this state, such firm or person shall maintain a copy of such wholesale distributor's license issued by the State Board of Pharmacy. Such firm or person shall maintain copies of all invoices, receipts, and other records regarding such products containing pseudoephedrine for a minimum of three years from the date of receipt, purchase, or access. Failure to maintain records to verify the presence of any and all products containing pseudoephedrine being held by a firm or person shall subject such products containing pseudoephedrine to being embargoed or seized by proper law enforcement authorities until such time as proof can be shown that such products containing pseudoephedrine were obtained from a Georgia licensed wholesale distributor.

(5) Agents of the Georgia Drugs and Narcotics Agency, agents of the Georgia Bureau of Investigation, and the sheriff of a county or the police chief of a county or municipality in this state in which a firm or person that receives, purchases, or otherwise gains access to products containing pseudoephedrine is located may request to review the receiving records for such products. Failure to provide such records within five business days following such request to account for the presence of such products shall result in the embargo or seizure of such products.

(c) A license or permit obtained pursuant to this Code section shall be denied, suspended, or revoked by the board of pharmacy upon finding that the licensee or permit holder has:

(1) Furnished false or fraudulent material information in any application filed under this Code section;

(2) Been convicted of a crime under any state or federal law relating to any controlled substance;

(3) Had his or her federal registration suspended or revoked to manufacture, distribute, or dispense controlled substances;

(4) Violated the provisions of Chapter 4 of Title 26; or

(5) Failed to maintain effective controls against the diversion of products containing pseudoephedrine to unauthorized persons or entities.

(d) The board of pharmacy may adopt reasonable rules and regulations to effectuate the provisions of this Code section. The board is further authorized to charge reasonable fees to defray expenses incurred in issuing any licenses or permits, maintaining any records or forms required by this Code section, and the administration of the provisions of this Code section.

(e) Notwithstanding any other provision of this Code section to the contrary, no person shall be required to obtain a license or permit for the sale, receipt, transfer, or possession of a product containing pseudoephedrine when:

(1) Such lawful distribution takes place in the usual course of business between agents or employees of a single regulated person or entity; or

(2) A product containing pseudoephedrine is delivered to or by a common or contract carrier for carriage in the lawful and usual course of the business of the common or contract carrier or to or by a warehouseman for storage in the lawful and usual course of the business of the warehouseman.

(f) Any products containing pseudoephedrine that have been or that are intended to be sold, transferred, purchased for resale, possessed, or otherwise transferred in violation of a provision of this Code section and any proceeds are declared to be contraband and no person shall have a property right in them and shall be forfeited according to the procedure set forth in Chapter 16 of Title 9. As used in this subsection, the term "proceeds" shall have the same meaning as set forth in Code Section 9-16-2.

(g)(1) Any person who sells, transfers, receives, or possesses a product containing pseudoephedrine violates this Code section if the person:

(A) Knowingly fails to comply with the reporting requirements of this Code section;

(B) Knowingly makes a false statement in a report or record required by this Code section or the rules adopted thereunder; or

(C) Is required by this Code section to have a license or permit and knowingly or deliberately fails to obtain such a license or permit.

(2) It shall be illegal for a person to possess, sell, transfer, or otherwise furnish a product containing pseudoephedrine if such person possesses, sells, transfers, or furnishes the substance with the knowledge or intent that the substance will be used in the unlawful manufacture of a controlled substance.

(3)(A) A person who violates paragraph (2) of this subsection shall be guilty of a felony and, upon conviction thereof, shall be punished by imprisonment for not less than one nor more than 15 years or by a fine not to exceed $100,000.00, or both.

(B) A person who violates any provision of this Code Section other than paragraph (2) of this subsection shall be guilty of a misdemeanor on the first offense and a misdemeanor of a high and aggravated nature on the second and subsequent offenses.

§ 16-13-30.5. Possession of substances with intent to use or convey such substances for the manufacture of Schedule I or Schedule II controlled substances

(a) It shall be illegal for a person to possess, whether acquired through theft or other means, any substance with the intent to:

(1) Use such substance in the manufacture of a Schedule I or Schedule II controlled substance; or

(2) Knowingly convey such substance to another for use in the manufacture of a Schedule I or Schedule II controlled substance.

(b) In determining whether a particular substance is possessed with the intent required to violate subsection (a) of this Code section, the court or other authority making such a determination may, in addition to all other logically relevant factors, consider the following:

(1) Statements by the owner or anyone in control of the substance concerning its use;

(2) Prior convictions, if any, of the owner or of anyone in control of the substance for violation of any state or federal law relating to the sale or manufacture of controlled substances;

(3) Instructions or descriptive materials of any kind accompanying the substance or found in the owner's or controlling person's possession concerning, explaining, or depicting its use;

(4) The manner in which the substance is displayed or offered for sale;

(5) The quantity and location of the substance considered in relation to the existence and scope of legitimate uses for the substance in the community; and

(6) Expert testimony concerning the substance's use.

(c) This Code section shall not apply where possession was by a person authorized by law to dispense, prescribe, manufacture, or possess the substance in question.

(d) A person who violates this Code section shall be guilty of a felony and, upon conviction thereof, shall be punished by imprisonment for not less than one nor more than 15 years or by a fine not to exceed $100,000.00, or both.

§ 16-13-30.6. Prohibition on purchase and sale of marijuana flavored products

(a) As used in this Code section, the term:

(1) "Marijuana flavored product" means any product, including lollipops, gumdrops, or other candy, which is flavored to taste like marijuana or hemp. The term shall include, but is not limited to, "Chronic Candy," "Kronic Kandy," or "Pot Suckers."

(2) "Minor" means any person under the age of 18 years.

(3) "Person" means any natural person, individual, corporation, unincorporated association, proprietorship, firm, partnership, limited liability company, joint venture, joint stock association, or other entity or business organization of any kind.

(b) The General Assembly finds and determines that:

(1) According to the "2004 Monitoring the Future Study" conducted by the University of Michigan, 16.3 percent of eighth graders, 35.1 percent of tenth graders, and 45.7 percent of twelfth graders reported using marijuana at least once during their lifetimes;

(2) According to a 2002 Substance Abuse and Mental Health Service Administration report, "Initiation of Marijuana Use: Trends, Patterns and Implications," the younger children are when they first use marijuana, the more likely they are to use cocaine and heroin and become drug dependent as adults;

(3) Marijuana abuse is associated with many negative health effects, including frequent respiratory infections, impaired memory and learning, increased heart rate, anxiety, and panic attacks;

(4) Marijuana users have many of the same respiratory problems that are associated with tobacco use;

(5) According to the "2001 National Household Survey on Drug Abuse," marijuana is the nation's most commonly used illicit drug, and more than 83,000,000 Americans aged 12 and older have tried marijuana at least once;

(6) Use of marijuana has been shown to lower test scores among high school students, and workers who smoke marijuana are more likely to have problems on their jobs;

(7) Federal, state, and local governments spend millions of dollars annually on programs educating people about the hazards of drugs, and the marketing of marijuana flavored substances would have an adverse impact upon these programs;

(8) The sale of marijuana flavored products, including lollipops and gum drops, which claim "every lick is like taking a hit" is a marketing ploy that perpetuates an unhealthy culture and should not be permitted in the State of Georgia;

(9) Marijuana flavored products are a threat to minors in the State of Georgia because such products give the false impression that marijuana is fun and safe;

(10) Marijuana flavored products packaged as candy or lollipops falling into the hands of unsuspecting minors may serve as a gateway to future use of marijuana and other drugs; and

(11) Merchants who sell marijuana flavored products are promoting marijuana use and creating new customers for drug dealers in the State of Georgia.

Therefore, the purpose of this Code section is to prohibit the purchase and sale of marijuana flavored products to minors in the State of Georgia.

(c) It shall be unlawful for any person knowingly to sell, deliver, distribute, or provide to a minor or knowingly possess with intent to sell, deliver, distribute, or provide to a minor any marijuana flavored product in the State of Georgia.

(d) It shall be unlawful for any minor falsely to represent to any person that such minor is 18 years of age or older with the intent to purchase or otherwise obtain any marijuana flavored product.

(e) Any person who violates subsection (c) of this Code section shall be guilty of a misdemeanor and shall be subject to a fine of $500.00 for each offense. Each sale in violation of this Code section shall constitute a separate offense.

§ 16-13-31. Trafficking in cocaine, illegal drugs, marijuana, or methamphetamine; penalties

(a) (1) Except as authorized by this article, any person who sells, manufactures, delivers, or brings into this state or who is in possession of 28 grams or more of cocaine or of any mixture with a purity of 10 percent or more of cocaine, as described in Schedule II, in violation of this article commits the felony offense of trafficking in cocaine and, upon conviction thereof, shall be punished as follows:

(A) If the quantity of the cocaine or the mixture involved is 28 grams or more, but less than 200 grams, the person shall be sentenced to a mandatory minimum term of imprisonment of ten years and shall pay a fine of $200,000.00;

(B) If the quantity of the cocaine or the mixture involved is 200 grams or more, but less than 400 grams, the person shall be sentenced to a mandatory minimum term of imprisonment of 15 years and shall pay a fine of $300,000.00; and

(C) If the quantity of the cocaine or the mixture involved is 400 grams or more, the person shall be sentenced to a mandatory minimum term of imprisonment of 25 years and shall pay a fine of $1 million.

(2) Except as authorized by this article, any person who sells, manufactures, delivers, or brings into this state or who is in possession of any mixture with a purity of less than 10 percent of cocaine, as described in Schedule II, in violation of this article commits the felony offense of trafficking in cocaine if the total weight of the mixture multiplied by the percentage of cocaine contained in the mixture exceeds any of the quantities of cocaine specified in paragraph (1) of this subsection. Upon conviction thereof, such person shall be punished as provided in paragraph (1) of this subsection, depending upon the quantity of cocaine such person is charged with selling, manufacturing, delivering, or bringing into this state or possessing.

(b) Except as authorized by this article, any person who sells, manufactures, delivers, brings into this state, or has possession of four grams or more of any morphine, opium, or substance identified in subparagraph (RR) or (SS) of paragraph (1) or paragraph (13), (14), or (15) of Code Section 16-13-25, or subparagraph (A), (C.5), (F), (U.1), (V), or (V.2) of paragraph (2) of

Code Section 16-13-26 or any salt, isomer, or salt of an isomer thereof, including heroin, as described in Schedules I and II, or four grams or more of any mixture containing any such substance in violation of this article commits the felony offense of trafficking in illegal drugs and, upon conviction thereof, shall be punished as follows:

(1) If the quantity of such substances involved is four grams or more, but less than 14 grams, the person shall be sentenced to a mandatory minimum term of imprisonment of five years and shall pay a fine of $50,000.00;

(2) If the quantity of such substances involved is 14 grams or more, but less than 28 grams, the person shall be sentenced to a mandatory minimum term of imprisonment of ten years and shall pay a fine of $100,000.00; and

(3) If the quantity of such substances involved is 28 grams or more, the person shall be sentenced to a mandatory minimum term of imprisonment of 25 years and shall pay a fine of $500,000.00.

(c) Except as authorized by this article, any person who sells, manufactures, grows, delivers, brings into this state, or has possession of a quantity of marijuana exceeding ten pounds commits the offense of trafficking in marijuana and, upon conviction thereof, shall be punished as follows:

(1) If the quantity of marijuana involved is in excess of ten pounds, but less than 2,000 pounds, the person shall be sentenced to a mandatory minimum term of imprisonment of five years and shall pay a fine of $100,000.00;

(2) If the quantity of marijuana involved is 2,000 pounds or more, but less than 10,000 pounds, the person shall be sentenced to a mandatory minimum term of imprisonment of seven years and shall pay a fine of $250,000.00; and

(3) If the quantity of marijuana involved is 10,000 pounds or more, the person shall be sentenced to a mandatory minimum term of imprisonment of 15 years and shall pay a fine of $1 million.

(d) Except as authorized by this article, any person who sells, manufactures, delivers, or brings into this state 200 grams or more of methaqualone or of any mixture containing methaqualone, as described in paragraph (6) of Code Section 16-13-25, in violation of this article commits the felony offense of trafficking in methaqualone and, upon conviction thereof, shall be punished as follows:

(1) If the quantity of the methaqualone or the mixture involved is 200 grams or more, but less than 400 grams, the person shall be sentenced to a mandatory minimum term of imprisonment of five years and shall pay a fine of $50,000.00; and

(2) If the quantity of the methaqualone or the mixture involved is 400 grams or more, the person shall be sentenced to a mandatory minimum term of imprisonment of 15 years and shall pay a fine of $250,000.00.

(e) Except as authorized by this article, any person who sells, delivers, or brings into this state or has possession of 28 grams or more of methamphetamine, amphetamine, or any mixture containing either methamphetamine or amphetamine, as described in Schedule II, in violation of this article commits the felony offense of trafficking in methamphetamine or amphetamine and, upon conviction thereof, shall be punished as follows:

(1) If the quantity of methamphetamine, amphetamine, or a mixture containing either substance involved is 28 grams or more, but less than 200 grams, the person shall be sentenced to a mandatory minimum term of imprisonment of ten years and shall pay a fine of $200,000.00;

(2) If the quantity of methamphetamine, amphetamine, or a mixture containing either substance involved is 200 grams or more, but less than 400 grams, the person shall be sentenced to a mandatory minimum term of imprisonment of 15 years and shall pay a fine of $300,000.00; and

(3) If the quantity of methamphetamine, amphetamine, or a mixture containing either substance involved is 400 grams or more, the person shall be sentenced to a mandatory minimum term of imprisonment of 25 years and shall pay a fine of $1 million.

(f) Except as authorized by this article, any person who manufactures methamphetamine, amphetamine, or any mixture containing either methamphetamine or amphetamine, as described in Schedule II, in violation of this article commits the felony offense of trafficking methamphetamine or amphetamine and, upon conviction thereof, shall be punished as follows:

(1) If the quantity of methamphetamine, amphetamine, or a mixture containing either substance involved is less than 200 grams, the person shall be sentenced to a mandatory minimum term of imprisonment of ten years and shall pay a fine of $200,000.00;

(2) If the quantity of methamphetamine, amphetamine, or a mixture containing either substance involved is 200 grams or more, but less than 400 grams, the person shall be sentenced to a mandatory minimum term of imprisonment of 15 years and shall pay a fine of $300,000.00; and

(3) If the quantity of methamphetamine, amphetamine, or a mixture containing either substance involved is 400 grams or more, the person shall be sentenced to a mandatory minimum term of imprisonment of 25 years and shall pay a fine of $1 million.

(g) (1) The district attorney may move the sentencing court to impose a reduced or suspended sentence upon any person who is convicted of a violation of this Code section who provides substantial assistance in the identification, arrest, or conviction of any of his or her accomplices, accessories, coconspirators, or principals. Upon good cause shown, the motion may be filed and heard in camera. The judge hearing the motion may impose a reduced or suspended sentence if he or she finds that the defendant has rendered such substantial assistance.

(2) (A) In the court's discretion, the judge may depart from the mandatory minimum sentence specified for a person who is convicted of a violation of this Code section as set forth in subparagraph (B) of this paragraph if the judge concludes that:

(i) The defendant was not a leader of the criminal conduct;

(ii) The defendant did not possess or use a firearm, dangerous weapon, or hazardous object during the crime;

(iii) The criminal conduct did not result in a death or serious bodily injury to a person other than to a person who is a party to the crime;

(iv) The defendant has no prior felony conviction; and

(v) The interests of justice will not be served by the imposition of the prescribed mandatory minimum sentence.

(B) The sentencing departure ranges pursuant to subparagraph (A) of this paragraph shall be as follows:

(i) Any person convicted of violating paragraph (1) of subsection (b) or (d) of this Code section, two years and six months to five years imprisonment and a fine of not less than $25,000.00 nor more than $50,000.00;

(ii) Any person convicted of violating paragraph (1) of subsection (c) of this Code section, two years and six months to five years imprisonment and a fine of not less than $50,000.00 nor more than $100,000.00;

(iii) Any person convicted of violating paragraph (2) of subsection (c) of this Code section, three years and six months to seven years imprisonment and a fine of not less than $125,000.00 nor more than $250,000.00;

(iv) Any person convicted of violating subparagraph (a)(1)(A), paragraph (2) of subsection (a), relating to the quantity of drugs specified in subparagraph (a)(1)(A) of this Code section, or paragraph (1) of subsection (e) or (f) of this Code section, five to ten years imprisonment and a fine of not less than $100,000.00 nor more than $200,000.00;

(v) Any person convicted of violating paragraph (2) of subsection (b) of this Code section, five to ten years imprisonment and a fine of not less than $50,000.00 nor more than $100,000.00;

(vi) Any person convicted of violating subparagraph (a)(1)(B), paragraph (2) of subsection (a), relating to the quantity of drugs specified in subparagraph (a)(1)(B) of this Code section, or paragraph (2) of subsection (e) or (f) of this Code section, seven years and six months to 15 years imprisonment and a fine of not less than $150,000.00 nor more than $300,000.00;

(vii) Any person convicted of violating paragraph (3) of subsection (c) of this Code section, seven years and six months to 15 years imprisonment and a fine of not less than $500,000.00 nor more than $1 million;

(viii) Any person convicted of violating paragraph (2) of subsection (d) of this Code section, seven years and six months to 15 years imprisonment and a fine of not less than $125,000.00 nor more than $250,000.00;

(ix) Any person convicted of violating paragraph (3) of subsection (b) of this Code section, 12 years and six months to 25 years imprisonment and a fine of not less than $250,000.00 nor more than $500,000.00; and

(x) Any person convicted of violating subparagraph (a)(1)(C), paragraph (2) of subsection (a), relating to the quantity of drugs specified in subparagraph (a)(1)(C) of this Code section, or paragraph (3) of subsection (e) or (f) of this Code section, 12 years and six months to 25 years imprisonment and a fine of not less than $500,000.00 nor more than $1 million.

(C) If a judge reduces the mandatory minimum sentence pursuant to this paragraph, the judge shall specify on the record the circumstances for the reduction and the interests served by such departure. Any such order shall be appealable by the State of Georgia pursuant to Code Section 5-7-1.

(D) As used in this paragraph, the term:

(i) "Dangerous weapon" shall have the same meaning as set forth in Code Section 16-11-121.

(ii) "Firearm" shall have the same meaning as set forth in Code Section 16-11-127.1.

(iii) "Hazardous object" shall have the same meaning as set forth in Code Section 20-2-751.

(iv) "Leader" means a person who planned and organized others and acted as a guiding force in order to achieve a common goal.

(3) In the court's discretion, the judge may depart from the mandatory minimum sentence specified in this Code section for a person who is convicted of a violation of this Code section when the prosecuting attorney and the defendant have agreed to a sentence that is below such mandatory minimum.

(h) Any person who violates any provision of this Code section shall be punished as provided for in the applicable mandatory minimum punishment and for not more than 30 years of imprisonment and by a fine not to exceed $1 million.

(i) Notwithstanding Code Section 16-13-2, any sentence imposed pursuant to subsection (g) of this Code section shall not be reduced by any earned time, early release, work release, leave, or other sentence-reducing measures under programs administered by the Department of Corrections, the effect of which would be to reduce the period of incarceration ordered by the sentencing court or any form of pardon, parole, or commutation of sentence by the State Board of Pardons and Paroles; provided, however, that during the final year of incarceration, a defendant so sentenced shall be eligible to be considered for participation in a Department of Corrections administered transitional center or work release program.

§ 16-13-31.1. Trafficking in ecstasy; sentencing; variation

(a) Any person who sells, manufactures, delivers, brings into this state, or has possession of 28 grams or more of 3, 4-methylenedioxyamphetamine or 3, 4-methylenedioxymetham-
phetamine, or any mixture containing 3, 4-methylenedioxyam
phetamine or 3, 4-methylenedioxymethamphetamine
as described in Schedule I, in violation of this article commits the felony offense of trafficking in 3, 4-methylenedioxyam-
phetamine or 3, 4-methylenedioxymethamphetamine and, upon conviction thereof, shall be punished as follows:

(1) If the quantity of such substance involved is 28 grams or more, but less than 200 grams, the person shall be sentenced to a mandatory minimum term of imprisonment of three years but not more than 30 years and shall pay a fine of not less than $25,000.00 nor more than $250,000.00;

(2) If the quantity of such substance involved is 200 grams or more, but less than 400 grams, the person shall be sentenced to a mandatory minimum term of imprisonment of five years but not more than 30 years and shall pay a fine of not less than $50,000.00 nor more than $250,000.00; and

(3) If the quantity of such substance involved is 400 grams or more, the person shall be sentenced to a mandatory minimum term of imprisonment of ten years but not more than 30 years and shall pay a fine of not less than $100,000.00 nor more than $250,000.00.

(b) (1) In the court's discretion, the judge may depart from the mandatory minimum sentence specified for a person who is convicted of a violation of this Code section as set forth in paragraph (2) of this subsection if the judge concludes that:

(A) The defendant was not a leader of the criminal conduct;

(B) The defendant did not possess or use a firearm, dangerous weapon, or hazardous object during the crime;

(C) The criminal conduct did not result in a death or serious bodily injury to a person other than to a person who is a party to the crime;

(D) The defendant has no prior felony conviction; and

(E) The interests of justice will not be served by the imposition of the prescribed mandatory minimum sentence.

(2) The sentencing departure ranges pursuant to paragraph (1) of this subsection shall be as follows:

(A) Any person convicted of violating paragraph (1) of subsection (a) of this Code section, one year and six months to 30 years imprisonment and a fine of not less than $12,500.00 nor more than $250,000.00;

(B) Any person convicted of violating paragraph (2) of subsection (a) of this Code section, two years and six months to 30 years imprisonment and a fine of not less than $25,000.00 nor more than $250,000.00; and

(C) Any person convicted of violating paragraph (3) of subsection (a) of this Code section, five to 30 years imprisonment and a fine of not less than $50,000.00 nor more than $250,000.00;

(3) If a judge reduces the mandatory minimum sentence pursuant to this subsection, the judge shall specify on the record the circumstances for the reduction and the interests served by such departure. Any such order shall be appealable by the State of Georgia pursuant to Code Section 5-7-1.

(4) As used in this subsection, the term:

(A) "Dangerous weapon" shall have the same meaning as set forth in Code Section 16-11-121.

(B) "Firearm" shall have the same meaning as set forth in Code Section 16-11-127.1.

(C) "Hazardous object" shall have the same meaning as set forth in Code Section 20-2-751.

(D) "Leader" means a person who planned and organized others and acted as a guiding force in order to achieve a common goal.

(c) The district attorney may move the sentencing court to impose a reduced or suspended sentence upon any person who is convicted of a violation of this Code section who provides substantial assistance in the identification, arrest, or conviction of any of his or her accomplices, accessories, coconspirators, or principals. Upon good cause shown, the motion may be filed and heard in camera. The judge hearing the motion may impose a reduced or suspended sentence if he or she finds that the defendant has rendered such substantial assistance.

(d) In the court's discretion, the judge may depart from the mandatory minimum sentence specified in this Code section for a person who is convicted of a violation of this Code section when the prosecuting attorney and the defendant have agreed to a sentence that is below such mandatory minimum.

(e) Notwithstanding Code Section 16-13-2, any sentence imposed pursuant to subsection (b) of this Code section shall not be reduced by any earned time, early release, work release, leave, or other sentence-reducing measures under programs administered by the Department of Corrections, the effect of which would be to reduce the period of incarceration ordered by the sentencing court or any form of pardon, parole, or commutation of sentence by the State Board of Pardons and Paroles; provided, however, that during the final year of incarceration, a defendant so sentenced shall be eligible to be considered for participation in a Department of Corrections administered transitional center or work release program.

§ 16-13-32. Transactions in drug related objects; civil forfeiture; penalties

(a) As used in this Code section, the term:

(1) "Drug related object" means any instrument, device, or object which is designed or marketed as useful primarily for one or more of the following purposes:

(A) To inject, ingest, inhale, or otherwise introduce marijuana or a controlled substance into the human body;

(B) To enhance the effect of marijuana or a controlled substance on the human body;

(C) To test the strength, effectiveness, or purity of marijuana or a controlled substance;

(D) To process or prepare marijuana or a controlled substance for introduction into the human body;

(E) To conceal any quantity of marijuana or a controlled substance; or

(F) To contain or hold marijuana or a controlled substance while it is being introduced into the human body.

(2) "Knowing" means either actual or constructive knowledge of the drug related nature of the object; and a person or corporation has constructive knowledge of the drug related nature of the object if he or it has knowledge of facts which would put a reasonable and prudent person on notice of the drug related nature of the object.

(b) It shall be unlawful for any person or corporation, knowing the drug related nature of the object, to sell, lend, rent, lease, give, exchange, or otherwise distribute to any person any drug related object. It shall also be unlawful for any person or corporation, knowing the drug related nature of the object, to display for sale, or possess with the intent to distribute any drug related object. Unless stated within the body of the advertisement or notice that the object that is advertised or about which information is disseminated is not available for distribution of any sort in this state, it shall be unlawful for any person or corporation, knowing the drug related nature of the object, to distribute or disseminate in any manner to any person any advertisement of any kind or notice of any kind which gives information, directly or indirectly, on where, how, from whom, or by what means any drug related object may be obtained or made.

(c) It shall be unlawful for any person or corporation, other than a licensed pharmacist, a pharmacy intern or pharmacy extern as defined in Code Section 26-4-5, or a practitioner licensed to dispense dangerous drugs, to sell, lend, rent, lease, give, exchange, or otherwise distribute to any person a hypodermic syringe or needle designed or marketed primarily for human use. It shall be an affirmative defense that the hypodermic syringe or needle was marketed for a legitimate medical purpose.

(d) For a first offense, any person or corporation which violates any provision of this Code section shall be guilty of a misdemeanor. For a second offense, the defendant shall be guilty of a misdemeanor of a high and aggravated nature. For a third or subsequent offense, the defendant shall be guilty of a felony and, upon conviction thereof, shall be imprisoned for not less than one year nor more than five years and shall be fined not more than $5,000.00.

(e) All instruments, devices, and objects which are distributed or possessed in violation of this Code section and any proceeds are declared to be contraband and no person shall have a property right in them and shall be forfeited according to the procedure set forth in Chapter 16 of Title 9. As used in this subsection, the term "proceeds" shall have the same meaning as set forth in Code Section 9-16-2.

§ 16-13-32.1. Transactions in drug related objects; evidence as to whether object is drug related; civil forfeiture; penalties

(a) It shall be unlawful for any person or corporation to sell, rent, lease, give, exchange, otherwise distribute, or possess with intent to distribute any object or materials of any kind which such person or corporation intends to be used for the purpose of planting, propagating, cultivating, growing, harvesting, manufacturing, compounding, converting, producing, processing, preparing, testing, analyzing, packaging, repackaging, storing, containing, concealing, injecting, ingesting, inhaling, or otherwise introducing into the human body marijuana or a controlled substance.

(b) Unless stated within the body of the advertisement or notice that the object or materials that are advertised or about which information is disseminated are not available for distribution of any sort in this state, it shall be unlawful for any person or corporation to sell, rent, lease, give, exchange, distribute, or possess with intent to distribute any advertisement of any kind or notice of any kind which gives information, directly or indirectly, on where, how, from whom, or by what means any object or materials may be obtained or made, which object or materials such person or corporation intends to be used for the purpose of planting, propagating, cultivating, growing, harvesting, manufacturing, compounding, converting, producing, processing, preparing, testing, analyzing, packaging, repackaging, storing, containing, concealing, injecting, ingesting, inhaling, or otherwise introducing into the human body marijuana or a controlled substance.

(c) In determining whether any object or materials are intended for any of the purposes listed in subsections (a) and (b) of this Code section, a court or other authority shall consider all logically relevant factors. In a trial under this Code section, any evidence admissible on this question under the rules of evidence shall be admitted. Subject to the rules of evidence, when they are the object of an offer of proof in a court proceeding, the following factors are among those that should be considered by a court or other authority on this question:

(1) Statements by an owner or anyone in control of the object or materials;

(2) Instructions provided with the object or materials;

(3) Descriptive materials accompanying the object or materials;

(4) National and local advertising or promotional materials concerning the object or materials;

(5) The appearance of, and any writing or other representations appearing on, the object or materials;

(6) The manner in which the object or materials are displayed for sale or other distribution;

(7) Expert testimony concerning the object or materials; and

(8) Any written or pictorial materials which are present in the place where the object is located.

(d) For a first offense, any person or corporation which violates any provision of this Code section shall be guilty of a misdemeanor. For a second offense, the defendant shall be guilty of a misdemeanor of a high and aggravated nature. For a third or subsequent offense, the defendant shall be guilty of a felony and, upon conviction thereof, shall be imprisoned for not less than one year nor more than five years and shall be fined not more than $5,000.00.

(e) All objects and materials which are distributed or possessed in violation of this Code section and any proceeds are declared to be contraband and no person shall have a property right in them and shall be forfeited according to the procedure set forth in Chapter 16 of Title 9. As used in this subsection, the term "proceeds" shall have the same meaning as set forth in Code Section 9-16-2.

§ 16-13-32.2. Possession and use of drug related objects

(a) It shall be unlawful for any person to use, or possess with the intent to use, any object or materials of any kind for the purpose of planting, propagating, cultivating, growing, harvesting, manufacturing, compounding, converting, producing, processing, preparing, testing, analyzing, packaging, repackaging, storing, containing, concealing, injecting, ingesting, inhaling, or otherwise introducing into the human body marijuana or a controlled substance.

(b) Any person or corporation which violates any provision of this Code section shall be guilty of a misdemeanor.

§ 16-13-32.3. Use of communication facility in committing or facilitating commission of act which constitutes felony under chapter; penalty

(a) It shall be unlawful for any person knowingly or intentionally to use any communication facility in committing or in causing or facilitating the commission of any act or acts constituting a felony under this chapter. Each separate use of a communication facility shall be a separate offense under this Code section. For purposes of this Code section, the term "communication facility" means any and all public and private instrumentalities used or useful in the transmission of writing, signs, signals, pictures, or sounds of all kinds and includes mail, telephone, wire, radio, computer or computer network, and all other means of communication.

(b) Any person who violates subsection (a) of this Code section shall be punished by a fine of not more than $30,000.00 or by imprisonment for not less than one nor more than four years, or both.

§ 16-13-32.4. Manufacturing, distributing, dispensing, or possessing controlled substances in, on, or near public or private schools

(a) It shall be unlawful for any person to manufacture, distribute, dispense, or possess with intent to distribute a controlled substance or marijuana in, on, or within 1,000 feet of any real property owned by or leased to any public or private elementary school, secondary school, or school board used for elementary or secondary education.

(b) Any person who violates or conspires to violate subsection (a) of this Code section shall be guilty of a felony and upon conviction shall receive the following punishment:

(1) Upon a first conviction, imprisonment for not more than 20 years or a fine of not more than $20,000.00, or both; or

(2) Upon a second or subsequent conviction, imprisonment for not less than five years nor more than 40 years or a fine of not more than $40,000.00, or both. It shall be mandatory for the court to impose a minimum sentence of five years which may not be suspended unless otherwise provided by law.

A sentence imposed under this Code section shall be served consecutively to any other sentence imposed.

(c) A conviction arising under this Code section shall not merge with a conviction arising under any other provision of this article.

(d) It shall be no defense to a prosecution for a violation of this Code section that:

(1) School was or was not in session at the time of the offense;

(2) The real property was being used for other purposes besides school purposes at the time of the offense; or

(3) The offense took place on a school vehicle.

(e) In a prosecution under this Code section, a map produced or reproduced by any municipal or county agency or department for the purpose of depicting the location and boundaries of the area on or within 1,000 feet of the real property of a school board or a private or public elementary or secondary school that is used for school purposes, or a true copy of the map, shall, if certified as a true copy by the custodian of the record, be admissible and shall constitute prima-facie evidence of the location and boundaries of the area, if the governing body of the municipality or county has approved the map as an official record of the location and boundaries of the area. A map approved under this Code section may be revised from time to time by the governing body of the municipality or county. The original of every map approved or revised under this subsection or a true copy of such original map shall be filed with the municipality or county and shall be maintained as an official record of the municipality or county. This subsection shall not preclude the prosecution from introducing or relying upon any other evidence or testimony to establish any element of this offense. This subsection shall not preclude the use or admissibility of a map or diagram other than the one which has been approved by the municipality or county.

(f) A county school board may adopt regulations requiring the posting of signs designating the areas within 1,000 feet of school boards and private or public elementary and secondary schools as "Drug-free School Zones."

(g) It is an affirmative defense to prosecution for a violation of this Code section that the prohibited conduct took place entirely within a private residence, that no person 17 years of age or younger was present in such private residence at any time during the commission of the offense, and that the prohibited conduct was not carried on for purposes of financial gain. Nothing in this subsection shall be construed to establish an affirmative defense with respect to any offense under this chapter other than the offense provided for in subsection (a) of this Code section.

§ 16-13-32.5. Manufacturing, distributing, dispensing, or possessing controlled substance, marijuana, or counterfeit substance near park or housing project; nonmerger of offenses; evidence of location and boundaries; posting; affirmative defenses

(a) It shall be unlawful for any person to manufacture, distribute, dispense, or possess with intent to distribute a controlled substance or marijuana or a counterfeit substance in, on, or within 1,000 feet of any real property which has been dedicated and set apart by the governing authority of any municipality, county, state authority, or the state for use as a park, playground, recreation center, or for any other recreation purposes, unless the manufacture, distribution, or dispensing is otherwise allowed by law.

(b) It shall be unlawful for any person to manufacture, distribute, dispense, or possess with intent to distribute a controlled substance or marijuana or a counterfeit substance in, on, or within 1,000 feet of any real property of any publicly owned or publicly operated housing project, unless the manufacture, distribution, or dispensing is otherwise allowed by law. For the purposes of this Code section, the term "housing project" means any facilities under the jurisdiction of a housing authority which constitute single or multifamily dwelling units occupied by low and moderate-income families pursuant to Chapter 3 of Title 8.

(c) Any person who violates or conspires to violate subsection (a) or (b) of this Code section shall be guilty of a felony and upon conviction shall receive the following punishment:

(1) Upon a first conviction, imprisonment for not more than 20 years or a fine of not more than $20,000.00, or both; or

(2) Upon a second or subsequent conviction, imprisonment for not less than five years nor more than 40 years or a fine of not more than $40,000.00, or both. It shall be mandatory for the court to impose a minimum sentence of five years which may not be suspended unless otherwise provided by law.

A sentence imposed under this Code section shall be served consecutively to any other sentence imposed.

(d) A conviction arising under this Code section shall not merge with a conviction arising under any other provision of this article.

(e) In a prosecution under this Code section, a map produced or reproduced by any municipal or county agency or department for the purpose of depicting the location and boundaries of the area on or within 1,000 feet of the real property of any publicly owned or publicly operated housing project or the real property set apart for use as a park, playground, recreation center, or for any other recreation purposes, or a true copy of the map, shall, if certified as a true copy by the custodian of the record, be admissible and shall constitute prima-facie evidence of the location and boundaries of the area, if the governing body of the municipality or county has approved the map as an official record of the location and boundaries of the area. A map approved under this Code section may be revised from time to time by the governing body of the municipality or county. The original of every map approved or revised under this subsection or a true copy of such original map shall be filed with the municipality or county and shall be maintained as an official record of the municipality or county. This subsection shall not preclude the prosecution from introducing or relying upon any other evidence or testimony to establish an element of this offense. This subsection shall not preclude the use or admissibility of a map or diagram other than the one which has been approved by the municipality or county.

(f) The governing authority of a municipality or county may adopt regulations requiring the posting of signs designating the areas within 1,000 feet of any lands or buildings set apart for use as parks, playgrounds, recreation centers, or any other recreation purposes as "Drug-free Recreation Zones" and designating the areas within 1,000 feet of the real property of any publicly owned or publicly operated housing project as "Drug-free Residential Zones."

(g) It is an affirmative defense to prosecution for a violation of this Code section that the prohibited conduct took place entirely within a private residence, that no person 17 years of age or younger was present in such private residence at any time during the commission of the offense, and that the prohibited conduct was not carried on for purposes of financial gain. Nothing in this subsection shall be construed to establish an affirmative defense with respect to any offense under this chapter other than the offense provided for in subsections (a) and (b) of this Code section.

§ 16-13-32.6. Manufacturing, distributing, dispensing, or possessing with intent to distribute controlled substance or marijuana in, on, or within drug-free commercial zone

(a) It shall be unlawful for any person to illegally manufacture, distribute, dispense, or possess with intent to distribute a controlled substance or marijuana in, on, or within any real property which has been designated under this Code section as a drug-free commercial zone.

(b)(1) Any person who violates or conspires to violate subsection (a) of this Code section shall be guilty of a felony and upon conviction shall receive the following punishment:

(A) Upon a first conviction, imprisonment for not more than 20 years or a fine of not more than $20,000.00, or both; or

(B) Upon a second or subsequent conviction, imprisonment for not less than five years nor more than 40 years or a fine of not more than $40,000.00, or both.

(2) A sentence imposed under this Code section shall be served consecutively to any other sentence imposed.

(3) Any person convicted of a violation of subsection (a) of this Code section may, as a condition of probation or parole, be required by the sentencing court or State Board of Pardons and Paroles to refrain for a period of not more than 24 months from entering or at any time being within the boundaries of the drug-free commercial zone wherein such person was arrested for a violation of this Code section. Any person arrested for violation of his or her terms of probation shall be governed by the provisions of Code Section 42-8-38 and any person arrested for a violation of his or her terms of parole shall be governed by the provisions of Article 2 of Chapter 9 of Title 42.

(c) A conviction arising under this Code section shall not merge with a conviction arising under any other provision of this article.

(d) Any municipality or county may designate one or more commercial areas where there is a high rate of drug related crime as drug-free commercial zones. A drug-free commercial zone may include only an area which the municipality or county has previously zoned commercial pursuant to its planning and zoning powers and any residential area contiguous to such commercially zoned area extending not more than one-half mile from the external boundary of any portion of the commercially zoned area. A municipality or county which designates one or more areas as drug-free commercial zones shall be required to make such designations by ordinance and shall be required to post prominent and conspicuous signs on the boundaries of and throughout any such drug-free commercial zone. A municipality or county shall be required to file with the Department of Community Affairs a copy of each ordinance which shall have attached a clearly defined map describing each drug-free commercial zone and a report evidencing all drug related crimes in such drug-free commercial zone area during the 12 months preceding the enactment of such ordinance. A municipality or county shall also be required to file with the Department of Community Affairs, during the period that a drug-free commercial zone is in effect, annual reports evidencing all drug related crimes in such drug-free commercial zone. Such ordinances, maps, and drug crime reports shall be maintained in a permanent register by such department, and copies of such ordinances, maps, and drug crime reports of drug-free commercial zones shall be made available to the public at a reasonable cost. A drug-free commercial zone shall not be effective and valid for the purposes of this Code section until it has been adopted by the General Assembly by general law. After the General Assembly has adopted one or more drug-free commercial zones, the governing authority of each municipality or county which has such a zone or zones designated and adopted shall be required to have a description of each such zone published in the legal organ of the municipality or county at least once a week for three weeks. A drug-free commercial zone adopted by the General Assembly shall remain in effect for five years and shall expire five years from the effective date of such adoption by the General Assembly. An area which has been a drug-free commercial zone may be continued as or again designated as a drug-free commercial zone upon the enactment of an ordinance and adoption thereof by the General Assembly in accordance with the provisions of this subsection. No arrest for a violation of this Code section shall be permissible for a period of 30 days immediately following the effective date of the adoption of such drug-free commercial zone by the General Assembly.

(e) In a prosecution under this Code section, a true copy of a map produced or reproduced by any municipal or county agency or department for the purpose of depicting the location and boundaries of any drug-free commercial zone and filed and on record at the Department of Community Affairs shall, if certified as a true copy by the custodian of such records at such department, be admissible and shall constitute prima-facie evidence of the location and boundaries of such zone. A map approved under this Code section may be revised from time to time by the governing body of the municipality or county; provided, however, that a revised map shall not become effective and the revised area shall not be a drug-free commercial zone until the revised map has been filed with the Department of Community Affairs and adopted by the General Assembly by general law; provided, further, that the revision of a drug-free commercial zone shall not extend the expiration date of such a drug-free commercial zone. The original copy of every map approved or revised under this subsection or a true copy of such original map shall be filed with the Department of Community Affairs and shall be maintained as an official record of the department. This subsection shall not preclude the prosecution from introducing or relying upon any other evidence or testimony to establish any element of this offense.

(f) The General Assembly hereby adopts and incorporates into this Code section all drug-free commercial zones which have been adopted by municipal or county ordinance and entered in the register of the Department of Community Affairs as provided for in subsection (d) of this Code section on or before July 1, 2015.

§ 16-13-33. Attempt or conspiracy to commit offense under this article

136

Any person who attempts or conspires to commit any offense defined in this article shall be, upon conviction thereof, punished by imprisonment not exceeding the maximum punishment prescribed for the offense, the commission of which was the object of the attempt or conspiracy.

§ 16-13-34. Promulgation of rules relating to registration and control of controlled substances; registration fees

The State Board of Pharmacy may promulgate rules and charge reasonable fees relating to the registration and control of the manufacture, distribution, and dispensing of controlled substances within this state.

§ 16-13-35. General registration requirements

(a) Every person who manufactures, distributes, or dispenses any controlled substances within this state or who proposes to engage in the manufacture, distribution, or dispensing of any controlled substance within this state must obtain annually a registration issued by the State Board of Pharmacy in accordance with its rules.
(b) Persons registered by the State Board of Pharmacy under this article to manufacture, distribute, dispense, or conduct research with controlled substances may possess, manufacture, distribute, dispense, or conduct research with those substances to the extent authorized by their registration and in conformity with this article.
(c) The following persons need not register and may lawfully possess controlled substances under this article:
(1) An agent or employee of any registered manufacturer, distributor, or dispenser of any controlled substance if he is acting in the usual course of his business or employment;
(2) A common or contract carrier or warehouseman, or any employee thereof, whose possession of any controlled substance is in the usual course of his business or employment;
(3) An ultimate user or a person in possession of any controlled substance pursuant to a lawful order of a practitioner or in lawful possession of a Schedule V substance; and
(4) Officers and employees of this state, or of a political subdivision of this state, or of the United States while acting in the course of their official duties.
(d) The State Board of Pharmacy may waive by rule the requirements for registration of certain manufacturers, distributors, or dispensers if it finds it consistent with the public health and safety.
(e) A separate registration is required at each principal place of business or professional practice where the applicant manufactures, distributes, or dispenses controlled substances.
(f) The State Board of Pharmacy, the director of the Georgia Drugs and Narcotics Agency, or other drug agents designated by the State Board of Pharmacy for this purpose may inspect the establishment of a registrant or applicant for registration in accordance with the State Board of Pharmacy rules and the provisions of this article.
(g) The following persons are registered under this article and are exempt from the registration fee and registration application requirements of this article:
(1) Persons licensed by the State Board of Pharmacy as a pharmacist or a pharmacy under Chapter 4 of Title 26;
(2) Persons licensed as a physician, dentist, or veterinarian under the laws of the state to use, mix, prepare, dispense, prescribe, and administer drugs in connection with medical treatment to the extent provided by the laws of this state; and
(3) An employee, agent, or representative of any person described in paragraph (1) or (2) of this subsection acting in the usual course of his employment or occupation and not on his own account, provided that suspension or revocation of licensure as set forth in paragraphs (1) and (2) of this subsection shall nullify the exemption as set forth in this subsection.

§ 16-13-36. Factors considered in determining whether to register manufacturer or distributor

(a) The State Board of Pharmacy shall register an applicant to manufacture or distribute controlled substances included in Code Sections 16-13-25 through 16-13-29 unless it determines that the issuance of that registration would be inconsistent with the public interest. In determining the public interest, the State Board of Pharmacy shall consider the following factors:
(1) Maintenance of effective controls against diversion of controlled substances into other than legitimate medical, scientific, or industrial channels;
(2) Compliance with applicable state and local law;
(3) Any convictions of the applicant under any federal or state laws relating to any controlled substance;
(4) Past experience in the manufacture or distribution of controlled substances and the existence in the applicant's establishment of effective controls against illegal diversion of controlled substances;
(5) Furnishing by the applicant of false or fraudulent material in any application filed under this article;
(6) Suspension or revocation of the applicant's federal registration to manufacture, distribute, or dispense controlled substances as authorized by federal law;
(7) Suspension or revocation of the applicant's registration or license to manufacture, distribute, or dispense controlled substances, drugs, or narcotics in this state or any other state of the United States; and
(8) Any other factors relevant to and consistent with the public health and safety.
(b) Registration under subsection (a) of this Code section does not entitle a registrant to manufacture and distribute controlled substances in Schedule I or II other than those specified in the registration.
(c) Practitioners must be registered under state law to dispense any controlled substances or to conduct research with controlled substances in Schedules II through V if they are authorized to dispense or conduct research under the law of this state. The State Board of Pharmacy need not require separate registration under this Code section for practitioners engaging in research with nonnarcotic controlled substances in Schedules II through V where the registrant is already registered under this article in another capacity. Practitioners registered under federal law to conduct research with Schedule I substances may conduct research with Schedule I substances within this state upon furnishing the State Board of Pharmacy satisfactory evidence of that federal registration. Any practitioner conducting research with Schedule I controlled substances must obtain a separate registration with the State Board of Pharmacy.
(d) Compliance by manufacturers and distributors with the provisions of federal law respecting registration (excluding fees) entitles them to be registered under this article.

§ 16-13-37. Grounds for suspending or revoking registration; disposition of controlled substances; notification to bureau

(a) A registration under Code Section 16-13-36 to manufacture, distribute, or dispense a controlled substance may be suspended or revoked by the State Board of Pharmacy upon a finding that the registrant:
(1) Has furnished false or fraudulent material information in any application filed under this article;
(2) Has been convicted of a felony under any state or federal law relating to any controlled substance;
(3) Has had his federal registration to manufacture, distribute, or dispense controlled substances suspended or revoked;
(4) Has violated any provision of this article or the rules and regulations promulgated under this article; or
(5) Has failed to maintain sufficient controls against diversion of controlled substances into other than legitimate medical, scientific, or industrial channels.
(b) The State Board of Pharmacy may limit revocation or suspension of a registration to the particular controlled substance with respect to which grounds for revocation or suspension exist.
(c) If the State Board of Pharmacy suspends or revokes a registration, all controlled substances owned or possessed by the registrant at the time of suspension or the effective date of the revocation order shall be placed under seal. No disposition may be made of substances under seal until the time for taking an appeal has elapsed or until all appeals have been concluded unless a court, upon application therefor, orders the sale of perishable substances and the deposit of the proceeds of the sale with the court. Upon a revocation order becoming final, all controlled substances shall be forfeited to the state.
(d) The State Board of Pharmacy shall promptly notify the bureau of all orders suspending or revoking registration and all forfeitures of controlled substances.

§ 16-13-38. Procedure for denying, suspending, revoking, or limiting registration; automatic suspension

(a) Before denying, suspending, revoking, or limiting registration, or refusing a renewal of registration, the State Board of Pharmacy shall serve upon the applicant or registrant an order to show cause why registration should not be denied, revoked, limited, or suspended, or why the renewal should not be refused. The order to show cause shall contain a statement of the basis therefor and shall call upon the applicant or registrant to appear before the State Board of Pharmacy at a time and place not less than 30 days after the date of service of the order; but in the case of a denial of renewal of registration the show cause order shall be served not later than 30 days before the expiration of the registration. These proceedings shall be conducted in accordance with Chapter 13 of Title 50, the "Georgia Administrative Procedure Act," without regard to any criminal prosecution or other proceeding. Proceedings to refuse renewal or registration shall not abate the existing registration, which shall remain in effect pending the outcome of the administrative hearing.

(b) The State Board of Pharmacy shall suspend, without an order to show cause, any registration simultaneously with the institution of proceedings under Code Section 16-13-37 or where renewal of registration is refused if it finds that there is an imminent danger to the public health or safety which warrants this action. The suspension shall continue in effect until the conclusion of the proceedings, including judicial review thereof, unless sooner withdrawn by the State Board of Pharmacy or dissolved by a court of competent jurisdiction.

§ 16-13-39. Manufacturers, distributors, and dispensers to maintain records of controlled substances

Persons registered to manufacture, distribute, or dispense controlled substances under this article shall keep a complete and accurate record of all controlled substances on hand, received, manufactured, sold, dispensed, or otherwise disposed of and shall maintain such records and inventories in conformance with the record-keeping and inventory requirements of federal law and with any rules issued by the State Board of Pharmacy.

§ 16-13-40. Distribution of Schedule I and II substances

Controlled substances in Schedules I and II shall be distributed by a registrant to another registrant only pursuant to an order form. Compliance with federal law respecting order forms shall be deemed compliance with this Code section.

§ 16-13-41. Prescriptions

(a) Except when dispensed directly by a registered practitioner, other than a pharmacy or pharmacist, to an ultimate user, no controlled substance in Schedule II may be dispensed without the written prescription of a registered practitioner.

(b) When a practitioner writes a prescription drug order to cause the dispensing of a Schedule II substance, he or she shall include the name and address of the person for whom it is prescribed, the kind and quantity of such Schedule II controlled substance, the directions for taking, the signature, and the name, address, telephone number, and DEA registration number of the prescribing practitioner. Such prescription shall be signed and dated by the practitioner on the date when issued, and the nature of such signature shall be defined in regulations promulgated by the State Board of Pharmacy. Prescription drug orders for Schedule II controlled substances may be transmitted via facsimile machine or other electronic means only in accordance with regulations promulgated by the State Board of Pharmacy in accordance with Code Section 26-4-80 or 26-4-80.1, or in accordance with DEA regulations at 21 C.F.R. 1306.

(c) In emergency situations, as defined by rule of the State Board of Pharmacy, Schedule II drugs may be dispensed upon oral prescription of a registered practitioner, reduced promptly to writing and filed by the pharmacy. Prescriptions shall be retained in conformity with the requirements of Code Section 16-13-39. No prescription for a Schedule II substance may be refilled.

(d)(1) Except when dispensed directly by a practitioner, other than a pharmacy or pharmacist, to an ultimate user, a controlled substance included in Schedule III, IV, or V, which is a prescription drug as determined under any law of this state or the Federal Food, Drug and Cosmetic Act, 21 U.S.C. Section 301, 52 Stat. 1040 (1938), shall not be dispensed without a written or oral prescription of a registered practitioner. The prescription shall not be filled or refilled more than six months after the date on which such prescription was issued or be refilled more than five times.

(2) When a practitioner writes a prescription drug order to cause the dispensing of a Schedule III, IV, or V controlled substance, he or she shall include the name and address of the person for whom it is prescribed, the kind and quantity of such controlled substance, the directions for taking, the signature, and the name, address, telephone number, and DEA registration number of the practitioner. Such prescription shall be signed and dated by the practitioner on the date when issued or may be issued orally, and the nature of the signature of the prescriber shall meet the guidelines set forth in Chapter 4 of Title 26, the regulations promulgated by the State Board of Pharmacy, or both such guidelines and regulations.

(e) A controlled substance included in Schedule V shall not be distributed or dispensed other than for a legitimate medical purpose.

(f) No person shall prescribe or order the dispensing of a controlled substance, except a registered practitioner who is:

(1) Licensed or otherwise authorized by this state to prescribe controlled substances;

(2) Acting in the usual course of his professional practice; and

(3) Prescribing or ordering such controlled substances for a legitimate medical purpose.

(g) No person shall fill or dispense a prescription for a controlled substance except a person who is licensed by this state as a pharmacist or a pharmacy intern acting under the immediate and direct personal supervision of a licensed pharmacist in a pharmacy licensed by the State Board of Pharmacy, provided that this subsection shall not prohibit a registered physician, dentist, veterinarian, or podiatrist authorized by this state to dispense controlled substances as provided in this article if such registered person complies with all record-keeping, labeling, packaging, and storage requirements regarding such controlled substances and imposed upon pharmacists and pharmacies in this chapter and in Chapter 4 of Title 26 and complies with the requirements of Code Section 26-4-130.

(h) It shall be unlawful for any practitioner to issue any prescription document signed in blank. The issuance of such document signed in blank shall be prima-facie evidence of a conspiracy to violate this article. The possession of a prescription document signed in blank by a person other than the person whose signature appears thereon shall be prima-facie evidence of a conspiracy between the possessor and the signer to violate the provisions of this article.

(i) (1) Pharmacists may dispense prescriptions from a remote location for the benefit of an institution that uses a remote automated medication system in accordance with the requirements set forth in the rules and regulations adopted by the State Board of Pharmacy pursuant to paragraph (12.1) of subsection (a) of Code Section 26-4-28.

(2) As used in this subsection, the term "institution" means a skilled nursing facility or a hospice licensed as such under Chapter 7 of Title 31.

§ 16-13-42. Unauthorized distribution and dispensation; refusal or failure to keep records; refusal to permit inspection; unlawfully maintaining structure or place; penalty

(a) It is unlawful for any person:

(1) Who is subject to the requirements of Code Section 16-13-35 to distribute or dispense a controlled substance in violation of Code Section 16-13-41;

(2) Who is a registrant to manufacture a controlled substance not authorized by his registration or to distribute or dispense a controlled substance not authorized by his registration to another registrant or other authorized person;

(3) To refuse or fail to make, keep, or furnish any record, notification, order form, statement, invoice, or information required under this article;

(4) To refuse an entry into any premises for any inspection authorized by this article; or

(5) Knowingly to keep or maintain any store, shop, warehouse, dwelling, building, vehicle, boat, aircraft, or other structure or place which is resorted to by persons using controlled substances in violation of this article for the purpose of using these substances, or which is used for keeping or selling them in violation of this article.

(b) Any person who violates this Code section is guilty of a felony and, upon conviction thereof, may be imprisoned for not more than five years, fined not more than $25,000.00, or both.

§ 16-13-43. Unauthorized distribution; penalties

(a) It is unlawful for any person:

(1) Who is a registrant to distribute a controlled substance classified in Schedule I or II, except pursuant to an order form as required by Code Section 16-13-40;

(2) To use, in the course of the manufacture or distribution of a controlled substance, a registration number which is fictitious, revoked, suspended, or issued to another person;

(3) To acquire or obtain possession of a controlled substance by misrepresentation, fraud, forgery, deception, subterfuge, or theft;

(4) To furnish false or fraudulent material information in, or omit any material information from, any application, report, or other document or record required to be kept or filed under this article;

(5) To make, distribute, or possess any punch, die, plate, stone, or other thing designed to print, imprint, or reproduce the trademark, trade name, or other identifying mark, imprint, or device of another or any likeness of any of the foregoing, upon any drug or container or labeling thereof so as to render the drug a counterfeit substance; or

(6) To withhold information from a practitioner that such person has obtained a controlled substance of a similar therapeutic use in a concurrent time period from another practitioner.

(b) Any person who violates this Code section is guilty of a felony and, upon conviction thereof, may be imprisoned for not more than eight years or fined not more than $50,000.00, or both.

§ 16-13-44. Penalties under other laws

Any penalty imposed for violation of this article is in addition to, and not in lieu of, any civil or administrative penalty or sanction otherwise authorized by law.

§ 16-13-45. Powers of enforcement personnel

Any officer or employee of the State Board of Pharmacy designated by the director of the Georgia Drugs and Narcotics Agency may:
(1) Carry firearms in the performance of his official duties;
(2) Execute and serve search warrants, arrest warrants, administrative inspection warrants, subpoenas, and summonses issued under the authority of this state;
(3) Make arrests without warrant for any offense under this article committed in his presence or if he has probable cause to believe that the person to be arrested has committed or is committing a violation of this article which may constitute a felony;
(4) Make seizures of property pursuant to this article; or
(5) Perform other law enforcement duties as the State Board of Pharmacy or the director of the Georgia Drugs and Narcotics Agency designates.

§ 16-13-46. Administrative inspections and warrants

(a) Issuance and execution of inspection warrants shall be as follows:
(1) A judge of the superior, state, city, or magistrate court, or any municipal officer clothed by law with the powers of a magistrate, upon proper oath or affirmation showing probable cause, may issue warrants for the purpose of conducting inspections authorized by this article, or rules promulgated under this article, and seizures of property appropriate to the inspections. For the purpose of the issuance of inspection warrants, probable cause exists upon showing a valid public interest in the effective enforcement of this article, or rules promulgated under this article, sufficient to justify inspection of the area, premises, building, or conveyance in the circumstances specified in the application for the warrant;
(2) A warrant shall issue only upon an affidavit of a designated officer, drug agent, or employee of the State Board of Pharmacy having knowledge of the facts alleged, sworn to before the judicial officer and establishing the grounds for issuing the warrant. If the judicial officer is satisfied that grounds for the application exist or that there is probable cause to believe they exist, he shall issue a warrant identifying the area, premises, building, registrant, or conveyance to be inspected, the purpose of the inspection, and, if appropriate, the type of property to be inspected, if any. The warrant shall:
(A) State the grounds for its issuance and the name of each person whose affidavit has been taken in support thereof;
(B) Be directed to persons authorized by Code Section 16-13-45 to execute it;
(C) Command the persons to whom it is directed to inspect the area, premises, building, registrant, or conveyance identified for the purpose specified and, if appropriate, direct the seizure of the property specified;
(D) Identify the item or types of property to be seized, if any; and
(E) Designate the judicial officer to whom it shall be returned;
(3) A warrant issued pursuant to this Code section must be executed and returned within ten days of its date unless, upon a showing of a need for additional time, the court orders otherwise. If property is seized pursuant to a warrant, a copy shall be provided upon request to the person from whom or from whose premises the property is taken, together with a receipt for the property taken. The return of the warrant shall be made promptly, accompanied by a written inventory of any property taken. A copy of the inventory shall be delivered upon request to the person from whom or from whose premises the property was taken and to the applicant for the warrant; and
(4) The judicial officer who has issued a warrant shall attach thereto a copy of the return and all papers returnable in connection therewith and file them with the clerk of the superior court for the county in which the inspection was made.
(b) The State Board of Pharmacy, the director of the Georgia Drugs and Narcotics Agency or drug agents may make inspections of controlled premises in accordance with the following provisions:
(1) For purposes of this Code section only, "controlled premises" means:
(A) Places where persons registered or exempted from registration requirements under this article are required to keep records; and
(B) Places, including factories, warehouses, establishments, and conveyances, in which persons registered or exempted from registration requirements under this article are permitted to hold, manufacture, compound, process, sell, deliver, or otherwise dispose of any controlled substance;
(2) When authorized by an inspection warrant issued pursuant to subsection (a) of this Code section, an officer or employee designated by the State Board of Pharmacy or the director of the Georgia Drugs and Narcotics Agency, upon presenting the warrant and appropriate credentials to the owner, operator, or agent in charge, may enter controlled premises for the purpose of conducting an inspection;
(3) When authorized by an inspection warrant, an officer or employee designated by the State Board of Pharmacy or the director of the Georgia Drugs and Narcotics Agency may:
(A) Inspect and copy records required by this article to be kept;
(B) Inspect, within reasonable limits and in a reasonable manner, controlled premises and all pertinent equipment, finished and unfinished material, containers, and labeling found therein, and, except as provided in paragraph (5) of subsection (b) of this Code section, all other things therein, including records, files, papers, processes, controls, and facilities bearing on violation of this article; and
(C) Inventory any stock of any controlled substance therein and obtain samples thereof;
(4) This Code section does not prevent the inspection without a warrant of books and records pursuant to an administrative inspection in accordance with subsection (c) of this Code section, nor does it prevent entries and inspections, including seizures of property, without a warrant:
(A) If the owner, operator, or agent in charge of the controlled premises consents;
(B) In situations presenting imminent danger to health or safety;
(C) In situations involving inspection of conveyance if there is reasonable cause to believe that the mobility of the conveyance makes it impracticable to obtain a warrant;
(D) In any other exceptional or emergency circumstance where time or opportunity to apply for a warrant is lacking; or
(E) In all other situations in which a warrant is not constitutionally required; and
(5) An inspection authorized by this Code section shall not extend to financial data, sales data other than shipment data, or pricing data unless the owner, operator, or agent in charge of the controlled premises consents in writing.
(c) The State Board of Pharmacy, its members, or duly authorized agents or drug agents shall have the power to inspect, without a warrant, in a lawful manner at all reasonable hours, any pharmacy or other place licensed by the State Board of Pharmacy pursuant to Chapter 4 of Title 26 for the purpose:
(1) Of determining if any of the provisions of this article or any rule or regulation promulgated under its authority is being violated;
(2) Of securing samples or specimens of any drug or medical supplies, after first paying or offering to pay for such samples or specimens; and
(3) Of securing other such evidence as may be needed for an administrative proceedings action, as provided by this article.

§ 16-13-47. Injunctions

(a) The superior courts of this state may exercise jurisdiction to restrain or enjoin violations of this article.
(b) The defendant may demand a trial by jury for an alleged violation of an injunction or restraining order under this Code section.

§ 16-13-48. Cooperative arrangements with federal and other state agencies

139

(a) The State Board of Pharmacy shall cooperate with federal and other state agencies in discharging its responsibilities concerning traffic in controlled substances and in suppressing the abuse of controlled substances. To this end, it may:

(1) Arrange for the exchange of information among governmental officials concerning the use and abuse of controlled substances;

(2) Coordinate and cooperate in training programs concerning controlled substance law enforcement at local and state levels;

(3) Cooperate with the bureau by establishing a centralized unit to accept, catalogue, file, and collect statistics, including records, other than medical treatment records, of drug dependent persons and other controlled substance law offenders within the state, and make the information available for federal, state, and local law enforcement purposes; and

(4) Conduct or promote programs of eradication aimed at destroying wild or illicit growth of plant species from which controlled substances may be extracted.

(b) Results, information, and evidence received from the bureau relating to the regulatory functions of this article, including results of inspections conducted by it, may be relied and acted upon by the State Board of Pharmacy or drug agents in the exercise of its or their regulatory functions under this article.

§ 16-13-48.1. Funds or property transferred to state or local agencies under federal drug laws

Repealed by Ga. L. 2015, p. 693, § 2-21/HB 233, effective July 1, 2015.

§ 16-13-49. Declared items of contraband; forfeiture

(a) As used in this Code section, the term:

(1) "Controlled substance" shall have the same meaning as set forth in Code Section 16-13-21 and shall include marijuana, as such term is defined in Code Section 16-13-21.

(2) "Enterprise" means any person, sole proprietorship, partnership, corporation, trust, association, or other legal entity created under the laws of the United States or any foreign nation or a group of individuals associated in fact although not a legal entity and includes illicit as well as licit enterprises and governmental as well as other entities.

(3) "Proceeds" shall have the same meaning as set forth in Code Section 9-16-2.

(4) "Property" shall have the same meaning as set forth in Code Section 9-16-2.

(5) "United States" shall have the same meaning as set forth in Code Section 9-16-2.

(b) Except as provided in subsection (d) of this Code section, the following are declared to be contraband and no person shall have a property right in them:

(1) Any controlled substances, raw materials, or controlled substance analogs that have been manufactured, distributed, dispensed, possessed, or acquired in violation of this article;

(2) Any property which is, directly or indirectly, used or intended for use in any manner to facilitate a violation of this article and any proceeds;

(3) Any property located in this state which was, directly or indirectly, used or intended for use in any manner to facilitate a violation of this article or the laws of the United States relating to controlled substances that is punishable by imprisonment for more than one year and any proceeds;

(4) Any interest, security, claim, or property or contractual right of any kind affording a source of influence over any enterprise that a person has established, operated, controlled, conducted, or participated in the conduct of in violation of this article or the laws of the United States relating to controlled substances that is punishable by imprisonment for more than one year and any proceeds;

(5) Any property found in close proximity to any controlled substance or other property subject to forfeiture under this Code section; and

(6) Any weapon available for any use in any manner to facilitate a violation of this article.

(c) Any property subject to forfeiture pursuant to subsection (b) of this Code section shall be forfeited in accordance with the procedures set forth in Chapter 16 of Title 9.

(d) Property shall not be subject to forfeiture under this Code section for a violation involving only one gram or less of a mixture containing cocaine or four ounces or less of marijuana unless such property was used to facilitate a transaction in or a purchase of or sale of a controlled substance.

(e) In addition to persons authorized to seize property pursuant to Code Section 9-16-6, property which is subject to forfeiture under this Code section may be seized by the director of the Georgia Drugs and Narcotics Agency or by any drug agent of this state or any political subdivision thereof who has power to make arrests or execute process or a search warrant issued by any court having jurisdiction over the property.

(f) Controlled substances included in Schedule I which are contraband and any controlled substance whose owners are unknown shall be summarily forfeited to the state. The court may include in any judgment of conviction under this article an order forfeiting any controlled substance involved in the offense to the extent of the defendant's interest.

§ 16-13-50. Burden of proof; liability of enforcement officers in lawful performance of duties

(a) It is not necessary for the state to negate any exemption or exception in this article in any complaint, accusation, indictment, or other pleading or in any trial, hearing, or other proceeding under this article. The burden of proof of any exemption or exception is upon the person claiming it.

(b) In the absence of proof that a person is the duly authorized holder of an appropriate registration or order form issued under this article, he is presumed not to be the holder of the registration or form. The burden of proof is upon him to rebut the presumption.

(c) No liability is imposed by this article upon any authorized state, county, or municipal officer engaged in the lawful performance of his duties.

§ 16-13-51. Judicial review of administrative determinations, findings, and conclusions

All final determinations, findings, and conclusions of the State Board of Pharmacy under this article are final and conclusive decisions of the matters involved. Any person aggrieved by the decision may obtain review of the decision in the Superior Court of Fulton County. Findings of fact by the State Board of Pharmacy, if supported by substantial evidence, are conclusive.

§ 16-13-52. Programs and research on prevention of abuse of controlled substances; confidentiality of research; exemption from penalties

(a) The State Board of Pharmacy and the Georgia Drugs and Narcotics Agency shall carry out programs designed to prevent and deter misuse and abuse of controlled substances.

(b) The State Board of Pharmacy and the Georgia Drugs and Narcotics Agency shall encourage research on misuse and abuse of controlled substances. In connection with the research and in furtherance of the enforcement of this article, they may:

(1) Establish methods to assess accurately the effects of controlled substances and identify and characterize those with potential for abuse;

(2) Make studies and undertake programs of research to:

(A) Develop new or improved approaches, techniques, systems, equipment, and devices to strengthen the enforcement of this article;

(B) Determine patterns of misuse and abuse of controlled substances and the social effects thereof;

(C) Improve methods for preventing, predicting, understanding, and dealing with the misuse and abuse of controlled substances; and

(3) Enter into agreements with public agencies, institutions of higher education, and private organizations or individuals for the purpose of conducting research, demonstrations, or special projects which bear directly on misuse and abuse of controlled substances.

(c) The State Board of Pharmacy, in the public interest, may authorize persons engaged in research on the use and effects of controlled substances to withhold the names and other identifying characteristics of individuals who are the subjects of the research. Persons who obtain this authorization are not to be compelled in any civil, criminal, administrative, legislative, or other proceeding to identify the individuals who are the subjects of research for which the authorization was obtained.

(d) The State Board of Pharmacy may authorize the possession and distribution of controlled substances by persons engaged in research. Persons who obtain this authorization are exempt from state prosecution for possession and distribution of controlled substances to the extent of the authorization.

§ 16-13-53. Pending proceedings

Reserved. Repealed by Ga. L. 2015, p. 693, § 2-23/HB 233, effective July 1, 2015.

§ 16-13-54. Orders and rules promulgated prior to July 1, 1974

Any orders and rules promulgated under any law affected by this article and in effect on July 1, 1974, and not in conflict with it shall continue in effect until modified, superseded, or repealed.

§ 16-13-54.1. Weight or quantity of controlled substance or marijuana not essential element of offense

When an offense in this part measures a controlled substance or marijuana by weight or quantity, the defendant's knowledge of such weight or quantity shall not be an essential element of the offense, and the state shall not have the burden of proving that a defendant knew the weight or quantity of the controlled substance or marijuana in order to be convicted of an offense.

§ 16-13-55. Construction of article

This article shall be so applied and construed as to effectuate its general purpose to make uniform the law with respect to the subject of this article among those states which enact it.

§ 16-13-56. Penalty for violation of article; restitution to the state for cleanup of environmental hazards; other remedies

(a) Unless otherwise specified with respect to a particular offense, any person who violates any provision of this article shall be guilty of a misdemeanor.
(b) In addition to any other penalty imposed by law for a violation of this article, if the sentencing court finds that in committing a violation of this article, the defendant contributed to a release of hazardous waste, a hazardous constituent, or a hazardous substance as such terms are defined by Code Sections 12-8-62 and 12-8-92, the court shall require such defendant to make restitution to the State of Georgia pursuant to subsection (a) of Code Section 12-8-96.1 for the reasonable costs of activities associated with the cleanup of environmental hazards, including legal expenses incurred by the state. Restitution made pursuant to this Code section shall not preclude the State of Georgia from obtaining any other civil or criminal remedy available under any other provision of law. The restitution authorized by this Code section is supplemental and not exclusive.

§ 16-13-56.1. Opioids defined; notification of addictive risks

(a) As used in this Code section, the term "opioids" means opiates, opioids, opioid analgesics, and opioid derivatives.
(b) A prescriber who issues a prescription for an opioid shall provide the patient receiving the prescription information on the addictive risks of using opioids and information on options available for safely disposing of any unused opioids where such options exist. Such information may be provided verbally or in writing.

§ 16-13-57. Program to record prescription information into electronic data base; administration and oversight

(a) As used in this part, the term:
(1) "Department" means the Department of Public Health.
(2) "PDMP" means the prescription drug monitoring program data base.
(b) Subject to funds as may be appropriated by the General Assembly or otherwise available for such purpose, the department shall, in consultation with members of the Georgia Composite Medical Board, the State Board of Pharmacy, and the agency, establish and maintain a program to electronically record into an electronic PDMP prescription information resulting from the dispensing of Schedule II, III, IV, or V controlled substances and to electronically review such prescription information that has been entered into such data base. The purpose of such PDMP shall be to assist in the reduction of the abuse of controlled substances; to improve, enhance, and encourage a better quality of health care by promoting the proper use of medications to treat pain and terminal illness; to reduce duplicative prescribing and overprescribing of controlled substance practices, for health oversight purposes; and to gather data for epidemiological research. The PDMP shall be administered by the department.
(c) Each prescriber who has a DEA registration number shall enroll to become a user of the PDMP as soon as possible, and no later than January 1, 2018; provided, however, that prescribers who attain a DEA registration number after such date shall enroll within 30 days of attaining such credentials. A prescriber who violates this subsection shall be held administratively accountable to the state regulatory board governing such prescriber for such violation.
(d) Between January 1, 2018, and May 31, 2018, the department shall randomly test the PDMP to determine if it is accessible and operational 99.5 percent of the time. If the department determines that the PDMP meets such standard, then between June 1, 2018, and June 20, 2018, the department shall certify in writing to each board that governs prescribers that it is operational. Each board that governs prescribers shall publish such information on its website.

§ 16-13-58. Funds for development and maintenance of program; granting of funds to dispensers

(a) The department shall be authorized to apply for available grants and may accept any gifts, grants, donations, and other funds to assist in developing and maintaining the PDMP; provided, however, that neither the department nor any other state entity shall accept a grant that requires as a condition of the grant any sharing of information that is inconsistent with this part.
(b) The department shall be authorized to grant funds to dispensers for the purpose of covering costs for dedicated equipment and software for dispensers to use in complying with the reporting requirements of Code Section 16-13-59. Such grants to dispensers shall be funded by gifts, grants, donations, or other funds received by the department for the operation of the PDMP. The department shall be authorized to establish standards and specifications for any equipment and software purchased pursuant to a grant received by a dispenser pursuant to this Code section. Nothing in this part shall be construed to require a dispenser to incur costs to purchase equipment or software to comply with this part.
(c) Nothing in this part shall be construed to require any appropriation of state funds.

§ 16-13-59. Information to include for each Schedule II, III, IV, or V controlled substance prescription; compliance

(a) For purposes of the PDMP, each dispenser shall submit to the department by electronic means information regarding each prescription dispensed for a Schedule II, III, IV, or V controlled substance. The information submitted for each prescription shall include at a minimum, but shall not be limited to:
(1) DEA permit number or approved dispenser facility controlled substance identification number;
(2) Date the prescription was dispensed;
(3) Prescription serial number;
(4) If the prescription is new or a refill;
(5) National Drug Code (NDC) for drug dispensed;
(6) Quantity and strength dispensed;
(7) Number of days supply of the drug;
(8) Patient's name;
(9) Patient's address;
(10) Patient's date of birth;
(11) Patient gender;
(12) Method of payment;
(13) Approved prescriber identification number or prescriber's DEA permit number;

(14) Date the prescription was issued by the prescriber; and

(15) Other data elements consistent with standards established by the American Society for Automation in Pharmacy, if designated by regulations of the department.

(b) Each dispenser shall submit the prescription information required in subsection (a) of this Code section in accordance with transmission methods established by the department at least every 24 hours. If a dispenser is temporarily unable to comply with this subsection due to an equipment failure or other circumstances, such dispenser shall immediately notify the board and department.

(c) The department may issue a waiver to a dispenser that is unable to submit prescription information by electronic means acceptable to the department. Such waiver may permit the dispenser to submit prescription information to the department by paper form or other means, provided all information required in subsection (a) of this Code section is submitted in this alternative format and in accordance with the frequency requirements established pursuant to subsection (b) of this Code section. Requests for waivers shall be submitted in writing to the department.

(d) The department shall not revise the information required to be submitted by dispensers pursuant to subsection (a) of this Code section more frequently than annually. Any such change to the required information shall neither be effective nor applicable to dispensers until six months after the adoption of such changes.

(e) The department shall not access or allow others to access any identifying prescription information from the PDMP after two years from the date such information was originally received by the department. The department may retain prescription information that has been processed to remove personal identifiers from the health information in compliance with the standard and implementation rules of the federal Health Insurance Portability and Accountability Act (HIPAA) of 1996, P.L. 104-191, for more than two years but shall promulgate regulations and procedures that will ensure that any identifying information the department receives from any dispenser or reporting entity that is two years old or older is deleted or destroyed on an ongoing basis in a timely and secure manner.

(f) A dispenser may apply to the department for an exemption to be excluded from compliance with this Code section if compliance would impose an undue hardship on such dispenser. The department shall provide guidelines and criteria for what constitutes an undue hardship.

(g) For purposes of this Code section, the term "dispenser" shall include any pharmacy or facility physically located in another state or foreign country that in any manner ships, mails, or delivers a dispensed controlled substance into this state.

§ 16-13-60. Privacy and confidentiality; use of data; security program

(a) Except as otherwise provided in subsections (c), (c.1), and (d) of this Code section, prescription information submitted pursuant to Code Section 16-13-59 shall be confidential and shall not be subject to open records requirements, as contained in Article 4 of Chapter 18 of Title 50.

(b) The department, in conjunction with the board, shall establish and maintain strict procedures to ensure that the privacy and confidentiality of patients, prescribers, and patient and prescriber information collected, recorded, transmitted, and maintained pursuant to this part are protected. Such information shall not be disclosed to any person or entity except as specifically provided in this part and only in a manner which in no way conflicts with the requirements of the federal Health Insurance Portability and Accountability Act (HIPAA) of 1996, P.L. 104-191. Nothing in this subsection shall be construed to prohibit the agency or department from accessing prescription information as a part of an investigation into suspected or reported abuses or regarding illegal access of the data. Such information may be used in the prosecution of an offender who has illegally obtained prescription information.

(c) The department shall be authorized to provide requested prescription information collected pursuant to this part only as follows:

(1) To persons authorized to prescribe or dispense controlled substances for the sole purpose of providing medical or pharmaceutical care to a specific patient;

(2) Upon the request of a patient, prescriber, or dispenser about whom the prescription information requested concerns or upon the request on his or her behalf of his or her attorney;

(3) To local or state law enforcement or prosecutorial officials pursuant to the issuance of a search warrant from an appropriate court or official in the county in which the office of such law enforcement or prosecutorial officials are located pursuant to Article 2 of Chapter 5 of Title 17 or to federal law enforcement or prosecutorial officials pursuant to the issuance of a search warrant pursuant to 21 U.S.C. or a grand jury subpoena pursuant to 18 U.S.C.;

(4) To the agency, the Georgia Composite Medical Board or any other state regulatory board governing prescribers or dispensers in this state, or the Department of Community Health for purposes of the state Medicaid program, for health oversight purposes, or upon the issuance of a subpoena by such agency, board, or Department of Community Health pursuant to their existing subpoena power or to the federal Centers for Medicare and Medicaid Services upon the issuance of a subpoena by the federal government pursuant to its existing subpoena powers;

(5) (A) To not more than two individuals who are members per shift or rotation of the prescriber's or dispenser's staff or employed at the health care facility in which the prescriber is practicing, provided that such individuals:

(i) Are licensed under Chapter 11, 30, 34, or 35 of Title 43;

(ii) Are registered under Title 26;

(iii) Are licensed under Chapter 26 of Title 43 and submit to the annual registration process required by subsection (a) of Code Section 16-13-35, and for purposes of this Code section, such individuals shall not be deemed exempted from registration as set forth in subsection (g) of Code Section 16-13-35; or

(iv) Submit to the annual registration process required by subsection (a) of Code Section 16-13-35, and for purposes of this Code section, such individuals shall not be deemed exempted from registration as set forth in subsection (g) of Code Section 16-13-35;

(B) Such individuals may retrieve and review such information strictly for the purpose of:

(i) Providing medical or pharmaceutical care to a specific patient; or

(ii) Informing the prescriber or dispenser of a patient's potential use, misuse, abuse, or underutilization of prescribed medication;

(C) All information retrieved and reviewed by such individuals shall be maintained in a secure and confidential manner in accordance with the requirements of subsection (f) of this Code section; and

(D) The delegating prescriber or dispenser may be held civilly liable and criminally responsible for the misuse of the prescription information obtained by such individuals;

(6) To not more than two individuals, per shift or rotation, who are employed or contracted by the health care facility in which the prescriber is practicing so long as the medical director of such health care facility has authorized the particular individuals for such access; and

(7) In any hospital which provides emergency services, each prescriber may designate two individuals, per shift or rotation, who are employed or contracted by such hospital so long as the medical director of such hospital has authorized the particular individuals for such access.

(c.1) An individual authorized to access PDMP prescription information pursuant to this part may:

(1) Communicate concerns about a patient's potential usage, misuse, abuse, or underutilization of a controlled substance with prescribers and dispensers that are involved in the patient's health care;

(2) Report potential violations of this article to the agency for review or investigation. Following such review or investigation, the agency shall:

(A) Refer instances of a patient's possible personal misuse or abuse of controlled substances to the patient's primary prescriber to allow for potential intervention and impairment treatment;

(B) Refer probable violations of controlled substances being acquired for illegal distribution, and not solely for a patient's personal use, to the appropriate authorities for further investigation and potential prosecution; or

(C) Refer probable regulatory violations by prescribers or dispensers to the regulatory board governing such person; or

(3) Include PDMP prescription information in a patient's electronic health or medical record.

(d) The department may provide data that has been processed to remove personal identifiers from the health information in compliance with the standard and implementation rules of the federal Health Insurance Portability and Accountability Act (HIPAA) of 1996, P.L. 104-191, to government entities and other entities for statistical, research, educational, instructional, drug abuse prevention, or grant application purposes after removing information that could be used to identify prescribers.

(e) Any person or entity that receives PDMP prescription information or related reports relating to this part from the department shall not disclose such information or reports to any other person or entity except by order of a court of competent jurisdiction or as otherwise permitted pursuant to this part.

(f) Any permissible user identified in this part who directly accesses PDMP prescription information shall implement and maintain a comprehensive information security program that contains administrative, technical, and physical safeguards that are substantially equivalent to the security measures of the department. The permissible user shall identify reasonably foreseeable internal and external risks to the security, confidentiality, and integrity of personal information that could result in the unauthorized disclosure, misuse, or other compromise of the information and shall assess the sufficiency of any safeguards in place to control the risks.

(g) No provision in this part shall be construed to modify, limit, diminish, or impliedly repeal any authority of a licensing or regulatory board or any other entity so authorized to obtain prescription information from sources other than the PDMP maintained pursuant to this part; provided, however, that the department shall be authorized to release information from the PDMP only in accordance with the provisions of this part.

§ 16-13-61. Electronic Database Review Advisory Committee; members; terms; officers; procedure; compensation

(a) There is established an Electronic Database Review Advisory Committee for the purposes of consulting with and advising the department on matters related to the establishment, maintenance, and operation of how prescriptions are electronically reviewed pursuant to this part. This shall include, but shall not be limited to, data collection, regulation of access to data, evaluation of data to identify benefits and outcomes of the reviews, communication to prescribers and dispensers as to the intent of the reviews and how to use the PDMP, and security of data collected.
(b) The advisory committee shall consist of 12 members as follows:
(1) A representative from the agency;
(2) A representative from the Georgia Composite Medical Board;
(3) A representative from the Georgia Board of Dentistry;
(4) A representative with expertise in personal privacy matters, appointed by the president of the State Bar of Georgia;
(5) A representative from a specialty profession that deals in addictive medicine, appointed by the Georgia Composite Medical Board;
(6) A pain management specialist, appointed by the Georgia Composite Medical Board;
(7) An oncologist, appointed by the Georgia Composite Medical Board;
(8) A representative from a hospice or hospice organization, appointed by the Georgia Composite Medical Board;
(9) A representative from the State Board of Optometry;
(10) The consumer member appointed by the Governor to the State Board of Pharmacy pursuant to subsection (b) of Code Section 26-4-21;
(11) A pharmacist from the State Board of Pharmacy; and
(12) A representative from the Department of Public Health.
(c) Each member of the advisory committee shall serve a three-year term or until the appointment and qualification of such member's successor.
(d) The advisory committee shall elect a chairperson and vice chairperson from among its membership to serve a term of one year. The vice chairperson shall serve as the chairperson at times when the chairperson is absent.
(e) The advisory committee shall meet at the call of the chairperson or upon request by at least three of the members and shall meet at least one time per year. Five members of the committee shall constitute a quorum.
(f) The members shall receive no compensation or reimbursement of expenses from the state for their services as members of the advisory committee.

§ 16-13-62. Rules and regulations

The department shall establish rules and regulations to implement the requirements of this part. Nothing in this part shall be construed to authorize the department to establish policies, rules, or regulations which limit, revise, or expand or purport to limit, revise, or expand any prescription or dispensing authority of any prescriber or dispenser subject to this part. Nothing in this part shall be construed to impede, impair, or limit a prescriber from prescribing pain medication in accordance with the pain management guidelines developed and adopted by the Georgia Composite Medical Board.

§ 16-13-63. (For effective date, see note.) Liability; review of PDMP data when filling certain prescriptions; cause of action for civil damages

(a) (1) Nothing in this part shall require a dispenser to obtain information about a patient from the PDMP; provided, however, that dispensers are encouraged to obtain such information while keeping in mind that the purpose of such data base includes reducing duplicative prescribing and overprescribing of controlled substances. A dispenser shall not have a duty and shall not be held civilly liable for damages to any person in any civil or administrative action or criminally responsible for injury, death, or loss to person or property on the basis that the dispenser did or did not seek or obtain information from the PDMP.
(2) (A) (For effective date, see note.) On and after July 1, 2018, when a prescriber is prescribing a controlled substance listed in paragraph (1) or (2) of Code Section 16-13-26 or benzodiazepines, he or she shall seek and review information from the PDMP the first time he or she issues such prescription to a patient and thereafter at least once every 90 days, unless the:
(i) Prescription is for no more than a three-day supply of such substance and no more than 26 pills;
(ii) Patient is in a hospital or health care facility, including, but not limited to, a nursing home, an intermediate care home, a personal care home, or a hospice program, which provides patient care and prescriptions to be administered and used by a patient on the premises of the facility;
(iii) Patient has had outpatient surgery at a hospital or ambulatory surgical center and the prescription is for no more than a ten-day supply of such substance and no more than 40 pills;
(iv) Patient is terminally ill or under the supervised care of an outpatient hospice program; or
(v) Patient is receiving treatment for cancer.
(B) This paragraph shall not become effective unless the department's certification required by subsection (d) of Code Section 16-13-57 has been issued.
(C) A prescriber who violates this paragraph shall be held administratively accountable to the state regulatory board governing such prescriber but shall not be held civilly liable for damages to any person in any civil or administrative action or criminally responsible for injury, death, or loss to person or property on the basis that such prescriber did or did not seek or obtain information from such data base when prescribing such substance.
(3) A prescriber who has reviewed information from the PDMP shall make or cause to be made a notation in the patient's medical record stating the date and time upon which such inquiry was made and identifying the individual's name who made such search and review. If the PDMP does not allow access to such individual, a notation to that effect shall also be made containing the same information of date, time, and individual's name.
(4) Nothing in this part shall require a prescriber to obtain information from the PDMP when he or she is prescribing a controlled substance that is classified as a Schedule II, III, IV, or V controlled substance for a patient other than those controlled substances listed in paragraph (1) or (2) of Code Section 16-13-26 and benzodiazepines. Such prescriber shall not have a duty and shall not be held civilly liable for damages to any person in any civil or administrative action or criminally responsible for injury, death, or loss to person or property on the basis that the prescriber did or did not seek or obtain information from such data base when prescribing such a substance.
(b) Except as provided in paragraphs (2) and (4) of subsection (a) of this Code section, a person who is injured by reason of any violation of this part shall have a cause of action for the actual damages sustained and, when appropriate, punitive damages; provided, however, that a dispenser or prescriber acting in good faith shall not be held civilly liable for damages to any person in any civil or administrative action or criminally responsible for injury, death, or loss to person or property for receiving or using information from the PDMP. Such injured person may also recover attorney's fees in the trial and appellate courts and the costs of investigation and litigation reasonably incurred.

§ 16-13-64. Violations; criminal penalties

(a) A dispenser who knowingly and intentionally fails to submit prescription information to the department as required by this part or knowingly and intentionally submits incorrect prescription information shall be guilty of a felony and, upon conviction thereof, shall be punished for each such offense by imprisonment for not less than one year nor more than five years, a fine not to exceed $50,000.00, or both, and such actions shall be reported to the licensing board responsible for issuing such dispenser's dispensing license for action to be taken against such dispenser's license.
(b) An individual authorized to access PDMP prescription information pursuant to this part who negligently uses, releases, or discloses such information in a manner or for a purpose in violation of this part shall be guilty of a misdemeanor. Any person who is convicted of negligently using, releasing, or disclosing such information in violation of this part shall, upon the second or subsequent conviction, be guilty of a felony and shall be punished by imprisonment for not less than one nor more than three years, a fine not to exceed $5,000.00, or both.

(c) (1) An individual authorized to access PDMP prescription information pursuant to this part who knowingly obtains or discloses such information in a manner or for a purpose in violation of this part shall be guilty of a felony and, upon conviction thereof, shall be punished by imprisonment for not less than one year nor more than five years, a fine not to exceed $50,000.00, or both.

(2) Any person who knowingly obtains, attempts to obtain, or discloses PDMP prescription information pursuant to this part under false pretenses shall be guilty of a felony and, upon conviction thereof, shall be punished by imprisonment for not less than one year nor more than five years, a fine not to exceed $100,000.00, or both.

(3) Any person who obtains or discloses PDMP prescription information not specifically authorized in this part with the intent to sell, transfer, or use such information for commercial advantage, personal gain, or malicious harm shall be guilty of a felony and, upon conviction thereof, shall be punished by imprisonment for not less than two years nor more than ten years, a fine not to exceed $250,000.00, or both.

(d) The penalties provided by this Code section are intended to be cumulative of other penalties which may be applicable and are not intended to repeal such other penalties.

§ 16-13-65. Exceptions

(a) This part shall not apply to any veterinarian.

(b) This part shall not apply to any drug, substance, or immediate precursor classified as an exempt over the counter (OTC) Schedule V controlled substance pursuant to this chapter or pursuant to board rules established in accordance with Code Section 16-13-29.2.

§ 16-13-70. Short title

This article shall be known and may be cited as the "Dangerous Drug Act."

§ 16-13-70.1. Definition of terms

Any term used in this article and not defined in this article but defined in Code Section 16-13-21 shall have the meaning provided for that term in Code Section 16-13-21.

§ 16-13-71. "Dangerous drug" defined

(a) A "dangerous drug" means any drug other than a drug contained in any schedule of Article 2 of this chapter, which, under the federal Food, Drug, and Cosmetic Act (52 Stat. 1040 (1938)), 21 U.S.C. Section 301, et seq., as amended, may be dispensed only upon prescription. In any civil or criminal action or other proceedings, a certification from the Food and Drug Administration of the United States Department of Health and Human Services attesting to the fact that a drug other than a drug contained in any schedule of Article 2 of this chapter involved in the action or proceeding is a dangerous drug that federal law prohibits dispensing of without a prescription pursuant to the federal Food, Drug, and Cosmetic Act shall be admissible as prima-facie proof that such drug is a "dangerous drug."

(b) In addition to subsection (a) of this Code section, a "dangerous drug" means any other drug or substance declared by the General Assembly to be a dangerous drug; to include any of the following drugs, chemicals, or substances; salts, isomers, esters, ethers, or derivatives of such drugs, chemicals, or substances which have essentially the same pharmacological action; all other salts, isomers, esters, ethers, and compounds of such drugs, chemicals, or substances unless specifically exempted and the following devices, identified as "dangerous drugs":

(.03) Abacavir;(.035) Abarelix;(.037) Abatacept;(.04) Abciximab;

(.042) Abiraterone;(.043) AbobotulinumtoxinA;(.045) Acamprostate;(.05) Acarbose;(.1) Acebutolol;(1) Acecarbromal;(2) Acenocoumarol;

(3) Acetazolamide;(3.5) Reserved;(4) Acetohexamide;(4.1) Aceto-hydroxamic acid;(5) Acetophenazine;(6) Acetosulfone;(7) Acetyl sulfamethoxypyridazine;

(8) Acetyl sulfisoxazole;(9) Acetylcarbromal;(10) Acetylcholine;(11) Acetylcysteine;(12) Acetyldigitoxin;(12.1) Acitretin;(12.5) Aclidinium bromide;

(13) Acrisorcin;(13.3) Acrivastine;(13.5) Acyclovir;(13.53) Adalimumab;(13.531) Adalimumab-atto;(13.55) Adapalene -- See exceptions;(13.6) Adenosine;

(14) Adenosine 5-monophosphate;(14.5) Adenovirus;(15) Adenylic acid;(16) Adiphenine hydrochloride;(16.5) Ado-trastuzumab;

(17) Adrenal cortex extracts;(17.1) Afatinib;(17.3) Aflibercept;(17.5) Albendazole;(17.6) Albiglutide;(17.7) Albiraterone;

(18) Albumin, normal human serum;(18.1) Albuterol;(19) Albutonium;(19.3) Alcaftadine;(19.5) Alclometasone dipropionate;

(19.57) Alectinib;(19.58) Alemtuzumab;(19.6) Alendronate;(19.65) Alfuzosin;(19.7) Alglucerase;

(19.75) Alglucosidase alfa;(19.76) Alirocumab;(19.77) Aliskiren;(19.8) Alitretinoin;(20) Alkavervir;(21) Alkaverir;(21.1) Alkyl nitrites;(22) Allopurinol;

(22.2) Almotriptan;(22.3) Alogliptin;(22.5) Alosetron;(23) Alpha amylase;(23.1) Alprostadil;(24) Alseroxylon;(24.1) Altenodol;(24.6) Altretamine;

(25) Aluminum nicotinate;(26) Alverine;(26.5) Alvimopan;(27) Amantadine;(28) Ambenonium chloride;(28.5) Ambrisentan;(29) Ambrosiacae follens;

(30) Amcinonide;(30.1) Amdinocillin;(30.5) Amifostine;(31) Amikacin;(31.1) Amiloride;(32) Aminacrine;(33) 4-amino-N-methyl-pteroylglutamic acid;

(34) Amino acid preparations for injection or vaginal use;(35) Aminocaproic acid;(36) Aminohippurate;(36.5) Aminolevulinic acid;

(37) Aminophylline;(38) Aminosalicylate -- See exceptions;(39) Aminosalicylate calcium -- See exceptions;(40) Aminosalicylate potassium -- See exceptions;

(41) Aminosalicylate sodium -- See exceptions;(42) Aminosalicylic acid -- See exceptions;(42.1) Amiodarone;(43) Amisometradine;(44) Amitriptyline;

(44.3) Amlexanox;(44.5) Amlodipine;(44.6) Ammonia, N-13;(44.7) Ammonium lactate;(45) Amodiaquin;(45.5) Amoxapine;

(46) Amoxicillin;(47) Amphotericin B;(48) Ampicillin;(48.2) Amprenavir;(48.6) Amrinone;(49) Amyl nitrite;(50) Amylolytic enzymes;

(50.1) Anabolic steroids, if listed in Code Section 16-13-27.1 as being exempt as Schedule III controlled substances;(50.3) Anagrelide;

(50.4) Anakinra;(50.5) Anastrozole;(51) Androgens, except those androgens listed in paragraph (6) of Code Section 16-13-27;

(52) Angiotensin amide;(52.5) Anidulafungin;(53) Anisindione;(54) Anisotropine;(55) Antazoline;

(56) Anterior pituitary hormones;(57) Anthralin;(58) Anti-coagulant acid:(A) Citrate dextrose;(59) Antigens:(A) Alternaria tenius;(B) Aqua ivy;(C) Ash mix;

(D) Aspergillus fumigatus;(E) Bacterial, Staphylococcus aureus, Type 1;(F) Bacterial, Staphylococcus aureus, Type 3;(G) Bacterial, Undenatured;

(H) Bee;(I) Beech;(J) Bermuda grass;(K) Birch;(L) California live oak;(M) Candida albicans;(N) Careless weed;(O) Cat epithelia;(P) Cattle epithelia;

(Q) Coccidioides immitis;(R) Cottonwood fremont;(S) Dog epithelia;(T) Elm mix;(U) English plantain;(V) Feather mix;(W) Gram negative bacterial;

(X) Helminthosporium sativum;(Y) Hickory;(Z) Hormodendrum hordei;(AA) Hornet;(BB) House dust;(CC) House dust mix;

(DD) Insects;(EE) Intradermal or scratching test;(FF) Johnson grass;(GG) Kentucky blue grass;(HH) Kochia;(II) Lamb quarters;(JJ) Maple;

(KK) Mesquite;(LL) Mixed epidermals;(MM) Mixed grass, ragweeds (spring-fall);(NN) Mixed grasses (spring);(OO) Mixed inhalants;(PP) Mixed molds;

(QQ) Mixed ragweed;(RR) Mixed ragweed -- mixed weeds (fall);(SS) Mixed weeds;(TT) Molds;(UU) Mountain cedar;(VV) Mugwort common;

(WW) National weed mix;(XX) Oak mix;(YY) Olive;(ZZ) Orchard grass;(AAA) Pecan;(BBB) Penicillium notatum;(CCC) Perennial rye;

(DDD) Poison oak and poison ivy;(EEE) Pollens;(FFF) Poplar mix;(GGG) Prescription;(HHH) Ragweed mix;(III) Red top grass;

(JJJ) Respiratory bacterial;(KKK) Rough pigweed;(LLL) Russian thistle;(MMM) Sagebrush common;(NNN) Scale mix;(OOO) Short ragweed;

(PPP) Simplified allergy screening set;(QQQ) Skin bacterial;(RRR) Southern grass;(SSS) Staphylococcal;(TTT) Stinging insect mix;(UUU) Stinging insects;

(VVV) Sweet vernal;(WWW) Sycamore;(XXX) Tall ragweed;(YYY) Timothy;(ZZZ) Tree mix;(AAAA) Trees (early spring);(BBBB) Walnut;

(CCCC) Wasp;(DDDD) West ragweed;(EEEE) West weed mix;(FFFF) Yellow jacket;(60) Antihemophilic factor, Human;(61) Antirabies serum;

(62) Antivenin;(62.05) Apixaban;(62.1) Apomorphine;(62.3) Apraclonidine;(62.38) Apremilast;(62.4) Aprepitant;

(62.5) Aprotinin;(62.7) Ardeparin;(62.75) Arformoterol tartrate;(62.8) Argatroban;(63) Arginine, L-;(63.5) Aripiprazole;

(64) Arsenic -- Preparation for human use;(64.1) Arsenic trioxide;(65) Artegraft;(65.5) Artemether;(66) Ascorbate sodium -- Injection;(66.5) Asenapine;

(66.7) Asfotase;(67) Asparaginase;(67.6) Astemizole;(67.67) Astenajavol;(67.72) Atazanavir;(68.1) Atenolol;(68.13) Atezolizumab;

(68.15) Atomoxetine;(68.2) Atorvastatin;(68.3) Atovaquone;(68.4) Atracurium besylate;(68.5) Atropine -- See exceptions;(68.6) Auranofin;

(69) Aurothioglucose;(69.1) Avanafil;(69.2) Avibactam;(69.3) Axitinib;(69.5) Azacitidine;(70) Azapetine;(71) Azatadine maleate;(72) Azathioprine;

(72.3) Azelaic acid;(72.4) Azelastine;(72.43) Azficel-T;(72.45) Azilsartan;(72.5) Azithromycin;(72.7) Azlocillin;(73) Azo-sulfisoxazole;(73.5) Aztreonam;
(74) Azuresin;(75) Bacitracin -- See exceptions;(76) Baclofen;(76.5) Balsalazide;(77) Barium -- See exceptions;(77.3) Bazedoxifene;(77.5) Beclomethasone;
(78) Bedaquiline;(78.3) Belatacept;(78.5) Belimumab;(78.7) Belinostat;(79) Belladonna;(80) Belladonna alkaloids;
(83.1) Benoxaprofen;(83.2) Bentiromide;(83.5) Bentoquatam -- See exceptions;(84) Benzestrol;(85) Benzonatate;(86) Benzoylpas;
(87) Benzquinamide;(88) Benzthiazide;(89) Benztropine;(90) Benzylpenicilloyl - polylysine;(91) Bephenium hydroxynaphthoate;(91.3) Bepotastine;
(91.5) Bepridil;(91.7) Beractant;(91.8) Besifloxacin;(92) Beta-carotene -- See exceptions;(93) Betadine vaginal gel;(94) Betahistine;
(94.5) Betaine, anhydrous;(95) Betamethasone;(95.1) Betaxolol;(96) Betazole;(97) Bethanechol;(97.1) Bethanidine sulfate;(97.2) Bevacizumab;
(97.3) Bexarotene;(97.4) Bezlotoxumab;(97.5) Bicalutamide;(98) Bile extract;(98.2) Bimatoprost;(99) Biperiden;(100) Bisacodyl tannex;
(101) Bishydroxycoumarin;(101.5) Biskalcitrate;(102) Bismuth sodium tartrate -- See exceptions;(102.05) Bisoprolol;(102.1) Bitolterol mesylate;
(102.5) Bivalirudin;(103) Blastomycine;(104) Bleomycin;(104.3) Blinatumomab;(104.5) Boceprevir;(105) Boroglycerin glycerite;(105.3) Bortezomib;
(105.5) Bosentan;(105.6) Bosutinib;(105.7) Botulinum toxin (B);(106) Botulism antitoxin;(106.5) Brentuxima vedotin;(107) Bretylium;
(107.2) Brexpaprazole;(107.3) Briazolamide;(108) Brimonidine;(108.5) Bromelains -- See exceptions;(108.5) Bromfenac;(109) Bromisovalum;
(110) Bromocriptine;(111) Bromodiphenhydramine;(112) Brompheniramine -- See exceptions;(113) Brucella antigen;
(114) Brucella protein nucleate;(115) Buclizine;(115.3) Budesonide -- See exceptions;(115.5) Bumetanide;(116) Bupivacaine;(116.05) Reserved;
(116.1) Bupropion;(116.5) Buspirone;(117) Busulfan;(118) Butacaine;(119) Butaperazine;(119.05) Butenafine -- See exceptions;
(119.1) Butoconazole -- See exceptions;(120) Reserved;(121) Butyl nitrite;(122) Butyrophenone;(122.3) Cabazitaxel;(122.5) Cabergoline;(122.7) Cabozantinib;
(123) Cadmium sulfide -- See exceptions;(124) Caffeine sodium benzoate;(124.3) Calcifediol;(124.7) Calcipotriene;(125) Calcitonin, Salmon;
(126) Calcitriol;(127) Calcium disodium edetate -- See exceptions;(128) Calcium gluconogalactogluconate;(129) Calcium levulinate;
(129.5) Calfactant;(130) Calusterone;(130.1) Canagliflozin;(130.3) Canakinumab;(130.5) Candesartan;(131) Candicidin;(131.5) Cangrelor;(132) Cantharidin;
(132.5) Capecitabine;(133) Capreomycin;(133.05) Capsaicin -- See exceptions;(133.1) Captopril;(134) Capyodiame;(135) Caramiphen;
(136) Carbachol;(137) Carbamazepine;(138) Carbazochrome;(139) Carbenicillin;(140) Carbetapentane;(141) Carbidopa;(142) Carbinoxamine;
(142.5) Carboplatin;(142.7) Carfilzomib;(143) Carglumic Acid;(143.5) Cariprazine;(144) Carmustine;(144.1) Carnitine;
(145) Carphenazine;(145.5) Carteolol;(145.8) Carvedilol;(146) Casein hydrolysate;(146.6) Caspofungin;(147) Catarrhalis combined vaccine;
(148) Catarrhalis vaccine mixed;(149) Cefaclor;(150) Cefadroxil;(151) Cefamandole;(151.3) Cefazolin;(151.4) Cefdinir;
(151.45) Cefditoren;(151.5) Cefepime;(151.6) Cefixime;(151.7) Cefmetazole;(151.8) Cefonicid;(152) Cefoperazone;(152.1) Ceforanide;
(152.2) Cefotaxime;(152.3) Cefotetan;(152.7) Cefotiam;(152.9) Cefoxitin;(153.1) Cefpiramide;(153.2) Cefpodoxime;(153.3) Cefprozil;(153.35) Ceftaroline;
(153.6) Ceftizoxime;(153.7) Ceftolozane;(153.8) Ceftriaxone;(153.9) Cefuroxime;(153.95) Celecoxib;(154) Cellulose, Oxadized, Regenerated -- See exceptions;
(154.5) Centruroides [Scorpion] Immune;(155) Cephalexin;(156) Cephaloglycin;(157) Cephaloridine;(158) Cephalothin;(159) Cephapirin;
(159.3) Cephradine;(159.6) Ceretec;(159.7) Cerivastatin;(159.8) Certolizumab;
(160.1) Ceruletide;(160.15) Cetirizine -- See exceptions;(160.16) Cetrorelix;(160.165) Cetuximab;(160.17) Cevimeline;(160.20) Chenodiol;(161) Chlophedianol;
(162) Chlorambucil;(163) Chloramphenicol;(164) Chloranil -- See exceptions;(165) Chlordantoin;
(166) Chlordiazepoxide in combination with clidinium bromide or water soluble esterified estrogens;
(166.5) Chlorhexidine -- See exceptions;
(167) Chlormadinone;(168) Chlormerodrin;(169) Chlormezanone;(170) Chloroacetic acid -- See exceptions;
(171) Chlorobutanol -- See exceptions;(172) Chloroform -- See exceptions;(173) Chloroguanide;(174) Chloroprocaine;(175) Chloroquine;
(176) Chlorothiazide;(177) Chlorotrianisene;(178) Chloroxine;(179) Chlorphenesin;(180) Chlorpheniramine -- See exceptions;
(181) Chlorphenoxamine;(182) Chlorpromazine;(183) Chlorpropamide;(184) Chlorprothixene;(185) Chlorquinaldol;
(186) Chlortetracycline;(187) Chlorthalidone;(188) Chlorzoxazone;(189) Cholera vaccine;(190) Cholestyramine resin;
(190.3) Cholic Acid;(190.5) Choline C 11;(191) Chondroitin;(191.5) Chymopapain;(192) Chymotrypsin;(192.02) Ciclesonide;
(192.03) Ciclopirox;(192.05) Cidofovir;(192.1) Cilastatin;(192.4) Cilexetil;(192.7) Cilostazol;(193) Cimetidine -- See exceptions;
(193.5) Cinacalcet;(194) Cinoxacin;(194.5) Ciprofloxacin;(194.7) Cisapride;(194.8) Cisatracurium;(195) Cisplatin;(195.2) Citalopram;
195.3) Cladribine;(195.5) Clarithromycin;(195.7) Clavulanate;(196) Clemastine -- See exceptions;
(196.5) Clevidipine;(197) Clidinium bromide;(198) Clindamycin;(198.1) Clobetasol propionate;(199) Clocortolone pivalate;
(200) Clofibrate;(201) Clomiphene;(201.5) Clomipramine;(202) Clonidine;(203) Clopidogerel;(204) Clostridiopeptidase;
(205) Clotrimazole -- See exceptions;(206) Cloxacillin;(206.5) Clozapine;(207) Coal tar solution topical;(207.5) Cobicistat;
(207.7) Cobimetinib;(208) Cobra venom;(208.5) Coccidioides immitis;(209) Colchicine -- See exceptions;
(209.5) Colesevelam;(210) Colestipol;(211) Colistimethate;(212) Colistin;(213) Collagenase;(213.1) Collagenase clostridium histolyticum;
(213.3) Conivaptan;(213.5) Corticorelin;(214) Corticotropin;(215) Corticotropin, Respository;(216) Cortisone;
(217) Cosyntropin;(217.4) Crisaborole;(217.5) Crixivan;(217.8) Crizotinib;(217.9) Crofelemer;(218) Cromolyn -- See exceptions;
(219) Crotaline antivenin, Polyvalent;(220) Crotamiton;(221) Cryptenamine;(221.5) Cupric chloride -- injectable;
(222) Cyanide antidote;(223) Cyclacillin;(224) Cyclandelate;(225) Reserved;(226) Cyclobenzaprine;(227) Cyclomethycaine;
(228) Cyclopentamine;(229) Cyclopentolate;(230) Cyclophosphamide;(231) Cycloserine;(231.5) Cyclosporine;(232) Cyclothiazide;
(233) Cycrimine;(234) Cyproheptadine;(234.5) Cysteamine;(235) Cytarabine;(235.5) Dabigatran;(235.7) Dabrafenib;
(236) Dacarbazine;(236.5) Daclatasvir;(236.6) Daclizumab;(237) Dactinomycin;(237.05) Dalbavancin;(237.1) Dalfampridine;
(237.2) Dalfopristin;(237.5) Dalteparin;(237.7) Danaparoid;(238) Danazol;(239) Dantrolene;(239.4) Dapagliflozin;(239.5) Dapiprazole;
(240) Dapsone -- See exceptions;(240.3) Daptomycin;(240.4) Daratumumab;(240.5) Darbepoetin alfa;(240.6) Darifenacin;
(240.7) Darunavir;(240.8) Dasabuvir;(240.9) Dasatinib;(241) Daunorubicin;(242) Deanol;(243) Decamethonium;
(243.3) Decitabine;(243.5) Deferasirox;(243.7) Deferiprone;(244) Deferoxamine;(244.2) Defibrotide;(244.4) Degarelix;
(244.5) Delavirdine;(245) Demecarium;(246) Demeclocycline;(247) Demethylchlortetracycline;(247.7) Denosumab;
(247.8) Deoxycholic Acid;(248) Deoxyribonuclease, Pancreatic;(249) Deserpidine;(249.5) Desflurane;(250) Desipramine;
(250.5) Desirudin;(251) Deslanoside;(251.5) Desloratadine;(252) Desmopressin;(252.5) Desogestrel;(253) Desonide;
(254) Desoximetasone;(255) Desoxycorticosterone;(256) Desoxyribonuclease;(256.5) Desvenlafaxine;(257) Dexamethasone;
(258) Dexbrompheniramine -- See exceptions;(259) Dexchlorpheniramine;(259.5) Dexlansoprazole;(260) Dexpanthenol;
(260.5) Dexrazoxane;(261) Dextran;(262) Reserved;(263) Dextriferron;(264) Dextroisoephedrine;(265) Dextrothyroxine;
(265.5) Dezocine;(266) Diatrizoate;(267) Diazoxide;(268) Dibucaine;(269) Dichloralphenazone;(270) Dichlorphenamide;
(270.5) Diclofenac;(271) Dicloxacillin;(272) Dicyclomine;(272.5) Didanosine;(273) Dienestrol;(273.5) Dienogest;
(274) Diethylcarbamazine;(275) Diethylstilbestrol;(276) Reserved;(277) Diflorasone diacetate;(277.5) Diflunisal;(277.57) Difluprednate;
(278) Digitalis;(279) Digitoxin;(280) Digoxin;(281) Dihydroergocornine;(282) Dihydroergocristine;(283) Dihydroergocryptine;
(284) Dihydroergotamine;(285) Dihydrostreptomycin;(286) Dihydrotachysterol;(287) Diiodohydroxyquin;(287.5) Diltiazem;
(288) Dimenhydrinate -- Injection or suppositories;(289) Dimercaprol;(290) Dimethindene;(291) Dimethisterone;
(291.5) Dimethyl fumarate;(292) Dimethyl sulfoxide -- See exceptions;(293) Dimethyl tubocurarine;(293.5) Dimyristoyl;
(294) Dinoprost;(295) Dinoprostone;(295.5) Dinutuximab;(296) Dioxyline;(297) Diphemanil;(298) Diphenadione;
(299) Diphenhydramine -- See exceptions;(300) Diphenidol;(301) Diphenylhydantoin;(302) Diphenylpyraline;
(303) Diphtheria antitoxin;(304) Diphtheria and tetanus toxoids;(305) Diphtheria and tetanus toxoids and pertussis vaccine;
(306) Diphtheria and tetanus toxoids, Absorbed;(307) Diphtheria and tetanus toxoids, Pertussis;(308) Diphtheria toxoid;

145

(309) Dipivefrin;(310) Dipyridamole;(311) Dipyron;(311.3) Dirithromycin;(311.5) Disibind;(312) Disodium edetate -- See exceptions;
(313) Disopyramide;(314) Disulfiram;(314.5) Divalproex;(315) Dobutamine;(315.5) Docetaxel;(315.7) Docosanol -- See exceptions;
(316) Doderlein bacilli;(316.2) Dofetilide;(316.3) Dolasetron;(316.4) Dolutegravir;(316.5) Donepezil;(317) Dopamine;
(317.2) Doripenem;(317.3) Dornase Alpha;(317.4) Dorzolamide;(317.5) Doxacurium;(318) Doxapram;(318.5) Doxazosin mesylate;
(319) Doxepin;(319.5) Doxercalciferol;(320) Doxorubicin;(321) Doxycycline;(322) Reserved;(323) Doxylamine;(324) Dromostanolone;
(324.5) Dronedarone;(325) Droperidol;(325.3) Drospirenone;(325.4) Drotrecogin alfa;(325.43) Droxidopa;(325.44) Dulaglutide;
(325.45) Duloxetine;(325.5) Dutasteride;(326) Dyclonine;(327) Dydrogesterone;(328) Dyphylline;(328.5) Ecallantide;(329) Echothiophate;
(329.5) Econazole;(330) Ectylurea;(330.3) Eculizumab;(330.5) Edetate -- See exceptions;(330.7) Edoxaban;(331) Edrophonium;
(331.03) Efavirenz;(331.04) Efinaconazole;(331.05) Eflornithine;(331.053) Elbasvir;(331.055) Eliglustat;(331.058) Elosulfase;(331.059) Elotuzumab;
(331.06) Eltrombopag;(331.065) Elvitegravir;(331.07) Emedastine;(331.071) Empagliflozin;(331.072) Emtricitabine;(331.1) Enalapril;
(331.6) Enalaprilat;(332) Enflurane;(332.2) Enfuvirtide;(332.5) Enoxacin;(332.7) Enoxaparin;(332.8) Entacapone;(332.85) Entecavir;
(332.87) Enzalutamide;(332.9) Epinastine;(333) Epinephrine;(334) Epinephryl borate;(334.3) Epirubicin;(334.4) Eplerenone;
(334.5) Epoprostenol;(334.7) Eprosartan;(334.8) Eptifibatide;(335) Ergocalciferol -- See exceptions;(335.5) Ergoloid mesylates;(336) Ergonovine;
(337) Ergotamine;(338) Ergosine;(339) Ergocristine;(340) Ergocryptine;(341) Ergocornine;(342) Ergotaminine;(343) Ergosinine;(344) Ergocristinine;
(345) Ergocryptinine;(346) Ergocorninine;(346.05) Eribulin;(346.1) Erlotinib;(346.5) Ertapenem;(347) Erythrityl tetranitrate;
(348) Erythromycin;(348.722) Escitalopram;(349) Eserine;(349.3) Eslicarbazepine;(349.4) Esmolol;(349.7) Esomeprazole -- See exceptions;
(350) Esterified estrogens;(351) Estradiol;(352) Estriol;(353) Estrogens;(354) Estrogenic substances;(355) Estrone;(355.5) Estropipate;
(355.6) Etanercept-szzs;(355.8) Eteplirsen;(356) Ethacrynate;(357) Ethacrynic acid(358) Ethambutol;(359) Ethamivan;(359.5) Ethanolamine oleate;
(360) Ethaverine;(361) Ether -- See exceptions;(361.5) Ethinamate;(362) Ethinyl estradiol;(363) Ethiodized oil;(364) Ethionamide;(365) Ethisterone;
(366) Ethoheptazine;(367) Ethopropazine;(368) Ethosuximide;(369) Ethotoin;(370) Ethoxazene -- See exceptions;(371) Ethoxyzolamide;
(372) Ethyl biscoumacetate;(373) Ethyl chloride -- See exceptions;(374) Ethyl nitrite spirit;(375) Reserved;(376) Ethylnorepinephrine;
(377) Ethynodiol diacetate;(378) Etidocaine;(379) Etidronate;(379.05) Etodolac;(379.07) Etomidate;(379.09) Etonogestrel;
(379.1) Etoposide;(379.5) Etravirine;(380) Eucatropine;(380.3) Everolimus;(380.4) Evolocumab;(380.5) Exemestane;
(380.6) Exenatide;(380.7) Ezetimibe;(381) Factor IX complex, Human;(381.1) Famciclovir;(381.2) Famotidine -- See exceptions;
(381.3) Felbamate;(381.5) Felodipine;(381.55) Fenfibrate;(381.6) Fenofenadine;(381.7) Fenofibrate;(381.75) Fenofibric acid;
(381.8) Fenoldopam;(382) Fenoprofen;(382.25) Febuxostat;(383) Ferric cacodylate;(383.15) Ferric Hexacyanoferrate;(383.3) Ferumoxides;
(383.4) Ferumoxsil;(383.43) Ferumoxytol;(383.45) Fesoterodine;(383.5) Fexofenadine -- See exceptions;(384) Fibrinogen;
(385) Fibrinogen/antihemophilic factor, Human;(386) Fibrinolysin, Human;(386.05) Fidaxomicin;(386.1) Filgrastim-SNDZ;(386.3) Finasteride;
(386.5) Filgrastin;(386.6) Finafloxacin;(386.7) Fingolimod;(387) Flavoxate;(387.1) Flecainide acetate;(387.7) Flibanserin;
(388) Florantyrone;(388.3) Florbetapir F 18;(388.5) Flosequinan;(389) Floxuridine;(389.5) Fluconazole;(390) Flucytosine;(390.5) Fludarabine;
(390.7) Fludeoxyglucose;(391) Fludrocortisone;(391.5) Flumazenil;(392) Flumethasone;(392.1) Flunisolide;(393) Fluocinonide;
(394) Fluocinolone;(395) Fluorescein;(396) Fluoride -- See exceptions;(396.5) Fluorometholone;(397) Fluorophosphates;
(398) Fluorouracil;(399) Fluoxetine;(399.5) Fluoxymesterone;(400) Fluphenazine;(401) Fluprednisolone;(402) Flurandrenolide;
(402.2) Flurbiprofen;(402.5) Flutamide;(402.6) Flutemetamol F18;(402.7) Fluticasone -- See exceptions;(402.8) Fluvastatin;(402.9) Fluvoxamine;
(403) Folate sodium;(404) Folic acid -- See exceptions;(404.3) Follitropin;(404.5) Fomivirsen;(404.7) Fondaparinux;(405) Foreign protein;
(406) Formaldehyde -- See exceptions;(406.2) Formoterol;(406.3) Fosamprenavir;(406.35) Fosaprepitant;(406.4) Foscarnet;(406.5) Fosfomycin;
(406.7) Fosinopril;(406.9) Fosphenytoin;(406.95) Frovatriptan;(407) Furazolidone;(408) Furosemide;(408.2) Gabapentin;(408.25) Gadobenate;
(408.27) Gadobutrol;(408.3) Gadodiamide;(408.35) Gadofosveset;(408.4) Gadopentetate dimeglumine;(408.5) Gadoterate meglumine;
(408.6) Gadoteridol;(408.8) Gadoversetamide;(408.85) Gadoxetate;(408.9) Galantamine;(409) Gallamine triethiodide;(409.3) Gallium citrate;
(409.5) Gallium nitrate;(409.8) Galsulfase;(410) Gamma benzene hexachloride;(411) Gamma globulin;(411.5) Ganciclovir;(411.7) Ganirelix;
(412) Gas gangrene polyvalent antitoxin;(412.03) Gatifloxacin;(412.04) Gefitinib;(412.05) Gemcitabine;(412.1) Gemfibrozil;(412.2) Gemifloxacin;
(412.3) Gemtuzumab ozogamicin;(412.5) Genotropin;(413) Gentamicin;(414) Gentian violet vaginal suppositories;(415) Gitalin;(415.03) Glatiramer;
(415.05) Glimepiride;(415.1) Glipizide;(416) Glucagon;(416.5) Glucarpidase;(417) Gluceptate;(418) Gluconate magnesium;
(419) Gluconate potassium -- See exceptions;(420) Glutamate arginine;(420.1) Glyburide;(420.2) Glycerol phenylbutyrate;(420.5) Glycine -- See exceptions;
(421) Glycobiarsol;(422) Glycopyrrolate;(423) Gold sodium thiomalate;(424) Gold thiosulfate -- See exceptions;(424.4) Golimumab;
(425) Gomenol Solution;(425.5) Gonadorelin acetate;(426) Gonadotropin, Chorionic;(427) Gonadotropin, Chorionic, Anti-human serum;
(428) Gonadotropin, Serum;(428.5) Goserelin;(429) Gramicidin;(430) Gramineae pollens;(430.3) Gramosetron;(430.5) Granisetron;(430.7) Grazoprevir;
(431) Griseofulvin;(431.5) Guanabenz;(432) Guanethidine;(432.4) Guanadrel;(432.7) Guanfacine;(432.9) Guanidine;
(433) Halcinonide;(433.5) Halobetasol Propionate;(433.7) Halofantrine;(434) Haloperidol;(435) Haloprogin;(436) Halothane;(437) Hartman's solution;
(438) Heparin;(439) Hetacillin;(440) Hexachlorophene -- See exceptions;(441) Hexafluorenium;(442) Hexocyclium;
(443) Hexylcaine;(444) Histamine;(445) Histoplasmin;(445.5) Histrelin acetate;(446) Homatropine;(446.4) Human secretin;
(446.6) Hyaluronan;(446.7) Hyaluronic acid;(447) Hyaluronidase;(448) Hydralazine;(449) Hydrocalciferol;(450) Hydrochlorothiazide;
(451) Hydrocortamate;(452) Hydrocortisone -- See exceptions;(453) Hydroflumethiazide;(454) Hydroquinone;(455) Hydroxocobalamin -- See exceptions;
(456) Hydroxyamphetamine;(457) Hydroxychloroquine;(458) Hydroxyprogesterone;(459) Hydroxyurea;(460) Hydroxyzine;
(461) Hyoscyamine;(462) Hyoscyamus alkaloids;(463) Hypophamine;(463.03) Ibandronate;(463.5) Ibrutinib;(464) Ibuprofen -- See exceptions;
(464.05) Ibutilide;(464.07) Icatibant;(464.1) Idarubicin;(464.15) Idarucizumab;(464.2) Idelalisib;(464.3) Idoxuridine;(464.5) Idursulfase;
(464.6) Ifosfamide;(464.67) Iloperidone;(464.7) Iloprost;(464.8) Imatinib;(465) Imiglucerase;(465.1) Imipenem/cilastatin;(466) Imipramine;
(466.5) Imiquimod;(467) Immune hepatitis B globulin, Human;(468) Immune poliomyelitis globulin, Human;(469) Immune serum globulin, Human;
(469.05) IncobotulinumtoxinA;(469.07) Indacaterol;(469.1) Indapamide;(469.5) Indecainide;(470) Indigotindisulfonate;(470.05) Indinavir;
(470.1) Indium IN-III oxyquinolone;(470.3) Indium IN-III pentetreotide;(471) Indocyanine green;(472) Indomethacin;(472.5) Infliximab;(472.51) Infliximab-dyyb;
(473) Influenza virus vaccines;(473.5) Ingenol mebutate;(474) Injections, All substances for human use -- See exceptions;(474.2) Insulin aspart;
(474.3) Insulin degludec;(474.4) Insulin glargine;(474.45) Insulin glulisine;(474.5) Interferon;(475) Intrinsic factor concentrate manufactured for human use;
(475.3) Inulin;(475.5) Iobenguane;(476) Iocetamic acid;(477) Iodamide;(478) Iodinated I-125 serum albumin;
(479) Iodinated I-131 serum albumin;(480) Iodinated glycerol-theophylline;(481) Iodine solution, Strong oral;(482) Iodipamide;(482.5) Iodixanol;(483) Iodized oil;
(484) Iodobenzoic acid -- See exceptions;(485) Iodobrassid;(485.1) Iodohippurate sodium;(486) Iodopyracet;(487) Iodothiouracil;
(487.05) Iofetamine;(487.06) Ioflupane;(487.08) Iohexol;(487.1) Iopamidol;(488) Iopanoic acid -- See exceptions;(489) Iophendylate;
(489.1) Iopromide;(489.2) Iothalamate;(489.3) Iothiouracil;(489.5) Iotrolan;(489.6) Ioversol;(490.1) Ioxaglate;(490.5) Ioxilan;(490.7) Ipilimumab;(491) Ipodate;
(491.5) Ipratropium;(491.6) Irbesartan;(491.7) Irinotecan;(492) Iron cacodylate;(493) Iron dextran injection;(494) Iron peptonized;(495) Iron sorbitex;
(495.5) Isavuconazonium;(496) Isocarboxazid;(497) Isoetharine;(498) Isoflurane;(499) Isoflurophate;(500) Isoniazid;
(502) Isopropamide;(503) Isoproterenol;(504) Isosorbide dinitrate;(504.05) Isosorbide mononitrate;(504.1) Isosulfan blue;
(505) Isothipendyl;(505.5) Isotretinoin;(506) Isoxsuprine;(506.5) Israidipine;(506.7) Itraconazole;(506.72) Ivabradine;
(506.75) Ivacaftor;(506.8) Ivermectin;(506.9) Ixabepilone;(506.95) Ixazomib;(506.97) Ixekizumab;(507) Kanamycin;(508) Reserved;(509) Ketocholanic acids;
(509.1) Ketoconazole -- See exceptions;(509.15) Ketoprofen -- See exceptions;(509.17) Ketorolac tromethamine;(509.18) Ketotifen -- See exceptions;
(509.2) Labetalol;(509.7) Lacosamide;(510) Lactated ringers solution;(511) Lactulose;(511.3) Lamivudine;(511.5) Lamotrigine;
(512) Lanatoside C;(512.3) Lanreotide;(512.5) Lansoprazole -- See exceptions;(512.6) Lanthanum;(512.67) Lapatinib;

(512.7) Latanoprost;(513) Latrodectus mactans;(513.3) Ledipasvir;(513.5) Leflunomide;(513.7) Lenalidomide;(513.74) Lenvatinib;(513.77) Lesinurad;
(513.8) Letrozole;(514) Leucovorin;(514.1) Leuprolide;(514.5) Levalbuterol;(515) Reserved;(515.5) Levamisole;(516) Levarterenol;
(516.05) Levetiracetam;(516.07) Levobetaxolol;(516.1) Levobunolol;(516.3) Levobupivacine;(516.5) Levocabastine;(516.7) Levocarnitine;
(516.75) Levocetirizine;(517) Levodopa;(517.2) Levofloxacin;(517.25) Levoleucovorin;(517.3) Levomethadyl;(517.35) Levomilnacipran;
(517.4) Levonordefrin;(518) Levopropoxyphene;(519) Levothyroxine;(520) Lidocaine -- See exceptions;(520.2) Lifitegrast;(520.3) Linaclotide;
(520.5) Linagliptin;(521) Lincomycin;(522) Lindane -- See exceptions;(522.5) Linezolid;(523) Linolenic acid;(524) Liothyronine;
(525) Liotrix;(525.2) Liraglutide;(525.5) Lisinopril;(526) Lithium carbonate -- See exceptions;(527) Lithium citrate;
(528) Liver extract;(528.1) Lixisenatide;(528.3) Lodoxamide;(528.5) Lomefloxacin;(528.7) Lomitapide;(529) Lomustine;
(529.1) Loperamide -- See exceptions;(529.5) Lopinavir;(529.7) Loracarbef;(529.9) Loratadine -- See exceptions;
529.93) Lorcaserin hydrochloride;(529.95) Losartan;(529.97) Loteprednol;(530) Lovastatin;(530.5) Loxapine;(530.7) Lubiprostone;
(530.8) Lucinactant;(531) Lugols solution;(531.3) Luliconazole;(531.4) Lumacaftor;(531.5) Lumefantrine;(531.7) Lurasidone;
(532) Lututrin;(533) Lymphogranuloma venereum antigen;(534) Lypressin synthetic;(534.5) Macitentan;
(535) Mafenide;(536) Magnesium gluconate -- See exceptions;(537) Magnesium salicylate;(538) Mandelic acid -- See exceptions;
(539) Mannitol -- See exceptions;(540) Mannitol hexanitrate;(540.1) Maprotiline;(540.3) Maraviroc;(540.5) Masoprocol;(541) Measles immune globulin, Human;
(542) Measles virus vaccines;(543) Mebendazole for human use;(544) Mecamylamine;(544.5) Mecasermin;
(545) Mechlorethamine;(546) Meclizine -- See exceptions;(546.5) Meclocycline;(547) Meclofenamate;(548) Medroxyprogesterone;
(551) Megestrol;(552) Meglumine;(552.5) Meloxicam;(553) Melphalan;(553.5) Memantine;(554) Menadiol;(555) Menadione;
(556) Meningococcal polysaccharide vaccine;(557) Menotropins;(558) Mepenzolate;(559) Mephenesin;(560) Mephentermine;(561) Mephenytoin;
(562) Mepivacaine;(562.5) Mepolizumab;(563) Meprednisone;(563.5) Mequinol;
(564) Meralluride;(565) Mercaptomerin;(566) Mercaptopurine;(567) Mercury bichloride -- See exceptions;(567.1) Meropenem;
(567.2) Mersalyl;(567.3) Mesalamine;(567.5) Mesna;(568) Mesoridazine;(569) Mestranol;(570) Metaproterenol;
(571) Metaraminol;(572) Metaxalone;(572.5) Metformin;(573) Methacholine;(574) Methacycline;
(575) Methallenestril;(576) Reserved;(577) Reserved;(578) Methantheline;(579) Methazolamide;(580) Methdilazine;
(581) Methenamine hippurate;(582) Methenamine mandelate;(583) Methenamine sulfosalicylate;
(584) Methicillin;(585) Methimazole;(586) Methiodal;(587) Methionine;(588) Methixene;(589) Methocarbamol;
(590) Methotrexate;(591) Methotrimeprazine;(592) Methoxamine;(593) Methoxsalen;(594) Methoxyflurane;
(595) Methoxyphenamine;(595.5) Methoxy polyethylene glycol-epoetin beta;(596) Methscopolamine;(597) Methsuximide;
(598) Methyclothiazide;(599) Methylandrostenediol;(600) Methylatropine;(601) Methyldopa;(602) Methyldopate;
(603) Methylene blue, Oral;(604) Methylergonovine;(604.5) Methylnaltrexone;(605) Methylprednisolone;(606) Reserved;
(607) Methysergide;(608) Metoclopramide;(609) Metocurine iodide injection;(610) Metolazone;(611) Metoprolol;(611.5) Metreleptin;
(612) Metrizamide;(612.5) Metrizoate;(613) Metronidazole;(614) Metyrapone;(615) Metyrosine;(615.01) Mexiletine;(615.1) Mezlocillin;
(615.6) Mibefradil;(615.9) Micafungin;(616) Miconazole -- See exceptions;(617) Microfibrillar collagen hemostat;
(617.1) Midodrine;(617.22) Midubosathol;(617.3) Mifepristone;(617.4) Miglitol;(617.44) Miglustat;
(617.47) Milnacipran;(617.5) Milrinone;(617.7) Miltefosine;(618) Minocycline;(619) Minoxidil -- See exceptions;
(619.05) Mipomersen;(619.1) Mirabegron;(619.3) Mirtazapine;(619.5) Misoprostol;(620) Mithramycin;(621) Mitomycin;
(622) Mitotane;(622.3) Mitoxantrone;(622.5) Mivacurium;(622.7) Moexipril;(623) Molindone;
(623.5) Mometasone;(624) Monobenzone;(624.1) Monooctanoin;(624.5) Montelukast;(624.7) Moricizine;
(625) Morrhuate;(625.1) Moxalactam;(625.3) Moxidectin;(625.5) Moxifloxacin;(626) Mumps virus vaccines;(626.5) Mupirocin;
(627) Mushroom spores which, when mature, contain either psilocybin or psilocin;(627.5) Mycophenolate;(628) N-acetyl-1-cysteine;
(629) N. cattarhalis antigen;(629.5) Nabumetone;(630) Nadolol;(630.5) Nafarelin;(631) Nafcillin;(631.5) Naftifine;(632) Nalbuphine;
(633) Reserved;(634) Nalidixic acid;(634.5) Nalmefene;(634.7) Naloxegol;(635) Naloxone -- See exceptions;
(635.1) Naltrexone;(636) Reserved;(637) Naphazoline -- See exceptions;(638) Naproxen -- See exceptions;
(638.3) Naratriptan;(638.4) Natalizumab;(638.45) Nebivolol;(638.47) Necitumumab;(638.5) Nedocromil;(638.7) Nefazodone;
(638.75) Nelarabine;(638.8) Nelfinavir;(639) Neomycin -- See exceptions;(640) Neostigmine;(640.1) Nepafenac;(640.2) Nesiritide;
(640.3) Netilmicin;(640.35) Netupitant;(640.4) Nevirapine;(640.5) Niacinamide -- See exceptions;(640.7) Nicardipine;(640.8) Niclosamide;
(641.1) Nicotine resin complex (polacrilex) -- See exceptions;(641.15) Nicotine transdermal system -- See exceptions;(642) Nicotinyl alcohol;
(642.1) Nifedipine;(643) Nifuroxime;(644) Nikethamide;(644.3) Nilotinib;(644.4) Nilutamide;(644.5) Nimodipine;
(644.6) Nintedanib;(644.7) Nisoldipine;(644.72) Nitazoxanide;(644.8) Nitisinone;(644.9) Nitric oxide -- for use in humans;
(645) Nitrofurantoin;(646) Nitrofurazone;(647) Nitroglycerin;(648) Nitroprusside -- See exceptions;
(648.3) Nitrous oxide -- See exceptions;(648.5) Nivolumab;(648.6) Nizatidine -- See exceptions;(649.1) Nomifensine maleate;
(650) Nonoxynol -- See exceptions;(651) Norepinephrine;(652) Norethindrone;(653) Norethynodrel;(653.5) Norfloxacin;(654) Norgestrel;
(655) Normal serum albumin, Human;(656) Nortriptyline;(657) Nositol;(658) Novobiocin;(658.7) Nusinersen;(659) Nux vomica;(660) Nylidrin;
(661) Nystatin;(661.03) Obeticholic acid;(661.05) Obiltoxaximab;(661.1) Obinutuzumab;(661.15) Ocilizumab;
(661.3) Ocriplasmin;(661.5) Octreotide acetate;(661.6) Ofatumumab;(661.7) Ofloxacin;(661.8) Olanzapine;
(661.9) Olaparib;(661.96) Olaratumab;(662) Old tuberculin;(663) Oleandomycin;(663.1) Olmesartan;(663.15) Olodaterol;
(663.2) Olopatadine;(663.3) Olsalazine Sodium;(663.35) Omacetaxine mepesuccinate;(663.36) Omalizumab;
(663.37) Ombitasvir;(663.4) Omega-3-acid;(663.5) Omeprazole -- See exceptions;(663.6) OnabotulinumtoxinA;
(663.7) Ondansetron;(663.73) Oritavancin;(663.75) Orlistat -- See exceptions;(664) Orphenadrine;
(665) Orthoiodobenzoic acid;(665.5) Oseltamivir;(665.55) Osimertinib;(665.6) Ospemifene;
(665.7) Ovine hyaluronidase;(666) Oxacillin;(666.4) Oxaliplatin;(666.6) Oxamniquine;(667) Oxaprozin;(667.5) Oxcarbazepine;
(668) Oxethazaine;(668.5) Oxiconazole;(669) Oxolinic acid;(669.1) Oxprenolol;(670) Oxtriphylline;
(671) Oxybutynin -- See exceptions;(672) Oxygen for human use -- See exceptions;(673) Oxymetazoline;
(674) Oxyphenbutazone;(675) Oxyphencyclimine;(676) Oxyphenisatin;(677) Oxyphenonium;
(678) Oxyquinoline;(679) Oxytetracycline;(680) Oxytocin;(680.5) Ozogamicin;(681) P-nitrosulfathiazole;
(681.3) Paclitaxel;(681.35) Palbociclib;(681.4) Palifermin;(681.45) Paliperidone;(681.5) Palonosetron;
(681.7) Pamidronate;(682) Pancreatin dornase;(683) Pancreatic enzyme;(684) Pancrelipase;(685) Pancuronium;
(685.5) Panidronate;(685.6) Panitumumab;(685.65) Panobinostat;(685.7) Pantoprazole;(686) Papaverine;
(687) Paramethadione;(688) Paramethasone;(689) Paranitrosulfathiazole;(690) Parathyroid injection;(691) Pargyline;
(691.5) Paricalcitol;(691.7) Paritaprevir;(692) Paromomycin;(692.2) Paroxetine;(692.25) Pasereotide;
(692.28) Pasireotide;(692.29) Patiromer;(692.3) Pazopanib;(692.4) Pegademase bovine;(692.5) Pegaspargase;
(692.51) Pegfilgrastim;(692.513) Peginesatide;(692.515) Peginterferon;(692.517) Pegloticase;
(692.52) Pegvisomant;(692.53) Pembrolizumab;(692.54) Pemetrexed;(692.55) Pemirolast;(692.6) Penbutolol;
(692.8) Penciclovir;(693) Penicillamine;(694) Penicillin G;(695) Penicillin G;(696) Penicillin O;(697) Penicillin V;(698) Penicillinase;
(699) Pentaerythritol tetranitrate;(700) Pentagastrin;(700.1) Pentamidine isethionate;(701) Pentapiperide;
(701.5) Pentetate calcium trisodium;(701.7) Pentetate zinc trisodium;(702) Penthienate;(703) Pentolinium;(703.03) Pentosan;

(703.05) Pentostatin;(703.1) Pentoxifylline;(703.4) Pentylenetetrazol;(703.42) Peramivir;(703.43) Perampanel;
(703.45) Perflexane;(703.5) Perflubron;(703.6) Perfluoroalkylpolyether;(703.65) Perflutren;(703.7) Pergolide;(704) Perindopril;
(704.1) Permethrin -- See exceptions;(705) Perphenazine;(706) Pertussis immune globulin, Human;
(706.5) Pertuzumab;(707) Phenacemide;(708) Phenaglycodol;(709) Phenaphthazine;
(710) Phenazopyridine -- See exceptions;(711) Phenelzine;(712) Phenethicillin;(713) Phenformin;(714) Phenindamine;
(715) Phenindione;(716) Pheniramine -- See exceptions;(717) Phenitramin;(718) Phenothiazine derivatives;
(719) Phenoxybenzamine;(720) Phenoxymethyl penicillin;(721) Phenuprocoumon;(722) Phensuximide;(723) Phentolamine;
(724) Phenylbutazone;(725) Phenylmercuric acetate;(726) Phenylmercuric nitrate;(726.5) Phenylpropanolamine;
(727) Phenyltoloxamine dihydrogen citrate;(727.2) Phenytoin;(728) Phthalylsulfacetamide;(729) Phthalylsulfathiazole;
(730) Physostigmine;(731) Phytonadione;(731.1) Pimozide;(732) Pilocarpine;(732.3) Pinacidil;(732.7) Pindolol;
(732.8) Pioglitazone;(732.9) Pimecrolimus;(733) Pipazethate;(733.5) Pipecuronium;(734) Pipenzolate;
(735) Piperacetazine;(735.1) Piperacillin;(736) Piperazine;(737) Piperidolate;(738) Piperocaine;(739) Pipobroman;
(740) Pipradrol;(740.05) Pirbuterol;(740.07) Pirfenidone;(740.1) Piroxicam;(740.5) Pitavastatin;
(741) Plague vaccine;(742) Plasma protein fraction;(742.3) Plerixafor;(742.5) Plicamycin;
(743) Pneumococcal polyvalent vaccine;
(743.3) Podofilox;(743.5) Podophyllotoxin;(744) Poison ivy extract;(745) Poison ivy oak extract;
(746) Poison ivy oak, sumac extract;(747) Poldine methylsulfate;(747.4) Polidocanol;(748) Poliomyelitis vaccine;
(749) Poliovirus vaccine, Live, Oral, All;(750) Polyestradiol;(751) Polymyxin B -- See exceptions;(751.5) Polytetrafluoroethylene;
(752) Polythiazide;(752.05) Pomalidomide;(752.1) Ponatinib;(752.2) Poractant alfa;(752.5) Porfimer;
(752.7) Posaconazole;(753) Posterior pituitary;(754) Potassium acetate injection;(755) Potassium acid phosphate -- See exceptions;
(756) Potassium p-aminobenzoate -- See exceptions;(757) Potassium aminosalicylate -- See exceptions;
(758) Potassium arsenite -- See exceptions;(759) Potassium bicarbonate -- See exceptions;
(760) Potassium carbonate -- See exceptions;(761) Potassium chloride -- See exceptions;
(762) Potassium citrate -- See exceptions;(763) Potassium gluconate -- See exceptions;(764) Potassium hetacillin;
(765) Potassium iodide -- See exceptions;(766) Reserved;(767) Potassium permanganate -- See exceptions;
(768) Povidone -- Iodine -- See exceptions;(768.8) Pralatrexate;(769) Pralidoxime;(769.2) Pramipexole;(769.3) Pramlintide;
(769.33) Prasterone;(769.35) Prasugrel;(769.4) Pravastatin;(769.7) Praziquantel;(770) Prazosin;(770.5) Prednicarbate;
(771) Prednisolone;(772) Prednisone;(773) Prilocaine;(774) Primaquine;(775) Primidone;(776) Probenecid;(777) Probucol;
(778) Procainamide;(779) Procaine;(780) Procaine penicillin;(781) Procaine penicillin G;(782) Procarbazine;
(783) Prochlorperazine;(784) Procyclidine;(785) Progesterone;(785.5) Proguanil;(786) Promazine;
(787) Promethazine;(788) Promethestrol;(788.5) Propafenone;(789) Propantheline;(790) Proparacaine;
(791) Prophenpyridamine -- See exceptions;(792) Propiolactone;(793) Propiomazine;(794) Propoxycaine;(795) Propranolol;
(795.5) Propylhexedrine;(796) Propylparaben;(797) Propylthiouracil;(798) Protamine sulfate injection;
(799) Protein hydrolysate injection;(800) Protein, Foreign injection;(801) Proteolytic enzyme;(802) Protirelin;(803) Protokylol;
(804) Protoveratrine A and B;(805) Protriptyline;(805.5) Prussian blue;(806) Reserved;(807) Pseudomonas polysaccharide complex;
(808) P-ureidobenzenearsonic acid;(809) Purified protein derivatives of tuberculin;(810) Pyrantel;(811) Pyrazinamide;
(812) Pyrazolon;(813) Pyridostigmine;(814) Pyrimethamine;(815) Pyrrobutamine;(816) Pyrvinium;(816.5) Quetiapine;
(817) Quinacrine;(817.5) Quinapril;(818) Quinestrol;(819) Quinethazone;(820) Quinidine;(821) Quinine hydrochloride;
(822) Quinine and urea hydrochloride;(822.3) Quinupristin;(822.5) Rabeprazole;(823) Rabies anti-serum;
(824) Rabies immune globulin, Human;(825) Rabies vaccine;(826) Radio-iodinated compounds;(827) Radio-iodine;(828) Radio-iron;
(829) Radioisotopes;(830) Radiopaque media;(831) Ragweed pollen extract;(831.02) Raloxifene;(831.03) Raltegravir;(831.04) Ramelteon;(831.05) Ramipril;
(831.06) Ramucirumab;(831.07) Ranibizumab;(831.1) Ranitidine -- See exceptions;(831.3) Ranolazine;(831.5) Rapacuronium;(831.7) Rasagiline;
(832) Rauwolfia serpentina;(832.1) Raxibacumab;(832.2) Reboparhamil;(832.5) Regadenoson;(832.7) Regorafenib;(833) Rescinnamine;
(834) Reserpine;(835) Reserpine alkaloids;(835.5) Reslizumab;(836) Resorcinol monoacetate -- See exceptions;
(836.3) Retapamulin;(836.5) Retinoic acid, all-trans;(837) Rhus toxicodendron antigen;(838) Rh D immune globulin, Human;
(838.5) Ribavirin;(839) Riboflavin -- See exceptions;(840) Ricinoleic acid;(840.5) Rifabutin;(841) Reserved;(842) Rifampin;
(842.1) Rifapentine;(842.15) Rifaximin;(842.17) Rilonacept;(842.18) Rilpivirine;(842.2) Riluzole;(842.4) Rimantadine;(842.7) Rimexolone;
(843) Ringer's injection;(843.1) Riociguat;(843.2) Risedronate;(843.3) Risperidone;(843.7) Ritodrine;(843.8) Ritonavir;
(843.82) Rituximab;(843.825) Rivaroxaban;(843.83) Rivastigmine;(843.9) Rizatritpan;(844) Rocky mountain spotted fever vaccine;
(844.5) Rocuronium;(844.7) Rofecoxib;(844.75) Roflumilast;(844.8) Rolapitant;(845) Rolitetracycline;
(845.1) Romidepsin;(845.15) Romiplostim;(845.3) Ropinirole;(845.5) Ropivacaine;(845.7) Rosiglitazone;(845.8) Rosuvastatin;
(845.9) Rotavirus vaccine;(845.95) Rotigotine;(846) Rotoxamine;(846.5) RSVIGIV;(847) Rubella and mumps virus vaccine;
(848) Rubella virus vaccine;(848.2) Rucaparib;(848.5) Rufinamide;(849) Rutin -- See exceptions;(849.5) Sacrosidase;
(849.7) Sacubitril;(850) Salicylazosulfapyridine;(850.5) Salmeterol;(851) Salmonella typhosa, Killed;
(851.02) Reserved;(851.03) Samarium SM 153 lexidronam;(851.04) Saneromazile;
(851.045) Sapropterin;(851.05) Saquinavir;(851.1) Saralasin acetate;(851.7) Saxagliptin;(852) Scopolamine;(852.05) Sebelipase;
(852.1) Secretin;(852.4) Secukinumab;(852.6) Selegiline;(853) Selenium sulfide -- See exceptions;(853.5) Selenomethionine;(853.7) Selexipag;
(854) Senecio cineraria extract ophthalmic solution;(855) Senega fluid extract;(855.3) Seractide acetate;(855.5) Sermorelin Acetate;
(855.6) Sertaconazole;(855.7) Sertraline;(855.74) Sevelamer;(855.8) Sevoflurane;(855.85) Sildenafil;(855.9) Silodosin;(855.95) Siltuximab;
(856) Silver nitrate ophthalmic solutions or suspensions;(857) Silver sulfadiazine cream;(857.1) Simeprevir;(857.3) Simethicone coated cellulose suspension;
(857.5) Simvastatin;(858) Sincalide;(858.3) Sinecatechins;(858.5) Sirolimus;(858.7) Sitagliptin;(859) Sitosterols;
(860) Solutions for injections, All;(861) Smallpox vaccine;(862) Sodium acetate injection;(863) Sodium acetrizoate;(864) Sodium ascorbate injection;
(865) Sodium biphosphate -- See exceptions;(866) Sodium cacodylate;(867) Sodium chloride injection;(868) Sodium dehydrocholate;
(869) Sodium dextrothyroxine;(870) Sodium estrone;(871) Sodium fluorescein -- See exceptions;(872) Sodium fluoride -- See exceptions;
(873) Sodium iothalamate;(873.5) Sodium nitroprusside;(873.7) Sodium phenylbutyrate;(873.8) Sodium picosulfate;
(874) Sodium polystyrene sulfonate;(875) Sodium propionated vaginal cream;(876) Sodium sulfacetamide;(877) Sodium sulfadiazine;
(878) Sodium sulfobromophthalein;(879) Sodium sulfoxone;(880) Sodium tetradecyl;(880.5) Sodium thiosulfate;(881) Sodium tyropanoate;
(881.03) Sofosbuvir;(881.05) Solifenacin;(881.1) Somatrem;(882) Somatropin;(882.3) Sonidegib;(882.5) Sorafenib;
(883) Sorbus extract;(883.5) Sotalol;(883.8) Sparfloxacin;(884) Sparteine;(885) Spectinomycin;(885.5) Spinosad;(886) Spirapril;
(887) Spironolactone;(888) Staphage lysate bacterial antigen;(889) Staphylococcus and streptococcus vaccine;
(890) Staphylococcus toxoid;(890.5) Stavudine;(891) Stibophen;(892) Stinging insect antigens -- Combined;
(893) Stockes expectorant;(894) Stramonium;(895) Streptococcus antigen;(896) Streptokinase-streptodornase;
(897) Streptomycin;(898) Strontium -- See exceptions;(899) Strophanthin-G;(900) Strychnine -- See exceptions;(901) Succimer;
(902) Succinylchloline;(903) Succinylsulfathiazole;(903.1) Sucralfate;(903.15) Sucroferric oxyhydroxide;(903.17) Sugammadex;(903.2) Sulconazole;
(904) Sulfabenzamide vaginal preparations;(905) Sulfacetamide;(906) Sulfachlorpyridazine;(907) Sulfacytine;(908) Sulfadiazine;(909) Sulfadimethoxine;

148

(909.1) Sulfadoxine;(910) Sulfaethidole;(911) Sulfaguanidine;(912) Sulfamerazine;(913) Sulfameter;(914) Sulfamethazine;(915) Sulfamethizole;(916) Sulfamethoxazole;

(917) Sulfamethoxypyridazine;(918) Sulfanilamide;(919) Sulfaphenazole;(920) Reserved;(921) Sulfapyridine;(922) Sulfasalazine;

(922.5) Sulfathiazole;(923) Sulfinpyrazone;(924) Sulfisomidine;(925) Sulfisoxazole;(926) Sulfur thioglycerol;(927) Sulindac;(927.5) Sumatriptan;(927.7) Sunitinib;

(928) Superinone;(928.1) Suprofen;(929) Sutilains;(930) Syrosingopine;(930.5) Tacrine;(930.7) Tacrolimus;(930.9) Tadalafil;(930.93) Tafluprost;

(930.97) Tagliglucerase alfa;(930.98) Talimogene;(931) Tamoxifen;(931.1) Tamsulosin;(931.2) Tasimelteon;(931.21) Tavaborole;

(931.3) Tazarotene;(931.35) Tazobactam;(931.37) Tbo-filgrastim;(931.5) Technetium;(931.52) Tedizolid;(931.53) Teduglutide;(931.55) Tegaserod;

(931.553) Telaprevir;(931.555) Telavancin;(931.56) Telbivudine;(931.57) Telithromycin;(931.6) Telmisartan;(931.7) Temafloxacin;

(931.75) Temozolomide;(931.77) Temsirolimus;(931.8) Teniposide;(931.85) Terazosin;(931.9) Tenofovir;(931.95) Terbinafine -- See exceptions;

(932) Terbutaline;(932.05) Terconazole;(932.1) Terfenadine;(932.2) Teriflunomide;(932.3) Teriparatide;(933) Terpin hydrate with codeine;(934) Reserved;

(935) Tesamorelin;(936) Tetanus and diphtheria toxoids;(937) Tetanus antitoxin;(938) Tetanus immune globulin;

(939) Tetanus toxoids;(939.5) Tetrabenazine;(940) Tetracaine;(941) Tetracycline;(942) Tetraethylammonium chloride;

(943) Tetrahydrozoline -- See exceptions;(943.5) Thalidomide;(944) Thallous chloride;(945) Theobromide;(945.5) Theobromine;

(946) Theobromine magnesium oleate;(947) Theophylline -- See exceptions;(948) Theophylline sodium glycinate;(949) Thiabendazole;

(950) Thiamylal;(951) Thiethylperazine;(952) Thiopropazate;(953) Thioguanine;(954) Thioridazine;(955) Thiosalicylate;(956) Thiotepa;(957) Thiothixene;

(958) Thiphenamil;(959) Thrombin;(960) Thyroglobulin;(961) Thyroid;(962) Thyrotropin;(963) Thyroxine;(964) Thyroxine fraction;(964.5) Tiagabine;(964.7) Ticagrelor;

(965) Ticarcillin;(965.5) Ticlopidine;(966) Ticrynafen;(966.3) Tigecycline;(966.6) Tiludronate;(967) Timolol;(967.1) Tinidazole;(967.2) Tinzaparin;

(967.3) Tioconazole -- See exceptions;(967.5) Tiopronin;(967.55) Tiotropium;(967.56) Tipiracil;(967.57) Tipranavir;(967.6) Tirofiban;(967.7) Tizanidine;

(968) Tobramycin;(968.1) Tocainide;(969) Tocamphyl;(969.6) Tocilizumab;(969.8) Tofacitinib;(970) Tolazamide;(971) Tolazoline;(972) Tolbutamide;

(972.5) Tolcapone;(973) Tolmetin;(973.05) Tolterodine;(973.07) Tolvaptan;(973.1) Topiramate;(973.3) Topotecan;(973.4) Toremifene;(973.5) Torsemide;

(973.6) Trabectedin;(973.7) Trametinib;(973.8) Trandolapril;(973.9) Tranexamic acid;(974) Tranylcypromine;(974.4) Travoprost;(974.5) Trazodone;

(974.7) Treprostinil;(975) Tretinoin;(976) Triamcinolone;(977) Triamterene;(978) Trichlormethiazide;(979) Trichloroacetic acid -- See exceptions;

(980) Trichloroethylene -- See exceptions;(981) Trichlobisonium;(982) Triclofos;(983) Tridihexethyl chloride;(983.1) Trientine;(984) Triethanolamine polypeptides;

(985) Triethylenethiophosphoramide;(986) Trifluoperazine;(987) Triflupromazine;(988) Trifluridine;(989) Trihexyphenidyl;

(990) Triiodothyronine;(990.1) Trilostane;(991) Trimeprazine;(992) Trimethadione;(993) Trimethaphan cansylate;(994) Trimethobenzamide;(995) Trimethoprim;

(995.5) Trimetrexate;(996) Trimipramine;(997) Triolein;(998) Trioxsalen;(999) Tripelennamine -- See exceptions;(1000) Triphenyltetrazolium;(1001) Triple sulfas;

(1002) Triprolidine -- See exceptions;(1002.5) Triptorelin;(1003) Trisulfapyrimidines;(1003.5) Troglitazone;(1004) Troleandomycin;(1005) Trolnitrate;

(1006) Tromethamine;(1007) Tropicamide;(1007.3) Trospium;(1007.5) Trovafloxacin;(1008) Trypsin;(1009) Trypsin-chymotrypsin;(1010) Tuaminoheptane;

(1011) Tuberculin, Purified protein derivatives;(1012) Tuberculin tine test;(1013) Tuberculin, Old;(1016) Typhoid and paratyphoid vaccine;

(1017) Typhus vaccine;(1018) Tyropanoate;(1018.5) Ulipristal;(1018.8) Umeclidinium;(1019) Undecoylium;(1019.5) Unoprostone;(1020) Uracil;

(1021) Urea -- See exceptions;(1021.1) Uridine;(1021.3) Urofollitropin;(1021.5) Ursodiol;(1021.6) Ustekinumab;(1021.7) Valacyclovir;

(1021.8) Valdecoxib;(1022) Valethamate;(1022.2) Valganciclovir;(1023) Valproate;(1024) Valproic acid -- See exceptions;(1024.3) Valrubicin;

(1024.5) Valsartan;(1025) Vancomycin;(1025.2) Vandetanib;(1025.5) Vardenafil;(1025.7) Varenicline;(1026) Vasopressin;

(1027) VDRL antigen;(1027.1) Vecuronium bromide;(1027.53) Velpatasvir;(1027.55) Vemuranfenib;(1027.57) Venetoclax;(1027.6) Venlafaxine;(1027.7) Verapamil;

(1028) Veratrum viride;(1029) Versenate;(1029.5) Verteporfin;(1030) Vidarabine;(1030.3) Vigabatrin;(1030.4) Vilanterol;(1030.5) Vilazodone;(1031) Vinblastine;

(1032) Vincristine;(1032.5) Vinorelbine;(1033) Vinyl ethyl -- See exceptions;(1034) Viomycin;(1034.5) Vismodegib;(1035) Vitamin K;(1036) Vitamin B12 injection;

(1037) Vitamine with fluoride;(1037.3) Vorapaxar;(1037.5) Voriconazole;(1037.7) Vorinostat;(1037.8) Vortioxetine;(1038) Warfarin;(1039) Wargarin;(1039.1) Xylocaine;

(1040) Yellow fever vaccine;(1041) Yohimbine;(1042) 4-chloro-3, 5-xylenol -- See exceptions;(1042.01) Zafirlukast;(1042.02) Zalcitabine;(1042.03) Zanamivir;(1042.05) Zidovudine;(1042.4) Zileuton;(1042.7)

 Zinc acetate -- See exceptions;(1042.75) Ziprasidone;(1042.78) Ziv-aflibercept;(1042.8) Zoledronic Acid;(1042.9) Zolmitriptan;(1042.92) Zonisamide;

(1043) Devices that require a prescription:

(A) Cellulose, Oxadized, Regenerated (surgical absorbable hemostat) -- See exceptions;

(B) Diaphragms for vaginal use;

(C) Hemodialysis solutions;

(D) Hemodialysis kits;

(E) Lippes loop intrauterine;

(F) Saf-T-Coil intrauterine device;

(G) Intrauterine devices, All;

(H) Absorbable hemostat;

(I) Gonorrhea test kit.

(b.1) A "restricted dangerous drug" means any other drug or substance declared by the General Assembly to have no medical use, which cannot be legally prescribed by a practitioner, and which cannot be manufactured, grown, produced, distributed, used, or otherwise possessed in this state; to include any of the following drugs, chemicals, or substances; salts, isomers, esters, ethers, or derivatives of such drugs, chemicals, or substances which have essentially the same pharmacological action; and all other salts, isomers, esters, ethers, and compounds of such drugs, chemicals, or substances unless specifically exempted, identified as "restricted dangerous drugs":

(1) Salvinorin A; and

(2) Salvia divinorum -- except as otherwise provided for in paragraph (4.3) of Code Section 16-13-72.

This subsection shall not prohibit a person from possessing a restricted dangerous drug for the purpose of conducting research approved by the federal Food and Drug Administration.

(c) The following are exceptions to and exemptions from subsection (b) of this Code section:

(0.5) Adapalene -- when used with a strength up to 0.1 percent in a topical skin product;

(1) Atropine sulfate -- where the oral dose is less than 1/200 gr. per unit;

(2) Bacitracin cream or ointment for topical use;

(3) Belladonna or belladonna alkaloids when in combination with other drugs and the dosage unit is less than 0.1 mg. of the alkaloids or its equivalent;

(3.5) Bentoquatam -- when used with a strength of 5 percent or less in topical preparations;

(4) Beta carotene -- all forms occurring in food products or lotions;

(5) Bromelain, pancreatic enzymes, trypsin and bile extract -- when labeled properly as digestive aids with appropriate dosage and in compliance with FDA labeling and restrictions;

(6) Brompheniramine -- where a single dosage unit is 4 mg. or less but with no more than 3 mg. of the dextrorotary optical isomer of racemic brompheniramine per released dose;

(6.1) Budesonide -- when used as a nasal spray in doses up to 32 mcg per spray;

(6.2) Butenafine -- when used with a strength of 1 percent or less as a topical preparation;

(6.4) Butoconazole -- when used with a strength up to 2 percent in a vaginal preparation;

(6.45) Capsaicin -- when in an external analgesic with concentration of 0.25 percent or less;

(6.5) Cetirizine -- when a single dosage unit is either 1mg per 1ml or less or 10mg or less;

(6.7) Chlorhexadine -- when used with a strength up to 4 percent in a topical skin product;

(7) Chlorpheniramine -- where a single dosage unit is 12 mg. or less;

(7.1) Cimetidine -- when a single dosage unit is 200 mg. or less;

(7.3) Clemastine -- where a single dose is 1.34 mg. or less;

(7.5) Clotrimazole -- when a single vaginal insert is 200 mg. or less or with a strength up to 2 percent in a topical skin, topical vaginal, or vaginal product;

(7.8) Cromolyn -- when used as cromolyn sodium in a nasal solution of 4 percent or less in strength;

(7.9) Dexbrompheniramine -- when a single dosage unit is 6 mg. or less;

(8) Diphenhydramine -- up to 12.5 mg. in each 5 cc's when used in cough preparations and up to 50 mg. per single dose when used as a nighttime sleep aid or used as an antihistamine and labeled in compliance with FDA requirements;

(8.5) Docosanol -- when used in 10 percent topical preparation to treat fever blisters, cold sores, or fever blisters and cold sores.

(9) Doxylamine succinate -- where a single dosage form is 25 mg. or less and when labeled to be used as a nighttime sedative;

(9.3) Edetate -- when used in any form other than an oral or parenteral;

(9.4) Esomeprazole -- when a single dosage unit is 20 mg. or less;

(9.5) Famotidine -- when a single dosage unit is 20 mg. or less;

(9.6) Fexofenadine -- when packaged for distribution as an over-the-counter (OTC) drug product;

(9.7) Fluoride -- when used with a strength up to 1,500 parts per million in an oral care or dentifrice product;

(9.75) Fluticasone -- when available in a device that delivers a metered spray of 0.05 mg and to be used for the temporary relief of symptoms due to hay fever or other upper respiratory allergies;

(9.8) Glycine -- when used with a strength up to 1.5 percent in an irrigation solution, when used in a topical skin product;

(10) Hydrocortisone topical skin preparations up to 1.0 percent in strength;

(11) Hydroxocobalamin, riboflavin, niacinamide, ergocalciferol (maximum of 400 I.U. per day), Folic acid (maximum of 0.4 mg. per day), and magnesium gluconate -- when as a source of vitamins and dietary supplement but must bear such labels and adhere to such restrictions of FDA regulations;

(11.1) Ibuprofen -- where a single dose is 200 mg. or less;

(11.6) Reserved;

(12) Insulin -- all injectable products which do not require a prescription drug order and bear a label which indicates "Rx Use Only" or are otherwise listed under subsection (b) of this Code section; and no injectable insulin product may be sold except by a pharmacy issued a permit by the State Board of Pharmacy or by a medical practitioner authorized to dispense medications;

(12.3) Ketoconazole -- when used with a strength of 1 percent or less in topical preparations;

(12.5) Ketoprofen -- when a single dosage unit is 12.5 mg. or less;

(12.7) Ketotifen -- when used with a strength of 0.025 percent or less in an ophthalmic solution;

(12.9) Lansoprazole -- when a single dosage unit is 15 mg. or less;

(13) Lidocaine topical ointment, 25 mg./gm. or less;

(13.5) Loperamide -- where a single dose is either 1 mg. per 5 ml. or 2 mg. per dosage unit;

(13.7) Loratadine -- when used in a single dose of 10 mg. or less, including doses used in combination with other drugs provided for under this subsection;

(14) Meclizine -- 25 mg. or less;

(14.1) Miconazole -- when used as antifungal powder or cream, or both, and containing not more than 4 percent of miconazole, or when used as a vaginal insert and containing not more than 1,200 mg. of miconazole;

(14.2) Minoxidil -- when used with a strength of 5 percent or less in topical preparations;

(14.25) Naloxone -- shall also be exempt from subsections (a) and (b) of this Code section when used for drug overdose prevention and when supplied by a dispenser as follows:

(A) Nasal adaptor rescue kits containing a minimum of two prefilled 2 ml. luer-lock syringes with each containing 1 mg./ml. of naloxone;

(B) Prepackaged nasal spray rescue kits containing single-use spray devices with each containing a minimum of 4 mg./0.1 ml. of naloxone;

(C) Muscle rescue kits containing a 10 ml. multidose fliptop vial or two 1 ml. vials with a strength of 0.4 mg./ml. of naloxone; or

(D) Prepackaged kits of two muscle autoinjectors with each containing a minimum of 0.4 mg./ml. of naloxone;

(14.3) Naphazoline -- when used in an ophthalmic solution in a concentration of 0.027 percent or less in combination with a pheniramine concentration of 0.315 percent or less;

(14.5) Naproxen -- where a single dosage unit is 220 mg. or less;

(15) Neomycin sulfate ointment or cream for topical use;

(15.5) Nicotine resin complex (polacrilex) -- when used as oral chewing gum where a single dose (piece of gum) is 4 mg. or less;

(15.55) Nicotine transdermal system -- when used in a strength of 21 mg. or less per transdermal patch (transdermal delivery system);

(16) Nitrous oxide -- air products suppliers shall not sell medical grade nitrous oxide to other than licensed practitioners or medical suppliers; industrial grade nitrous oxide shall only be sold when mixed with not less than 100 parts per million of sulfur dioxide and used as a fuel additive for combustion engines or when used in industrial laboratory equipment;

(16.3) Nizatidine -- when a single dosage unit is 75 mg. or less;

(16.8) Nonoxynol -- when used with a strength up to 12.5 percent or 1 gram per dose in a vaginal product;

(16.9) Omeprazole -- when a single dosage unit is 20.6 mg. or less;

(16.95) Orlistat -- when a single dosage unit is 60 mg. or less;

(16.97) Oxybutynin -- when a single dose is delivered as 3.9 mg. per day using a transdermal system patch;

(17) Oxygen -- compressed oxygen which is not labeled "CAUTION: Federal law prohibits dispensing without prescription" or similar wording;

(17.3) Permethrin -- when used as a topical preparation in a strength of 1 percent or less;

(17.5) Phenazopyridine -- where a single dose is 100 mg. or less, as approved by the federal Food and Drug Administration;

(18) Pheniramine -- when the oral dose is 25 mg. or less, or when used in an ophthalmic solution in a concentration of 0.315 percent or less in combination with a naphazoline concentration of 0.027 percent or less;

(19) Polymyxin B when in combination with other drugs in an ointment or cream for topical use;

(20) Any potassium electrolyte when manufactured for use as a dietary supplement, food additive for industrial, scientific, or commercial use, or when added to other drug products when the product is not intended as a potassium supplement but must bear such labels and adhere to such restrictions of FDA regulations;

(21) Povidone -- Iodine solutions and suspensions;

(22) Reserved;

(23) Reserved;

(23.5) Ranitidine -- when a single dosage unit is 150 mg. or less;

(24) Rutin -- where the dosage unit is less than 60 mg.;

(25) Selenium sulfide suspension 1 percent or less in strength;

(25.1) Strychnine -- when used in combination with other active ingredients in a rodent killer, and when not bearing a label containing the words "CAUTION: Federal law prohibits dispensing without prescription" or other similar wording;

(25.5) Terbinafine -- when used with a strength of 1 percent or less in a topical antifungal cream;

(26) Tetrahydrozoline for ophthalmic or topical use;

(27) Theophylline preparations alone or in combination with other drugs prepared for and approved for OTC (over the counter) sale by FDA; example -- tedral tablets (plain) or oral suspension;

(27.5) Tioconazole -- when used with a strength of 1 percent or less in topical preparations or when used with a strength of 6.5 percent or less in vaginal preparations;

(28) Tripelennamine cream or ointment for topical use;

(28.5) Triprolidine -- when a single dose is 5 mg. or less when combined in the same preparation as one or more other drug products for use as an antihistamine or decongestant or an antihistamine and decongestant;

(29) Urea -- except when the manufacturer's label contains the wording "CAUTION: Federal law prohibits dispensing without prescription" or similar wording;

(29.5) Zinc acetate -- when used in topical preparations;

(30) Any drug approved by FDA for animal use and the package does not bear the statement "CAUTION: Federal law prohibits dispensing without prescription" or similar wording; or

(31) Loperamide Oral Liquid (1.00 mg/5.00 ml).

(d) The following list of compounds or preparations may be purchased without a prescription, provided the products are manufactured for industrial, scientific, or commercial sale or use, unless they are intended for human use or contain the label "CAUTION: Federal law prohibits dispensing without prescription" or similar wording:

(1) Aminosalicylate;(2) Aminosalicylate calcium;(3) Aminosalicylate potassium;

(4) Aminosalicylate sodium;(5) Aminosalicylic acid;(6) Barium;

(7) Beta-carotene;(8) Bismuth sodium tartrate;(9) Cadmium sulfide;

(10) Calcium disodium edetate;(11) Cellulose, Oxadized, Regenerated;(12) Chlorabutanol;

(13) Chloranil;(14) Chloroacetic acid;(15) Chloroform;

(16) Colchicine;(17) Dapsone;(18) Dimethyl sulfoxide;

(19) Disodium edetate;(20) Edetate disodium;(21) Ether;(22) Ethoxazene;

(23) Ethyl chloride;(24) Fluoride;(25) Formaldehyde;(26) Gold thiosulfate;

(27) Hexachlorophene;(28) Iodobenzoic acid;(29) Iopanoic acid;(30) Lindane;

(31) Lithium carbonate;(32) Mandelic acid;(33) Mannitol;(34) Mercury bichloride;

(35) Nitroprusside;(36) Potassium aminosalicylate;(37) Potassium p-aminobenzoate;

(37.5) Potassium perchlorate;(38) Potassium permanganate;(39) Resorcinol monoacetate;

(40) Selenium sulfide;(41) Sodium biphosphate;(42) Sodium fluorescein;

(43) Sodium fluoride;(44) Strontium;(45) Trichloroacetic acid;(46) Trichloroethylene;

(47) Valproic acid;(48) Vinyl ether;(49) 4-chloro-3, 5-xylenol.

(e) The State Board of Pharmacy may delete drugs from the dangerous drug list set forth in this Code section. In making such deletions the board shall consider, with respect to each drug, the following factors:

(1) The actual or relative potential for abuse;

(2) The scientific evidence of its pharmacological effect, if known;

(3) The state of current scientific knowledge regarding the drug;

(4) The history and current pattern of abuse, if any;

(5) The scope, duration, and significance of abuse;

(6) Reserved;

(7) The potential of the drug to produce psychic or physiological dependence liability; and

(8) Whether such drug is included under the federal Food, Drug, and Cosmetic Act, 52 Stat. 1040 (1938), 21 U.S.C. Section 301, et seq., as amended.

§ 16-13-71.1. "Anabolic steroid" defined

Repealed by Ga. L. 1991, p. 312, § 3, effective April 4, 1991.

§ 16-13-72. Sale, distribution, or possession of dangerous drugs

Except as provided for in this article, it shall be unlawful for any person, firm, corporation, or association to sell, give away, barter, exchange, distribute, or possess in this state any dangerous drug, except under the following conditions:

(1) A drug manufacturer, wholesaler, distributor, or supplier holding a license or registration issued in accordance with the Federal Food, Drug, and Cosmetic Act and authorizing the holder to possess dangerous drugs may possess dangerous drugs within this state but may not distribute, sell, exchange, give away, or by any other means supply dangerous drugs without a permit issued by the State Board of Pharmacy. Any drug manufacturer, wholesaler, distributor, or supplier holding a permit issued by the State Board of Pharmacy may sell, give away, exchange, or distribute dangerous drugs within this state, but only to a pharmacy, pharmacist, a practitioner of the healing arts, and educational institutions licensed by the state, or to a drug wholesaler, distributor, or supplier, and only if such distribution is made in the normal course of employment;

(2) A pharmacy may possess dangerous drugs, but the same shall not be sold, given away, bartered, exchanged, or distributed except by a licensed pharmacist in accordance with this article;

(3) A pharmacist may possess dangerous drugs but may sell, give away, barter, exchange, or distribute the same only when he compounds or dispenses the same upon the prescription of a practitioner of the healing arts. No such prescription shall be refilled except upon the authorization of the practitioner who prescribed it;

(4) A practitioner of the healing arts may possess dangerous drugs and may sell, give away, barter, exchange, or distribute the same in accordance with Code Section 16-13-74;

(4.1) A physician in conformity with Code Section 43-34-23 may delegate to a nurse or a physician assistant the authority to possess vaccines and such other drugs as specified by the physician for adverse reactions to those vaccines, and a nurse or physician assistant may possess such drugs pursuant to that delegation; provided, however, that nothing in this paragraph shall be construed to restrict any authority of nurses or physician assistants existing under other provisions of law;

(4.2) A registered professional nurse licensed under Article 1 of Chapter 26 of Title 43 who is employed or engaged by a licensed home health agency may possess sterile saline, sterile water, and diluted heparin for use as intravenous maintenance for use in a home health setting, and such nurse may administer such items to patients of the home health agency upon the order of a licensed physician. The State Board of Pharmacy shall be authorized to adopt regulations governing the storage, quantity, use, and administration of such items; provided, however, nothing in this paragraph or in such regulations shall be construed to restrict any authority of nurses existing under other provisions of law;

(4.3) Possession, planting, cultivation, growing, or harvesting of Salvia divinorum or Salvia divinorum A strictly for aesthetic, landscaping, or decorative purposes;

(5) A manufacturer's sales representative may distribute a dangerous drug as a complimentary sample only upon the written request of a practitioner. The request must be made for each distribution and shall contain the names and addresses of the supplier and the requestor and the name and quantity of the specific dangerous drug requested. The written request shall be preserved by the manufacturer for a period of two years; and

(6) Such person, firm, corporation, or association shall keep a complete and accurate record of all dangerous drugs received, purchased, manufactured, sold, dispensed, or otherwise disposed of and shall maintain such records for at least two years or in conformance with any other state or federal law or rule issued by the State Board of Pharmacy.

§ 16-13-72.1. Revocation of dangerous drug permit; forfeiture

(a) A permit issued by the State Board of Pharmacy under paragraph (1) of Code Section 16-13-72 may be suspended or revoked by the State Board of Pharmacy upon a finding that the drug manufacturer, wholesaler, distributor, or supplier:

(1) Has furnished false or fraudulent material information in any application filed under this article;

(2) Has been convicted of a felony under any state or federal law relating to any controlled substance or has been convicted of a felony or misdemeanor under any state or federal law relating to any dangerous drug;

(3) Has violated any provision of this article or the rules and regulations promulgated under this article; or

(4) Has failed to maintain sufficient controls against diversion of dangerous drugs into other than legitimate medical, scientific, or industrial channels.

(b) The State Board of Pharmacy may limit revocation or suspension of a permit to the particular dangerous drug with respect to which grounds for revocation or suspension exist.

(c) Instead of suspending or revoking a permit as authorized by subsection (a) or (b) of this Code section, the State Board of Pharmacy may impose a fine in an amount not to exceed $1,500.00.

(d) If the State Board of Pharmacy suspends or revokes a permit, all dangerous drugs owned or possessed by the permittee at the time of suspension or the effective date of the revocation order shall be placed under seal. No disposition may be made of drugs under seal until the time for taking an appeal has elapsed or until all appeals have been concluded unless a court, upon application therefor, orders the sale of perishable drugs and the deposit of the proceeds of the sale with the court. Upon a revocation order becoming final, all dangerous drugs shall be forfeited to the state.

§ 16-13-73. Labeling prescription containers of dangerous drugs

(a) Whenever a pharmacist dispenses a dangerous drug, he shall, in each case, place upon the container the following information:
(1) Name of the patient;
(2) Name of the practitioner prescribing the drug;
(3) The expiration date, if any, of the drug;
(4) Name and address of the pharmacy from which the drug was dispensed; and
(5) The date of the prescription.
(b) Any pharmacist who dispenses a dangerous drug and fails to place the label required by subsection (a) of this Code section upon the container of such drug shall be guilty of a misdemeanor.

§ 16-13-74. Written prescriptions for dangerous drugs; content; signature

(a) All written prescription drug orders for dangerous drugs shall be dated as of, and be signed on, the date when issued and shall bear the name and address of the patient, together with the name and strength of the drug, the quantity to be dispensed, complete directions for administration, the printed name, address, and telephone number of the practitioner, and the number of permitted refills. A prescription drug order for a dangerous drug is not required to bear the DEA permit number of the prescribing practitioner. A prescription drug order for a dangerous drug may be prepared by the practitioner or the practitioner's agent. The practitioner's signature must appear on each prescription prepared by the practitioner or the practitioner's agent and the nature of the practitioner's signature must meet the guidelines set forth in Chapter 4 of Title 26, the regulations promulgated by the State Board of Pharmacy, or both such guidelines and regulations. Any practitioner who shall dispense dangerous drugs shall comply with the provisions of Code Section 16-13-73.
(b) Any practitioner of the healing arts who fails to comply with subsection (a) of this Code section shall be guilty of a misdemeanor.

§ 16-13-75. Drugs to be kept in original container; exception

(a) Possession and control of controlled substances or dangerous drugs by anyone other than the individuals specified in Code Section 16-13-35 or 16-13-72 shall be legal only if such drugs are in the original container in which they were dispensed by the pharmacist or the practitioner of the healing arts and are labeled according to Code Section 26-3-8.
(b) The possession, filling, and use of canisters for remote automated medication systems pursuant to subsection (i) of Code Section 16-13-41 shall not be considered a violation of this Code section.

§ 16-13-76. Use of fictitious name or false address when obtaining drugs

No person shall obtain or attempt to obtain any dangerous drug by use of a fictitious name or by the giving of a false address.

§ 16-13-77. Applicability of article to practitioner of the healing arts

Nothing in this article shall be construed to prohibit the administration of dangerous drugs by or under the direction of a practitioner of the healing arts.

§ 16-13-78. Obtaining or attempting to obtain dangerous drugs by fraud, forgery, or concealment of material fact

(a) No person shall obtain or attempt to obtain any dangerous drug or attempt to procure the administration of any such drug by:
(1) Fraud, deceit, misrepresentation, or subterfuge;
(2) The forgery or alteration of any prescription or of any written order;
(3) The concealment of a material fact; or
(4) The use of a false name or the giving of a false address.
(b) Any person violating subsection (a) of this Code section shall be guilty of a misdemeanor.
(c) Nothing in this Code section shall apply to drug manufacturers or their agents or employees when such manufacturers or their agents or employees are authorized to engage in and are actually engaged in investigative activities directed toward the safeguarding of the manufacturer's trademark.

§ 16-13-78.1. Prescribing or ordering dangerous drugs

(a) No person shall prescribe or order the dispensing of a dangerous drug, except a registered practitioner who is:
(1) Licensed or otherwise authorized by this state to prescribe dangerous drugs;
(2) Acting in the usual course of his professional practice; and
(3) Prescribing or ordering such dangerous drug for a legitimate medical purpose.
(b) Any person violating subsection (a) of this Code section shall be guilty of a misdemeanor.

§ 16-13-78.2. Possession, manufacture, delivery, distribution, or sale of counterfeit substances

Except as authorized by this article, it is unlawful for any person to possess, have under his control, manufacture, deliver, distribute, dispense, administer, sell, or possess with intent to distribute a counterfeit substance. Any person who violates this Code section shall be guilty of a misdemeanor.

§ 16-13-79. Violations

(a) Except as provided in subsections (b), (c), and (d) of this Code section, any person who violates this article shall be guilty of a misdemeanor.
(b) Any person who distributes or possesses with the intent to distribute nitrous oxide for any use other than for a medical treatment prescribed by the order of a licensed medical practitioner, except as provided for by paragraph (16) of subsection (c) of Code Section 16-13-71, shall be guilty of a felony and upon conviction thereof shall be punished by imprisonment for not less than one year nor more than three years or by a fine not to exceed $5,000.00 or both.
(c) Any person who distributes or possesses with the intent to distribute to any person under 18 years of age nitrous oxide for any use other than for a medical treatment prescribed by the order of a licensed medical practitioner, except as provided for by paragraph (16) of subsection (c) of Code Section 16-13-71, shall be guilty of a felony and upon conviction thereof shall be punished for not less than two years nor more than six years or by a fine not to exceed $10,000.00 or both.
(d) This article shall not apply to any person who possesses, distributes, sells, or uses nitrous oxide for food preparation in a restaurant, for food service, or in household products.
(e) Any person who knowingly distributes or resells any nonprescription injectable insulin product which was first obtained through an over-the-counter sale made to a patient from any pharmacy, practitioner, or other source shall be guilty of a misdemeanor. All such injectable insulin distributed or sold in this manner is considered to be an adulterated dangerous drug and unsalable, making it subject to seizure under the laws of this state.

§ 16-13-90. "Model glue" defined

As used in this article, the term "model glue" means any glue, cement, solvent, or chemical substance containing one or more of the following chemicals: acetone, amyl chloride (iso- and tertiary), benzene, carbon disulfide, carbon tetrachloride, chloroform, ether, ethyl acetate, ethyl alcohol, ethylene dichloride, isopropyl acetate, isopropyl alcohol, isopropyl ether, methyl acetate, methyl alcohol, propylene dichloride, propylene oxide, trichlorethylene, amyl acetate, amyl alcohol, butyl acetate, butyl alcohol, butyl ether, diethylcarbonate, diethylene oxide (dioxane), dipropyl ketone, ethyl butyrate, ethylene glycol monoethyl ether (cellosolve), ethylene glycol monomethyl ether acetate (methyl cellosolve acetate), isobutyl alcohol, methyl amyl acetate, methyl amyl alcohol, methyl isobutyl ketone, or toluene.

§ 16-13-91. Intentional inhalation of model glue; application of article to anesthesia

No person shall, for the purpose of causing a condition of intoxication, stupefaction, euphoria, excitement, exhilaration, or dulling of the senses or nervous system, intentionally smell or inhale the fumes from any model glue, provided that this Code section shall not apply to the inhalation of any anesthesia for medical or dental purposes.

§ 16-13-92. Possession, sale, or transfer of model glue

No person shall intentionally possess, buy, sell, transfer possession, or receive possession of any model glue for the purpose of violating or aiding another person to violate this article.

§ 16-13-93. Sale or transfer of model glue to minors

No person shall sell or transfer possession of any model glue to another person under 18 years of age, nor shall any person under 18 years of age possess or buy any model glue unless the purchase is for model building or other lawful use and the person under 18 years of age has in his possession and exhibits to the seller or transferor the written consent of his parent or legal guardian to make such purchase or take possession of the model glue, provided any minor who shall transfer possession of model glue to another minor for model building or other lawful purpose shall not be held criminally liable for failing to require exhibition of the written consent of the transferee-minor's parents or for failing to keep same available for inspection by law enforcement officials.

§ 16-13-94. Maintenance of records of sales to minors

The person making a sale or transfer of possession of model glue to a person under 18 years of age must require the purchaser to exhibit the written consent of his parent or guardian and the name and address of the consenting parent or guardian. All data required by this Code section shall be kept available by the seller for inspection by law enforcement officials for a period of six months.

§ 16-13-95. Effect of article on laws or ordinances of counties and municipalities

No provisions in this article shall be construed to repeal or limit laws or ordinances of the governing authority of any county or municipality regulating, restricting, or prohibiting the sale of model glue to any person under the age of 18, nor shall this article restrict the governing authority of any county or municipality from enacting ordinances or regulations governing the regulation of model glue not inconsistent with this article.

§ 16-13-96. Penalty for violation of article; separate offenses

Any person who violates this article shall be guilty of a misdemeanor. Each violation of this article shall be deemed a separate and distinct offense.

§ 16-13-110. Definitions

(a) As used in this article, the term:
(1) "Controlled substance" means any drug, substance, or immediate precursor included in the definition of the term "controlled substance" in paragraph (4) of Code Section 16-13-21.
(2) "Convicted" or "conviction" refers to a final conviction in a court of competent jurisdiction, or the acceptance of a plea of guilty or nolo contendere or affording of first offender treatment by a court of competent jurisdiction.
(3) "Licensed individual" means any individual to whom any department, agency, board, bureau, or other entity of state government has issued any license, permit, registration, certification, or other authorization to conduct a licensed occupation.
(4) "Licensed occupation" means any occupation, profession, business, trade, or other commercial activity which requires for its lawful conduct the issuance to an individual of any license, permit, registration, certification, or other authorization by any department, agency, board, bureau, or other entity of state government.
(5) "Licensing authority" means any department, agency, board, bureau, or other entity of state government which issues to individuals any license, permit, registration, certification, or other authorization to conduct a licensed occupation.
(6) "Marijuana" means any substance included in the definition of the term "marijuana" in paragraph (16) of Code Section 16-13-21.
(b) Without limiting the generality of the provisions of subsection (a) of this Code section, the practice of law shall constitute a licensed occupation for purposes of this article and the Supreme Court of Georgia shall be the licensing authority for the practice of law.

§ 16-13-111. Notification of conviction of licensed individual to licensing authority; reinstatement of license; imposition of more stringent sanctions

(a) Any licensed individual who is convicted under the laws of this state, the United States, or any other state of any criminal offense involving the manufacture, distribution, trafficking, sale, or possession of a controlled substance or marijuana shall notify the appropriate licensing authority of the conviction within ten days following the conviction.
(b) Upon being notified of a conviction of a licensed individual, the appropriate licensing authority shall suspend or revoke the license, permit, registration, certification, or other authorization to conduct a licensed occupation of such individual as follows:
(1) Upon the first conviction, the licensed individual shall have his or her license, permit, registration, certification, or other authorization to conduct a licensed occupation suspended for a period of not less than three months; provided, however, that in the case of a first conviction for a misdemeanor the licensing authority shall be authorized to impose a lesser sanction or no sanction upon the licensed individual; and
(2) Upon the second or subsequent conviction, the licensed individual shall have his or her license, permit, registration, certification, or other authorization to conduct a licensed occupation revoked.
(c) The failure of a licensed individual to notify the appropriate licensing authority of a conviction as required in subsection (a) of this Code section shall be considered grounds for revocation of his or her license, permit, registration, certification, or other authorization to conduct a licensed occupation.
(d) A licensed individual sanctioned under subsection (b) or (c) of this Code section may be entitled to reinstatement of his or her license, permit, registration, certification, or other authorization to conduct a licensed occupation upon successful completion of a drug abuse treatment and education program approved by the licensing authority.

(e) The suspension and revocation sanctions prescribed in this Code section are intended as minimum sanctions, and nothing in this Code section shall be construed to prohibit any licensing authority from establishing and implementing additional or more stringent sanctions for criminal offenses and other conduct involving the unlawful manufacture, distribution, trafficking, sale, or possession of a controlled substance or marijuana.

§ 16-13-112. Applicability of administrative procedures

Administrative procedures for the implementation of this article for each licensed occupation shall be governed by the appropriate provisions applicable to each licensing authority.

§ 16-13-113. Article as supplement to power of licensing authority

The provisions of this article shall be supplemental to and shall not operate to prohibit any licensing authority from acting pursuant to those provisions of law which may now or hereafter authorize other sanctions and actions for that particular licensing authority.

§ 16-13-114. Period of applicability of article

This article shall apply only with respect to criminal offenses committed on or after July 1, 1990; provided, however, that nothing in this Code section shall prevent any licensing authority from implementing sanctions additional to or other than those provided for in this article with respect to offenses committed prior to July 1, 1990.

CHAPTER 14. RACKETEER INFLUENCED AND CORRUPT ORGANIZATIONS

§ 16-14-1. Short title

This chapter shall be known and may be cited as the "Georgia RICO (Racketeer Influenced and Corrupt Organizations) Act."

§ 16-14-2. Findings and intent of General Assembly

(a) The General Assembly finds that a severe problem is posed in this state by the increasing sophistication of various criminal elements and the increasing extent to which the state and its citizens are harmed as a result of the activities of these elements.
(b) The General Assembly declares that the intent of this chapter is to impose sanctions against those who violate this chapter and to provide compensation to persons injured or aggrieved by such violations. It is not the intent of the General Assembly that isolated incidents of misdemeanor conduct or acts of civil disobedience be prosecuted under this chapter. It is the intent of the General Assembly, however, that this chapter apply to an interrelated pattern of criminal activity motivated by or the effect of which is pecuniary gain or economic or physical threat or injury. This chapter shall be liberally construed to effectuate the remedial purposes embodied in its operative provisions.

§ 16-14-3. Definitions

As used in this chapter, the term:
(1) "Civil forfeiture proceeding" shall have the same meaning as set forth in Code Section 9-16-2.
(2) "Criminal proceeding" means any criminal proceeding commenced by the Department of Law or the office of any district attorney under any provision of this chapter.
(3) "Enterprise" means any person, sole proprietorship, partnership, corporation, business trust, union chartered under the laws of this state, or other legal entity; or any unchartered union, association, or group of individuals associated in fact although not a legal entity; and it includes illicit as well as licit enterprises and governmental as well as other entities.
(4) "Pattern of racketeering activity" means:
(A) Engaging in at least two acts of racketeering activity in furtherance of one or more incidents, schemes, or transactions that have the same or similar intents, results, accomplices, victims, or methods of commission or otherwise are interrelated by distinguishing characteristics and are not isolated incidents, provided at least one of such acts occurred after July 1, 1980, and that the last of such acts occurred within four years, excluding any periods of imprisonment, after the commission of a prior act of racketeering activity; or
(B) Engaging in any one or more acts of domestic terrorism as described in subsection (a) of Code Section 16-4-10 or any criminal attempt, criminal solicitation, or criminal conspiracy related thereto.
(5) (A) "Racketeering activity" means to commit, to attempt to commit, or to solicit, coerce, or intimidate another person to commit any crime which is chargeable by indictment under the laws of this state involving:
(i) Unlawful distillation, manufacture, and transportation of alcoholic beverages in violation of Code Section 3-3-27;
(ii) Records and reports of currency transactions in violation of Article 11 of Chapter 1 of Title 7;
(iii) The "Georgia Uniform Securities Act of 2008" in violation of Chapter 5 of Title 10;
(iv) Homicide in violation of Article 1 of Chapter 5 of this title;
(v) Assault and battery in violation of Article 2 of Chapter 5 of this title;
(vi) Kidnapping, false imprisonment, and related offenses in violation of Article 3 of Chapter 5 of this title;
(vii) Prostitution, keeping a place of prostitution, pimping, pandering, and pandering by compulsion in violation of Code Sections 16-6-9 through 16-6-12 and 16-6-14;
(viii) Burglary in violation of Code Section 16-7-1;
(ix) Smash and grab burglary in violation of Code Section 16-7-2;
(x) Arson and explosives in violation of Article 3 of Chapter 7 of this title;
(xi) Bombs, explosives, and chemical and biological weapons in violation of Article 4 of Chapter 7 of this title;
(xii) Theft in violation of Article 1 of Chapter 8 of this title;
(xiii) Robbery in violation of Article 2 of Chapter 8 of this title;
(xiv) Criminal reproduction and sale of recorded material in violation of Article 3 of Chapter 8 of this title;
(xv) The "Georgia Residential Mortgage Fraud Act" in violation of Article 5 of Chapter 8 of this title;
(xvi) Forgery in any degree in violation of Code Section 16-9-1;
(xvii) Illegal use of financial transaction cards in violation of Code Sections 16-9-31, 16-9-32, 16-9-33, and 16-9-34;
(xviii) Use of an article with an altered identification mark in violation of Code Section 16-9-70;
(xix) The "Georgia Computer Systems Protection Act" in violation of Article 6 of Chapter 9 of this title;
(xx) Identity fraud in violation of Article 8 of Chapter 9 of this title;
(xxi) Bribery in violation of Code Section 16-10-2;
(xxii) False statements and writings or false lien statements against public officers or public employees in violation of Code Section 16-10-20 or 16-10-20.1;
(xxiii) Impersonating a public officer or employee in violation of Code Section 16-10-23;

(xxiv) Attempted murder or threatening of witnesses in official proceedings in violation of Code Section 16-10-32;

(xxv) Perjury and other related offenses in violation of Article 4 of Chapter 10 of this title;

(xxvi) Embracery in violation of Code Section 16-10-91;

(xxvii) Influencing witnesses in violation of Code Section 16-10-93;

(xxviii) Tampering with evidence in violation of Code Section 16-10-94;

(xxix) Intimidation or injury of grand or trial juror or court officer in violation of Code Section 16-10-97;

(xxx) Terroristic threats and acts in violation of Code Section 16-11-37;

(xxxi) The "Georgia Firearms and Weapons Act" in violation of Part 2 of Article 4 of Chapter 11 of this title;

(xxxii) Commercial gambling in violation of Code Section 16-12-22;

(xxxiii) Distributing obscene materials in violation of Code Section 16-12-80;

(xxxiv) The "Georgia Controlled Substances Act" in violation of Article 2 of Chapter 13 of this title;

(xxxv) The "Dangerous Drug Act" in violation of Article 3 of Chapter 13 of this title;

(xxxvi) Marijuana in violation of subsection (j) of Code Section 16-13-30;

(xxxvii) Payday loans in violation of Chapter 17 of this title;

(xxxviii) Insurance fraud in violation of Code Section 33-1-9;

(xxxix) Certain felonies involving certificates of title, security interest, or liens in violation of Code Section 40-3-90;

(xl) Removal or falsification of identification numbers in violation of Code Section 40-4-21;

(xli) Possession of motor vehicle parts from which the identification has been removed in violation of Code Section 40-4-22; or

(xlii) Article 8 of Chapter 5 of Title 16, relating to protection of elder persons.

(B) "Racketeering activity" shall also mean any act or threat involving murder, kidnapping, gambling, arson, robbery, theft, receipt of stolen property, bribery, extortion, obstruction of justice, dealing in narcotic or dangerous drugs, or dealing in securities which is chargeable under the laws of the United States, any territory of the United States, or any state and which is punishable by imprisonment for more than one year.

(C) "Racketeering activity" shall also mean any conduct defined as "racketeering activity" under 18 U.S.C. Section 1961 (1), any violation of 18 U.S.C. Section 1028, or any violation of 31 U.S.C. Sections 5311 through 5330.

(6) "Real property" means any real property situated in this state or any interest in such real property, including, but not limited to, any lease of or mortgage upon such real property.

§ 16-14-4. Prohibited activities

(a) It shall be unlawful for any person, through a pattern of racketeering activity or proceeds derived therefrom, to acquire or maintain, directly or indirectly, any interest in or control of any enterprise, real property, or personal property of any nature, including money.

(b) It shall be unlawful for any person employed by or associated with any enterprise to conduct or participate in, directly or indirectly, such enterprise through a pattern of racketeering activity.

(c) It shall be unlawful for any person to conspire or endeavor to violate any of the provisions of subsection (a) or (b) of this Code section. A person violates this subsection when:

(1) He or she together with one or more persons conspires to violate any of the provisions of subsection (a) or (b) of this Code section and any one or more of such persons commits any overt act to effect the object of the conspiracy; or

(2) He or she endeavors to violate any of the provisions of subsection (a) or (b) of this Code section and commits any overt act to effect the object of the endeavor.

§ 16-14-5. Criminal penalties for violation of Code Section 16-14-4

(a) Any person convicted of the offense of engaging in activity in violation of Code Section 16-14-4 shall be guilty of a felony and shall be punished by not less than five nor more than 20 years' imprisonment or the fine specified in subsection (b) of this Code section, or both.

(b) In lieu of any fine otherwise authorized by law, any person convicted of the offense of engaging in conduct in violation of Code Section 16-14-4 may be sentenced to pay a fine that does not exceed the greater of $25,000.00 or three times the amount of any pecuniary value gained by him or her from such violation.

(c) The court shall hold a hearing to determine the amount of the fine authorized by subsection (b) of this Code section.

(d) For the purposes of subsection (b) of this Code section, the term "pecuniary value" means:

(1) Anything of value in the form of money, a negotiable instrument, a commercial interest, or anything else, the primary significance of which is economic advantage; or

(2) Any other property or service that has a value in excess of $100.00.

§ 16-14-6. Civil remedies

(a) Any superior court may, after making due provisions for the rights of innocent persons, enjoin violations of Code Section 16-14-4 by issuing appropriate orders and judgments, including, but not limited to:

(1) Ordering any defendant to divest himself or herself of any interest in any enterprise, real property, or personal property;

(2) Imposing reasonable restrictions upon the future activities or investments of any defendant, including, but not limited to, prohibiting any defendant from engaging in the same type of endeavor as the enterprise in which he or she was engaged in violation of Code Section 16-14-4;

(3) Ordering the dissolution or reorganization of any enterprise;

(4) Ordering the suspension or revocation of any license, permit, or prior approval granted to any enterprise by any agency of the state; or

(5) Ordering the forfeiture of the charter of a corporation organized under the laws of this state or the revocation of a certificate authorizing a foreign corporation to conduct business within this state upon a finding that the board of directors or a managerial agent acting on behalf of the corporation, in conducting affairs of the corporation, has authorized or engaged in conduct in violation of Code Section 16-14-4 and that, for the prevention of future criminal activity, the public interest requires that the charter of the corporation be forfeited and that the corporation be dissolved or the certificate be revoked.

(b) Any aggrieved person or the state may institute a civil action under subsection (a) of this Code section. In such civil action, relief shall be granted in conformity with the principles that govern the granting of injunctive relief from threatened loss or damage in other civil cases, provided that no showing of special or irreparable damage to the person shall have to be made. Upon the execution of proper bond against damages for an injunction improvidently granted and a showing of immediate danger of significant loss or damage, a temporary restraining order and a preliminary injunction may be issued in any such action before a final determination on the merits.

(c) Any person who is injured by reason of any violation of Code Section 16-14-4 shall have a cause of action for three times the actual damages sustained and, where appropriate, punitive damages. Such person shall also recover attorney's fees in the trial and appellate courts and costs of investigation and litigation reasonably incurred. The defendant or any injured person may demand a trial by jury in any civil action brought pursuant to this Code section.

(d) Any injured person shall have a right or claim to forfeited property or to the proceeds derived therefrom as set forth in Code Section 9-16-16.

(e) A conviction in any criminal proceeding shall estop the defendant in any subsequent civil action or civil forfeiture proceeding under this chapter as to all matters proved in the criminal proceeding.

§ 16-14-7. Civil forfeiture proceedings

(a) All property of every kind used or intended for use in the course of, derived from, or realized through a pattern of racketeering activity shall be subject to forfeiture to the state. The Attorney General shall be specifically authorized to commence any civil forfeiture proceeding under this chapter in matters arising under Code Section 45-15-10.

155

(b) Any property subject to forfeiture pursuant to subsection (a) of this Code section and any proceeds are declared to be contraband and no person shall have a property right in them and shall be forfeited in accordance with the procedure set forth in Chapter 16 of Title 9.

§ 16-14-8. Period of limitations as to criminal proceedings or civil actions under this chapter

Notwithstanding any other provision of law setting forth a statute of limitations, a criminal proceeding or civil action brought pursuant to Code Section 16-14-6 shall be commenced up until five years after the conduct in violation of a provision of this chapter terminates. If a criminal proceeding or civil forfeiture proceeding is brought by the state pursuant to this chapter, then the running of this period of limitations, with respect to any cause of action arising under subsection (b) or (c) of Code Section 16-14-6 which is based upon any matter complained of in such criminal proceeding or civil forfeiture proceeding by the state, shall be suspended during the pendency of the criminal proceeding or civil forfeiture proceeding by the state and for two years thereafter.

§ 16-14-9. Civil remedies as supplemental and not mutually exclusive

The application of one civil remedy under this chapter shall not preclude the application of any other remedy, civil or criminal, under this chapter or any other provision of law. Civil remedies under this chapter are supplemental and not mutually exclusive.

§ 16-14-10. Recognition and enforcement of judgments of other states; reciprocal agreements with other states

(a) A valid judgment rendered by a court of a jurisdiction having a law substantially similar to this chapter shall be recognized and enforced by the courts of this state to the extent that a judgment rendered by a court of this state pursuant to this chapter would be enforced in such other jurisdiction.
(b) The Attorney General shall be authorized to enter into reciprocal agreements with the attorney general or chief prosecuting attorney of any jurisdiction having a law substantially similar to this chapter so as to further the purposes of this chapter.

§ 16-14-11. Venue

In any criminal proceeding, the crime shall be considered to have been committed in any county in which an incident of racketeering occurred or in which an interest or control of an enterprise or real or personal property is acquired or maintained.

§ 16-14-12. Cases of special public importance

The state may, in any civil action or civil forfeiture proceeding brought pursuant to this chapter, file with the clerk of the court a certificate stating that the case is of special public importance. A copy of such certificate shall be furnished immediately by such clerk to the chief judge or, in his or her absence, the presiding chief judge of the court in which such civil action or civil forfeiture proceeding is pending; and, upon receipt of such certificate, the judge shall immediately designate a judge to hear and determine such civil action or civil forfeiture proceeding. The judge so designated shall promptly assign such civil action or civil forfeiture proceeding for hearing, participate in the hearings and determination, and cause such civil action or civil forfeiture proceeding to be expedited.

§§ 16-14-13 through 16-14-15

Repealed by Ga. L. 2015, p. 693, § 2-25/HB 233, effective July 1, 2015.

CHAPTER 15. STREET GANG TERRORISM AND PREVENTION

§ 16-15-1. Short title

This chapter shall be known and may be cited as the "Georgia Street Gang Terrorism and Prevention Act."

§ 16-15-2. Legislative findings and intent

(a) The General Assembly finds and declares that it is the right of every person to be secure and protected from fear, intimidation, and physical harm caused by the activities of violent groups and individuals. It is not the intent of this chapter to interfere with the exercise of the constitutionally protected rights of freedom of expression and association. The General Assembly recognizes the constitutional right of every citizen to harbor and express beliefs on any lawful subject whatsoever, to associate lawfully with others who share similar beliefs, to petition lawfully constituted authority for a redress of perceived grievances, and to participate in the electoral process.
(b) The General Assembly, however, further finds that the State of Georgia is in a state of crisis which has been caused by violent criminal street gangs whose members threaten, terrorize, and commit a multitude of crimes against the peaceful citizens of their neighborhoods. These activities, both individually and collectively, present a clear and present danger to public order and safety and are not constitutionally protected.
(c) The General Assembly finds that there are criminal street gangs operating in Georgia and that the number of gang related murders is increasing. It is the intent of the General Assembly in enacting this chapter to seek the eradication of criminal activity by criminal street gangs by focusing upon criminal gang activity and upon the organized nature of criminal street gangs which together are the chief source of terror created by criminal street gangs.
(d) The General Assembly further finds that an effective means of punishing and deterring the criminal activities of criminal street gangs is through forfeiture of the profits, proceeds, and instrumentalities acquired, accumulated, or used by criminal street gangs.

§ 16-15-3. Definitions

As used in this chapter, the term:
(1) "Criminal gang activity" means the commission, attempted commission, conspiracy to commit, or solicitation, coercion, or intimidation of another person to commit any of the following offenses on or after July 1, 2006:
(A) Any offense defined as racketeering activity by Code Section 16-14-3;
(B) Any offense defined in Article 7 of Chapter 5 of this title, relating to stalking;
(C) Any offense defined in Code Section 16-6-1 as rape, 16-6-2 as aggravated sodomy, 16-6-3 as statutory rape, or 16-6-22.2 as aggravated sexual battery;
(D) Any offense defined in Article 3 of Chapter 10 of this title, relating to escape and other offenses related to confinement;
(E) Any offense defined in Article 4 of Chapter 11 of this title, relating to dangerous instrumentalities and practices;
(F) Any offense defined in Code Section 42-5-15, 42-5-16, 42-5-17, 42-5-18, or 42-5-19, relating to the security of state or county correctional facilities;

(G) Any offense defined in Code Section 49-4A-11, relating to aiding or encouraging a child to escape from custody;

(H) Any offense of criminal trespass or criminal damage to property resulting from any act of gang related painting on, tagging, marking on, writing on, or creating any form of graffiti on the property of another;

(I) Any criminal offense committed in violation of the laws of the United States or its territories, dominions, or possessions, any of the several states, or any foreign nation which, if committed in this state, would be considered criminal gang activity under this Code section; and

(J) Any criminal offense in the State of Georgia, any other state, or the United States that involves violence, possession of a weapon, or use of a weapon, whether designated as a felony or not, and regardless of the maximum sentence that could be imposed or actually was imposed.

(2) "Criminal street gang" means any organization, association, or group of three or more persons associated in fact, whether formal or informal, which engages in criminal gang activity as defined in paragraph (1) of this Code section. The existence of such organization, association, or group of individuals associated in fact may be established by evidence of a common name or common identifying signs, symbols, tattoos, graffiti, or attire or other distinguishing characteristics, including, but not limited to, common activities, customs, or behaviors. Such term shall not include three or more persons, associated in fact, whether formal or informal, who are not engaged in criminal gang activity.

§ 16-15-4. Participation in criminal gang activity prohibited

(a) It shall be unlawful for any person employed by or associated with a criminal street gang to conduct or participate in criminal gang activity through the commission of any offense enumerated in paragraph (1) of Code Section 16-15-3.

(b) It shall be unlawful for any person to commit any offense enumerated in paragraph (1) of Code Section 16-15-3 with the intent to obtain or earn membership or maintain or increase his or her status or position in a criminal street gang.

(c) It shall be unlawful for any person to acquire or maintain, directly or indirectly, through criminal gang activity or proceeds derived therefrom any interest in or control of any real or personal property of any nature, including money.

(d) It shall be unlawful for any person who occupies a position of organizer, supervisory position, or any other position of management or leadership with regard to a criminal street gang to engage in, directly or indirectly, or conspire to engage in criminal gang activity.

(e) It shall be unlawful for any person to cause, encourage, solicit, recruit, or coerce another to become a member or associate of a criminal street gang, to participate in a criminal street gang, or to conduct or participate in criminal gang activity.

(f) It shall be unlawful for any person to communicate, directly or indirectly, with another any threat of injury or damage to the person or property of the other person or of any associate or relative of the other person with the intent to deter such person from assisting a member or associate of a criminal street gang to withdraw from such criminal street gang.

(g) It shall be unlawful for any person to communicate, directly or indirectly, with another any threat of injury or damage to the person or property of the other person or of any associate or relative of the other person with the intent to punish or retaliate against such person for having withdrawn from a criminal street gang.

(h) It shall be unlawful for any person to communicate, directly or indirectly, with another any threat of injury or damage to the person or property of the other person or of any associate or relative of the other person with the intent to punish or retaliate against such person for refusing to or encouraging another to refuse to become or obtain the status of a member or associate of a criminal street gang.

(i) It shall be unlawful for any person to communicate, directly or indirectly, with another any threat of injury or damage to the person or property of the other person or of any associate or relative of the other person with the intent to punish or retaliate against such person for providing statements or testimony against criminal street gangs or any criminal street gang member or associate.

(j) In addition to the prohibitions set forth in Code Section 16-10-93, it shall be unlawful for any person to communicate, directly or indirectly, with another any threat of injury or damage to the person or property of the other person or of any associate or relative of the other person with the intent to intimidate, deter, or prevent such person from communicating to any law enforcement or corrections officer, prosecuting attorney, or judge information relating to criminal street gangs, criminal street gang members or associates, or criminal gang activity.

(k) (1) Any person who violates subsection (a), (b), or (c) of this Code section shall be guilty of a felony and upon conviction thereof, in addition to any other penalty imposed, shall be sentenced to imprisonment for five years but not more than 20 years or pay a fine of not less than $10,000.00 nor more than $15,000.00, or both.

(2) Any person who violates subsection (a) of this Code section through the commission of a violation of Code Section 42-5-18 shall be guilty of a felony and upon conviction thereof, in addition to any other penalty imposed, shall be sentenced to a mandatory minimum term of imprisonment of two years but not more than 20 years which shall be served consecutively to any other sentence imposed, and no portion of the mandatory minimum sentence imposed shall be suspended, stayed, probated, deferred, or withheld by the sentencing court.

(3) Any person who violates subsection (d) of this Code section shall be guilty of a felony and upon conviction thereof, in addition to any other penalty imposed, shall be sentenced to imprisonment for five years but not more than 20 years which shall be served consecutively to any other sentence imposed.

(4) Any person who violates subsection (e), (f), (g), (h), (i), or (j) of this Code section shall be guilty of a felony and upon conviction thereof, in addition to any other penalty imposed, shall be sentenced to imprisonment for five years but not more than 20 years.

(l) In addition to any other penalty provided by this Code section, all sentences imposed under this Code section shall require as a special condition of the sentence that the person sentenced shall not knowingly have contact of any kind or character with any other member or associate of a criminal street gang, shall not participate in any criminal gang activity, and, in cases involving a victim, shall not knowingly have contact of any kind or character with any such victim or any member of any such victim's family or household.

(m) Any crime committed in violation of this Code section shall be considered a separate offense.

§ 16-15-5. Civil forfeiture

(a) As used in this Code section, the terms "proceeds" and "property" shall have the same meanings as set forth in Code Section 9-16-2.

(b) Any property which is, directly or indirectly, used or intended for use in any manner to facilitate a violation of this chapter and proceeds are declared to be contraband and no person shall have a property right in them.

(c) Any property subject to forfeiture pursuant to subsection (b) of this Code section shall be forfeited in accordance with Chapter 16 of Title 9.

§ 16-15-6. Local ordinances not preempted by state law

Nothing in this chapter shall prevent a local governing body from adopting and enforcing ordinances relating to gangs and gang violence which are consistent with this chapter. Where local laws duplicate or supplement the provisions of this chapter, this chapter shall be construed as providing alternative remedies and not as preempting the field.

§ 16-15-7. Real property used by criminal street gangs declared public nuisance; abatement; persons injured by gangs entitled to treble damages

(a) Any real property which is erected, established, maintained, owned, leased, or used by any criminal street gang for the purpose of conducting criminal gang activity shall constitute a public nuisance and may be abated as provided by Title 41, relating to nuisances.

(b) An action to abate a nuisance pursuant to this Code section may be brought by the district attorney, solicitor-general, prosecuting attorney of a municipal court or city, or county attorney in any superior, state, or municipal court.

(c) Any person who is injured by reason of criminal gang activity shall have a cause of action for three times the actual damages sustained and, where appropriate, punitive damages; provided, however, that no cause of action shall arise under this subsection as a result of an otherwise legitimate commercial transaction between parties to a contract or agreement for the sale of lawful goods or property or the sale of securities regulated by Chapter 5 of Title 10 or by the federal Securities and Exchange Commission. Such person shall also recover attorney's fees in the trial and appellate court and costs of investigation and litigation reasonably incurred. All averments of a cause of action under this subsection shall be stated with particularity. No judgment shall be awarded unless the finder of fact determines that the action is consistent with the intent of the General Assembly as set forth in Code Section 16-15-2.

(d) The state, any political subdivision thereof, or any person aggrieved by a criminal street gang or criminal gang activity may bring an action to enjoin violations of this chapter in the same manner as provided in Code Section 16-14-6.

§ 16-15-8. Matters proved in criminal trial

A conviction of an offense defined as criminal gang activity shall estop the defendant in any subsequent civil action or proceeding as to matters proved in the criminal proceeding.

§ 16-15-9. Commission of offense admissible as evidence of existence of criminal street gang

For the purpose of proving the existence of a criminal street gang and criminal gang activity, the commission, adjudication, or conviction of any offense enumerated in paragraph (1) of Code Section 16-15-3 by any member or associate of a criminal street gang shall be admissible in any trial or proceeding. Evidence offered under this Code section shall not be subject to the restrictions in paragraph (22) of Code Section 24-8-803.

§ 16-15-10. Criminal Street Gang Reward Fund

There shall be established as part of the Prosecuting Attorneys' Council of the State of Georgia the Criminal Street Gang Reward Fund. The chief of police, sheriff, or chairperson of any county governing authority may request the posting of up to a $5,000.00 reward for information leading to the arrest and conviction of any person involved in criminal gang activity that leads to the death or maiming of another person or property damage in the amount of $2,500.00 or more.

§ 16-15-11. Georgia Criminal Street Gang Database; uniform reporting format; confidentiality

(a) Subject to funds as may be appropriated by the General Assembly or otherwise available for such purpose, the Georgia Bureau of Investigation shall be authorized to establish, develop, manage, and maintain a state-wide criminal street gang data base, to be known as the Georgia Criminal Street Gang Database, to facilitate the exchange of information between federal, state, county, and municipal law enforcement, prosecution and corrections agencies, offices, and departments. The Georgia Bureau of Investigation shall be authorized to solicit input from law enforcement and prosecuting attorneys in determining useful information for such data base so that information may be used by law enforcement, prosecution and corrections agencies, and other agencies, offices, and departments for investigative, prosecutorial, and corrections purposes.
(b) Once the Georgia Criminal Street Gang Database is created and operational, the Georgia Bureau of Investigation shall be authorized to notify all federal, state, county, and municipal law enforcement, prosecution and corrections agencies, offices, and departments located in this state that information regarding criminal street gangs and their members and associates shall be entered into the Georgia Criminal Street Gang Database.
(c) The Georgia Bureau of Investigation shall be authorized to create and promulgate a uniform reporting format for the entry of pertinent information received from law enforcement, prosecution and corrections agencies, offices, and departments for use in the Georgia Criminal Street Gang Database.
(d) All state, county, and municipal law enforcement, prosecution and corrections agencies, offices, and departments may timely furnish information acquired relating to criminal street gangs and criminal gang activity to the Georgia Bureau of Investigation to be included in the Georgia Criminal Street Gang Database according to the reporting format developed by the Georgia Bureau of Investigation.
(e) Notwithstanding the provisions of Article 4 of Chapter 18 of Title 50, the information and related records associated with the Georgia Criminal Street Gang Database shall not be open to inspection by or made available to the public.

CHAPTER 16. CIVIL FORFEITURE OF PROPERTY USED IN BURGLARY, ARMED ROBBERY, OR HOME INVASION

§ 16-16-1. Definitions

As used in this chapter, the term:
(1) "Armed robbery" means the offense defined in subsection (a) of Code Section 16-8-41.
(2) "Burglary" means the offense defined in Code Section 16-7-1 in any degree.
(3) "Home invasion" means the offense defined in Code Section 16-7-5 in any degree.

§ 16-16-2. Civil forfeiture of property used to commit property related offenses

(a) As used in this Code section, the terms "proceeds" and "property" shall have the same meanings as set forth in Code Section 9-16-2.
(b) Any property which is, directly or indirectly, used or intended for use in any manner to facilitate the commission of a burglary, home invasion, or armed robbery and any proceeds are declared to be contraband and no person shall have a property right in them.
(c) Any property subject to forfeiture pursuant to subsection (b) of this Code section shall be forfeited in accordance with the procedures set forth in Chapter 16 of Title 9.

CHAPTER 17. PAYDAY LENDING

§ 16-17-1. "Payday lending" defined; legislative findings; prohibited activity; no impairment of agencies with concurrent jurisdiction

(a) Without limiting in any manner the scope of this chapter, "payday lending" as used in this chapter encompasses all transactions in which funds are advanced to be repaid at a later date, notwithstanding the fact that the transaction contains one or more other elements and a "payday lender" shall be one who engages in such transactions. This definition of "payday lending" expressly incorporates the exceptions and examples contained in subsections (a) and (b) of Code Section 16-17-2.
(b) Despite the fact that the Attorney General of the State of Georgia has opined in Official Opinion 2002-3 entered on June 27, 2002, that payday lending is in violation of Georgia law and despite the fact that the Industrial Loan Commissioner has issued cease and desist orders against various payday lenders in the State of Georgia, the General Assembly has determined that payday lending continues in the State of Georgia and that there are not sufficient deterrents in the State of Georgia to cause this illegal activity to cease.
(c) The General Assembly has determined that various payday lenders have created certain schemes and methods in order to attempt to disguise these transactions or to cause these transactions to appear to be "loans" made by a national or state bank chartered in another state in which this type of lending is unregulated, even though the majority of the revenues in this lending method are paid to the payday lender. The General Assembly has further determined that payday lending, despite the illegality of such activity, continues to grow in the State of Georgia and is having an adverse effect upon military personnel, the elderly, the economically disadvantaged, and other citizens of the State of Georgia. The General Assembly has further determined that

substantial criminal and civil penalties over and above those currently existing under state law are necessary in order to prohibit this activity in the State of Georgia and to cause the cessation of this activity once and for all. The General Assembly further declares that these types of loans are currently illegal and are in violation of Code Section 7-4-2. The General Assembly declares that the use of agency or partnership agreements between in-state entities and out-of-state banks, whereby the in-state agent holds a predominant economic interest in the revenues generated by payday loans made to Georgia residents, is a scheme or contrivance by which the agent seeks to circumvent Chapter 3 of Title 7, the "Georgia Industrial Loan Act," and the usury statutes of this state.

(d) Payday lending involves relatively small loans and does not encompass loans that involve interstate commerce. Certain payday lenders have attempted to use forum selection clauses contained in payday loan documents in order to avoid the courts of the State of Georgia, and the General Assembly has determined that such practices are unconscionable and should be prohibited.

(e) Without limiting in any manner the scope of this chapter, the General Assembly declares that it is the general intent of this chapter to reiterate that in the State of Georgia the practice of engaging in activities commonly referred to as payday lending, deferred presentment services, or advance cash services and other similar activities are currently illegal and to strengthen the penalties for those engaging in such activities.

(f) This chapter in no way impairs or restricts the authority granted to the commissioner of banking and finance, the Industrial Loan Commissioner, or any other regulatory authority with concurrent jurisdiction over the matters stated in this chapter.

§ 16-17-2. Prohibition on loans of less than $3,000.00; exceptions; penalty for violations

(a) It shall be unlawful for any person to engage in any business, in whatever form transacted, including, but not limited to, by mail, electronic means, the Internet, or telephonic means, which consists in whole or in part of making, offering, arranging, or acting as an agent in the making of loans of $3,000.00 or less unless:

(1) Such person is engaging in financial transactions permitted pursuant to:

(A) The laws regulating financial institutions as defined under Chapter 1 of Title 7, the "Financial Institutions Code of Georgia";

(B) The laws regulating state and federally chartered credit unions;

(C) Article 13 of Chapter 1 of Title 7, relating to Georgia residential mortgages;

(D) Chapter 3 of Title 7, the "Georgia Industrial Loan Act";

(E) Chapter 4 of Title 7, relating to interest and usury;

(F) Chapter 5 of Title 7, "The Credit Card and Credit Card Bank Act," including financial institutions and their assignees who are not operating in violation of said chapter; or

(G) Paragraph (2) of subsection (a) of Code Section 7-4-2 in which the simple interest rate is not greater than 16 percent per annum;

(2) Such loans are lawful under the terms of:

(A) Article 1 of Chapter 1 of Title 10, "The Retail Installment and Home Solicitation Sales Act";

(B) Article 2 of Chapter 1 of Title 10, the "Motor Vehicle Sales Finance Act"; or

(C) Part 5 of Article 3 of Chapter 12 of Title 44, relating to pawnbrokers;

(3) Subject to the provisions of paragraph (4) of subsection (b) of this Code section, such person is a bank or thrift chartered under the laws of the United States, a bank chartered under the laws of another state and insured by the Federal Deposit Insurance Corporation, or a credit card bank and is not operating in violation of the federal and state laws applicable to its charter; or

(4) Such loan is made as a tax refund anticipation loan. In order to be exempt under this paragraph the tax refund anticipation loan must be issued using a borrower's filed tax return and the loan cannot be for more than the amount of the borrower's anticipated tax refund. Tax returns that are prepared but not filed with the proper government agency will not qualify for a loan exemption under this paragraph.

(b) Subject to the exceptions in subsection (a) of this Code section, this Code section shall apply with respect to all transactions in which funds are advanced to be repaid at a later date, notwithstanding the fact that the transaction contains one or more other elements. Without limiting the generality of the foregoing, the advance of funds to be repaid at a later date shall be subject to this Code section, notwithstanding the fact that the transaction also involves:

(1) The cashing or deferred presentment of a check or other instrument;

(2) The selling or providing of an item, service, or commodity incidental to the advance of funds;

(3) Any other element introduced to disguise the true nature of the transaction as an extension of credit; or

(4) Any arrangement by which a de facto lender purports to act as the agent for an exempt entity. A purported agent shall be considered a de facto lender if the entire circumstances of the transaction show that the purported agent holds, acquires, or maintains a predominant economic interest in the revenues generated by the loan.

(c)(1) A payday lender shall not include in any loan contract made with a resident of this state any provision by which the laws of a state other than Georgia shall govern the terms and enforcement of the contract, nor shall the loan contract designate a court for the resolution of disputes concerning the contract other than a court of competent jurisdiction in and for the county in which the borrower resides or the loan office is located.

(2) An arbitration clause in a payday loan contract shall not be enforceable if the contract is unconscionable. In determining whether the contract is unconscionable, the court shall consider the circumstances of the transaction as a whole, including but not limited to:

(A) The relative bargaining power of the parties;

(B) Whether arbitration would be prohibitively expensive to the borrower in view of the amounts in controversy;

(C) Whether the contract restricts or excludes damages or remedies that would be available to the borrower in court, including the right to participate in a class action;

(D) Whether the arbitration would take place outside the county in which the loan office is located or any other place that would be unduly inconvenient or expensive in view of the amounts in controversy; and

(E) Any other circumstance that might render the contract oppressive.

(d) Any person who violates subsection (a) or (b) of this Code section shall be guilty of a misdemeanor of a high and aggravated nature and upon conviction thereof shall be punished by imprisonment for not more than one year or by a fine not to exceed $5,000.00 or both. Each loan transaction shall be deemed a separate violation of this Code section. Any person who aids or abets such a violation, including any arbiter or arbitration company, shall likewise be guilty of a misdemeanor of a high and aggravated nature and shall be punished as set forth in this subsection. If a person has been convicted of violations of subsection (a) or (b) of this Code section on three prior occasions, then all subsequent convictions shall be considered felonies punishable by a fine of $10,000.00 or five years' imprisonment or both.

§ 16-17-3. Collection of indebtedness barred; civil action permitted by borrowers

Any person who violates subsection (a) or (b) of Code Section 16-17-2 shall be barred from the collection of any indebtedness created by said loan transaction and said transaction shall be void ab initio, and any person violating the provisions of subsection (a) or (b) of Code Section 16-17-2 shall in addition be liable to the borrower in each unlawful transaction for three times the amount of any interest or other charges to the borrower. A civil action under Code Section 16-17-2 may be brought on behalf of an individual borrower or on behalf of an ascertainable class of borrowers. In a successful action to enforce the provisions of this chapter, a court shall award a borrower, or class of borrowers, costs including reasonable attorneys' fees.

§ 16-17-4. Liability for civil penalty to state; distribution of proceeds

(a) Any person who violates subsection (a) or (b) of Code Section 16-17-2 shall be liable to the state for a civil penalty equal to three times the amount of any interest or charges to the borrowers in the unlawful transactions.

(b) A civil action under Code Section 16-17-2 may be brought by the Attorney General, any district attorney, or a private party. Where a successful civil action is brought by a district attorney, one-half of the damages recovered on behalf of the state shall be distributed to the office of the district attorney of the judicial circuit of such district attorney to be used by the district attorney in order to fund the budget of that office.

§ 16-17-5. Tax on loans

(a) There is imposed a state tax on all loans made in violation of this chapter. Such tax shall be administered and collected in connection with the Georgia income taxation of the person making such loans and shall be in addition to any other tax liability of such person.
(b) The tax imposed by this Code section shall be at the rate of 50 percent of all proceeds received by a person from loans made in violation of this chapter.
(c) A person making loans in violation of this chapter shall declare and return the proceeds subject to taxation under this Code section as a part of such person's Georgia income tax return.
(d) The state revenue commissioner shall retain returns under this Code section apart from all other returns and shall not disclose any part of such a return for any purpose other than the collection of tax owed or a criminal prosecution involving tax matters. In a criminal proceeding under this chapter, a person's return of proceeds under this Code section and any evidence derived as a result of such return shall not be admissible.

§ 16-17-6. Evidence and investigation in pursuit of prosecutions

In regard to any loan transaction that is alleged to be in violation of subsection (a) of Code Section 16-17-2, the trial court shall be authorized to review the terms of the transaction in their entirety in order to determine if there has been any contrivance, device, or scheme used by the lender in order to avoid the provisions of subsection (a) of Code Section 16-17-2. The trial court shall not be bound in making such determination by the parol evidence rule or by any written contract but shall be authorized to determine exactly whether the loan transaction includes the use of a scheme, device, or contrivance and whether in reality the loan is in violation of the provisions of subsection (a) of Code Section 16-17-2 based upon the facts and evidence relating to that transaction and similar transactions being made in the State of Georgia. If any entity involved in soliciting or facilitating the making of payday loans purports to be acting as an agent of a bank or thrift, then the court shall be authorized to determine whether the entity claiming to act as agent is in fact the lender. Such entity shall be presumed to be the lender if, under the totality of the circumstances, it holds, acquires, or maintains a predominant economic interest in the revenues generated by the loan. Furthermore, the trial court shall further be authorized to investigate all transactions involving gift cards, telephone cards, the sale of goods or services, computer services, or the like which may be tied to such loan transactions and are an integral part thereof in order to determine whether any such transaction is in fact a contrivance, scheme, or device used by the payday lender in order to evade the provisions of subsection (a) of Code Section 16-17-2.

§ 16-17-7. Prohibition against issuance of certificate of authority from Secretary of State

All corporations, limited liability companies, and other business entities which are engaged in payday lending in the State of Georgia are prohibited from obtaining any certificate of authority from the Secretary of State or from the Department of Banking and Finance, and engaging in such payday lending activity in the State of Georgia shall result in the revocation of any existing certificate of authority.

§ 16-17-8. Site of payday lending is public nuisance

The site or location of a place of business where payday lending takes place in the State of Georgia is declared a public nuisance.

§ 16-17-9. Special provisions for borrowers who are members of the military or their respective spouses

(a) In addition to the other obligations and duties required under this chapter, if the customer is a member of the military services of the United States or a spouse of a member of the military services of the United States, the following duties and obligations apply to any payday lender:
(1) The lender is prohibited from garnishment of any military wages or salaries;
(2) The lender is prohibited from conducting any collection activity against a military customer or his or her spouse when the military member has been deployed to a combat or combat support posting for the duration of the deployment;
(3) The lender is prohibited from contacting the commanding officer of a military customer in an effort to collect on a loan to the military member or his or her spouse;
(4) The lender agrees to be bound by the terms of any repayment agreement that it negotiates through military counselors or third-party credit counselors; and
(5) The lender agrees to honor any statement or proclamation by a military base commander that a specific payday lender branch location has been declared off limits to military personnel and their spouses.
(b) If the customer is a member of the military services of the United States or a spouse of a member of the military services of the United States, the following disclosures shall be made in writing by the payday lender:
(1) A notice that the lender is prohibited from garnishment of any military wages or salaries;
(2) A notice that the lender is prohibited from conducting any collection activity against a military customer or his or her spouse when the military member has been deployed to a combat or combat support posting for the duration of the deployment;
(3) A notice that the lender is prohibited from contacting the commanding officer of a military customer in an effort to collect on a loan to the military member or his or her spouse;
(4) A notice that the lender agrees to be bound by the terms of any repayment agreement that it negotiates through military counselors or third-party credit counselors; and
(5) A notice that the lender agrees to honor any statement or proclamation by a military base commander that a specific payday lending branch location has been declared off limits to military personnel and their spouses.

§ 16-17-10. Severability

If any provision of this chapter or the application of such provision is found by a court of competent jurisdiction in the United States to be invalid or is found to be superseded by federal law, then the remaining provisions of this chapter shall not be affected, and this chapter shall continue to apply to any other person or circumstance.

CPSIA information can be obtained
at www.ICGtesting.com
Printed in the USA
LVHW061255071119
636663LV00012B/256/P

9 781717 843715